CULTURAL ANTHROPOLOGY
A CONTEMPORARY PERSPECTIVE
THIRD EDITION

Harcourt College Publishers

Where Learning Comes to Life

TECHNOLOGY

Technology is changing the learning experience, by increasing the power of your textbook and other learning materials; by allowing you to access more information, more quickly; and by bringing a wider array of choices in your course and content information sources.

Harcourt College Publishers has developed the most comprehensive Web sites, e-books, and electronic learning materials on the market to help you use technology to achieve your goals.

PARTNERS IN LEARNING

Harcourt partners with other companies to make technology work for you and to supply the learning resources you want and need. More importantly, Harcourt and its partners provide avenues to help you reduce your research time of numerous information sources.

Harcourt College Publishers and its partners offer increased opportunities to enhance your learning resources and address your learning style. With quick access to chapter-specific Web sites and e-books . . . from interactive study materials to quizzing, testing, and career advice . . . Harcourt and its partners bring learning to life.

Harcourt's partnership with Digital:Convergence™ brings :CRQ™ technology and the :CueCat™ reader to you and allows Harcourt to provide you with a complete and dynamic list of resources designed to help you achieve your learning goals. You can download the free :CRQ software from www.crq.com. Visit any of the 7,100 RadioShack stores nationwide to obtain a free :CueCat reader. Just swipe the cue with the :CueCat reader to view a list of Harcourt's partners and Harcourt's print and electronic learning solutions.

http://www.harcourtcollege.com/partners

CULTURAL ANTHROPOLOGY

A CONTEMPORARY PERSPECTIVE

THIRD EDITION

ROGER M. KEESING

LATE OF McGILL UNIVERSITY

ANDREW J. STRATHERN

UNIVERSITY OF PITTSBURGH

HARCOURT BRACE COLLEGE PUBLISHERS

Fort Worth   Philadelphia   San Diego   New York   Orlando   Austin   San Antonio
Toronto   Montreal   London   Sydney   Tokyo

Publisher	Earl McPeek
Acquisitions Editor	Brenda Weeks
Product Manager	Julie McBurney
Developmental Editor	Margaret McAndrew Beasley
Project Editor	Angela Williams Urquhart
Production Managers	Cindy Young, Debra A. Jenkin
Art Director	Don Fujimoto

Cover image © Art Wolfe / Art Wolfe, Inc.
Part-opening illustrations by Sueo Fujimoto.

Address for Editorial Correspondence
Harcourt Brace College Publishers, 301 Commerce Street, Suite 3700, Fort Worth, TX 76102

Address for Orders
Harcourt Brace & Company, 6277 Sea Harbor Drive, Orlando, FL 32887-6777
1-800-782-4479

Web site address:
http://www.hbcollege.com

Harcourt Brace & Company will provide complimentary supplements or supplement packages to those adopters qualified under our adoption policy. Please contact your sales representative to learn how you qualify. If as an adopter or potential user you receive supplements you do not need, please return them to your sales representative or send them to:
      ATTN: Returns Department
      Troy Warehouse
      165 South Lincoln Drive
      Troy, MO 63379

ISBN: 0-03-047582-1

Library of Congress Catalogue Number: 97-74500

Printed in the United States of America

8 9 0 1 2 3 4 5 6   039   10 9 8 7 6 5 4 3 2

Contents

Part 4
Anthropology and the
Present

List of Cases

Preface to the Third Edition

THE THIRD EDITION

George and Louise Spindler kindly suggested me as someone who could step partially into Roger Keesing's shoes in order to effect the revision which he had planned but not executed. Because I am an anthropologist trained in the British social anthropological tradition, whose fieldwork was in the Pacific, and whose more recent experience had acquainted me with American cultural anthropology, it was thought that I could bridge the continents somewhat as Roger had done. In the fall of 1996, I was joined by a collaborator, Dr. Pamela J. Stewart. In rereading each page of Keesing's text together, it became evident to us that piecemeal alterations of the text ran the danger of destroying the very vision that informs the whole book and gives it unity. What we decided to do, then, was to preserve all the parts of the book's argument and the ethnographies presented at its heart as the descriptive illustrations of his theories, while examining closely every sentence to determine whether its assertions needed to be updated, modified, or abandoned. Small changes made from time to time in this way incorporate a larger aim of updating and recasting the statements of the book to fit better with a world 20 years

or more on from the time when the second edition was published.

This deliberately unobtrusive, but detailed approach was followed also with regard to the ethnographic case histories. We have left these as they were, but provided updated references wherever appropriate or feasible. These new references usually indicate something about the subsequent history of the group and/or a different approach to the analysis of their social life.

Two examples of terminologies that have proved difficult to alter systematically and consistently are *tribe* and *Third World*. Keesing himself used the term *tribal* to refer to a range of societies seen as outside the hierarchical contexts of capitalist society, thus using it as equivalent in some senses to the term *precapitalist*. At the same time, he noted that a society may be "tribal" in this sense but not be a "tribe," a term that sometimes has been found unacceptable. Because his usage of *tribal* (e.g., "the tribal world") is so integral to his whole text, we have kept it where necessary. The term *tribe* may be quite applicable also in reference to a kind of political unit, so we have not avoided it in principle. Often, where *tribal* was superfluous we have simply omitted it. The same holds with regard to *Third World*. We have kept it where necessary, and otherwise either substituted other terms or omitted it.

There are a few areas of Keesing's text which have been altered more substantially—for example, contexts where he touches on issues of medical anthropology, on gender relations, and on the meanings of forms of taboo in Melanesian contexts (i.e., notions of ritual pollution). Sentences have been added in clarification of theoretical discussions on cultural materialism, and on Marxist approaches themselves, as well as to the discussions of the former Soviet Union, Communism, and the like.

Another area of substantial revision is the significant reduction of the material on physical anthropology and on archaeology and prehistory. This change is in response to professional reviewers' feedback regarding the relative value of this material to the introductory student in Cultural Anthropology. The validity of Keesing's original intentions in including these chapters is recognized, but his arguments regarding the evolutionary correlates of the forms of societies he discusses do not form such a central part of his work that the chapters are indispensable. The book does not therefore lose its unity by reduction of this material.

NEW TO THIS EDITION

- Chapter summaries synthesize key points of discussion and assist students in understanding the concepts presented.
- Revised material on the worlds of women recognizes the ongoing changes in the sphere of gender studies as it applies to cultural anthropology.
- A postscript discusses the shifts in anthropology (most notably postmodernism) and global relations, placing

Keesing's theories in the context of contemporary society.
- Case updates and related recommended readings bring currency to the original 85 case studies which illustrate the theories and concepts discussed.
- Updated further reading lists and bibliography provide current resources for additional study.

EXTENDING ROGER KEESING'S VISION

Roger Keesing had a very particular vision for his book *Cultural Anthropology*. In recreating it from the earlier introductory work by his father, Felix M. Keesing, he wanted to instill the viewpoints he had developed in his own research work in the Pacific, notably a concern with the political and ethical implications of anthropological fieldwork and a recognition of worldwide conditions of inequality caused by the spread of capitalist relations of production. In his general writings, Keesing combined this focus on economic and moral issues with loyalty to the established ethnographic virtues of detailed local description and analysis in terms of the actors' own values and forms of expression. This combination of interests is shown very well in one of his last publications, *Custom and Confrontation* (Chicago University Press, 1992). This book, which explores the forms of reaction and resistance to the historical impingement of the Europeans on the part of the Kwaio people of the Solomon Islands whom he had studied throughout his career, shows clearly his dual insistence on the need to understand the Kwaio on their own terms and the need, in part contradictory to the first need, to analyze their history in terms of their resistance to colonialism and its agents and their reformulations of their culture in this historical process. Interpretation *plus* explanation was what he sought in this work, as in others. These same orientations are shown also in his responses during the late 1980s and early 1990s to the various inroads into, and suggestions for, anthropological work by writers who adopted a stance of post-modernism.

Postmodernism means different things to different people. Basically, its significance as a term varies in the balance of positive and negative connotations it conveys. As a reaction within anthropology to some of the modes of theorizing that were prevalent up to and through the 1970s, postmodernism implies the rejection of overall explanatory theories of social life such as structuralism or Marxism. In a positive sense, however, the term may connote a variety of flexible new approaches by means of which authors can critically engage with a changing world: reflexivity, which means under-standing one's own position and subjectiv-ity in relation to the experience of fieldwork and the production of knowledge and infor-mation; irony, which means being able to see the unexpected turns that history may take and in so doing may force us to recon-sider our theories of it; and an appreciation of history itself as the crucible in which all of our hypotheses and theories are sub-jected to testing. The overall effect of post-modernist questioning is to instill a certain degree of doubt and skepticism into our work, while suggesting new ways in which we may be able to reconceptualize our ac-counts. Although we may not be able to synthesize these accounts into systemic "truths" we can certainly produce interest-ing and productive new statements.

Keesing was well aware of all these de-velopments, and his contributions to the collected volume of papers edited by James Carrier, *History and Tradition in Melanesian Anthropology* (University of California Press, 1992), demonstrate this. In particular he used postmodernist ideas to produce a sub-

stantive questioning of the ideas of tradi-tion and custom that had been the stock in trade of an earlier anthropology, argu-ing that "the static, self-contained, self-reproducing 'authentic' ancestral cultures of the past are themselves in some ways fic-tions" (*History*, p. 189, see also p. 239). And in the epilogue to the book, Margaret Jolly and he asked "How do we get individuals, time, outside forces, and *ourselves* back into the picture?" (p. 229).

In spite of suggestions and questions of this sort, Keesing, like some other cultural anthropologists, also resisted certain as-pects of what he understood to be postmod-ernism. His resistance was founded on the same two points that formed his vision for *Cultural Anthropology*: postmodernism can be used to aestheticise other cultures and remove us from the moral implications of our work in the world; and it can be used also to justify a concentration only on local details at the expense of the larger picture of social forces that can help us to explain why things happen the way they do in particular places (Keesing and Jolly, *History*, p. 237). In seeking for such explanations Keesing re-mained faithful to materialist forms of theo-rizing derived from the thinking of Marx and therefore opposed the postmodernist notion that such grand forms of explana-tory theory are dead. There is little doubt that he would have carried this vision for-ward into his own projected revision of this work, mooted in 1987, had he not died sud-denly in 1993. Little doubt, either, that he would have combined it with attention to both local ethnography and linguistic theory.

It is perhaps less clear how he would have handled the specific question of the validity and utility of Marxist theory today. Criticisms of Marxist theory have been made that are independent from the general postmodernist handling of "grand theory" as such in anthropology. (For a defense of Marxist thinking and a polemic against postmodernism see A. Callinicos, *Against Postmodernism*, New York: St. Martin's Press, 1989). These criticisms stemmed from what was initially a powerful entry of Marxist thought into anthropology by way of a criticism of the colonial contexts of anthropological theorizing (see, e.g., T. Asad, ed., *Anthropology and the Colonial Encounter*, London: Ithaca Press, 1973) and a concomitant reanalysis of monographs written in a structural-functional mode emphasizing the stability and coherence of indigenous social structures. In the neo-Marxist approach pioneered in African ethnography by writers such as Emmanuel Terray and Claude Meillassoux, authors pointed to themes of domination and inequality, structural contradictions, and the inroads made by colonial forces into indigenous societies. Certain gender biases in early versions of the neo-Marxist recension of ethnographies were identified and corrected and Marxist approaches merged into those of dependency theory and world systems theory, as discussed by Keesing himself in this book. Where neo-Marxist approaches began to founder was with respect to the argument regarding the determination of social forms "in the last instance" by economics. Instead of such a linear view of the relationship between infrastructure and superstructure, many theorists began to emphasize the power of symbolic and ideological forms themselves. One well-known theorist of Melanesian societies, Maurice Godelier, exemplifies this pathway in the trajectory of his work, from *Perspectives in Marxist Anthropology* (Cambridge University Press, 1977) through to his 1996 book *L'Enigme du Don* (Paris: Fayard). From a concern to argue that elements of structure such as religion are dominant in a society only when they also function as "relations of produc-

tion," Godelier has moved increasingly toward a broad interest in symbolic forms of expression at work in society without regard to a lineal argument regarding causation. He thus reclaims a vigorous interest in contexts of production and exchange and the influence of capitalism while abandoning or modifying the original arguments regarding the determination of social forms in general.

Godelier's position is one which enables us to retain some of Marx's own ideas as a source of fertile hypotheses and ways of thinking about data without being bound to the more dogmatic assertions of Marxist theory as it developed out of Marx's own work. By recognizing also that capitalism exerts a strong influence but that this influence is always locally mediated, we are also able to take into account both culture and history in portraying the trajectories of contemporary societies. Though we cannot be sure, this is perhaps also the pathway that Keesing would have taken as a productive intellectual strategy of a post-Marxist kind.

ACKNOWLEDGMENTS

The work of preparing this revision, in addition to being shared with Dr. Pamela J. Stewart, has also been greatly facilitated by the inputs of two graduate student assistants funded through the auspices of the office of the Dean, Faculty of Arts and Sciences, University of Pittsburgh. In 1995–96, Jane Thomas prepared a complete photocopy of the second edition with interleaved blank pages for comments by line number and column, and made an initial set of such comments throughout, as well as making photocopies of materials for use in the revision. In 1996–97 Joan Paluzzi read each chapter again, made comments, and prepared a folder for it with further references and suggestions, as background to the actual revision. She has also been greatly instrumental in revising the Glossary and working on the Instructor's Manual. I thank Jane and Joan most sincerely for their enthusiastic help overall.

Individual chapters of the second edition were professionally reviewed through the kind offices of Professors Jeffrey Schwartz and Marc Bermann in the Department of Anthropology at the University of Pittsburgh. Two rounds of general reviews (in 1987 and 1996) provided many useful suggestions for the revision.

I thank these reviewers for their insights:

1987

Michael S. Billig, Franklin & Marshall College

E. Paul Durrenberger, University of South Alabama

Ellen R. Kintz, State University of New York, Genesco

Frank McGlynn, University of Pittsburgh

1996

Greg Acciaioli, University of Western Australia

Richard Curley, University of California, Davis

Michael Hoffman, University of Arkansas

Dan Jorgensen, University of Western Ontario

Nancy Levine, University of California, Los Angeles

Frances Rothstein, Towson State University

Robert Tonkinson, University of Western Australia

My greatest debt remains to Pamela, who provided much of the driving force and commitment to revive the project and see it to completion. For all substantive matters that are in error, I alone remain responsible.

Preface to the Second Edition

I would never have set about to write a general anthropology book. It had its beginnings, I suppose, when as a Stanford sophomore in 1954 I turned up in the back row of a large auditorium in my father's introductory anthropology course. Observing my apparent diligence in taking notes, he expressed enthusiasm that the lectures he hoped to put together into an introductory text were being so carefully recorded. He never saw my notebook, which during a warm California spring was being filled more with scurrilous drawings and outrageous puns than the distilled wisdom of anthropology.

But 15 years later I was persuaded that—having become a practicing professional—I should revise and up-date the book he had published in 1958, 3 years before his death. I was teaching introductory anthropology courses myself then, at the University of California, Santa Cruz; and it was that, as well as a sense of filial obligation, that overcame my reluctance and led me into what I thought then would be a one-time updating of a widely used text. My father's book has been left far behind. The 1971 version, of which he was billed as co-author, was mainly mine, but written within the original framework. The 1976 book, retitled, was solely mine. It represented a fairly drastic rethinking of the premises of the field, one that moved—some found, opaquely—to the edges of knowledge, in some cases well

beyond the boundaries of anthropology as an established discipline. It was also difficult—perhaps too difficult, in introducing grammatical theory and some other problems. And in trying to give an overview of theoretical developments, it left some students dissatisfied: I was not telling them what I thought, but presented too many competing views. It did succeed, perhaps as well as it then could have, in being a serious synthesis of theory, a book that an intelligent lay person or a scholar in another discipline could read. I had tried to avoid what I saw as serious problems of most existing introductory texts: a kind of unreflective cataloguing of kinds of kinship systems and modes of political organization that conveys a false impression that everything important is known about the field, and talks down to students without demanding their serious intellectual engagement.

The new edition represents a further progression of my own thinking. It is, I think, less difficult than the previous edition in some sections (such as the chapter on language). But it is probably as demanding of serious intellectual engagement. Although I try to characterize the alternative theoretical positions of the discipline, I make more explicit my own theoretical commitments. The internal organization of the book has been constructed more directly around a theoretical argument, and has been reworked and tightened considerably.

The book is focused more directly on the core areas of sociocultural anthropology. I have reduced considerably the space and detail devoted to human evolution and prehistory—a narrowing motivated by considerations of theory and by the increasing availability of excellent texts in these areas where a nonspecialist treads at great risk. Topics such as medical anthropology and the anthropology of art, although important in their own right, are outside the area of my focus as well.

It is a politically committed book, critical of many aspects of the international economic and political order, past and present. Some readers will find my questioning of sacrosanct premises about "the free world," "free enterprise," and the historic rectitude of the United States disturbing, or worse. I ask only that the reader think deeply about the issues, not necessarily agree with my positions.

Finally, writing a text undergraduates will read is a partial substitute, in my working life, for the intensive immersion in teaching undergraduates I experienced, enjoyed, and learned from in my first 9 years in academia, at the University of California, Santa Cruz. For the last 6 years, in a research institute where I do very little classroom teaching, I have found the reviews of the field an introductory text demands a partial but often unsatisfying substitute for the face-to-face interaction of teaching introductory students. Some sense of the unseen readers has emerged in the dozen or so letters I have received from student users of the book, and in the student evaluations of the text provided to me by some instructors. I would welcome more of both, whether positive or negative.

In addition to these mainly anonymous users, I have benefited from the suggestions of Talal Asad, Athol Chase, Boudhayan Chattopadhay, Ann Chowning, Joseph Collins, Shelton Davis, Susan George, John and Leslie Haviland, Edwin Hutchins, Grant Jones, Dharma Kumar, Martha Macintyre, John Messenger, William Murphy, Phillip Newman, Michael Olien, Peter Reynolds, Pierre Spitz, and Annette Weiner. I am also indebted to those who have helped me with photographs, and in particular to Donald D. Mitchell and Anneliese Stucki, whose splendid photographs appear on the front and back covers [of the second edition] respectively.

George and Louise Spindler have given of their time and ideas so generously that the book owes an enormous debt to them. David Boynton and Ruth Stark of Holt, Rinehart and Winston have been instrumental in the creation of the new edition, as have Judith Wilson, Ann Buller, Ita Pead, and Ria Van de Zandt of the Department of Anthropology, Australian National University.

My greatest debts, intellectual and personal, are to Shelley Schreiner, co-researcher in Solomon Islands and Himalayan India: my strongest supporter and sternest critic.

R.M.K.
Canberra, Australia
March 1981

CULTURAL
ANTHROPOLOGY
A CONTEMPORARY
PERSPECTIVE
THIRD EDITION

1

The Anthropological Approach

This journey through anthropology will take us to remote corners of the world— African deserts and coral lagoons in the South Pacific—and then will take us back to the crises and complexities of the 1990s and the challenges of the century that dawns. We may well pause before embarking to ask why such a circuitous route, which will take us through ways of life now vanished or transformed, is worth taking.

The journey to remote and remarkable peoples and places, and back to the present, is the route anthropologists themselves have taken. To do so now still has a compelling importance if we are to understand present complexities and if we are to find paths ahead to viable human futures, for the material which anthropologists command represents a cumulation of human experience in different times and places: the accumulated wisdom, and folly, of humankind. In this accumulation of experience, in its diverse cultural forms, lies crucial evidence about human differences and the similarities that underlie them, about human natures and institutional possibilities. If our collective future is not illuminated by our separate pasts, it will be impoverished and doubly hazardous.

It once could be said that anthropology was the study of "primitive" peoples. (We

will come back shortly to that word, with its unfortunate connotations—and will acquire a better one.) But anthropologists no longer work only, or even predominantly, in such societies: they study peasant villagers, including those in Europe; they study cities, at home as well as in the Third World; they study multinational corporations and law courts as well as lineages. This makes it harder than it was many years ago, when the classic studies by Margaret Mead, Ruth Benedict, and Bronislaw Malinowski first attracted popular attention to the anthropology of remote societies, to define what is distinctive about anthropology, what distinguishes it from sociology and other social sciences. Moreover, anthropology is internally diverse, covering a spectrum from specialized studies of human biology and evolution to studies of the social life of contemporary peoples, rural and urban. Some sorting out is in order.

1. ANTHROPOLOGY AS A FIELD OF KNOWLEDGE

Anthropology means "human study." But obviously anthropologists are not the only scholars concerned with human beings: so are specialists on Beethoven, Euripides, the

Ceremonial village of longhouses built for a pig-killing festival near Ialibu, Papua New Guinea.

Oedipus complex, and the Vietnam War. Nor do anthropologists study only human beings; some spend their time chasing through African thickets in pursuit of primates. Cultural anthropologists, however, are committed to engaging languages and traditions that are initially alien.

Subfields of Anthropology

In a large anthropology department, it would not be strange to find a human biologist specializing in the fossil bones of early humans; an archaeologist excavating ancient communities in the Middle East; a linguist analyzing the structure of West African languages; a folklorist studying Inuit mythology; a specialist in kinship and marriage in New Guinea; and an expert on Mexican American farm laborers in California. Each of them would probably have a Ph.D. in anthropology.

What do these different kinds of anthropologists have in common? What makes anthropologists different from sociologists, psychologists, linguists, or historians? To sort out what anthropology is, what anthropologists do, and how things got that way is by no means simple.

That anthropology includes specialists in human biology—in evolution, in primate behavior—as well as specialists in diverse facets of society and culture is partly a peculiar turn of academic history. The *physical anthropologist,* or human biologist, has for decades stood quite apart from colleagues concerned with cultural behavior. Yet the wide gulf between physical anthropology and cultural anthropology has recently been bridged in many places.

This text will be mainly concerned with *cultural anthropology.* In sketching the field of anthropology in the paragraphs to follow, we will focus on scholars like the Middle Eastern archaeologist, African linguist, Inuit folklorist, and New Guinea kinship specialist in our hypothetical department. In sorting them out we will describe the subfields of cultural anthropology and the common ground that unites them.

One major subfield of cultural anthropology is *prehistoric archaeology* or *prehistory.* Unlike classical archaeologists, on whom popular stereotypes of excavating ancient ruins and temples are based, prehistorians study mainly peoples without written records. Their attempts to reconstruct ancient ways of life take them through old rubbish heaps more often than through temples. Nowadays their studies extend to the emergence of urban states in the Near East, middle America, and other regions; but their concern is with theories of social process, not classical civilizations. Increasingly their investigations have been linked, in theory and method, with anthropological studies of living peoples.

Anthropological linguistics focuses on the (previously unwritten) languages of non-Western peoples. It puts to the test theories of language based mainly on European languages and examines languages in the full range of social and cultural settings. Two of the fathers of modern American anthropology, Franz Boas and Edward Sapir, were specialists in the languages, as well as the cultures, of Native Americans; as we will see, the way language and culture are related has been a major theme in American anthropology.

Cultural anthropology is often used to label a narrower field concerned with the study of human customs—that is, the comparative study of cultures and societies. In the nineteenth and early twentieth centuries, anthropology had been concerned with comparison of the peoples discovered on the frontiers of European expansion, but with goals in mind rather different from those that guide modern studies. These comparisons were used to reconstruct, speculatively, the historical connections between peoples in the ancient past (a task now pursued, with solid evidence, by prehistorians and historical linguists) and to reconstruct the stages through which human cultures have evolved. But since 1920, cultural anthropology in this narrower sense has increasingly taken as its central problem the search for generalizations and theories about human social behavior and cultures. For this core area of cultural anthropology, the term **social anthropology** is most appropriately and widely used. Figure 1.1 diagrams these relationships between the major subfields of anthropology.

As the diagram suggests, social anthropology in turn is loosely divided into a number of more specialized subject areas, although the exact number and labels would be matters of debate among scholars in the field. These are defined partly by subject areas: *legal* anthropology, *economic* anthropology, *political* anthropology. They are defined partly by kinds of theoretical focus:

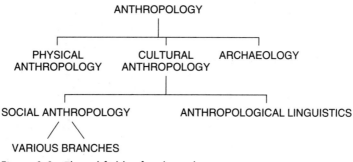

Figure 1.1 The subfields of anthropology.

psychological anthropology, *symbolic* anthropology, *cognitive* anthropology, *ecological* anthropology. The fields of *folklore* and *ethnohistory* (the history of peoples and their cultural traditions, especially in the last few centuries) spill over into other disciplines. An emerging subfield, *medical* anthropology, connects biological aspects of health and disease with their cultural conceptualization and treatment.

The Distinctiveness of Anthropology

As we have noted, anthropologists could once be distinguished from sociologists and political scientists because it was their special role in the academic division of labor to study "primitive" peoples—or, as I shall refer to them in the chapters to follow, "tribal" peoples. (The term *primitive*, although in anthropological usage intended to refer only to relatively simple technologies, has unfortunate pejorative connotations. I use the term **tribal** in a broad and relatively loose sense to cover the spectrum of peoples and cultures for which "primitive" has been used, but without implying that "tribe" could appropriately be used to describe any of them. For further discussion, please see Chapter 5.) But now anthropologists work with peasants and urbanites, in Western settings as well as elsewhere. Sociologists, political scientists, and other social scientists

have increasingly turned their attention to non-Western societies.

Yet anthropological approaches and perspectives remain distinctive. Anthropologists not only have specialist knowledge of the accumulated evidence on peoples around the world—by virtue of the tradition of work in small-scale communities, on the basis of intimate participation in people's daily lives, they have an orientation, a set of research styles and methods, that distinguishes anthropology within the social sciences. This anthropological orientation, deeply humanistic, concerned with meanings, with the texture of everyday life in communities rather than formal abstractions, remains valuable and even urgent in a world increasingly dominated by technocracy.

If the tradition of research in anthropology tends to narrow its view to local communities, the breadth of training required of anthropologists also gives them the power of generalists, whose knowledge spans the social and biological sciences. A return to our hypothetical anthropology department will illustrate the point. Each of the anthropologists, in the course of Ph.D. training, is likely to have studied—and passed examinations in—physical anthropology, archaeology, and linguistics, even though most of them are specialists in cultural anthropology. Although the cultural anthropologists may no longer remember what they learned about fossil teeth, most of them know a good deal about human biology, human evolution, and the behavior of our primate relatives. The African language specialist could probably talk intelligently about marriage systems in New Guinea, and would share with colleagues who specialize in Chinese and Inuit studies many ideas about how to study farm workers in California anthropologically. This breadth of training in human biology as well as human social life, and in the full range of cultures, past and present, equips anthropologists, in a way almost unique in the academic world, to generalize about the human condition. I have encountered people who consider themselves experts on "human nature" in every walk of life, and in settings as diverse as jungle hamlets in the Solomon Islands and remote Himalayan villages. But if there are professional specialists on "human nature" (or, we might better say, on "human natures") in the full range of cultural settings, they are anthropologists or are students of anthropology. This breadth of view that anthropology gives can help us assess "human nature" better than the street-corner or jungle philosopher, and wisely to understand human differences and human possibilities.

2. MODES OF ANTHROPOLOGICAL UNDERSTANDING: THEORY, INTERPRETATION, AND SCIENCE

Anthropology, Social Science, and Natural Science

Including anthropology within the social sciences raises questions about whether anthropologists are entitled to wear the sacred mantle of "science." Here it is difficult to disengage ourselves from stereotypes about science related to white coats and laboratories, and ideas about precision, prediction, and the "scientific method" that relate more to the nineteenth century than modern scientific practice. Contemporary astronomers spin out vast theories of the evolution of the universe; physicists work in a realm of subatomic particles; biologists model small segments of systems too vastly complex to comprehend. Each realm of natural science faces mysteries of its own, and works by guesswork and approximation as well as by precise experiment.

In some of the social sciences it has been imagined that systematic knowledge leading to theory can be gained by painstaking "experimental designs" that test hypotheses statistically in laboratory situations or through gathering of survey data. This approach is appropriate to some problems, but its general consequence has been to distort the *nature* of the phenomena under study, which are complex, social, and contextural (see Harré and Secord 1973). By seeking to simplify situations so as to isolate and measure one variable at a time, researchers have very often, inadvertently, radically changed the context, and hence the nature, of the behavior under study. Ironically, these approaches, in their concern with experimental rigor, systematic inference, laboratories, prediction, measurement, and so on, have very often emulated—even parodied—latter nineteenth-century natural science. As LaBarre puts it, the social scientist has been

> the invisible man desperately trying not to be seen *seeing* other men. . . . Fatuously "experimental"-manipulative social scientists have lacked both the humility and the wit to recognize that they are feeding . . . man-contaminated data into their "Truth Machines." (LaBarre 1967: viii)

Anthropologists have been less preoccupied with being scientific than many of their colleagues in psychology, sociology, and political science, and by and large this has probably been a blessing. Anthropologists have had to struggle with problems of communication as they have worked across gulfs of cultural differences. Finding it sometimes difficult to use tests, questionnaires, polls, experiments, and the like, in human communities where they were guests and where Western instruments of "objectivity" were inappropriate, anthropologists have fallen back on human powers to learn, understand, and communicate.

In any case, anthropologists have often dealt with phenomena for which classical scientific methods were clearly inappropriate. Trying to understand the symbolism and meaning of a myth or a ritual is not like predicting who will win an election or testing experimentally how a rat learns or how a psychology student can be tricked. There is nothing to measure, count, or predict. The task is much more like that of trying to interpret *Hamlet*. One cannot dig up, measure, and test Shakespeare to find out whether one's interpretation is "true" and everybody else's is wrong. Much cultural anthropology, guided by a search for *meaning*, has been squarely interpretive, hence in many ways closer to the humanities than to the natural sciences. Anthropology, like history, has modes in which it explores and interprets phenomena as unique, and seeks to interpret them—and modes in which it seeks to generalize and theorize in ways that place it squarely in the social sciences. The approaches brought to bear are those appropriate to the task, whether primarily interpretive or primarily generalizing and theoretical. But in the case of anthropology, they are shaped very directly by the nature of the encounters in which

anthropologists observe and learn, since as observers we are always an integral part of the picture.

Fieldwork

For most anthropologists, the immediate problems of understanding and the sources of data come from what has come to be known as **fieldwork:** intimate participation in a community and observation of modes of behavior and the organization of social life. The process of recording and interpreting another people's way of life is called **ethnography.**

What fieldwork actually entails depends in part on where the anthropologist goes to study. In the 1920s and 1930s, when little-known peoples lay along almost every colonial frontier and the ranks of anthropologists were thin, fieldwork usually meant going into an isolated society armed with notebooks, camera, and quinine, and setting up residence in a village for a year or longer. By the time an anthropologist arrived on the scene there were usually colonial administrators collecting taxes and imposing peace, as well as trade stores and missionaries. But the ethnographer set up housekeeping with the locals and did his or her best to ignore these intrusive influences. Since World War II, with new nations emerging on these frontiers and rapid transformation in people's lives, fieldwork is increasingly done in less isolated settings. An Anatolian or Mexican village, an African port town, a Haitian market town, or an American suburb may be the setting for fieldwork.

Whether the setting is city, town, village, or jungle hamlet, the mode of anthropological research is in many important respects the same. Most essentially, it entails a deep immersion into the life of a people. Instead of studying large samples of people, the anthropologist enters as fully as possible into the everyday life of a community, neighborhood, or group. These people become a microcosm of the whole. One learns their language and tries to learn their mode of life. One learns by participant observation, by living as well as viewing the new patterns of life. Successful fieldwork is seldom possible in a period much shorter than a year, especially where a new language and culture must be learned. Ideally, the researcher stays a good deal longer, sometimes on several successive field trips. The value of fieldwork sustained over a long period is beginning to come clearly into view (Colson et al. 1979). Sustained and deep research yields insights into a culture, and into the processes of continuity and change, scarcely attainable any other way. Central to this process is the need to stay long enough in a community to obtain a practical command of everyday linguistic usage.

The ethnographer brings to the task techniques of mapping and census-taking and skills of interviewing and observation. But one's position is usually radically different from that of political scientists, economists, or sociologists studying events in their own society. In the "classic" fieldwork situation in which one cannot learn a local language in advance, and little is known of the society and culture, a fieldworker's place and tasks are in many ways more like those of an infant. Like an infant, the anthropologist does not understand the noises, the visual images, the smells that carry rich meanings for the people being studied. One's learning must be of the same magnitude, and one's involvement correspondingly deep. Time, deep involvement, a lot of guessing, a lot of practice, and a lot of mistakes enable one to begin to make sense of the scenes and events of this new cultural world.

But the anthropologist is not an infant, and that makes the task harder as well as easier. Unlike an infant, the fieldworker has adult competence (though only partial in a jungle or desert) and can often use an interpreter to find out something about what is going on. The difficulty is that the anthropologist, unlike the infant, already knows a native language and set of patterns for thinking, perceiving, and acting. Instead of filling in an open framework with the design of one's people, as an infant does, the anthropologist must organize knowledge in terms of an existing design and interpret new experiences in terms of familar ones. This renders the fieldworker's learning slower and harder (consider how much harder it is for an adult to learn a new language), and it inevitably distorts his or her perception.

Consider the encounter from the other side. A people's lives are interrupted by a strange foreigner, often with a family, who moves into the community, bringing all manner of new and strange things. This person seldom fits the types of foreigners the people have learned to deal with previously—missionaries, traders, government officers, politicians, or whatever. The newcomer is insatiably curious about things private, sacred, and personal, for reasons and motives that are incomprehensible. The person must be accorded a role of some sort; clumsy efforts to speak, bad manners, and intrusions into daily life must be tolerated. All this attention may be flattering, but it may breed suspicion, hostility, and jealousy. In a less isolated and more sophisticated community, "being studied" may smack of condescension and may offend pride, not arouse it. (We will see how the anthropologist has, usually unwittingly, been aligned with colonial, and now neocolonial, forces; and how the politics of ethnography have become a focus of debate.)

On the anthropologist's side, ethical problems loom large. Should one try to protect the identity of the community and its people by disguising names and places? Can one intervene in matters of custom and health? Can one betray the confidence of one's informants in some grave violation of the law?

And how deeply can one really penetrate into another way of life? Sitting in a Solomon Islands mountain hamlet chewing betel with my friends, and bantering in their language, I feel a oneness with them, a bond of common humanity and shared experience. But can they feel that with me? Can I be more than a visiting curiosity and celebrity, a rich white man who will soon go back to his own world?

Through all this, the anthropologist goes through routines of gathering data—taking a census, recording genealogies, learning about the local cast of characters, and querying informants about matters of custom and belief. What goes into notebooks comes mainly from such routines. Advances have been made in recent years in minimizing the distorting effect of the ethnographer's own conceptual scheme and in analyzing another way of life in terms of the categories and premises of the people being studied. But as we learn more about learning, it seems increasingly likely that much of what the ethnographer learns never goes into the notebooks; it is in the realm, that for lack of a better term, we can call the "unconscious"—a knowledge of scenes and people and sounds and smells that cannot be captured in the written word.

What informants can tell the ethnographer about their customs may be a similarly inaccurate and partial rendering of what they see, do, think, and feel. Sometimes their reports are distorted by the intent to deceive or by linguistic misunderstanding. In any case, what people tell the ethnographer about their way of life must be cross-checked, substantiated, and filled out by detailed records of actual events and transactions. A modern anthropological study is a far cry from the older style where one simply said "descent is patrilineal" and left it at that. Detailed statistical tables, and often maps and genealogies, enable anthropologists to reconstruct the network of people and events from which generalizations are worked out.

In the past, recording the way of life of a small-scale and relatively self-contained society seemed to pose few problems of sampling. The community in which the ethnographer lived—a village or hamlet—promised to constitute a reasonable sample of the society's way of life, and it was assumed that within that society, customs, ideas, and beliefs were shared by all or most people. More detailed observation, more careful derivation of ethnographic generalizations from actual events, more concern with statistical patterns, and use of a wider range of informants have made it clear that things were never this simple. Ideal standards are more uniform than patterns of actual behavior. When deeply probed, the conceptual worlds of different individuals in a given society show wide variation. Most anthropologists for years paid more attention to adult men than to adult women or children. (A major advance in modern anthropology has come indirectly from the women's movement: a revelation and growing understanding of women's worlds in non-Western societies.) Anthropologists need to be trained in detailed behavioral observation and close study of the actual behavior and emotional states of people as they enact customs.

The problem of sampling has become much more acute in larger-scale, more complex societies. Cultural diversity, large populations, social stratification, and rapid change have made fieldwork in large-scale modern societies, whether in the West or elsewhere, a complicated business in which more concern with sampling, statistics, and methodological precision is needed.

Limitations of the Fieldwork Perspective

The tradition of fieldwork, and with it a conceptual repertoire derived from deep immersion in local ways of life, has been the source of anthropology's strength. But it is becoming evident that it has also been a source of anthropology's weakness. First, this fieldwork tradition, in which one studied a village or cluster of local communities to document "a culture," has produced a very misleading stereotype of some cultures, depicting each one as an integrated, unique experiment in human possibility—one that had been there for centuries until the anthropologist arrived. We will see in the chapters to follow that this stereotypic view, largely created by anthropologists, exaggerates the diversity of cultures—exaggerating their integration as coherent and unchanging "total systems" and minimizing individual diversity, conflict, and change. It exaggerates their stability, and their separateness—when in fact local peoples were in many areas tied into vast regional systems of trade and exchange, and were often tied into states and empires.

This anthropological innocence of history and regional systems, which were hidden from view in a local village, has led to conceptual schemes that embody a naïveté about internal diversity and dynamics, about regional organization and historical processes. Anthropologists have been prone to explain local phenomena in terms of other local phenomena, to show with a flourish how everything fits together neatly, to account for the global and general as

local particularities. Anthropology has been a discipline good at seeing local trees, but often inadequate in seeing the forests that lie beyond.

The directions in which anthropological theories and methods have moved—amid heated argument—are toward better views of the forest, a turn which brings anthropologists closer to colleagues in history, geography, economics, sociology, and political science. In the latter chapters of this book, where we turn attention from small-scale societies toward the massive complexities of the modern world and the emergence of world economic systems, we will see both a widening of anthropology's field of vision and a blurring of the lines that separate anthropology from other disciplines. We will find anthropologists using modes of analysis more akin to those of the economic historian or urban sociologist than those of the traditional fieldworker.*

Despite these directions of development, anthropology has retained its humanistic vision. In the chapters that follow we will examine ways of life in comparative perspective, building up foundations of theoretical understanding. In the final chapters, we will turn to the transformations of the modern world. Throughout this journey, the underlying concerns will be humanistic as well as scientific—with the natures and potentials of humankind, with the structures of past and present societies as they illumine the search for viable futures. For our futures, if we are to survive present crises and those that loom ahead, we will have to build creatively on the strengths of the past, and at the same time learn from and transcend histories of oppression and folly.

*Note: For further reading on issues of cross-cultural translation and meaning, see Keesing 1989. For a discussion on integrating local studies with wider regional and national-level analyses, see Eriksen 1993.

SUMMARY

The study of different peoples around the world can be a way of better understanding ourselves. As it is studied in the U.S.A., anthropology is conventionally divided into cultural anthropology, physical anthropology, archaeology, and anthropological linguistics. Anthropologists nowadays work with all kinds of societies, and their methods vary from the more humanistic to the more scientific. For cultural anthropologists ethnographic fieldwork is important, involving the detailed study of local situations in their wider contexts. Fieldwork must take into account the fact that local societies are not isolated entities but belong to wider regional and transnational contexts.

SUGGESTIONS FOR FURTHER READING

SECTION 1

Clifton, J. 1968. Cultural Anthropology: Aspirations and Approaches. In J. Clifton, ed., *Introduction to Cultural Anthropology*. Boston: Houghton Mifflin Company.

Frantz, C. 1972. *The Student Anthropologist's Handbook*. Cambridge, Mass.: Schenkman Publishing Company.

Fried, M. 1972. *The Study of Anthropology*. New York: Thomas Y. Crowell Company.

Hatch E. 1973. *Theories of Man and Culture*. New York: Columbia University Press.

Honigmann, J. J. 1976. *The Development of Anthropological Ideas*. Homewood, Ill.: Dorsey Press.

Langness, L. L. 1974. *The Study of Culture*. Novato, Calif.: Chandler and Sharp.

Sturtevant, W. 1968. The Fields of Anthropology. In M. H. Fried, ed. *Readings in Anthropology*, 2nd ed., Vol. 1. New York: Thomas Y. Crowell Company.

Tax, S., ed. 1964. *Horizons of Anthropology*. Chicago: Aldine Publishing Company.

SECTION 2

Berreman, G. D. 1962. *Behind Many Masks: Ethnography and Impression Management in a Himalayan Village*. Ithaca, N. Y.: Society for Applied Anthropology, Monograph No. 4.

————. 1968. Ethnography: Method and Product. In J. Clifton, ed., *Introduction to Cultural Anthropology*. Boston: Houghton Mifflin Company.

Bowen, E. S. 1954. *Return to Laughter*. New York: Harcourt Brace Jovanovich, Inc.

Casagrande, J. B., ed. 1960. *In the Company of Man*. New York: Harper & Row, Publishers.

Crane, J. G., and M. V. Angrosino. 1974. *Field Projects in Anthropology*. Morristown, N. J.: General Learning Press.

Edgerton, R. B., and L. L. Langness. 1974. *Methods and Styles in the Study of Culture*. San Francisco: Chandler and Sharp.

Epstein A. L., ed. 1967. *The Craft of Social Anthropology*. London: Tavistock.

Freilich, M., ed. 1970. *Marginal Natives: Anthropologists at Work*. New York: Harper & Row, Publishers.

Golde, P., ed. 1970. *Women in the Field*. Chicago: Aldine Publishing Company.

Hentry, F., and S. Saberwal, eds. 1969. *Stress and Response in Fieldwork*. New York: Holt, Rinehart and Winston.

Hunter, D. E., and M. B. Foley. 1976. *Doing Anthropology: A Student Centered Approach to Cultural Anthropology*. New York: Harper & Row, Publishers.

Jongmans, D. G., and P. C. Gutkind, eds. 1967. *Anthropologists in the Field*. Assen: Van Gorcum.

Paul, B. 1963. Interview Techniques and Field Relationships. In A. L. Kroeber, ed., *Anthropology Today*. Chicago: University of Chicago Press.

Spindler, G. D., ed. 1970. *Being an Anthropologist: Fieldwork in Eleven Cultures*. New York: Holt, Rinehart and Winston.

Spradley, J. P. 1979. *The Ethnographic Interview*. New York: Holt, Rinehart and Winston.

Williams, T. R. 1967. *Field Methods in the Study of Culture*. New York: Holt, Rinehart and Winston.

In Part 1 we will first look at the concepts of culture and society. We will then consider language; the organization of languages provides insights into the structure of the mind and gives important conceptual guidelines for thinking about other systems of cultural knowledge. Then in Chapter 4 we will look at the relationship between individuals (their personalities, their orientations to the world) and the cultural heritages of the communities in which they live.

Part 1

Culture, Society, and the Individual

Culture and People: Some Basic Concepts

We have reached a state now where greater precision is needed if understanding is to deepen. We need to know more clearly what social scientists mean by culture and society, and how the two are related. In this chapter and the next four, a way of thinking about individuals and groups, ideas and meanings, and stability and change will be developed. This way of thinking can then be brought to bear in the broadest comparative perspective, in hopes of obtaining some clear vision of what humans are and can be.

Anthropologists, like other social scientists, are far from agreement on how best to conceptualize the complex facets of social life. The way of thinking about culture, society, and the individual that we will sketch here builds on a substantial consensus about general principles among such theorists as Geertz, Lévi-Strauss, Victor Turner, and Goodenough. We will also glimpse in passing several issues, some more philosophical than substantive, that divide these scholars. This theoretical approach views the realm of ideas, the force of symbols, as centrally important in shaping human behavior—not simply as secondary reflections of the material conditions of social life.

The reader should be forewarned that not all anthropologists agree with this view. Other theoretical approaches will be touched upon in the chapters to follow. But to give them all equal stress would leave matters muddled and vague. We need sharp conceptual tools.

3. THE ANTHROPOLOGICAL CONCEPT OF CULTURE

Anthropological Views of Culture

The anthropological concept of culture has been one of the most important and influential ideas in twentieth-century thought. Usage of the term *culture* adopted by nineteenth-century anthropologists has spread to other fields of thought with profound impact; it is now commonplace for humanists and other social scientists to speak, say, of "Japanese culture."

Yet, paradoxically, the notion of culture implied in such usages has proven too broad and too blunt for carving out the essential elements in human behavior. The reaction of some scholars has been to abandon the term as a central conceptual tool;

Man holding cluster of pearl shells with woven handles to make a payment to his mother's kin, near Ialibu, Papua New Guinea.

the response of others has been to sharpen and narrow the instrument to render it more precise.

Culture in the usage of anthropology does not, of course, mean cultivation in the arts and social graces. It refers, rather, to learned, accumulated experience. A culture—say, Japanese culture—refers to those socially transmitted patterns for behavior characteristic of a particular social group.

Anthropologists have not been totally precise, or totally consistent, in their usages of this crucial concept. Some earlier representative attempts at definition reveal different facets of culture:

> That complex whole which includes knowledge, belief, art, morals, law, custom, and any other capabilities and habits acquired by man as a member of society. (Tylor 1871)

> The sum total of knowledge, attitudes and habitual behavior patterns shared and transmitted by the members of a particular society. (Linton 1940)

> [All the] historically created designs for living, explicit and implicit, rational, irrational, and nonrational, which exist at any given time as potential guides for the behavior of man. (Kluckhohn and Kelly 1945)

> The mass of learned and transmitted motor reactions, habits, techniques, ideas, and values—and the behavior they induce. (Kroeber 1948)

> The man-made part of the environment. (Herskovits 1955)

> Patterns, explicit and implicit, of and for behavior acquired and transmitted by symbols, constituting the distinctive achievement of human groups, including their embodiments in artifacts. (Kroeber and Kluckhohn 1952)

An Ideational Concept of Culture

Goodenough (1957, 1961) has pointed out that most such definitions and usages have blurred a crucial distinction between patterns *for* behavior and patterns *of* behavior. In fact, Goodenough says, anthropologists have been talking about two quite different orders of things when they have used the term *culture*—and too often they have moved back and forth between the two sorts of meanings. First, culture has been used to refer to the "pattern of life within a community—the regularly recurring activities and material and social arrangements" characteristic of a particular human group (Goodenough 1961:521). In this sense, culture has referred to the realm of observable phenomena, of things and events "out there" in the world. Second, culture has been used to refer to the organized system of knowledge and belief whereby people structure their experience and perceptions, formulate acts, and choose between alternatives. This sense of culture refers to the realm of ideas. (See also Goodenough 1990.)

When archaeologists talk about the culture of an early Near Eastern farming community as an adaptive system, they are using the concept in its first sense. It is the way-of-life-in-ecosystem characteristic of a particular people: "Culture is all those means whose forms are not under genetic control which serve to adjust individuals and groups within their ecological communities" (Binford 1968:323). We will, when the need arises, use the cumbersome term **sociocultural system** to refer to the pattern of residence, resource exploitation, and so on, characteristic of people. (There is, it turns out, an odd sort of advantage in having a clumsy, composite term for a complex, composite phenomenon: short and easy labels often lead to conceptual sloppiness, to a logical fallacy of "misplaced concrete-

ness" or "reification" whereby an abstraction is talked about as if it were a "thing".)

We will restrict the term *culture* to an **ideational** system. Cultures in this sense comprise systems of shared ideas, systems of concepts and rules and meanings that underlie and are expressed in the ways that humans live. Culture, so defined, refers to what humans *learn*, not what they do and make. As Goodenough (1961:522) expressed it, this knowledge provides "standards for deciding what is, . . . for deciding what can be, . . . for deciding how one feels about it, . . . for deciding what to do about it, and . . . for deciding how to go about doing it."

This ideational notion of culture is not radically new. For example, Kluckhohn and Kelly's 1945 definition of culture in terms of "designs for living" follows a similar course. Nor is it without problems, since ideas are not simply shared equally, but are distributed and controlled through the structure of society.

Perceiving Cultural Codes

An initial difficulty in the study of culture is that we are not in the habit of analyzing cultural patterns; we seldom are even aware of them. It is as though we—or the people of any other society—grow up perceiving the world through glasses with distorting lenses. The things, events, and relationships we assume to be "out there" are in fact filtered through this perceptual screen. The first reaction, inevitably, on encountering people who wear a different kind of glasses is to dismiss their behavior as strange or wrong. To view other ways of life in terms of our own cultural glasses is called **ethnocentrism.** Becoming conscious of, and analytic about, our own cultural glasses is a painful business. We do so best by learning about other people's glasses. Although we can never take our glasses off to find out what the world is "really like," or try looking through anyone else's without ours on as well, we can at least learn a good deal about our own prescription.

With some mental effort we can begin to become conscious of the codes that normally lie hidden beneath our everyday behavior. Consider the mental operations you perform when you go into an unfamiliar supermarket with a shopping list. You have a generalized mental guide to the sections a supermarket will have: one with fresh fruits and vegetables, one with bread, one with fresh meats, one with ice creams and frozen desserts, and so on. On the shelves somewhere will be spices; and somewhere among the canned fruits and vegetables one is likely to find canned juices. So a first challenge in an unfamiliar supermarket is to orient yourself, perhaps simply by traversing the aisles with your shopping cart, picking out the items you are looking for as you pass them. In all this, you are matching your set of mental categories, your generalized mental guidebook, against the one actually used in laying out this supermarket.

But when your first pass through is finished, you are likely still to have some items on your list: perhaps the yogurt, which was not next to the milk where you expected to find it, and the Worcestershire sauce, which was not next to the ketchup, where you looked. You look at the list of categories on the wall or along the aisles, comparing their scheme with yours and wondering how they are classifying the items you are looking for. And then there is the chop suey or enchilada sauce, which must be in some ethnic food section you haven't found.

In all this, you are drawing on a vastly intricate system of knowledge that is stored in your brain but is only partly accessible to your consciousness. The knowledge in your mental guidebook is not quite like that of any other shopper's. But your knowledge

and theirs are sufficiently similar that you avoid bumping into one another most of the time, and you avoid violating implicit codes of physical intimacy, eye contact, and orientation in space—as well as eventually finding the groceries you are looking for.

When it comes to going through a queue at the checkout stand, another set of implicit codes comes into play. And finally, your transaction with the cashier involves a complex set of shared understandings. (You can perceive such implicit rules more vividly if you deliberately break them and watch the reactions: try putting pebbles down on the checkout counter instead of money, or bargain with the cashier by offering 50 cents for a 79-cent tube of toothpaste.)

Project from the supermarket to the vast body of other shared understandings we need in order to eat in a restaurant, drive in traffic, dress so as to convey the desired impression, or play a game of tennis—and what the anthropologist means by culture will begin to come into view. We are not, in our everyday lives, simply choosing appropriate alternatives for acting; we are interpreting one another, placing constructions on one another's actions and meanings. Cashing a check at the bank or going to the doctor's office is not simply an enactment of culturally "programmed" routines, but a *social* process in which the bank teller and customer, or doctor and patient, communicate in ways that require shared understandings. In many settings the capacities in which we relate to one another are less clear-cut, so that social interaction entails negotiating and defining relationships with one another (not simply enacting appropriate roles). Is a lecturer met off campus to be related to by a student formally or informally, as teacher or as acquaintance? How are people who were once lovers to relate to one another? One way when they are alone, another when they are with others? When they are with present lovers? The clues and cues and understandings are at once cultural and individual matters of shared (though unconscious) convention and personal style.

Cultures as Systems of Shared Meanings

Culture consists not of things and events that we can observe, count, and measure: It consists of shared ideas and meanings. Clifford Geertz, borrowing from the philosopher Gilbert Ryle, provides an interesting example. Consider a wink and an involuntary eye twitch. As physical events, they may be identical—measuring them will not distinguish the two. One is a signal, in a code of meanings Americans share (but which presumably would be unintelligible to Inuits or Australian Aborigines); the other is not. Only in a universe of shared meaning do physical sounds and events become intelligible and convey information.

An anthropological parable—one that happens to be true—will usefully illustrate the nature of cultural meanings. A Bulgarian woman was serving dinner to a group of her American husband's friends, including an Asian student. After her guests had cleaned their plates, she asked if any would like a second helping—a Bulgarian hostess who let a guest go hungry would be disgraced. The Asian student accepted a second helping, and then a third, as the hostess anxiously prepared another batch in the kitchen. Finally, in the midst of his fourth helping, the Asian student slumped to the floor; but better that, in his country, than to insult his hostess by refusing food that had been offered. A Bulgarian hostess serving a second or third helping is not part of Bulgarian culture; but the conceptual principles that lie behind her acts, the patterns of meaning that make them intelligible, are. Bulgarian culture is something learned,

something in the minds of Bulgarians, and thus it cannot be studied or observed directly. Nor could our Bulgarian woman tell us all the premises and principles on which her behavior is based. Many are as hidden from her perception as they are from ours.

When we say that Bulgarian culture is an ideational system, that it is manifest in the minds of Bulgarians, we raise a thorny philosophical issue. Does that mean that a culture is ultimately a psychological system that exists in individual minds? Is Bulgarian culture "in the heads" of individual Bulgarians?

Goodenough would say that it is—and many of his colleagues would agree. But that gets us into sticky philosophical questions. Geertz's position is that cultural meanings are *public,* and transcend their realization in individual minds. A code for communicating exists in a sense that goes beyond any individual's knowledge of it. A Beethoven quartet exists in a sense that transcends individuals knowing it, performing it, or printing the score.

Some Guidelines From Language

The issues become more clear, perhaps, if we turn to one subsystem of cultural knowledge—language. Think about "the English language." Does "the English language" consist of all the partly different versions and dialects that individuals know, or is it somehow, as a system, above and beyond the knowledge of individuals?

Let us line up some arguments for the "above and beyond" position. First, English exists prior to (and irrespective of) any individual's being born into an English-speaking community and learning the language. English is, so to speak, *among* individuals rather than *in* them. Second, no indivudual knows all the words of English or their uses. Third, English as a *system* in some ways transcends the individual versions people have, which may incorporate pronunciations, grammatical usages, and so forth, which are uniquely personal, not part of the language. Fourth, the way language changes seems to be largely independent of what individuals know and how they use it. Finally, English as a code could well, through books and recordings, survive the death of all its speakers.

But writing is a fairly recent human invention and sound-recording a very recent one. Many Native American and Australian languages have disappeared completely: they survived only as systems of knowledge in the minds of individuals, and died when the last speakers died. And many modern linguists now believe that to understand how languages (including English) change, we do indeed have to look at the variant versions in what individuals "know" (unconsciously) about their languages. So in some important senses language is situated in the minds of individuals, not hovering above the community.

A final important point, one to which we will return in the next two chapters, is that all languages apparently have the same underlying organizational design; and there are strong reasons to infer that this design is based to a substantial degree on the organization and logical programming of our brains. If we supposed that languages were situated in communities, rather than individual brains, we would be tempted to believe that any imaginable language is possible. In fact, only a very small segment of languages that might conceivably have been invented in human communities could be learned and used by animals with human brains.

Culture as Public, Culture as Private

To go beyond this we will need to learn more about language in the next chapter. But these are precisely the issues that are debated with regard to culture by anthropologists. Those who, like Geertz, argue that cultures are systems of public meanings, not private codes in the minds of individual members, point to the way "Bulgarian culture" exists prior to (and irrespective of) the birth of any individual Bulgarian. They point to the way that—like the Bulgarian language—it consists of rules and meanings that transcend individual minds. They argue that as a conceptual system, Bulgarian culture is structured in (and changes in) ways that cannot be grasped if we take it to be a composite of what individual Bulgarians know.

The counter-arguments in favor of what Schwartz (1978) calls a "distributive model of culture" are equally compelling. Such a view takes as fundamental the distribution of partial versions of a cultural tradition, among members of society:

> The distribution of a culture among the members of a society transcends the limitations of the individual in the storage, creation, and use of the cultural mass. A distributive model of culture must take into account both diversity and commonality. It is diversity that increases the cultural inventory, but it is commonality that answers a degree of communicability and coordination. (Schwartz 1978:423)

Such a distributive view of culture can take into account the different perspectives on a way of life of women and men, young and old, specialists and nonspecialists. "A culture" is seen as a pool of knowledge to which individuals contribute in different ways and degrees:

> The knowledge of a genealogical expert, in Manus [an island in Papua New Guinea,] . . . was available for the structuring of events, and when he died, without transmitting this knowledge to a protégé, the culture was importantly altered. (Schwartz 1978:429)

Anthropologists advancing such a distributive view of culture would argue that it gives better means for conceptualizing change than depicting "a culture" ("Manus culture," "Bulgarian culture") as a system external to and transcending individual members of the society.

Here we get to the heart of the problem. In the real communities of Manus and Bulgaria, the knowledge of the world organized in the minds of individuals varies from person to person, from subgroup to subgroup, from region to region, and varies according to age and sex and life experience and perspective. Yet individuals share a common code, mainly submerged beneath consciousness, that enables them to communicate, to live and work in groups, to anticipate and interpret one another's behavior. They share a world of common meanings, even though the vantage points individuals have on it are different. In describing "a culture," anthropologists are trying to capture what is shared, the code of shared "rules" and common meanings. We describe a cultural system or a culture when our focus is on the common elements of the code in the community (just as linguists speak of "the English language," rather than a local dialect or individual variations). In the real world, the knowledge we describe as cultural is always distributed among individuals in communities.

Moreover, the organization of individuals' knowledge of the world, like the organization of language, is limited and shaped by the structures of mind and brain. A community's heritage of cultural knowledge is subject to many "real world" constraints: it must lead people to reproduce, raise children, provide food, and organize their social life in ways that sustain the population within an ecosystem, or it will not survive as a cultural tradition. But a cultural tradition, as a composite of individuals' conceptualizations of their world, must also (like a language) be learnable and us-

able. If we describe a culture as above and beyond the individuals who participate in it, we run the risk of inventing a spurious system that could not be learned and used by human individuals.

The Dangers of Reification

"A culture" is always a composite, an *abstraction* created as an analytical simplification. (For other purposes we, like linguists, may want to describe as a "subculture" some regional, local, or subgroup variation; and that, too, is an abstraction from the variant versions of individual knowledge.) We make such a simplification in order to capture and describe as a system the shared elements of socially distributed knowledge. But there is a danger of taking this abstraction we have created as having a concreteness, an existence as an entity and causal agent "it" cannot have. Both specialists and nonspecialists are prone to talk about "a culture" as if it could be a causative agent ("their culture leads them to go on vision quests") or a conscious being ("X culture values individuality"). They are prone to talk as if "a culture" could *do* things ("their culture has adapted to a harsh environment") or to talk as if "a culture" were, like a group, something one could "belong to" ("a member of another culture"). We need to guard against the temptation to reify and falsely concretize culture as a "thing," to remember that "it" is a strategically useful abstraction from the distributed knowledge of individuals in communities.

Cultural Meanings as Social Process

Although culture refers to knowledge distributed among individuals in communities, the sharing of meanings in people's daily lives is a social process, not a private one. Here again we have to force ourselves to think about familiar experiences in unfamiliar ways. If we imagine a community of individuals, each with his or her private conceptualization of the social world, and each enacting routines and interpreting meanings on the basis of this private conceptualization of reality, we fail to grasp the social process whereby shared meanings are created and sustained—a process which happens, as it were, *between* people, not simply in their private thought worlds. (It is this social construction of shared meanings that has led Geertz to criticize mentalistic views of culture.)

A familiar example of this social construction of shared meanings will illustrate. If I pick up a stick and throw it for my dog, I have defined a little world of meanings the dog and I (at least temporarily) share—in which the stick is a token of a social relationship, not merely a physical object. My dog may initiate the game by dropping a stick or a tennis ball at my feet. The dog's private psychological world is separated from mine by millions of years of evolution. We cannot share a "common culture." Yet we together create a system of meanings we share, in which the stick or the ball has become imbued with a magic we have together given to it. (One might object that my dog and I have through time worked out something like a common culture of our own; but I have had a stranger's dog drop a ball or a stick at my feet to incorporate me fleetingly into its system of meanings.) To say that the meanings are "in my head" and "in the dog's head" may be neurologically correct, but it misses or distorts the way the meanings are created *between* us, as a social process.

The challenge in the years to come will, I think, be to capture the sharedness of meanings and the social construction of symbolic

worlds—which are illuminated by "above andbeyond"theoriesofculture—while at the same time perceiving the distribution of cultural knowledge within communities, to enable us to conceptualize the processes of cultural transmission and change and to relate them to political and economic realities. In the meantime, debate about what culture "really is" is not likely to be fruitful. For some purposes, it is useful to view a peoples' cultural knowledge *as if* it were a single coherent system; for other purposes, we need to take into account its distribution within a community. The importance of taking a distributive view in interpreting the dynamics of culture, the way cultural knowledge is socially situated, will be a recurrent theme in the chapters to follow.

Although actual behavior, what people say and do, can be observed, their ideas cannot. Why worry about culture at all if it leads us into a never-never land of unobservables and shadowy mentalistic formulations? Some scholars believe that anthropologists should focus on *behavior*, on things observable and measurable, and leave "the mind" to philosophers. There are compelling reasons why we cannot understand human behavior without postulating an ideational code beneath it. We can measure to our hearts' content without capturing the meanings of a wink and distinguishing it from a twitch. The most compelling reasons to interpret social action in terms of ideational codes, not simply to analyze the stream of behavior, come from the study of language. We will see in the next chapter that much of what we perceive in the world and cloak with meaning is not in the physical world at all. We put it there in our "mind's eye." Nevertheless, it is a synthesis of the experiences of individuals and populations encoded over time (Schwartz 1992:324).

...fine and deepen our under-
...ure in the next five chapters,
... other tools to our concep-
...ve need to see how culture
......y, and how cultural structure and social structure are interwoven.

4. THE RELATION OF CULTURE TO SOCIETY

We need now to look at a second, and complementary, set of abstractions social scientists make from the complex realities of
social life. Let us begin with a community—
say, a town in Bulgaria or a village in
Manus. We find people organized in families, and in other collectivities—a soccer
club in Bulgaria, groups of people sharing
common descent in Manus. We find people
acting in various capacities toward one another; as physician or shopkeeper or political leader in Bulgaria, as curer or artisan or
fish-seller in Manus. From these capacities
in which people act, and the groups that
they form, we can draw another set of abstractions (complementary to those we
drew from the ideational codes that enable
Bulgarians or Manus Islanders to communicate and live together). The second set of
abstractions focuses on social relationships
and collectivities.

Roles, Identities, and Groups

First, we can view Bulgarians or Manus
Islanders as interacting in a system of capacities or **social identities,** enacting **roles.**
The relationships between a physician and
patient, and between physician and nurse,
comprise *identity relationships*; the behavior
appropriate between people in these capacities is a *role relationship*. (Identity focuses
on the capacities; role describes the behavior appropriate to an actor in a particular

capacity.) Note that as in the case of culture,
we are abstracting out what is common to
physicians, and patients, and glossing over
variations between individuals. A **social
group** is a collectivity of individuals who
recurrently interact in a set of connected
identity relationships. We can narrow our
focus down to a single family in one Manus
village and describe it as a group, or we
can generalize about "the family" as a kind
of social group in Manus.

If we look at a community, at some segment of it (a hospital, a family), or at a set of
communities as a system of identity relationships and groups, we describe it as a
social system. What level we carve out depends on what we are looking at. One
might want to talk about "the Bulgarian
tractor factory," in which case a fairly abstract and idealized depiction of a social
system would suffice. Or one might want to
talk about a particular tractor factory, in
which case the special characteristics of that
factory come into view. The organization of
a social system, in groups and identity relationships, comprises its **social structure.**

The Boundedness of Society and Culture

All the communities that are connected politically and economically (and hence comprise a kind of total social system) can be
taken as comprising a **society.** Characteristically, a society comprises a total social system whose members share a common
language and cultural tradition. But in a
complex social system such as that of
Bulgaria, we find ethnic minorities and outsiders, so we need to talk about a dominant
cultural and linguistic tradition. Anthropologists traditionally left to sociologists
the study of complex societies; and they
looked at fairly small-scale settings like
Manus, where it could be assumed that

everyone shared the same culture, and the "edges" of the society were neatly and unambiguously defined. In recent years our understanding of the world has deepened, and the edges now seem less neat than they once did. Here Schwartz's reflections on Manus, within the regional system of the Admirality Islands, will illustrate:

> Delimiting a culture spatially and demographically is . . . problematic. . . . The Manus people are rather easily bounded ecologically, linguistically, and in other cultural respects. . . . [But] theirs is a culture specialized in fishing and trade, interlaced in exchange relations with all other peoples of the Archipelago. . . . Manus culture [has] . . . to be seen as part of a simple interactive areal culture encompassing the whole of the Admiralty Islands. (Schwartz 1978:422)

We will return to these problems of societal boundedness in Chapter 5.

The Cultural and the Social

What is the relationship between the set of abstractions built from social relationships and the set of abstractions built from the conceptions and meanings a people broadly share? They are complementary ways of looking at the same reality, each illuminating a different side. As Geertz has written:

> Culture is the fabric of meaning in terms of which human beings interpret their experience and guide their action; social structure is the form that action takes, the . . . network of social relations. Culture and social structure are . . . different abstractions from the same phenomena. (Geertz 1957:33–34)

The two modes of abstraction from the events in communities serve complementary purposes. However, it is possible to place primary emphasis on either the culture of a community or on its social structure. American anthropology, working for decades in the footsteps of Franz Boas and led by his students, Kroeber, Linton, Sapir, Benedict, Mead, Lowie, Herskovits, and Kluckhohn, long placed primary emphasis on cultures, as the ideational heritages of communities.

In contrast, British anthropology, viewing its task as a comparative sociology, laid primary emphasis on social structure as an organizing framework for theory. More recently, the partial intellectual isolation of the two academic communities has largely been transcended, to the benefit of both; and each has been profoundly affected by trends in French anthropology that take as a central problem the relationship between the structures of the mind and the structures of society, particularly in the work of Claude Lévi-Strauss. Culture and social structure have been taking their rightful place as complementary and mutually reinforcing abstractions from complex reality.

An analogy used by Victor Turner, in analyzing Mukanda, an initiation ritual of the Ndembu of Zambia, will further clarify the relationship between cultural and social as complementary abstractions, and the challenge of analyzing the interplay between them:

> A simile that occurred to me likened the cultural structure of Mukanda to a musical score, and its performers to an orchestra. I wanted to find some way of expressing and analyzing the dynamic interdependence of score and orchestra manifested in the unique performance. Furthermore, I wanted to find a theoretical framework which would have enabled me to understand why it was that certain persons and sections of the orchestra were obviously out of sympathy with the conductor or with one another, though all were obviously skilled musicians, and well

rehearsed in the details of the score. Neither the properties of the orchestra qua social group, nor the properties of the score, taken in isolation from one another seemed able to account fully for the observed behavior, the hesitancies in certain passages, the lapses in rapport between conductor and strings, or the exchanged grimaces and sympathetic smiles between performers. (Turner 1968a: 135–136).

The quest for a way of understanding the interplay between orchestra and score—between social system and culture—so as to give a wider understanding of social processes, has been a major theme in recent anthropology (see also V. Turner 1992).

Both the conception of culture developed here and the conceptions of society and social structure have limitations as instruments for understanding the internal organization of social systems—especially complex systems—and the processes of change. But they are essential elements we will need in developing a conceptual system adequate to our task. In the chapters of Part 3, as we examine the internal organization of societies and their cultures, we will build up a more powerful conceptual system, step by step. At the very end of that section, we will pause to put together and summarize this inventory of theoretical tools. Then, as in Part 4 we examine the vast complexity of contemporary societies, we will put this theoretical system to the test, and will add further dimensions of understanding.

But now, in Chapter 3, we need to increase our knowledge of the nature and organization of ideational systems by looking at the best-charted sector of culture—language. Then, in Chapter 4, we will look at the relationship between cultures as the ideational heritages of societies and the psychology of individuals.

SUMMARY

This chapter discussed the anthropological concept of *culture* as a learned accumulation of life experiences and presented several definitions of how various anthropologists have described culture. Cultures are systems of shared ideas. Thus, culture can be referred to as an *ideational* system; in contrast, a *sociocultural* system can refer to the patterns of residence, resource exploitation, and day-to-day life ways characteristic of a particular group of people. One difficulty that arises in studying a culture occurs in properly analyzing the cultural patterns of the society. To view other ways of life in terms of our own cultural perspectives is called *ethnocentrism* and produces biased results which can be partially avoided if we carefully examine the cultural codes—the clues and cues of how a particular culture differs from or is similar to cultural patterns that we are familiar with from our own life experience or our education.

One must remember that "a culture" is dynamic and always changing as new and/or reoccurring pressures are placed on it. Although culture refers to knowledge differentially distributed among individuals in communities, the sharing of meanings in people's daily life is a social process, not a private one. People within a society play certain roles and acquire social identities as part of a social group.

SUGGESTIONS FOR FURTHER READING

SECTION 3
Freilich, M., ed. 1972. *The Meaning of Culture.* Lexington, Mass.: Rand Xerox Publishing.
Geertz, C. 1973. *The Interpretation of Cultures.* New York: Basic Books.

Goodenough, W. H. 1961. Comment on Cultural Evolution. *Daedalus* 90: 521–528.

———. 1971. *Culture, Language, and Society.* McCaleb Module in Anthropology. Reading, Mass.: Addison-Wesley Publishing Company.

Langness, L. L. 1974. *The Study of Culture.* Novato, Calif.: Chandler and Sharp.

Spradley, J. P. 1972. Foundations of Cultural Knowledge. In J. P. Spradley, ed. *Culture and Cognition: Rules, Maps, and Plans.* San Francisco: Chandler Publishing Company.

Wagner, R. 1975. *The Invention of Culture.* Englewood Cliffs, N. J.: Prentice-Hall, Inc.

SECTION 4

Biddle, B. J. 1979. *Role Theory: Expectations, Identities and Behaviors.* New York: Academic Press, Inc.

Goodenough, W. H. 1971. *Culture, Language, and Society.* McCaleb Module in Anthropology. Reading, Mass.: Addison-Wesley Publishing Company.

Language and Communication

The capacity humans have to build up local cultural traditions, to create symbolically constituted conceptions of reality and transmit them across generations, depends centrally on language. Language is the essence of our humanity. Yet human languages are so incredibly complex that scientific understanding of our faculties of language, and of the ways languages are organized, is still partial and provisional. The more linguists learn about languages, the more their awesome complexity emerges into view; each advance reveals to us the further complexities involved in analyzing how humans speak and understand one another.

5. THE NATURE AND ORGANIZATION OF LANGUAGE

Human Linguistic Capacities: Miracles and Mysteries

We will begin by looking at some of the remarkable aspects of our linguistic capacities. First, we do not simply produce sentences we have heard or used before. We continually produce sentences we have never heard and understand sentences we have never encountered; some of them have never been used before in the history of the language.

Second, deciphering the meaning of sentences we hear—something we do unconsciously and almost instantaneously—entails immensely complex analytical feats. Looking at a pair of contrived sentences will bring the analytical process partly to consciousness:

Time flies like an arrow.
Fruit flies like a banana.

How do we decode the underlying meanings? Trying to account for the way we produce and interpret sentences has led linguists to invent thousands of complex "rules" for English. (Most of them turn out not to work; one grammatical theorist observed that the life span of a theory in linguistics is 17 minutes, except late on Friday afternoons.) The incredibly complex logical operations used in speaking and understanding speech are almost totally hidden from consciousness.

Third, when someone speaks to you, you hear it as a sequence of sounds, segmented into words and constructed into sentences. But if the actual sound waves you hear are analyzed with a sound spectrograph, the flow of sound is continuous; acoustically, the separate sounds and words all run into one another. That means that you are doing the

Orator making a speech over pork at a funerary occasion, Melpa, Papua New Guinea. The pork will be given to kin of the deceased. Note the yellow clay of mourning on the speaker's face.

separating in your mind; you are creating, in your mind, linguistic structures that are in the mind of the person who is speaking to you, but not in the sounds themselves.

Finally, consider the subtle ways in which what you know about the world allows you to express and understand ideas through language. Look at these two sentences:

A cellist got on the bus ahead of me today.

A cellist asked some interesting questions in our music theory class.

"A cellist" in the first sentence evokes an image of a person carrying a cello; "a cellist" in the second sentence does not. What do we know about the world and the language that enables us to evoke understandings and achieve them in such subtle ways? If someone says to you that "It's cold in here," are they making small talk or are they telling you to close the window?

Linguistics and Anthropology

Linguists working with non-Western languages—for example, Native American languages, or African or Pacific languages—were for several decades as closely associated with anthropology as with linguistics. From 1960 onward, a conceptual revolution in linguistics forced the abandonment of many assumptions about language and its relationship to other realms of culture. This conceptual revolution, known as "transformational" or "generative" grammar, took as its goal a formal description of a speaker's linguistic knowledge as a set of explicit logical rules. For several reasons, this movement created a wide gulf between anthropology and the study of language.

First, the main languages with which linguistic theorists worked were European (mainly English, German, and Russian). One of the underlying assumptions was that, as formal systems, all languages are, beneath surface differences, relatively similar; and since the intuitions of a native speaker are a crucial element in testing linguistic rules, it made apparent sense to take the linguist's native language as target for analysis. That left anthropologists and anthropological linguists, with their "exotic" languages, standing on the sidelines. Second, the sheer formal complexity of linguistic rules made linguistics unintelligible to most anthropologists. Perhaps more important, treating languages as *formal systems*, as vastly complex schemes of rules, pulled them out of social and cultural context—precisely the realm where anthropologists encountered language in their research.

Anthropologists and linguists studying the cultural uses of languages were concerned with how knowledge of the world and the organization of language were interrelated, with how language is used to express familiarity or respect, to convey meaning in metaphor. Linguists concerned with the grammatical knowledge of an idealized speaker-hearer were more concerned with contrived sentences (such as "Fruit flies like a banana") than with who says what to whom in the real world, and how meaning is conveyed in social situations.

Fortunately, new winds have been blowing in linguistics. The idea that linguistic knowledge could be expressed in a system of formal rules has been questioned. Transformational-generative linguistics has separated into dozens of alternative attempts either to patch up the wreckage or to start putting it together in some different way. The disintegration of formal linguistics has come not simply from the growing mountain of discarded rules that failed, but from a realization that the understanding of language as a system was deeply flawed from the outset. The mistake was in thinking that a speaker's (unconscious) knowledge of the grammar of the language could be separated from knowledge about people, situations, and the world. What we know about cellos and bus passengers, about cold rooms and subtle ways of giving commands, can no longer be left out of the study of language. Linguists, hoping to make their task manageable by staying out of the messy realm of odd customs and beliefs where anthropologists work, had built a conceptual wall between linguistic knowledge and cultural knowledge. But what speakers know about the world, and draw on to evoke and interpret meanings, cannot be sealed off from their grammatical knowledge; it has been seeping, dripping, and now pouring through cracks in the wall. That makes studying language more difficult; but it brings anthropology and linguistics together again.

Linguistic Structures: Some First Principles

Linguists distinguish between *language* and *speech*. Language is the conceptual code, the system of (mainly unconscious) knowledge that enables a speaker-hearer to produce and understand speech. Speech is actual behavior—people making noises. The goal of linguistic theory has been a theory of language, of how languages are organized. In the long run, linguists and psychologists would want to be able to understand the process of speaking. But though language as a conceptual system is part of this process, so are other aspects of psychology (such as memory and attention) and the physiology of producing and hearing sounds.

Prior to the transformational revolution in linguistics, most linguists assumed that languages contrasted greatly in grammatical structure. Some languages have complicated systems of case-marking (like Latin and Russian); others, like English, rely heavily on word order to distinguish, say, the subject of a verb from the object. Some have incredibly complex verb systems, or noun classes, while in these respects others are simple. Some are "agglutinative," putting together long strings of linguistic units to express compound meanings.

One of the basic reorientations of the transformational revolution was the discovery that these differences are less extreme than they appeared to be. Beneath the many ways of expressing ideas through different languages lie the logical structures of the ideas themselves; and these logical structures are fundamentally the same in all languages. The nature of this logical structure, and how detailed, or general and abstract, it may turn out to be has been a central theme in modern linguistics.

Sentence Structures

The grammatical differences between languages lie in the ways in which the underlying logical structure are given conventional form as sentences that make propositions, ask questions, give instructions and commands. In transformational grammar, a sentence is conceived as having an inner-face and an outer-face. The inner-face is the underlying logical structure which conveys meanings; the outer-face is the way the sentence is actually expressed in a language. One might imagine what goes on in the translation room of the United Nations General Assembly when a speaker produces a sentence in French. One translator mentally (and almost instantaneously) strips the sentence back to its underlying logical pattern and then reencodes the sentence into Russian; another does the same into English; and another into Chinese. What the French sentence is mentally decoded into is its inner-face or **deep structure.** It is then reencoded into a Chinese **surface structure,** a quite different string of words and wordlike elements.

Languages differ in the ways they express the relationships between the nouns (or noun phrases) in sentences. Thus, a sentence, uttered in English in a U.N. debate, that

> In the future the government of the Soviet Union will have to cease supplying weapons to the guerrillas in Fungoolistan.

will, when translated into the other four official languages, reveal different means of distinguishing between the agent (government), the object of the verb (weapons), and the target of the action (guerrillas).

Languages also differ in the ways they mark *tense* and *aspect* of verbs. In the sentence about supplying weapons, the action is a hypothetical future occurrence; how this relationship in time, and the hypothetical nature of the act, are marked (if at all) in different languages will vary widely. In some Native American languages, a speaker reporting any event must mark the verb according to whether he or she witnessed it directly or heard about it from someone who witnessed it, or is reporting hearsay. Languages also differ in patterns of word order, rules for pluralization, and so on—differences that in an earlier linguistics had been viewed as expressions of the uniqueness of each language, and in the newer linguistics appear as different ways of building on the underlying framework.

The sentence about supplying weapons to guerrillas, although internally complicated, consists of only a single clause. Further orders of complexity, and further contrasts between languages, come into view when we look at more complex sentences consisting of two or more clauses, nested inside one another or strung together. The English sentence

> The woman who left her purse in the store yesterday will be able to get it from the manager if she sees him and identifies herself.

would be converted into very different strings in Turkish, or Inuit, or Chinese. Different languages would use different means to connect the embedded clause "who left her purse in the store yesterday" to the clause "the woman will be able to get it"; they will use different means to specify and distinguish the "it," "him," and "herself," and to specify the relations between the event that happened in the past and the hypothetical event in the future.

Such a complex sentence is conceived by linguists as made up of clauses ("The woman will be . . . "; "She left her purse"; "She sees him"; "She identifies herself"). The complexity of encoding or decoding involved in producing or understanding such

a complicated sentence, and the complexity of the mental logical operations this implies, are illustrated by another English sentence:

> Because the boy had been talking to the old lady he met at the laundry he got home late and was scolded.

Here a series of propositions is made:

1. The boy talked to a lady.
2. The lady is old.
3. The boy met the lady at the laundry.
4. The boy got home late.
5. (Someone) scolded the boy.

Moreover, a series of logical relationships between these propositions is proposed (4 occurred because of 1; 5 occurred because of 4; they occurred temporally in the sequence 2, 3, 1, 4, 5). How are these five propositions articulated together to express the appropriate relationships between each proposition? "Because" serves to embed the clause "the boy had been talking to the old lady" and specifies that "he got home late" as a result. The "and" before "he was scolded" serves to conjoin "he got home late" and "he was scolded" and to imply that the second was a result of the first. The conventions of **syntax,** or sentence structure, in a language prune out redundant words ("he" serves through the rest of the sentence to designate "the boy"; the someone who scolded the boy is unspecified; the lady the boy was talking to is the lady he met at the laundry); they embed and conjoin sentences; they rearrange word order ("someone scolded the boy" → "[he] was scolded"); and they add such outward trim as marking past tenses.

Despite years of concerted effort to formalize the rules of syntax that connect the inner-face or deep structure of a sentence with its outer-face or surface structure, and to show the logical relationship between the clauses from which sentences are built, the path is strewn with abandoned rules. The logic of the mind would seem to be different from and more powerful than the formal logics linguists and philosophers are using.

Functional Approaches to Syntax

The many competing theories of grammar make it both impossible and unnecessary to go into detail about the organization of syntax. The most promising developments are concerns with languages as communicative systems whose primary functions are social rather than formal. Humans are concerned with communicating about one another and the world. In these emerging functional approaches to language,

> syntax is viewed as the outcome of the interplay between the speaker's intent to communicate . . . information and the constraints imposed by the social and linguistic context in which the utterance occurs. (Van Valin and Foley 1980)

One promising direction of exploration follows the suggestion by Charles Fillmore (1968, 1977) that languages be analyzed in terms of an underlying system of **case** relationships. That is, the nouns (or noun phrases) within a clause are distinguishable by their functional relationships. In English, the sentence

He gave Mary a book.

establishes a relationship among the giver, the recipient, and the object given. In English, this is marked partly by word order, partly by the form of the pronoun. Compare "Mary gave him a book." The pronoun "he" in the first sentence identifies the male person as the agent (or subject); the "him" in the second sentence identifies the male person as the object of the predicate.

In other languages, the relationships between nouns (or pronouns) and their functional roles (e.g., object of predicate versus object of preposition, etc.) may be marked in more complex ways (as students of Latin or Russian may recall with discomfort). Fillmore and other explorers of case grammars have been seeking a scheme in terms of which the case relationships of any language can be described. Thus, the "subject" of a clause may, depending on the predicate, be distinguished as any of the following:

Agent	*Max* shot the duck.
Source	The *sun* emits radiation.
Experiencer	The *boy* felt chilled.
Instrument	The *key* opened the door.

The "object" of the predicate may similarly be classified according to its functional role. Thus "duck" in the first sentence is *goal*, "radiation" (in the second sentence) is *factitive*, "door" (in the fourth) is *patient*. In

Harry sold a book to John.

"Harry" is *source*, "book" is *patient*, and "John" is *goal* (Van Valin and Foley 1980).

Such an approach to grammars in terms of the functional role nouns play in sentences allows the linguist to deal with the way formally synonymous sentences can be selected to express different perspectives. Thus we can convey the same information about Harry, John, and the book with "John bought a book from Harry"—but the speaker is taking a different perspective on the event described.

Case grammars lead linguists to look at linguistic diversity from a somewhat different direction than transformational grammars. They look at an underlying set of relationships between predicates (verbs), their subjects, and their objects as sorted out and expressed in different ways in different languages. Distinctions that are overt in one language are, as it were, latent in another. We are led to see sentences not so much as formal objects but as ways of accomplishing the work of communicating. The work one language accomplishes at the level of morphological marking (by attaching a suffix or shifting a vowel) another language accomplishes in a different way. We are led to ask fewer questions about the innate structures of the mind, and more questions about the social worlds in which humans communicate. And that brings linguistics back again in the direction of anthropology.

Languages are not simply incredibly complex systems of grammar. In speaking, we produce sequences of sounds, using the vocal tract as sound chamber. And in speaking, we express *meanings*. How sound systems are organized—the **phonology** of language—is an important concern of linguistics; and so is **semantics,** the study of how meaning is carried by words and expressed in sentences. But these aspects of language, and some others, will be most relevant to this journey into anthropology if we look at how they are related to other aspects of culture. We will see that anthropologists have often turned to language for models of how humans organize perceptions, how cultures encode a view of the world, and how communication is embedded in social life.

6. FROM LANGUAGE TO CULTURE

Here we will look at a series of extensions that have been made from the realm of language to the realm of culture—a series of theoretical positions within anthropology which in various ways have drawn on language as a source of philosophical guidelines and analytical tools and concepts.

Phonology and Structuralism

The ways languages divide the spectrum of sound that can be produced by the human vocal chamber, and the ways they use systems of sound contrast to convey meaning, have had a strong impact on modern anthropology. The study of sound systems has provided important insights on human thought and perception.

First, sound systems depend on *contrasts.* What matters is not the acoustic quality of, say, b's and p's in English, but rather, the difference between them that distinguishes "bit" from "pit," "bin" from "pin," "ban" from "pan," and so on. A sound system is an organized system of differences that make a difference (Bateson 1972). English speakers may produce a considerable range of noises, all of which pass as b's. The differences between these b's are irrelevant: we do not hear them. Second, as with b's and p's sound systems build on *binary oppositions:* b's are *voiced,* p's are *unvoiced.* The same distinction is used to contrast "din" and "tin," "gill" and "kill," "van" and "fan." Another cross-cutting distinction (nasalized–nonnasalized) distinguishes "mat" from "bat" and "not" from "dot." The distinctive sounds, **phonemes,** of a language are "compartments" defined by the intersection of binary oppositions.

In **structuralism,** as applied in cultural analysis by the French anthropologist Claude Lévi-Strauss, the sound systems of language have been taken as conceptual models for understanding cultures, perception, and the very nature of the human mind. Humans, Lévi-Strauss argues, impose a logical order on experience in the way they perceive order in the stream of sound—in terms of differences that make a difference. In the symbolic realms of culture, notably myth and ritual, the human mind uses contrasts and explores contradictions.

In everyday thought and perception, humans impose a logical order on experience—create a logical, compartmentalized world in their minds—in ways formally similar to the organization of sound systems. We will look at Lévi-Strauss's modes of interpretation in the chapters ahead. Although the direct use of phonological models for cultural analysis is somewhat precarious (see Keesing 1974), we can use the way humans interpret speech as a more general model of the way the mind creates a world from sensory experience: we do not see objects, in the sense that they are presented as images on the retina of the eye. We see patterns of light and color, and we use them to create objects in our minds. Perception and thought are creative, constructive processes. On the basis of internal models of reality, models built in our minds, we construct the things and events we see.

> *Man does not see in the way he thinks he sees.* Instead of a passive-receptive act in which scenes . . . are simply recorded . . . the act of perceiving is one in which man is totally involved and in which he participates actively, screening and structuring. . . . The visual process is therefore *active* and *creative.* (Hall 1972:54)

> The visual perception system . . . "reads" from optical images non-optical properties of surrounding objects. For example, we "see" that a table is solid, hard, easily scratched. It is these non-optical physical properties which are important. . . . The perceptual system "infers" the existence of optically hidden features. We "see" the legs of the table, though hidden. (Gregory 1970:77)

> Perception . . . does not mediate behavior directly from current sensory information, but always via the internal models of reality. (Gregory 1969:239)

It is the anthropologist's special insight that these internal models we use to create a world of perceived things and events are largely learned and largely cultural. What we see is what we, through cultural experience, have learned to see.

Semantics and "The New Ethnography"

How is *meaning* conveyed in language? Philosophers have struggled for decades with the meaning of meaning. Linguists have explored meaning zealously for many years. Anthropologists have, partly independently, sought to find ways to capture and define meanings in the languages they encounter in the field. How words carry meaning and how sentences encode messages are rather different, though related, questions. Progress has been made on both fronts.

It is assumed that we each have some kind of mental dictionary, a **lexicon.** In it we somehow must store our knowledge of what words mean, of how they fit into grammatical designs, and of their sound patterns. But here again, linguists have encountered unexpected complexities—the further they probe, the more complicated matters get. Anthropologists, meanwhile, have, after an early burst of enthusiasm, discovered that the analysis of semantics in alien languages is neither simple nor a shortcut to cultural understanding.

Many linguists have assumed or hoped that (like phonological systems) semantic systems would turn out to be constructed from a universal set of distinctive features ultimately rooted in universal human experience and the structures of the mind. A set of semantic primitives, or ultimate defining features, with reference to which all words can be defined has been sought (Wierzbicka 1972, 1991). The essential goal has been to define words with reference to one another and such ultimate primitives, rather than with reference to the world of cultural experience. Yet there are increasing reasons to doubt that such a self-contained and relatively culture-free semantic analysis will be possible (see Haiman 1980, Keesing 1979).

Meanwhile anthropologists working in non-Western languages have sought to use them to explore the structure of other people's conceptual worlds. In **ethnoscience** the aim has been to analyze folk taxonomies. A **folk taxonomy** is a conceptual system organized hierarchically, in "kind of" relationships. That is, a Monterey pine is a kind of pine, a pine is a kind of tree, and so on:

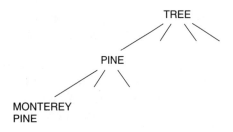

Note that in some contexts an intermediate category of "evergreen" would categorize together pines, firs, spruces, and so on. This is one of the problems—in different contexts, people use different taxonomies (in some contexts, for example, "Christmas tree" would be a generic category that would include many varieties of evergreens, but would exclude some pines).

Having sorted out a folk taxonomy, the analyst seeks a means to define the contrasts between words ("Monterey pine" versus other kinds of pines) that fit into the same level of the hierarchy. The most widely explored method has been **componential analysis.** This method seeks to find distinctive features that, in combination, would serve to define uniquely each

term within such a set of contrasting terms. Thus we might define "chair," "stool," and "bench" in terms of three aspects—seating capacity, padding, and backrest:

A. Seating Capacity   "chair" A_1C_1
  A_1 single
  A_2 multiple

B. Padding   "stool" A_1C_2
  B_1 upholstered   "couch" A_2B_1
  B_2 bare

C. Backrest   "bench" A_2B_2
  C_1 present
  C_2 absent

Unfortunately, the choice of dimensions is often quite arbitrary, so there are often dozens of possible solutions. Many English speakers probably use shape to distinguish stools from benches and chairs. Especially in dealing with another culture, there is little assurance that the analyst's distinctive features mean anything to the people he or she is studying. Moreover, increasing evidence suggests that we class things by what they are, not simply by the outer boundaries of categories. It is impossible to produce an intuitively convincing distinctive-feature definition of a weed (in contrast to a flower), a dog, or a chair (in contrast to the other objects in the room). The intersection of features seems far too simple a model to deal with the human ability to recognize patterns. We instantly perceive the relations between a great many features as forming a coherent and recognizable pattern. Thus we perceive a pattern of "dogness," whether the dog is large or small, black or white, barks or does not, wags tail or has none, has four legs visible or none, and so on. Moreover, for some words there seem to be focal meanings: weediest weeds, reddest reds, even perhaps chairiest chairs (Rosch 1974, 1978a, 1978b).

The problems of semantics highlighted by the difficulty of distinguishing chairs, stools, benches, and couches illustrate a deeper scientific problem that is emerging along many sectors of the frontiers of research on the human mind. Methods for analyzing structure are most efficient in dealing with phenomena in sequences of steps—in treating features, rules, or processes one at a time. Yet humans seem to think and perceive in terms of simultaneous relationships between features as patterns. An analogy may be useful. When a witness sees a bank robber, he or she perceives the robber's face and appearance as total patterns of features. Yet when a police artist tries to draw a composite picture of the robber, the witness must pick out nose, eyebrows, mouth, chin, and so on, one after another. Recognizing meanings probably depends partly on the same kinds of mental processes as recognizing faces; yet linguists and anthropologists are forced to pull features apart, as do the witness and police artist, and treat them one at a time.

These problems also confront semanticists as they seek to account for the way the same word has different senses in different contexts. Thus gardens flower, and so do civilizations; the blood that is thicker than water is different from the blood people sacrifice for their country or the blood you wipe from a cut; and what makes your blood boil is different from what makes water on the stove boil. To sort out and define the different senses of "flower," "blood," and "boil" here is far from easy. The different senses of a word often have no common denominator, only a "family resemblance" (see Basso 1976, Fernandez 1991).

Languages may indeed be logical systems. But as the limitations of our formal devices for describing patterns and relationships come increasingly into view, a realization is spreading that the logics of the mind may be more powerful, and simpler, than the logics of the logicians. As

Haugeland (1974:33) has observed, "A science of the mind may . . . require a new conceptual revolution. . . . We await our Galileo." In anthropology the optimism of the "ethnoscience" or "new ethnography" of the early 1960s has substantially receded. What one knows, in using a language and culture, is incredibly rich, complex, and subtle. The early attempts to reduce this richness to tree diagrams and algebraic formulae seem—in the light of the vast mysteries of mind and the preliminary state of the sciences of cognition (Sloan Foundation 1978)—both trivial and naive. These early attempts also, in exaggerating diversity in the thought-worlds of other peoples, deflected us from seeing underlying processes and patterns.

On the surface, it is true that there are striking differences between the ways peoples classify their worlds. Thus the Kwaio of the Solomon Islands label fresh water as one substance, salt water as another; they place birds and bats in one category, in contrast to moths, butterflies, and other flying insects; they class fish and marine mammals together; and they label with a single term most colors we would call blue and black. But whereas early ethnoscience stressed such radical differences between the ways different peoples divided up their world of experience into labeled categories, the pendulum has swung back in the direction of universals.

In some domains, notably the classification of color, modes of categorizing exhibit regularities across cultures. Languages may distinguish as few as three primary colors, or may make much finer discriminations; but if one focuses on the centers of categories (the reddest reds) rather than the boundaries, the distinctions are far from arbitrary—if you know how many primary colors are distinguished in a language, you can predict (with one or two alternative possibilities) which colors they will be and what their focal points (in terms of wavelengths of light) will be. In other realms, less physiologically restricted, categorizations now are turning out to be less radically varied than they appeared when only the widest category boundaries were taken into account (e.g., when the least typical chair was still considered a chair, and when robins, penguins, and ostriches were looked at as equally "birdy").

Even the notion that taxonomies are a natural mode whereby the human mind classifies things, an assumption basic to early ethnoscience, has taken on a new light. Subsequent research suggests that humans use taxonomies primarily to classify phenomena that are products of evolution. Taxonomies seem to be a "natural" way for humans to conceptualize the species- and family-resemblances of biological evolution. We humans may, then, use the same kinds of classification schemes to conceptualize the things we create—tools, kinds of gardens, kinds of houses. But we need not. Recent research on folk classification suggests that the way we conceptualize our world is less directly a reflection of the structures of the mind, and more a reflection of the organization of the phenomena being conceptualized, than the early explorers of folk classification had anticipated.

Careful research on how humans conceptualize the world around them continues, and yields deepening insights. But hopes that such analysis would capture the distinctive conceptual universe of a people, and render other modes of anthropological understanding obsolete and impressionistic, have faded. Comparative study of semantic systems contributes importantly to both linguistic theory and anthropological theory (see Keesing 1979). But it is not a shortcut to understanding a culture, or understanding the mind.

Language Acquisition and Cultural Acquisition

How children acquire language has become a focal area of recent research, spurred by developments in both linguistics and cognitive psychology. There are several amazing facets of a child's acquisition of his or her native language:

1. It takes place very quickly, with the major burst coming between 2 and 3½ years.
2. It apparently follows generally uniform stages of unfolding development for all normal children in all societies.
3. It is based on a very partial, limited, fragmented, and usually poor sample of adult speech; that is, the child builds an amazingly good and systematic theory of the language incredibly quickly with only limited and rough evidence to build with.
4. Acquiring linguistic competence seems largely unrelated to cognitive skills.
5. The rapid burst of language acquisition is demonstrably tied to sequences of biological maturation.

All this has led Chomsky to conclude that children begin the process of language acquisition with a big headstart: that a universal grammatical system is biologically programmed in the brain. The child knows language, but not *a* language. Exposure to a sample of adult speech enables the child—once biological maturation activates the necessary neural circuitry—to acquire quickly the special conventions of his or her speech community. The child is programmed to build the right kinds of theories with great efficiency. The difficulty of learning a second language in adolescence and afterwards comes partly from code interference, but probably more seriously from deactivation of the neural circuitry for efficient language learning—for some of us probably more drastically than for others.

Chomsky further concludes that this linguistic faculty is specialized and quite independent from other cognitive faculties for learning, problem-solving, and so on. All children of anywhere near normal intelligence acquire language seemingly almost automatically, regardless of their struggles and differential abilities in acquiring other skills.

This view seems biologically plausible. Consider the fact that the communicative codes of other animals are mainly coded genetically in quite fine detail, though augmentation by learning is often required. Evolution is capable of generating species-specific codes; and the evolutionary time span of hominids and early humans would probably be long enough for the grammatical structures to evolve gradually.

Though Chomsky's view may be biologically plausible, it may not be right; at least it may well be overstated. From various cognitive psychologists, notably Piaget and his associates, have come two main thrusts of criticism:

1. Linguistic competence may be closely related to other kinds of cognitive competence. Thus a child may use the same general cognitive strategies—ways of building theories about the world—to learn about his or her language and to learn about the social environment, to build theories about family relationships, physical objects, causality, and so on.
2. These genetic programs for building theories need not be as detailed as the theories they produce.

As Piaget has argued, a very complex system can develop from the cyclical operation of relatively simple organizing principles. Moreover, the shift in linguistics away from concern with languages as formal systems, toward concern with languages as means for humans to communicate in and about the world, makes Chomsky's patterns of inference suspect. If we find that languages share some characteristic pattern, the source of that commonality may lie in the ways languages are used rather than the organization of the brains of the creatures who learn them. There almost certainly are some innate language faculties, more detailed and extensive than researchers previously imagined. But the path to discovering them is slippery and indirect. We cannot know in advance to what extent universals of language derive from the biological programming of our linguistic faculties, more general faculties of mind, and the practical constraints of animals like us communicating about a world like the one we live in.

Nor can we know in advance the extent to which our faculties to acquire language are related to our faculties to acquire other forms of cultural competence. Are we programmed as culture-learners as well as language-learners? If so, how and to what degree? Could there be important cultural universals hidden beneath surface diversity? Could universal modes of logic and thought, universal organizations of knowledge, be based heavily on genetic programming? Or, to turn the questions around, could an infant learn a culture if he or she began with a blank slate, with no genetically programmed "knowledge" of what kind of world it was, of how it should be responded to, and of how to construct and organize theories of a particular cultural milieu?

Piaget for years argued that children progressively put together theories, then reorganize them at a higher and more sophisticated level: cultural knowledge unfolds in stages. But as with language, the genetic programming may well be much more extensive than Piaget believed. Biological maturation may activate detailed programs that, interacting with culturally patterned experience, enable the child to create progressively more complex models of the world. These questions remain open—central though they are to understanding how humans become human and to interpreting the diverse cultural worlds humans have created. We will come back to them in the next chapter. These questions raise a related set of questions about language and thought.

Language, Culture, and World View

Anthropologists in the 1940s and 1950s were very much concerned with "language and culture." Does a people's language shape their ways of thinking and perceiving? Is a people's world view encoded in their language and structured by its unique grammar?

At the turn of the century, von Humboldt hypothesized that the unique design of each language encoded a distinctive view of the world. This idea was elaborated in the 1920s by the brilliant anthropologist Edward Sapir, who argued that "the worlds in which different societies live are distinct worlds, not merely the same world with different labels attached." He advanced the view that language patterns are centrally important in structuring these distinct cultural worlds. This idea was carried further by Sapir's student Benjamin Lee Whorf. Whorf produced a series of papers based mainly on his research on the Hopi Indian language (published in Whorf 1956). He argued that the European languages embody not only ways of speaking about the world,

but also embody a *model* of that world. Contrasting "Standard Average European" with Hopi, he sought to show how our ideas of "thingness" are shaped by the grammatical treatment of nouns, and how our models of time as past, present, and future—ticking past like an endless belt—reflect the tense system of our language structure. Hopi concepts of time and space, as built into their language structure, represent a different model of the universe: a model, Whorf argues, that should make the theory of relativity more intuitively meaningful to a Hopi than to a European.

This powerful and plausible hypothesis has been pursued by other writers as well, notably Dorothy Lee. She drew on data from the Wintu Indian language of California and the Trobriand language of Melanesia to distinguish between "lineal and non-lineal codifications of reality" and other linguistically structured contrasts in world view (see Case 55).

The hypothesis has been tested extensively, yet the results have consistently been ambiguous. This is partly because, like a jellyfish, it is hard to get hold of—you grab it and it slithers somewhere else. Does Whorf mean that it is the grammatical framework that structures thought? How can you find out, because both are in the realm of ideas, which is by definition unobservable? You can get at language structure only through speech and can get at thought only through speech (or introspection). This imposes both a circularity and a consistent impression that the "test" is missing Whorf's point. The hypothesis remains largely impregnable because it has been untestable (see Black 1959, Fishman 1960).

The Whorfian hypothesis has been eroded more by the shifting tides of intellectual fashion and the waves of linguistic theory than by empirical disproof. The Whorfian thesis is a somewhat ethereal expression of a conviction that languages and cultures are unique. If our focus is on how different peoples are, how diverse their conceptual worlds and how variable their cultures, then the Whorfian thesis is both an expression and a partial explanation of that diversity. (For a further discussion see Lucy 1992a, Lucy 1992b.)

Yet both anthropologists and linguists, having taken for granted a great variation in the content of custom and the details of language, have focused increasingly on how similar are languages and cultures. A quest for universals and similarities in basic design and underlying structure became in the latter 1960s and 1970s both fashionable and theoretically necessary. Transformational linguists, as we have seen, argue that the deepest structures of syntax and the basic linguistic design are the same in all languages, and that the kinds of linguistic features Whorf used to illustrate the contrasts between European and Hopi reflect differences in surface structure. They imply differences not in thought but in ways of expressing the same thoughts. (If this were not so, it would seem impossible to move between different linguistic codes the way some bilinguals can—as with the simultaneous translation used in the United Nations.)

Further erosion has come from evidence and increasing conviction that thinking and manipulating language are not ultimately the same thing. To interpret Whorf as trying to find correlations between linguistic structures and modes of thinking is inevitably misleading; rather, he saw linguistic categories and classes as the units or vehicles of thinking itself. Since these linguistic elements are organized into grammatical systems, so the organization of thought must inevitably mirror this structure. Yet the basic assumption that the elements of perception and thought *are* the elements of language now seem tenuous and misleading at best. We should not reject Whorf's ideas out of hand. They are exciting partial truths, and they make us vividly aware of variability on a level where many do not expect it. Linguists would mainly agree that "the categories and distinctions inextricably interwoven in the fabric of the language system . . . [introduce] unconscious or pre-perceptual distortion" (Grinder and Elgin 1973:8), that they set up a filter between a human being and the world he or she perceives. But the distortions now seem less deep, less pervasive, and less binding than they did in Whorf's day.

There is a serious problem an anthropologist faces, working in an alien language, in trying to understand another people's world view. Suppose that language uses conventions for talking about time, where the future is behind, rather than in front of, the speaker. Or suppose that they have ways of talking about connections of cause and effect, or emotions, that are very different from ours. Does that mean that their world view is very different from ours, that their view of time or causality is culturally defined and unique?

Linguist George Lakoff and philosopher Mark Johnson have explored the ways in which everyday experience is talked about (in English and other languages) metaphorically. These are not "dead metaphors," but living, conventionalized ones. We talk, for example, as though time were a commodity, like money—as in the expressions "save time," "waste time," "budget time," and so on. We talk about emotions in terms of space ("high spirits," "feeling low"), temperature ("heated discussion"), or color ("blue," "green with envy," "seeing red"). These represent neither arbitrary, meaningless, "dead" conventions nor deeply meaningful views of the universe (Johnson 1987, Lakoff 1987). Rather, they represent culturally conventional ways of talking about realms of experience (of time, emotion, etc.) that are by their nature not easily conveyed directly in language.

Anthropologists, it seems, have often exaggerated the differences between cultures by taking the conventional metaphoric schemes of other languages (languages they usually learn with much less than a native speaker's competence) too literally—by attributing a mystical world view or some notion of causality or mystical substance to another people on the basis of their ways of talking about experiences which, it seems likely, are much the same to them as to us.

The Social Uses of Language

The ways language is used to communicate in social situations has increasingly been a focus of theoretical concern. Transformational linguistic theory assumed that the primary function of language is *referential:* to make propositions about the world. Yet curiously, "the world" largely got left out. Linguistic theory was basically concerned not with which utterances were appropriate, given particular situations in the world, but with the relationship of sentences to one another (that is, which sentences were propositionally equivalent to one another, as rearrangements or paraphrases—"John hit the ball" = "The ball was hit by John").

Linguists have increasingly had to deal with the world to which language refers. Thus, for example, *deictics* or "pointers" (in English, words like "here" or "there," referring to space, and "then" and "now" referring to time) convey information only with reference to situations in the real world. Once such questions were opened, it became clear that language did not simply make statements about the world, or ask questions about it. We use **speech acts** to give directions or commands, and even to make changes in the world ("I christen thee USS *Guppy*," or "I now pronounce you man

and wife"). Magical spells, curses, and oaths may be deemed by speakers to make more sweeping changes in the world or relations with the spirits (Keesing 1979).

It has also been noticed increasingly that sentences that are propositionally equivalent are not interchangeable. "Would you please open the door?" and "Open the damn door" are appropriate to very different contexts and social relationships. In the choices speakers make, they communicate about social relations in subtle ways.

In many languages, changes in the pronoun system are used to express formality or respect. There may be different *vertical dialects* within a language, appropriate to different social classes, to addressing status equals, superiors, or inferiors, or to different situations. (We may shift into different dialects in moving from the locker room to the dinner table, or from our own place to our parental home.)

Particularly interesting have been patterns of such dialects in non-Western settings. Two examples will illustrate. To use the Javanese language in a particular situation, a speaker must choose one of three levels or styles of speech—a "lowest" (and most rough and informal), a "highest" (or most formal and elegant), or a middle level. There are also ways to make the lowest style even lower and the highest even higher. What levels a speaker of Javanese knows will depend on his or her social class, but each speaker will have some repertoire to choose from. The choice depends not only on the speaker's status but also on that of the person spoken to, the relationship between them, and the situation.

A single sentence illustrated by Geertz (1960)—"Are you going to eat rice and cassava now?"—is so completely transformed when spoken on different levels in Javanese that only one word, the one for "cassava," is the same on both the highest and lowest levels. Even more radical code switching occurs in Paraguay. Guarani, an Indian language, has remained the dominant language of the people. Yet Spanish is the official language and is used in government, schools, and commerce. More than half of the Paraguayans are bilingual in Spanish and Guarani. They use Spanish in formal social relationships, official business, and to express respect; they use Guarani with friends and relatives, in making love, and in talking with status inferiors (Rubin 1968).

Nonlinguistic Communication

Studying the social uses of language leads in the long run, then, beyond a concern with the internal organization of language to the organization of the societies in which languages are situated. It also leads beyond language to other codes of communication. Communicating through speech becomes part of a wider phenomenon that includes nonlinguistic communication. Systems of nonlinguistic communication have, in humans, developed alongside language. These have old evolutionary roots (as witness the highly complex communication of chimpanzees); but humans have, in systems of gestures or conventional signs, added to them, and augmented them with cultural patterning. Some authors have, for example, explored the way humans communicate subtly and unconsciously through "body language" (Birdwhistell 1970, Scheflen 1973).

Hall (1966), in his study of the way cultures use physical space to communicate about social relationships, brings to consciousness many patterns we normally take for granted. Americans surround themselves with a kind of envelope of private space, a sort of invisible plastic bag. This space is normally inviolate in everyday interaction. Try, for instance, in talking to people, to move gradually closer and closer to them; you will find them retreating to preserve their envelopes intact. Only in a few contexts, such as lovemaking and contact sports, do we invade one another's envelopes. Even in a crowded bus or subway, when our envelopes get all squished together, we go to considerable lengths to affirm to one another that we are not really invading private space; we depersonalize the close physical encounters by staring into space, reading tabloid newspapers and so on.

Many of the messages we exchange tell us how other messages are to be interpreted—whether they are "true," "serious," "joking," "threatening," and so on. Bateson (1955) calls these messages about messages **metacommunication.** By metacommunication, we put "frames" around messages that tell others how to interpret them: "You old son of a bitch" may be dire insult or friendly camaraderie among age mates. We had best be careful to make that clear ("Smile when you say that . . . ").

Bateson has argued that such framing, evolutionarily at least as old as mammalian play, reaches new and important complexity in human communication (Bateson 1955, 1972). Paradoxes in which the framing messages contradict the messages within the frame are basic to this process. Animals biting one another, but at the same time framing or labeling it as "just play," show the simplest form of such contradiction: the bite is not what it seems to be. But in art, fantasy, symbolism, and ritual, humans develop these paradoxes more fully (see also Eibl-Eibesfeldt 1989). Much of the richness of cultural structure lies in such framing of contexts. Our ability to participate in the events of our cultural world and understand what is going on depends not so much on knowing what will happen next—we often do not know that—as on knowing the right frames.

We have gone far enough for our purposes in exploring the study of language and communication to reinforce our conceptual foundations. However, it is worth pausing for a brief conceptual review.

Language and the Conceptualization of Culture

When we talk about "a language" or "a culture," we confront the difficulty we can call code variability. Your theory for speaking English (as well as the way you actually speak, which is not the same thing) is different from everyone else's. Your theory for shaking hands—how, when, and with whom—is not the same as everyone else's. Furthermore, there are things you probably do not know about electrical wiring, pole vaulting, and nuclear physics that are part of our language and culture. How, then, can we speak of "the English language" or "American culture" as a common code? The same problem confronts us when we talk of Hopi Indian language or Hopi culture.

Linguists manage the problem by talking about *dialects* (of regions and social classes) and finally *idiolects,* the special versions of a language characteristic of each speaker. For most purposes, it has been useful to focus on the common features of the code that all speakers share and to ignore dialect and idiolect variations. "English" (or "German") is thus an abstract model of a language, an idealized standardization. It is also a composite, since it includes the special vocabularies of the electrician, pole vaulter, and physicist. In addition, the edges of "French" and "German" are not sharp. French blends into Italian, and German into Dutch, along country borders. But linguists have found it conceptually useful to ignore the "marginal speaker" most of the time.

For many purposes the cultural anthropologist can usefully follow the simplifying assumptions linguists make about code variability. One can speak of Hopi culture, ignoring code variation and messy cultural borders and lumping together the knowledge of Hopi wife, Hopi artisan, and Hopi priest. But there are problems lurking here.

As we noted in the last chapter, we need to remember that in the real world—as distinct from the imaginary world of conceptual abstractions and scientific simplifications—cultural knowledge is distributive. Linguists have found it necessary for interpreting certain problems to take code diversity into account. Anthropologists—studying social systems where men and women, old and young, rulers and ruled may have very different perspectives on (and commitments to) cultural ideologies—will more and more often have to take the distribution of cultural models of reality within communities into account. One way to go further in this direction and further refine our conceptual tools will be to narrow our focus down to the individual.

═══════ SUMMARY ═══════

Human culture depends to a considerable extent on the human capacity for creating language. Linguists since 1960 have studied language in terms of a theory of generative grammar, which produced a multiplicity of formal rules and also seemed to remove language from the rest of culture. Languages do, of course, have patterns of phonology, grammar, and syntax—and distinctions between the meanings of words are built up from phonological contrasts. Structuralist anthropologists have argued that cultural meanings are also built in terms of contrasts such as between "left" and "right." Anthropologists working in the domain of ethnoscience have concentrated on folk taxonomies, in which binary contrasts build up into more elaborate nesting hierarchies of concepts. Not all forms of classification, however, need be taxonomic and there may be cross-culturally shared patterns that transcend particular taxonomies. Noam Chomsky argued that a universal grammatical system is biologically programmed in the human brain. It is not clear, however, how such a system interacts with experience in the life cycle and whether there are similar programs for learning other aspects of culture. Benjamin Lee Whorf argued further that language structures world view as a whole, and Lakoff and Johnson have pointed to the importance of broad metaphors in the expression of experience. We have also to compare linguistic with non-linguistic communication by means of gesture, movement, and the use of space. We must also remember that cultural and linguistic knowledge is shared distributively and that code diversities have to be taken into account within broad unities.

SUGGESTIONS FOR FURTHER READING

SECTION 5

Bolinger, D. 1975. *Aspects of Language,* 2nd ed. New York: Harcourt Brace Jovanovich, Inc.

Chomsky, N. 1973. *Language and Mind,* 2nd ed. New York: Harcourt Brace Jovanovich, Inc.

Grinder, J., and S. Elgin. 1973. *Transformational Grammar: History, Theory, Practice.* New York: Holt, Rinehart and Winston.

Langacker, R. W. 1973. *Language and Its Structure,* 2nd ed. New York: Harcourt Brace Jovanovich, Inc.

SECTION 6

Problems in the use of the "linguistic model" as a way of understanding cultural knowledge are explored further in Keesing 1979. Discussion of language pragmatics and speech acts, in relation to Samoa, can be found in Duranti 1990, and general reviews are given in Sherzer 1987 and DeBernardi 1994.

Bower, T. G. 1974. *Development in Infancy.* San Francisco: W. F. Freeman and Company.

Brown, R. 1973. *A First Language.* Cambridge, Mass.: Harvard University Press.

Burling, R. 1970. *Man's Many Voices: Language in Its Cultural Context.* New York: Holt, Rinehart and Winston.

DeBernardi, J. 1994. Social Aspects of Language Use. In T. Ingold, ed. *Companion Encyclopedia of Anthropology,* pp. 861–890. London and New York: Routledge.

Duranti, A. 1990. Politics and Grammar: Agency in Samoan Political Discourse. *American Ethnologist* 17:646–666.

Ferguson, C. A., and D. Slobin, eds. 1973. *Readings in Child Language Acquisition.* New York: Holt, Rinehart and Winston.

Gumperz, J. J., and D. Hymes, eds. 1972. *Directions in Sociolinguistics.* New York: Holt, Rinehart and Winston.

Hutt, S. J., and C. Hutt, eds. 1973. *Early Human Development.* London: Oxford University Press.

Hymes, D., ed. 1964. *Language in Culture and Society.* New York: Harper & Row, Publishers.

———, 1974. *Foundations in Sociolinguistics: An Ethnographic Approach.* Philadelphia: University of Pennsylvania Press.

Kagan, J. 1972, March. Do Infants Think? *Scientific American.*

Keesing, R. M. 1979. Linguistic Knowledge and Cultural Knowledge: Some Doubts and Speculations. *American Anthropologist* 81:14–36.

McCormack, W. C., and S. A. Wurm, 1977. Language and Thought: Anthropological Issues. *World Anthropology.* The Hague: Mouton and Company.

McNeill, D. 1970. *The Acquisition of Language.* New York: Harper & Row, Publishers.

Piaget, J. 1970. Piaget's Theory. In P. H. Mussen, ed. *Carmichael's Manual of Child Psychology,* 3d ed., Vol. 1. New York: John Wiley & Sons, Inc., pp. 703–732.

Sherzer, J. 1987. A Discourse-Centered Approach to Language and Culture. *American Anthropologist* 89:295–309.

Spradley, J. P. 1972. *Culture and Cognition: Rules, Maps and Plans.* New York: Chandler Publishing Company.

Tyler, S., ed. 1969. *Cognitive Anthropology.* New York: Holt, Rinehart and Winston.

Whorf, B. L. 1956. *Language, Thought and Reality.* Cambridge, Mass.: MIT Press.

Culture and the Individual

A New Guinea man, gravely examining the inkblot patterns on a Rorschach plate proffered by an anthropologist, describes what he sees in them: a swirl of moving birds, bats, and mythical creatures of the forest where he lives. If a resident of Los Angeles responded to Rorschach inkblots in this way, it would be very odd—and would point to deep psychological problems. But what if the other inhabitants of the New Guinea community all saw spirit beings in the inkblot plates?

There are standard psychiatric techniques for interpreting Rorschach tests. But can we apply them in New Guinea? What does it mean if remote mountain villagers, propitiating ancestral ghosts and spirit beings, produce responses that, in Los Angeles, would indicate psychosis or severe neurosis? Does it mean that the scoring techniques are correct in measuring severe psychological stress, but that men in this New Guinea society are culturally conditioned to experience such stress by the traumatic initiation rites and cults of dangerous secrecy through which they have been raised to manhood? And what about the ancestral ghosts, dangerous and punitive? Are they psychologically projected fantasy images of punitive fathers and male authority figures? Is the culture of this New Guinea

people a cumulative creation of adults that reflects their common experience in infancy and childhood?

Or is the process whereby cultural traditions cumulate and change only remotely connected to the psychological conflicts and fantasies of individuals growing up in a society? If the New Guinean sees birds, bats, and mythical creatures in the inkblots, is he simply responding to these ambiguous splotches on the basis of the symbolic traditions of his community, only secondarily related to the underlying dynamics of his personality? And how, once we pose such questions, are we to distinguish between the culture of the community and the psychology of the individual?

These questions point to basic conceptual issues about private meanings and public meanings, personality and culture, and how cultural traditions within a community are built up, and progressively change. Unless we sort out these issues in a preliminary way, our examinations of the ways of life of other peoples will begin on very slippery ground.

Yet in trying to sort them out, we face a problem. In the 1930s, 1940s, and 1950s, anthropologists—mainly Americans, of whom Margaret Mead, Ruth Benedict, and Ralph Linton are best known—addressed

Young girl at *moka* exchange festival with head-dress of eagle feathers and pearl shell pendant, Melpa, Papua New Guinea.

these questions directly. A tradition of research in "culture and personality" became centrally established in the discipline, acquiring a special urgency during World War II through attempts to delineate the "national character" of friends and enemies. Because the field was plagued with deep conceptual problems and methodological circularities and paradoxes, it fell into disfavor. Since 1960, research in "culture and personality" has become unfashionable and somewhat disreputable. One unfortunate consequence is that many of the critical conceptual and empirical issues have too often been swept under the rug and ignored. A kind of glib faith in the old methodological dictum of the French sociologist Émile Durkheim that psychological explanations of social facts are always wrong has sustained anthropological analysis for too long. More recently, however, advances in psychological and cognitive research have led to a reexamination of many of these issues (Bock 1988).

In the sections to follow, we will look back at the old conceptual and methodological impasses and paradoxes, look across at the new developments in psychology and biology, and look ahead to emerging better answers to the old questions.

7. CULTURE AND PERSONALITY: BEYOND CULTURAL DETERMINISM

Cultural Determinism: Personality and the Internalization of Culture

The assumption that guided research on culture and personality through the 1930s, 1940s, and 1950s was that adult behavior is determined primarily by culture: an infant growing up in a particular society is molded by the impress of cultural experience. For instance, how often and under what circumstances an infant is fed and bathed, how it is held, how and when it is disciplined, how and when it is weaned and toilet-trained depend on the customs of a particular people. Common patterns of childhood experience create a characteristic personality orientation; and in learning a culture, a child acquires motives and values, a distinctive world view. Personality, in this view, represents the "internalization" of a culture (see Gaines 1992).

In this framework there could be no universal pattern of human nature. There would be no significant variations between individuals created by innate differences in temperament. There could scarcely be a clear dividing line between the culture of a community and the personality of individuals.

Methodologically as well as conceptually, this approach presented impenetrable tangles. If personality were the internalization of culture, and culture were the projection of personality, then one could infer personality orientations from cultural beliefs and practices. If the New Guineans with whom this chapter began fear the dangerous spirits of the forest, and if our psychological theories tell us that such symbolic creations represent particular kinds of fantasies and personality conflicts, then we can, as it were, diagnose their psychology from their myths and rituals. But how, then, is one testing the psychological theory? Can we say we have found a correlation between individual psychology and cultural tradition unless we have some way to assess psychological patterns other than through cultural symbols? Yet—as with the inkblots in which the New Guineans saw bats and birds and spirits—the methods psychologists in Los Angeles or London use to assess personality are dependent on, and expressed through, cultural symbols.

Other conceptual and methodological problems lie in the concept of culture; some of them we have already encountered. If the analyst progressively builds up a composite and idealized model of the culture of the community out of what the individuals do and say, is it legitimate then to ask how this "culture" shapes, or is shaped by, the behavior of individuals? There are some paths out of these tangled thickets; they lead us back to basic assumptions.

Personality, Ethogram, and Individual Variation

A partial untangling of those assumptions has come with the recognition of substantial biological shaping of human behavior. Some of the biological components are characteristic of our species; others, factors of **temperament,** vary widely between individuals. Recognition of the importance of these biological factors erodes the foundations of cultural determinism. On the one hand, an **ethogram** characteristic of our species may underlie and limit cultural diversity; and on the other, innate differences in temperament and variations in individual experience preclude the cultural standardization of personality that had been assumed.

The change in point of view can be illustrated with an anecdote. In the 1930s, Gregory Bateson and Margaret Mead (1942) carried out a well-known photographic study and film on Balinese childhood. How, they asked, did Balinese infants grow up to act like Balinese, with their exquisite sense of restraint, harmony, balance, and grace? Their assumption was that Balinese infants, like infants everywhere, were plastic to whatever impress of cultural experience shaped their early lives. The child who appears most often in the photographic series and film is a young boy named Karba.

How was Karba being shaped into standard Balinese ways of experiencing and acting? Psychologist Daniel Freedman, a specialist on human infancy and childhood, comments that in Bateson and Mead's film,

> One can see [on] film the Balinese boy, Karba, growing from a universal infancy into a withholding, muted, graceful, expressionless child, a typical Balinese. (Freedman 1974:145)

But Freedman notes that he and Gregory Bateson later observed the following:

> [We] recently visited the highland village of Bajung Gede in Bali and met Karba, who is now the village priest. I was struck by the fact that Karba was, even in his forties, a contained and rather expressionless person, . . . in contrast to his more outgoing fellow villagers. . . . Karba, upon whom so great a theoretical point rested ("culture determines personality"), may be a constitutionally reticent individual. (Freedman 1974:145; see Freedman and DeBoer 1979, Wikan 1990)

An interactionist theory that sees personality as the outcome of an interplay between biological potentialities or predispositions and experience opens the way to serious study of individual differences within a cultural tradition. It also opens the way to serious study of possible universal patterns of "human nature" which are differently channeled, expressed, and valued in different cultural traditions. Spiro (1978) argues strongly that universals of human nature, of our emotional and behavioral repertoire, underlie cultural differences. In one place competitiveness and aggressiveness may be valued and culturally reinforced; in another place (such as Bali) they may be disvalued, with emphasis on control of the emotions. Cultural traditions may enjoin the pursuit of different goals in different styles—the free indulgence or repression of sexuality, the dramatic display or suppression of anger. But beneath these codes of cultural expectation, Spiro argues, lie human tendencies to anger, to competition, to positive attachment and solidarity that cultural codes may channel, push beneath the surface, and differentially express—but can never eliminate or ultimately deny (see also Jordan and Schwartz 1990, Spiro 1982).

Such a perspective is useful, but it calls for caution. Once we start talking about a biologically structured "human nature" we can too easily slip into the errors of earlier scholars who talked about "instincts"—against whom the cultural determinists were reacting, in a way that has turned out to be exaggerated. If humans as a species have innate behavioral propensities, they are "open-ended" ones. That is, they are not innately specified programs for behavior, but are propensities that depend on cultural learning for their expression. They represent one side of a pattern, with the other part left blank to be filled in by cultural learning. Every population comprises a reservoir of diversity in temperament. A cultural tradition that positively reinforces and enjoins gentleness and restraint will be congruent with the temperament of some individuals and will be repressive for others; a tradition that values warrior bravado will be congruent with the temperament of some individuals, not of others.

So in their differential valuation and channeling of elements in the human behavioral repertoire, cultural traditions select out and reinforce some of our potentials and restrict others. But all these elements—propensities to compete and cooperate, to be violent or gentle—are open-ended and incomplete unless given cultural meanings and channels of expression. This expression may be overt in some societies, relatively hidden in others. Thus the supposedly gentle Hopi express hostility in ways that usually remain below the surface of outward restraint; it surfaces when witches are driven into the desert. The outwardly gentle Balinese exploded in orgies of murderous violence in 1965 when they killed tens of thousands of their fellows in political purges. The Semai of Malaya, pictured by Dentan (1968) as "the gentle people," committed terrifying acts of cruelty and violence during civil riots in an urban setting. As Spiro observes:

> The Hopi may be no less hostile than the Sioux, despite the fact that the latter exhibit much more social aggression, and . . . their cultural values concerning aggression are . . . different. (Spiro 1978:358)

The errors in the traditional view of culture and personality have been well summarized by Spiro (1978), reflecting about the course of his own intellectual career:

> When anthropologists began to view culture as internalized by social actors, they . . . began to argue that culture was the exclusive . . . content of the . . . organism. . . . Since culture is found in a bewildering variety of local manifestations, anthropologists came to view each culture as a more or less historically unique creation, each producing a culturally unique human nature. (Spiro 1978:353)

The "internalization-of-culture" model had, by simplistic conceptual assumptions, at once ruled out any effective search for a universal and biologically grounded human nature and any effective study of how individuals in a society differ in motives and orientations to the world. In addition, many of the characterizations of people must be regarded as stereotypes rather than as descriptive generalizations.

Personality as a Psychobiological System

We need a way of conceptualizing personality and a way of conceptualizing culture that do not entrap us in circularity. **Personality** is the psychobiological world of an individual viewed as a system. A person's personality includes his or her knowledge (largely unconscious) of the way of life of the community, but it includes more than that. First, an individual has a sense of **identity,** a sense of self in relation to fellow members of the community and their way of life. He or she has motives and goals that are partly distinctive, private fantasies and meanings and memories. An individual also has inclinations to behavior—to be gentle or aggressive, reflective or impulsive, intense or relaxed, introspective or gregarious—that have substantial biological components. This is partly a matter of innate predisposition; but one's temperament is affected by one's state of health and nutrition, by stress or relaxation. "Personality" conventionally refers to a kind of ongoing integration of an individual's psychological world rather than to temporary moods and motives.

Seen this way, personality can be conceptually distinguished from the cultural tradition of the community, even though they are closely interconnected. Both the partial separation and the interconnections emerge if we look at mental illness cross-culturally. Again an anecdote will be illuminating. The late William Caudill told of a visit to a Japanese mental hospital during which he was taken by the senior psychiatrist to see a "severe and incurable catatonic schizophrenic." When they entered, the patient was frozen in a rigid pose familiar to Caudill from observation of Western patients. But when the psychiatrist entered, the patient got up, bowed to him, and then reverted to his previous state.

Here we have an individual whose private construction of reality, a world of fears and conflicts and meanings, can in no sense be equated with "Japanese culture." The patient perhaps became schizophrenic through a complex interplay of genetic predispositions, biochemical reactions to certain kinds of stress that disrupt brain functioning in characteristic ways, and kinds of family experience that created stress and pushed him beyond the breaking point. Yet the patient was culturally Japanese, and in constructing a private world of withdrawal, his building blocks were Japanese concepts and values. Even in his terrible withdrawal from the world, he was interacting with it in a culturally defined role in a culturally appropriate way; withdrawing completely would possibly have been the greater anguish. The patient's personality and "Japanese culture" are conceptually separable. "Japanese culture" has no genetic predispositions, biochemical reactions, or fears. Yet the patient's unique private world was intimately linked to the ideas, values, and behavioral codes that are broadly shared by people in Japanese communities.

One of the difficulties in understanding and comparing the interaction of psychobiological systems across different cultures and societies lies in culturally dependent constructions of what is considered to be "normal" and what is considered to be "abnormal" behavior. Additionally, the concept of the physical processes of the body can differ and that will in turn influence perceptions of normative versus disease processes. For example, Sudir Kakar (1991), in his discussion of whether Freudian concepts of mind and body were expressions of universally constant laws or subject to cultural modifications, relates that the Hindu concept of "subtle body," while analogous in some respects to the Western concept of "psyche," is not considered to be a psychological category in India.

Attempting then to apply diagnostic criteria for specific disease states between cultures that may define such basic concepts as wellness and illness in different ways and in differing contexts becomes difficult at best. The diagnosis of schizophrenia again serves as a model to illustrate this point. It is recognized that there are inconsistencies in applying any kind of standardized criteria in the diagnosis of this complex condition. Blue and Gaines (1992) in noting the difficulties of cross-cultural comparisons of schizophrenia (or any mental illness) report that these studies often assume "universality of syndromes" and that the models from which these emerge develop for the most part from Western concepts of the disorders. They demonstrate the hazards of these assumptions by citing a 1975 study by Jablensky and Sartorius who observed that symptoms associated with schizophrenia, such as some sensory hallucinations, while rarely reported in the European patient populations, appear with some frequency in patients from other countries.

Attempts to standardize diagnostic criteria lead to standardization of treatment methods and goals. Again, the cultural ideas, values, and behavioral codes make standardization virtually impossible. Even the logistical constraints imposed by the lack of trained personnel and facilities to care for the mentally ill in some areas, often itself the result of cultural conditioning, make comparison between cultures difficult.

The interplay between the private and the social, the individual and collective, the biological and the cultural, emerges strikingly in forms of mental illness quite different from those familiar to Western psychiatry. Culture-bound disorders have been described, in which apparently psychotic episodes take on standardized patterns quite different from those of the West and incorporate belief systems that have become part of the cultural tradition. In these disorders, a person may express a psychotic break with everyday reality in a highly conventionalized way.

Helman (1994) sees these disorders as an effective, culturally sanctioned way for individuals to express and resolve both personal and intersocietal conflict. The list of these disorders is extensive and contains such relatively well-known manifestations as a hyper-suggestibility state called *latah*, found primarily in Southeast Asia; *windigo*, described as a cannibalistic compulsion manifest among the Algonkian-speaking cultures of Canada; and *susto*, the belief in loss of soul caused by a sudden, traumatic physical or emotional event, found throughout Latin America. In Western culture it has been suggested that commonly seen behavior patterns and diagnoses such as anorexia nervosa and agoraphobia are examples of culture-bound syndromes (Helman 1994).

Once we conceptualize personality so that it is not simply an internalization of the culture, but also incorporates biological as well as cultural factors, then we can ask new questions about culturally patterned mental illness. Thus Wallace (1960, 1978) and his students (notably Foulks 1972) have asked whether dietary deficiencies or other chemical imbalances—particularly calcium deficiency—could contribute to the stress that triggers windigo. Similarly, culturally patterned aggression, seemingly endemic in some societies, may represent biochemical deficiencies as well as cultural learning. A possible case from the Andes, still only partially documented, is illustrated in Case 1. (This is the first of many case examples that will be scattered through the chapters to follow, numbered so that related cases can be cross-referenced.)

The close interconnection between biological factors and cultural conventions also appears in the cultural meanings and social roles accorded to biologically abnormal individuals.

Even those diagnosed with major mental disorders such as schizophrenia may find productive and crucially important niches as shamans, seers, visionaries (Silverman 1967). Whether the talk of a schizophrenic, seemingly divorced from the realities of the physical world, comes from a disordered mind or a divine source is something our cultures tell us. Whether a schizophrenic ends up as a mental patient or a religious prophet depends on the circumstances of time and place and his or her talents in conveying a unique vision of self and of the world to other people.

One development, then, that allows us to begin sorting out the conceptual and methodological tangles of earlier culture and personality research is the emergence of a serious study of psychobiology, of the interplay between biological processes and psychological development, between innate proclivities—those all humans share, and those unique to individuals—and experience. Personality as the ongoing integration of an individual's orientation to self and the world, the outcome of this interplay between biological and psychological, private and social, is thus distinguishable from the cultural heritages of communities. Another important development in psychology that enables us to sort out the earlier confusions is the emergence of a science of **cognition**—the processes of thinking and knowing, the organization of knowledge and memory.

8. CULTURE AS INTERNAL MODELS OF REALITY

Internal Models of Reality: Perception and Memory

The development of a science of cognition since the decline of studies of culture and personality has revolutionized our understanding of the mind. We have touched on some elements of this emerging understanding in the last two chapters—the way humans construct in their minds the things they see and hear, the nature of concepts such as "chairness" in relation to meaning, and the seemingly universal and partly innate patterns of logic that underlie linguistic diversity.

In the realm of perception, R. L. Gregory has explored the way what we see is constructed out of what we know. We do not "see" wet pavement: rather, what our retinas pass through our optic nerves are patterns which we interpret as reflections; knowing that streets are not made of glass, and that they reflect light only when covered with water, we "see" the wet street and drive accordingly. The knowledge of the world we draw on to construct perceptions of it has been described by Gregory as our "internal models of reality" (1969, 1970).

If we broaden the term a bit, it will include not only our knowledge of wet pavement

and tables and chairs, but our knowledge of events and acts, and what they mean. Thus, our internal models of reality enable us to supply meaning to a quick closing of one eye (a wink) and to a right hand extended to us (something to be grasped and "shaken" in greeting). What we know about the world, these "internal models," are staggeringly complex. What we know that allows us to speak and understand speech is only a small segment of what we know that enables us to participate in our social worlds.

How is that vastly complex "knowledge" organized? Cognitive psychologists have mainly approached the question by looking at *memory*. Experimentally, one can study the processes of acquiring information and retrieving it. Researchers working in the field of artificial intelligence have constructed mathematical representations of memory, including the knowledge of what words mean. Others, seeking to program robotlike automata, have created increasingly complex internal representations of the external environment, and ways of interacting with it. Despite these important advances, our understanding of how internal models of reality are organized is still developing. There are several reasons that this interdisciplinary assault on the mysteries of mind and brain is crucial anthropologically.

Culture as an Internal Model

Recall that in Chapter 2 we looked at culture from two directions. Like physicists who must view light both in terms of particles and in terms of waves—because each vantage point requires and implies the other—anthropologists must view culture both as a cognitive system organized in individual minds and as a system shared within a community, a system of public and collective meanings.

CASE

1

Qolla Aggression

The Qolla of the South American Andes and other Aymara-speaking peoples have been described by many observers for more than a century as highly aggressive, hostile, violent, treacherous—the list of derogatory adjectives goes on. Various observers have attributed the social and psychological turbulence of the Aymara to their harsh high-altitude environment, impoverished existence, and cruel domination by other South American groups and then Spanish and mestizo ruling classes.

Bolton regards these interpretations as only partial: they do not account for individual variations in aggressiveness among the Qolla, for the mechanisms whereby social and psychological stress is translated into aggressive behavior, and for the quite different behavior exhibited by other populations subject to seemingly similar pressures. There must be a missing element and a way to break out of the circularity of explanation.

Bolton hypothesized that high altitude and poor diet place many individuals far below the optimal levels of blood sugar (glucose), though individual biochemistry and diet lead to different degrees of such hypoglycemia. Drawing on extensive neurophysiological and biochemical

evidence, Bolton suggests that moderate hypoglycemia may activate aggressive response patterns in the neural system so that individuals so affected are prone to excitability and violence and are easily triggered by normally innocuous stimuli of everyday social life. Bolton tested blood sugar levels of Qolla men, and independently, had Qolla rate one another on a four-point scale of aggressiveness. In the sample, Bolton's hunch was strikingly supported: of the 13 men ranked by the Qolla as highly aggressive, 11 showed moderate blood sugar deficiency, while 1 was normal and 1 was low. Among the 13 at the low end of the aggressiveness scale, 8 had normal blood sugar, 3 had moderate deficiency, and 2 had a severe deficiency (Bolton had hypothesized that a severe deficiency would lead to low energy and hence perhaps would limit aggressiveness).

The sample is fairly small, the measurements inevitably less than ideal, and biological knowledge of the mechanisms involved still unfortunately somewhat limited. But this example does suggest that there is a physiological link in a complex web of variables—involving diet, altitude, and social stress—that makes the Qolla

Seeing culture as a system of meanings above and beyond individuals allows us to see how reality is socially defined and constructed. As Geertz (1973) expressed it:

> From the point of view of any particular individual, [cultural] symbols are largely given. He finds them already current in the community when he is born, and they remain, with some additions, subtractions, and partial alterations he may or may not have had a hand in, in circulation there after he dies. While he

lives he uses them, or some of them . . . to put a construction upon the events through which he lives.

Looking at culture as a cognitive system, as internal models of reality distributed within the community, enables us to ask about the diversity of individual models and about the politics of knowledge. But at least equally important, it allows us to explore the constraints on cultural knowledge imposed by biology—to ask what kinds of

vulnerable to interpersonal conflict and socially and psychologically disruptive bursts of hostility (Bolton 1973). The probability that such a physiological linkage, involving hypoglycemia, contributes to aggression among individual Qolla has been strengthened by further research. Administering the Sentence Completion Test to Qolla, Bolton (1976) discovered differences in the test responses of individuals with moderate blood sugar deficiency and normal blood sugars. Hypoglycemic individuals gave aggressive responses to the test significantly more often. But it is illustrative of the complex interplay between physiological and cultural factors that the aggressive responses were elicited most often when the sentences dealt with special areas in which aggression is focused in Qolla society: land, women, authority figures, male relatives, and money. (See Bolton 1976, 1978.)

Case Update

The Qolla (or Colla) are part of the Aymara, a South American indigenous population that traditionally lived in the Lake Titicaca region of Peru and Bolivia. Today, in addition to these areas, they can also be found in Argentina.

Throughout the 1970s, Ralph Bolton continued the investigation of his hypothesis that there is a causal link between chronic hypoglycemia and aggressive behavior. Recent (1994–1995) studies of the behavior of imprisoned violent offenders in Finland has also postulated a correlation between hypoglycemia and irritable, impulsive, and aggressive behavior.

For More Information

Bolton, R. 1976. Hostility in Fantasy: A Further Test of the Hypoglycemic-Aggression Hypothesis. *Journal of Aggressive Behavior* 2(4): 257–274.

Sallnow, M. J. 1989. Cooperation and Contradiction: The Dialectics of Everyday Practice. *Dialectical Anthropology* 14(4): 241–257.

Virkkunen, M., E. Kallio, R. Rawlings, R. Tokola, R. E. Poland, A. Guidotti, C. Nemeroff, G. Bissetti, K. Kalogeras, S. L. Karonen, and M. Linnoila. 1994. Personality Profiles and State Aggressiveness in Finnish Alcoholic, Violent Offenders, Fire Setters, and Healthy Volunteers. *Archives of General Psychiatry* 51(1): 28–33.

internal models of reality can be learned and used by animals like us.

Culture as an internal model of reality does not consist of everything an individual "knows" about the world (Keesing 1974). What I know about the most comfortable chair in the living room, the peculiarities of Uncle Jake, and the dietary preferences of my dog are part of my model of reality, perhaps, but they are hardly part of my culture. Here again we get a dividing line between the realm of "personality," in the sense of

my psychological integration and orientation to the world as a unique individual and biological organism, and that segment of my model of reality which it is useful to call my version of the culture. The latter consists of my theory about meanings and codes for behavior that others in the community are using.

Thus, when one learns what clothes to wear, or where and how to shake hands, it is with reference to a code others are presumed to be following. When one learns what a

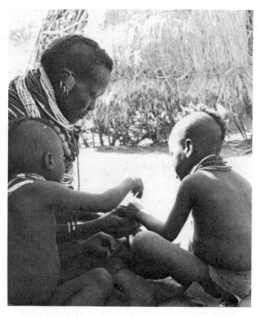

Learning a culture: A Turkana (Kenya) mother instructs her children.

word means, it is with reference to the way others are presumed to be using and understanding it. One's knowledge of one's culture comprises one's model of this code being used in one's community. Whereas one's memory consists of knowledge of the particular, of experiences and events, cultural knowledge is generalized. It consists of principles and meanings and "rules" built up as theories from particular experiences. Taking this vantage point on cultural meanings—which does not preclude, and indeed requires that we take Geertz's vantage point as well—we can ask about how cultural theories of the world are learned, how they are organized, and how widely they vary from one society to the next.

The Acquisition of Internal Models

To ask how culture as a cognitive model is built up by a child brings us back to the questions we raised at the end of the last chapter with regard to language. To what degree an infant is preprogrammed with the underlying logics and organizing structures of language remains an open question. Some who challenge Chomsky's view of the language faculty as resting heavily on innate structures do so from the direction of Piaget—denying that a child has *any* significant preprogramming of ways to think, learn, and reason. Others would challenge the Chomskyan view as too narrow, and see the acquisition of language as an application of more general learning strategies, logics, and theory-building capacities the child brings to other tasks as well. In other words, one can deny that there are innate mental faculties, or one can deny that they are specific to the realm of language.

It seems increasingly likely that innate capacities to represent concepts, to reason, to perceive logical relationships *do* make possible the dramatic rapid acquisition of linguistic competence—but that they are less specialized, less specifically linguistic, more generalized and abstract than Chomsky inferred. They are brought to bear both in learning language and in acquiring other elements of cultural knowledge. But how detailed they are, and how they operate in the building up of internal models of reality, remain mysterious.

Although an infant is, once the circuitry of the brain is fully formed, a formidable theory-builder, the task of progressively creating the vastly complex internal models of reality needed to operate in society is awesome. Undoubtedly, this entails progressive stages of reformulation, transformation, and reintegration. This process depends apparently on the ability to generalize from the particular, to reason abstractly and formulate abstract concepts, to perceive logical connections. Some of these capacities humans share with other mammals; some they share with their closest relatives, chimps and gorillas; and some are uniquely human.

To what extent, and in what ways, the internal models of reality humans acquire are structured by the physical organization of our brains is a question still being investigated. If anthropologists were content to catalogue the customs of other peoples these questions might not matter. But anthropologists inevitably try to do more: to characterize the world view or ways of thinking of other peoples, to assess the diversity of cultures. And when they enter this realm, even when they write in terms of culture as transcending individuals, in terms of shared meanings and symbolic systems, their footing becomes precarious.

Cognitive Systems and Cultural Variability

These questions of how a child builds up an internal model of reality are crucial in assessing cultural diversity. Are all cultural traditions, viewed as models of reality built up within populations over time (and learned by each child born into the society), the same in basic structure? Are ways of experiencing time, space, and perhaps causality substantially determined by our evolutionary heritage? Cultural traditions may differ in their idioms and metaphors for talking about time, space, and causality; but our experience of them may be fundamentally structured by our perceptual-conceptual equipment. These are among the most crucial questions addressed by anthropology. But the evidence anthropologists gather is by its nature open to interpretation in either direction. That is, it can be interpreted as indicating that the thought worlds of different peoples are radically diverse and culturally shaped, or as indicating that these experiential worlds are fundamentally the same despite different cultural idioms for talking about

the same experiences. Anthropologists, although they tend to have heated opinions in these matters, have no way of knowing the right answers.

There are growing reasons to think that cultural logics and world views are much less diverse than they once seemed. Some of the evidence comes from linguistics, where underlying universal logics increasingly emerge. Some come from studies of the behavioral repertoires and cognitive potential of our primate relatives. Some anthropologists have argued, for example, that the ability to recognize two-dimensional images as pictures of people and objects is a special Western cultural skill. Some peoples in New Guinea seemed unable to recognize the images in pictures when these were first shown to them. Later they learned how to do this, showing that the capacity to recognize two-dimensional representations of objects is clearly part of our perceptual equipment, not a cultural peculiarity.

The accumulating evidence seems now to point to a kind of everyday "reality" orientation, a sense of space and time and causality, which is essentially biologically structured, a product of mammalian and primate evolution, and common to humans everywhere. Our linguistic faculties, a product of recent evolution, overlie these capacities and enable us—in our various ways—to talk about them.

Cultural Development of Cognitive Capacities

To this everyday "reality" orientation, various cultural traditions have added elaborations: mystical moods and fantasy worlds, vision quests and mythic journeys, possession states and religious frenzies. The "dreamtime" rites of Australian Aborigines, the trances of Bali, the voodoo seances of Haiti, the hallucinogen-induced visions of Mesoamerica or Amazonia, are expressions of panhuman capacities for altered-heightened states of consciousness. These may represent the development and cultural valuation of mental faculties—for mystical, holistic thought—which are undeveloped and disvalued in the Western rational tradition. Many may be expressions of faculties centered in the brain, complementary to the faculties of language and analytic logic. But this is not to say that some people walk around all day in a state of mystical oneness with the cosmos. When they hunt, cook dinner, and scratch their rear ends they are being as rational and pragmatic as humans everywhere are most of the time.

The special cultural development of mental capacities emerges in other realms of mind as well. Since the emergence of mass literacy, humans have become dismally poor at tasks of memory that were commonplace for their ancestors. Special skills of visual perception, direction-finding, problem-solving, or navigation may be fostered by training and experience, culturally reinforced. Thus Micronesian seafarers who navigate by stars and tides, or African or Australian hunters tracking game, or Polynesians reciting vastly long genealogies are all using skills sharpened in particular cultural traditions.

These skills are not shared equally by all: every society has its experts and its clods, whatever the skill in question. Differences in cognitive style have been extensively studied cross-culturally in recent years—though as with tests of personality, difficulties of rapport and cultural bias in the test instruments make findings difficult to interpret (see Cole and Scribner 1974).

At this stage, having looked at cultures as systems of knowledge, as internal models of reality, we need to balance this emphasis on cognition by looking at the other side of personality, the realm of emotions.

9. THE PSYCHODYNAMICS OF PERSONALITY IN EVOLUTIONARY PERSPECTIVE

The emotional side of human mental life, as contrasted with the cognitive side, has been conventionally referred to by the term **psychodynamics.** The image here is of the emotions as a driving force in behavior, as providing the motive power behind fantasy and action. Here we will look at older theories of psychodynamics in the light of new explorations of mind and biological heritage.

Psychoanalytic Theory and Culture

The most influential stream of thought in modern personality research has been psychoanalytic theory—the work of Freud and his students and successors. Since the first two decades of this century anthropologists have had a continuing dialogue with psychoanalysts, through such figures as Kroeber, Linton, Mead, Kluckhohn, LaBarre, Leach, and Fortes. The anthropological side of these dialogues has ranged from sympathetic borrowing to critical skepticism. A few scholars whose primary training or commitment was in psychoanalysis, notably Roheim, Kardiner, and Erikson, have worked directly with anthropological materials.

One element in this dialogue has been to ask whether psychoanalytic theories of the unconscious could illuminate custom, belief, and behavior in non-Western societies. Might the supernatural spirits of a people represent projections of parental figures, hence of the conflicts of primary experi-

A Micronesian master navigator teaches apprentices the star compass with pebbles, on Puluwat, Central Caroline Islands.

ence? Such questions have been a continuing theme in psychoanalytically oriented anthropology.

Another element has been the effort to broaden psychoanalytic theory, rendering it less culture-bound. Could the repression of overt sexuality by the Viennese patients he treated have misled Freud into overly limited models of the unconscious? Is the Oedipus complex really universal in human experience? Does the hostility of father and infant son, and rivalry over the mother's sexuality which Freud viewed as central in human psychology everywhere, take the same form, and have the same importance, where—as in the Trobriand Islands—a boy's maternal uncle, not his father, is the stern disciplinarian? (See Obeyesekere 1984, Spiro 1982.)

Anthropological interest in psychoanalysis has been limited, especially in British social anthropology, by a relatively narrow concern with social relations and how societies worked. And after a burst of interest in "depth" psychology in American culture and personality research, there was widespread disillusionment with the apparent chicken-or-egg circularities of interpretation and the lack of firm evidence on the processes of mind. A very large proportion of modern anthropologists are relatively untrained in, skeptical about, and generally uninterested in psychoanalysis and other related theories of personality.

Some scholars, such as George Devereux (1978) and Weston LaBarre (1978), stuck to their psychoanalytic orientations through the years; and they have been joined by

Micronesian navigators use cognitive skills fostered by study of the stars and detailed knowledge and experience of currents, winds, and tiny islands.

others who have been drawn into psychoanalytic theory after more conventional social anthropological training (see Hook 1979, Spindler 1978). There are now signs of a resurgence in the continuous but long-attenuated stream of psychoanalytic anthropology; and there are strong signs that this resurgence will now yield deeper insights than have yet been possible.

Evolutionary Perspectives on the Unconscious Mind

It would be premature even to sketch the shape of a more powerful and anthropologically useful theory of the unconscious mind. However, we can at least examine why deepened understanding is becoming possible, and can glimpse some partial outlines of an emerging theory.

A theory of the human unconscious and its relationship to the cultural products of mind can now become biologically grounded in a way that has never before been possible. It is not that Freud was uninterested in biology; he was first a neurophysiologist and always an explorer of the biological roots of human mental life. But unfortunately, in Freud's day almost nothing was known about human evolution, about the evolution of behavior, about the behavior of primates and other mammals in natural settings, and about the brain. Freudian theory, seeking to be a biological theory of the mind, had to be created virtually in a biological vacuum.

Freud, in the absence of an adequate knowledge of animal behavior and its evolution, drew on inference and on clinical data: he saw animals as driven by biological urges to eat and to reproduce, and thus to the killing and combat of hunting and mating. Since humans are animals, such biological urges must lie deep in the brain and be overlain by the mechanisms of the conscious mind. Cultural learning must provide the controls whereby animal nature is kept within bounds and bonds, for without cultural controls, our drives of sex, hunger, and aggression would break loose and ordered social life would be impossible. But Freud believed that our true animal nature and the wellsprings of our psychic and hence physical energy lie beneath these conscious overlays.

Human mental life is, Freud thought, a continuing dynamic of conflict and control, of channeled expression, redirection, and the repression of basic instinctual urges and energies; cultural control and hence social life exacts a severe cost in anxiety, conflict, and often neurosis. The normal processes of the psyche—of dreams and other fantasy, of symbolizing, of everyday social interaction—express the blockage, redirection, and disguised expression of the energies of our natural life forces. Freud asserted that, since we are unable, due to cultural convention, to deal directly and consciously with the sexual and aggressive drives so central in the unconscious mind, we repress, we sublimate, we disguise in symbols, we deny, we redirect. Though the costs of psychic health are severe and are manifest in neurosis or at worst in psychosis, these processes of fantasy and repression also underlie the cultural creations of art and religion.

This seems now not to be all wrong, but to be partly wrong. In the light of modern ethology, it substantially distorts our animal nature. First, all mammals are, in varying degree, social animals. They are biologically programmed not simply to satisfy individual urges, but to live in groups. Behavior patterns that are transmitted biologically and shaped by evolution are orchestrated so as to produce group behaviors that are adaptive.

The model of conscious mind superimposed on primal nature is partly supported by modern knowledge of the brain in evolutionary perspective, but it is too simple. The evolutionarily ancient limbic system of the brain is geared to survival and reproduction, and it is the neural source of surges of rage and other emotions. In the course of mammalian evolution, it has not been superseded and eliminated, but with the development of the mammalian neocortex, it has been connected into a more complicated system where the old limbic system continues to serve the basic demands of survival (McLean 1964, 1968, 1969, 1970).

In mammalian and hominid evolution, limbic system and neocortex have been evolving together as a system—a system that must be adaptive if species are to survive. Humans, in evolving massive cortical capacities for problem-solving and symbolic elaboration, have also evolved a complex circuitry that connects with older parts of the brain. Cortical control of limbic processes is a product of evolution, not a cultural imposition on our biological nature (see Damasio 1994).

Thus the modern neurosciences point to serious inadequacies in Freudian and other psychoanalytic conceptions of consciousness and unconscious. Mind and brain are staggeringly complex. No dichotomy of the Freudian sort between unconscious and conscious, or between primary and secondary process, or any other *stratigraphic* theory of mind that sees "levels" as deeper and shallower, can be adequate. The structures of the brain whereby left and right cerebral hemispheres are complementary—the left normally performing predominantly linguistic, logical, and sequential operations and the right performing primarily holistic, integrative operations—render any stratigraphic conception of mind inadequate. So too do the results of brain damage, which point to different brain locations and different processing and organization of the programs for language, for dealing with the natural environment, and for dealing with the social environment.

For example, some brain-damaged patients are severely handicapped in their social relations due to an inability to "read" the responses and moods of others, yet can read newspapers or perform manual operations unimpaired; in other cases patients' social relations are unimpaired but their ability to manipulate the physical environment is severely impaired by brain damage. In one celebrated case, a Soviet composer totally lost the powers of language due to massive brain damage, but continued to compose music.

Conscious and unconscious, therefore, must be viewed as an extreme over simplification of a vastly complex system science is only beginning to understand.

Psychological Development and Social Relationships

Psychoanalytic theory viewed the **Oedipus complex,** the sexual attachment between mother and son, with father as rival and authority figure, as a crucial phase in the development of adult personality. (The female mirror image, the **Electra complex,** whereby a girl develops a sexual attachment to her father, has received less attention; see Chodorow 1979, Mitchell 1974, Strouse 1974 for reflections on the sex biases of psychoanalytic theory.)

In the light of modern behavior studies of humans and their closest animal relatives, this emphasis takes on a new significance. The work of John Bowlby and his colleagues (Bowlby 1969) indicates that long before Oedipus and Electra complexes develop, an infant (of either sex) forms a deep psychological bond with the mother (or a substitute caretaker). The key psychoattachment system, for the infant, comes into operation between the ages of 3 and 7 months. This *primary bond,* most basic and formatively crucial of the human psychoattachments, colors emotional attachments in later life. Oedipus and Electra complexes are developments out of this earlier (and nonsexual) bond. Both in its emphasis on the subsequent "sexualized" phases of parent-child psychoattachment and its relatively undeveloped treatment of the other psychoattachment systems (peer bonding, pair bonding), psychoanalytic theory is too narrow in its view of psychosocial development. The findings of ethology demand that we see our animal nature as fundamentally oriented to living in social groups, and

that we see human psychoattachment systems as adaptations to and bases of life in groups, and to the prolonged dependence that prolonged maturation and culture-learning require.

The diverse modes of family organization and custom in different times and places provide varied settings in which human proclivities and potentials, partly common to our species and partly unique to individuals, are expressed and developed. And they also provide, then, laboratories for theoretical exploration.

Cultural Expression of Psychobiological Themes

The broadened view anthropologists get of the family situation in comparative perspective has led Fortes (1974), Devereux (1953), and others to see the threat and ambivalence of parent-child relations from the standpoint of the parents as well as the children. Humans, foreseeing their own demise, can hardly avoid seeing in their children their eventual successors, survivors, and replacements. Culturally patterned ambivalence and tension is a common theme (Fortes 1974). Here the evidence from anthropology is particularly vivid: conflicts and emotional dramas that are probably universal in human experience, yet in our society may be openly acted out only by psychiatric patients, may in other societies become a focus of ritual practice and cultural convention. As Fortes (1974:93) observed, "What may appear as idiosyncratic or even bizarre individual responses . . . in one culture will be embodied in public and normal custom in some other culture."

Consider the example in Case 2. Some elements in the ritual symbolism of the Tallensi and other groups are somewhat transparent—the phallic bow, explicitly a

The First-Born Among the Tallensi

Among the Tallensi, a people of Ghana, descent and inheritance pass from father to son. The Tallensi strikingly dramatize and ritualize the tensions between parents and the children who will replace them. The focus of customary observance is the first-born son, who culturally bears the brunt of ambivalence of a father toward being supplanted by his sons.

It is important, first, that the Tallensi marry and have children—in fact, a man must have a son if he is to attain fulfillment psychologically and culturally. Children are desired and sought; without a male heir one cannot become an ancestor and hence be assured of a permanent place in the Tallensi cosmos.

Tallensi consider the crowning glory, indeed the only worthwhile object of life, to be assurance of leaving descendants, ideally in the male line. . . . To have lived successfully one must die with the hope of achieving ancestorhood and that is possible only if one leaves male descendants. (Fortes 1974:84)

But it is the first-born son, and secondarily the first-born daughter, whose birth signals the end of the uphill path of a person's life and the beginning of the downhill path leading to senility and death (the Tallensi are not really anxious to hurry into ancestorhood). From the age of 5 or 6, the first-born son may not eat from the same dish as his father, may not wear his father's cap or tunic, carry his quiver, or use his bow; and he may not look into his father's granary. After the first-born son reaches adolescence, he and his father may not meet in the entrance to the house compound. Parallel taboos restrict the relations of a first-born daughter with her mother, with the mother's storage pot being forbidden to the daughter.

When the parents die, the replacement by the first-born children is ritually dramatized. First-born son and first-born daughter take the lead in

A first-born Tallensi son is ritually shown the inside of his father's granary for the first time as part of the funeral ceremony.

the mortuary rites: the son puts on his dead father's cap and tunic. An elder holding the dead man's bow leads the son to the forbidden granary and guides him inside. And only when his father is dead does the son assume full ritual maturity and make sacrifices—especially to his dead father, as mediator between those still living and more remote ancestors.

Case Update

Today, the Tallensi people continue their primarily agrarian life in northern Ghana on the coast of West Africa. Meyer Fortes's work with the Tallensi from the 1940s through the 1970s is a classic anthropological study and continues to provide insight into a way of life that still endures in many parts of the world.

Some Suggested Readings

Fortes, M. 1987. In J. R. Goody, ed., *Religion, Morality, and the Person.* Cambridge: Cambridge University Press.

Hart, K. 1971. Migration and Tribal Identity Among the Frafras of Ghana. *Journal of Asian and African Studies* 6(1): 21–36.

cultural symbol of manhood, the granary as repository of seed and fertility. But more important are the ways in which the taboos and rites dramatize changes of status built into the human life cycle and give them cultural expression (the transition to the status of parenthood, the founding of a sibling group in which the oldest assume responsibility); and even more important are the ways in which these rites and restrictions express psychological ambivalence and hostility along socially channeled paths.

All parents in all societies are ambivalent toward the children that drain their energies and will eventually replace them; inevitably they feel hostility and resentment as well as love and attachment. In all societies, these negative feelings must be transcended: a society where parents were encouraged to kill or desert their children (except under the very special exigencies of culturally enjoined infanticide) or simply not to have any could hardly be well equipped for long-term survival. But the ambivalence can be dramatized in ritual avoidance and **taboo,** and thus to some extent stripped of guilt and relieved of tension. Among the Tallensi, the making of first-born son and daughter so directly into symbolic replacements focuses and at the same time defuses the hostility of parents and the thwarted rivalry (for example, the Oedipal conflict) of children. The cultural creation of ancestors at the same time denies the finality of death and the loss of loved ones.

Private Symbols, Public Symbols

If religious institutions or rites may in part be expressions of psychological conflicts, is it possible that deities or other supernaturals are psychological projections? Is a punishing deity a psychological projection of a disciplining father? The psychoanalyst Abram Kardiner, the psychoanalytic anthropologist Geza Roheim, and others have long argued that supernaturals are indeed creations of projection. Relations with supernaturals in propiation or expiation reenact or express conflicts or guilt toward parental figures. Most anthropologists would reject such interpretations. The private and personal fantasy of an individual may be subject to interpretation in terms of individual psychological experience, many would say, but beliefs and rites that are shared and public cannot be interpreted in terms of the individual psyche. Many would cite Émile Durkheim's dictum that shared patterns of culture—"collective representations"—cannot be accounted for through the psychology of individuals. The converse has been forcefully argued by LaBarre (1970), Devereux (1975), and others. Belief systems, bodies of myth, and ritual sequences all have histories in time and space. The illusion that they do not derives from the anthropological study of societies for which there are no historical records. A particular myth or ritual procedure has a history that can have begun only through private ideas that were communicated. Each modification in retelling (or borrowing) of a myth or alteration of a rite is similarly the product of individual minds.

To become shared and hence part of the culture, a religious or ritual element must be socially communicated and must be accepted by others. These characteristics, LaBarre and Devereux argue, distinguish a private fantasy that serves only the private psychological needs of its creator from the private fantasy that strikes a responsive chord in others, and draws on psychological experience shared with others as well as on a cultural repertorie of symbolic elements.

The process whereby one person's dream becomes a society's myth, and one persons' private compulsion becomes a society's ritual, is little understood. A culture apparently includes a body of symbolic material out of which myths and rites are constructed and modified. The creation or modification of rites or myths may be more culturally channeled and formally structured than many of the creations of private fantasy; but they are ultimately created or modified by individual minds and become shared or borrowed from the neighbors only if they are psychologically meaningful to other people (Kracke 1978).

What about the stock of symbols? Freud's work suggests universal themes in symbolism, and anthropologists of both Freudian and non-Freudian bent have similarly noted recurrent themes. But the contrast between scholars who interpret these in terms of individual psychodynamics and those who (following Durkheim) interpret them as collective representations is wide.

Do we have to choose between psychoanalytic interpretations of cultural symbols and interpretations that see collective and social meanings? Victor Turner's (1978) essay on a social anthropologist's encounter with Freudian psychology suggests an answer to which we will return in a later chapter. We cannot simplistically equate "intrapsychic" (i.e., private) symbols with "interpsychic" (i.e., public) symbols.

> Cultural symbols, . . . transmitted from generation to generation by precept, teaching, and example, [are] not—at least for all practical purposes—psychogenic in origin. (Turner 1978:573)

But at the same time, cultural symbols cover a spectrum of reference, have different senses or meanings, that extend from social and collective ones to private and physical ones. Thus in the course of a single ritual the Ndembu *mudyi* tree (which exudes a milky white sap) "stands for" a whole range of referents:

> breasts, breast milk, the mother-child relationship, the novice's [lineage], matriliny [descent in the female line], womanhood in general, married womanhood, childbearing, and even . . . Ndembuhood. (Turner 1978:577; also see Case 51, Chapter 15)

Whereas psychoanalytic theory would see physical meanings, especially sexual ones, as primary in ritual, myth and art, the social meanings may be the more salient. Physical sex or the genitals may serve as symbols of the creative forces of the universe, as in Hindu symbology. What is important is the connection between physical meanings related to primary experience and social and religious meanings. Collective, cultural symbols may "work" precisely because they relate social meanings to individual psychodynamics. If so, the apparent conflict between psychoanalytic theories of how symbols are created and used and social anthropologists' theories of cultural meanings may be an artifact of faulty conceptualization and theoretical overstatement. One of the many important challenges of the anthropological frontier is to find ways to conceptualize and explore the interconnection between individual experience and collective meanings that do not force us to try—as both psychoanalysts and social theorists have—to reduce one to the other. A biologically sophisticated conceptualization of the multiple modes of unconsciousness, and the depths of motivation, will be an important element in a more powerful understanding of the symbolic process (see Obeyesekere 1984).

In looking at culture and society, at language, and at personality, we have acquired the refined conceptual equipment we need to carry further our exploration of human ways, equipped now to think more precisely and analytically about the organization of culture and society, and how sociocultural systems change.

SUMMARY

This chapter looked more closely at how culture is shaped by the behavior of individuals who have widely ranging temperaments and definite senses of unique identities.

What shapes a particular personality within a culture is determined by multiple factors. Cultural traditions select from a wide range of human potentialities and encourage or discourage particular ways of self-expression, such as gentleness or violence, according to contexts. It is possible that certain propensities, such as an inclination toward aggressive behavior, may be triggered by ecological factors (high altitude and poor diet, as Ralph Bolton suggested for the Qolla people). But these tendencies are always modulated culturally through perception and knowledge. Cognitive studies have improved our understanding of how memory, for example, is acquired and used by individuals and is at the same time shared communally. Culture can therefore be looked at as a cognitive system of internalized models of reality distributed within a community. By examining the processes by which a person organizes knowledge and memory we can better understand how personalities develop within a cultural milieu.

Cross-cultural evidence also suggests that world views are not as diverse as the "mosaic" view of cultures would suggest.

Finally, we need to balance the study of cognition with the study of emotions. Psychoanalytic theory can contribute here, but there are problems with its universal applicability. Studies of linkages within the brain can help us define more clearly the interplay between cognition and emotion in a way that transcends the Freudian picture of the unconscious and the conscious. The case study of the Tallensi people of Ghana shows that there is tension between father and eldest son, because in their family structure it is this son who succeeds to his father's place in the household when the father dies. The son must observe elaborate taboos that both express and obviate this tension. Cultural symbols are used in this process to link social meanings and individual psychodynamics.

SUGGESTIONS FOR FURTHER READING

SECTIONS 7, 8, 9

Barnouw, V. 1973. *Culture and Personality*, rev. ed. Homewood, Ill: Dorsey Press.

Bourguignon, E. 1979. *Psychological Anthropology: An Introduction to Human Nature and Cultural Difference.* New York: Holt, Rinehart and Winston.

Cole, M., and S. Scribner. 1974. *Culture and Thought: A Psychological Introduction.* New York: John Wiley & Sons, Inc.

Edgerton, R. B. 1971. *The Individual in Cultural Adaptation: A Study of Four East African Peoples.* Berkeley: University of California Press.

Hook, R. H., ed. 1979. *Fantasy and Symbol: Studies in Anthropological Interpretation.* New York: Academic Press, Inc.

Hsu, F. L. K., ed. 1972. *Psychological Anthropology,* 2nd ed. Cambridge, Mass: Schenkman Publishing Company.

Hunt, R., ed. 1967. *Personalities and Cultures.* Garden City, N.Y.: Natural History Press.

Lebra, W. P., ed. 1976. *Culture-Bound Syndromes, Ethnopsychiatry and Alternate Therapies.* Honolulu: University of Hawaii Press.

Le Vine, R. A. 1973. *Culture, Behavior, and Personality.* Chicago: Aldine Publishing Co.

————, ed. 1974. *Culture and Personality: Contemporary Readings.* Chicago: Aldine Publishing Co.

Spindler, G. D., ed. 1978. *The Making of Psychological Anthropology.* Berkeley: University of California Press.

Wallace, A. F. C. 1970. *Culture and Personality,* 2nd ed. New York: Random House, Inc.

Anthropologists have created an image of the tribal* world which existed at the time of European intrusion as a kind of mosaic of peoples, each with a distinctive culture. Each culture represents a separate instance of human possibility, a different way of being human. This image has been profoundly influential in the social sciences and in shaping popular views of cultural variation. In anthropology itself, it has been complemented by alternative views of societies in evolutionary perspective, as representing successive stages in the emergence of complex societies: from hunter-gatherers to horticulturalists, to chiefdoms, and, eventually, to states.

In Chapter 5, I will argue that this world as often depicted anthropologically never existed. Taking a regional and systemic point of view, I will argue that the societies described by anthropologists and more complex societies (including states) coexisted and evolved together. "Primitive" cultures do not represent earlier or simpler stages; most ways of life have emerged only in the last 3,000 years. Many of them had existed for only a few centuries when Europeans arrived. Rather than being separate, isolated "pieces," most were parts of complex regional systems. The "ethnographic present," considered to be the supposed baseline point of first European contact, before which societies were in pristine isolation, is a myth as well as a simplification.

Part 2

Tribal Peoples: Toward a Systemic View

*Here, recall that I am using *tribal* in a broad and loose sense, as an alternative to *primitive*. In this usage "tribal" peoples include hunter-gatherers as well as peoples who produce food using relatively simple technologies. In some places, where this is quite clear from context, I shall use *tribal* in a narrowed sense to include these tribal food-producers, but contrast them with hunter-gatherers (this usage is a rather more conventional one anthropologically; but so far no adequate alternative to the pejorative *primitive* has emerged). Recall that neither the broad and loose nor the somewhat narrowed sense of *tribal* implies that the societies involved can properly be called "tribes" (see § 11; also see the discussion of this term in the Introduction to this revised edition).

The Tribal World as Mosaic, as Ladder, and as System

In this brief chapter, we will take a closer look at the stereotypic views of the tribal world that have been created by anthropology—and then will point to the kind of corrective picture, of this world as a system, that is emerging. Then, in Chapter 6, we will look more closely at the ecological settings of modern hunter-gatherers, tribal horticulturalists, and pastoralists. In doing so, the systemic view of the world prior to European expansion will be reinforced: peoples and their cultures lived in environments that were not isolated and self-contained, but were parts of regional systems that (in most parts of the world) included other societies, often very different in scale, complexity, and economy.

10. MOSAIC AND LADDER STEREOTYPES

The Mosaic Stereotype

Two ways of depicting tribal peoples have been prominent in the anthropology of the last 60 years. I will label the first as a "mosaic" view. In this view, small-scale tribal societies (mainly in the tropical zone of the world—in Africa, Southeast Asia, Oceania, and South America—and in its Arctic margins) constitute a kind of mosaic of cultures. Each culture is seen as a separate and unique experiment in human possibility—as if each were a differently colored, separate piece in a mosaic of human diversity, to be studied, and valued, in its own right.

In this view, developed in the United States by students of Franz Boas, and popularized by scholars such as Margaret Mead and Ruth Benedict, one studied tribal cultures to see the widest reaches of human possibility, to subject some proposed generalization about human behavior to the ultimate test. Thus one studied adolescence in Samoa or sex roles in New Guinea using these societies as natural laboratories for studying the cultural natures possible for humans. In the British tradition, Malinowski's studies of the Trobriand Islanders of the Southwest Pacific similarly used the tribal world as a laboratory for studying cultural variations; and the pioneers of social anthropology in Africa made similar assumptions, although they saw the tribal world as a laboratory for comparative study of kinship and political institutions.

Men wearing brown cassowary feather head-dresses receive sticks of sugar cane as a promise of pork to be given later, Pangia, Papua New Guinea.

The mosaic view taken in both the American and the British approaches was a reaction against nineteenth-century speculation in which armchair scholars drew on reports of missionaries and explorers to construct schemes abut how civilization emerged from the ancient depths of savagery and barbarism. But the mosaic view has been challenged by the return of such evolutionary schemes in more sophisticated form (and supported by more substantial evidence). In such **neoevolutionary** approaches, hunting and gathering people are viewed as the first rung on a ladder of societal scale and complexity.

The Ladder Stereotype

The "ladder" view sets out a series of developmental stages or levels, characterized by different subsistence economies and accompanying levels of sociopolitical integration. (Depending on the theoretical predilection of a particular author, the economic or the sociopolitical side may be emphasized; and since there are many alternative depictions of the ladder, we will have to make do with a quite generalized set of levels.)

The band organization of hunting and gathering peoples is a starting point for virtually all modern ladder schemes. The scattered resource base and necessary mobility of hunter-gatherers militates against sedentary residence and large residence groups; the flexibility of band organization is taken to be an adaptive response to these constraints.

With horticulture and neolithic stone technology, sedentary residence and larger groups become feasible. But society remains classless, full-time specialization is absent or rare, and the accumulation and redistribution of surplus production is limited. Concomitantly, there is no strongly hierarchical political organization, there are no true chiefs, no polity. "A society" comprises a congeries of separate local, autonomous sociopolitical units, united by a common language and culture. The societies of Melanesia, the Philippines and other parts of Southeast Asia, much of tropical South America, and parts of tropical Africa fall into this "level."

In some parts of the world, a higher development of political stratification and intensification of production are represented in "chiefdoms"—in Polynesia, parts of Africa, parts of Southeast Asia. Here social classes or incipient social classes and societywide political structures begin to emerge.

A kind of sideways step of the ladder is represented by pastoral societies, depicted as limited by sharp ecological constraints imposed by animal husbandry, to which flexible and characteristically relatively egalitarian modes of political organization are adaptive solutions. From the level or rung of chiefdoms, a further step up the ladder of evolutionary scale and complexity is the emergence of state societies. Thus, the factors that engen-

dered the rise of early states in some parts of the ancient world, and the constraints that precluded the emergence of states in others (e.g., Polynesia), have been much debated.

"Ladder" theories do not in fact assume that each particular society has a history of moving upwards from one rung to the next—that a particular state emerged out of a particular chiefdom, which in turn had developed out of a "tribe." But they do, by implication if not intention, imply that these have been successive developments in the broad sweep of societal development. And they do assume or imply that successive developments in the technology of production (which in some sense have been worldwide and cumulative) have been associated with the successive emergence of more complex modes of sociopolitical organization.

"Ladder" theories predispose us to look at the world of the "ethnographic present," the world described by explorers and missionaries and ethnographers, in a particular way. First, we are led to look at modern hunter-gatherers or horticultural peoples as sources of evidence about ancient stages in societal evolution. Second, we are led to see different parts of the world as having gone more or less far along a sequence of transformations. Thus Melanesians were further along in this progression than Australian Aborigines, but not as far as Polynesians. When we find hunters and gatherers surviving (as in parts of mainland and island Southeast Asia) surrounded by horticulturalists, we are led to view them as survivors from an ancient past, living in marginal isolation.

Defects in Mosaic and Ladder Stereotypes

The crucial point from which we must proceed to understand the flaws in both the mosaic and the ladder views is chronological. Let us take as our time frame the 3,000 or 4,000 years prior to the European "age of discovery" when (beginning around 1500) the Americas, Africa, Asia, and the Pacific were transformed by invasion.

In this time period the ancient states crystallized in the Middle East, in India and China, and in Mesoamerica—and other states derivative from them emerged in Africa, Southeast Asia, Asia, and the Americas. And it is in this period that most of the societies of sub-Saharan Africa, Southeast Asia, and the Pacific diversified. Much of sub-Saharan Africa was only sparsely occupied by hunters and gatherers before about the beginning of the Christian era; most of the Pacific (except for the Sahul continent, including what are now Australia and New Guinea) was not inhabited by humans until, in the last 3,000 to 4,000 years, they were progressively settled. Parts of Polynesia were settled only within the last thousand years. The point is that the ancestors of the hunting and gathering peoples of whom we have direct ethnographic evidence, the peoples of New Guinea or Borneo or central Africa or Amazonia, and the urbanites of Ur and Mohenjodaro existed contemporaneously.

How sharply separated were peoples from one another, developing as independent human experiments, different colored pieces in the mosaic? The emerging evidence suggests now that hunters and gatherers have in this time frame been closely interdependent with surrounding horticultural and agricultural peoples, and that the latter were in this period closely tied to one another by economic complementarity, trade, and exchange. Pastoralists and agriculturalists had complementary and symbiotic relationships; as we will see, there was often shifting of population between the villages of the farmers and the camps of the nomads. Peoples were in many parts of the world tied directly or indirectly into the margins of state societies.

If we look at the tribal world as a mosaic of cultural variation, we are led to attribute a spurious ancientness and stability to these ways of life. In some places, the "life span" of "a culture" as a coherent tradition may well have been a century or two, or less. And we are led to attribute a spurious separateness and self-containment to these "cultures," to overlook the way peoples were tied into regional systems of trade, exchange, and politics, through which ideas as well as objects flowed.

If we look at this world as a ladder of progressive evolutionary stages, we are prone to make spurious inferences about the ancient past from the present. Modern hunters and gatherers whose economy is closely tied to that of surrounding cultivators are used as evidence of the Paleolithic past; a tribal people using iron tools, and Chinese jars or brass gongs as valuables, is used to make inference about a "level" that existed only in relation to more complex societies.

In criticizing the mosaic and ladder views, I do not mean to dismiss the value of the studies carried on in these frameworks or to suggest that my colleagues have been grossly naive about the sorts of connections in time and space to which I will point. Margaret Mead, whose popular books helped to spread the mosaic view of tribal peoples, vividly described the Mountain Arapesh of the coastal mountains of New Guinea as having an "importing culture" pieced together from the ideas and practices of neighboring peoples in a distinctive way.

Bronislaw Malinowski's first major account of the Trobriand Islanders of Melanesia—a people in whose way of life we ourselves will become deeply immersed in Part 3—described a remarkable circle of ceremonial exchange and accompanying trade that connects culturally diverse people across a wide expanse of water. Nor do connections between neighboring peoples imply that each has not developed and maintained distinctive customs and beliefs—or that we cannot learn about human possibility and human variation by studying diverse cultural ways. The point is that studies of local cultural traditions have cumulatively produced an *image* of a mosaic—an image anthropologists have often drawn on and hence reinforced in conveying ideas about cultural variation to the lay public, to students, and to colleagues in other disciplines. And that image, that stereotype, is of a world that never existed.

A similar reservation must be made in criticizing the ladder stereotype. Theorists of cultural evolution have often made painstaking use of historical, ethnographic, and archaeological evidence in piecing together regional sequences of development. Looking at the gradual evolution of states and urbanism in Mesoamerica, for example, we do find peoples passing through a series of developmental stages of increasing societal complexity, for which ladder-climbing is a quite reasonable image. Having looked at such a developmental sequence in Mesoamerica, it is an obvious next step to compare it with sequences in the Near East and China to seek regularities and test theories of the developmental process.

Similarly, if we want to test a theory about the interrelationship among hunter-gatherers, between the mode of subsistence and demography, the division of labor, or political organization, it makes quite reasonable sense to compare South African San with Australian Aborigines, or African rain forest dwellers with Malaysians. I am not arguing against comparison, against classification, or against theory. What is dangerous and misleading about images of evolutionary ladders (as they are used in teaching, in popularizations, and in conveying the findings of anthropology to other disciplines) are the implications they carry that

the lower rungs on the ladder are earlier than the higher rungs, that peoples of a region typically progress up such ladders (until at some level they are interrupted by European intrusion), or that the task of anthropology is to classify societies according to the level they have reached.

The transition from food-gathering to food-producing in the Near East was not made by people whose mode of life resembled in the slightest that of contemporary Australian Aborigines or San or Inuit, but by sedentary villagers collecting wild grains and hunting wild ungulates in a temperate zone. The village farmers of subsequent millennia had ways of life that did not resemble in the slightest those of the peoples of tropical Africa or New Guinea who are supposed to be one rung higher on the ladder than Australian Aborigines. When more complex forms of political organization emerged in the Near East, they did not resemble Polynesian or African chiefdoms. The actual sequences of societal transformation toward greater complexity often took place long before the societies arrayed on hypothetical ladders by anthropologists even existed, and occurred in very different ecological zones, among peoples whose modes of economy and social life were radically different from those of the tribal world described by ethnographers.

There have been, in the tribal world, developments of more complex modes of societal organization out of simpler ones—the emergence of social classes and other forms of social stratification, the emergence of hierarchical, centralized political systems from egalitarian ones. But I will argue in the chapters to follow that we do better to examine these processes regionally, in real time and space, than in terms of ladder typologies. A system of political hierarchy and hereditary chiefs on South Malaita in the Solomon Islands or among the Mekeo of coastal New Guinea is better compared with the political systems of surrounding societies without centralized authority—to ask how and why it might have evolved there—than arrayed on the same rung with African or Polynesian chiefdoms. To go beyond mosaic and ladder views, we need to begin to look at the tribal world in terms of real history and regional systems.

11. THE TRIBAL WORLD AS SYSTEM

A first element in a corrective view comes from looking more closely at the recent culture history of some of the parts of the world where indigenous peoples were encountered by explorers and colonialists, and described by anthropologists. Let us look first at sub-Saharan Africa.

The Complexities of Regional History

Linguistic and archaeological evidence points to the dispersion of Bantu-speaking peoples from a West or Central African center beginning about 2,000 years ago, accelerated by iron tools which permitted efficient clearing of forest and savannah. The descendants of these early Bantu-speakers spread over much of sub-Saharan Africa, developing cultivation and pastoral adaptations, absorbing or displacing previous populations, and diversifying into the scores of groups described by anthropologists. The late spread of Bantu-speakers and other African populations is suggested by historical evidence cited by Fage:

> The inference . . . is . . . that in the first century A.D. there were no Negroes on the east coast of Africa to as far south as about Zanzibar [an island opposite what is now Tanzania]; that they were first seen south of Zanzibar in the fourth century; and that they then expanded northwards, reaching their present limits by about the tenth century.
>
> [At] the end of the fifteenth century [when] Europeans got to know southern

Africa . . . Negro speakers of Bantu languages . . . were still expanding southwards [into what is now South Africa] at the expense of the Khoisan peoples [indigenous hunters and gatherers, including the San]. (1978:21–22)

The cultural map of sub-Saharan Africa is highly complicated, and the movements of population and the adoption of new subsistence technologies and ecological adaptations were going on into the period when European and Arab traders, then explorers, and finally colonialists disrupted and transformed these processes. If we look at pastoral adaptations in relation to the expanding Bantu (some of whom became pastoralists) and the ancient Khoisan-speaking hunters and gatherers, we glimpse this complexity:

> The Khoikhoi [Hottentots] were the product of . . . contact between different cultures in southern Africa. . . . Their ancestors were predominantly indigenous southern African hunters who at some stage had acquired sheep and cattle from neighbors and modified their social and political institutions as a result of this change in their material culture. . . . The crucial transfers of sheep and cattle . . . must have happened comparatively recently, perhaps early in the second millenium A.D. The hunting communities which first acquired sheep and cattle in southern Africa probably did so in central Botswana. The donors would have been Bantu-speaking mixed farmers. Once this change started, it developed a momentum. Pastoralists formed larger-scale communities than hunting bands had, and they expanded into the better pasturelands throughout the western half of southern Africa. . . . They generated a series of new political units . . . and also incorporated members of the hunting communities. . . . In good seasons, hunters acquired cattle and sheep and became pastoralists; but in time of drought and warfare, people lost their livestock and again became wholly dependent on hunting and collecting. (Curtin, Feierman, Thompson, and Vansina 1978:292–293)

The Bantu-speakers may themselves have acquired cattle by way of Khoisan peoples:

> The linguistic evidence . . . suggests that the Bantu acquired cattle from eastern Africa speakers of Afro-Asiatic, Cushitic, languages, and that they may have done this through the mediation of Khoisan-speaking peoples who could have been ancestral to the modern Sandawe. (Fage 1978:32)

Because these processes of expansion, absorption, displacement, and transformation were still going on when European and Arab trade and slave-raiding penetrated the African interior, the patterns of the "ethnographic present" were heavily shaped by these alien forces (see, e.g., Ekholm 1977). But the impact of Europeans was a continuation of influences from outside sub-Saharan Africa that go back to dynastic Egypt, and include the spread of Indonesian peoples to Madagascar, bringing Southeast Asian food crops and technology, and the spread of Islam. There is no time in the last 4,000 years when the map of Africa has been static, rather it has consisted of a mosaic of different cultures.

The possibility raised by Fage that agriculturalists were introduced to pastoralism by Khoisan hunter-gatherers strikes a jarring note to the tidy-minded builder of cultural ladders. But such muddling of technology and "cultural level" was widespread, a concomitant of the fact that in the last several thousand years pastoralism, hunting and gathering, advanced metallurgy, and the construction of cities and irrigation canals were going on simultaneously. If one thinks in terms of levels, one would like to imagine tribal peoples in the tropical zones of the world as Neolithic—that is, as users of advanced stone tools—and in some places they were. But in large zones of southeast Asia and Africa, iron tools were a major shaping force in the distribution of peoples

and economies (as with the Bantu cultivators of African forest and savannah). In Southeast Asia and tropical Africa, some hunting and gathering peoples became specialized in smelting iron tools and supplying them to neighboring farming peoples. This is true of some of the rain forest peoples of central Africa and Malaysia (see, e.g., Schebesta 1954:150).

Economic Complementarity in Regional Systems

This kind of interdependence between modern hunter-gatherers and cultivators is not a rare situation. The close relationships between peoples who stand on different rungs of an imaginary ladder call for a close look. Hutterer (1976:223) notes that virtually all known groups of extant hunter-gatherers in Southeast Asia are in regular and relatively intensive communication and exchange with neighboring cultivators. Hutterer asks whether this is a relatively recent situation or an old one—and finds good evidence that this complementarity between peoples on different "levels" is very old:

> Such exchange of goods and services exists . . . not only between agriculturalists and hunters, but also between agriculturalists and horticulturalists and between horticulturalists and hunters. . . . The continuing survival of hunter-gatherers in Southeast Asia has been in the interests of agricultural populations. . . . Interaction between hunting and agricultural populations has also introduced an element of specialization among the hunters and made them dependent . . . upon agriculturalists. (Hutterer 1976:226; the distinction between *horticulture* and *agriculture* Hutterer draws is between the use of hand-cultivation and cultivation using ploughs and draught animals.)

Such interdependence is not confined to Southeast Asia, as Bronson comments in relation to Hutterer's paper:

> The overall pattern exemplified by the economic integration of Southeast Asian hunter-gatherers with culturally and ethnically distinct farming groups is almost worldwide. Nomads and agriculturalists in southwestern Asia are often culturally distinct but economically interdependent, as are swiddeners [shifting horticulturalists] and irrigators in northern Thailand and farmers and fishermen in the Admiralties [Melanesia].
>
> [Hunter-gatherers] may . . . be groups of economic specialists who make their living by virtue of their superior ability to extract from the forest goods utilized in a wider regional economy—in short . . . they exist not in spite of but because of contacts with the outside world. (Bronson 1976:230)

Because hunting and gathering peoples in the last several millennia have in most areas coexisted with and traded with cultivators, their occupancy of a specialized ecological niche cannot be understood in terms of "survivals" from an ancient past. There is strong and accumulating evidence that there is no inherent drive to technological "advance" that leads people either to strive to improve their technology or to adopt a "better" technology when they are exposed to it, when doing so would force a substantial change in the organization of subsistence. Hunting and gathering is highly labor-efficient and permits a relatively unconstrained and mobile life. To practice cultivation requires more work and sharply constrains options of mobility. Humans seem to have made these sacrifices only when they have had to, because of demographic or ecological or political pressures. Even Australian Aborigines, long assumed to have been cut off by isolation from revolutions in world technology, and hence "trapped" in the Paleolithic, turn out to have had, at least in the north, knowledge of and access to Neolithic horticultural technology; they had what one might call "proto-agricultural" patterns of resource management (e.g., the distribution of fruit and plant seeds in environments where they could sprout). Australian Aborigines could have adopted horticulture, but had no reason to.

This view of economies in the tribal world enables us to understand why the edges between hunting-and-gathering and food production are blurred, not neat, as the ladder model would suggest they should be. Thus many Amazonian peoples and some Southeast Asian peoples have economies predominantly organized in terms of food-collecting, but augmented by seasonal or small-scale cultivation. The Batek, forest people of Malaysia, who are primarily hunter-gatherers living in small, mobile bands, sometimes clear gardens in the forest and plant root crops. But instead of tending and weeding the gardens, as good horticulturalists should, they leave them and go off for months on their mobile quest for wild foods. They come back past their garden after counting off the months, and harvest whatever bird, animal, and insect predators have not already gathered—treating the garden as if it were a richer-than-usual stand of wild foods.

All this means partly that—contrary to both the mosaic and ladder stereotypes—we have to look at regional economic systems that include peoples with different subsistence economies, occupying complementary ecological niches. Barth's (1956) classic description of how pastoralists and farmers occupy complementary niches in Swat, Pakistan, is now being augmented with data on similar patterns in many parts of the world, evidence being gleaned from both ethnography and archaeology. Such complementarity and diversity in subsistence economies may represent the coexistence of peoples very different in their culture and historic origins, or peoples whose cultural heritage is fundamentally similar but who have become specialized economically or have adapted differentially to microvariation in the ecosystem. Thus Allen notes as follows:

> New Guinea represents a patchwork quilt of subsistence strategies, from almost totally wild-food dependence to a totally domesticated-food base; amongst gardeners, technology similarly reveals a spectrum from simple house-plot horticulture to complex agriculture which transforms natural ecosystems into artificial ones. (1976:227–228)

Extensive patterns of trade and economic interdependence in New Guinea and island Melanesia have been documented in recent years (see especially Specht and White 1978). Thus, for instance, the Amphlett islanders of the d'Entrecasteaux Islands off New Guinea specialized in the production of pots for export; the Langalanga people of Malaita in the Solomon Islands exported ground shell-disc valuables in exchange for foodstuffs (nowadays, they export them by air to Papua New Guinea). Such trade and specialization are old in the region. Some 3,500 years ago, obsidian adze blades from the Bismarck Archipelago were being traded up to 500 miles into the southern Solomons.

Processes of Transformation

The coexistence of peoples supposed to be at different "levels" of societal evolution in the same time frame also casts doubt on models whereby a people advance from one level to the next. Even where, say, a chiefdom is transformed into a more complex system, that may not represent a simple developmental sequence in an evolutionary sense. People who are "evolving" from one "level" to another may be doing so under direct influence of a civilization on whose margins they lie. Paul Wheatley cites an interesting case from Southeast Asia, where

brahmanic influence emanating from India provided the models for transformation of older political systems:

> Political power in Southeast Asia traditionally derived from control over labor, and . . . chieftains . . . doubtless sought to extend their authority so as to be able to draw on labor rights in as many neighboring settlements as possible. [Under the influence of brahmanic culture] there . . . evolved the city-state, the *nāgara*, focused on . . . the temple. The whole complex represented the outcome of a series of social and political transformations that replaced the tribal chief by a divine king, the shaman by a brahmana [priest], the tribesman as warrior by a Ksatriya, and the tribesman as cultivator by a peasant. . . . Occupational specialization assumed the character of *jāti* [subcaste], age-sets were transmuted into *āsrama*, the tribal meeting was formalized in an assembly on the model of the [Indian] *sabha*, and custom hardened into law. . . . These institutional transformations . . . were manifested . . . in the conversion of the chief's hut into a palace, the spirit house into a temple, . . . the boundary marker into the city wall. (1975:246–247)

The impetus for the transformation of sub-Saharan African political systems in the direction of centralization, the trappings of kingship, and the development of statelike bureaucratic structures, partly has come from within, as warfare, the intensification of production, and demographic expansion have provided foundations for increased complexity. But the models for such developments have been emanating southward from the Mediterranean world since the pharaohs of Eygpt, through the emperors of Rome, and to the sultans and caliphs of expanding Islam.

"Tribes"

We can usefully come back at this stage to the concept of "tribe," and the disputes surrounding it. The issue was brought to the foreground most compellingly by Morton Fried in 1975. The term *tribe,* Fried argued, has been applied loosely in anthropology (and other fields) to refer to a discrete ethnic group distinguished from its neighbors by a separate language and culture, commonly referred to by a distinctive name, whose members have some sense of common identity. "Tribe" has tended to imply some political coherence and economic organization as well. Fried, reviewing the evidence, suggests that communities in stateless societies rarely if ever had this kind of political or economic organization, except as a secondary response to invasion or domination by a state-organized society. Even the linguistic and cultural separation supposed to characterize "tribes" breaks down under close examination (Béteille 1986:304). What emerges as "tribal" units in the colonial period, such as the Yoruba of Nigeria or the Tolai of Papua New Guinea, turn out to have been crystallized out of separate communities and dialect groups . Such apparent "tribal" unity, and even the sense of identity and of loyalty to one's tribe (so often cited by, say, political scientists as an obstacle to unity at a national level in Africa), are—Fried argues—artifacts of colonial rule. State societies, particularly those of the expanding West, have created tribes, intentionally or not, in the process of subjugating, controlling, and/or exploiting peoples of the hinterlands; these peoples develop modes of internal organization in response to (or sometimes struggle against) outside domination. Tribalism, in short, is a secondary phenomenon, not a mode of organization that develops in a world where one's neighbors are similar in scale, technology, and political organization (see Ferguson and Whitehead 1992).

Fried would dismiss, on these grounds and those of vagueness, use of the term *tribal* to describe a range of societies or a level of sociopolitical organization. Sahlins had used "tribal" to label

> a notable range of evolutionary developments . . . which counterposes at the extremes two radically different types. At the underdeveloped end of the spectrum . . . stand tribes socially and politically fragmented and in their economics undiversified and modestly endowed. . . . In its most developed expression, the *chiefdom,* tribal culture anticipates statehood in its complexities. . . . Between the most advanced chiefdom and the simplest segmentary tribe stand many intermediate arrangements. (Sahlins 1968:20–21)

Fried takes exception not only to the label "tribe" but to the range of social systems it covers: he remains a ladder-builder at heart, and wants to be sure to get the rungs properly arranged and labeled:

> There is no "tribal level" of polity. The concept of tribe has been used in connection with totally acephalous organization and with . . . structures at the veritable level of kingdoms, or at least of emirates. A terminology that implicitly equates one of the old men . . . given to haranguing the young among the Ona [of Tierra Del Fuego at the southern tip of South America] with the *Khan* of the Mongols, cannot be of much use. (Fried 1975:65)

But one can avoid using "tribe" for the reasons advanced by Fried and still have need of an intentionally broad and vague term to label the range to which Sahlins refers. "Tribal" remains preferable to "primitive," or the other available alternatives, I think. It need not imply that either Ona or Mongols comprise "tribes" in any precise sense, or had anything important in common: they are classed together because of what they are *not.*

Tribal Peoples and States

More interesting than quarrels about labels are Fried's observations about the relationships between stateless ethnic groups and state societies. Long before the European invasion of the Americas, Asia, and the Pacific, peoples of the hinterlands were cast into relationships of subjugation, trade, and tribute with state societies. Even in the island Pacific, where no states emerged in pre-European times, highly stratified societies in Tonga, Yap, and other areas extended control outward to form what were virtual empires. At or beyond the margins of the ancient states, peoples were caught up into foreign relations, often unwillingly (as with the Nubian slaves captured by the pharaohs of Egypt). Paying tribute, providing slaves or sacrificial victims, serving as soldiers, providing valuables or raw materials in trade, the peoples of the hinterlands were an integral part of the processes of ancient state formation and economy. Fox (1967) and Sinha have suggested that many of the peoples of Indian forest zones were not—as conventional assumptions would have it—isolated remnants surviving between the margins of civilization. Rather, they were incorporated within state economic and political systems, maintained as "primitives" for the special economic services they provided as catchers and tamers of elephants, suppliers of honey, and collectors of other forest products. Hunter-gatherers in the ancient central zone of what is now the Sudan seem similarly to have been maintained within the economic and political orbit of Old Kingdom dynastic Egypt. In some parts of the anthropologically recorded world, tribal groups may represent a product of *devolution*, as now-separated remnant pieces that were once marginally tied into former state systems.

Cultural Diversity in Regional Perspective

At this stage we can return to the question of cultural distinctiveness. If tribal societies had open boundaries, why and how have distinctive cultural traditions evolved and been maintained? Fredrik Barth (1969), in his introductory essay on *Ethnic Groups and Boundaries,* suggests that commonsense ideas that different cultural groups have separate origins, or have drifted apart by isolation, need radical rethinking. Becoming distinctive in customs, in dress, in dialect, is an ongoing social and political process within regional systems (see also Barth 1992, Descola 1992). One's "world view" or religious rituals are not simply a closed view of the cosmos, but a commentary on one's identity vis-à-vis the neighbors. Just why the boundaries form where they do, so that this group is marked by a particular mode of dress, house style, dialect, and kinship system while that group several miles away has distinctive modes, is commonly a puzzle, in areas with no sharp geographical separations or ecological contrasts, and in the absence of historical evidence. But it is clear that to account for and understand such ethnic boundaries we need to look at cultural differences as symbolic assertions of separateness, not simply as diverse pieces in a mosaic. And because maintaining, developing, or erasing cultural boundary lines is a political process, we cannot assume (as Fried's warning about "tribes" indicates) that the lines we find are either old or stable—or that they should be the boundaries for our analysis.

Does that mean that we cannot learn, from these cultural differences, about human nature, possibility, and variation? Not at all. Each venture in customary distinctiveness, cumulated across generations and maintained along its boundaries, does give insights into the possible paths of humankind, and their consequences.

Are the customs people develop in a particular setting arbitrary cumulations? Or is there a hidden logic that leads a particular cultural practice to develop in this valley, and not the next? We will come to this central question in the next two chapters.

We have gone far enough to see that popular stereotypes of the tribal world, anthropologically reinforced if not anthropologically created, are highly misleading. Tribal cultures had not been as they were when Europeans discovered them "since time immemorial." They were not neatly separated from one another, nor (in most regions) from the influence of states and civilizations. When we do find surviving groups of hunters and gatherers we cannot treat them as windows on the ancient past, survivors from the dawn of humanity. We can learn from these and other small-scale societies about the myriad ways and potentials of humankind, about the nature and organization of societies. But we will have to seek to do so with a wise and discerning eye.

from each other and stable over time, which may not be true. Regional history in sub-Saharan Africa shows a complex historical relationship between Bantu- and Khoisan-speaking peoples. Horticulturalists and hunter-gathers or pastoralists exchanged products through networks of trade. Such networks extended over hundreds of miles in New Guinea also, linking populations. Groups we label "tribes" may owe their current form of existence to interactions with centralized chiefships or kingdoms, and chiefships have also been influenced by their less stratified neighbor societies.

Categories such as that of "tribe" itself are also to some extent artifacts of colonial policy and labeling. Nevertheless, peoples have differentiated themselves from one another, and Fredrik Barth's observation regarding ethnic groups applies: boundaries exist in spite of transactions across them and a flow of transactions exists in spite of boundaries.

=========== SUMMARY ===========

The societies we have called "tribal" should not be thought of as isolated, self-sufficient entities. They usually belonged at one time to regional systems of exchange and interacted for economic, religious, and political purposes with other groups. In evolutionary terms, these societies have previously been looked on as belonging to a "ladder" of development, consisting of different stages, starting with bands of hunter-gatherers and ending with hierarchical chiefdoms as precursors of the state. "Ladder" views are contrasted with "mosaic" views, in which each culture is treated as a unique, separate experiment in a way of life, to be compared on the same level with every other such experiment. Both viewpoints are deficient. The "ladder" view presupposes a smooth series of evolutionary progressions; the "mosaic" view tends to depict cultures as isolated

SUGGESTIONS FOR
FURTHER READING

SECTION 10

Fried, M. 1967. *The Evolution of Political Society.* New York: Random House, Inc.

Honigmann, J. J. 1976. *The Development of Anthropological Ideas.* Homewood, Ill.: Dorsey Press.

Langness, L. L. 1974. *The Study of Culture.* Novato, Calif.: Chandler and Sharp.

Service, E. R. 1971. *Primitive Social Organization: An Evolutionary Perspective.* 2nd ed. New York: Random House, Inc.

SECTION 11

Fagan, B. M. 1980. *People of the Earth: An Introduction to World Prehistory.* 3rd ed. Boston: Little, Brown and Company.

Fried, M. 1975. *The Notion of Tribe.* Menlo Park, Calif.: Cummings Publishing Company.

Friedman, J., and M. J. Rowlands. 1977. *The Evolution of Social Systems.* Pittsburgh: University of Pittsburgh Press.

CHAPTER

6

Modes of Subsistence, Modes of Adaptation

The systemic view we have taken warns us not to be cavalier about placing hunter-gatherers, horticulturalists, or herders into imaginary chronologies and developmental scales. But we do not want to miss seeing the interconnections between modes of subsistence and modes of social and political structure, between ecological settings and the way humans, given a particular technology, organize their lives. In this chapter we will glimpse the subsistence economies of modern hunter-gatherers, tropical horticulturalists, and pastoralists, and begin to ask how economy and the organization of society are related.

12. CONTEMPORARY HUNTER-GATHERERS

What Can Contemporary Hunter-Gatherers Tell Us—and Not Tell Us?

The hunter-gatherers who survived and maintained their ways of life long enough to be recorded anthropologically are not a direct source of evidence on the vast span of the Paleolithic past. First, their technologies

reflect relatively recent technological advances:

> In the last few thousand years before agriculture, both hunting and gathering became much more complex. This final adaptation, including the use of products of river and sea and the grinding and cooking of otherwise inedible seeds and nuts, was worldwide, laid the basis for the discovery of agriculture, and was much more effective and diversified than the previously existing hunting and gathering adaptations. (Washburn and Lancaster 1968:295)

Most modern hunter-gatherers had access to fairly recent complexes of technological advance. In some cases, as in marginal societies of tropical South America, modern hunting and gathering peoples may previously have had agriculture and lost or abandoned this technology.

Second, the marginal environments in which modern hunter-gatherers have survived hardly give an adequate view of hunting and gathering ways of life in the much richer environments of Paleolithic Europe or the early savannas of Africa where hominids evolved. Even for Australia, our stereotypes

Woman using heavy digging stick to till soil in swidden garden, Pangia, Papua New Guinea.

are based on remote deserts, not on the temperate and well-watered forests of the east coast.

> We must not model our thinking about the Paleolithic world on the world as we know it today. . . . The Paleolithic world [was] . . . swarming with game. The zones in which the last tribes of hunters and gatherers have taken refuge today only serve to put wrong ideas in our heads. (Bordes 1968:235)

Nor can the residual hunter-gatherers, and their social and political relations, necessarily instruct us well about social organization in a world in which all peoples were hunters and gatherers (Kelly 1995:333ff.).

As we will see, the degree to which the social and political systems recorded among modern hunting and gathering peoples reflect the impact of Western intrusion is a matter of continuing debate. Fortunately, the question is more important to those who want to know (or worse yet, who think they know, and want to prove) what was at the bottom rung of the ladder than to us. The systemic view we have taken assumes that for several thousand years the "environments" of most hunter-gatherers have included surrounding agriculturalists, pastoralists, and in many cases kingdoms and empires. Questions about their adaptation become questions about their place in regional systems.

Subsistence Economies of Contemporary Hunter-Gatherers

That said, we can begin to ask about the subsistence economy of modern hunter-gatherers. First, there is a long continuum between peoples who rely mainly or solely on hunting (some Inuit groups constituted the limiting case of virtually complete subsistence on animal products) and peoples who rely very heavily on gathering wild vegetable foods. As a worldwide generalization, the further removed from the equator, the greater tends to be the importance of animal foods. In tropical zones, the diverse vegetable environment opens the way to a heavy reliance on wild tubers, shoots, fruits, nuts, and so forth. Since few hunting and gathering peoples survived into the twentieth century in the temperate zone between equatorial rain forests and the frozen north—except in arid deserts of southern Africa and Australia—we have little information on the middle range. We particularly lack evidence for resource-rich temperate zones where rich marine or land resources permitted sedentary residence of large populations, and complex social and political structures. What we can glimpse from the evidence of the Upper Paleolithic in Europe, the northwest coast of North America, and even the scant records of Australian Aborigines living in favored temperate environments suggests the dangers of talking about hunting and gathering as a single and uniform subsistence mode, or generalizing about the social forms adaptive to "it."

We can say that, in the areas we know about, subsistence techniques are intricate and diverse, showing intimate familiarity with microenvironments. We can also say that, despite preconceptions one might have about the hardships of survival in a hunting and gathering way of life, the food quest seems not to be a constant and exhausting business. For hunting and gathering bands, unable to do very much to control their natural world, the possibilities of material comfort and accumulation are quite limited. And given these limits to the feasible goals of life, hunter-gatherers seem to have a surprisingly easy time of it, and to have considerable time for leisure and relaxation. Sahlins (1972), reflecting on the implications of detailed evidence on the subsistence of the San of southern Africa, and similar findings from other hunter-gatherers, dubbed the hunting and gathering band as "the first affluent society":

> An affluent society is one where all the people's material wants are easily satisfied. To assert that the hunters are affluent is to deny ... that the human condition [must keep] man the prisoner at hard labor of a perpetual disparity between his unlimited wants and his insufficient means. ...
>
> There is [instead] a road to affluence, departing from premises ... that human wants are finite and few, and technical means unchanging but on the whole adequate. Adopting the Zen strategy, a people can enjoy an unparalleled material plenty. (Sahlins 1972:1–2)

At least for the modern hunter-gatherers living in tropical or arid zones, a stereotype of "man the hunter" is quite misleading. Among such peoples in Australia, Central and South Africa, and Malaysia, collecting of wild vegetable foods and hunting of small animals by women is centrally important to everyday subsistence. That men are usually the ones who engage in hunting

Australian Aboriginal technology: Fire-making.

Australian Aboriginal technology: Trimming the edge of a digging stick.

larger animals presumably partly reflects their physical advantages in size, strength, and endurance, and their greater independence from care of infants and young children. But such hunting, however it may be practically valued and symbolically rewarded, is also an uncertain and risky pursuit. Game, to be sure, provides the times of plenty and contributes crucially to the diet; but humans as hunters, bereft of great speed or a keen sense of smell and dependent on limited weapons, are hard pressed in what for any carnivore is a difficult game of chance. Modern evidence reveals that among such hunter-gatherers as the San, roots, fruits, nuts, seeds, berries, and other vegetable foods collected by women provide the staple base needed for survival (R. Lee 1969). For hunting and gathering peoples of tropical forest zones, a sharp and hard division of labor between the sexes is not universal. Hunting and gathering may be less clearly separated activities

when a foraging expedition turns up a cluster of wild yam vines, an edible monitor lizard or turtle, and a treeful of monkeys within a stone's throw of one another. Thus Karen and Kirk Endicott's data on the Batek of the Malaysian forest indicate that virtually every subsistence activity can be, and often is, performed by either men or women (K. A. L. Endicott 1979).

At this stage, we need to remember that we are not—at least for the period in which modern ethnographic studies have been done—dealing with peoples living in pristine isolation, but rather with peoples living among settled farmers (and very often now with development agencies in their midst). The foraging strategies used by the Batek include returning to the neat villages they have been induced to construct by the

A Batek mother (Malaysia) and her daughter dig for wild yams.

or the nature of society. Hunter-gatherers are ourselves, as it were, in a *natural state*. We look at them to find out our true nature, which for us is submerged beneath or transformed by the institutions of a complex society and a powerful technology:

> In their questionable status as ancestors, modern hunter-gatherers have been analyzed to discover "elementary" social forms and/or basic human nature, uncontaminated by disparities in wealth and power that result from food-producing adaptations. . . . Most investigators have been less concerned with understanding the quality of hunter-gatherer life than with discovering how hunter-gatherers are, or are not, like ourselves. . . . Gatherer-hunters emerge either as pure "ideologues" who act out innate mental structures, . . . or as barely cultural animals whose ideas are simple reflections of social groupings dictated by biological needs. (Rosaldo and Collier 1981)

Malaysian government, so as to gather foodstuffs dropped to them by parachute—after which they return to the forest. The parachutes may be recent, but the Batek and other Southeast Asian hunter-gatherers have been dealing with the "outside world" of settled and sometimes urban peoples for centuries, and their economies are specialized accordingly (in the Batek case, for trade in rattan and other forest products).

Hunter-Gatherers and the "Natural State" of Humankind

How are hunting and gathering societies organized? How are these patterns shaped by these modes of subsisting? Interpretations of hunter-gatherer society, in regard to such questions as relationships between the sexes and concepts of property, have been heavily shaped by ideologies. Those who see contemporary hunter-gatherers as direct sources of evidence about the earliest forms of human society seek in them some confirmation of assumptions about human nature

Both Marxist and feminist scholars have seen hunter-gatherers as reflecting a fundamental egalitarianism and a lack of asymmetry in male-female power and status: without private property, without surplus to accumulate, and without labor beyond subsistence needs to appropriate, there are no bases for social stratification or sexual inequality (see Leacock 1978). Where institutions of private property or sexual inequality are reported, they reflect either faulty ethnographic interpretation or the impact of capitalist-colonialist intrusion. (A long debate in anthropology has revolved around whether apparent institutions of "private property" among northeastern Native Americans such as the Montaignais are indigenous or reflect the impact of the European fur trade.)

We will seek (following suggestions of Rosaldo and Collier 1981) to characterize social relations and symbolic systems in hunter-gatherer societies, and their ecological-economic bases, in more positive terms—not in terms of human nature or what such societies lack, but in terms of the way social life is ordered and given meaning.

Social Organization

The "classic" model of the social organization of hunters and gatherers is the **patrilocal band.** In this social arrangement, the men of a band form the political core; men spend their lives hunting in the territory where they grew up. Daughters, however, leave the band at marriage. Thus wives come into the band at marriage, leaving their childhood home territory. This means changing their foraging grounds, but that is less precarious as a mode of ecological adaptation than having young men move to a new hunting territory. Such patrilocal bands were seen as characteristic of Australian Aborigines and many other hunter-gatherers. In Australia and some other areas, marriage rules went far beyond a rule of out-marriage to posit complex rules for the exchange of women between bands.

Sparse and scattered resources in some ecological settings made fairly stable and concentrated bands maladaptive. In such marginal areas, nuclear families might disperse for all or part of the year. The Basin Shoshoni, who continued into historic times to follow the desert mode of Archaic adaptations in North America, are a striking example. (See Case 3.)

A number of modern studies of hunter-gatherers in Australia, North America, and Africa have suggested that the classic patrilocal band model may be too simple. Bands tend to be diverse and heterogeneous, there is considerable mobility and individual and subgroup shifting from band to band, and bands hunt extensively on one another's territory. Even out-marriage is often less neat than in the classic model. In Case 4, the San illustrate some aspects of this flexibility and diversity.

Whether such flexibility and diversity were characteristic of hunter-gatherers in the Upper Paleolithic, or even in the recent past, has been hotly debated. Some experts urge that this flexibility represents an effective mode of ecological adaptation and political relations and therefore is old and basic; others counter that it is a recent by-product of colonialism and intrusion by the external world.

Political Systems

The political organization of hunting and gathering societies runs a wide gamut. Where the environment was rich and the population relatively large and sedentary, a degree of political centralization far beyond that of contemporary marginal hunter-gatherers is revealed in the early records. Even bearing in mind the tendency to promote leaders met along early colonial frontiers into "kings" and "chiefs," one is struck by early accounts of leadership in ecologically rich southeastern Australia. A party of early colonists near what is now Melbourne "were met by a number of natives who, on a shot being fired over their heads, ran a small distance but soon approached again with the king, who wore a very elaborate turban crown and was always carried on the shoulders of the men" (Howitt 1904, quoting Shillinglaw 1870). Elaborate hierarchical structures involving clan chiefs, formal clan and tribal councils, and tribal paramount chiefs are reliably reported.

Among the surviving marginal hunting and gathering people, with smaller, often scattered, populations and often forced subservience to surrounding peoples, political leadership tends to be much less formal and

CASE

3

Shoshoni Social Organization

The Shoshoni of Nevada, and other Shoshonean-speaking peoples of the Great Basin of the western United States (Ute and Paiute), had an extremely simple and fragmented social organization, classed by Steward (1955) as a "family level of sociocultural integration."

The Shoshoni environment was extremely arid, harsh, diversified, and unpredictable. It included desert and near-desert, lakes and streams, high pine forests, and a range of intermediate settings at different elevations. Winter was cold and severe, summer hot and dry. The sparse food resources, mainly rabbits and other small game, and even more important, pine nuts and other wild vegetable foods, were scattered and unpredictable.

In such a setting, human settlement was sparse—one person to every 5, 10, or even 50 or 100 square miles. Mobility was necessary, so that no permanent settlements were possible, and only tiny groups could make ends meet in the business of subsistence.

The Shoshoni and their neighbors developed an adaptation whereby a family (either a couple and their children or a man, his several wives, and their children) lived alone for most of the year—perhaps 80 percent of the time. They moved in pursuit of food, following the seasons. Only when resources such as fish or pine nuts were temporarily abundant did several families live together. In winter, they sometimes camped together, living largely on whatever dried nuts and seeds they had been able to store. At other times, they joined together in communal hunts for rabbits or antelope. Such gatherings were times for dancing and collective religious rites.

Spouses had to come from outside the family. Characteristically, however, marriage alliances would be worked out between two families, so that when a young man from one family married a young woman from another, the younger children of the two families would also marry when the time came. When a man took two or more wives, they were supposed to be sisters. If a spouse died, his or her surviving sibling was supposed, if possible, to marry the widow or widower. The several families united by such marriages would usually be the ones that coordinated their movements so as to group together seasonally when resources permitted. (Steward 1938, 1955)

stratified, based primarily on personal powers—whether of hunting, ritual, peacekeeping, oratory, or general leadership—and carried out by egalitarian decision-making or consensual support. The San case is a typical example.

Fighting within and between groups was undoubtedly more widespread and often more violent than some recent stereotypes of a primitive Eden imply. In the surge of literature on hunter-gatherers in the 1960s, conflict and warfare were often underplayed. Records of warfare among Australian Aborigines and similar clues from the recent and more remote past should make us wary of projecting too much peace and harmony into our conceptions of human life during the distant Paleolithic past. Further, for aboriginal Australia and North America, most of the evidence we have comes from time periods when the indirect pressures of colonial intrusion were

Australian Aboriginal religion is rich in symbolism and in relating the visible present to the mystical dreamtime of the past.

considerable and patterns of conflict had altered accordingly.

Religion and World View

In Chapter 15 we will look at religion and world view among tribal peoples, including hunting and gathering peoples. Here we can pause only for the most general observations.

The various religious systems of hunter-gatherers, diverse though they are, are characterized by a oneness with nature. In a world you cannot control, a natural balance you must study and adjust to, a human environment dominated by climate, the cycling of the days and the years, your kinship with nature is compelling and sacred. It may be expressed in mystical personification of natural forces; by belief in supernatural beings; by belief in a divine creator; or by conceptu-

alizing relations between social groups in terms of relations between animals, birds, or natural forces. Colin Turnbull's picture of the BaMbuti of the Ituri forest—the immediacy and vividness of their perceptions of the natural world, the intimacy of their knowledge of it, and their mystical oneness with the spirit of the forest—gives a compelling sense of humans in nature, not against it (Turnbull 1961).

The religions of contemporary hunter-gatherers do not necessarily provide windows on the ancient human past. But they usefully remind us that when humans do not have a technology that permits or requires them to transform or control nature, they develop philosophies that situate them *within* the processes and forces of nature, not on top of them. Such philosophies can well serve as sources of wisdom at a time when our efforts to control and dominate

!Kung San Social Organization

The !Kung San are hunter-gatherers living in the forbidding Kalahari Desert of southern Africa. The arid environment permits survival only in small, scattered bands. These bands, ranging in size from about 20 to 60, are spread over some 10,000 square miles; the total population is only about 1,000.

Each band has a territory. Within a territory, rights to gather wild vegetable foods, the everyday staples on which existence depends, are limited to band members. Water is another scarce good, and each band has primary rights to the waterhole or holes on which it depends (though outsiders may use the water with permission).

A !Kung San band.

Hunters of large animals may cross into the territories of other bands quite freely in pursuit of game. If a band's waterhole goes dry, its component families move temporarily to live with other bands where they have relatives.

Each band is made up of a cluster of families. Some consist only of husband, wife, and children; other families are augmented by the presence of one or more married children and their families. Other families consist of a man and two or more wives and their children. Marriage is forbidden within the immediate family, between certain close kin, and between a man and a girl whose name is the same as his mother's (there is only a limited set of names for men and women, transmitted along family lines; name-sharing is taken to imply distant kinship). But marriages are allowed within a band. When a man takes his first wife, he goes to reside with his bride's father until two or three children have been born. During this time he contributes his labor to the relatives of the bride, adding to the larder of his father-in-law and his band. Since marriage often takes place well before the bride reaches puberty, this may cover a span of 8 or 10 years, during which the husband is absent from his band. After that, the husband may take his wife

and children back to his father's band or may choose to remain with his wife's people.

Each band has a headman, chosen by consensus. He has formal authority over the disposition of a band's resources and its movements; but his political powers are in fact quite limited. Group action is usually based on consensus of its members. In some ways the headman's stewardship is symbolic. His de facto power depends on his personal skills at leading, organizing, planning, and maintaining internal harmony. Headship of the band passes through family lines, from a headman to his oldest son.

Internal conflicts, as between a headman and his younger brother or another kinsman, are resolved either by the dissident member moving to another band where he has relatives or by the dissident faction splitting off to form a new band.

Persons related to the band by marriage may join a band and enjoy equal rights with persons born into the band, but these rights lapse if they leave. The rights of a person born into the band to live in band territory and share in its resources remain even though he or she may live elsewhere; the option to return remains open (Marshall 1959, 1960, 1965).

nature have placed our environment, and our entire planet, gravely at risk. One distinguished geneticist who spent time studying peoples of the Amazonian forest put it this way:

The intellectual arrogance cr,eated by our small scientific successes must now be replaced by a profound humility based on the new knowledge of how complex is the system of which we are a part. . . . In the most sophisticated way we can summon, we must return to the awe, and even fear, in which primitive man held the mysterious world

about him, and like him we must strive to live in harmony with the biosphere. (Neel 1970)

13. TROPICAL HORTICULTURISTS

Swidden Cultivation

One distinctive development out of the early food-producing technologies was their adaptation to tropical rain forest. In Mesoamerica, Africa, and Southeast Asia, the crops adapted to tropical forest cultivation included ones propagated by seed: maize, millet, rice. But the most distinctive development of tropical horticulture was the domestication, in different parts of the world, of crops propagated by roots, shoots, and cuttings (which we can lump together as *vegetative* propagation). The contrast is not a trivial one. Coursey (1978) has argued that seed propagation and vegetative propagation engender different kinds of view of oneself in relation to the plant world and ecosystem: the former more manipulative and interventionist, the latter more perceptive of continuities between natural and cultural worlds, stressing harmony with, rather than control over, the natural environment.

To adopt either seed crops (usually originally domesticated in temperate zones) or root crops (yams, taro, manioc, sweet potatoes, whose wild precursors are tropical) to rain forest entails a close cooperation with the forces of nature. We think of a tropical rain forest as a lush and fertile place. But this is seldom true, except where volcanic soil creates a rich environment. Under the towering forest canopy, primary rain forest is by no means the lush tangle of vegetation of Hollywood's stereotype. Not enough sunlight penetrates to support thick undergrowth, except where rivers or other openings break the canopy. What fertility there is comes from the thick layer of decaying vegetation fallen from above. When the giant forest trees are cleared—an immense task with stone tools and fire—the ground is opened for planting yams, taro, maize, dry rice, and manioc. Burning the leaves and branches accumulated in clearing the area temporarily enriches the soil. But then the problems set in. Torrential rains and hot sun leach out the nutrients quickly and can laterize the soil into infertile crusts. By the time a crop has been harvested, the soil is often exhausted. After a second crop, if one

is possible at all, the soil is likely to be useless for cultivation. (Meanwhile, hungry insects and birds from the surrounding crops aheadforest have done their best to harvest the of the humans who planted them.)

The solution worked out by peoples in the tropics was a system known as **shifting cultivation** or **swidden cultivation.** A family or kin group must have considerably more land than is needed for gardens at any time. As a crop is harvested in one garden, a new garden is cleared and planted. The old garden is allowed to lie fallow, and secondary growth of grasses, bushes, and then forest covers it. At some optimum point— often 10 to 20 years if land is sufficient—a balance is struck between renewed fertility of the land and the difficulty of clearing it again for a new garden. Such a system depends on a relatively low population density (Russell 1988).

Usually the ground is worked only by simple digging sticks, often improvised and at best hardened by fire. Polished axes and adzes, the original cutting and felling tools of Neolithic peoples, were supplanted by iron in Africa and Southeast Asia, reducing the labor investment of felling and fencing and making it more feasible to clear virgin forest where it was available.

Many European observers have commented on the wastefulness of shifting cultivation. They have often been misled by the seeming lushness and fertility of tropical rain forests into assuming that land lying fallow is wasted and that more intensive agriculture would support larger, more sedentary populations with a higher standard of living. But in fact, shifting cultivation usually is a highly effective and balanced ecological adaptation; and efforts to introduce intensive agriculture in tropical forest have usually been disastrous. *Balance* is a crucially important element in swidden horticulture:

In ecological terms, the most distinctive positive characteristic of swidden agriculture . . . is that it is integrated into and, when genuinely adaptive maintains the general structure of, the preexisting natural ecosystem. . . . Any form of agriculture represents an effort to alter a given ecosystem in such a way as to increase the flow of energy to man: but a wet-rice terrace accomplishes this through a bold reworking of the natural landscape; a swidden through a canny imitation of it. (Geertz 1963:16)

Production of root and/or seed crops is often augmented by the raising of pigs, chickens, or other domesticated animals. Where possible, aquatic resources and small game augment a monotonously starchy diet low in protein. The swiddens of horticulturalists usually contain not only the staple crops but also a wide range of supplementary cultigens, including bananas, leafy greens, squashes, beans, sugarcane, and the like. Thus, in a single 3-acre swidden among the Hanunoo of the Philippines, Conklin (1957) recorded more than 40 species of plants under cultivation at once. (The Hanunoo have separate labels for more than 400 cultivated plants.)

The nature of swidden horticulture as a mode of adaptation is well illustrated by the Tsembaga Maring of New Guinea, in Case 5.

Economic Entailments of Swidden Cultivation

We are on firmer ground if we ask, as we did for hunter-gatherers, how the organization of production structures social life, politics, and relations between the sexes among horticulturalists such as the Maring. First, there are more possibilities for the production and accumulation of surplus than in the day-to-day economies of hunter-gatherers. Some tropical crops (yams, rice)

can be stored, others (manioc, taro, plantains) cannot. But they can be produced in quantities well beyond subsistence needs, and used in feasting and exchange. Thus among the Maring, cycles of pig production can similarly be planned and orchestrated in relation to a prestige economy of feasting and exchange.

Among the Maring, as for many other swidden cultivators, the bulk of continuous labor in producing vegetable foods is done by women, but felling, fencing, and other tasks require sporadic bursts of heavy work by men. This means that a domestic group of an adult man and woman and their children constitutes a food-producing unit capable of meeting subsistence needs. But it, in conjunction with the potential to produce surpluses (and as in the Maring case, to "bank" them in the form of pigs as living capital), means that male control over female labor can become an instrument of politics—through men acquiring multiple wives, or controlling the financing of marriage and hence the flow of women's labor.

Another concomitant of swidden horticulture is that *land* becomes an essential resource of local groups, in a quite different sense than the hunting and foraging territoriality of hunter-gatherers. Whereas peoples such as Aboriginal Australians and San seldom maintained an exclusive and defensive control over a territory and its resources, for tropical cultivators the land has a different character. As we will see for the Maring, defense and conquest of territory are common. Even where occupation of territory by warfare does not occur, land rights are a constant issue for horticultural peoples. This is particularly true for swidden horticulturalists, such as those in Melanesia, who traditionally used stone tools. Clearing of primary forest was a massive task; and the secondary growth, once cleared, constituted *property*, controlled by the successors of those who

The Ecology of Tsembaga Maring Subsistence

The Maring are a people living in two large river valleys, the Simbai and Jimi, of mountainous highland New Guinea. There are about 20 local groups of Maring-speakers, varying in size from a little more than 100 to 900. We are fortunate that three detailed studies of Maring ecology have been carried out in different local groups, by Rappaport (1967, 1968, 1971c), Clarke (1971), and Vayda et al. (1961), giving us unusually rich information. Here we will examine the Tsembaga Maring, a local group of 200 studied by Rappaport.

The Tsembaga are shifting horticulturalists. Though their steep valley habitat rises in less than 3 miles from the Simbai River (2,200 feet) to a mountain ridge of 7,200 feet (a territory of 3.2 square miles), only the slopes from the river to about 5,000 feet can be effectively cultivated. About 1,000 acres of this sloping land were used as gardens or were lying fallow. Forty-six acres had been planted during the year of study; about 100 acres (10 percent of the total garden land) were in gardens that year, since some gardens are used for 2 years or longer. Rappaport

Tsembaga Maring cultivations: (left) A new garden is planted.
(right) A mature garden from which taro and sweet potatoes have been harvested.

considered that the potential carrying capacity of the land might be about 200 persons per square mile of arable land; the actual density was 124.

Horticulture provides 99 percent of the everyday Tsembaga diet. But they also eat wild pigs, marsupials, reptiles, and grubs from the surrounding forest. A typical garden contains not only the main staples, sweet potatoes and taro, but also other starchy crops such as yams, manioc, and bananas; and a wide range of legumes, leafy greens, and other vegetables, plus sugarcane. The intricate intermingling of garden crops creates a kind of miniature garden version of a tropical rain forest (Geertz 1963).

To build a garden a Tsembaga family must first clear secondary forest. Men and women begin by clearing undergrowth (now with machetes, previously with stone adzes). After about 2 weeks, men fell most of the trees; they leave the largest ones stripped but standing. Clearing, Rappaport estimated, requires more than two and a half times as much energy investment per acre as felling the trees. The gardens are then fenced to keep out wild and domestic pigs—an incentive to cluster gardens together to minimize fencing. Fencing requires somewhat less than half the energy investment per acre of the initial clearing, and again is done by men. When the garden litter dries it is stacked and burned, and the garden is weeded; this work is divided between women and men. Preparing the garden requires a relatively brief investment of work, but keeping it weeded over the months that the crops are maturing requires sustained effort—more than three times the total energy of initial clearance.

Harvesting and hauling crops are also demanding, though visibly rewarding, tasks. Rappaport estimated that about 300,000 calories per acre are invested in gardening, and that about 5 million calories of food per acre are harvested—somewhat more than 16 to 1 as a return on energy invested. Rappaport (1971c) estimated that in a more typical year than the one he observed when residences were scattered through the gardens, the yield ratio would probably be around 20 to 1. This ratio is more than double the return on subsistence energy invested by the hunting and gathering San of southern Africa (R. Lee 1969, Harris 1971; cf. Kemp 1971 for the Inuit)—evidence of the progressively more efficient investment of energy made possible by human technological advance.*

A factor in gardening strategies is the number of domestic pigs to be fed. Tsembaga pig husbandry runs in cycles. When a family is feeding only one or two pigs, one major garden at middle altitude, sufficient to feed the animals and their owners, is cultivated. When the number of pigs is increased, a garden containing mainly sweet potatoes (fed to the pigs as well as eaten by humans) is cultivated high on the slopes above 4,500 feet; and a second, lower-altitude garden is planted with mainly taro and yams.

We will see in the next chapter how this cycle of pig husbandry is geared to Tsembaga religious ritual and politics. There we will look in detail at Rappaport's sophisticated and persuasive argument that Tsembaga Maring culture—its religious rites as well as its social organization and economy—represents an intricate and balanced adaptive system that adjusts Maring life to the exigencies of their difficult environment.

*This, as Sahlin's "primitive affluence" depiction suggests, does not necessarily mean that hunter-gatherers have to work harder to earn a livelihood than swidden cultivators. The Tsembaga make very heavy energy investments to raise pigs, while the San hunt wild game animals as a source of animal protein; moreover, the vast quantities of starchy tubers the Tsembaga must eat to stay alive constitute high calories but thin nutrition. The San survive well on far lower caloric intake. The point is that you can double the return on energy invested—and depending on what form the caloric return takes and how it is used, you may still have to work harder and longer to survive.

had cleared the land. We will see in Chapter 9 how groups based on descent from founding ancestors exercised control, in such societies, not unlike that of corporations.

Entailments of Iron Technology

Southeast Asian peoples practicing swidden cultivation using iron tools contrast in several ways with horticulturalists such as the Maring. First, their primary dependence on a seasonal seed-crop, rice, imposed different constraints on social life. Second, iron technology led to different divisions of labor and different relationships to land and forest, to which different sorts of social groupings were adaptive. The Iban of Sarawak in Borneo (see Case 6) illustrate these contrasts. They further serve to remind us that the distributions of peoples in the tribal world were constantly shifting, not ancient, and that stable, adaptive, and ecologically reverent relationships to the environment were far from universal.

Here we can turn to a brief look at the ecology and economy of pastoral peoples, and the ways in which production shapes social relations and institutions. Then, in the next chapter, we will step back to look in more general terms at the processes that shape the development of sociocultural systems.

14. PASTORAL ADAPTATIONS

Pastoral Adaptations in Time and Space

The early food producers of the Near East had mixed economies of cultivation and herding. While it was agriculture that in the long run made possible revolutionary changes in the organization of society, herding of sheep and goats provided the possibility for specialized adaptation to arid areas

where cultivation was limited or impossible. In the arid mountain belt across south-central Asia, from near the Mediterranean to the Himalayas, these pastoral adaptations enabled relatively sparse populations to inhabit zones, such as those in Iran and Afghanistan, that had become too dry for agriculture.

Historically, pastoralism thus represents an offshoot of the early mixed agriculture and herding complexes, in adaptation to dry grasslands. Whereas Neolithic cultivation enabled humans to create miniature environments where plant domesticates could thrive, herding of domestic animals allowed no such control. It was humans who had to conform to the patterns of rainfall and natural vegetation, and to substantial degree, to the biological cycles and needs of the animals they herded. Often this required seasonal migration, or **transhumance.** Domestication of the horse, probably in central Eurasia about 2000 B.C., opened new possibilities—for an enormous new mobility, in the vast, grassy slopes of central Asia, and a fully nomadic life. Cattle herding, widespread in the Old World, represents another mode of adaptation. As we will shortly see, the centrality of cattle in human life is particularly striking in some parts of east Africa.

Pastoral economies, developing in marginal zones around those where settled agriculture predominated, have for several millennia been closely tied to those of sedentary peasants and of states on whose peripheries they lay. Understanding pastoralists requires that we keep a kind of double field of vision—seeing at once the internal organization of pastoral life and the external system in which it is set. Even the boundaries between sedentarism and nomadism, and between pastoralism and cultivation, are by no means neat. Movement between sedentary and pastoral groups has historically

A Hindu shepherd in the Himalayas. These pastoralists take their flocks of sheep and goats to high pastures in summer and to the Punjab plains in winter.

been common; nomads may settle, then move again; and pastoralists often cultivate crops as well. Even fully nomadic peoples like the Mongols represent not an independence from settled agricultural communities but a kind of symbiotic interdependence with them. The horsemen who were the scourge of Egypt, of medieval Europe, and of China depended on settled communities for many of the products they needed to survive. In turn, the herds of the nomads contributed centrally to the economy of settled groups during the periods of peace. Nomadic life offered an escape from poverty for peoples on the margins; yet in times of drought the settled communities provided a refuge for nomads.

Pastoral Adaptations: Southwest Asia and East Africa

We will look briefly at two modes of pastoral adaptation: one from the zone of southwest Asia where herding of sheep and goats has been practiced for millennia (Case 7), and one from the East African zone, where specialized traditions of cattle herding have long been a focus of anthropological interest (Case 8). We will then come back to a more general look at the relationship between pastoral ecology, the ways production is structured, and the organization of social and political life.

The African complex of pastoralism is based on cattle herding. The symbiosis between humans and cattle, and the symbolic elaborations of the "cattle complex," have long attracted anthropological interest. These elaborations are carried to most remarkable lengths in East Africa. The Karimojong of Uganda provide a vivid illustration.

Pastoralism and the Structure of Society

How are we to interpret more generally the relationship between ecological constraints imposed by animal husbandry in marginal environments and the organization of pastoral societies? Two themes have been prominent in the literature. One has been to view the ecological pressures and biological constraints of animal husbandry as the active forces, and the organization of pastoral societies as a sort of passive adaptation to these natural exigencies. Another has been to take an imagined "pure nomadic" society developing in isolation as the ideal model, and to regard departures from this—such as partial sedentarism or partial agriculture, as among Karimojong and Basseri—as a consequence of outside influences. Thus, the fundamentally egalitarian nature of pastoral

Iban Agriculture

Iban communities consist of long-houses, the component apartments of which are occupied by separate families. We will trace this pattern of family organization in Case 26. Here the system of cultivating dry rice will give important ecological insights.

An Iban "tribe" is a population occupying a series of long-house communities in a single river

An Iban swidden: This steep hillside, cleared and burned, will be planted with rice and harvested. If it is planted with a second crop, severe erosion and deforestation may result.

system. Marriage normally takes place only within a tribe; head-hunting is directed outside. The tribes are not permanently settled, however. The Iban have proliferated and greatly expanded their territory in historic times—moving steadily into the vast virgin forests of the Baleh region and displacing alien peoples that stood in their way, including hunter-gatherers and other horticulturalists, with "fierce attacks":

The "rich, untouched vegetation" of the Baleh was, to the Iban, the most inviting of prizes, and their desire to exploit it was the overruling incentive of their advance and an important motive in prompting their fierce attacks on alien tribes that stood in the way. Head-hunting and a craving for virgin land went hand in hand. (Freeman 1955:111)

The desire for virgin land expresses a knowledge of the rich subsistence it provides. In prayers, the Iban ask for land:

Land that is fat, fat in deep layers, luxuriant land, land that is fruitful, soil soft and fecund, land richly fertile. (Freeman 1955:115)

By cultivating virgin forest—feasible with their homemade iron tools—the Iban secure rights over the forest territory that is created. But the drive is not only to secure land, where "land is wealth" (Freeman 1955:115), but to keep pressing onward, with an "insatiable appetite."

Iban fell virgin forest, clear, and burn in ways not dissimilar to Tsembaga practices. But growing dry rice imposes a seasonality, in which planting, weeding, harvest, and threshing of the rice structure the annual round of life. This round can be ecologically balanced, if the scrub vegetation *(krukoh)* that grows in old gardens is allowed to return to secondary forest and lie fallow. But Iban prefer to maximize short-term rewards, not long-term balance. Their more usual strategy is to cut and clear the *krukoh* scrub vegetation and to plant a second year's rice crop in the same garden. This makes weeding, burning, and other tasks easier; and it yields a maximum return, since the second year's crop is often better than the first. But the 2-year cycle leaves the land plundered, and the family carves deeper into the virgin forest again—leaving erosion, deforestation, and ecological devastation in their wake.

The reason for this overcultivation . . . [includes] an historically rooted conviction that there are always other forests to conquer, a warrior's view of natural resources as plunder to be exploited, a large village settlement pattern which makes shifting between plots a more than usually onerous task, and, perhaps, a superior indifference toward agricultural proficiency. (Geertz 1963:16)

Productive relationships contrast with those of the Maring. Economic independence of component family units, political unity of the long-house group in matters of warfare and internal order, and an egalitarianism and individualism as fierce as their foreign policy are keystones of Iban life. Here it is worth emphasizing the characteristic pattern, for Southeast Asian iron-using peoples, that the forest itself is a "free good." In clearing primary forest, one does not gain title over the secondary forest that is created. And correspondingly, the relevance of a descent-based corporation-like group controlling title over an estate in land falls away.

CASE

7

Basseri Nomads of Southern Iran

The Basseri of southern Iran are pastoral, tent-dwelling nomads numbering some 16,000. They migrate seasonally through a strip of land some 300 miles long, an area of about 2,000 square miles. Some of the villagers through whose areas the Basseri move claim a common origin with the nomads; the mosaic of languages and cultures of agricultural villagers and nomads is quite complicated.

The seasonal migration pattern is shaped by the physical environment. There is winter snow in the northern mountains, a well-watered middle region around 5,000 feet elevation (where most of the agriculturalists are settled), and lower pasture land to the south that becomes arid in summer. Each of the nomadic tribes of south Iran has its own traditional migration pattern.

The Basseri economy rests squarely on their large herds of sheep and goats. Milk, meat, wool, and hides come from these herds and can be traded with villagers to meet other needs. Transportation is provided by horses, donkeys, and camels. Sheep's and goat's milk are mixed at the time of milking, and soured; sour milk, jun-ket, and cheese are the primary foods. During the summer, when pastures are rich, the Basseri remain temporarily settled. Food surpluses are built up in the form of cheese and meat on the hoof, which provide subsistence in the leaner winter months. The Basseri also eat agricultural products. Most are obtained by trade, but the Basseri grow some wheat at their summer camps. Hunting and collecting contribute minimally to the economy.

The mobility of the Basseri is reflected in the realm of social organization. Family groups, conceived as "tents," are the main units of production and consumption. These tent groups, represented by their male heads, hold full rights over property and sometimes act as independent political units. All of the property of a tent group—tents, bedding, cooking equipment—must be moved, along with the herds, when the group migrates. An average family would have 6 to 12 donkeys and somewhat less than 100 sheep and goats. In winter, the families separate into small clusters of 2 to 5 tents, associated as herding units. The rest of the year, larger camps of 10 to 40 tents

societies has been stressed by many writers. Where one finds social stratification among pastoralists, then, it must ipso facto be a result of the influence of outside forces.

These rather simplistic perspectives have been clarified considerably in the last several years. First, much more detailed and critical studies of the ecology and economics of pastoral production have become available (notably Dahl and Hjort 1976). They point both to the complexity of these systems—which rules out glib interpretations or sweeping generalizations—and to their diversity. As Dahl notes,

Pastoralism is not one single type of ecological adaptation. It is fallacious to equate all livestock-oriented societies, even all pastoralists who must move regularly. . . .

Under certain circumstances, notably those in pastoral East Africa, ecology has made a greater impact on society than in other contexts. . . . [But although] many general—and often vague—references are made in the literature to the "harshness of nature," and even though specific constraints occasionally enter into the anthropological analysis, little has been done in the systematic study of the exact nature of these constraints . . . and . . . their restricting effects on society. (Dahl 1979:263)

move together. Members of these camps comprise solidary communities; but because of their mobile patterns, quarreling may lead to temporary or even permanent fission.

At higher levels, the Basseri are divided into *Tira* or "sections"—units that are structurally equivalent but of different size. Most of them are divided into "families" or *oulads* (as many as six), each with a headman, and with a particular grazing area and migration route. *Oulads* of the same section have closely linked migration routes and schedules.

The sections . . . differ somewhat in prestige—partly because of differences in wealth, partly because of different genealogical traditions, especially the fact that the chiefly dynasty sprang from a branch of one of them. (Barth 1961:50)

Membership in an *oulad* is determined by descent in the male line, and the structure of sections is—at least in idealized versions—based on connections of descent in the male line.

The scattered and constantly shifting tent camps of the Basseri are held together and welded into a unit by their centralized political system, culmi-

nating in the single office of the chief. . . . The chief . . . is the central, autocratic leader of the tribe. (Barth 1961:71)

The chief and his immediate relatives belong in a category entirely apart from the rest of the Basseri. . . . Subject to the approval of the ruling chief, they are free to associate with any oulad and to utilize any of the Basseri pastures. Most of them, however, own lands and take little part in nomadic life. . . . The chief and his brothers . . . are sophisticated members of the *elite* on a . . . national level. . . . In wealth they are also in a class entirely apart from other Basseri, each owning several villages as well as flocks of many thousand head of sheep and goats. (Barth 1961:73–74)

As we will shortly see, one of the central issues in the contemporary interpretation of pastoralists is how to treat the seeming contradiction whereby among nomads such as the Basseri some social relations are fiercely egalitarian yet the people as a whole are closely incorporated within wider national and regional systems in ways that reveal great disparities of class, wealth, and power.

These and other issues were debated in a 1976 conference (1Équipe Écologie et Anthropologie des Sociétés Pastorales 1979). Both the ideal typification of "nomad society" and the supposed ecological determination of egalitarian society came under concerted scrutiny—particularly as the many documented cases of social stratification in pastoral societies were examined.

The ideal type of the "nonstratified nomadic pastoral society" has perhaps survived the critical scrutiny—but not unscathed. Lefébure (1979:2) characterizes such societies by a "particular combination

of domestic and community patterns of production." First, production is centered in family groups. These supply the labor of herding and depend on the multiple products of livestock (milk, meat, wool, etc.) for their survival. When family producing units cooperate, as in guarding or moving flocks, they do so in temporary and shifting groups, as among the Basseri. Second, there is a close relationship between the cyclical growth and dissolution of herds and the cycles families themselves go through:

Each stockbreeder seeking to found a new production unit and to ensure its

CASE
8

Karimojong Pastoralism

The Karimojong comprise some 60,000 pastoralists occupying about 4,000 square miles of semiarid plain in northeastern Uganda. The position of cattle among the Karimojong is best introduced by their ethnographers, the Dyson-Hudsons:

Cattle are property, and accordingly they represent variable degrees of wealth, of social status, and of community influence. They are a man's legacy to his sons. They can be exchanged to symbolize formal contracts of friendship and mutual assistance. The transfer of cattle from the groom's family to the bride's is needed to validate a marriage. The sacrifice of cattle is a vital feature of religious observances. The focus of Karimojong aspirations is the acquisition of cattle, and disputed cattle ownership is at the root of most Karimojong quarrels. Cattle are considered proper objects of man's affection, and this conviction is an integral part of each man's life cycle. (Dyson-Hudson and Dyson-Hudson 1969:359)

Yet first and foremost cattle provide subsistence, by transforming the energy stored in the grasses, herbs, and shrubs of a difficult environment.

Blood and milk products, not meat, provide the primary subsistence. Cattle are bled once every 3 to 5 months. Cows are milked morning and night; ghee (butter and curdled milk) can be stored and is centrally important in the diet. Milk, often mixed with blood, provides the main diet, especially for the men who move with the herds.

Cultivation of sorghum provides secondary subsistence. Women, based in the permanent settlements in the center of Karimojong land, do the cultivation, while men follow the sparse rainfall to find grazing lands. Cultivation and collecting of wild foods provide important daily subsistence for the women, and also give some insurance-in-diversity in a harsh environment where droughts and cattle diseases pose a recurring threat. Cattle are slaughtered rarely, mainly for initiations and sacrifices; and those are mainly performed when drought forces reductions in the herd.

With a limited technology that precludes bringing food or water to their herds, or storing most foods, the Karimojong must follow strategies that minimize risk in a harsh and unpredictable environment as well as maximize subsistence production. Rather than modifying their environment, the Karimojong must adapt their lives to it; but in doing so, they build a rich world of cultural symbols and social arrangements (see, for example, the account of Karimojong age sets in Case 32, Chapter 10).

reproduction is faced with two requirements: first, he needs to acquire livestock and one or more wives; second, he must be able to maintain the size of his herd and to beget heirs. The controlled circulation of women through marriage ... implies the circulation of a portion of the herd through different matrimonial payments [to obtain wives for his sons]. . . . The size of the herd corresponds to a moment in the domestic group's developmental cycle; in other words, this group's food requirements having been satisfied in one way or another, herd-size is a function of the intensity, at the time in question, of the technico-economic, matrimonial, political and symbolic prac-

East African pastoralist: Samburu man with his cattle, Masai National Park, Kenya.

tices designed to ensure the group's reproduction. (Lefébure 1979:3)

But nomadic domestic groups are also organized into wider communities. The interconnections between these groups are established through temporary alliances in herding, through marital alliances and exchanges, and their need for collective access to grazing land and natural resources. Lefébure characterizes the "collective" identity of pastoralist societies, as expressed in societywide structures based on kinship or age or religious rites, as in some sense fictional—disguising the fundamental atomism of the units of production and consumption. The egalitarianism of such societies refers not to the equality of young with old, or of men to women. They may be sharply separated in rights and roles. Rather, it is the male heads of domestic units who are equals—in terms of their place in the system, not necessarily in wealth. (See also Dahl 1987 on women's roles in the productive process in pastoral societies.)

Lefébure goes on to show the imbalances in such systems, which—even apart from the impact of the state societies on whose margins pastoralists lie—can move them in the direction of stratification. The prosperous household head can

> weave around himself a web of economic and social relations that can subsequently prove of great advantage. He will be more resilient, recovering more quickly from the consequences of drought, animal epidemics, enemy raids, etc. . . . He will have access to a choice of grazing lands and wells, so much so that among the Karimojong [see Case 8] . . . one herdsman may enjoy access to as much as four or five times the amount of space . . . as the least-favoured of his peers. He is in the position to pay or otherwise secure the services of a shepherd. Above all, his wealth will affect his social status, giving him greater influence in the council of elders. A newly rich herdsman may therefore acquire the rank of notable or leader. (Lefébure 1979:7)

Stratification may go much further than this, as many of the papers of the 1976 conference indicate. And it will not suffice to say that this is a consequence of outside contamination. At least in central and southwest Asia, such "contamination" is fundamental to the history of pastoral peoples (Krader 1979).

The issues about pastoral societies— whether they can be understood in terms of ecological shaping of social structure, whether they can properly be analyzed in terms of ideal types free from "contamination," whether they can properly be understood at all as separate cultural units—have wider theoretical ramifications. We will trace them out in the chapters to follow. At this stage, one particular set of questions is crucial.

These are questions we have touched on since they were raised at the end of the last chapter. To what extent is the organization of hunting and gathering societies shaped by ecological constraints? To what extent is the social organization of tropical horticulturalists an adaptation to their ecosystems? With pastoralists, the shaping force of ecology would seem to be more immediate, because humans have to organize their lives so directly around the food and water supplies and habits of their animals and the exigencies of climate. Is ecological adaptation then the primary factor shaping the organization of human societies, at least of those with limited technologies? If so, does this process of adaptation operate directly in some realms of culture, and weakly if at all in others? Does ecological adaptation shape the organization and distribution of social groups and their economic life, leaving free reign to religious beliefs and rituals and other symbolic elaborations of a culture? Or are these other areas of culture also shaped, in hidden ways, by processes of ecological adaptation? We are facing here some of the most basic issues in anthropological theory. We need to look at them in further detail.

SUMMARY

Hunter-gatherer populations in the contemporary world are not necessarily identical in their lifeways with those who lived in richer Paleolithic environments, but they do appear to have time for leisure and relaxation. They are generally organized into patrilocal bands whose families may disperse over wide areas in the subsistence quest (examples are the Shoshoni and the San). Fighting could take place between bands. Their religions tend to reflect their close relationship with the resources of the natural world.

Tropical horticulturists practicing swidden cultivation have a more sedentary way of life and engage in varying degrees of intensification of labor inputs on their land (examples are the Tsembaga Maring and the Iban).

Pastoralists are usually seasonally transhumant, moving between ecological niches according to the availability of food for their animals (examples are the Basseri nomads and the Karimojong). Production is centered in domestic groups, but wider collective identities are constructed on the basis of descent and age sets. Inequality between households can develop.

Anthropologists debate the extent of influence that ecological factors can have on the culture, social organization, and religion of the peoples they study.

SUGGESTIONS FOR FURTHER READING

SECTION 12

Bicchieri, M. G., ed. 1972. *Hunters and Gatherers Today: A Socioeconomic Study of Eleven Such Cultures in the Twentieth Century.* New York: Holt, Rinehart and Winston.

Coon, C. S. 1971. *The Hunting Peoples.* Boston: Little, Brown and Company.

Crum, S. J. 1994. *The Road on Which We Came: A History of the Western Shoshone.* Salt Lake City: University of Utah Press.

Graburn, N. H. H., and B. S. Strong. 1973. *Circumpolar Peoples: An Anthropological Perspective.* Pacific Palisades, Calif.: Goodyear Publishing Company.

Kelly, R. L. 1995. *The Foraging Spectrum. Diversity in Hunter-Gatherer Lifeways.* Washington: Smithsonian Institution Press.

Lee, R. B., and I. DeVore, eds., 1968. *Man the Hunter.* Chicago: Aldine Publsihing Company.

————. 1974. *Kalahari Hunter-Gatherers.* Cambridge, Mass.: Harvard University Press.

Oswalt, W. H. 1973. *Habitat and Technology: The Evolution of Hunting.* New York: Holt, Rinehart and Winston.

Service, E. R. 1979. *The Hunters,* 2nd ed. Englewood Cliffs, N.J.: Prentice-Hall, Inc.

Testart, A. 1988. Some Major Problems in the Social Anthropology of Hunter-Gatherers. *Current Anthropology* 29(10): 1–31.

SECTION 13

Clarke, W. C. 1971. *Place and People: An Ecology of a New Guinea Community.* Berkeley: University of California Press.

Conklin, H. C. 1954. An Ethnoecological Approach to Shifting Agriculture. *Transcripts of New York Academy of Sciences* 17(2): 133–142.

De Schlippe, P. 1956. *Shifting Cultivation in Africa.* London: Routledge & Kegan Paul Ltd.

Geertz, C. 1963. *Agricultural Involution.* Berkeley: University of California Press.

Healey, C. 1990. *Maring Hunters and Traders.* Berkeley: University of California Press.

Kuntstadter, P., et al., eds., 1978. *Farmers in the Forest.* Honolulu: University of Hawaii Press.

SECTION 14

Beck, L. 1991. *Nomad: A Year in the Life of a Qashqa'i Tribesman in Iran.* Berkeley: University of California Press.

Galaty, J. G., and D. L. Johnson, eds. 1990. *The World of Pastoralism: Herding Systems in Comparative Perspective.* London: Guilford Press.

Irons, W., and N. Dyson-Hudson, eds. 1972. *Perspectives on Nomadism.* Leiden. W. J. Brill. (International Studies in Sociology and Social Anthropology, Vol. 13.)

Weissleder, W., ed. 1978. *The Nomadic Alternative: Modes and Models of Interaction in the African-Asian Deserts and Steppes.* The Hague: Mouton and Company.

How Cultures Change

The importance of ecological adaptation in shaping cultural heritages has been a central theme in anthropology since the pioneering explorations of the American anthropologist Julian Steward and the British anthropologist-geographer Daryll Forde. A theory of cultures as adaptive responses to ecosystems has been given modern form by social anthropologists such as Roy Rappaport and A. P. Vayda, in terms of sophisticated **systems theory** models; and by theoretically minded archaeologists looking at humans-in-environments over long time spans. The theory that cultures serve adaptive ends, often in ways disguised by a people's own religious or sociological explanations, has been flamboyantly argued by American anthropologist Marvin Harris, in a series of popular books and technical works. Arguing for a theory of "cultural materialism," Harris sees the primary shaping forces in the development of local cultural traditions to be the biological imperatives of survival in ecosystems, particularly the need for high-quality protein and the need to regulate population increase. For every seemingly exotic custom there is some material, biological rationality, if we probe beneath cultural ideologies to find it.

In this chapter I will illustrate the sophisticated systems-theoretic interpretations of cultures as adaptive systems, and will set out the argument of cultural materialism in two case studies about which controversy has arisen.

I will suggest that despite the plausibility and scientific guise of these theories that see cultures as responses to biological pressures, they are defective in some major respects. I will argue that biological constraints do indeed play an important part in the development of sociocultural systems—but that the processes through which they operate are much less simple and direct than those postulated by cultural materialists.

At the end of the chapter, I will point briefly to the need for a more powerful theory of sociocultural change, and will suggest what I take to be the sources for such a theory—a theory that will represent a synthesis of several streams of anthropological thought, and is barely yet emerging. This preliminary sketch of the sources and scope of an emerging theory of sociocultural change (and stability) will then progressively be given substance in later chapters. In these chapters, examining the "tribal" world (as very broadly defined) in terms of economics, kinship, politics, law, religion, and so on, I will try to establish both the conceptual tools and the foundations of concrete evidence that will make a more

Man butchering a pig by removing its innards, Melpa, Papua New Guinea.

sophisticated view of sociocultural process possible. First, we need to look carefully at theories of cultures as adaptive systems.

15. CULTURAL ECOLOGY, CULTURAL MATERIALISM

Evolution—Biological and Sociocultural

Humans are animals, and like all other animals must maintain an adaptive relationship with their ecosystems in order to survive—although they achieve this adaptation principally through the medium of culture.

A crucial starting point is to ask ourselves how cultures change over time. We have defined a culture as a system of more or less shared ideational designs for a living characteristic of a particular people. These ideational designs are only one set of elements shaping the behavior of a population in an ecosystem; it is on these *behavior patterns* that evolutionary processes operate. We are not asking, then, simply how cultures evolve, but how sociocultural systems-in-environments evolve.

When we place the behavior of human populations in this broadened biological perspective, we risk a misunderstanding. It is true that human populations are ultimately subject to the biological laws that affect any animal population: they must reproduce in adequate numbers and not irreversibly degrade their ecosystem.

But this is not to say that the processes of change in the cultural (that is, learned) components of human behavior are necessarily identical to the processes of natural selection that shape the genetic information in a population. Woodpeckers cannot decide not to peck holes in trees. If their feeding patterns degraded the vegetable components of their ecosystem, their population would be affected accordingly—and their genes would change only by an indirect process of gradual adaptation. A people can change their customs: they can prohibit hunting a totem animal or decide not to build nuclear power plants. The *consequences* of such changes are subject to biological laws; the *processes* of change may be quite different.

Ecological Approaches in Anthropology

Julian Steward (1955) postulated that there is a core area of sociocultural systems that is particularly responsive to ecological adaptation: the division of labor; the size and stability of local groups, and their distribution in space; and residence rules. Adjustments to ecological pressures directly affect these core elements of social structure; thus, the seasonality of climate, availability of water, or fertility of the soil would shape how many people could live in settlements, how permanent these could be, how they would be scattered, and how the population would organize their productive efforts. These influences on social structure then ramify through a culture so as to promote changes in realms only secondarily related to ecology—in cosmological ideas, patterns of political succession, art, and the like.

Subsequent theorists of cultural adaptation have mainly followed Steward in viewing subsistence technology and production and the social organization whereby foods and other scarce material goods are produced, controlled, and distributed as the core areas of sociocultural systems where selective pressures are most direct. We can look at these processes of ecological adaptation either across long time spans or across short time spans. That is, we can look at the long-run processes through which more complex sociocultural systems evolve out of simpler ones. (This is one path pioneered by Steward and, in a different way, by the American cultural-evolutionist Leslie White, who looked at this long-range emergence of increasing complexity in terms of the development of progressively greater thermodynamic efficiency.) Or we can take a closer-range look over shorter time spans, seeking to account for processes of what we might call sociocultural "microevolution." Taking a close-up view of microevolutionary processes, we may seek to explain why a particular complex of customs—say, a rule of descent, a pattern of local-group formation, a mode of warfare, or a system of marriage—appears in some societies (in say, New Guinea) and not in others.

Some cultural anthropologists concerned with evolutionary processes and the ecological shaping of sociocultural systems have taken the longer-range view, joining prehistorians in interpreting state formation and the emergence of higher degrees of societal complexity (see, e.g., Carneiro 1970, Cohen 1978a, Cohen 1978b, Service 1975). Other ecologically oriented anthropologists have viewed different settings as ecological niches in which diverse ways of life have evolved through adaptation.

It may be reasonable to account for the "core" of some New Guinea peoples' socio-cultural systems, in Steward's sense—that is, the size and composition and settlement pattern of local groups, their patterns of economy and resource exploitation, their political relations and warfare. But is it reasonable to expect that their religious beliefs, their initiation rites or the lack of them, would be shaped by physical pressures such as those that arise from environmental conditions?

Systems-Theoretic Anthropological Ecology

Roy Rappaport, one the most sophisticated proponents of ecological anthropology, would argue that the answer to the foregoing question is yes. Drawing on his detailed ethnography of the Tsembaga Maring, which we glimpsed in Chapter 6 (Case 5), Rappaport uses a systems theory model to argue for a hidden rationality in Maring culture. His position is that Maring rituals have a number of unintended adaptive results that are beneficial for individuals and communities, as shown in Case 9.

Rappaport's view of humans-in-environment as an incredibly complex network of circuits through which information passes, a network that includes cultural beliefs and their consequences as well as ecological events, is boldly innovative and at first hard to grasp. It leads him to see ritual operating as a "homeostat" (like a heating thermostat), and as a "transducer" (converting complex information about the number of pigs, state of human relations, preparedness for war, or strength of allies into a simple binary or "yes-no" signal the neighbors can easily "read": the *rumbim* is uprooted). It leads him to speculate that *sanctity*, the unquestioned

ultimate truth of religious belief, may have a major adaptive significance in human life. Our elevation of science and rationality, our loss of ultimate faith, may be more directly related to our ecological crisis than most have realized (Rappaport 1970, 1971a, 1971b).

But can systems of cultural belief be adaptive rather than maladaptive, if these beliefs lack empirical foundations? Scientific accuracy of a cosmological belief is not the crucial matter—only "whether or not it elicits behavior contributing to the well-being of the actors and to the maintenance of the ecosystem of which they are parts" (Rappaport 1971d:261). Accurate, naturalistic (that is, scientific) explanation may even have negative survival value in the long run:

> It is by no means certain that the representations of nature provided us by science are more adaptive or functional than those images of the world, inhabited by spirits whom men respect, that guide the action of the Maring and other "primitives." Indeed they may be less so, for to drape nature in supernatural veils is perhaps to provide her with some protection against human parochialism and destruction. (Rappaport 1971d:262).

Interpretations similar to Rappaport's have been advanced regarding the way beliefs about the relationships between women and men—especially in New Guinea and elsewhere in Melanesia—may serve ecologically adaptive ends. In many New Guinea societies, men's and women's domains are widely separated. There may be separate initiation rites for the sexes. Men may organize for war and ceremonial exchange, which they claim is their domain (although there is usually a reliance on cooperation between the sexes to achieve these aims). Women raise pigs that they contribute to festivals where men play prominent roles. The sexes may occupy separate houses, and this may partly be explained by the people as

CASE

9

Tsembaga Culture as an Adaptive System

Rappaport (1967, 1968) begins by noting the role of pig-raising in Tsembaga life. Normally, when few pigs are being raised, pigs root freely in the day and return to the owners' houses at night to be fed the substandard sweet potatoes. The pigs are then sacrificed to ancestors at times of intergroup fighting or illness. Rappaport notes that these sacrifices have physiologically adaptive consequences, even though the participants are presumably unaware of them. When a pig is sacrificed to ancestors to cure a patient's illness, the patient (as well as his immediate kin)

receives high-quality protein badly needed at a time of physical stress (where the normal diet is marginally protein deficient). So too do the warriors, when a sacrifice is made before a fight.

More interesting in their ecological ramifications are the elaborate ritual cycles that bring the number of pigs far above the normal level. To understand these pig cycles, Rappaport suggests, we need to look at political relations. Maring local groups live in alternating states of hostility and peace. When warfare breaks out between groups, usually ones occupying adjoining

Tsembaga Maring magic: Objects to be used in the purification of the dance ground are bespelled. The stake is to pierce corruption, the cordyline-leaf broom is to sweep it away.

A visiting group charges onto the Tsembaga Maring dance ground.

territory, the fighting may continue sporadically for weeks. Often it is more or less balanced, and there is no decisive victory. But sometimes one of the groups is routed. The survivors take refuge with relatives in other groups; their houses, gardens, and pigs are destroyed. But the territory laid waste cannot at that stage be occupied by the victors; it is still guarded by the ancestors of the vanquished.

When hostilities end, a group that has not been driven from its territory performs a ritual in which a *rumbim*, a sacred cordyline shrub, is ritually planted. All their pigs, other than juveniles, are killed and dedicated to the ancestors. Most of the pork goes to allies from surrounding groups who took part in the fighting. Stringent taboos in force during hostilities are partially lifted, but

material and spiritual debts to allies and ancestors remain unpaid. This state of debt and danger—though of formal truce—remains until the *rumbim* can be ritually uprooted and a pig festival *(kaiko)* can be staged. And that takes a great many pigs. It takes time and great effort to raise large herds, perhaps 5 or 10 years.

As the pig herd builds up, the burden of feeding them requires great expansion of gardens and major investment of effort. The Tsembaga herd of 169 animals Rappaport recorded just before their *kaiko* pig festival was getting 54 percent of the sweet potatoes harvested and 82 percent of the manioc. The gardens were 36.1 percent larger before the pig festival than they were afterwards.

Continued

Case 9 continued

Pressure to uproot the *rumbim* and slaughter the pigs predictably comes from the women on whose shoulders rests most of the burden of feeding expanding herds. It also comes from quarreling and often violence triggered by pigs breaking into gardens; to minimize this, the settlement pattern becomes increasingly dispersed.

The *kaiko* festival begins with planting of stakes at the boundary. If a vanquished and dispersed neighboring group has remained elsewhere as refugees, and has not been strong enough in the intervening years to reoccupy their territory and plant their own *rumbim*, the victors may at this stage extend their boundaries to incorporate the conquered territory: since no *rumbim* has been planted there, the territory is officially unoccupied. Moreover, the participation by the vanquished in the ritual life of the group where they have taken refuge—especially in planting *rumbim* elsewhere—moves their own ancestors and their own group affiliation to those territories.

When the *rumbim* is uprooted, many pigs (in the case observed, 32 out of 169) are slaughtered and distributed to allies and in-laws in other groups. The *kaiko* continues for about a year. During this time, the host group entertains neighboring friendly groups from time to time, and dancing and food distributions take place. Rappaport speculates that these dances function as "courtship displays"; but more important, by bringing together the potential allies of a group, they serve to display to the outside world (like a modern political-conference of allied nations) the strength of a potential coalition in the event of war. Rappaport notes that invitations to dance are extended by individuals, recruiting relatives, in-laws, and friends in other groups, along the same lines as invitations to fight:

Dancing and fighting are regarded as in some sense equivalent. Their equivalence is expressed in the similarity of some pre-fight or pre-dance rituals, and the Maring say that those who come to dance come to fight. The size of a visiting dancing contingent is consequently taken [by the group and its potential enemies] as a measure of the size of the contingent of warriors whose assistance may be expected in the next round of warfare. (Rappaport 1967:196)

After a night of dancing, the participants trade: the *kaiko* thus provides a setting for peaceful exchange of scarce goods, including salt and stone tools as well as symbolic wealth.

The *kaiko* concludes with major sacrifices of the remaining adult pigs, which are distributed to members of other local groups following lines of kinship and alliance. An estimated 2,000 to 3,000 Maring in 17 local groups received pork from the Tsembaga *kaiko* distribution Rappaport

resulting from ideas that their bodily substances can be dangerous to each other.

One behavioral consequence of such a set of ideas can be that husband and wife avoid sexual intercourse until a child is weaned, after 2 years or more. The cultural explanation may be that semen and mother's milk must be kept separate: but by spacing childbirth, the adaptive consequences may include ensuring maximum protein for infants in a society subsisting dangerously close to the margins of protein deficiency (Whiting 1964). The same practices may also help to ensure that the woman's body is able to recover from her pregnancy and enhance the likelihood of a healthy birth the next time.

Lindenbaum (1972, 1976) and others have also viewed sexual taboos as, among other things, symbolic means of regulating population. Lindenbaum notes that such taboos are most commonly found where population pressures are extreme, as observed. This was also an occasion for the distribution of wealth between groups in connection with marriage transactions.

When the *kaiko* festival is concluded, fighting could break out again. And usually it did. But a second ritual cycle could eventually be performed if peace was preserved that long; and then the two local groups that had been warring were supposed to be permanently at peace.

Rappaport believes that the ritual cycles of the Maring have a number of consequences, of which the participants are not aware, that help to preserve the balance of the ecosystem, maintain ordered relations between local groups, redistribute land resources in relation to population, and distribute resources—including traded scarce goods and badly needed animal protein:

Ritual cycles . . . play an important part in regulating the relations of these groups with both the non-human components of their immediate environments and the human components of their less immediate environments. (Rappaport 1968:182)

In later analyses, Rappaport has extended this model by tracing the cybernetic interconnections* between Tsembaga culture and ecosystem. He has looked in detail at cosmology—the classes of spirits the Maring believe to exist and

play a part in human affairs. And he notes not only adaptive value in some of these beliefs, but even a kind of parallel between the world as conceived in supernatural terms and the ecosystem. "The behavior of certain spirits, who the Tsembaga say occupy the lower portion of their territory, and the consequences of their behavior, correspond closely to that of the anopheles mosquito whom the Tsembaga do not understand to be a malaria vector" (Rappaport 1970:49). But such parallelism is not necessary for the cultural beliefs to have adaptive consequences—that is, to trigger and channel "messages" through the "circuits" of the system of humans-in-environment so as to correct imbalances in the system.

*Cybernetic interconnections are loops or circuits in an information system through which messages are transmitted—a process called *feedback*. A simple physical example of *negative feedback*—that is, feedback that preserves the stable balance of the system—is a thermostat. As the temperature goes down, the thermostat activates a heating system; as the heat rises, the thermostat shuts it off. But a cybernetic system need not be mechanical—a tightrope walker's pole operates as a circuit that maintains balance through negative feedback. Cybernetic systems may also include *positive feedback* circuits: more of A produces more of B which in turn produces more of A—an armaments race is a dramatic example (see Gregory Bateson's paper "Cybernetic Explanation" in Bateson 1972).

among the Enga of highland New Guinea. Prohibitions on sexual intercourse, found under conditions of population pressure, may serve as "a form of ideological birth control" (Lindenbaum 1972:148).

Cultural Materialism

Marvin Harris and his students have attempted to generalize studies such as Rappaport's analysis of Tsembaga Maring adaptation into a general theory of sociocultural change. Harris calls this general theory *cultural materialism.* The analytical strategy of cultural materialism includes the following expectation:

Similar technologies applied to similar environments tend to produce similar arrangements of labor in production and distribution, and . . . these in turn call forth similar kinds of social groupings, which justify and coordinate their activities by means of similar systems of values and beliefs. (Harris 1968:4)

CASE

10

Warfare, Male Supremacy, Protein Scarcity, and Population in Amazonia

Studies of tropical forest peoples of greater Amazonia, of whom the Yanomamö of Venezuela have become best known, have revealed high levels of murderous warfare between villages: A 1976 incident will serve to illustrate continuing intercommunity violence:

The male members of Toropo-teri [village] participated in an ambush at the nearby village of Yamaho-teri, their friends and allies. The two groups invited the members of a distant village, Kobariwä-teri (4-days walk away) to a feast at Yamaho-teri. When the unsuspecting visitors arrived, they were treacherously attacked by their hosts and five men were killed. Several weeks later, the men from Toropo-teri and Yamaho-teri, supported by additional allies, made the arduous trip to Kobariwä-teri to attack them again. (Chagnon and Hames 1979:912)

Associated with such murderous raiding and ambush is a high level of intra group violence, between males (often in stylized chest-pounding duels) and directed by men at their wives (Chagnon 1968, 1977). Siskind (1973), Harris (1974), and Gross (1975), looking at comparative data on Amazonian societies, have sug-

gested correlations between levels of population, protein availability, settlement patterns, and intergroup conflict. Siskind hypothesized that cultural limits on population through infanticide lead to "an artificially or culturally produced scarcity of women" that throws men into continuous raiding and bloody competition. This, in turn, serves to disperse populations in small, scattered settlements, a pattern which preserves fragile supplies of animal protein. Gross, estimating protein consumption for eight Amazonian populations, hypothesized that the factor limiting the population densities possible in Amazonia is scarcity of animal protein. In doing so, he pointed both to the cultural controls on population that have evolved and to the ecological consequences of intergroup raiding. Harris has suggested that the raiding of the Yanomamö is an indirect adaptation to protein scarcity, with infanticide (and hence imbalances in the sex ratio) throwing men into competition and conflict.

Subsequently, Harris and W. T. Divale broadened the argument, in defining what they call the "male supremacist complex." It is characterized

Harris, as the most thoroughgoing proponent of cultural materialism, has taken it upon himself to examine critically virtually every important anthropological case where customs or institutions have been interpreted in symbolic terms—religious ideologies, value systems, cognitive organization—and to produce a materialist counterinterpretation. In his popular books *Cows, Pigs, Wars, and Witches: The Riddles of*

Culture (1974) and *Cannibals and Kings* (1977), in his general text (1975), and in numerous technical publications, Harris has advanced materialist explanations that suggest a hidden rationality, in terms of ecological adaptation, for a series of cultural practices that on the surface epitomize human irrationality in cultural guise. Sacred cattle in India, pig herding in New Guinea, the Kwakiutl Indian potlatch in which

by male "material, domestic, politic, and military subordination of women . . . matched in the ritual and ideological spheres by pervasive beliefs and practices that emphasize the inferiority of females" (Divale and Harris 1976:525). They postulated warfare as the linchpin of the male supremacy complex and associated its occurrence in band and village societies with population control. Population increase which would degrade the environment is prevented by cultural selection against female children, through infanticide or neglect; a premium is placed on male dominance, bravery, and aggression, with systems of sexual reward through polygyny (multiple wives) for successful men.

Although Harris and Divale set out worldwide patterns of correlation between warfare and component elements of the "male supremacy complex," they came back to Amazonia—in fact to the Yanomamö—for a specific illustration of the causal claims they postulate:

Any sudden shift from high-protein, low-calorie diets to low-protein, high-calorie diets, should produce a spurt of population growth, followed by an increase in female infanticide and the intensification of warfare. The Yanomamö of Amazonia may be the classic case. Expansion of their investment in banana and plantain gardens probably provided the starchy calorie supply for a . . . population explosion among the central villages. This expansion may have adversely affected the fragile animal-protein ecology typical of interriverine Amazonian habitats. Female infanticide produced junior-age sex ratios of 148:100 for 11 Yanomamö villages in the intensive warfare zone, and an intense male supremacist-warfare complex developed. But in 12 Yanomamö villages that were peripher-ally located, junior-age sex ratios were only 118:100 and warfare was less intense. . . . Recently fissioned groups fought each other for possession of . . . garden sites, as well as for possession of the proportionately decreas- ing number of women and protein resources. (Divale and Harris 1976:532–533)

Case Update

The Yanomamö data have recently been reanalyzed from a different perspective (see Ferguson 1989, 1995). Ferguson argues that colonial history has greatly influenced patterns of warfare in this part of the world. See also Westen (1984) for a further consideration of cultural materialism.

blankets and valuables are flamboyantly destroyed, and other customs emerge as ways of regulating resources, acquiring protein, controlling population, or otherwise adapting to material and biological exigencies.

Two major problems facing peoples in small-scale societies emerge as focal themes in Harris's work. The first is the tendency to population growth—which, if not controlled by cultural means, will threaten a people's relationship with their ecosystem. The second is limitation in protein supply. The two, Harris suggests, are closely linked. (See Case 10.)

Do such ecological pressures structure institutions and belief systems only for peoples with relatively simple technologies and social systems? No, say Harris and other cultural materialists such as Harner (1977). A key and controversial case is the Aztec

CASE 11

Aztec Human Sacrifice and Cannibalism

Harner (1977) has argued that religious explanations of Aztec human sacrifice by such distinguished scholars as Caso, Sòustelle, and Vaillant are inadequate to account for "why this particular form of religion demanding large-scale human sacrifice should have evolved where and when it did" (Harner 1977:118). Harner suggests that the development of Aztec human sacrifice is a consequence of heavy population pressure in the Valley of Mexico, the concomitant decrease in availability of wild game, and the absence of a domesticated herbivore as a source of animal protein:

This made the ecological situation of the Aztecs and their neighbors unique among the world's major civilizations. . . . Large-scale cannibalism, disguised as sacrifice, was the natural consequence of this situation. (Harner 1977:119)

Harner notes that whereas human sacrifice among the Aztecs has attracted the attention of many commentators, few have commented on the accompanying cannibalism.

The scale of human sacrifice is appalling. Some 70,000 to 80,000 victims were sacrificed at the dedication of the main pyramid in Tenochtitlan in 1487. Whereas earlier estimates had pointed to an average annual sacrifice of about 15,000 human victims in central Mexico (out of a population of 2 million), recent estimates push the total population as high as 25 million, and suggest that as many as 250,000—1 percent of the total population—were sacrificed each year (Harner 1977, citing W. W. Borah).

That sacrificial victims had their hearts torn out and offered by the priests to the sun god is well known. But what was done with the bodies? Harner cites evidence from contemporaneous Spanish authors that the arms and legs of the butchered bodies were usually eaten:

At least three of the limbs were normally property of the captor, who formally retained ownership of the victim. He then hosted a feast at his quarters, of which the central dish was a stew of tomatoes, peppers, and the limbs of the victim. The torso of the victim, in Tenochtitlan at least, went to the royal zoo to feed carnivorous mammals, birds, and snakes. (Harner 1977:120)

civilization of the Valley of Mexico, whose religious rites, described in Case 11, horrified Spanish invaders.

Cultural materialist-adaptationist interpretations are inherently persuasive. They have a strong aura of being scientific. This comes partly from their phrasing in terms of measurements, numbers, and biological calculations, partly from the nature of the argument. Social phenomena are explained not with reference to the mind, or symbols, but in reference to energy calculations, amino acids, the biology of fertility, and other "hard" data. This persuasive scientism casts cultural explanations in an unfavorable light as unscientific, insubstantial, diffuse, and circular—in contrast to "real" explanations grounded in hard facts of the real world.

But how hard are the facts? And how valid are the assumptions on which they rest (since "facts" can be used to construct a theory only within a framework of assumption)? Is change in sociocultural systems

Commoners were forbidden to partake of human flesh. But Harner infers that the contribution of meat protein to the diet of the upper classes would have been significant. He further speculates that one reason commoners supported and participated in warfare (and risked becoming sacrificial victims of the enemy) was that success in war through the capture of prisoners was a way to rise to noble status. The complex of human sacrifice not only sustained—and provided meat for—the priests; it also provided a reinforcement for the dogmas that the priests were necessary, as mediators in sacrifice, to make the crops grow. When the crops did not grow well, they could claim that more sacrifices were needed. When the crops grew well, they could claim credit.

Either way, the gods could be seen as the benefactors of the population. . . . The maintenance of the religious myth was thus in the interest of the self-preservation of the upper class. (Harner 1977:131)

Harner's hypothesis has been endorsed by Harris (1977), but challenged by others, notably Ortiz de Montellano (1978) and Sahlins (1979).* The grounds for dissent include counterclaims that the Aztec diet was adequate in protein without human flesh, that the lurid ac-

counts of the contemporaneous Spanish observers may reflect propaganda efforts (to induce the king to bring civilization and Christianity to such a cruel and barbarous land), and that the religious motivations of sacrifice have been misunderstood and undervalued. Sahlins writes of sacrifice as communion of priest and victim, and Ortiz de Montellano writes of

the acquiescence of the sacrificed victims to their fate. . . . Only sacrificial victims and battle casualties could go to a heaven associated with the sun and later be reborn as hummingbirds and butterflies. (1978:615)

For a further reconsideration of Aztec materials, see Hassig in Ferguson and Whitehead (1992).

*Arens (1979) in fact claims that the Aztec did not practice cannibalism at all—and that cannibalism has never existed as a human custom, only as a fantasy peoples attribute to their neighbors and enemies. Arens claims that there are no solidly documented cases of institutionalized cannibalism, and that people always attribute it to others, not to themselves. Having read my own great-grandfather's reliable eyewitness accounts of cannibal feasts in Fiji, and myself spent hours talking to Kwaio friends in the Solomon Islands who cheerfully described the culinary delights of the people they ate when they were young, I regard Arens's claims as simply wrong.

guided by an unseen hand of ecological rationality? And if so, how? And how precisely?

16. BEYOND ECOLOGICAL EXPLANATION

We need to look closely at a series of assumptions implicit in the materialist interpretations of Amazonia, Aztec sacrifice, Maring religion, and pollution systems.

The Adequacy of Ecological Data

How solid are the "hard" biological facts on which ecological interpretations rest? Ecosystems are fantastically complex. Can one or two ethnographers record enough data about the intricate webs of interconnection in ecosystems to establish with any certainty the causal relations they seek?

Critical analyses and restudies, in some cases involving interdisciplinary research teams, cast increasing doubts on the adequacy of studies such as the classic one by Rappaport among the Tsembaga Maring. Such studies entailed herculean labor by one or two ethnographers in mapping gardens, weighing crop yields, sampling soil, recording rainfall, recording food consumption, counting pigs, collecting botanical data, and so on. But does this tell us enough? Careful scrutiny reveals that sweeping approximations and extrapolations are used in estimating nutritional yields, energy expenditures, and environmental patterns. Small samples taken over short time periods from a few sectors of a vastly complex system are used to draw inferences about the total system (see McArthur 1974 for a critique of Rappaport's study on such grounds). More sophisticated follow-up studies (such as that by Chagnon and his colleagues for the Amazonian Yanomamö; see Chagnon and Hames 1979) sometimes indicate that the earlier inferences were radically in error.

Here cultural materialism, in aspiring to be a scientific anthropology, may seek too optimistically and glibly to borrow methods and models from biology.

> The concepts of environmental degradation and carrying capacity are indiscriminately used whenever an explanation for the presence or function of some cultural pattern is needed. But when is an environment degraded or when is carrying capacity exceeded? . . . The use of ecological terminology and analysis in anthropology . . . borrows heavily from older, more established fields with richer conceptual heritages. Like pack rats, we have foraged about looking for shiny and glittering things to take back to our nests. (Nietschmann 1975:165)

The Passivity of Cultural Response

The view advanced by Rappaport of Tsembaga Maring ritual cycles as following the natural cycle of pig populations—so that as pigs build up to a troublesome number,

the ritualized pig-killings provide the cultural occasion for thinning them out again—follows a more general argument made earlier by Vayda, Leeds, and Smith (1961) for the New Guinea highlands. That is, pig populations progressively build up (because their breeding is beyond effective human control); and the humans who raise them have created cultural occasions for killing them off in massive numbers in the name of prestige feasting and regional exchange.

But data gathered by Robin Hide (1974) among the Simbu show very clearly that New Guinea highlanders are able to control and plan pig populations very carefully. When the populations build up, it is not through "natural" processes beyond human control, but through systematic breeding strategies directed at building up herds so that feasts and exchanges can be staged. Salisbury has made the same point, drawing comparative data from his own work among the Siane:

> The population dynamics of pigs, which Rappaport takes as "natural" or inherent in pigs and something to which humans adapt, are, in fact, the result of deliberate planning by pig breeders. Pig feasts, and the crises which trigger the final slaughters, are all matters of deliberate long-range planning. . . . [The] final year [of the pig-breeding cycle] that Rappaport witnessed [was] a year for which the Maring had deliberately planned years in advance, knowing that the huge pig population would create huge demands on garden production of sweet potatoes to keep them fed until slaughter, and knowing what demands and problems to plan for. . . . The crises, human and porcine, which Rappaport saw the pig feasts as being a ritual adaptation to, are best seen as the predictable working out of breeding programmes, planned to produce crises. (1975:130–131)

The view of humans passively adjusting their religious institutions or exchange systems to adapt to the natural demands of their protein supply is no longer tenable. Humans, as we will see clearly in the next chapter, organize their productive efforts around culturally defined goals—not the reverse.

The Assumption of Equilibrium

To establish that a sociocultural system brings a population into stable equilibrium within an ecosystem requires both highly detailed ecological data and evidence on ecological relationships over long time spans. To look at a population over a span of 2, 3, or even 10 years, and infer that doing what they do preserves a balance (that is, that they are not degrading the ecosystem, that their population is stable, that they have been in this environment for long enough for their culture to have become adapted to it, etc.) is never enough. Diachronic (long-time-period) evidence, not synchronic (single-time-period) evidence, is always needed. Otherwise, all one can say is that a population is well enough adjusted to an ecosystem to have survived long enough to be observed:

> Diachrony is necessary to distinguish the adaptive from the maladaptive and the selective forces from neutral process. A synchronic account of survival is merely an existential statement. (Morton 1978:50–51)

Let us give these warnings some substance by considering the Maring. How do we know that the ancestors of the present Maring were living in an environment such as the one Rappaport observed when customs of planting the *rumbim,* or patterns of warfare and ritual, evolved? How do we know that they are not seriously degrading their present environment? How do we know whether they are dwindling in number, or proliferating?

Are Maring local groups really that well adapted to their environment? Other studies in the same area by Georgeda Buchbinder (1973) and William Clarke (1971) suggest that they may not be. Buchbinder's demographic and nutritional study of the Maring suggests that they are threatened by demographic decline. Moreover, the subsistence they extract from their relatively infertile environment may be much less adequate than Rappaport believed (see McArthur 1977). Buchbinder's data suggest that a diet marginally deficient in protein and drastically deficient in iodine may have severe consequences for Maring health and reproduction. Female fertility seems to be curtailed by dietary deficiencies; the onset of menstruation, in particular, seems to be long delayed. The Maring may in fact be clinging as best they can to survival in a difficult environment. But this can by no means be comfortably assumed. Nor is there any solid evidence that the Maring have been in this marginal environment for a long time period. Maring culture may well have evolved in a different ecosystem, more fertile and less precipitous.

Population increase and pressure from neighboring peoples may have driven at least some Maring groups into a setting where their diets, and hence demography, have gone into decline. Here we can note that the interpretations of most cultural ecologists in assuming equilibrium and seeking the "functional" interconnectedness of social, religious, and economic organization have rested implicitly on a "mosaic" view—one that assumes the relative separateness, stability, and long time span of cultural traditions. This lack of a dynamic view, that would take into account the impact of the outside world, makes interpretations based on present subsistence economies doubly suspect. There are some curious contradictions in the assumption that because a system exists it is adaptive. How do adaptive changes evolve? Because if a people developed maladaptive customs, such that their population expanded or their protein supplies were threatened, they would lose out in the struggle for survival to surrounding peoples who had developed customs that prevented overpopulation or malnutrition. So if we find people surviving, they must be the ones with adaptive customs; so it is our job to find out their hidden rationality.

"Evolutionary Success" and Stable Adaptations

When we do have historical records, they often show that the peoples who "succeed" in the struggle for existence are precisely the ones whose populations are expanding, such as the Iban of Sarawak (Case 6)—who in historic times were busily wiping out surrounding peoples and primary forest. The very power to expand, to displace neighboring peoples, may often be an expression of a cultural instability and disequilibrium, often one that contains the seeds of its own destruction. In Case 12, another example from New Guinea will illustrate the complexity of interpreting success or adaptiveness in the realm of culture.

This case underlines the oversimplification and danger of assuming that the customs of a people are ecologically adaptive, as products of natural selection, and that their consequences are to maintain balanced relations with an ecosystem. Salisbury, after reviewing several hundred years of probable rapid population expansion and sociocultural change among the people of New Britain Island who became the Tolai, suggests the following:

> It seems likely that at any one time more societies are in phases of expansion lasting several centuries, than are in states of dynamic equilibrium, mediated by feedback mechanisms, with their environment. (Salisbury 1975: 143)

Salisbury also makes this warning:

> When the social anthropologist quantitatively records social behavior at one particular time and in one place, he is not describing a balanced adaptation to a specific environment, but one specific realisation of the cultural rules, by particular people who modify their behavior to cope with particular . . . constraints of time and place. (Salisbury 1975:141)

A Regional Systems View: Peoples in Time and Space

Here, the need for a systemic view of the "tribal" world such as we glimpsed in Chapter 5 becomes urgent. The anthropologist in the field, working in a single village or cluster of settlements and taking this area as a microcosm of a culture and a society, has often gotten too limited a view in space as well as in time. The ecosystem approach to human populations can probably be most productive if we do not simply consider (as Rappaport did for the Tsembaga Maring) how a particular local group or even a tribal group is adapted to its environment; but rather if we see a series of contiguous (or interpenetrating) human populations within a wider ecosystem. Thus, the Marind Anim and their neighbors would constitute a regional system, as would the peoples of the Melanesian Massim, the islands off eastern New Guinea, who trade valuables around a large ring of islands (see Case 15). The Maring and neighboring peoples, the Iban of Borneo and their neighbors (whose heads they hunted and whose land they invaded; see Case 6), the Amazonian Yanomamö and their cultural relatives would each be seen as constituting regional systems whose populations, boundaries, resources, and strength *might* be in stable equilibrium, but might be highly unstable and imbalanced in the direction of absorption, conquest, extinction, and so on. Each people would to some extent be competing for land and resources (see Sahlins 1961, Vayda et al., 1961) and hence be more or less successful. But their relationship might also be complementary and symbiotic—as with the Basseri pastoralists (Case 7) and the peoples of Swat, northern Pakistan, occupying complementary ecological niches in the same region (Barth 1956).

In most parts of the tribal world the regional environment has for several centuries been directly or indirectly tied to European economy and colonial expansion. Firearms, the ivory trade, and slave-raiding were part of the "environment" to which sub-Saharan Africans have been "adapting" for several centuries; the Borneo of nineteenth-century Iban expansion was the Borneo of the British "White Rajahs."

Ecological anthropology needs to look at regional systems in historical perspective, not imaginary mosaics. But what, then, about protein? Can people, in Amazonia or elsewhere, depend equally well on animal or vegetable foods? Is protein the prime mover?

The Need for Protein

The assumption that human populations need high protein intakes to achieve full potentials and health has been increasingly challenged in nutritional studies. Many specialists on nutrition argue that we are victims of a "protein myth" that has led even experts to exaggerate the need and value of animal protein intake. The main issue has not been whether Amazonians stage raids for the sake of protein, but whether they—and other Third World peoples—die and suffer for lack of it. A main

thrust of development effort in the Third World has been to provide more protein, to eliminate the protein starvation that is supposed to afflict the poor.

But studies suggest three things. First, virtually no human populations have levels of protein intake below the range of nutritional adequacy—which are turning out to be considerably lower than most experts had thought. Humans evolved as omnivores, and they appear to be able to survive admirably at very high or surprisingly low levels of protein intake. This protein component can come from either animal or vegetable protein, as long as a needed spectrum of amino acids is covered. Evidence suggests the following:

> If a diet has 5 percent of its calories from good quality protein, such as in egg, the individual's needs for protein will be met regardless of whether the individual is a preschool child or an adult man *provided the individual eats enough to meet his energy needs* [emphasis added]. . . . Relative to energy a child will undoubtedly need more dietary protein than an adult . . . [but] even human milk contains only 5 to 6 percent of its calories as protein. (Sukhatme 1975:57)

The second important finding is evidence that the phrase "provided the individual eats enough to meet his energy needs" is crucial. Malnutrition and such protein-deficiency diseases as Kwashiorkor are not myths. But the crucial factor seems to be not absolute deficiencies of protein, in most cases, but rather insufficient caloric consumption:

> Unless a diet provides the energy cost of synthesizing and retaining protein, a person must lose protein. (Sukhatme 1975:59)

That is, the body processing of protein requires a heavy investment of energy. A person who is on a starvation diet cannot

The Marind Anim

The Marind Anim of the southern coast of New Guinea had a remarkable culture that had apparently been going through an efflorescence—in the sense of artistic creativity and collective ritual, and also in the sense of expansion at the expense of neighboring peoples—in the century or more before European contact.

Marind Anim culture centered around cults of male homosexuality, ritual license, and head-hunting. Marind Anim boys were led into a set of initiatory grades, where they were introduced to an orgiastic cult of sodomy in which they were the passive partners, sustained by the cultural dogma that semen is essential to growth.

The elaborate ceremonial cycle was built around the male fiction of sexual supremacy and independence, but involved ritual intercourse with women in what amounted to gang rape: the semen was collected and mixed with food or used in ritual decoration. Van Baal's interpretation bears on issues we will touch on in subsequent sections and hence is worth quoting:

The great secret is that the venerated power [of male potency and hence of males in general] is not really as powerful as it pretended to be. The source of all life, sperma, is effective only . . . if produced in copulation. These self-sufficient males need the females and they know it. . . . In secret in the celebration of the rites, they will allow their dependence and immediately afterwards they go out head-hunting. It is as if by that time their rage has mounted to such a pitch that they have to find an outlet for it. (Van Baal 1966:949)

Marriage begins with such a gang rape of the bride by the husband's kin group; and this is repeated with young married women, at a cost of their physical suffering—a cost that is validated by the cultural dogma of fertility, where the mingled sperm of the men of the community is supposed to sustain fertility. Though there are few data on marital intercourse, it is clear that homosexuality remains a central theme in most married men's lives.

The cultural concern with fertility was not without substance, since infertility was very high (subsequently exacerbated by venereal disease) and the population was threatened with demographic collapse. A South Pacific Commission demographic study concluded that the custom of collective sexual assault—in part, a cultural response to infertility—was in fact a major factor in perpetuating and worsening that problem.

Yet even though Marind Anim sexual practices did not provide demographically for reproduction of the population, this was a center of efflorescence in ceremonialism, art, and myth. Moreover, the Marind Anim sustained successfully an expansionist "foreign policy" that decimated surrounding populations. The power of the Marind Anim was sustained by rich sago resources that permitted large populations to concentrate in sedentary villages.

But what about demographic decline? Apparently in the period for which evidence can be pieced together, the Marind Anim maintained their population by capturing children in their head-hunting raids. They literally drained the reproductive capacities of neighboring peoples to support a predatory and expansionist "foreign policy" and an orgiastic lifestyle (Van Baal 1966).

This practice in turn underlines the long-range imbalance of Marind Anim adaptation. As in imperialist Europe, prosperity at home was sustained by exploitation and murder abroad; and the expansiveness and success were inevitably limited. This pattern of Marind Anim adaptation probably had not been maintained for very long; and had Europeans not intruded, it would probably have collapsed, if only through the wiping out of surrounding populations within the feasible limits of warfare. For a further discussion of the Marind Anim case, see Knauft (1993).

Marind Anim: (top) A man is given an elaborate hairdo. (left) A warrior in full regalia. (right) Men's house.

process protein, and suffers protein starvation even though the needed absolute amounts of protein are being consumed.

A third discovery about the role of protein is that vegetable proteins can be sufficient to meet human needs if other dietary components are adequate. Here Western prejudices in favor of meat proteins are misleading. But our own biology may be misleading as well. Some evidence is accumulating that in areas such as Melanesia, where diets centered around starchy root vegetables and (by Western standards) very low in animal protein have prevailed for more than a hundred generations, humans have become physically adapted to extracting and processing protein from vegetables. Thus, for example, Watson (1977) in discussing possible protein stress in highlands New Guinea, cites a study by Oomen (1970) that "suggests an organic adaptation in some New Guineans enabling them to subsist with a markedly lower protein intake than has been judged normal in man" (Watson 1977:62).

> [Oomen] draws attention to the health, growth, and vigor of the subjects of his study, chosen from a generally robust population. Based on nitrogen measurements of intake and excretion, he infers that local peoples may possess a specialized intestinal flora that benefits its host in this respect, as well as having the capacity to move a large bulk of starchy food. (Watson 1977:63)

All this suggests that to view scarcity of protein, and competition for "high quality" animal protein, as prime movers shaping patterns of warfare or social structure is tenuous and precarious.

It is worth returning briefly to the case of Aztec cannibalism. Price notes that whereas animal protein seems to be a limiting factor in Amazonia among hunting peoples who cultivate starchy root crops, the "protein deprivation hypothesis" cannot be directly transferred to the Aztec situation, in the light of the subsistence economies of contemporary peasants:

> In the Basin of Mexico the carbohydrate staple was and remains maize, which is regularly and consistently consumed with beans. The two are effectively co-staples; the source of the bulk of caloric intake is also the source of most protein consumed. Only occasionally is there supplementation with protein from animal sources. (1978:99)

Price remains committed to cultural materialist explanation, but she views cannibalism as a by-product of expansionist warfare, for which she advances an ecological interpretation. For the Amazonian case, she remains convinced that the protein deprivation hypothesis is apt:

> Population size and the distributions of entire settlements, population mobility, and competition within and between groups all show close and powerful linkage with the quality and distribution of wild protein sources. (Price 1978:99)

Yet evidence casts doubt on the adequacy of comparative studies of the connection between animal protein and Amazonian social organization by Siskind (1973), Gross (1975), Ross (1978), and Ferguson (1989). A careful study of protein consumption among the Yanomamö (whose high intergroup warfare is claimed to reflect competition for scarce animal protein) shows that Yanomamö protein consumption is high, far above stipulated levels of adequacy for human populations. Their protein intake

> would put them on a par with national populations from the world's most developed countries. . . . From the protein consumption data . . . Harris's general hypothesis about the relation between protein availability and

warfare practices would permit the prediction that the Yanomamö of the Padamo River basin should be pacific and unlikely to engage in warfare. (Chagnon and Hames 1979:912)

Similar data emerge in detailed studies of another Yanomamö area by Lizot (1978). The picture of the Yanomamö emerging from biomedical studies that "the Yanomamö are in good physical condition, are well nourished by world standards, and show no signs of protein deficiency" (Chagnon and Hames 1979:911) contrasts sharply with Harris's description of the Yanomamö as a people who

> have "eaten the forest"—not its trees, but its animals—and . . . are suffering the consequences in terms of increased warfare, treachery, and infanticide and a brutal sex life. (Harris 1977:102)

The sex life of the Yanomamö can well bring us back to Harris's other preoccupation, the control of population.

The Regulation of Population

How did the small-scale populations with hunting-gathering and horticultural subsistence economies maintain demographic stability, avoiding population increase that outstripped resources? There is little doubt that peoples with finite space and resources in many parts of the world practiced infanticide, of both sexes or of females, so as to restrict population numbers. This was true, for example, of some Pacific islanders living on small islands; and of some tropical forest and arid zone hunter-gatherers. Some peoples deliberately controlled pregnancy through abortion and through consciously controlled child-spacing techniques such as postpartum sex taboos and prolonging of lactation (which inhibits conception through suppression of ovulation). We can

surmise that most peoples had a sufficiently coherent sense of themselves in relation to their environment that they knew whether numbers were rising in such a way as to threaten resources, and a sufficient understanding of reproductive biology to make *some* interventions when threatened by population growth.

But contra Harris, we do not yet know nearly enough about the demography of small-scale human populations and the biology of fertility and disease to make strong claims about the "natural" demographic tendencies of human populations, in the absence of direct human interventions. Biologists do not yet fully understand the regulating mechanisms that usually—though not always—keep populations in other mammalian species stabilized well below the carrying capacity of their ecosystems. Natural balances between predator and predated species are part of this process. But there apparently are subtle mechanisms of self-regulation in the reproductive process itself that help to maintain balances. Such mechanisms demonstrably exist in humans, as well as other mammals.

Fertility of human females appears to be highly responsive to diet. One important mechanism here is the level of body fat. Low female body fat to body weight ratios (characteristic of hunter-gatherer populations and intensified by prolonged lactation) retard the onset of menstruation and the resumption of ovulation after birth (Frisch and McArthur 1974). It seems likely that the dramatic increases in population that followed food production reflected a relaxation of this constraint on fertility. Birth-spacing from prolonging lactation in itself does not seem a sufficient factor to prevent steady population growth (Van Ginneken 1974). But there are other biological constraints at work. Under conditions of marginal diet in horticultural societies, the onset of menstruation may be very late. In the Maring case, Buchbinder's data suggest an average age of menarche as late as 18 or 19. Moreover, there are widespread reports from other horticultural societies of irregularity in menstrual cycles, and presumably sharply reduced fertility, under conditions of inadequate diet. These mechanisms may regulate fertility when populations rise to levels that begin to threaten food supplies, but before deficient diets begin to cause neurological damage in young children. There is some evidence of other fertility-suppressing processes, as yet poorly documented. For example, nonnutritive suckling of nursing infants by women who are not themselves lactating may activate hormonal controls of ovulation.

A further complexity here is the role of diseases in maintaining population balance. Diseases widespread in the tropical world—notably malaria, which seems for several thousand years to have been closely tied to human demography and ecology (Livingstone 1958)—appear to have played an important part in regulating population. Where malaria has been eradicated or sharply curtailed in the tropics, populations have risen sharply. Humans and the microorganisms and insects that evolved with them as disease agents and vectors may have been locked into mutually regulating balances. Many of the threats to population balance assumed by Harris and his colleagues may be imaginary. (See also McElroy and Townsend 1985.)

Adaptive When?

If we find a people practicing infanticide or holding a complex of religious beliefs that limits population growth (such as Lindenbaum's "supernatural birth control"), does that mean the group is now experiencing population pressure? Or that they were 20 or 50 years ago when Europeans intruded? Or that they were 500 or a 1,000 years earlier when these customs were adopted? If we opt for the latter choice, then we are in a poor position to find the hidden rationality in people's present customs by mapping their gardens, taking censuses, or weighing their dinner. As Nietschmann expresses it,

> One can show the function of a particular system-maintaining and system-regulating mechanism in a present-day primitive society, but how and why did it evolve? . . . Did the ecologically adaptive "lifeways" evolve some time in the past when the ancestors' society actually exceeded carrying capacity? (1975:165).

And if customs outlive the conditions in which they evolved, how can we understand their continuing meaning to the people who practice them without according a motive force to symbolic systems in their own right—what ardent cultural materialists most want to avoid?

The custom of infanticide of the first-born child among the Melanesians of San Cristobal, Solomon Islands, may possibly have evolved historically as a device for population regulation (though there is no evidence for any such population pressure in the past*). But even if this was the case, we cannot account in terms of a materialist rationality for the way the people of San Cristobal, when as much as 80 percent of the population was wiped out by introduced epidemic diseases in the late nineteenth and early twentieth centuries, continued to kill first-born infants—because their custom required it—and then sought

---

*We cannot assume that the need for population regulation at a community level is a sufficient explanation for people killing their own infants.

to adopt infants from nearby Malaita to re-place the ones they had killed.

The Unseen Hand of Rationality

If humans perceive the threat of overpopulation or the destruction of valued food sources, they may well invent customs that serve as corrective forces. But what about the emergence of customs—such as the planting of the *rumbim*, or the belief in red spirits, among the Maring—that have a positive effect of which the population itself is unaware? How is it that humans invent adaptive customs, and not maladaptive ones? Is it, as Nietschmann wonders, the unseen hand of the "Big Ecologist in the Sky"?

Or is it that humans invent both maladaptive and adaptive—and neutral—customs and beliefs, and the maladaptive ones get weeded out? How? What selective pressures eliminate ritual rules that lead to malnutrition or illness, beliefs that inefficiently disperse population, or social customs that reduce subsistence production? How efficient are such weeding and pruning mechanisms? And thus, how comfortably can we assume that the ritual we observe or the belief we encounter is not ecologically maladaptive?

Is it that peoples who adopt maladaptive cultural practices get out-competed by their neighbors, and either get killed off or are absorbed into a more viable sociocultural tradition? Perhaps so, if we take adequate account of the regional systems in which peoples have lived for centuries (which may include state societies, European invaders, etc.), and if we have adequate historical evidence to assess the case. But otherwise the operating asumption that has guided most cultural materialist ethnography—that whatever *is* is adaptive—leads us into error. The customs we record may be maladaptive: doomed, perhaps, to ex-tinction if they were carried on long enough, but still (like Marind Anim sexual practices and warfare) "there" to be "explained." The most striking case also comes from New Guinea. Involving a disease known as *kuru*, it is described in Case 13.

Kuru and the ritual cannibalism that transmits it are relatively recent among the Fore. Eventually, by trial and error, they might have abandoned the practice of ritual cannibalism and broken the cycle themselves. But the response in the meantime—building an elaborate and further maladaptive theory of sorcery to explain the disease—is itself revealing. It lends weight to Lindenbaum's hypothesis that rituals are partly symbolic statements about the body politic and a people's perceived demographic situation. But it hardly lends confidence to the notion of efficient pruning mechanisms chopping out maladaptive customs or of humans inadvertently and fortuitously creating only adaptive ones. And it hardly lends confidence to the working assumption of cultural materialists that the customs they find must be adaptive or they would not be there, or to Harris's quest to find the hidden rationality in the most "bizarre" of customs.

It does reinforce, however, the notion that within regional ecosystems, populations, and hence their cultures, are to substantial degree in competition. While all populations probably have a complex tangle of adaptive, partly maladaptive, drastically maladaptive, and adaptively neutral customs, the organizational, economic, and demographic success of different populations will vary—and with this differential success, culture-bearing populations will spread, contract, dwindle, conquer, or be absorbed. The Fore may have been doomed ultimately to absorption by their neighbors, whose less maladaptive culture the survivors would eventually have adopted.

CASE
13

Kuru and Its Consequences

Among the New Guinea Fore, about 1 percent of the population, mainly women, died annually from an inevitably fatal degenerative disease of the nervous system called *kuru*. The consequences demographically were catastrophic: a sex ratio imbalanced in favor of males by as much as 3 to 1 in some areas and a declining and fragile population structure.

The Fore explain *kuru* as caused by sorcery. Not only did *kuru* generate a rather frantic system of marriage and social organization, be-

The fatal outcome of *kuru*: A Fore girl in the terminal stage of the disease.

cause of the imbalanced sex ratio and frequent death of wives and mothers, but when a group's women died of *kuru* the men were likely to make war on their neighbors to avenge sorcery, further disrupting the social order and decimating population.

Yet studies* have shown that *kuru* is a disease caused by an agent (now known as a prion) that attacks the central nervous system after a long incubation period that may last 15 years or more. The agent, which concentrates in the brain tissues of the victim, was transmitted by a special Fore custom: Fore women and children ritually ate the bodies of their own dead relatives, including their brains. Only by eating the brain of a victim can a person become a future victim. The colonial administration, by prohibiting cannibalism, broke the cycle.

But the point is that natural selection did not weed out a desperately maladaptive ritual practice. Natural selection does not automatically eliminate customs that have harmful consequences: *human beings must change them*. And since people most often do not consciously perceive directly the ecological consequences of their customs, the process of their consciously changing the customs into more adaptive ones is haphazard at best. Lindenbaum (1972:251) suggests that, ironically, Fore ritual cannibalism may be a symbolic attempt at self-regeneration in a society whose members perceive the threat of depopulation (see Lindenbaum 1979, Zelenietz and Lindenbaum 1981).

*Dr. Carlton Gajdusek was instrumental in identifying the mechanism that causes *kuru*. However, it is noteworthy that the detective work that initially pointed to the mode of transmission, at a time when this was a mystery, was done by anthropologists Shirley Lindenbaum and Robert Glasse (see Lindenbaum 1979).

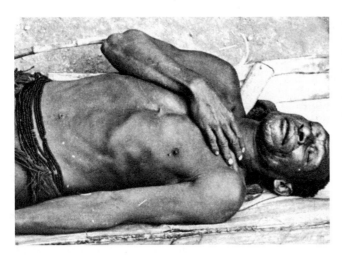

Fore vengeance: A Fore man lies brutally beaten by the relatives of a *kuru* victim who have accused him of sorcery. Often fatal vengeance against men suspected of sorcery compounds the catastrophic demographic consequences of *kuru*.

The most urgent point—one that could be illustrated with scores of less dramatic cases—is that a great many societies practice rituals, follow customs, and hold beliefs that have harmful or at best neutral ecological or demographic consequences. And they do so with a persistent faith and commitment to the ways of the past that is as characteristically human as flexibility and pragmatism. The garden magician uttering spells over crops is carrying on in the style of his ancestors despite the fact that empirically the spells have no effect and ecologically his energy might be better spent making a better fence or digging drainage ditches. However, the magician may also be a leader who organizes and motivates the workers on a garden, so that his spells do have a beneficial effect in that regard. In all cases we have to consider the "net balance" of consequences of action, as the sociologist Robert Merton (1968) pointed out.

This leads us in a less negative direction than the critique of a deterministic cultural ecology. We can begin to set out in more positive terms the processes that generate sociocultural change—processes that include but are not limited to or necessarily dominated by ecological adaptation. Ecological pressures can be seen as constraining, not determining, factors; and they operate through systems of human motive and meaning. We can begin to sketch the elements of a more complex and multidimensional theory of sociocultural change.

Ecological Constraints as Limiting Factors

We can begin with the general principle that adaptation operates through *negative constraints*. Ecological and demographic constraints (whether of diet, population, soil fertility, etc.) set limits to what is viable. They pose problems. But these negative constraints never create solutions, never produce cultural forms. A protein shortage and population explosion in the Valley of Mexico did not and could not create a religious system in which the gods demanded human sacrifice.

In biological evolution, the constraints are similarly negative. The processes whereby new possibilities are generated are essentially negative as well: random genetic mutation, which most often produces nonviable or less viable forms but sometimes produces new and adaptive possibilities; and random reshuffling of the cards dealt genetically through the matings in each generation. But in humans the processes are radically different. The forces that create new forms are positive, not negative; and they are products of choice, not random biological processes.

Rationality, Choice, and Innovation

Humans can perceive a problem and do something to solve it. That, presumably, was a major payoff in the evolution of human intelligence over hundreds of thousands of years. As intelligent problem-solvers, our ancestors could plan hunts, create weapons, and build shelters to stay dry. The ability to assess problems and devise solutions remains a crucial element in sociocultural change.

In engaging the world, even in the most practical and goal-directed ways, humans make choices. These choices depend not simply on the material payoffs of alternate courses, but on values and symbolic meanings. Energy is expended not simply hunting for proteins but hunting for the ochre used in ritual body painting. To dismiss the symbolic motives and values through which humans orient their lives as hiding some covert ecological rationality is to misconstrue drastically the nature of the animal one is trying to understand. Rationality is in the eye of the cultural actor, not the Big Ecologist in the Sky.

Human intellect seems to be given almost compulsively to making *rules*. And these proclivities (as well as the nature of social life) lead us not simply to solve prob-

lems and transmit the solutions to our fellows, but also to define ways of doing things as *the* ways of doing things, as customs. We seem also to be given to observing, classifying, sorting out, labeling the things of the world. Human problem-solving depends, for its power, on this restless searching, sorting, classifying, and theorizing in realms beyond the immediately practical. This year's idle curiosity may provide the means to solve next year's problem. Folk science, going far beyond the immediately practical, often provides the means to it. (Imagine how many generations of sky-gazing and observation were needed, without writing, to provide the foundations for a calendar of practical value). The human capacity to solve problems, to classify and theorize, and to convert prevailing practice or new ideas into custom, are interconnected elements of our capacity to develop locally viable ways of life.

Cultures as ideational systems are distributed within communities, among individuals who command different versions of, and perspectives on, the ways of their people. A model of change needs to deal with this level of individual meanings and choices. Thus Salisbury points to the importance of

individual inventiveness in modifying rules to fit personal circumstances. Culture . . . does not itself adapt to environments but is the means through which *individuals* adapt to their environment. . . . Culture develops, elaborates, or stagnates in a process of individual cultural innovation. The vast majority of innovations, like minor genetic mutations, are unrelated to survival, either by individuals or by culture. But the richness in number of innovations . . . leads[s] to a . . . probability that *some* survival-related behaviours will occur. (1975:145)

Individuals making choices, then, are a major mechanism of long-run sociocultural change and of adaptive response to the material circumstances of life. Members of a population who have developed a set of rules about possible marriage partners, and who then generations later, through changed circumstances, find that fewer and fewer people have permissible spouses, may begin to circumvent the rules or change them in a way that solves the problem. A people faced with severe population pressure may start to kill newborn infants, and later—finding that only a few need to be killed to avoid the problem, may define a custom of killing the first-born, or of killing one or two infant daughters once a family has reached an acceptable size. Or they may prohibit burning the forest to hunt animals because they find the burned growth may revert to grassland or suffers from erosion. In these realms, humans (with a measure of trial and error, success and failure) perceive problems and take steps to solve them. Ecological constraints shape (but never determine) such cultural solutions. But the people who change marriage rules or hunting patterns also invent deities and create rituals.

Beyond Rationality

For humans, the nonrational faculties of mind—dream, fantasy, senses of form, pattern, and rhythm—are just as essential as the rationality that invents bows and arrows, plows and machines. Rappaport tells us that the Tsembaga Maring massed dancers communicate about the strength and readiness of a kin group, and as a courtship display to potential mates. The important thing is to dance or not to dance. Whether the dancers go clockwise or counterclockwise, in the center of the settlement or in a dance ground away from it, wearing white feathers or green leaves, presumably does not matter ecologically. Yet it is precisely such details of symbolic arrangement that distinguish the creations of the mind.

The mind imposes demands of its own. In the face of anxiety, uncertainty, and tragedy, the mind demands explanation and security, and projects fantasy. Garden magic may, as Malinowski argued, be psychologically adaptive rather than ecologically adaptive; so too may be a theory of illness.

A people's symbolic elaborations may or may not have hidden adaptive consequences. A people may kill a particular species of bird in order to use the brightly colored feathers as decorations in rituals, not knowing that these birds feed on the insects that are the vector for a contagious disease that afflicts them—a disease for which they use magical remedies that might, in turn, have harmful health consequences. Few people live so close to the margins of survival that their existence would be threatened by a substantial collection of customs that have neutral or negative consequences.

It is the essence of our humanity to pursue symbolically defined goals in our seemingly practical moments (in working and eating), as well as our more ethereal moments (in painting designs or performing rituals). These symbolic patterns may be ultimately constrained by ecological viability. But except in the most hostile of environments, these negative constraints allow wide latitude for cultural elaborations.

Ecological Constraints and Cultural Meanings

Depicting cultures as adaptations to ecological and demographic pressures—ways of preserving protein intake, population balance, or environmental equilibrium—radically underestimates the importance of the symbolic systems through which humans engage the world. Humans are hungry for food as they conceive it, not protein. They modify dwellings in terms of their ideas

Solomon Islands' Magic: Does it serve adaptive ends? A Siuai magician (Bougainville Island) rides atop an enormous slit drum to lighten the load magically.

about social relations, not simply to keep dry and warm. They modify their sexual practices in terms of their conceptions of marriage, not simply the exigencies of reproduction and demography. Humans perceive problems and solve them within the framework of an ideational system. They experience rainfall, temperature, soil, birth, death, plans, and animals through systems of classification and interpretation—never directly. And it is through such mediating systems of symbols that changes must take place. The "spirits of rot" the Tsembaga Maring see as inhabiting the lower reaches of their valleys and causing harm and illness to humans may indeed be in some sense personifications of the invisible agents of malaria, which in reality are anopheles mosquitoes. But the spirits, and the actions the Maring take in relation to them, are elaborations of an ancient symbolic tradition through which New Guinea peoples attribute order and meaning to the events of an environment they can do little to control. Some of these symbolic responses—magic to ensure success in war or to cure fever and chills—may be quite useless in affecting the outcome of events. Some, like avoiding the realm of the spirits of rot, may be useful. Some, like the widespread New Guinea custom of men sticking reeds up their nostrils to induce bleeding—

in symbolic imitation of menstruation—are physiologically harmful and sometimes cause fatal hemorrhaging. But all are deeply meaningful to those who enact these practices. Further, even though such practices may or may not be in themselves medically efficacious, they may nevertheless have a beneficial physiological effect owing to neurological and immunological responses that are regulated by the emotions. Humans, as Sahlins (1977) insists, never engage the physical environment directly; they always encounter nature *through* culture, through systems of symbols, meanings, and values.

Social Processes of Change

A theory of sociocultural change that seeks to find answers within the nature of the mind and the webs of cultural meanings humans have created is as partial, and hence misleading, as cultural materialism. For cultural forms are not simply spun out by the human mind. They are produced within *social systems*.

Humans do not simply encounter the physical world through systems of cultural symbols; they encounter the world in systems of social relationships. These relationships change, and partly in response to practical considerations. If, given a particular agricultural technology, environmental conditions provide opportunities for a mode of terracing or a system of irrigation, then new modes of collective labor or cooperation are likely to emerge. But they are created out of, and through, existing social relationships.

The impact of ecological constraints and environmental possibilities thus operates both in terms of cultural meanings, values, and goals, and through systems of social relations through which humans pursue these values and goals. This raises a further and crucial question. Are the values and goals of Maring men and Maring women necessarily the same? In the hypothetical society in which irrigation systems are constructed, some people may own the land, while others are tenant farmers who must give a large share of the crop to the owners. Are their interests and values, in relation to intensifying production and working to create an irrigation system, the same?

The members of a society may have different rights and privileges, in relation to the resources of the environment and in relation to one another. Consider even a society such as the Maring or the Marind Anim (Case 12) of New Guinea, where everyone is, in effect, a landowner, and where there are no social classes. A Maring woman must labor in the gardens to feed the pigs her husband will use to advance his prestige. A Marind Anim woman is not only subordinated and symbolically demeaned (while she labors to produce the sago flour that is the staple of life), but when she is married, she is gang-raped. If she should chance to see a secret male cult object, she will be gang-raped or killed.

Do we really want, as Sahlins (1977) would seem to imply, to see these as symbolic outpourings of the human mind? Or do we want to be able to see internal conflicts of interest within a society, even a classless society such as that of the Marind Anim or Maring? Where men oppress women, or elders oppress juniors (as in the sexual exploitation and domination of Marind Anim boys by their elders), we must be prepared to probe beneath cultural ideologies and apparent shared commitment to meanings and values to see the conflicts and contradictions they disguise.

There is one major body of social theory that has focused both on the way humans engage the world through systems of social relationships, and on the way conflicts and contradictions underlie apparent consensus and integration. It will, I think, provide a major component of the composite theory of social change we need. That body of theory derives from Marx.

Neo-Marxist Contributions to a Theory of Change

Some explanations are in order. Marx formulated his social theories during the nineteenth century, seeking both to work out a general model of societal process and to understand the historical forces and hidden dynamics that had shaped the Europe in which he lived. In the twentieth century, revolutions fought in his name, and states reorganized in his name, transformed world political relations. These events—most strikingly the creation of the Stalinist police state in the former Soviet Union—were separated by a vast gulf from the new world, freed from oppression, that Marx had envisioned. Moreover, in the process Marxism as state ideology became a crude economic determinism far from the subtle, multidimensional understandings Marx himself brought to bear in analyzing European feudalism: the Paris communes, the Bordeaux wine industry, and the economic relations of British factory owners and workers.*

The Marxism to which some anthropologists and other social scientists turned for theoretical inspiration was the Marx of the nineteenth century as illuminated by the twentieth. This renewal of Marxist social science, which I shall refer to as **neo-Marxism,** sought to broaden the understandings reached by Marx, on the basis of both the events of subsequent decades and the radical advances in human knowledge,

---

*Marx himself was better at applying his method than at summarizing it: so that some of his own general statements of his theoretical tenets have served as texts for crude and one-dimensional materialist interpretations.

in the physical, biological, and social sciences, since Marx wrote. These include the findings of anthropology, which in Marx's day were rudimentary and often mistaken.

Despite the generally open and exploratory spirit of neo-Marxist social science, there is still too often a slavish use of the technical concepts Marx devised to analyze very different social systems, and a preoccupation with textual orthodoxy—with what Marx really said or really meant. In seeking to incorporate neo-Marxist perspectives and conceptualizations into a composite model of societal process, I shall not be bound by nineteenth-century terms when twentieth-century ones are better, or by a concern with textual orthodoxy. Intellectual schemes are always partial and provisional: we cannot afford to make them objects of reverence when that impedes our discarding conceptual tools when better ones come to hand. All that said, we can begin to ask what neo-Marxist perspectives might tell us about the organization of societies such as the Tsembaga Maring and Aztecs, and about the processes of social change.

Neo-Marxists agree with cultural materialists that the material circumstances of human life are in some sense primary and social institutions and belief systems are in some sense secondary. But Marxists begin with the premise to which I have already pointed: that in producing the material means of life, humans engage the world in and through a system of social relations. Marxism focuses on *economy,* as a system of social relations and values as well as technology.

Nor do neo-Marxists assume a simple economic determinism. In a particular form of society, economic relationships may not dominate other sorts of relations and institutions (such as kinship or religion) as they do in a complex capitalist society. Among the Tsembaga Maring and other peoples of New Guinea, social relations are based primarily on *kinship*, not on economic relationships. In traditional Hindu India, or Medieval Europe, *religion* provided the idiom through which social relations were organized. Neo-Marxist theory—unlike the old Soviet version of Marxism—does *not* assume that an economic system directly determines the way a society is organized, or that ideational systems can be directly inferred from, or attributed to, material circumstances (see Kahn and Llobera 1981).

Marx's own work was primarily concerned with understanding the nature and historical emergence of nineteenth-century European capitalist society out of its feudal antecedents. Marxist theory is most fully developed with regard to conflicts between social classes, and with the structure of complex societies. The emergence of a neo-Marxist anthropology, within a wider front of social theory, has represented an attempt to broaden this developed body of Marxist theory to deal with the full range of societies—a task Marx himself had envisioned, but had pursued only sketchily with the meager evidence then at hand.

Even in small-scale and classless societies, we find internal cleavages and conflicts of interest of the sort to which I have pointed for the Maring and Marind Anim. Ideologies of women as polluting and dangerous, systems that subordinate them and extract their labor to serve the political interests of men, unquestionably have cultural meanings—meanings to which the women, as well as the men, may be committed. But these ideologies may nonetheless be instruments of male domination. That they may have consequences of limiting population may be quite true, and may be one of the factors that lead one population to adopt or invent such a set of practices, and another population to reject this path or leave it

unexplored. But the political interests that underlie such symbolic elaborations can never be ignored; and the ecological and demographic consequences of such practices can never be taken as a necessary and sufficient explanation for their existence.

Harris's depiction of the "male supremacy complex" aptly characterizes the sexual-political conflicts underlying Amazonian warfare and male aggression. But why, then, do we have to move back outside the social system to find the hidden rationality of brutal sexual politics in the politically neutral realms of population biology and nutrition?

The same contradiction emerges in an exchange between Harris and Sahlins (1979) about Aztec sacrifice. Sahlins argued that Aztec sacrifice entailed a happy communion between priests and victims, united in their religious pursuit of symbolic meanings and collective goals. To this Harris provided a retort that would fit well into the Marxist tradition:

> Sahlins claims that what mattered to the victims whose screams ended 500 years ago was that they were part of a sacrament and not that they were part of a meal . . . as if labeling human sacrifice "communion" transubstantiates obsidian knives and human meat. . . . Anthropologists should certainly try to understand why people think they behave the way they do, but we cannot stop at that understanding. It is imperative that we have the right not to believe some explanations. Most of all we must reserve the right not to believe ruling-class explanations. A ruling class that says it is eating some people out of concern for the welfare of all is not telling the whole story. . . . Aztec cannibalism was the "highest form of communion" for the eaters but not the eaten. (Harris 1979b:52)

But why, if we are to look for the vested interests of ruling classes (or their equivalent among African tribal elders, New Guinea men's cultists, or Yanomamö wife-beaters),

...ave to find some hidden ecological ...onality of protein deficiency or population regulation in religious ideologies, systems of property, or patterns of warfare?

Looking Ahead: Toward a Composite Theory of Sociocultural Change

What we need is a theoretical perspective that accounts for the shaping and constraining forces of ecological adaptation, but sees them as operating through systems of cultural meanings and social relationships; that sees internal conflict and contradiction within social systems, as well as adaptation to material circumstances, as dynamic forces; and that incorporates the human imperative to create and elaborate a world of symbols, a web of meanings, far beyond any practical necessities or material goals. A doctrinaire Marxism that saw only conflict and vested interest would not account for the shared commitments to cultural goals and meanings anthropologists have encountered in the real communities of New Guinea or Africa; an anthropology that focused on the integration of society and culture could not account for conflict and change; and a symbolist anthropology that saw only a communion of shared meanings would be blind to their political consequences, and their history. We will need a conceptual system that accounts for internal dynamics and conflicts, for cultures as shared systems of cultural meaning, and for the constraints and pressures imposed by the material circumstances of people's lives. In the chapters to follow, we will build up progressively the conceptualizations we need. And, before we turn to the complexity of the modern world, we will pause to pull these conceptualizations together, as best possible, into a coherent system.

=== SUMMARY ===

Ecological constraints play a part in constraining social systems but do not determine them in any simple way. Ecology clearly plays a part in shaping economic practices, but its role in other spheres, such as religion, may be harder to discern. Roy Rappaport, in his study of the Tsembaga Maring people in Papua New Guinea, argued that the large periodic pig-killing festivals, known as *kaiko*, were instrumental among these people in regulating adaptation by reducing pig herds to manageable sizes as well as in regulating warfare, territory, and population dispersal. Marvin Harris has argued that warfare patterns among the Yanomamö of Venezuela represent an indirect adaptation to protein scarcity where game reserves are depleted. Harner and Harris have claimed that Aztec human sacrifices and cannibalism were also based on protein shortages.

All of the foregoing interpretations of data, however, have been challenged, and we also cannot assume that populations have been in a state of stable equilibrium with their environments. The Marind Anim of southern New Guinea were successful warriors and head-hunters but their sexual practices, designed to increase human fertility, actually reduced it. Among the Fore people of the eastern highlands of Papua New Guinea, the practice of eating the brains of deceased relatives enabled the transmission of a severe neurological condition, known as *kuru*, resulting in many deaths. Customs can therefore be maladaptive as well as adaptive. Neo-Marxist theorists recognize the complexities involved in the determination of social practices, without implying any necessary ecological rationality behind them. More complex and composite theories are needed to examine the problems of cultural change.

SUGGESTIONS FOR FURTHER READING

SECTION 15

Burnham, P. C., and R. F. Ellen, eds. 1979. *Social and Ecological Systems.* New York: Academic Press, Inc.

Damas, D., ed. 1969. *Contributions to Anthropology: Ecological Essays.* National Museum of Canada Anthropological Bulletin No. 86. Ottawa.

Ferguson, R. B., and N. L. Whitehead, eds. 1992. *War in the Tribal Zone: Expanding States and Indigenous Warfare.* Santa Fe: School of American Research Press.

Harris, M. 1974. *Cows, Pigs, Wars, and Witches: The Riddles of Culture.* New York: Harper & Row, Publishers.

————. 1993. *Culture, People, Nature: An Introduction to General Anthropology,* 6th ed. New York: HarperCollins College Publishers.

Heider, K. G. 1972. Environment, Subsistence, and Society. *Annual Review of Anthropology* 1: 207–226.

Kottak, C. P. 1974. *Anthropology: The Exploration of Human Diversity.* New York: Random House, Inc.

Meggers, B. J. 1971. *Amazonia: Man and Nature in a Counterfeit Paradise.* Chicago: Aldine Publishing Company.

Moran, E. F. 1979. *Human Adaptability: An Introduction to Ecological Anthropology.* North Scituate, Mass.: Duxbury Press.

Netting, R. M. 1971. *The Ecological Approach in Cultural Study.* Reading, Pa.: Addison-Wesley Publishing Company, Inc.

Rappaport, R. A. 1968. *Pigs for the Ancestors: Ritual in the Ecology of a New Guinea People.* New Haven, Conn.: Yale University Press.

————. 1971. Nature, Culture and Ecological Anthropology. In H. Shapiro, ed., *Man, Culture, and Society.* London: Oxford University Press, pp. 237–267.

————. 1979. *Ecology, Meaning, and Religion.* Richmond, Calif: North Atlantic Books.

Steward, J. H. 1977. *Evolution and Ecology: Essays on Social Transformation,* ed. by J. C. Steward and R. F. Murphy. Urbana: University of Illinois Press.

Vayda, A. P., ed. 1969. *Environment and Cultural Behavior: Ecological Studies in Cultural Anthropology.* Garden City, N.Y.: Natural History Press.

————, and R. Rappaport. 1968. Ecology, Cultural and Noncultural. In J. A. Clifton, ed., *Introduction to Cultural Anthropology.* Boston: Houghton Mifflin Company.

SECTION 16

Friedman, J. 1974. Marxism, Structuralism, and Vulgar Materialism, *Man* 9: 444–469.

Gajdusek, D. C. 1980. *Journal of Further Explorations in the Kuru Region and in the Kukukuku Country, Eastern Highlands of Eastern New Guinea, and of a Return to West New Guinea: December 25, 1963, to May 4, 1964.* Bethesda, Md.: National Institutes of Health.

Nietschmann, B. 1975. Beyond the Bizarre with Rumplestiltskin. *Reviews in Anthropology.* May: 157–168.

Sahlins, M. 1977. *Culture and Practical Reason.* Chicago: University of Chicago Press.

Salisbury, R. F. 1975. Non-Equilibrium Models in New Guinea Ecology: Possibilities of Cultural Extrapolation. *Anthropologica* 17(2): 127–147.

We have, at this stage, begun to reach a deepened understanding of diverse ways and institutions; and of the nature of humankind. But there is much still to be learned from the social systems and customs of the tribal world. It is worth pausing at this stage to consider again why it is worth seeking to understand dispute settlement in an African society, family structure in Borneo, religious beliefs in the Solomon Islands, or the production of yams in the Trobriand Islands.

To interpret such diverse customs and institutions, we are led to ask fundamental questions about society and human nature. Like Aztec human sacrifice and Amazonian men's cults, they lead us to seek the cultural logic whereby seemingly bizarre customs are meaningful and rational to those who participate in them. But they lead us beyond these cultural meanings as well, to fundamental questions of social theory. Should we, like the Marxists, seek to find conflicts and opposing "class" interests separating rulers and ruled, men and women? Or should we, like Sahlins, assume a consensus of commitment to cultural symbols? Do we begin with the assumption that the natural inclination of humans is to be autonomous individuals, and ask what leads them to sacrifice their freedom so as to live in society? Or do we assume it is humans' natural state to live in groups with a shared commitment to their cultural heritage and social institutions? Are war or the subordination of women inevitable expressions of our biological nature, or products of particular kinds of social institutions? To seek to understand the Trobriand islanders of Melanesia, whom we are about to encounter, or other

Part 3

The Tribal World: The Legacy of Human Diversity

non-Western peoples is to seek to understand ourselves.

These fundamental questions about society and human nature are not confined to the arcane debates of social theorists and philosophers working in the shadow of Plato and Aristotle, Hobbes and Rousseau, Spencer, Marx, Durkheim, and Weber: They pervade the everyday practice of Western social science, law, and politics. Economists seeking to control inflation work with a theoretical system erected on assumptions about human nature and society. So do political scientists and sociologists.

Anthropology seeks to pose these fundamental questions squarely; and, in asking them against the whole range of human ways in different times and places, to seek to provide more solid foundations for a comparative social science.

In the chapters to follow we will explore, through a series of strategic steps, the path to a deepened understanding of social institutions in this broadest perspective. We will begin with humans engaging the world in work, within a setting far from ours in space and far from ours in its logic of cultural meanings. To get there we will take a classic anthropological voyage.

8

Economic Systems

Leaving the bronzed rocks and the dark jungle of the Amphletts . . . we sail north into an entirely different world of flat coral islands. . . . We . . . enter an opaque, greenish sea, whose monotony is broken only by a few sandbanks, some bare and awash, others with a few pandanus trees squatting on their air roots. . . . Further ahead through the misty spray the line of horizon thickens here and there, as if faint pencil marks had been drawn upon it. These become more substantial, one of them lengthens and broadens, the others spring into the distinct shapes of small islands, and we find ourselves in the big lagoon of the Trobriands. . . . (Malinowski 1922:49)

So one of the most famous anthropological voyages began, as Bronislaw Malinowski conveyed his readers across the Southwest Pacific seas east of New Guinea to the Trobriand Islands. From this vantage point, in a world of lush gardens, lagoons, and shallow seas, Malinowski did battle with what he took to be the myths of a culture-bound social science: "economic man" maximizing values like an automaton, the Oedipus complex, the "primitive mentality."

We will follow Malinowski's intellectual voyage to the Trobriands in this chapter and those to follow in search of a more generalized and powerful social science perspec-

tive and a deepened understanding of human diversity and the oneness that underlies it. Such an odyssey back to the Trobriands is not a matter of anthropological sentiment: there are special elaborations and complexities in that far corner of Melanesia that challenge anthropological interpretation now as they did when Malinowski first described them in the years following World War I. There is a sense in which understanding the Trobriand islanders is understanding the full richness of human symbol systems, the full intricacy of social institutions, the full subtlety of human values and motives.

The Trobriand islanders, still growing their yams and exchanging their armshells and necklaces as they did in Malinowski's day, will challenge our analytical powers and sharpen them. In this chapter we will look at Trobriand systems of production and exchange, and will place them in comparative perspective. This will set out the issues of anthropological economics. But it will leave us with a host of further questions. In the chapters to follow we will progressively acquire better means to conceptualize and analyze the ways of Trobriand islanders—and thus of Basseri nomads, San, Tsembaga Maring—and through them, ourselves.

Banknotes arranged in decorative circles and adorned with flowers at a compensation payment for a killing, Melpa, Papua New Guinea.

17. SYSTEMS OF PRODUCTION

Production as Technical and Social

Production is the process whereby the world is engaged and transformed by human labor. It always has both a physical side—the tools and technology of work, the resources on which production depends—and a social side. Humans work in groups, for ends that are collective as well as individual; and the products of their work pass through social networks, are given meaning and value by and within groups.

Both the physical-technological side and the social side of production will come more clearly into focus if we follow Malinowski's voyage to the Trobriands in Case 14—first, to take an overview of the setting, then to go to the heart of Trobriand production, and indeed of Trobriand life: the gardens.

The Trobriander is above all a gardener, who digs with pleasure and collects with pride, to

CASE

14

Trobriand Systems of Production

The Setting

The Trobriand Islands consist of a flat coral island about 30 miles long and several smaller surrounding islands (Figure 8.1). Trobriand villages are scattered along the west coast, with its shallow lagoons, and in the interior. No single village has access to all the material goods its people need; and nowhere in the Trobriands can one obtain some crucial materials. These supplies include the greenstone needed for blades of adzes and axes, which comes from Murua Island to the east; rattan for lashing, and bamboo, which come from Fergusson Island to the south; and clay for pottery, most of which is made in the Amphlett Islands to the south (see Figure 8.3, Case 15).

Furthermore, there are broad regions of specialization on the main island of the Trobriands. Along the western coast, circling the lagoon, are villages that specialize in fishing. The northern section of the island is a rich agricultural area, with villages scattered through the interior. Some villages specialize in a special craft: one in polishing stone tools, another in woodcarving, another in decorating lime pots—all for export. Yet less handsome, everyday articles of almost all kinds can be produced within any Trobriand village—dependent at most on the import of raw materials (Malinowski 1935, I:21–22).

Gardens

We can usefully focus, as Malinowski did, on the rich agricultural districts of the north. He gives a vivid word picture of the yam gardens that are the Trobrianders' pride and joy, as they are at harvest time:

Walking across the country at that season, you would see some gardens in all the glory of their green foliage, just turning to gold. These would be some of the principal plantations of yams. . . . Then again you would see some of next season's gardens being started, and from time through a flat stretch of broad green leaves—the taro gardens. During my first rough inspection of the gardens . . . I was astonished by the bewildering variety of garden scenery, garden work, and garden significance. In one place a harvest was going on, men and women cutting vines, digging up roots, cleaning them and stacking them in heaps; in some of the taro plantations women were weeding; men were clearing away the low bush with axes in parts of the garden, in others they were laying out the ground in small squares like a chessboard. (Malinowski 1935, I:10)

The major crop is the yam, though taro is an important secondary subsistence food. Because yams can be stored, a regular seasonal cycle of planting and harvest is possible, based on the cycle of winds and rainfall. This annual cycling of the yam season structures many aspects of Trobriand life: trading expeditions, warfare, ceremonies, and even sexual life.

The Organization of Work

Let us begin the cycle when an area is chosen for the year's cultivation, in this system of swidden horticulture. Here we can begin to sort out social units of production. The *gardening team* that will work the large area chosen for gardens usually consists of all residents of a village. Villages may be relatively small—20 households—or may be much larger. A village may consist of one "subclan"—a group of men and women descended in the female line from a common ancestress, which holds collective title to land. Or a village may be composed of two or more subclans. When there are two or more subclans, their members usually work together as a single gardening team:

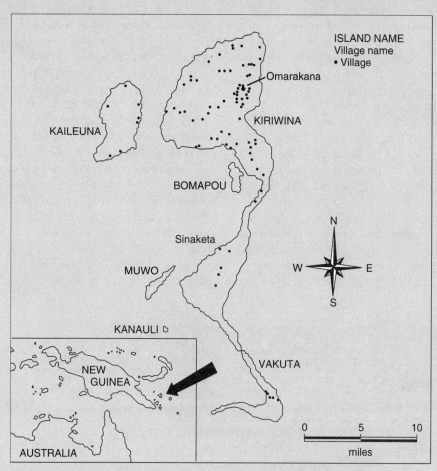

Figure 8.1   The Trobriand Islands. (After a map by Powell)

The village . . . is the effective unit of economic activities. . . . In the making of gardens, whole villages . . . operate as organized corporate bodies under the direction of subclan leaders and garden magicians. (Powell 1969b:581)

The gardening team does some of its work collectively, under the direction of a garden *magician* who is also its technical expert. The whole garden is divided into smaller squares. This phase of collective labor by the village gardening team is called *tamgogula*. Each man has several squares within the large garden, which his *household group* cultivates. Daily tasks are done separately by each family, consisting of father, mother, and children; this household labor is called *tavile'i*.

Continued

Case 14 continued

For other tasks, larger work groups form. In some cases, members of several households, or sometimes the entire gardening team, may pool their labor to do tasks collectively which each household group could, with less speed and camaraderie, do for itself. Such communal labor "takes place whenever a number of villagers agree to do one stage of gardening in common, on the basis of reciprocity" (Malinowski 1922:161). Usually the household whose work of many days is being done in a single day by a large work team provides rations for the workers, who go from plot to plot; but "no great or special payments take place" (1922:161).

Another form of communal labor entails an individual summoning kin, in-laws, and neighbors to work for him. He then has to distribute food to them. An ordinary man may do so, in what is called kabutu labor, to build a house or a yam house. But kabutu is also used by leaders of high rank—who hold wealth in surplus food—to mobilize followers. Such surpluses are, as we will see, contributed by villagers along lines of kinship obligation; the surpluses enable leaders to use redistribution to maintain support of kin and mobilize "retainers" and allies. Through kabutu, an important leader commands a communal labor force, which erects yam houses, builds canoes, and undertakes other large-scale projects through which he, and they, derive prestige. Being able to feed a work force, with vegetables that have been contributed by followers, is the prerequisite to such mobilizations of communal labor.

All adults in the Trobriands take a full part in agricultural production. Apart from the special

Trobriand production: Fishermen net mullet using traditional methods on the north coast of Kiriwina Island (1971).

A Trobriand gardener uses a wooden digging stick to plant yams.

services of the garden magician, who may be the leader of the village or his designated close relative, the division of labor is mainly by sex and age. Men cut the scrub; men and women clear ground and prepare for planting; men plant and women weed; men train yam vines, and thin roots; and both sexes take part in the harvest. Tools are simple: sharpened poles for digging and weeding and stone axes and adzes for tree-felling.

Yam Production
Each household group produces yams individually on its plots. Two factors of this production

are crucial here. First, probably the most important sphere of life to a Trobriand couple is their garden production. Vast piles of accumulated yams, far above what they need to feed their household, are their pride and joy—the more the better. They work extremely hard to produce great and "useless" quantities of food in an environment where a livelihood could be won with far more limited efforts.

Second, about half of the yams produced by a household go to the households of the husband's sister and other close female kin. The yams the household gives away, to other households and to the leader of the subclan, are the best and largest it produces. The more and better the yams one presents, the greater is one's prestige. There even are spectacular "giveaway" contests of yams that are duels for prestige between subclans and villages. The symbolic side of Trobriand yam production comes out clearly if we note that many of the yams most highly prized and conspicuously displayed are not used as domestic food at all, and may simply rot. Furthermore, the high-value yams, displayed in storehouses, especially by leaders of high rank, become symbols of prestige and power. A high-ranking leader, such as the "Paramount Chief" of prosperous Omarakana in the north, receives enormous quantities of yams as tribute from villages within a wide region—and this in turn provides the means of mobilizing an obligated labor force in collective enterprises.

whom accumulated food gives the sense of safety and pleasure in achievement, to whom the rich foliage of yam-vines or taro leaves is a direct expression of beauty. (Malinowski 1935, I:10)

We could go further in setting out the nature, organization, and apparent motivation of production—in looking at fishing, craft industries, domestic work such as cutting firewood and cooking, and so on. But our brief sketch of Trobriand horticulture goes far enough to pose important questions about the nature and logic of Trobriand economic life, and to begin to raise the most central issues in anthropological economics. Let us look first at the puzzles posed by the Trobriands, then step back for comparative implications.

Seeking the Logic of Production

Some of these problems were set out by Malinowski decades ago. Why do Trobriand islanders produce so many more yams than they need for subsistence, then let many of them rot? And why does a household give a large proportion of its yam harvest, including the most valued yams, to the householder's sister and brother-in-law?

Other questions are organizational. Why are villages comprised of subclans that trace descent in the female line from their founding ancestresses? Is this a matriarchy? How is it that these subclans hold collective title to lands—a matter of great emotional significance and mythological importance to Trobrianders? There are more complicated organizational puzzles here, as we will see.

What about the high-ranking leaders such as the "Paramount Chief" of Omarakana? On the one hand, these leaders receive vast quantities of produce as tribute, and play a central part in the exchange of prestige valuables (as we will shortly see); and they command deference from "common-

ers," who have to prostrate themselves before leaders of high rank. But on the other hand, there are no state institutions maintaining the power of a ruling class, no army or police to exact surplus produce as tribute or demand deference. And the "chiefs," however commanding their presence, themselves work in their own gardens, paddle their own canoes. Why do Trobrianders present yams to leaders of high rank? How much real power do these leaders have?

What are we to make of the garden magician, who performs important rites at every stage of the procedure? As analysts of the Trobriand economy, are we to treat magic as if it were an important component of technology, or as useless mumbo jumbo?

First Issues in Comparative Economics

This leads us toward a more general problem. In Trobriand terms, gardeners are being highly rational in performing magic or hiring a specialist to do it. They are being completely rational in producing far more yams than they or anyone else could eat, giving away the best ones, displaying surplus yams and letting them rot. An economist's definition of economic behavior as making choices about the allocation of scarce means—that is, as *maximizing*—fits the Trobriands as it fits all human societies, if we look at choices in Trobriand terms. But that tells us nothing, unless we understand "Trobriand terms": the meanings and motives that guide choice, and the institutional framework within which choices take place.

Here we begin to face a need to take a stance toward the major controversies in anthropological economics. Can we apply the models of formal economics, from the neo-classical tradition that dominates Western economics departments, to tribal economies? Or are they different in kind and basic structure from those of modern capitalist societies dominated by market principles? Even to characterize what is economic means taking a stance toward these questions. The view I will take derives mainly from neo-Marxist anthropology, but it draws inspiration as well from complementary perspectives.

Production in Tribal Societies

We can step back from the Trobriands to take a wider comparative view. Recall that the Tsembaga Maring of New Guinea studied by Rappaport (Cases 5 and 9) are, like the Trobrianders, swidden horticulturalists. Like the Trobrianders, they are organized in groups based on descent that act like corporations in holding collective title to land. (The Maring constitute these groups through descent in the male line, the Trobrianders through descent in the female line.)

But for the Maring, cultivating swiddens is not an affair of the whole community. Swiddens are cleared, planted, and harvested separately by each household group. Sweet potatoes, unlike yams, cannot be stored for long periods. They are harvested continuously. Like the Trobrianders, the Maring grow more tubers than they need for daily subsistence. But those they do not eat are neither stored nor given away, but are fed to pigs. These pigs, which we glimpsed in Case 9, are used in cycles of exchange and feasting, with power and prestige as the stakes. (To understand Maring rationality, we would be led, as we are in the Trobriand case, into a cultural world of symbolic goals, motives, and meanings.)

In comparison with European feudalism or capitalism, or the ancient states, Maring and Trobriand economies are relatively similar. Both mobilize **surplus labor,** if we define that as work beyond that needed to sustain the worker; by that means, the young, the elderly, the ill, and injured are provided for, and community needs (the construction of a dance-ground or path by the Maring, or the scaffoldings used in ritual by the Trobrianders) are met. Surplus labor is required among the Maring to produce the sweet potatoes used to feed pigs raised for exchange and feasting cycles; and among the Trobrianders, to produce yams for presentation and display.

Both the Maring and Trobrianders have a division of labor that is relatively simple, based mainly on sex and age. The tasks of producing staple root crops are divided rather differently in the two societies, although in each case men do more of the sporadic tasks of felling and fencing that require bursts of heavy labor in which sheer strength is called for, and women do more of the time-consuming and continuous tasks, as well as the daily domestic work of food preparation, carrying water, and so on.

If we look at craft production, we find that the skills needed to produce virtually all utilitarian items made in the Trobriands are widely distributed. Moreover, the people who produce craft goods also work in the gardens. There is a specialization among communities in fishing or horticulture in the Trobriands, and specialization in the production of craft items that go beyond everyday utilitarian standards. Among the Maring, in a less diverse environment, all communities within the region are producers of sweet potatoes and pigs, and all command equivalent craft skills. In the Trobriand case, then, **trade** of the products of labor flourishes along with **exchange.** In the Maring case, exchange predominates.

If we look at the distribution of the products of labor, we find in both cases that it is structured quite directly by systems of kinship and marriage. (Even the tribute yams given to a high-ranking leader are presented in terms of the obligations between in-laws, as we will see.) We will shortly examine categories of transactions within the highly complex Trobriand system of distribution and exchange. The point for the moment is that there are no state institutions regulating the production and distribution of surplus—such as those that, in the early states of the Middle East or Mesoamerica, exacted surplus from farmers in the form of taxation. The political processes of both the Maring and Trobrianders are carried on within structures and idioms of kinship and community.

Means and Modes of Production

The **means of production**—in these societies, land, tools, planting materials, technical and magical knowledge—are mainly collectively held by groups. Land is held, among the Maring and Trobrianders, by groups whose membership is based on descent from common ancestors. Such groupings, acting as legal individuals in a way analogous to corporations, will be a central theme in the next chapter. Tools and planting materials may be nominally owned by individuals, but control over them is held within the household groups that are—for both the Maring and Trobrianders—the main units of everyday production. Magical knowledge may be held by individuals, but usually as custodians who use it in the interest of their household, sibling group, descent group, or community. The Trobriand garden magician acts on behalf of the whole gardening team, while lesser everyday magic is known to many more people. The means of production are then, in general, accessible to every Trobriand household.

Such a complex of relations between production and distribution, command over surplus labor and its products, and access to the means of production comprises a

mode of production. Neo-Marxist theorists have struggled with the question of how (or whether) to use this technical concept, created mainly for analyzing feudalism and capitalism, to analyze other societies. Marx analyzed particular periods of European society in terms of two or more modes of production occurring simultaneously (he pointed out that there was a time in England when it was against the law to paint one's house or work in one's garden on the Sabbath, while at the same time it was against the law for a worker to refuse to work in a factory on the Sabbath: this represented the conjunction of an old and a new mode of production, and the laws appropriate to each). Are we then to analyze a society like that of the Trobriands, where one day a household is working on its own plots and the next day all members of the village gardening team are working together on collective tasks within the whole village garden, as having two (or more) modes of production? Or are they both manifestations of a single mode of production?

And if there is a single mode of production, of which there are alternative expressions or phases, what are we to call it? Some usages have emphasized the channeling of surplus labor and its products within structures of kinship and community (Hindess and Hirst 1975). Others have emphasized the importance of groupings based on descent in corporately controlling land, as with Terray's "lineage mode of production" (1972). Yet others have emphasized the way that the primary social unit, in both production and consumption, is the household, as with Sahlins's and Meillassoux's "domestic mode of production" (Meillassoux 1975, Sahlins 1972).

For our purposes the term **tribal communal mode of production** will serve well enough. But to imagine that labeling such a broad family of production systems as those of the Iban, the Maring, and the Trobrianders with any single term would take us very far in analysis would be to succumb to naive typology-building—we would simply end up with a somewhat different "ladder." For some purposes it will be useful to lump the Maring, the Trobrianders, the Iban, and hundreds of other peoples together and contrast them with the Aztec, Inca, and Maya, or with peasants in Mexico and Thailand. More commonly, in anthropological economics, we will be seeking to understand the differences between the Maring and Trobrianders and the internal operation of each system. To class them as having the same mode of production does not give us a promising start.

One important question that has grown out of protracted debate by neo-Marxist anthropologists about modes of production in tribal societies is whether it is appropriate to talk about *exploitation* in such societies. The debate has mainly been focused on tribal elders in African societies, and whether they can be said to exploit juniors (or "cadets"). It can be generalized to other societies that lack social classes (see Chapter 13), but where surplus labor is extracted from women to advance the prestige and power of men. Do Maring men, especially those who seek power and prestige through pig feasting and exchange, exploit the women who work to feed the pigs? Do Trobriand leaders who control the prestige economy, and exercise power by redistributing the yams produced by others, exploit these producers? These questions take us to the heart of tribal societies—into the realm of politics, of sexual politics, and even religion. We will have to work toward the answers.

A people's system of production constitutes the way they engage and transform their physical environment. Note, then, how we have shifted our focus from ecosystems (the biological context) to economic systems (the *social* context). We have gone from a view of the environment as a natural system that shapes human adaptations, toward a view of humans organized in groups engaging and transforming the natural world through work.

This natural world sets limits to, but cannot determine, the economic organization of a society. The economic system, viewed in these terms, is not neatly separable from kinship institutions (which organize the processes of production and distribution) or from beliefs about ancestors and magical powers (which legitimize title to the means of production and provide crucial elements of technology).

Base and Superstructure

There has been much debate and misunderstanding about Marxist and neo-Marxist conceptions of how economic systems and the social, political, and religious institutions of societies are interrelated. I have noted that Marxism has often been portrayed as economic determinism, a view that the political and religious institutions of a society are a reflection of its economic system. Marx himself repeatedly asserted that the economic relations determined only "in the last instance" the forms of law, politics, or religion; and he noted how in ancient Rome legal institutions had played a dominant part in the organization of society, and in the Middle Ages in Europe religious institutions had been central. But why, he asked, were legal institutions dominant in one case, religious institutions in another? The ultimate underlying reasons, he argued, lay in the dominant modes of production in the two cases. But what does determination "in the last instance" mean?

Marxist theory distinguishes the economic system—the social relations and technology of production—from the political-legal institution and ideologies that sustain it. The metaphor of a physical structure is used. The economic system constitutes the **base** (or **infrastructure**). The institutions that sustain and perpetuate the forces and relations of production constitute the **superstructure.**

But when it comes to applying this conceptual scheme to real historical societies—and especially to the full range of societies anthropologists study—there has been much room for debate. I have noted that in the last century interpretations of Marx have themselves been institutionalized. The orthodox Soviet interpretation of Marx took "determination in the last instance" to be a quite direct economic determinism, comparable to the ecological determinism of cultural materialists like Harris. It is against this doctrinaire Marxism that many refutations have been directed, from anthropology, history, and other fields that take a broad, comparative view of human ways.

> For Radcliffe Brown, it was enough to show that kinship was the dominant factor among Australian Aborigines. . . . Dumont sees this refutation as furnished by the blatant domination of religion in India and by the fact that the caste system takes the form of an ideological opposition between pure and impure. For the historian Will, the domination of politics in ancient Greece shows clearly that economics did not play the determining role. . . . How can Marxists reconcile the hypothesis that it is the infrastructure which is determinant in the last analysis with the fact that in certain historical societies one finds a superstructure occupying a dominant position? (Godelier 1978:765)

Determination "in the Last Instance"

Neo-Marxists such as Godelier (1978), seeking in Marx's own work a more viable basis for anthropological economics, reject economic determinisms. Godelier notes that in

the societies, past and present, that anthropologists have mainly studied, there is no clear separation between economic institutions and the institutions of kinship, politics, or religion. If there is any distinction to be drawn between base and infrastructure, it must be drawn on the basis of *functions*. If kinship relations or religious rituals serve to organize production and distribution, then in these respects they are elements in the economic system.

Kinship relations and religious rituals seem, on the surface, to function as part of the superstructure of a social system. That is, they sustain a prevailing system of social relations, or in Marxist terms *reproduce* the means for the existence of the system. Kinship, by regulating marriage and descent, reproduces the labor force. Religion, through the eyes of its participants, sustains the cosmos—the seasons, the fertility of crops, the powers of magic—without which human productive effort could not be realized. But, Godelier argues, in a tribal society kinship does more than physically reproduce the labor force through birth, nurturance, and subsistence, a function kinship serves in an industrial society or feudal system. In a tribal society, kinship provides the system through which production itself is organized, and through which distribution takes place. In Hindu India, in contrast, religious institutions not only "reproduce" the cosmos and reinforce the social relations of production; through the caste system, a religious order based on purity and pollution establishes relations of production. Untouchables do menial labor because it would be polluting for others to do it.

But why is kinship dominant—that is, central in structuring relations of production—in a tribal society? And why is religion dominant in Hindu India, as it was in Europe in the Middle Ages? Here we come back to Marx's notion of determination " in the last instance." As Godelier (1978:766) observes, "We must seek to explain how it is that kinship (or religion) comes to function as a relation of production and hence to dominate." In complex social systems, the products of human labor are accumulated in the form of wealth, in physical structures of buildings, towns, waterworks, in livestock, tools, and so on. In a system of **social classes** (say, peasants, slaves, warriors, artisans, priests, rulers), the ruling class controls the system through state ap-paratuses of repression and force that ex-tract food surpluses and keep control over the means of production (and through religious ideologies that define observances such as Aztec human sacrifices as necessary for the fertility of crops and the favor of the gods).

But in tribal societies, without social classes, there is only a very limited accumulation of the products of past human labor—little wealth, no giant temples or cities, few tools beyond what each household can produce itself. What matters, Godelier suggests, is living human labor; hence, he suggests, the dominant role in production of the kinship institutions, of marriage and descent, that physically reproduce the labor force (Godelier 1978:766).

The crucial point is that if we are to use Marxist-derived conceptions of base and superstructure to analyze the range of societies anthropologists study, it cannot be by finding separate compartments—"the economic system," "the kinship system," "the religion"—with the economy as base and the rest as superstructure. The compartmentalization into such functionally specialized subsystems is peculiar to certain kinds of complex societies. We must look at the customs and institutions of the tribal world not simply in terms of the symbolic modes in which they are expressed (obligations of kinship, beliefs in the pollutedness of women, the demands of the ancestors) but in terms of what they *do*, in terms of organizing relations of humans toward one another and toward the world of nature. (For later treatments by Godelier on these and related issues, see Godelier 1986, 1996.)

Reproduction of Social Relations

The concept of "reproduction" still needs examination. To avoid confusion with the biological sense, we can best distinguish this as **social reproduction.** A system of production is not automatically sustained and perpetuated across generations. We have glimpsed how, in an ancient state, mechanisms of state repression and a religious system served to sustain the power of nobles and priests, their control over the means of production, and their extraction of surpluses. Such state mechanisms sustain an existing social order; so do the marriage systems and household organization of peasant families, through which the labor force is perpetuated. These superstructural mechanisms reproduce the system.

What about a tribal society? Even where there are no classes, women may do the bulk of daily horticultural labor (which may include, as among the Tsembaga Maring, producing a food surplus to feed pigs used for male prestige purposes). Senior men may command the labor of several cowives, and of junior men, through their control over prestige valuables used in marriage payments. A religious ideology that defines women as polluted, hence excluding them from religious ritual and politics, consigns them, as producers, to the domestic realm. All of these mechanisms reproduce a system of relations of production. The focus on reproduction of a social system across generations also enables us to see how labor that may be surplus in terms of meeting subsistence needs may in the longer run be necessary to sustain the system:

> Human social production requires reproduction—of labor and of the means of production. Tools must be replaced, seed kept for a new planting, land renewed through fallowing or fertilization, children borne and nourished, new units of production formed. What appears to be surplus from the point of view of immediate production may in fact be necessary for social reproduction. (O'Laughlin 1975:360–361)

If we see the reproduction of a social system as problematic, if we view all societies as processes over time, then we have the conceptual means to deal with progressive changes of one system into another. Such transformation may occur in tribal societies, as in the emergence of chiefs and social hierarchy in the Trobriands, as well as in complex class-stratified societies. If a productive system provides, say, an opening for the accumulation of capital resources, then a gradual and cumulative seizing of these opportunities may lead to the gradual emergence of a new class of merchants or landlords. As they gain power, the system of productive relations is transformed— and so are the ideologies, legal institutions, and other superstructural elements of the old system. Any social system contains the seeds of its own transformation.

Reproduction and System Boundaries

Recall the depiction by Sahlins (1972) and Meillassoux (1975) of tribal societies as representing a "domestic mode of production." It is true that in most tribal societies, the social groups that perform the everyday labor of production comprise households. A widow and her children may not be an independent producing unit; they may have to depend on male kin to do some tasks. But an intact household group in a tribal community characteristically can perform all or most of the necessary productive tasks (perhaps with the exception of magic), and does so on a day-to-day basis—periodically, perhaps, enlisting or participating in wider work groups, as in the Trobriands. Why, then, is this not adequately characterized as a "domestic mode of production"?

Households may be independent, or relatively so, at "the level of immediate production." But when we look at the economics of distribution and particularly when we look at the processes whereby the system of social relations is reproduced, we find that households are necessarily tied together within a wider system: a system within which households are created and perpetuated by marriage, and through which products flow. It is a fundamental analytical flaw to look at the groups of people who actually work together in day-to-day production and to infer that these groups and the social relations *within* them adequately characterize the mode of production.

The need to see the process of reproduction operating within a wider system than the units within which work is performed has a further implication. What constitutes an appropriate social system for analysis is never an easy or immediately answerable question. Is it a Trobriand village? A Trobriand region? All of the Trobriand Islands? Or could the system we want to analyze include the surrounding islands and peoples as well? That depends partly on what questions we want to answer. This dilemma will confront us squarely when we look at the modern world system in Part 4. Trobriand villages, and virtually all communities on earth, are at least indirectly connected into a single global system. For the purposes of analysis, we must draw lines somewhere, not include "the whole world."

But the appropriate place to draw a line, if we are looking at how a system of social and economic relations is reproduced, may well not coincide with the boundaries of a language and culture. We often need to analyze as a single system a regional complex of ethnic groups. The question is particularly crucial theoretically when we consider pastoralists—and whether there is such a thing as a "pastoral mode of production." We can illustrate with reference to the nomads of central Asia. As Krader observes:

> In north China and neighboring central Asia . . . there has been a great specialization of social production on either side of the Great Wall of China, whereby the nomadic Turks and Mongols have had a major concern with stock-breeding, but a minor concern with agriculture, and the Chinese, predominantly agriculturalists, devote only a small part of their social labor and land to cattle, camel, sheep, or horse raising. Each side was dependent . . . on . . . the other. (Krader 1979: 225–226)

One cannot assume, then, that a pastoral people constitute the significant unit of analysis, in relation to surrounding sedentary ones: that must be discovered by a careful sorting out of relations of production and appropriation and distribution of surplus within the regional system of which pastoralists are a part. Talal Asad notes the following in the case of China and the Mongols:

> By the beginning of the twentieth century . . . a vast quantity of surplus product was being extracted from the producers [Mongolian herdsmen] through an alliance of Chinese merchants and Mongolian lords. The critical relationship in such a case is that between the direct producer from whom surplus labor is extracted and its appropriators (both "nomadic" princes and nonnomadic "outsiders"). (Asad 1979:423)

> The point is to identify the nature of the total social system within which nomads exist and reproduce themselves as a distinctive cultural, political, and economic entity. . . . And since the conditions, and the system which reproduces [perpetuates] them, vary radically according to time and place, there cannot be an essential "pastoral nomadic society." (Asad 1979:422)

As Asad's observations about the appropriation and distribution of surplus and O'Laughlin's cautions against preoccupation with "the level of immediate production" suggest, we can understand the organization and bounds of an economic system only by looking at the process of distribution as well as the process of production.

18. THE ECONOMICS OF DISTRIBUTION

Gudeman (1978) argues that neither neo-Marxists nor other students of anthropological economics have developed sufficiently broad and systematic theories of distribution. He notes that an anthropological theory of distribution must at once be formal, in the sense of dealing systematically with the allocation of the products of labor, and cultural, in comprehending in the terms of the people under study, the meaning of time, work and leisure, of consuming, giving, and receiving, of the symbolic as well as nutritive value of products. We must find out and analyze the cultural meanings of work—as with "the time spent in the service of the saints or making large canoes to carry argonauts on their expeditions of trade" (Gudeman 1978:369). And with that, we find ourselves back in the Trobriands. (See Case 15.)

Distribution, Consumption, and Exchange in the Trobriands

The fame of the Trobriand islanders in anthropology began with the "argonauts on their expeditions of trade" on which Malinowski's first account was centered. But to understand the economics of distribution and consumption, we need to begin not on the green seas of the "Sea Arm of Pilolu," realm of flying witches, mythic voyages, and dangerous adventure; but in the less dramatic realm of hearth and home. In working from the domestic setting outward into the public realm of prestige and exchange, we will glimpse a complexity far beyond what Malinowski described—a complexity coming to light from recent restudies of the Trobriands, notably Annette Weiner's *Women of Value, Men of Renown* (1976). Fortunately for our purposes we need not seek to comprehend the entire system, but to learn some needed insights from it.

Domestic Labor, Domestic Consumption

A Trobriand household, primary unit of subsistence production, is also the setting for everyday subsistence consumption. Malinowski tells us less about this than we would like to know:

The division of functions within the household is . . . quite definite. The woman has to cook the food, which is simple, and does not require much preparation. The main meal is taken at sunset, and consists of yams, taro, or other tubers, roasted in the open fire—or, less frequently, boiled in a small pot or baked in the ground— with the occasional addition of fish or meat. Next morning the remains are eaten cold, and sometimes, though not regularly, fruit, shellfish, or some other light snack may be taken at midday. (1929:19)

Collection of wild foods, animal and vegetable, is apparently women's work—a side of labor missed in our glimpse of gardening: "The women may have gone collecting shellfish or wild fruits," Malinowski (1929:18) tells us. Fishing and hunting are done by men.

Here, we can note that such humdrum domestic labor is not simply marked by a division of labor by sex, but by symbolic elaborations. Women carry loads on their heads, in a "special feminine receptacle, the bell-shaped basket"(1929:19); men carry objects only on the shoulder. Only women carry water bottles, made of coconut shells; and these bottles, as well as heads, are laden with sexual symbolism, as we will see in Case 54. This symbolically laden women's task helps to create a separate realm controlled by women, the water-hole. "The water-hole is the woman's club and center of gossip, and as such is important, for there is a distinct woman's public opinion and point of view in a Trobriand village" (1929:20). We will see shortly that this women's side of Trobriand life remained largely hidden for 50 years.

Food, Gardens, and Exchange

Gardens

What is the relationship between yams produced for exchange and the yams and taro grown for everyday subsistence? Malinowski indicated that more than half of a household's yam produce was presented to other households, especially that of the husband's sister; and Powell's (1960) subsequent data indicated that this pairing of households was done according to systematic planning: the responsibility to grow yams for particular sisters of subclan members was carefully assigned by the group's leaders. Weiner's evidence shows that matters went even further. From the moment a garden plot is laid out, it is considered to be either a *food garden*—one from which a household will derive everyday subsistence needs—or an *exchange garden*—one with which the household will meet its obligations.

A man who plants and tends an exchange garden does not own any of the yams. From the time of planting, the yams belong to the person to whom the harvest will be presented. (Weiner 1976:138)

Moreover, the planting materials are provided by the eventual recipient of the yams (from the previous year's crop), so that what the man who plants and tends an exchange garden and his wife are presenting is *labor* embodied in yams (Weiner 1976:147).

Malinowski failed to distinguish clearly between food gardens and exchange gardens (because he was so much more interested in the latter). This led him to overlook a puzzling fact:

A man uses garden magic *only* in those gardens which he grows for someone else; no one uses magic in subsistence gardens, for this produce is immediately converted into food and does not facilitate the maintenance of extended formalized social relationships. (Weiner 1976:217)

But *which* social relationships? And why?

Harvest Presentations

Malinowski used the Trobriand term *urigubu* to refer to the annual presentation of the best yams a household produces to another household—ideally, to the household of the husband's sister and brother-in-law. It now seems that Malinowski may have used the wrong word, so we will simply call these *harvest presentations*.

The presentation of yams to another household—which stores them in a building specially constructed for display purposes, where they will be kept for up to 6 months and sometimes allowed to rot—is a very different matter from cooking them for food. As long as a yam is uncooked it is an item of wealth that can be invested. Once it is cooked, it can only be eaten. Converting raw yams into cooked food is, in Trobriand terms, not the realization of productive effort, but a succumbing to practical necessity one avoids if possible:

Once the yam houses are filled, the villagers eat very few yams as part of their daily diet. Yams neatly stacked inside a yam house are a man's capital—they are a display of his potential. Conversely, the rotting of yams means that a man has fulfilled all his yam exchange obligations, that he has land enough that he has seed yams and subsistence for himself. The natural process of decay is a visual public statement of a man's total control over his social, financial, and ecological environment. (Weiner 1974)

When members of a Trobriand household labor in an exchange garden to produce as many yams as possible, what are they getting out of it? Is it "rational" to work harder to produce for someone else than for oneself?

The organizational side of these harvest presentations must remain fuzzy until we explore, in the next two chapters, the organization of Trobriand subclans, and the structures of descent, kinship, and marriage that are so central in production, distribution, and reproduction in tribal societies. At this point, however, we can go part way.

Continued

Case 15 continued

Harvest presentation yams are carried to their recipient by the producer and immediate relatives (1974).

Reciprocation for Harvest Presentations

What comes back to the household that gives its yams to another household? When a Trobriand gardener piles for display the yams harvested from an exchange garden, most of them are allocated to the particular sister and brother-in-law for whom it is his responsibility to provide; some smaller amounts are set aside to be presented to other sisters (or equivalent close female relatives) and their husbands. A basket of such yams, and perhaps a pig and some areca nuts for betel

chewing, is presented to the sister; and the latter's husband reciprocates by presenting the donor with a polished green-stone ax blade or a clay pot. The next year, the original donor presents a larger pile of yams "as reciprocation for the valuable"—that is, the ax blade or pot. But why stone ax blades or pots, neither of which was put to practical use, even in the days before Western technology? The recipient of an unusually large harvest presentation may similarly present a valuable—an ax blade, a pot, an ornament—in recognition for the extra hard work

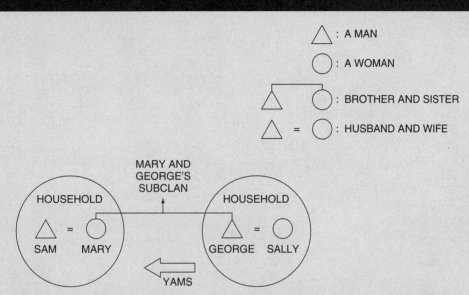

Figure 8.2 Hypothetical households linked through harvest presentations. (For fuller explication of kinship diagrams, see Figure 9.1, p.181.)

that has been put in. That, in turn, will elicit more hard work in future years. But why work extra hard in exchange for useless objects?

Another element in the reciprocation for harvest yams emerges if we look at women's mortuary feasts. These are spectacular events in which women distribute large quantities of fiber skirts and banana-leaf bundles—items that in practical terms are as useless as ax blades and pots that are kept apart and not used. When a woman is making a mortuary distribution, the women to whom her husband has presented harvest yams parade up to her and present her with leaf bundles and skirts.

Here an example using Western names* will help (see Figure 8.2). George and his wife Sally make exchange gardens for George's sister Mary and her husband Sam. George and Sally

also present yams to George's other sisters and female cousins (Elizabeth, Pam, Laura . . .). When these yams are presented, they are considered to be "from" George "to" Mary, Elizabeth, and so forth (although if valuables are given in reciprocation they are presented by Sam, by Elizabeth's husband, by Pam's husband, etc.—the men into whose yam houses the yams are put). Now what about the leaf packets and skirts? When Sally's brother or close subclan relative dies, Sally takes the lead in mortuary rites. And Mary, Elizabeth, Pam, and Laura (whose husband's yam houses Sally's labor helped to fill) present Sally with bundles and skirts.

There is another even more important kind of reciprocation for harvest presentations. Imagine that now it is Mary who is taking the lead in a mortuary ceremony for the death of someone in her subclan (descent is through the female line, so this could be for the death of George's

*The Western names may seem out of place, but Trobriand names are often four, five, or six syllables long.

Continued

Case 15 continued

A Trobriand yam house, symbol of pride and wealth.

brother or maternal uncle). The person who above all is responsible for financing the lavish distributions of symbolic wealth, in bundles and skirts, which Mary will distribute at the mortuary rite, is her husband Sam. Here Sam is investing his resources to support his wife Mary, in reciprocation for the labor of growing yams provided by Mary's brother George. George might make a statement something like this, as one of Weiner's Trobriand informants did:

We watch our sister's husband carefully to see how fast he helps her get ready for the women's mortuary ceremony. If he does not help her quickly to collect her things, then we say that man [Sam] is not a good husband and we do not want to make a garden for our sister [Mary] any more. (Weiner 1976:198)

Harvest Presentations and the Power of Chiefs

Malinowski noted that harvest presentations are a major mechanism whereby powerful leaders of high rank maintain their power. Only chiefs are entitled to polygamous marriages. In fact, the chief's representatives will be sent to the leader of a subclan with which he and his advisers seek a marriage alliance. They throw down a spear with four coconuts tied on top. If they decide to go ahead with a marriage, this subclan will provide a wife; but they then must assign men to make four large exchange gardens for this "sister" and her husband (Weiner 1976:201–202).

This puts the wife's subclan in what Malinowski described as a "tribute" relationship to a prominent chief: his yam houses are filled to overflowing by subclans around a whole district. But as Weiner (1976:202) points out, "these chiefs must use their resources to provision their wives with women's wealth [as part of] the formal reciprocity which every man has for his wife's kinsmen."

To understand these strands of kinship and obligation, we need to know more about how ties of birth, marriage, and descent weave tribal peoples into groups and networks—a task that lies ahead in the next two chapters. It reinforces again Godelier's point that production and distribution in tribal societies are organized in terms of kinship—which then is an

A *sagali* yam distribution in the Trobriands.

integral part of economic base as well as superstructure.

But the cultural logic of *meanings;* as well as the organizational logic of groups, still eludes us. Why objects like leaf bundles and ceremonial ax blades? We need to look more widely at other categories of exchange. First, there is a general category of distribution, *sagali,* of which women's mortuary distributions are one subtype. These provide further mechanisms for the redistribution of the wealth in yams concentrated in the hands of prominent leaders.

Sagali

A *sagali* is a distribution of food in connection with some ceremonial or special occasion—a mortuary feast, a commemorative feast, a competitive enterprise, or the like. Prestige in the system is achieved, expressed, and validated by being able to give away large quantities of food, to sponsor a feast, a war, a work project. Thus an important leader of a village or district gives away in *sagali* much of what he receives.

The most spectacular distributions of food and valuables apparently come in the mortuary

Continued

distributions after a death. Here, as we have glimpsed, women play a dramatic and central role, even though neither Malinowski nor H. A. Powell, who did a restudy, published any detailed information on women's exchange systems. Only with Weiner's research in the Trobriands in the early 1970s did it become clear that the men's world of high finance and exchange is complemented by and intertwined with a system where women publicly exchange symbolically female valuables and compete for high stakes of prestige.

When a person from a woman's own subclan dies, she and her fellow subclan women give away vast quantities of women's skirts and especially of banana-leaf bundles (as many as 15,000 of them) at a special *sagali* mortuary distribution, one of long series of mortuary distributions. "In this ceremony women are the major actresses on-stage in the center of the hamlet playing a role every bit as tough and aggressive and competitive as a . . . man" (Weiner 1974). A woman also plays a central part in the distribution after her father's death, and a lesser part after the death of another person in her father's subclan. We have seen how a woman acquires skirts and bundles from her husband and from her husband's kinswomen to whom she has given baskets of yams. She also acquires wealth to finance lavish mortuary distributions by strategically investing yams she and her husband have received as harvest presentations from her male subclan relatives, and by making salable craft goods.

Pokala

Another important category of transaction is *pokala,* an asymmetrical presentation to one's status-superior. The term *pokala* covers a range of conceptually related transactions. First, it cov-

ers the presentation of gifts and services from junior members of a subclan or clan to senior members in exchange for anticipated material benefits and status advantage. Thus *pokala* gifts are a means of securing future political advantage, validating rights to matrilineal inheritance, or rendering tribute to one's ranking leader. It thus implies giving by one of lower status to one of higher status in exchange for obligations—obligations of protection, future status, future material advantage, and so on. In Chapter 11 we will look more closely at the politics of rank and prestige validated by such transactions.

Pokala in a different sense also refers to tribute to a district chief or some other notable. The essentials of *pokala* are (1) that it implies status asymmetry, with the giver below the receiver, and (2) that it creates a diffuse or specific obligation, so the giver improves his position vis-à-vis his rivals (even when the "giver" is a village sending tribute).

Two other forms of distribution should be mentioned before we examine Trobriand valuables laden with symbolic value, and the remarkable pattern of overseas voyaging which was Malinowski's original focus. These are important because both are mechanisms for the exchange of specialized products, which play parts in the regional organization of the Trobriand economy.

Wasi

A formalized exchange between coastal villages that specialize in fishing and inland villages producing yam surpluses is called *wasi*. Here there are traditional alliances between villages, and within them there are "partnerships" between a particular fisherman and particular gardeners. After the harvest, the gardeners will take a bunch of taro or yams to their coastal opposite numbers. As soon afterwards as possible, the lagoon dwellers will stage a large fishing expedition. The haul of fish is taken directly to the inland village, where fish bundles are presented in exchange for the earlier yam presentation, according to fixed standards of equivalence.

Gimwali

Gimwali comprises Trobriand forms of barter—nonmoney transactions according to market principles. Here haggling and publicly acknowledged efforts to get the better of the other man prevail. Within or between Trobriand villages, gimwali entails irregular barter of fish for vegetables or of newly manufactured items of various sorts. Our knowledge of the flow of agricultural produce and the exchange of root vegetables for fish has been colored and limited by Malinowski's (and the Trobrianders' own) emphasis on dramatic, formal, and ritualized transactions at the expense of more mundane, impersonal, or informal transactions. Thus we know much more about formal wasi exchange of vegetables for fish partners than about vava, a form of gimwali where vegetables are bartered directly for fish.

The everyday barter of yams or manufactured items—skirts, lime, spatulas, combs—for other valuables is clearly crucial in Trobriand economics, but the data give only rare glimpses of such exchange. The symbolic value of ax blades, pots, and shell ornaments remains a puzzle. We will look first at the axes and pots; the shell ornaments will take us overseas onto the green seas of myth and danger.

Vaygu'a

Vaygu'a (Weiner: veguwa) are valuables used in ceremonial presentations and exchanges.

Of all objects of exchange, shell and stone valuables are inherently the most durable and permanent. Within the internal exchange system in Kiriwina [main island of the Trobriand group], stone ax blades (beku) are the most valued. A man is called wealthy . . . if he owns such blades. The general term for beku is veguwa. Clay pots manufactured in the Amphlett Islands are used as utilitarian cooking pots, but they are also used as veguwa for exchange. . . . Beku is . . . considered the primary wealth object. . . .

Stone ax blades can be converted through exchanges into a wide variety of other objects and services. . . . Beku can be exchanged for pigs, magic spells, seed yams, and raw yams. Unlike yams, the virtually indestructible ax blade circulates for generations. Moreover, ax blades, unlike yams, are not homegrown. As with certain other valuables—for example, clay pots and shell decorations—ax blades are manufactured by specialists. Access to these manufactured goods within Kiriwina comes about primarily through exchanges of pigs, yams, and magic spells. (Weiner 1976:179–180)

These vaygu'a may have purely symbolic value, but it is a power that moves men and women.

Access to valuables is of the utmost political importance. Hamlet managers, whether of high or low rank, constantly need valuables in order to keep making payments for continuing land use. Men who control workpower need valuables to repay other men for large yam gardens [that is, harvest presentations]. Men need valuables for the marriages of their sons, brothers, and sisters' sons, and men need valuables when a death occurs. (Weiner 1976:181)

The quest for the power conveyed by symbolic objects takes Trobriand men out onto the seas, and into one of the most remarkable regional systems of the tribal world.

Kula

The Trobriand Islands form part of the d'Entrecasteaux Archipelago (Figure 8.3) lying off the southeastern end of New Guinea. Though

Continued

Case 15 continued

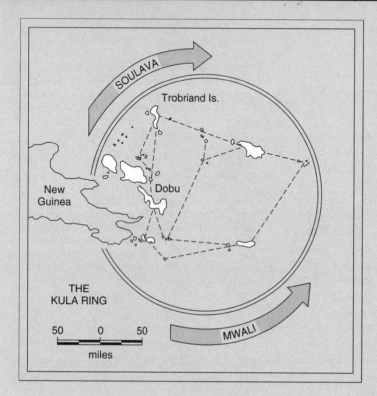

Figure 8.3 The *Kula* ring: Necklaces (*soulava*) are exchanged clockwise from island group to island group around the ring; armshells (*mwali*) are exchanged from them, in a counterclockwise direction. Paths of exchange are shown in broken lines. (Map by Gilbert Hendren)

the cultures of these islands form a related family, the customs and languages of each group are quite different. Yet they are united into a giant ring of ceremonial exchange several hundred miles across, so that each tribal group is a unit within the whole circle.

What they exchange around the ring are two kinds of ceremonial valuables also classed by Trobrianders as *vaygu'a*. Each kind is exchanged around the ring of islands in a different direction. *Soulava*, long necklaces of shell discs, move clockwise around the circle. *Mwali*, white armshells (Figure 8.4), travel counterclockwise. But what does "travel" mean? Who gets the objects? How are they exchanged?

Let us look from the viewpoint of the Trobrianders, one link in this chain. The essential rule is that I ceremonially and publicly present you, my partner, with a necklace. You are obligated to give me, some time later, an equally valuable armshell. Our relationship, as partners, is lifelong, maintained by our periodic exchange of *vaygu'a*. From any point in the Trobriands, a man receives necklaces from partners to the south and west, and armshells from partners to the north and east.

An average man has a number of *kula* partners, at home and overseas. His partners at home are mainly friends and in-laws; and their exchange of *vaygu'a* is part of a relationship entail-

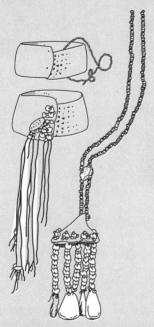

Figure 8.4 *Kula* valuables: The armshells (left) are made from the spiral trochus shell. The necklaces (right) are made primarily of pink spondylus shell discs strung on fiber.

ing different forms of exchange and assistance. He will also *kula* (that is, exchange *vaygu'a*) with one or two important leaders of high rank.

Kula partnerships within a single district (like the Trobriands) constitute the "inland *kula*." Exchanges in the inland *kula* are smaller-scale, individual, and treated with less ceremonial formality than the overseas *kula* exchange, which involves large-scale voyages and great complexes of magic and ceremony. The strategies and principles of overseas *kula* transactions, as seen from the perspective of the important coastal Trobriand village of Sinaketa, are well summed up by Malinowski:

Let us suppose that I, a Sinaketa man, am in possession of a pair of big armshells. An overseas expedition from Dobu [in the d'Entrecasteaux Archipelago] arrives at my village. Blowing a conch shell, I take my armshell pair and I offer it to my overseas partner, with some such words. "This is a *vaga* [initial gift]—in due time, thou returnest to me a big *soulava* [necklace] for it!" Next year, when I visit my partner's village he either is in possession of an equivalent necklace, and this he gives to me as *yotile* [restoration gift], or he has not a necklace good enough to repay my last gift. In this case he will give me a smaller necklace—avowedly not equivalent to my gift—and will give it to me as *basi* [intermediary gift]. This means that the main gift has to be repaid on a future occasion and the *basi* is given in token of good faith—but it, in turn, must be repaid by me in the meantime by a gift of small armshells. The final gift, which will be given to me to clinch the whole transaction, would be then called *kudu* [equivalent gift] in contrast to *basi*. . . .

If I . . . happen to be in possession of a pair of armshells more than usually good, the fame of it spreads. It must be noted that each one of the first-class armshells and necklaces has a personal name and history of its own, and as they all circulate around the big ring of the *kula,* they are all well known, and their appearance in a given district always creates a sensation. Now all my partners—whether from overseas or from within the district—compete for the favor of receiving this particular article of mine, and those who are specially keen try to obtain by giving me *pokala* [offerings] and *kaributu* [solicitory gifts]. (1922:99–100)

A man tries to maintain a reputation as a generous *kula* partner. The more important and numerous the valuables that pass through his hands (for he cannot keep them long or do much with them), the greater his prestige. This requires him both to *give* generously and to *obtain* strategically: he clearly cannot do one

Continued

Case 15 continued

Women of Vakuta, Trobriand Islands, prepare for a mortuary distribution.

without the other. But the Melanesian prestige strategist, like the Western capitalist, sometimes cuts a few corners. Here is how a Dobuan explained his strategies:

Suppose I, Kisian of Tewara, go to the Trobriands and secure an armshell named Monitor Lizard. I then go to Sanaroa and in four different places secure four different shell necklaces, promising each man who gives me a shell necklace a Monitor Lizard in return later. I, Kisian, do not have to be very specific in my promise. It will be conveyed by implication and assumption for the most part. Later, when four men appear in my home at Tewara each expecting Monitor Lizard, only one will get it. The other three are not defrauded permanently, however. They are furious it is true, and their exchange is blocked for the year. Next year, when I, Kisian, go again to the Trobriands I shall represent that I have four necklaces at home waiting for those who will give me four armshells. I obtain more armshells than I obtained previously, and pay my debts a year late. The three men who did not get

Monitor Lizard are at a disadvantage in my place, Tewara. Later when they return to their homes they are too far off to be dangerous to me. They are likely to attempt to kill their successful rival, who did get the armshell, Monitor Lizard, by the black art. That is true enough. But that is their own business. I have become a great man by enlarging my exchanges at the expense of blocking theirs for a year. I cannot afford to block their exchange for too long, or my exchanges will never be trusted by anyone again. I am honest in the final issue. (Fortune 1932:217)

Kula exchange is intimately bound up with the system of social stratification we will later look at more closely.

A leader of chiefly subclan builds, reinforces, and validates his political power not only by accumulating and redistributing yams and other foodstuffs, but also by his participation in the *kula*. The number of *kula* partnerships a high-ranking man possesses, the prestige and power of his partners, and the renown of the valuables that he acquires and passes on constitute symbolic validations of status and power. Note that it is only men who participate in the *kula*.

Gimwali also takes place, on a large scale, on *kula* expeditions. It is by this means that raw materials and manufactured goods from some segments of the *kula* ring are exchanged through the system to places that lack these objects and resources. Trobrianders thus get pottery, rattan, bamboo, greenstones, and other items through the *gimwali* that accompanies the *kula*. Both items of everyday use and items of high symbolic value get to the Trobriands through the overseas *kula*:

In overseas *kula,* men have the opportunity to find . . . clay pots, shell variables, and stone ax blades. . . . Necklaces and armshells [that] are *not yet* part of the *kula* provide some of the keenest competition in *kula.* . . . Success presents a man not only with prestige but also with [the option of putting them] into the *kula* ring, thereby establishing new partners or strengthening old ones, [or using them] as wealth within Kiriwina. . . . The search for valuables remains a driving force behind the *kula* exchange or an armshell or a necklace. (Weiner 1976:180–181)

While *kula* partners are going through their dramatic interchanges, barter is going on around them. The rule is that no *kula* partners can barter—that would mix haggling with ceremonial; but everyone can barter with everyone else's partner.

Kula canoes being launched.

Continued

Case 15 continued

Inspecting the lashings of a *kula* canoe before facing the open sea.

It has been argued that among other things the *kula* constitutes a kind of regional peace pact under which otherwise hostile peoples can carry out the trade essential in their ecological setting. Such networks and chains of regional trade were common in Melanesia. A crucial element in such trade systems is the production of pottery, widely used in Melanesia, but made in only a few specialized "exporting" centers. In the d'Entrecasteaux, the people of the neighboring Amphlett Islands were the pottery producers; and they, like their counterparts in other Melanesian trading networks, commanded a strategic position (Harding 1967, Sahlins 1972); much of their food was imported from their agriculturally richer neighbors. Large canoes were imported from the islands to the east, as were the greenstones used for axes and adzes. The *gimwali* trade accompanying the *kula* apparently involved a large volume of coconuts, areca nuts for betel chewing, lime, sago, building materials, and manufactured goods such as combs, baskets, and betel-chewing accessories. It is unfortunate that because of the focus of ethnographers on the more spectacular and symbolically central *kula* exchanges, we know too little about the volume and nature of accompanying trade.

The *kula* in action: Valuables on the beach at Vakuta.

More data have emerged on the *kula* as a regional system, and on perspectives on the exchange ring from other islands. The collection of papers edited by Leach and Leach (1983) not only attests to the continuing fascination of the *kula* but to its historical resilience in the face of colonialism and now independence. The *kula* is still going on, though outboard motors and even airplanes now serve, along with decorated canoes of ancient design, as vessels of the argonauts.

Case Update

Beginning with Malinowski and continuing to the present day, the systems of exchange, trade, and reciprocity in the Trobriand Islands have been the focus of a great deal of valuable anthropological research.

Suggested Readings

Battaglia, D. 1995. Problematizing the Self: A Thematic Introduction. In D. Battaglia, ed., *Rhetorics of Self-Making*. Berkeley: University of California Press.

Bell-Krannhals, I. 1990. *Haben um zu Geben: Eigentum und Besitz auf den Trobiand-Inseln Papua Neu Guinea*. Basel: Wepf and Company.

Damon, F. H., and R. Wagner, eds. 1989. *Death Rituals and Life in the Societies of the Kula Ring*. DeKalb: Northern Illinois University Press.

Weiner, A. 1992. *Inalienable Possessions: The Paradox of Keeping-While-Giving*. Berkeley: University of California Press.

19. COMPETING VIEWS OF ANTHROPOLOGICAL ECONOMICS

How, we can well wonder, can one construct an economics that will comprehend the complexity and the cultural particularity of Trobriand distribution and exchange? The system clearly makes sense to the Trobrianders and their immediate neigh-bors—compelling sense, judging by the endurance of traditional exchange. Given Trobriand motives, participants producing yams and presenting them, seeking valuables and giving them away are acting rationally. An important man or woman emerges from the pages of the ethnographic accounts as a master chess player moving pieces according to subtle and global strategies. But how do we grasp analytically the values that motivate the game and guide the strategies?

Formalist and Substantivist Economic Anthropology

Such questions raise the issues that have divided economic anthropologists into warring camps since the early 1960s. One important position—argued in various ways by H. K. Schneider (1974), Belshaw (1965), Cook (1973), and Nash (1966)—has come to be known as *formalist*. This position assumes that the formal theories of mainstream neoclassical economics are applicable in principle to an economy such as that of the Trobriands. Economics is the study of choices—choices that maximize values. When a Trobriander with a pile of yams chooses whether to use them in *sagali* distribution or present them to a sister's husband in expectation of receiving a valuable, whether to eat them or give them away or let them rot, he is making a rational economic choice, allocating his scare means strategically. Deciding which of several claimants among one's *kula* partners to give one's armshells to is an economic decision, even though the shells are intrinsically useless and will just keep going around in a circle. The values Trobriand strategists seek to maximize may include such intangibles as prestige, but after all, a wealthy American buys a "prestige" car, and that is behavior the economist can interpret without difficulty. The nature of exchange systems should allow us to find transactions where scarce goods of measurable value are exchanged with intangibles, allowing us to "measure" the latter. In doing so, we can not only depict in formal terms the rationality of economic behavior in non-Western settings such as the Trobriands; but as anthropologists, we can borrow methods and formal models from the most precise and

methodologically sophisticated of the social sciences, and bring them to bear on behavior in non-Western societies.

Not so, say their adversaries, taking a position that has come to be called *substantivist*. These economic anthropologists, notably George Dalton (1961, 1965, 1972), take their inspiration from the economic historian Karl Polanyi (1957, 1959). Polanyi argues that there are three major modes of exchange in human societies: *reciprocity, redistribution,* and *market exchange.* Market exchange is the exchange of goods at prices based on supply and demand. Redistribution is the movement of goods up to an administrative center and their reallotment downward to consumers. Reciprocity is the exchange of goods that takes place neither through markets nor through administrative hierarchies.

Polanyi sharply contrasts these modes of exchange as reflecting fundamentally different social means to distribute the material goods of a society. Though Polanyi argued at times as though any society could be characterized by the predominance of one of these three modes, his followers in economic anthropology have recognized that all three modes can occur in the same society. Reciprocity and redistribution may well be universal. Still, they argue, one mode is likely to be dominant while others are peripheral. (Update: for a retrospective on the formalist-substantivist debate, see Isaac 1993.)

Polanyi's theories, introduced into anthropology most forcefully by George Dalton (1961), have been brought to bear on such phenomena of the tribal world as market exchange (which appears in limited form in Trobriand *gimwali* and is more elaborately developed—but still, in Polanyi's sense, peripheral—in some other Melanesian areas), and to the use of valuables in ways that resemble money. There are no

CASE

16

Tolai *Tambu*

The people of the Melanesian island of New Britain who emerged as the Tolai in the colonial period, and have become a prosperous and powerful cultural force in the emergence of modern Papua New Guinea, originally comprised a chain of communities of cultural close cousins, tied together by regional trade, intermarriage, feast-giving, and ceremonial observance.

The networks of trade and marketing, the transactions of marriage that interlinked communities, and the mortuary feasts that were a focus of political power and prestige (as in the Trobriands) depended on *tambu,* strung shell discs that served as currency and ceremonial valuables. The standard length of *tambu* was a fathom, but there were shorter lengths that served as set denominations. There were standard prices for many items purchased with *tambu* (Danks 1887; A. L. Epstein 1963, 1968, 1969, 1979; T. S. Epstein 1964; Salisbury 1966, 1970; Simet 1992).

Tolai *tambu* were closely tied up with the cultural treatment of death: one's worth in life was affirmed by the distribution of *tambu* at one's death. Though strings of *tambu* were used in a wide range of transactions, from the purchase of foodstuffs in markets to payment of bridewealth, it was in these mortuary distributions that their full symbolic significance was expressed. In their preoccupation with *tambu,* Tolai have not behaved as economists of development would anticipate, in response to the impact of cash-cropping and substantial Western wealth in recent decades. Although the Tolai are centrally involved in cash-crop production, and many have amassed considerable wealth and are quite Westernized, *tambu* remain centrally important in Tolai life. Even in commercial transactions such as trade in urban markets, *tambu* are interchangeable with national currency; Tolai can choose between alternative modes of payment. In bridewealth, mortuary distribution, and other traditional transactions, *tambu* retain a central position. *Tambu* have come to serve as a symbol of cultural identity.

moneylike valuables in the Trobriands (ax blades, pots, and *kula* valuables are too specialized in their use). But in other parts of Melanesia, shell valuables are much more "moneylike," such as the *tambu* described in Case 16.

Because *tambu* were used in such a wide range of transactions, because anything one could own could be bought and sold either at fixed or negotiated prices, and because *tambu* were interchangeable, in standard denominations, these strung shell valuables resemble Western money in many ways. Yet as

Dalton (1965) points out, the more peripheral function of markets in a Melanesian society and their central significance as ceremonial valuables call for caution in equating such "currency" with Western money.

Polanyi (1957, 1959) and Dalton (1961) have proceeded to argue that the basic models of economics, and notions like scarcity, economizing, allocation, and maximizing, properly apply to systems of market exchange. To talk in such terms about tribal economics is to superimpose notions based on the market onto social institutions that differ *in kind,* not merely in degree and the nature of scarce goods. They argue for a comparative economics based on different modes of organization and exchange of the means of material subsistence.

Rationality and Anthropological Economics

The nature of rationality in economic systems is an issue that highlights the triangular relationship between neoclassical (formalist) economics, the substantivist challenge to it, and the neo-Marxist opposition to both. Neoclassical economics assumes that "the system" represents the outcome of market forces; and that these, in turn, reflect the cumulative result of acts of maximization by individuals and firms. Substantivist economic anthropologists accept the applicability of these models to market-governed sectors of the economy, but challenge their applicability to economies where reciprocity and/or redistribution are dominant. The rationality of economic systems sinks too often, in substantivist analyses, into a kind of soggy relativism. The Marxist challenge to formalist economics is more radical and general. The rationality of economic action is not, from the Marxist point of view, at issue. All humans, including Trobrianders, act rationally much of the time, in choosing among alternative courses and options. But to say that Trobrianders, in choosing among *kula* partners, in allowing yams to rot, in deciding whether to barter fish or eat them, are acting rationally is to tell us nothing—unless we understand the historically created structure of institutions and cultural meanings within which these alternatives emerge (Godelier 1974). The assumption that the system is the cumulative product of individual acts of maximization is, in the Marxist view, an ideological rationalization

of capitalist economic relationships: an implicit depiction of maximization as human nature (Rowthorn 1974). Marxist conceptions of value in terms of labor, not commodities, and views of exploitative class relationships, pose a more sweeping challenge to mainstream economic theory.

Analysis of Distribution

Gudeman (1978) urges that in the creation of an anthropological economics, more attention to systems of distribution is needed. Marxists have paid primary attention to production in tribal societies, and only secondary attention to the distribution processes which are assumed to correspond to them. The Trobriand case, where yams are produced according to the pathways along which they will be given away, attests to the importance of distribution in shaping pro-duction and the reproduction of social relations.

Gudeman suggests that neo-Marxist attempts to generalize Marx's analysis of class relations under feudalism and capitalism so as to fit the range of economies anthropologists study have not yet developed appropriate ways of dealing with the logics and processes of distribution. It is too simplistic to use Marx's conception of "exploitation" to analyze the way Tsembaga Maring men draw upon the labor of women to produce pigs they use to derive prestige through exchange (Cases 5 and 9) or to analyze the way surplus yams sustain the power of high-ranking Trobriand leaders.

> The Marxian notion of exploitation provides a foreshortened view of the variability of distributive patterns. . . . Exploitation as explanation is posited on an unidimensional view of human nature. (Gudeman 1978:374)

We need a conceptualization that will take fully into account the symbolic goals pursued and advanced in a society such as the Trobriands where you seek valuables in order to give them away.

We also, Gudeman suggests, need formal models of distribution and exchange that will do the things the models of mainstream economics do, but are based on more solid foundations of assumption. He points to the neo-Ricardian critique of neoclassical economics as a possible source for an anthropologically useful model. The details need not concern us. But it is worth noting that in economics itself, the seemingly solidly established models which formalist economic anthropology has sought to borrow are under concerted attack, by critics arguing in the traditions of Marx and Ricardo. Gudeman's general perspective is important to us:

> What is the relation between anthropology and economics? . . . Anthropology's greatest [potential] offering—and here its role is complementary to history—lies in its capacity to elucidate different economies as *systems*. (1978:373; emphasis added)

What an anthropological economics needs is to comprehend the cultural and organizational logic of production in terms of "the context of the total, and culturally unique, distribution pattern" (Gudeman 1978:374). This, then, leads to an effort to perceive and analyze the integration of an economic system in terms of both its cultural meanings and its embeddedness in the real material world. (See also the essays in Landa 1994.)

20. THE INTEGRATION OF ECONOMIC SYSTEMS

Economies as Systems

We can begin by returning briefly to the Trobriands to ask how the forms of distribution and exchange sketched in Case 15 fit together into a coherent system. This process is discussed in Case 17.

Cultural Logic and Hidden Dynamics

Neo-Marxist theories of tribal economies, perhaps as expanded along the lines suggested by Gudeman, should increasingly make possible a conceptualization that does not assume such systems are in neatly balanced equilibrium, but that views them in terms of historical processes (even where, as in the Trobriands, little history is known), and that comprehends both their hidden dynamics and their cultural meanings. The latter element can usefully be clarified. As Sahlins (1976) argues, humans encounter nature not as a physical array of potential products to meet human needs for nutrition, clothing, and housing. Rather, they encounter nature through a system of cultural meanings. To a Trobriander diving in the lagoon, a spondylus shell is meaningful as a potential part of a *kula* necklace, not as a physical object. Even a fish is not a piece of swimming protein, but has economic meaning in terms of the uses it might have in *wasi* exchange or in *gimwali* barter or in a meal—a meal structured by cultural assumptions about food, about eating, and about social relationships.

At the same time, we must look underneath cultural conceptualizations about armshells and ax blades, skirts, bundles, and yams, to see the relations to production and distribution they express and even disguise. A neo-Marxist perspective leads one to ask how the token of prestige and obligation serve to sustain relations of power and control over labor. To show that in cultural terms Aztec priests control the seasons and fertility of the crops, or a Trobriand chief of the Tabalu subclan commands deference and tribute because of the ancient emergence of his subclan ancestors is not an analysis of "how the system works" or of how it got that way.

The Integration of the Trobriand Economy

Here we can pause only to illustrate the questions we would explore in a global analysis of Trobriand economics, and to glimpse some of the mechanisms that connect the economy into a single coherent system. We saw in Case 15 a range of modes of exchange. Some are ceremonial and transacted at set standards of equivalence with an obligation of direct return. Others entail much less specific return obligations, such as *pokala,* or entail the supply and demand adjustments of the market, as in *gimwali.* For some, the return may simply be prestige, as in some forms of *sagali.*

To understand Trobriand economic systems, we need urgently to know how the exchange subsystems fit together. This would entail knowing more about the following:

1. How values or valuables are converted from one sphere of exchange to another, and according to what standards of value.

2. How valuables, foodstuffs, raw materials, and manufactured goods flow through the system, and how that flow relates to power, prestige, kinship, and so on.

3. What strategies lead to transactions between, as well as within, the exchange subsystems and to investment in one subsystem rather than another.

Data gathered by Annette Weiner provide important clues. She described a "main road of exchange" traveled by all Trobriand men and women and connected by side paths to other cycles of exchange. This road connects not only men's wealth and women's wealth but connects agricultural production with the web of social relations and with the mortuary rites that are a major focus of Trobriand culture.

The crucial valued exchange items on the main road are exchange yams. Yams constitute the all-important goods convertible into other

Equilibrium and Change

"How it got that way" reminds us that we can make no assumptions about equilibrium. A system such as that of the Trobriands may "reproduce itself" in the short run. An analysis in terms of production and distribution must identify these mechanisms of social reproduction. But peoples of the surrounding islands, the closest cultural relatives of the Trobrianders, have less complex prestige economies and less marked social stratification. The Trobriand system almost certainly evolved out of a simpler, more egalitarian one. How, and why? The potential for surplus yam

production in the Trobriands exceeds that of surrounding islands less rich in agricultural land. But what are the mechanisms and processes through which a system of production oriented most strongly toward subsistence production by household groups is transformed into a system of production geared to production of surplus for exchange, organized at a subclan or village level, in which high-ranking leaders serve as nodes through which surplus and valuables are accumulated, then dispersed?

Yet Trobriand leaders are not as secure in their chiefly powers as Polynesian chiefs. Their claims are hereditary, but their control of valuables and yams and the labor power

forms of wealth and ultimately into prestige and power. "If a man has yams he can find everything else that he needs," the Trobrianders told Weiner, And even in these days when cash has penetrated many areas of the Trobriand economy, "nothing takes the place of distribution of yams at mortuary ceremonies or feasts—nor can cash take the place of giving yams to women—or giving yams in marriage exchanges. . . . Exchanges which involve the creation or maintenance of important relationships have not been replaced [by cash]" (Weiner 1974).

The circulation of . . . exchange yams . . . produces access to other objects of wealth and other comestibles as well as access to immediate and future obligations. . . . A basket of yams given produces objects received which in turn provide additional roads to other things and people. (Weiner 1974)

Thus a woman can take harvest yams presented to her husband by her brother or matrilineal kin and convert them through exchange into grass skirts or leaf bundles. She can further convert between subsystems by bartering items she

manufactures, for example woven bags, either into women's wealth or into yams that can be further converted. The ultimate goal is enhancement of prestige through the ceremonial presentation of exchange objects (skirts and leaf bundles for women, *kula* valuables and *sagali* for men) and also by the ultimate conversion of exchange yams back to the realm of nature when they rot.

The main road of exchange through which every man and woman converts yams into a measure of prestige leads by side paths into the roads to the *kula* and other subsystems; and through these paths, it opens roads to great power and wealth for men of rank. (We will view the system of rank and politics in Chapter 11.) The web of connection between these exchange subsystems renders any model of gift exchange focusing on direct reciprocity overly simple: "One kind of gift given to A leads to another kind of gift given to B and that in turn leads to another object given to C" (Weiner 1974).

they represent is tenuous and vulnerable. If the Trobriand system had become more stratified, was it in the process of evolving into a chiefdom? If not, what constraints prevented the highest-ranking chiefs from gaining a monopoly over the most valuable valuables, and securing power over their subjects and their labor? What about the balance of power between the sexes? As we have glimpsed, Trobriand women play a prominent part in the prestige economy. Do they have power? Was it increasing or decreasing? What part was money and the commercialization of products playing in the historical process? (Also see Jolly 1992.)

Questions about power, about stratification, about men and women, will engage us in the chapters to come. We will gain progressively deepened insights about the Trobrianders and other tribal peoples.

Capitalist Penetration of the Tribal World

A final point about the Trobrianders can lead us to look further ahead. Even when Malinowski was in the Trobriands during World War I, the islands had a resident population of pearl traders and other Europeans. They sought to recruit Trobrianders to dive for pearls in the lagoon.

The gulf between Trobriand economics and capitalist economics emerged in these encounters: Trobrianders would exchange fine pearls only for traditional ceremonial trade goods, not money; they would refuse to dive for pearls when the gardens were in full swing; and they would fish rather than dive for pearls, even when the payment for pearls was 10 or 20 times as great in exchange value as the fish they would barter (Malinowski 1935, I:20). A wide gulf separated the Trobriand logic of value and the capitalist logic of value. By World War I, the Trobriands were being invaded by a colonial system that brought wage labor, money, and class relationships between employer and employee—a different mode of production. In the intervening years, money has increasing penetrated the Trobriand world, juxtaposed with the traditional mode of production and distribution. The emergence of individualist entrepreneurship and the spread of market principles into traditional economies is viewed by mainstream development economists (and their anthropological counterparts) as a take-off stage necessary to modernization. Marxist critics have provided a counter-interpretation: the spread of capitalist institutions into colonial and postcolonial societies constitutes part of a global design whereby the tropical periphery provides cheap labor and raw materials and markets, and the industrial metropolitan countries maintain industrial prosperity and global control (see, for example, Dupré and Rey 1973, Rey 1971). We will return to these questions in Part 4.

Before we go on to look at political power, social stratification, relations between men and women, and religious systems—and then move on to look at the impact of the West on other peoples—we need to look at systems of descent, kinship, and marriage. Through groups such as the Trobriand subclan, and relations established by marriage and defined by kinship, tribal peoples organize their social worlds and reproduce the conditions of their existence.

SUMMARY

The complexities and ramifications of agricultural production are shown in the case of the Trobriand Islanders of Papua New Guinea. Gardening work is led by a village magician and is conducted by both sexes, sometimes on a communal basis. Each household group produces yams on its own plots, but about half the produce goes to the sister and other female kin of the male householder. There is pride in gardening and in the production of a surplus above subsistence needs. A system like this is referred to as a tribal communal mode of production. In such a structure there is no definite separation between economics and kinship, politics, or religion. These institutions reproduce the means of existence for the society and also regulate spheres of equality and inequality between categories of people through the symbolic values accorded to goods. Harvest presentations, funeral distributions (sagali), and gifts or services (pokala) from junior to senior men among the Trobrianders contribute to the wider reproduction of social relations. In addition, the kula exchange of shell valuables is a venue for prestige competition between men. The kula tradition continues today, but the Trobriands and society as a whole have been deeply influenced by the capitalist world, and relations between the sexes as well as between chiefs and their people have been altered.

SUGGESTIONS FOR FURTHER READING

SECTIONS 17–20

Belshaw, C. 1965. *Traditional Exchange and Modern Markets.* Englewood Cliffs, N.J.: Prentice-Hall, Inc.

Bohannan, P., and G. Dalton, eds. 1962. *Markets in Africa.* Evanston, Ill.: Northwestern University Press.

Clammer, J., ed. 1978. *The New Economic Anthropology.* London: Macmillan & International Ltd.

Dalton, G., ed. 1967. *Tribal and Peasant Economics.* Garden City, N.Y.: Natural History Press.

Firth, R., ed. 1967. *Themes in Economic Anthropology.* ASA Monographs, 6. London: Tavistock.

Godelier, M. 1972. *Rationality and Irrationality in Economics.* Trans. by B. Pearce. New York: Monthly Review Press.

———. 1977. *Perspectives in Marxist Anthropology.* Cambridge: Cambridge University Press.

LeClair, E. F., and H. Schneider. 1968. *Economic Anthropology.* New York: Holt, Rinehart and Winston.

Sahlins, M. 1971. Economic Anthropology and Anthropological Economics, *Social Science Information* 8(5): 13–33.

Schneider, H. K. 1974. *Economic Man: The Economics of Anthropology.* New York: The Free Press.

Seddon, D., ed. 1978. *Relations of Production: Marxist Approaches to Economic Anthropology.* London: Frank Class.

Kinship, Descent, and Social Structure

In many societies, a person's place in the scheme of things has been structured by the circumstances of birth. Being born of particular parents defines membership in a group, places you in a network of obligation and cooperation within which your life will be lived, from birth to death (and often beyond as well, as ancestral spirit). As in the Trobriands, production and distribution in a society can be organized through **kinship** and **descent.** It is within and through such structures that marriage, and hence the reproduction of a social system, is organized.

But how are we to interpret a system, such as the one we glimpsed in the Trobriands, where descent is traced through lines of women? Among the Tsembaga Maring of New Guinea, descent is usually traced through lines of men. How do these systems of descent, through female and male lines, contrast? How and why did they evolve in different settings?

21. SOCIAL STRUCTURE: SOME FIRST PRINCIPLES

Social Structure and Cultural Structure

When anthropologists speak of the "social structure" or "social organization" of a community, they are taking a theoretical perspective introduced briefly in Chapter 2. That is, they are looking at a social system as comprised of *groups,* looking at social relations in terms of interlocking positions and roles. Because in the communities where anthropologists developed their conceptual tools these groups and role relationships are based so centrally on kinship and marriage that anthropological study of social structure has been almost synonymous with the study of kinship. When we say that the social structure of a community comprises its systems of social relationships, we run the risk of some conceptual confusion. It is worth pausing, before we look at systems of kinship and marriage, to underline the distinction drawn in Chapter 2 between cultural system and social system.

To study social structure, it is often said, one begins with *social relationships.* But what is a social relationship? If we take two people, A and B, we can see two sides or facets to their "relationship." First, there are the ways they interact, the things they do and say in their dealings with one another. But there are also their ideas about their relationship, their conceptions of one another, the understandings and strategies and expectations that guide their behavior.

Woman with child beside a dry stream bed. Her face is decorated for attendance at a festival. She has her netbag beside her for carrying the child, Melpa, Papua New Guinea.

Both patterns of behavior and conceptual systems have "structure," in the sense that they are not helter-skelter or random. But they are different kinds of structure. Imagine an intersection governed by traffic lights. If we observed it for a while, we could record the "behavior" of the cars in terms of the density of traffic in various directions at various times and the number of cars that stop, go through, and slow down, according to sequences of changing lights. From these records would crystallize patterns of regularity, the "social structure" of the intersection. We would probably find the social structure of a North American intersection quite different from a South American one. But alternatively, we could describe the principles for making decisions used by drivers when they cross the intersection—not only the laws that are written down, but the unwritten "rules" about honking horns and going through while the lights are changing. These rules also have a structure, but it is quite different from the patterns of traffic flow: it consists of organized *knowledge*. We need to perceive and study both social and cultural structure if we are to understand the processes of social life and the ways social systems are perpetuated and transformed across the generations.

Categories and Groups

Here and in the chapters that follow, this distinction between the cultural (ideas, categories, and "rules") and the social (people, acts, events, and groups) will be centrally important. It enables us to see at the outset a contrast between *cultural categories* and *social groups*. A cultural category is a set of entities in the world—people, things, events, supernaturals—that are classed as similar for some purposes, because they have in common one or more culturally relevant attributes. Thus trees, weeds, bachelors, and left-handed baseball pitchers are categories in our culture. As categories, they exist only in human minds. Note also that not all categories have one-word labels in our language. Nor are they sets of entities we keep in separate "chunks" in our mental schemas. Rather, they are sets we draw mental lines around in particular contexts. Women who wear size 7 dresses comprise a relevant category in only a very few contexts (mainly for people who make or sell dresses, while they happen to be at work). Thus any single entity can be classed, in varying contexts, as belonging to dozens of different cultural categories. A category of human beings, grouped conceptually because of some socially relevant features they share (like men or warriors or descendants of ancestor X), we can call a *social category* (i.e., a type of cultural category).

A *social group*, on the other hand, consists of actual warm-blooded human beings. What distinguishes a social group from a temporary gathering is their organization. First of all, the members interact recurrently. Secondly, they do so in a set of (culturally defined) capacities or positions. Such positions or capacities are technically called *social identities*. They are defined in relation to matching social identities: doctor-nurse; salesperson-customer; employer-employee, etc.; the behaviors appropriate to such capacities comprise roles (so that one can speak of the role of a nurse vis-à-vis patients, doctors, and other nurses). A social group is an aggregation of human beings, then, who recurrently interact within an interconnected set of social identities. Thus groups can be distinguished from forms of aggregation which are temporary and limited. Members of a social group need not all interact face to face, though such *primary groups* are common in all small-scale communities anthropologists usually study. What defines a group is its internal organization, the connection of its members in a set of interconnected roles. Thus the stockholders of General Motors comprise a *secondary group*. Although most of its members do not interact with one another, they are bound into a group through their relationships with the management.

Who belongs to a group is seldom neatly defined by some cultural principle such as being descended from the same ancestor or being the right age or social class. Such membership in a social category usually defines *eligibility* to be a member of a group. Whether an eligible person actually takes part in a group is likely to depend on the circumstances of life history, on economic interests and resources, on personal choice.

To illustrate some basic points about categories and groups, we will look at a hypothetical example from our own society—one that parallels closely the kinship-based categories and groups of other societies.

Imagine that three generations ago, in a New England community, 10 men founded a music festival which has taken place ever since. Priority for tickets to the festival now goes to the festival patrons, who comprise all those descendants of the 10 founders who take part in meetings and maintain an active interest. Many of the descendants *eligible* to be patrons have, of course, moved away and lost touch. But if they ever moved back, they could become active again, and if they happened to visit on the day of a performance, a good seat would always be found for them. At any performance, there will also be persons in the audience who come as guests of patrons or who are simply filling in the remaining seats.

What sorts of social units have we here? First, all descendants of the founders, whether patrons or those who have moved away or lost interest, form a *social category.* Their descent status makes them eligible to activate a set of rights if they can and wish. Second, those descendants who are patrons comprise a *corporate group,* which ultimately controls the activities of the festival—and whose members enjoy the attendant privileges, though they may well not turn up at a particular performance. Finally, the audience actually attending a performance comprises a *gathering.* But if they gathered in some more organized fashion to perform a common task—to erect a new stage, for example—we could call the mixed bunch who actually came an *action group* or *task group.* The anthropological literature is full of confusions about "clans" and "moieties" and "lineages" and "kindreds" where these distinctions between groups and categories, corporations and action groups, have been blurred or overlooked.

22. KINSHIP IN TRIBAL SOCIETIES

It is hard for us to understand a way of life where relationships with people are preeminently relationships with relatives. In many societies, all members of the community trace connections of blood or marriage with one another; in some places, a person is either your relative or your enemy. Such systems have probably prevailed through most of the human time span on earth.

Study of the forms of social arrangement built around kinship has been a dominant theme in anthropology for almost a century. Almost all the leading figures in anthropology have participated at one time or another in debates about kinship, and a very extensive body of technical literature continues to expand. Even those who are not specialists in this area must lead their readers through the intricacies of kinship—in a jargon incomprehensible to the uninitiated—in describing life in a small-scale society. We will not attempt here to cover all the technical concepts and controversies, though the reader who makes his or her way through the pages that follow will be well on the way toward understanding more technical works in the field (Keesing 1975 and 1990 seek to take the interested anthropological initiate further into the cult of kinship mysteries). Before we begin, it will be rewarding to ask why anthropologists have worried so much for so long about the intricacies of kinship.

Kinship as the Basic Idiom of Social Relations

In analyzing a tribal community, one has to make sense of kinship to make sense of anything else. Even where people in a tribal society are competing for economic advantage or political power, they are likely to talk about what they are doing in terms of kinship. Moreover, kinship ties serve as models or templates for relationships to nonrelatives and often to deities.

The anthropologist who studies a community can anticipate that people do not always live up to the ideal standards of behavior between relatives, and that they act toward one another in many roles other than those based on blood relationship. Yet a first challenge is to sort out the cast of characters, and it has usually been useful to begin with complex webs of connection by blood and marriage. Having done so, one can proceed to decipher the complex social processes carried out in this idiom and perceive how kinship serves as a basic model for relating to other people. The anthropologist often finds that he or she must be assigned a place, albeit fictional, in this scheme of kinship, in order to take part in the life of the community.

Obligations between relatives are viewed as morally binding, and their fulfillment ranks high among the paramount virtues. The obligations of kinship have a central symbolic significance we can understand in the light of the hominid transformations whereby a nuclear family group based on the pair bond, incest avoidance, and sharing of food emerged. Kinship obligations symbolize the collective as opposed to the individual, social obligation rather than self-gratification; and they symbolize the cultural in contrast to the biological. In the light of our primate heritage, it is not surprising that kinship has been central in the thought worlds of tribal peoples, as expression and symbol of what makes humans human; and it is not surprising that emotionally, blood is so much thicker than water.

Kinship and the Organization of Economic Relations

As Godelier's (1978) analysis of modes of production makes explicit (see Chapter 8), and as the Trobriand case amply illustrates,

there is a compelling theoretical reason for focusing on kinship in these small-scale communities. In contemporary New York, Moscow, or Tokyo, the reproduction of labor force and social system depends on bearing and rearing of children in domestic groups created by marriage. Kinship and marriage are, in this sense, universally important elements in the "superstructuure" (in neo-Marxist terms) of a society. But in New York, Moscow, and Tokyo, these domestic groups are not central in the organization of production and distribution.

But in the Trobriands or among the Tsembaga Maring or among Australian Aborigines, domestic groups and larger structures based on kinship, descent, and marriage are crucial not only in reproducing the labor force but in organizing production and distribution—and, as the Trobriand case illustrates, even in creating the motivation for production. The social relations of production are organized in terms of lineages, households, and networks of obligation defined by kinship and marriage.

To say that kinship, descent, and marriage are central in organizing economic relations as well as in perpetuating them is not to explain why this should be so. In the next two chapters, both the organizational patterns and the reasons for their pervasive importance will become more clear.

Recurrent Puzzles: Limited Variations in Kinship Systems

We will see that kinship and descent systems are not only pervasively important, but that the range of variation we encounter is much less wide than it might be. Formally similar patterns turn up in widely separated parts of the world. Thus, the same specific, complicated, and, by our standards, bizarre way of classing relatives is used by the Trobrianders and by the Cow Creek Seminole Indians—even though they

CASE

18

Nuer "Ghost Marriage"

In two uncommon but perfectly legitimate forms of marriage among the Nuer, the socially recognized father (*pater* in the Latin sense) of a child is not the man whose sexual intercourse with the mother is presumed to have led to the pregnancy (the *genitor*). A Nuer woman whose husband has died remains subject to a legal contract through which rights to the children she bears were transferred to her husband's group. By giving cattle to her father's group, the husband's group acquires right in perpetuity to her reproductive powers. Ideally, if the husband dies, the contract will be sustained by her remarrying, to her deceased husband's brother or some other member of his group. But the children she bears from sexual relations with her second husband are socially defined as the offspring of her dead first husband (hence, "ghost marriage"). The widow, rather than remarrying, may simply take

lovers; but then again, the children she bears from her sexual relations with them are defined as offspring of her dead husband.

In a more rare form, an old and important woman may (by acquiring cattle) "marry" a girl. The senior woman finances the marriage transactions as if she were a man. The young woman then bears children by lovers. They are socially defined as the children of the female "husband," who in turn is their "father" (hence they belong to *her* father's group, even though membership in it is transmitted in the male line).

Case Update

More recent studies shed further light on these arrangements. For instance, see Hutchinson (1996) on these and other Nuer practices in contemporary and past times.

---

are separated by thousands of miles, have had no contact with one another, and speak unrelated languages. The Kwara'ae-speakers of Malaita, in the Melanesian Solomon Islands, have a complex and quite different system of classing relatives; and it turns out to be almost identical to the system used by the Seneca Indians of what is now upstate New York. There are systematic logics and recurrent patterns to be deciphered in this realm of kinship; that has been one of the challenges that has led generations of anthropologists to seek to solve these puzzles.

What Is Kinship?

What *is* kinship? Here, we face a recurrent conceptual dilemma in anthropology of

trying to make a term from one cultural and linguistic tradition—our own—elastic enough that it fits the range of cultural variations, yet preserve its essential meaning. Kinship, to us, intuitively refers to "blood relationships." Our relatives are those connected to us by bonds of "blood." Our in-laws, to be sure, are related by marriage and not blood—and so are some of our aunts and uncles. But it is successive links between parents and children that are the essential strands of kinship (see again Keesing 1990).

Is this true in other societies? Case 18 considers the Nuer, a pastoral people of the Sudan who became anthropologically famous through the work of the British anthropologist E. E. Evans-Pritchard.

In the Nuer system and many other forms of socially defined parenthood there is a gap between presumed physical paternity (or even *maternity*) and socially assigned parentage (even leaving aside customs that, as with adoption in Western societies, *transfer* assignment of parentage). How, then, are we to define *parentage*? And how can we talk about "blood" relationship between father and child, or mother and child, in cultures that have quite different theories or metaphors about the connection between parent and child? In some, the mother is thought to contribute no substance to the child, but only to provide a container for its growth. The Lakher of Myanmar (Burma), for example, believe that two children with the same mother and different fathers are not relatives at all.

Moreover, the Trobriand islanders and some Australian Aborigines staunchly deny that copulation between father and mother is the cause of pregnancy—hence seemingly denying the father a physical connection to the child. In each case, pregnancy is asserted to have been brought about by spiritual beings—in the Trobriand case, through a *baloma* spirit of the mother's subclan ancestor entering her vagina. A physical relationship is, however, posited because the husband's semen and acts of intercourse are said to "mold"*(kopo'i)* the fetus in the womb. We are dealing, probably in both cases and certainly in that of the Trobriands, with a theological dogma. Sexual intercourse with a man is a necessary condition for pregnancy; but the *animation* of the potential child created by synthesis of semen and female fluids is a spiritual, not a physical, matter (Scheffler 1973).

Such variations must lead us at the outset to be wary of assuming that kinship is simply a matter of "blood relationship." It is safest to broaden our scope considerably to say that relations of kinship are connections modeled on those conceived to exist between a father and child and between a mother and child. In a particular culture these connections may be viewed as the same for father and mother (as with our "blood" relations) or as different—based on metaphors of seed and soil, of bone and flesh, or substance and container. Moreover, "modeled on" leaves room for those cases like the Nuer where a socially defined parent is known not to have actually fathered or borne the child. (Adoptive parenthood in our society and many others would similarly be modeled on "natural" parenthood.)

We conceive kinship relations, based on "blood," to be natural and immutable; they entail diffuse obligations of solidarity (what Fortes calls the "axiom of amity"). They contrast with relationships "in-law"—that is, contingent and legal relations established by the marriage contract. D M. Schneider (1972, 1984) has argued that this symbolic system is only indirectly related to sex and reproduction, and that other peoples may have quite different conceptualizations of the realm of kinship similarly related only indirectly to perceived relations of biological parenthood.

But the contrast in this realm seems less wide than it might be. However a people conceptualize the biological connection between presumed father and child and between mother and child, it is this relationship—inalienable and deep—that is the basis of kinship bonds. And even where the contributions of father and mother are thought to be different, these bonds of kinship are extended, in almost all societies, through both father and mother as though they were equivalent. We are sometimes misled, as with Nuer woman-woman marriage, because parents characteristically occupy several different roles toward their children. And some of these roles, such as having custody, caring for and nurturing the child, or being socially recognized in terms of descent or inheritance, may be contingent on the natural parents being married or on some legal validation of the connection of parenthood.

Tracing Kinship

Tracing kin relations out through father and mother creates networks of kinship ties (Figure 9.1). The greater importance of these networks of kinship ties in tribal societies has been underlined already. But the ways tribal peoples use networks of kinship very often parallel the ways we use them. Our ties with relatives appear most clearly on special occasions like Christmas or birthdays, when presents or cards are given or exchanged, and especially on the major events in our lives—our christening or bar mitzvah, our wedding, our funeral.

So too in many societies the ties of kinship between individuals come out most dramatically in the focal points of a persons's life—birth, initiation, feasts, marriage, death. The action group that mobilizes around a person in support, celebration, or mourning is in almost all societies crystallized from networks of the individual's relatives and in-laws. Where these relatives, or some close network of them, are conceptually recognized as a special cultural category, it is called a **kindred** or **personal kindred**. An idealized kindred is diagrammed in Figure 9.2.

The descending arrows in Figure 9.2 indicate that the descendants of siblings of grandparents (or of great-grandparents and more distant relatives) may be included for some purposes within a kindred category. Since in real life families often include many, many siblings, not simply two, the actual kindred may include dozens of relatives. The number who actually participate in kindred-based action groups may be much smaller—since many potential members live far away, have competing obligations, belong to the opposite political factions, and so on.

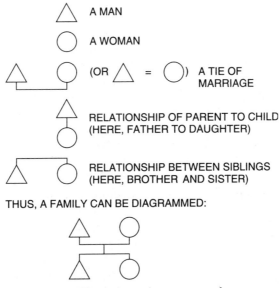

Figure 9.1 Anthropological conventions for diagramming kinship relations.

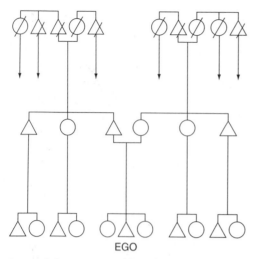

Figure 9.2   A personal kindred. (The diagonal slash indicates "deceased.") (From Keesing 1975:15)

Kindreds cannot serve as the basis of ongoing corporations; the groups crystallized from them are always temporary and mobilized in particular situations (as at a wedding or christening or funeral in our society). The reason is that each individual has a unique set of relatives, and kindreds overlap in their membership. Your Uncle George is also someone else's father, another person's brother, still another person's cousin. George can act in each of these capacities on different occasions, but he cannot act in all of them all the time. If you get married on the day Uncle George's oldest son graduates, he is likely to miss your wedding.

Kinship ties in many societies play a part in numerous spheres of life. The people who live in a community, the people who work together, the people who compete and quarrel are, as we will see, mainly relatives. Before we can understand how kinship shapes social groups, we must examine some organizational problems and see ways in which kinship is used to solve them.

23. DESCENT SYSTEMS

Descent, Corporations, and Continuity

Some hunting and gathering peoples define their relationships to territories in terms of spiritual connections through lines of ancestors into the ancient, myth-shrouded past. Thus, many Aboriginal Australian peoples define relationships of living people to the landscape in terms of sacred sites where ancient events celebrated in myth and enacted in ritual took place—events that bind the living spiritually to ancestors and to one another.

With the advent of Neolithic cultivation, land became transformed in nature and value. The connection of the living to the ancestral past acquires compelling new importance. Land as *property* becomes the central means of production; and title to it must be passed across the generations. Especially in the tropical zones where shifting cultivation prevailed, land did not have to be partitioned, or title assigned to each plot according to rules of inheritance. Rather, an estate in land could be kept together, with title to it held by a *corporation* (not unlike the patrons of our imaginary New England music festival earlier in this chapter).

To make such a system work requires a rule or principle defining (as with the imaginary patrons) who is eligible to be a corporation member. Consider a system in which you are eligible to be a member of both your mother's and your father's corporation (assuming they are different). But then your father would in turn have been eligible to belong to two different corporations (his father's and his mother's); and your mother, too, would have had ties to two different corporations. How can corporations be formed such that one is a member of only one?

A crucial innovation here is **unilineal descent.** That is, a right to corporation membership is acquired (in each generation) *only* through father—or only through mother. A culturally recognized line of descent thus passes either through a line of men:

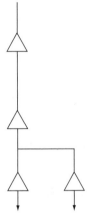

or through a line of women:

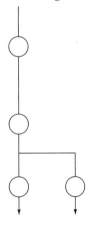

In the former case, the children of female members do not belong to the corporation; in the latter case, the children of male members do not belong to the corporation. The former alternative, **patrilineal** (or **agnatic**) **descent,** serves partly to form descent groups among the Tsembaga Maring (Cases 5 and 9) and many other tribal peoples. The latter, **matrilineal descent,** serves to form the Trobriand subclans we glimpsed in the last chapter. We will take a closer look at them shortly.

Descent is a *process* across time. The descendants of an ancestor or ancestress proliferate, the lines of descent branch. Patrilineal descent has been an effective organizing principle among pastoralists, as well as cultivators—as with the tribes of the Israelites in biblical times, or the Basseri nomads of Iran we glimpsed in Case 7 (Chapter 6).

Descent systems are means of defining continuity with the past, of specifying relations among the living in terms of relationships to long-dead ancestors. In New Guinea or Africa, they bind humans to land by traditions of ancient origin; in the arid zones of North Africa, the Near East, and central Asia, they tie pastoralists, spread over vast areas and moving widely, to one another—allowing them to disperse and regroup, allowing larger groupings to crystallize and dissolve again.

Patrilineal and Matrilineal Descent as Organizational Schemes

We can usefully look at an idealized blueprint of a corporation defined by patrilineal descent, and its apparent mirror-image, a corporation defined by matrilineal descent. In a corporation defined by patrilineal descent, members include both men and women (see Figure 9.3). But note that only the men have transmitted corporation membership to their children. Of course, in the real world numbers of children do not work out so neatly; some lines of descent die out, others proliferate and branch across the span of generations. The mirror-image (at least on a diagram; see Figure 9.4) is a corporation defined by matrilineal descent. Here both men and women are corporation

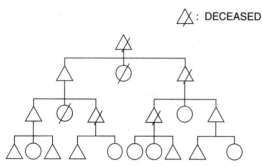

△X : DECEASED

Figure 9.3 Corporation defined by patrilineal descent.

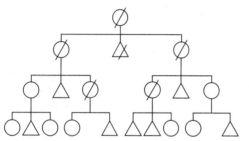

Figure 9.4 Corporation defined by matrilineal descent.

members, but only the women transmit this membership to their children.

Some cautions are needed. First, patrilineal or matrilineal descent from the founding ancestor does not usually make a person a member of a descent corporation, an actual social group. Being descended in the correct line *entitles* a person to be a member of a descent corporation: that is, patrilineal or matrilineal descent defines a category of persons entitled to be members. Whether they actually *are* members depends on the circumstances of life history and often on individual strategy and choice. In this respect, descent groups are like the corporation controlling our New England music festival: not all those eligible to be members actually are members. Moreover, in many such societies, many people actually act as members of descent corporations even though they do not

have the proper descent "credentials." This gap between descent entitlement and corporation membership—between being in a cultural category and being in a social group—is often important in making such forms of organization flexible and adaptive.

Second, once we perceive this gulf between descent entitlement and corporation membership, we can understand another mode of forming descent corporations. This is to say that *all* descendants of a founding ancestor, through any combination of male and female links, comprise a descent category. Such a nonexclusive mode of tracing descent is called **cognatic descent.** An individual then belongs to many cognatic descent categories—each of us had 8 great-grandparents, 16 great-great-grandparents, and so on. If we had acquired some descent entitlement through our connection to each of them, how could we belong to a single corporation? The organizational problem is then to use patterns of residential history, strategy, and choice to narrow any particular individual's corporation membership down to a single group, despite his or her eligibility and secondary interests in the other groups and territories from whose founders he or she can trace cognatic descent.

Third, chains of descent often serve to define rules and rights other than corporation membership. Thus, succession to a position or office might be determined by descent in the male line; or individually owned property might be inherited in the female line. Some anthropologists would not want to call this descent. But in any case, descent *categories*—patrilineal, matrilineal, or cognatic—may be accorded cultural relevance even where no corporate groups are involved.

Finally, this enables us to understand how, in a single society, different modes of tracing descent may be used for different purposes. Thus we must be wary of talking about a society as "patrilineal" or "matrilineal," as many anthropologists have done for typological classification or shorthand reference. In addition, there can be other modes of conceptualizing solidarity and continuity over time—for example, through concepts of "the house" or of the places where the dead are buried (Bloch 1971, Carsten and Hugh-Jones 1995).

Case 19 outlines Tallensi descent. Here, in a single society seemingly dominated by patrilineal descent, we find—used in different ways for different purposes—the three major modes of conceptualizing descent, as well as widespread webs of bilateral kinship.

Patrilineal Descent Systems

There are two reasons why it is useful to begin a brief look at descent systems by looking first at those based on patrilineal descent. First, patrilineal forms of social organization are much more widespread and more common—roughly three times as common—as matrilineal forms. Second, matrilineal systems are subject to fairly severe structural constraints, so that the range of organizational possibility is considerably narrower. It is strategically useful to identify these constraints in terms of the wider range of variation in patrilineal systems.

It is hard for students who live in Western industrialized societies, whose closest social ties are to friends and neighbors, not relatives, to visualize social life in a society where the scale of community is drastically reduced and where kinship and descent define where you live and how you relate to the people in your social world. It is useful to introduce unfamiliar modes of organizing social relations by phrasing them in more familiar terms: to describe a hypothetical descent system in terms with which the Western reader is familiar.

Having viewed an idealized imaginary system in these terms, we will command a model against which to contrast the many forms found in the real world. The imaginary society is here given English labels for people and places; but its counterparts in the real world are societies in Africa, Asia, the Americas, and the Pacific.

A Hypothetical Patrilineage System

Imagine a town of some 10,000 people, composed of six districts. Each district is made up of some five or ten small neighborhoods. All of the people in the town have one of a dozen names—Smith, Jones, Brown, and so on. (Those who find these names too WASPish can substitute others: they have the advantage of being short and familiar.) Children, as in contemporary Western society, have the same last name as their father. No two people with the same last name are supposed to marry.

In a particular *neighborhood*, the houses and land on a particular street are all owned by people with one name. Let us narrow our focus to the Smiths living on Elm Street (Figure 9.5). All of them are descended from Sam Smith, the grandfather of the oldest men now living. They own their Elm Street land collectively. Each Smith has a separate household for his family, though families assist one another in their work.

John Smith, one of the older men, acts as spokesman for these Elm Street Smiths in business and property matters and leads them at religious services in the shrine at his house. One of the peculiarities of the legal system is that should one of the Elm Street Smiths get married, injure someone, or commit a crime, all of the Elm Street Smiths join together to bear the costs, or are all held accountable. To an outsider, one Elm Street Smith is as good as another. Note that it is only the Smith men, their wives (who are

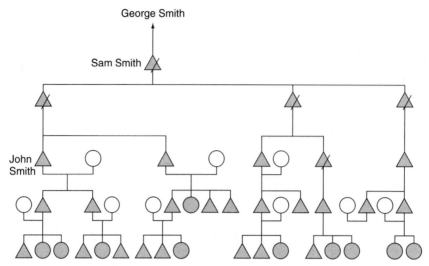

Figure 9.5 The Elm Street Smiths: The hypothetical genealogy shows the men, women, and children living on Elm Street. Note that most grown Smith women have married out, and non-Smith women have married in. (From Keesing 1975:29)

not Smiths), and their unmarried children who live on Elm Street. The married daughters of Smiths have gone to live with their husbands.

On the next street lives a group of Joneses, and on the other side a group of Browns. But within this neighborhood, there are six other streets of Smiths. All of these Smiths are descended from a common great-great-grandfather; and they recognize this common descent (from George Smith) at a neighborhood Smith church. There George Smith is buried, and there they occasionally gather for collective rites. The neighborhood Joneses, Browns, and others also have their own churches. The people with a common name and a common church own only church property collectively, and although they do a few nonreligious activities together, they are not a tight little group like the Elm Street Smiths. All of the Smiths within the district seldom see one another, except at a yearly religious outing, but they have a general feeling of unity based on the common descent they trace from a Smith ancestor seven generations ago.

Finally, all Smiths in the town believe that they are descended from a founding Smith, though they do not know how they are related. They have a few common religious symbols, but have no further social unity. Recall that no two Smiths—however remotely related—are ideally supposed to marry. In fact, Smiths from different districts rarely do marry, despite some disapproval. But marriage between two Smiths in the same district is regarded as very wrong, and marriage between Smiths in the same neighborhood would be strictly prohibited.

In everyday circumstances the Smiths on Elm Street are a separate corporation and deal with other Smiths, even those in the same neighborhood church, as they would with anyone else. But if the Elm Street Smiths quarrel with Browns on a nearby street, or another neighborhood, matters can escalate so that the Elm Street Smiths are joined by some or all Smiths of the neighborhood, and the Browns are backed by other Browns. But such alliances, which may sometimes unite Smiths of the same *district* (but different neighborhoods), are temporary and limited to the particular dispute at hand. When things are settled—and this often comes from the arbitration of Smiths whose mothers are Browns and Browns whose mothers are Smiths—these alliances dissolve.

Conceptual Refinements and Points of Variation

There are many variations on this pattern, and we will glimpse a few of them. First, some important features of patrilineal descent systems can be illustrated in terms of the Smiths and Joneses, and some needed technical terms defined.

First, note that the Elm Street Smiths are related by common descent; but so too are all the Smiths in the neighborhood and all the Smiths in the district, and—according to tradition—all the Smiths in town. That is, descent categories can be formed at higher

and higher levels, with more and more remote "apical" ancestors serving as the point of reference. But note that the Elm Street Smiths form a *descent group*, while all the Smiths in town form only a descent category. The Smiths on Elm Street form a solid little local corporation, with collective property, collective legal responsibility, and so on. The Smiths in the neighborhood form a group too, but the things they do and own as a group are much less important. The more inclusive descent categories serve to define rules of marriage and provide the bases for political alliances. Such descent groups and categories, based on descent from more and more remote ancestors, are called **segmentary.** A look at a wider hypothetical genealogy of Smiths will illustrate (Figure 9.6).

Such systems are called segmentary because they are divided at each level into segments (the descendants of Sam, Joe, and Ed Smith; and, as higher-order segments,

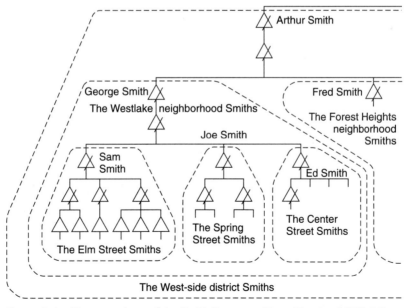

Figure 9.6   The genealogy of the Smith lineages. (From Keesing 1975:30)

CASE

19

Tallensi Descent and Kinship

The Tallensi of Ghana, whose system of restrictions involving first-born children we examined in Case 2, have a complicated social and ritual organization in which patrilineal descent is central (Fortes 1945, 1949). Thus corporate groups of Tallensi society are composed of persons patrilineally descended from a common ancestor. The Tallensi so emphasize patrilineal descent that they have often been cited as a classic example of a "patrilineal society." Yet Tallensi individuals are bound together by complex webs of kinship on the maternal as well as paternal side. A man sacrifices to the spirits of his mother and close maternal relatives, as well as to those on his father's side.

Furthermore, a Tallensi man has an interest not only in his father's corporate descent group; he also has secondary interests in his mother's group, his father's mother's group, and others to which he is more distantly related through a female link. When members of a patrilineal descent group sacrifice to their ancestors, any descendant through female as well as male links is entitled to partake of the sacrificial meal.

Moreover, not only are members of a patrilineal descent group forbidden to marry one another (as in many such systems), but any man and woman who are descended from the same ancestor by any chain of male *or* female links are forbidden to marry. Such patterns suggest that the Tallensi may conceptualize their relatedness in terms of cognatic descent, as well as patrilineal descent and bilateral kinship (Keesing 1970).

Finally, the Tallensi also attribute importance to relationship in the female line. Thus two persons who are descended, even distantly, through a chain of female links from a pair of sisters are conceived to have special and close ties; and witchcraft powers are specifically believed to be passed through such lines of matrilineal connection.

Case Update
See Verdun (1982) for a study of variations in Tallensi social organization and a questioning of the overall concept of a "segmentary lineage system." Verdun's study does not, however, invalidate the points made here.

the descendants of George and Fred Smith). Their genealogical structure is hierarchical. But this view of them one gets at any time is "frozen," like one frame of a movie film. To understand how such a system works, and how groups form and change, we must look at it in terms of processes in time. Consider the Elm Street Smiths, a group based on common descent from grandfather Sam Smith. If we visited Elm Street three generations later, Sam Smith would be a great-great-grandfather, and far too many Smiths would be descended from him to live on Elm Street. How then can the system work?

It works because what looks at any single point in time as though it were a stable and permanent arrangement of people, territories, and genealogical connections is in fact only a temporary crystallization. Over longer periods new groups are forming and old ones are dying out. When we look three generations later, John Smith, who was leader of the Smiths before, may now be treated as the founder of the Elm Street Smiths, who now will include his descendants but not those of the other men who lived with John Smith on Elm Street (see Figure 9.6). Some of John Smith's brothers

A Tallensi lineage sacrifice. The baobab tree is a shrine to lineage ancestors. Here pots of beer are assembled; they will be used for ritual libations, then shared by those present—who include both lineage members and cognatic descendants of the ancestors.

and cousins may by this time have no living descendants; others may have had only daughters, or granddaughters, who married and left. The descendants of others may have proliferated, but moved elsewhere to found new corporations, often due to internal quarrels or feuding. After the span of three generations, what had been a Jones Street may now be a Smith Street. All the Browns in the whole neighborhood may now have disappeared.

Another important feature of such a system of patrilineal descent groupings is that for any particular corporation and terri-

tory—say the Elm Street Smiths—there are actually two partly overlapping categories of membership. First, there are all those men, women, and children whose fathers were Elm Street Smiths, and hence are members of the corporation by birth. But not all of them live there. The adult Elm Street Smith women have mainly left to live with their husbands, and hence are scattered around other streets and neighborhoods. Second, there is the group of persons actually living on Elm Street: Smith men, their wives (who are not Smiths), and their children. The descent group, which is only partly localized, and the *local group,* which is only partly based on descent, are usually both important in different contexts—and it is dangerously easy to get them confused.

Finally, some technical terms are needed. A **lineage** is a descent group consisting of people patrilineally or matrilineally descended from a known ancestor through a series of links they can trace. When descent is in the male line (as with Smiths and Joneses), we can call these **patrilineages.** When descent is in the female line, we speak of **matrilineages.** A larger descent category like all the Smiths in the town, who believe they are descended from a common ancestor but do not know the actual connections, is called a **clan.**

In-laws are more commonly referred to in anthropology as **affines.** Thus Mary Brown, who has married one of the Elm Street Smiths is an affine of the other Elm Street Smiths (and they are her affines). Her husband is an affine of her Lake Street Brown relatives. In some systems of this type all of the Elm Street Smiths have an affinal relationship with all the Lake Street Browns based on this marriage.

A rule that requires marriage outside a particular group or category is technically called a rule of **exogamy** ("out-marriage"). A group or category whose members are prohibited from marrying one another is **exogamous.** Patrilineages (and matrilineages) like those of the Smiths and Joneses are usually exogamous (although the level of segmentation at which a rule of exogamy is strictly enforced varies considerably from society to society). Rules of exogamy are often extended to prohibit a person marrying a member of his mother's lineage, as well as his own.

Patrilineal Descent Systems in the Real World

There are many variations on the "typical" system of segmentary patrilineages illus-

trated by the Smiths and Joneses. In most real segmentary patrilineage systems, the people do not, of course, live in towns, but are scattered over large areas. The equivalent of Elm Street occupied by a corporate patrilineage is likely to be a territory of several square miles, with the people clustered in villages, hamlets, or scattered homesteads.

One variant, represented by such people as the Tiv of Nigeria or the Nuer of the Sudan (whose marriage system we glimpsed in Case 18), is a correspondence between the layout of territories in space and the structure of a segmentary genealogy. Each level of the segmentary hierarchy corresponds to a separate territorial segment. It is as though instead of Smith lineages being scattered around a neighborhood also occupied by Joneses, Browns, and others, a whole neighborhood was made up of Smiths, and a whole district was made up of Smiths, Browns, and Joneses, all of whom traced common descent from the same distant ancestor, and so on. Figure 9.7 illustrates this mode of segmentary organization among the Tiv. All the Tiv—who number in the hundreds of thousands—are regarded as descended in the male line from a traditional founding ancestor. But note then that as with Smiths and Joneses, rules prohibiting marriage between codescendants must apply only at lineage or clan level—or no Tiv could marry another Tiv.

A somewhat similar expression of the patrilineage model, but without its attachment to land, occurs among Islamic peoples such as the Basseri. It is possible to conceive widely dispersed nomadic groups as connected in a single vast patrilineal genealogy, with "tents," "families," and "lineages" corresponding to local lineages, clans, and so on—even though the only "territories" at stake may be pasture lands or migration routes.

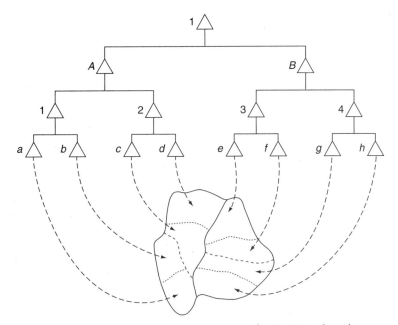

Figure 9.7 Segmentary organization among the Tiv: Note here how the geographical distribution of lineages corresponds to their genealogical relationships. (From P. Bohannan 1954, by permission of the International African Institute)

Lineages, Production, and Politics

At this point, it is useful to come back to a theoretical focus of the last chapter: modes of production. Recall that some scholars in the neo-Marxist tradition (mainly French specialists on Africa) have talked about the "lineage mode of production." What *is* the role of lineages in production?

Recall that for the Tsembaga Maring, the household group is the main unit both of production and consumption. The same is true of the Tiv or the Tallensi in Africa, if we take as the household a compound group consisting of cowives and their children, filling with their joint productive labor a granary from which they subsist (recall Case 2, which described the ritual rules preventing a first-born Tallensi boy from seeing the inside of his father's granary). The

Trobriand case is complicated by frequent communal labor within a large garden. But most of the time a family does subsistence labor separately on its own plot, and it is within this household that everyday consumption takes place. What, then, is the productive role of lineages?

The most important element of the means of production is territorial control of land. A family may hold title to the *garden* that represents the cumulation of their labor. But they would be hard-pressed, by themselves, to keep others from seizing control over it. Control over land by a corporate group of a size adequate to its collective defense assures that individual households will be able to work on the land to meet their needs. It further means that title to the land is not fractionated; should one family die out, title to the land—which is held by the whole corporation—remains intact. In creating corporations which are also locally sovereign political units, lineage or clan organization is crucial in reproducing a system of production even though lineages do not themselves comprise a collective labor force.

In a pastoral society, domestic groups such as the Basseri "tent" constitute the main units of production and consumption. But as with lineage organization among horticulturalists, the larger groupings at higher segmentary levels (in the case of the Basseri, "families" and "sections") provide collective defense of pasture land or migration routes—crucial elements in production, among pastoralists, which individual domestic groups could not effectively control.

In segmentary patrilineage systems, the genealogical relations between segments may provide an idiom in which the political relations between segments are expressed and the results of conflict are rationalized. The intertwining of patrilineal descent with politics is explored in § 32. There the political processes within the Nuer segmentary system (Case 34) and the intertwining of patrilineal descent groups with centralized kingship (the Bunyoro, Case 38) are illustrated. These will provide further substantive background.

How big the local corporations are is an important axis of variation: they may consist of 20 or 30 individuals or several hundred. Systems also vary in the depth of segmentary hierarchies. The Tiv, all tracing descent from a single ancestor, illustrate one extreme. At the other extreme, local lineages may trace no higher-level connections of common descent with one another.

The relative importance of descent groups, including out-marrying sisters, and descent-based local groups, excluding sisters and including wives, also varies. At one extreme are systems where the wife loses all legal interests in her patrilineage of birth and acquires full interests in the corporation into which she marries. Among the early Romans, when a girl married she was ritually removed from her lineage, and was ritually introduced into her husband's lineage—even acquiring a new set of ancestors, those of her husband. The husband's legal rights over her then replaced those of her father (Fustel de Coulanges 1864). In some other systems, ties to the husband are very weak, marriage is fragile, and the wife retains full legal interests in the lineage of her birth. Usually a balance is struck between the strength of a woman's ties to her brother and the lineage of her birth and her ties to her husband and his group.

Ideal Blueprints and Social Realities: Flexibility and Adaptation

Even if we look only at male members, not the in- and out-marrying women, the correspondence between membership in a descent category and membership in a local group is sometimes far less neat than our example of Smiths and Joneses suggests. This is where our distinction between categories and groups—between those entitled to rights in a corporation and those who actually exercise them—is badly needed. In many "patrilineal" systems, notably those in the highlands of New Guinea, a very large proportion of men (sometimes more than half) are not living in the territory to which they have rights through patrilineal descent. Instead, they are scattered around, some living in their mother's territories, others in their fathers' mothers' territories, and so on. Some of a person's legal rights and ritual relationships may be based squarely on patrilineal descent, so that a person retains them no matter where he or she lives, but these then have no direct correspondence with local groupings.

The same lack of neat correspondence between local groupings and the scheme of patrilineal descent emphasized in the "official charter" occurs in some African societies, like the Nuer, who seem on the surface to be very much like the Smiths and Joneses, and who conceive their political relationships in terms of patrilineal descent.

Our quick look at patrilineal modes of solving the organizational problems of societies can well end on this note of disorder, this lack of neat correspondence between the formal model of descent and the realities of who actually lives where and does what with whom. Patrilineal descent seems a beautiful formal solution to major organizational problems—maintaining ordered political relations without central institutions of government and maintaining corporate title to land as the most crucial means of production. But there are hidden problems here. How does "the system" adjust to the shifting tides of warfare, feuding, and politics? And how are relations of humans to land adjusted, given the inevitable imbalances that arise when one group proliferates, another dwindles. We have seen how, among the Tsembaga Maring of New Guinea, occupation of the neighbor's territory through war may give an answer. But many other mechanisms for redistributing land and for redistributing humans on the land were at work in different parts of the world.

These problems prevent any unilineal descent system from being as neat and stable as its formal blueprint. There must be flexibility to accommodate demographic shifts, adapt human groupings to the resources and pressures of an ecosystem, follow the tides of politics, and allow room for the strivings and foibles of human individuals. The question is not, as some have posed it, whether a society is "neat" or "messy"—for all social life is a layer cake of order and disorder. It is, rather, by what mechanisms are flexibility and adaptibility maintained and how are they justified, ignored, rationalized, or disguised ideologically? (See A. J. Strathern 1972 for a discussion of these issues in relation to the Melpa or Mt. Hagen people of Papua New Guinea.)

Matrilineal Descent

On a diagram, matrilineal descent—the tracing of descent from an ancestress through a line of daughters—is a mirror-image of patrilineal descent. But in practice, they are not mirror-images; and that has to do with the battlelines of sexual politics.

If women in a matrilineally organized society occupied the key positions of political power within descent corporations, then men could go off in marriage to other lineages or clans. The matrilineal equivalent of the Elm Street Smiths would consist of a line of matrilineally related Smith women (say, an elderly great-grandmother as matriarch and her daughters and granddaughters). These Smith women would control the corporation; their husbands, living on Elm Street, would be Joneses and Browns and Greens—outsiders in the local community. Such a system seems, on the surface of things, to be represented among a number of matrilineally organized peoples, such as the Hopi of Arizona, as discussed in Case 20.

A form of postmarital residence like that of the Hopi is the mirror-image of postmarital residence with the husband's people. But does the Hopi case, and others like it, really constitute a mirror-image of the Smiths and Joneses of our original example, or its real-world counterparts such as the Tiv? The key issue is political control of the descent corporation, both in its internal affairs and in its relationship to other

CASE

20

Hopi Social Organization

The pueblo-dwelling Hopi Indians have a highly intricate social and ceremonial organization. The major groupings are exogamous matrilineal clans, each tracing relationship to a particular animal, plant, or natural phenomenon. These clans are land-owning corporations. They are also central in the elaborate ceremonial cycles, in which each has a special part to play and a special set of ritual paraphernalia.

These clans are segmented into unnamed matrilineages, localized in sections of the pueblo. The core of these local groupings is a line of matrilineally related women. A Hopi man joins his wife's household—and she can send him packing any time she pleases. A typical household consists of an older woman and her husband, if she still has one; her daughters and their husbands and children; and her unmarried sons.

Note that the husbands are outsiders and that the senior woman's grown sons have married and moved elsewhere. Thus, while the lineage retains effective control over its women and their children, the adult men are scattered as outsiders in their wives' households. Women have considerable power in the public realm and preeminent power in the domestic sphere.

Case Update

See Whiteley (1985) for a reconsideration of the role of matrilineal descent in Hopi society. Whiteley questions whether Hopi descent units are true corporations. W. Adams (1983) has also argued for the Navaho people that groups are the products of situational residence decisions rather than simple reflections of descent rules.

descent groups. In his introduction to an important comparative study in which matrilineal systems belatedly received careful attention, D. M. Schneider (1961) argues that in all recorded matrilineal systems, control over descent corporations remains in the hands of men. In the Hopi case, and others like it, Schneider argues, men ultimately control lineage affairs despite the dominance of women within domestic groups. The board of directors of the corporation, as it were, is composed of men.

But how? A Hopi man is an outsider in his household, vulnerable to expulsion at any time through divorce. He lives with his wife's lineage, but he is a member of the board of directors in his own lineage—where his sisters live. How can a clan leader live in one place and act effectively in politics in another place? The answer for the Hopi is that "another place" is within the same pueblo, often only across the plaza. A descent corporation would be hard-pressed to maintain its strength if all or most of its adult men were widely scattered. Most often the potential problem is avoided, as with the Hopi, because the population is clustered into sizable communities; and in any single community, several different matrilineages or matrilineal clans are clustered together. "Marrying out" is likely to mean marrying into a nearby group. The men are close enough at hand to take an active part in corporation affairs.

Schneider underlines what A. I. Richards (1950) had earlier called "the matrilineal puzzle." Either the men marry out, as with the Hopi, so that the male "board of directors" must be reconstituted when the need arises; or the women marry out (as with the patrilineal Smiths and Joneses), in which case the matrilineal corporation must regain control of children born in their fathers' places. In either case, a woman's ties to her husband are potentially at odds with her ties to her brother; and if the corporation is to endure and be strong, her ties to her brother must prevail over those to her husband at the crucial times. It is her brother who must keep primary control over her children. Her sons must be her brother's heirs. In such a situation of structural conflict, marriage is almost inevitably fragile. Divorce rates are likely to be high.

Matrilineal Descent, "Matriarchy," and Women's Power

But all this rests on the assumption that men, not women, control the "board of directors" in a matrilineal society. Are there no matriarchies? Very probably Hopi women exercise more power than some anthropological theorists have conceded (see Schlegel 1973 and Udall 1969). So too did women among some of the matrilineally organized peoples of the American southeast such as the Choctaw and Creek, and among the Iroquois, as described in Case 21.

Just how we should interpret the political power of Iroquois women, extending from their power in the longhouse corporations, has been a matter of some controversy. Richards (1957) argues that the power of women in the political arena has

been exaggerated. She sees the interpretation of the Iroquois system as "matriarchal" as misleading; and she sees in the historical records evidence of an increasing role of Iroquois women in the political realm due to two centuries of bitter warfare and a resulting dwindling of the male population. We cannot confidently assess the political role of Iroquois women prior to European contact. It was clearly not "matriarchal"; but it is equally clear that the male "board of directors" was strongly shaped and guided by senior women. Assessing the political power of women in a society such as the Iroquois is a complicated matter. How much weight does one give to formal institutions and rules, how much weight to the actual political relationships between individuals? How much importance do we accord to a woman as "the power behind the throne," if men take the lead in formal, public settings? As we will see, assessing the "status of women" in any society entails deep and still unresolved problems.

Why Matrilineal Descent?

The question of political power of women usefully raises a further question. If matrilineal descent is not an expression of "matriarchy," what does it express? The answers revolve at least partly around the conceptualization of women's reproductive powers. Physically, women have the more obvious and compelling role in the creation of life. Through pregnancy, the umbilical bond between mother and infant, the drama of birth, and suckling, women literally and visibly create new lives. Male ideologists may portray women as passive containers and nurturers of a life created by male seed, but it is a rather shallow denial of the world as humans experience it. Matrilineal descent represents

CASE

21

Iroquois Matriliny and the Power of Women

The Iroquois tribes of the American Northeast are a striking example of a "kinship state." The famous League of the Iroquois, a political confederacy the writers of the U.S. Constitution drew on as a model, was conceptualized as an extension of the matrilineal extended family and matrilineage.

The Iroquois confederacy consisted of five culturally related "tribes," the Onondaga, Mohawk, Seneca, Oneida, and Cayuga. Our knowledge of their social organization is clouded by a lack of details about precolonial times, and by diversity between and within tribes that makes simple generalization difficult. But a relatively clear composite emerges from the scattered and large literature.

The precolonial Iroquois tribes lived, at least for most of the year, in 12 or 13 large villages of between 300 and 600 (Fenton 1957:41). Seasonally, the component families left the villages to hunt and fish in smaller groups. The core of Iroquois kin groupings was the household group, comprising several matrilineally related nuclear families that together occupied a longhouse (pairs of families shared a fireplace in the central aisle). The women of this extended family collectively held tools and garden plots and worked together in the cultivation of maize and other staple crops. The men hunted and fished. However, the household was controlled by its senior women; because of the residence pattern, the men were unrelated outsiders who belonged to different matriclans.

A cluster of these matrilineally related households comprised a matrilineage, which in turn was localized in a section of a village. As we will see, all or most lineages had male leaders chosen by their senior women. Matrilineages were in turn grouped into exogamous matrilineal clans.

However, the clans—ideally, eight in each tribe—were apparently not localized in a single village: each village had matrilineages from several clans, each clan included matrilineages localized in two or more villages. Matrilineages were strongly corporate; belonging to the same matriceian entailed ties and obligations of kinship, including mutual assistance in time of conflict.

Among the Western Iroquois, the matriclans were divided into tribal *moieties*—that is, divisions of the "tribe" into two halves, according to descent. Each moiety was represented in each village, and in many ritual contexts—notably mourning ceremonies—the two moieties had important and complementary roles. The potential fission between matrilineages and between clans was checked in part by this ritual dependence on members of the opposite moiety. Moreover, the pattern of clan exogamy and a man's residence with his wife's people meant that men of different lineages were united in a single household corporation. And it meant that a man or woman had strong kinship ties with his or her father's matrilineage as well; that lineage also played an important part in a person's life, ritually and socially. The component lineages of a community were thus bound together by webs of intermarriage, hence of kinship, ritual obligation, and common interest.

Iroquois society was also held together by a remarkable political system, one in which women played a prominent part commensurate with their power in the domestic realm and their central role in the subsistence economy. The Iroquois Confederacy that united the five tribes was governed by a council of 50 *sachems*. These male chiefs, who acted to maintain peace and conduct "foreign" relations, held positions or titles that belonged hereditarily to particular tribes; and within tribes, to particular matriclans or matrilineages. Succession to a sachem title, when an incumbent died, followed matrilineal lines. But the actual successor was nominated by the women of the lineage or clan. Among the Western Iroquois, the nomination of a sachem was confirmed by the moiety to which he belonged, then by the opposite moiety. In the event that the new sachem was too young to perform his duties, they were performed in his stead by a senior woman acting as regent. The sachem titles were not all equal in power and prestige. The Onondaga tribe had the three most important sachem titles, including that of wampum-keeper (keeper of trade goods, especially beads—the name comes from the Algonkian language). Holders of lesser sachem titles also had specific duties assigned to them.

The organization was remarkably simple yet efficient. The component tribes each had separate councils, composed of the sachems of the particular tribe. The council dealt with the internal affairs of the tribe. As in the League council, discussion was open, with a premium on oratorical skill; and council decisions were unanimous.

It is worth assessing the status and power of women in Iroquois society (see Randle 1951). Randle's summary is useful:

The extended family structure of the Longhouse, symbolized in the League, accounts for the function of the matrons to hold the chiefs' names in their clans and their consequent right to appoint and depose chiefs. Death feasts and mourning were the responsibility of the women. Women kept the white wampum belts which signified the chiefly names. [They had] the ability . . . to influence decisions of the council both directly through their speaker and indirectly through the weight of public opinion. . . . Since unanimity was necessary for decision to act, any proposal unpopular with the matrons could be hindered by their disapproval. Indirectly, too, it is stated

that the women could hinder or actually prevent a war party which lacked their approval by not giving the supplies of dried corn and the moccasins which the warriors required. Village headwomen are mentioned in myth, and though they may not actually have ruled villages, this concept reflects the power that women were thought to possess. The importance of clan matrons in deciding the fate of captives . . . is well known. (1951: 171–172)

The base of female power lay largely in their central role in subsistence: "Economically, the maintenance of the household was a joint undertaking, but the women had the chief responsibility in the care of the fields and the raising of the staple foods. Men and women cooperated in the clearing of new fields, after that the womens' group took over" (Randle 1951:172).

In the nineteenth century, Morgan had observed that "the Indian regarded woman as the inferior, the dependent, and the servant of man, and from nurture and habit, she actually considered herself to be so" (Morgan 1851:315). An early feminist took a different point of view: "by comparison with the restrictions . . . obtaining among civilized people, the Iroquois woman had a superior position and superior rights" (Converse 1908:138). Randle's observations—in 1951—sound as though they had been made 20 years later: "Behind the feminist movement as well as behind most male chauvinism is the concept that the difference between the sexes is always to be interpreted as inferiority. . . . Iroquois men and women had separate and different culture patterns, different values and different life goals" (Randle 1951:173–174).

Case Update
See also Thomas R. Trautmann (1987) for a review of Lewis H. Morgan's work on Iroquois society. On gender relations in Native American societies, see also Leacock (1981, 1983).

a cultural recognition of the mother-child bond as the basis of continuities across the generations. Such a cultural construction of biology, used to form groups, does not define the nature of women and men as social beings. It is compatible with a definition of men as the essential political actors in successive generations, with their connection running from a man to his sister's child (that is, connected by a sister's powers of fertility); and it would be equally compatible with a transfer of power from a matriarch to her daughter(s) and then granddaughter(s).

Matrilineal descent groups characteristically are found in societies with the following characteristics:

1. They are predominantly agricultural.
2. They have sufficiently high productivity to permit the sedentary residence of substantial populations.
3. They have a division of labor in which women perform many of the key productive tasks and/or have substantial control over what is produced.

But here, as in most comparative questions of social structure, there are no perfect correlations. Thus, many societies within this range of scale, technology, and productivity have patrilineal descent systems.

These correlations are more consistent when we look at negative constraints. Thus, atrilineal descent seems generally incompatible with pastoral subsistence economies, and is rare among hunter-gatherers and in societies with developed class systems and centralized political institutions.

Descent, Residence, and Flexibility

We have reached a stage where we can usefully return to an organizational puzzle of the last chapter: The Trobriand subclan, described in Case 22. As with patrilineal descent among the Smiths and Joneses, matrilineal descent is used in the Trobriands to form strong corporate groups that solve many of the organizational problems of tribal life in this setting. By allowing flexibility, choice, and readjustment of living arrangements, it also permits effective adaptation to the changing pressures of an environment and the processes of politics.

Near the Trobriands, on the Melanesian island of Dobu, an even more fascinating compromise of residence was adopted. Husband and wife alternated annually between residence in her matrilineage village (where he was a feared and insecure alien) and residence in his matrilineage village (where she was an outsider). Fortune's (1932) description of the tensions involved is an anthropological classic.

In many societies with matrilineal descent groups, the wife goes to live with her husband; yet the husband lives in his father's place, not in his matrilineage territory. If one traces out the implications of such a scheme, it would seem that lineages could not be localized. Neither the men nor the women of the corporation live together. Such systems, common in Melanesia and parts of Africa, are conventionally viewed as representing a late stage in the disintegration of a matrilineal system into a patrilineal or cognatic system; the matrilineage is no longer a strong corporation, but a kind of remnant category or debating society. But some detailed studies have shown that lineages in such societies can be localized and powerful to a surprising degree despite a residence rule that ostensibly prevents localization (see, for example, Case 14; also, Keesing 1975).

Other Forms of Descent Organization

Recall that two or more modes of descent may be relevant in different contexts in the same society. **Double descent,** where corporate patrilineal descent groups and corporate matrilineal descent groups occur in the same society, provides the most dramatic illustration, as illustrated in Case 23.

Another descent organization is *cognatic descent,* mentioned earlier in this section. Kinship specialists have realized rather recently that cognatic descent, where any series of male or female links to the founding ancestor establishes descent entitlement, can also produce workable descent corporations. The problem is to narrow down, from the many groups where a person could be a member, the one where he actually is a member. Here a number of mechanisms are possible. One is to specify that a couple can live with either the husband's or wife's group; but whichever they choose, their children belong to that group. Another is to give privileged status, among those persons eligible for membership, to those who trace descent in the male line. Thus, other things being equal, a chain of affiliations with the father's group will be made, though some people in each generation will affiliate with their mother's group due to economic strategies or the circumstances of life history. A person seldom has as much freedom to choose or change his or her membership as the formal rules seem to imply. In practice, cognatic descent can produce corporations similar to those based on unilineal descent, and just as efficient organizationally. In a sense, the difference is that cognatic descent builds into the rules a great range of flexibility and then uses only a portion of that range, while unilineal descent gives little flexibility in the rules yet allows it, as needed, in some disguised form. Case 24 describes cognatic descent as practiced by the Kwaio in the Solomon Islands.

Families, Kindreds, and Bilateral Organization

Descent-based corporations provide effective solutions to the organizational problems of many societies. Hunting and gathering peoples may conceive the relatedness of band members in their territory as based on descent (as with many Australian Aboriginal peoples), but the pressures toward corporate control of resources mainly arose with the advent of food production. With the urban revolution and advanced technologies, nonkinship forms of social groupings have come to the fore. However, anthropologists working in peasant communities often encounter important social groupings based on descent (Chapter 18).

Corporate groups based on descent turn out to be far from universal. There are other, equally adaptive solutions to the same problems. Many swidden horticulturists of Southeast Asia, in particular, and some pastoralists such as the Lapps, use bilateral kinship as the major principle of social organization. Thus in many parts of the Philippines, Borneo, and Indonesia, property is owned by family groups, and social structure is built up out of local groupings—families, settlement, and neighborhoods. (See Cases 25 and 26.) Here, bilateral kinship provides solutions to many of the organizational problems which in other parts of the world are solved through descent groups. Local groups are made up of consanguineal and affinal kin, and action groups are crystallized temporarily out of personal kindreds. (See also again, for example, Carsten and Hugh-Jones 1995.)

CASE

22

The Trobriand Subclan

The Trobriand landscape is divided into territories. Each territory contains sacred places from which, mythologically, its ancestress is supposed to have emerged. From her are descended, in the female line, the members of a *dala*. Since the precise genealogical links are not known but the groups are strongly corporate, *dala* are known in the Trobriand literature as *subclans*. A Trobriand subclan is a matrilineal descent group consisting of the following members:

1. Men related through their mothers, their mothers' mothers, their mothers' mothers' mothers, and so on
2. The sisters of men, and other women similarly related in the female line
3. The children of these women (but not the children of the men)

The *dala* is conceived as perpetually regenerated:

In the Trobriands the inner substance of a child is *dala* blood, conceived through the union of a woman and a spirit child who itself has been reincarnated from an old *baloma* [*baloma* are spirits of the dead, which inhabit the underworld of *Tuma*]. (Weiner 1976:122)

A child belongs to his or her mother's *dala*, but has close lifelong bonds with the father's *dala* as well (Robinson 1962, Weiner 1976):

In the Trobriands, children are created and nurtured by their own *dala* and by their father and his *dala*. Children benefit from their place within their own *dala* and from their position in another *dala*. . . . As a child represents an amalgamation of female essence and male provisioning, both a woman's *dala* and her husband's *dala* are infused with new life and new potential. (Weiner 1976: 130)

Cultural notions about conception, and the notions of time and causality expressed through them, do not exist as abstract ideas about the universe, but as ideas about the crucial groups in which human lives are lived, about the connections between humans over time—humans that, as in the Trobriands, include both the living and the dead. In many parts of the world, people think of lineages or clans as including both living and dead members, who at times of sacrifice or other rites participate together. We will see in Case 53 how the *baloma* spirits come back to their villages each year.

A *dala* is a corporation that controls land. At any time, a *dala*'s corporate land interests are represented by what Weiner calls its "manager":

Theoretically managerial status . . . passes from the manager to his youngest brother until the last sibling set [of men in a generation] has died. Then the status of manager passes to the oldest sister's oldest son. . . . The sons of younger sisters in a sibling set have very little chance of becoming managers. (1976:154)

The manager and other male leaders of the subclan (the Trobriand version of what we earlier likened to a "board of directors") make collective decisions about how a *dala*'s obligations of harvest presentations to its female members and their husbands will be assigned—that is, who will make exchange gardens for whom (Powell 1969b). They also plan and stage mortuary rites and other collective assertions of their prestige and kinship duty. In this sense, political power rests mainly in the hands of men. But the Trobriand system celebrates symbolically the nature and powers of women and their essential role in the connections between the generations.

And as we saw in Case 15, women take center stage in mortuary rites; women of wealth and rank have great prestige and considerable power. And compared to women in many patrilineally organized societies, women enjoy substantial autonomy over their personal lives and sexuality.

Postmarital residence in the Trobriands contrasts sharply with the Hopi system described in Case 20. Wives go to live with their husbands at marriage. But how, then, are *dala* constituted as local groups? If the women of the subclan do not stay on their *dala* land, then it must be the men who stay and run the subclan's affairs. But how can this be? Here a diagram will be useful:

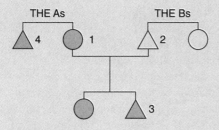

An A woman, number 1, marries a B man, 2, and goes to live with him. Their children then grow up in their father's hamlet. How, then, does the son, 3, end up in his mother's (therefore, his own) *dala* territory? The answer Malinowski gave was that when a son such as 3 reached adolescence, he would leave his father's hamlet and go to live with his maternal uncle, 4. This pattern, repeated across the generations, would mean that the adult men of a subclan would live on their own land, while its young boys would be growing up with their fathers.

Powell's Trobriand data from the 1950s made it clear that residence was more varied and flexible than Malinowski had suggested. Many men were living in their fathers', fathers' mothers', or other hamlets (Powell 1960, 1969a). Weiner's data further clarify the situation. She notes that it is only potential managers who need to leave their fathers' places and move to their own subclan land with their maternal uncles (a pattern of residence technically called "avunculocal"):

If a man's son is next in line to inherit the control of his own *dala* land, he is sent by his father to live with his mother's brother. Often, a sibling set will be sent to live avunculocally so that a man will have support from his younger brother. . . . If a man "returns home" to live with his mother's brother, he is potentially in a position to become an influential man. (Weiner 1976:154–155)

A subclan is ranked as either "chiefly" or "commoner" (as we will see in Case 36). Within these ranks the actual prestige and power of subclans varies considerably. But whatever its status, the Trobriand subclan is a strong and enduring landowning corporation, with strict rules of exogamy.

Each subclan is said to belong to one of four *clans*. The importance of these clans is obscure, but it is clear that they are social categories, each comprising a cluster of subclans traditionally associated by matrilineal descent and having symbolic connections with a particular bird or animal species. They are not corporate groups; and a single clan may include some of the highest-ranking and lowest-ranking subclans. The rule of subclan exogamy is extended in theory to all members of the same clan, but some marriages to clan members from other subclans do in fact take place. Sexual affairs between

Continued

Case 22 continued

members of the same clan, but different sub-clans, are regarded as wrong but not outra-geous.

The system as it has been outlined is simple and stable—one subclan owning one territory with one village in it, where male members and their families live. That relationship, validated by the myths of origin, implies great stability and permanence. But as we saw in dealing with pa-trilineal descent groupings, the real social world of real people is always less neat and stable than that. Descent corporations do not stay the same size: proliferation, dwindling, and extinc-tion of lineages require mechanisms for groups hiving off, collapsing, and taking over one an-other's lands. At any time, the interests, strate-gies, and alliances of individuals and groups, and the variations of demography, require that residence and affiliation be more flexible and variable than the dogma would have it.

In reality, if we could look at the Trobriand so-cial scene over a period of a century or two, the identity and arrangement of subclans and their territories would almost certainly shift drastically over that time span. One mechanism whereby this occurs is the branching off of a segment of a proliferating subclan (usually, an important one) so that it attaches to the village and territory of another subclan. This can take place when a woman from subclan B marries an important man from subclan A, who then—to bolster his strength and prestige—gives his sons a foothold in the A village. The sisters' children and matrilin-eal descendants of these sons who stayed put then establish a branch of subclan B in the vil-lage of subclan A.

By this mechanism, many local segments of subclans are living in different territories from those where their ancestors are supposed to have emerged. Moreover, many villages are com-posed of two, three, or more subclan segments. Sometimes the attached "immigrant" subclan segments outrank and politically dominate the original "owners." This upsets our neat earlier equation: 1 village = 1 subclan. For one village can contain its original subclan plus segments of one or two other subclans. And conversely, segments of a single subclan may be attached in several different territories, so that the subclan segment, not the whole subclan, is the locally based corporate group. In fact, in many respects the village (when composed of two or more subclan segments) is as important as the subclan in Trobriand life (as we will see in Case 31).

The flexibility of residential arrangements pro-vides a further adjustment to the shifting pres-sures of demography, land, and the tides of political fortune. The option to remain on one's father's land—or even for a father to go and live with a politically successful son on the land of the latter's *dala*. (Weiner 1976:155)—provides options of residence that can be pursued in rela-tion to the availability of land, to personal predilection, and political advantage.

Finally, the whims of demography are subject to human rearrangement, since a great many children are adopted into households other than those of their birth. This does not affect their subclan membership, but it shifts them into dif-ferent households—often those of subclans other than their father's or mother's—during their childhood.

CASE

2 3

Double Descent Among the Yakö

The Yakö of Nigeria, living in large towns of as many as 11,000 people, are organized in a way very similar, at first glance, to our patrilineal Smiths and Joneses. A small patrilineal group, like the Elm Street Smiths, reside together in a compound. But whereas Smith streets were scattered among Jones and Brown streets, Yakö compounds are grouped together into a cluster, a large local patrilineage that corporately owns land. Finally, a series of patrilineage clusters are grouped together into a clan, occupying a single "district" of the town. This correspondence between territories and segmentary levels recalls the Tiv (Figure 9.7). The clans are exogamous, so a Yakö man's wives (he often has several) come from other districts.

Yet at the same time, the Yakö trace matrilineal descent, and any Yakö belongs to his mother's matrilineal clan. Whereas the patrilin-

eages are concerned with real estate and ritual involving lands and first fruits, the corporate matrilineal clans are concerned with movable property, with legal responsibility for their members and rights to payments for their death, and with ritual involving fertility spirits. Any Yakö belongs to both his or her father's patrilineage and mother's matrilineage.

Thus two different modes of corporate group organization, through patrilineal and matrilineal descent, fulfill complementary functions in different spheres of Yakö life. Since only full siblings normally belong to both the same patrilineage and the same matrilineal clan, people opposed in one situation may well be allies in another—hence helping to bind together the large Yakö communities (Forde 1950).

For a further classic study of double descent in an African society, see Goody (1962).

It is well to end this section with a cautionary note. Descent groupings are obvious and easily recorded, and they lend themselves neatly to comparative schemes. Yet anthropologists may often have overestimated the importance of descent at the expense of more subtle principles of social groupings. Focusing on descent categories, they have used great ingenuity to explain why people who are not patrilineally related to a place happen to be living there. We might do better to focus on local groups rather than descent categories, on the strate-

gies of gardening, friendship, property interest, and the like, that lead people to live where they do. A people may talk about the cumulative outcomes of individual choices in terms of ideologies of descent, even though "descent rules" actually have little to do with who decides to live where and do what. Descent may be, in some societies, more a way of thinking about local groups than of forming them. Descent can also provide an important rhetoric in terms of which to mobilize action and solidarity (A. J. Strathern 1972). The theoretical

CASE

2 4

Cognatic Descent Among the Kwaio

The Melanesian Kwaio of the Solomon Islands divide their mountainous terrain into dozens of small territories. Each is believed to have been founded by known ancestors some 9 to 12 generations ago. All cognatic descendants of the founding ancestor of a territory have rights to live there and use the land, and most of them raise pigs for sacrifice to the ancestors associated with that territory.

Yet a person obviously cannot live in, and have equally strong rights to, all the many territories (often a dozen or more) to which that person is related by cognatic descent. Usually there is a strongest affiliation to only one territory and to a descent group based there. Those who are affiliated with the descent group form the nucleus of the landowning corporation; they are, so to speak, voting members with full rights. The other cognatic descendants, affiliated somewhere else, have secondary rights and lesser ritual interests.

How then does a person come to have a primary affiliation out of the large number of potential ones through the father and mother? In practice, he or she seldom affiliates with a descent group other than that of father or mother. But which? First, a person who is patrilineally descended from the founding ancestor of a territory is considered to have the strongest rights in the corporation and the greatest say in its ritual affairs. Second, a woman normally resides in her husband's territory; and a person usually affili-

ates with the group with which he or she grew up as a child. All of these factors combine so that most people affiliate with their father's descent group. Cumulatively, most descent groups are made up mostly of patrilineal descendants of the founding ancestor. Cognatic descendants who live somewhere else have a secondary interest in the corporation. Yet in every generation, due to the circumstances of life history, some people grow up with their maternal relatives and affiliate with the mother's descent group. As long as they maintain an active participation in the corporation, they are treated as full members.

However, many men do not live in the territory where they have primary interests. In fact, Kwaio residence is quite fluid, and many men live in four or five territories or more during the course of their lives. They take an active, though secondary, interest in the ritual and secular affairs of several different descent groups. Depending on the context of the moment, a member of group A and a member of group B may both be participating in the ritual affairs or feast of group C, in which both have secondary interests based on cognatic descent. Here the interplay of cognatic descent and patrilineal descent, and the strategies of feasting and gardening and the circumstances of life history, produce solidly corporate yet flexible and adaptive descent groups (Keesing 1970).

framework set out in the last chapter, in which we look at the organization of production and distribution, allows us to sort out the way ideas about descent and kinship are

used—and at the same time, to perceive the role of ideologies about clans or the reincarnation of ancestors in reproducing a system of social relations across the generations.

CASE
2 5

The Subanun of the Philippines

The Subanun are swidden horticulturists scattered through the mountains of the Philippine island of Mindanao. They lack any formal political structure and are organized in no enduring kinship groups larger than the family. Yet they maintain complex networks of kinship relations and legal rights that weave families together. A family, consisting of parents and unmarried children, forms an independent corporation—owning property, sharing legal accountability, and producing and consuming its own subsistence crops.

Two families arrange a marriage between their children through prolonged legal negotiations. Until an agreed bridewealth payment is completed, the married couple must contribute labor to the bride's parents, but in marrying they leave the parental families and found a new independent corporation. The family corporation formed by a marriage, like a legal partnership, is dissolved by the death of either partner (or by divorce), and its property is divided. Surviving members or divorced partners—even a widow or widower with no unmarried children—form a new corporation, however fragmentary, that is economically self-reliant and legally independent. Only remarriage or adoption can incorporate survivors of a dissolved family into a new one. Once married, a Subanun can never return to his or her natal household. However, the contractual obligations between parental families

that sponsored the marriage is strong and enduring: if one spouse dies, his or her household is legally obligated to supply another spouse if they can.

Marriage between close kin, even first cousins, is common. Given the independence of every family and the absence of larger corporate groupings, marriage of close kin entails few problems; every marriage is by its nature an "out-marriage." Each household lives in a separate clearing, as far from others as the arrangement of fields permits. Though 3 to 12 neighboring households comprise a dispersed "settlement," these alignments are only temporary. Any family is the center of a unique cluster of neighbors and kinsmen, bound first to the two families that sponsored its formation and later to the families with which it is contractually linked through marriage sponsorship. Ethnographer Charles Frake makes this observation:

Despite [the] network of formal and informal social ties among families, there have emerged no large, stable, discrete sociopolitical units. . . . The Subanun family [is] . . . largely a "sovereign nation." But . . . the Subanun family is not a descent group. Its corporate unity endures only as long as does the marriage tie of its founders. The continuity of Subanun society must be sought in the continuous process of corporate group formation and dissolution rather than in the permanency of the groups themselves. (1960:63)

24. THE CLASSIFICATION OF RELATIVES

Alternative Theories of Kinship Terminology

How kinds of relatives are classified is an old anthropological preoccupation. As we noted, the same formal schemes for classifying relatives turn up in widely separated parts of the world, among peoples whose languages are unrelated and who have no historical contact. Moreover, there are visible correlations between the ways in which relatives are classified and the organization of descent groups and systems of marriage.

CASE

26

Iban Social Organization

The Iban of Borneo, whose expansionist shifting cultivation of dry rice we examined in Case 6, have a social organization apparently highly adaptive to their mode of life and ecosystem. Yet they, like many Southeast Asians, organize corporate groups without reference to unilineal descent, though in a manner very different from the Subanun.

The Iban live in sizable communities, each one politically independent and occupying a defined territory. These communities include from as few as 30 to as many as 350 people. They are striking in that the inhabitants reside together in a single longhouse. The families in a longhouse are mainly cognatically related, but they do not comprise a corporate group. Their unity is expressed in ritual observances.

Each of the component families, or *bilek* is strongly corporate. A *bilek* is a separate economic unit, cultivating rice and other crops and owning heirloom property. It is also a separate ritual unit, performing its own rites and having a separate set of magical charms and ritual prohibitions. Each *bilek* lives in an apartment in the longhouse.

A *bilek* typically contains three generations: a pair of grandparents, a son or daughter and the spouse, and grandchildren. The *bilek* continues (unlike the Subanun family) as a corporation across generations. The device whereby this is accomplished is simple: at least one son or daughter in each generation stays put, brings in a spouse, and perpetuates the corporation. The other children characteristically marry into other households. Fission of a *bilek* can occur when two of the children marry and bring their spouses in; one of the married children can claim his or her (equal) share in the family estate and move the new nuclear family out to form a new corporation.

A newly built Iban longhouse surrounded by rice fields.

Kinship terminologies are ways of classifying "kinds of people" that are socially relevant in a person's life; and that depends on how a society is organized into groups, and how these groups are connected to one another.

Consider the hypothetical Smiths and Joneses. The Elm Street Smiths, from the

A marrying couple face a choice of whether to live with the bride's or groom's *bilek* group. That choice determines which corporation their children will belong to (Freeman 1960:67). Sons and daughters, in fact, stay in the family home at marriage with approximately equal frequency. They must marry an outsider, since the *bilek* is exogamous. However, any first cousins or other more distant relatives who are in a different *bilek* are allowed to marry. Marriage is very much a matter of personal choice, and after the early years of marriage divorce is rare.

Larger action groups are predominantly recruited from within the longhouse, according to the context of the moment. As among the Subanun, this recruitment is usually along kindred lines. The personal kindred is an important social category for the Iban, including a bilaterally expanding range of kin. In theory, it includes all an individual's known blood relatives; in practice, only fairly close kin are likely to be socially relevant. Kindreds, of course, overlap; they are not corporate groups. When life cycle rites, feuds, or other intermittent events place a particular person on center stage, his or her kindred rally to provide the supporting cast (Freeman 1955, 1958, 1960).

An Iban family: Members of a *bilek* eat their mid-day meal.

standpoint of outsiders, comprise a solidary corporation. Members of the lineage have collective accountability and substitutability (so that if one man commits a misdeed, the others are held responsible). Younger brothers step into the shoes of older brothers. (In many systems of this type, a younger brother will take his older brother's widow as wife; recall Nuer "ghost marriage," Case 18.) How might this be expressed in the classification of relatives?

One very common pattern is for a person's father's brothers to be classed together with father, and a person's mother's sisters to be classed together with mother. In the case of the Smiths and Joneses, if "ego" (the person doing the classifying) is an Elm Street Smith, his or her father and father's brothers are Elm Street Smiths as well. In fact all Elm Street Smiths of father's generation are lumped together terminologically as "fathers." Ego's mother may be a Spring Street Brown, and all the Brown women or mother's generation are classed as "mothers."

There have been two sharply contrasting positions in the study of modes of classifying relatives. One major position, most strongly articulated by the Americans Lounsbury and Scheffler, is that kinship terminologies are always genealogically structured. The term by which father is classed may be extended to include other male relatives of the father's generation (and perhaps to distant relatives whose actual relationship is unknown, but who fall in a socially equivalent relation to father on the basis of, say, clan membership). This reflects patterns of social equivalence, substitutability, or potential succession that render these relatives "fatherlike" in some important respect. Ego's articulation to the system of classification, or point of reference, is always his or her own mother and father; hence, the system is always ultimately genealogical even if, in classing distant relatives, group membership or age may take precedence over actual genealogical connection. Lounsbury and Scheffler have explored, using formal rules for expressing equivalences between kinship positions, alternative modes of classifying kin, such as the highly complex "Crow" type terminology of the Trobrianders (Lounsbury 1965).

A counter-position in the study of kinship (emanating mainly from England, and represented most notably by Needham and Leach) is that our own way of classing relatives seriously distorts our understanding of a system, such as that of Smiths and Joneses or Trobrianders, based on unilineal descent. Because some systems found in Europe and North America are bilateral, have no descent groups, and distinguish *lineal* relatives from *collateral* ones (that is, siblings from cousins, parents from aunts and uncles), we may think of kinship in terms of chains of genealogical connection between individuals. Peoples whose social world is organized in terms of descent corporations do not classify individuals on the basis of their genealogical connection to ego, but on the basis of their membership in broad social categories and groups defined by descent and marriage. A term may mean, say, "man of father's clan" or "marriageable woman"; but because of our genealogical bias, we are misled into trying to define it in genealogical terms, as "father" or as "mother's brother's daughter."

For our purposes, it is unnecessary either to go into the very complicated technical issues involved, or to introduce a typology of ways of classifying kin. The interested reader should turn to an introductory book on kinship such as Keesing (1975). (See also Kipp 1984 for a reconciliation of the two viewpoints here discussed.) It will be worth pausing to ask why so much anthropological attention has been paid to kinship terminology over more than a century of comparative study.

Why Study Kinship Terms?

The long-standing motivation behind studies of kinship terminologies has been that if we could find out how they map the social universe of a people, we could acquire a key to comparative analysis. Although the search for systematic correspondences between modes of descent or forms of marriage and ways of classing kin has gone on for many decades, there are increasing reasons to think that the correspondences are not as neat as had been expected (Keesing 1975). More recently, the formal symmetry and algebraic possibilities of kinship terminologies have made them a focal concern in ethnographic semantics (see Read et al. 1984). Attempts to use componential analysis in semantics have mainly dealt with kinship terms (recall the attempt in § 6 to define "chair," "stool," and "bench" in terms of the intersection of distinctive features). When componential analysis is used to define the meaning of a kinship term, such criteria as generation, sex, or relative age are used as distinctive features.

Unfortunately, analyzing kinship terms in only their genealogical senses, pulled out of social contexts, affords the analyst a spurious kind of freedom (see Keesing 1972b). It too easily becomes a kind of algebraic game, where solutions tell us very little either about the meanings of the terms to those who use them (in metaphorical and nongenealogical senses as well as genealogical ones) or about how words convey meanings.

Our primary goal has been to see how kinship and descent intertwine to form the fabric of social order in societies. It is worth pausing briefly to assess the importance of kinship and descent in shaping social relations.

25. KINSHIP AND SOCIAL RELATIONS

An earlier generation of ethnographers usually recorded the formal outlines of a society's "kinship system"—the kin terms, the residence rule, the rule of descent, the number and names of clans, rules of ex-

ogamy and forms of marriage, special rules of kinship avoidance, and such matters. When a finer grained detail began to be recorded, these ideal blueprints turned out to correspond only quite loosely to actual patterns of social relations. Local groups turned out not to be made up exclusively of lineal descendants, as rules of thumb would have it; "wrong marriages" were common, and postmarital residence often "violated" the "rule"; and kin competed and quarreled as the ideology insisted they should not. What to do about this emerging gulf between what people actually do in a society and the idealized version of their kinship system they presented to the ethnographer has been a major theme of modern social anthropology.

Kinship Ideologies and Political Processes

To some anthropologists, it seems best to focus on individual goals and strategies and the way coalitions are formed to advance collective ends and manipulate power, wealth, and status. The "rules" then show up as ideologies that are manipulated to advance political goals. When they are pulled out of these contexts and presented in codified form to the ethnographer they not only give too neat a picture of "the system" (and hence create the illusion of a gulf between the rules and actual behavior), but they also create a false picture of how rules operate: the rules are seen as moral dictates constraining behavior. Such critics as Leach (1961) and Barth (1966a) would argue that statements of the supposed "rules" in real social contexts are political acts; the ideologies are by-products and instruments of the processes of economics and politics. Thus a Kwaio man (Case 24) may argue eloquently in the course of litigation that agnates have primary rights in a custody case, citing the

CASE

27

Kwaio "Descent Groups" and Social Relations

The Kwaio "descent system" is comprehensible only if we see how the role a person is enacting in a particular situation determines the part he or she will play, and how this may not neatly correspond with "membership" in a descent group. Consider the following:

One of my subjects is an agnate in descent group A and he is priest for the A's though he has not lived with them since infancy. He grew up and has always lived with his mother's kin, from descent group B. In the course of a mortuary feast our man was giving, a leader from group A approached from the left and presented him with a major valuable, which he accepted with his left hand. At the same moment, a man from B approached from the right and presented another valuable to him—which he accepted simultaneously with his right hand. Our subject was acting at the same moment as both an A and a B—and no one was confused.

This is, of course, the limiting case where dual membership is expressed simultaneously. Yet in the course of a feast or marriage, an individual often acts as a member not only of more than one descent group, but of half a dozen other [descent categories]. Status in each case is clearly labeled, according to context. (Keesing 1968b:83)

Confusion and conflict of interest are avoided because ego's status is defined by context. One day ego behaves as a member of [group] A, another day he may behave as a member of B, C, or D. Descent-group membership does not, at most times, demand some exclusive allegiance, such as residence. It merely includes ego in a social category from which groups are crystallized in certain defined contexts. What is required to make such a system work is a situational sorting out, or clear labeling, of statuses, and a set of principles for making decisions in those situations where two

In Kwaio ritual roles are tightly structured by descent: Women of a descent group hold an "ancestral skull"—a sprouting coconut—in a rite renewing the group's skull repository *(previous page, left)*; and men and boys of the group perform an accompanying sacred dance *(previous page, right)*; however, in everday social relations and work the parts people play depend as much on friendship and ties between neighbors as on descent and kinship *(left)*.

Continued

Case 27 continued

---

allegiances conflict or where presence is required in two different places at once. (Keesing 1968b:83)

I have analyzed the action groups that crystallize in different settings—in feast-giving, in fighting, in ritual, and so on—as the enactment of different *roles*. A person acts as feast-giver one day, as member of fighting party the next. In both situations, which descent corporation he belongs to may partly account for his taking part, and for what he does with whom. Yet the group that joins together to fight will predictably only partly overlap with the group that sponsored the feast; and neither will correspond neatly to the group that joins together in ritual, which most nearly corresponds to the Kwaio "descent group":

The category of persons whose primary descent affiliation is to a particular named territory (for example, "Kwangafi"), because they are agnatically descended from its founder, is relatively clear. But this category does not define a "localized descent group," since adult women are mainly scattered in their husbands' territories and some male members live in territories other than Kwangafi. "The Kwangafi people," in this neat sense of a descent category, are crystal-

lized into a social group only in a few contexts, mainly involving ritual; they comprise a dispersed ritual community, not a local group. On the other hand, in different contexts "the Kwangafi people" refers to the people domiciled in Kwangafi and their families; that is, it includes in-marrying wives not related to Kwangafi and excludes Kwangafi women living elsewhere. "The Kwangafi people" may refer also to a much wider category of all those people *cognatically* descended from the founders of Kwangafi who sacrifice to Kwangafi ancestors. In still other contexts, "the Kwangafi people" may refer to an action group temporarily crystallized around the men of Kwangafi for some purpose such as feuding or feasting; these may include a broad scattering of cognates, affines, neighbors, and political allies. . . .

The component elements that contribute to being a "Kwangafi person" in different contexts (descent category membership, domicile, actual residence, sex, neighborhood cluster membership, etc.) can be analytically untangled. Distinguishing the different contexts where descent status is relevant and analyzing the roles involved enables us to make sense of much of the apparent flux of social interaction. One can anticipate fairly accurately, as Kwaio can, what group or category will comprise "the Kwangafi people" in a particular setting or event. (Keesing 1972b:23)

ideology of agnatic descent—and everyone understands that he is doing so because he and his allies are the child's agnates. The next day he may insist on receiving a share of sexual compensation for his sister's errant daughter—and may with equal vehemence cite the ideology of cognatic kinship.

Kinship Ideologies and Implicit Rules

But there is another equally revealing approach to the apparent gulf between ideal rules and ideologies and what people actually do. The Kwaio, like other tribal peoples, do not expect one another to follow the "ideal" rules. (See Case 27.) But they do manage to understand, interpret, and even anticipate such acts as I have described. If they can do so, there must be some more subtle code they share. A major theme in recent anthropology has been to probe beneath rules of thumb and ideal rules and categories to discover and describe as best as possible this shared knowledge that makes communication and ordered social relations possible.

My efforts to describe such shared knowledge among the Kwaio vividly illustrate how "lineages" and other kin groupings have been given a false concreteness. Many of the things people do, places they go, and action groups they temporarily join have little or nothing to do with their membership in descent corporations. Thus, when we study social organization we must look more carefully than we usually have at the groups that form temporarily to make gardens together, hunt together, fetch water from the stream, or sit and gossip; and hence must give more adequate emphasis to the role of friendship and personal choice, as well as kinship or descent status, in the fabric of everyday social life (see Holy 1976).

This usefully serves as a warning against a danger in the neo-Marxist theoretical framework outlined in the last chapter, as well as the more traditional "structural-functional" approaches that have dominated social anthropology. One can too easily give a lineage or clan—or even a household—a spurious concreteness in talking about systems of production. What is a conceptual category in the minds of a people, in terms of which they create groups in particular contexts to do work together, can be "reified" into the fundamental unit of production. Much of the Marxist literature on African lineages suffers from this false concreteness, a matter to which Fortes has referred:

> When Terray . . . instances "the lineage mode of production" in which "the lineage and the segment . . . are simultaneously units of production, consumption, political organization, and religion," it is evident that he has not caught up with modern studies. (1978:17)

The anthropologist analyzing social relations of production and distribution must pay careful attention to who is doing what with whom, as well as to the conceptual categories in terms of which they talk about what they are doing. (Such a stress on real people engaging the world in work, as opposed to sweeping categories and classes, will inevitably be dismissed by the most ideologically committed as "empiricism." It is true that events in the world do not speak for themselves as facts, and that we must explain them in terms of a theory. But theory, if it is not ultimately grounded in real humans and real events, refers only to an imaginary world in which abstractions do battle with one another.)

We have illuminated further some facets of the organization of societies such as the Trobriands. But other facets—the constitution of domestic groups, the alliances between descent corporations created through marriage, and the organization of communities—still remain to be explored.

SUMMARY

A distinction is made between cultural categories, as classificatory entities, and social groups, consisting of people who interact and carry out activities in an organized fashion. Groups may be based on kinship rules which define who should belong to them and how they should cooperate. Kinship itself may be complex, based either on putative physical links through procreation or through other principles, such as coresidence or transactions in wealth. Ties of filiation between persons can become the basis for the formation of personal kindreds or of corporate groups founded on principles of descent, either patrilineal, matrilineal, or cognatic. Descent may entitle a person to membership in such a group, but not determine it. Groups based on processes of affiliation other than descent may use a rhetoric of shared descent as the means of maintaining their solidarity. In social life there has to be flexibility, enabling people to move around and reaffiliate if they are short of resources or have quarrels.

Patrilineal descent groups are more commonly found than matrilineal ones. Matriliny does not necessarily entail power or high status for women, although it may do so. Complex rules and practices of residence may emerge in matrilineal systems (example: the Trobriands). Sometimes both patrilineal and matrilineal descent groups are found in the same society, with different functions such as in regard to immovable versus movable property (example: the Yakö). With cognatic descent, an individual has a choice of which group to affiliate with and may maintain an interest in more than one (example: the Kwaio). Societies may be based not on descent groups but on kindreds and family groups with rules of recruitment over the generations (example: the Iban).

SUGGESTIONS FOR FURTHER READING

SECTIONS 21–25

Bohannan, P. J., and J. Middleton, eds. 1968. *Kinship and Social Organization.* Garden City, N.Y.: Natural History Press.

Chun, A., J. Clammer, P. Ebrey, D. Faure, S. Feuchtwang, Y. K. Huang, P. S. Sangren, and M. Yang. 1996. The Lineage-Village Complex in Southeastern China: A Long Footnote in the Anthropology of Kinship. *Current Anthropology* 37(3): 429–440.

Eggan, F. 1968. Kinship: An Introduction. *International Encyclopedia of the Social Sciences* 8: 390–401. New York: The Macmillan Company.

Fox, R. 1967. *Kinship and Marriage.* Baltimore: Penguin Books, Inc.

Goody, J. R. 1968. Kinship: Descent Groups. *International Encyclopedia of the Social Sciences* 8: 401–408.

———, ed. 1971. *Kinship: Selected Readings.* Baltimore: Penguin Books, Inc.

Graburn, N. H. H. 1971. *Readings in Kinship and Social Structure.* New York: Harper & Row, Publishers.

Pasternak, B. 1976. *Introduction to Kinship and Social Organization.* Englewood Cliffs, N.J.: Prentice-Hall, Inc.

Sahlins, M. 1968. *Tribesmen.* Englewood Cliffs, N.J.: Prentice-Hall, Inc.

Scheffler, H. W. 1977. Kinship, Descent, and Alliance. In J. J. Honigmann, ed., *Handbook of Social and Cultural Anthropology.* Skokie, Ill.: Rand McNally & Company.

Schneider, D. 1968. *American Kinship: A Cultural Account.* Englewood Cliffs, N.J.: Prentice-Hall, Inc.

————, and K. Gough, eds. 1961. *Matrilineal Kinship.* Berkeley: University of California Press.

Schusky, E. L. 1974. *Variation in Kinship.* New York: Holt, Rinehart and Winston.

Marriage, Family, and Community

We have sorted out some of the organizational complexities of societies where kinship plays a dominant role. But the organization of domestic groups, which are the primary units of both production and consumption in many societies, has not yet been explored. And the processes of marriage through which families are formed, and in which children are born and raised, remain to be examined.

In fact it might seem that marriage and family organization would be more logical starting places for understanding kinship structures than corporations based on descent. But as we will see, marriage in many societies entails contracts or alliances between corporate descent groups; and domestic groups are often formed along lines of descent. So the path we have followed is, for the societies we are looking at, more direct than it might seem.

Finally, the organization of *communities*, which may be larger than descent groups and formed in complex ways, remains to be examined. We have fleetingly encountered Trobriand hamlets and villages, which take precedence over subclans in many contexts of community work, collective enterprise in quest of prestige, and

conflict or warfare. In looking at Trobriand communities, and others, we will further add to our analytical powers. We need first to turn to marriage, the process through which domestic groups are formed, descent groups are interlinked, and the reproduction of society, biologically and socially, is achieved.

26. MARRIAGE IN COMPARATIVE PERSPECTIVE

Does marriage occur in all societies? Anthropologists trying to compare customs are always caught in a dilemma: how far to stretch the meaning of a term like *marriage* so that it covers many different customs without losing its shape altogether. Some anthropologists, notably Gough (1959) and Goodenough (1970), have sought to find common denominators of marriage in different societies so as to distinguish essential features from inessential ones and to distinguish marriage from other forms of liaison that may be socially recognized. Others, such as Leach (1955, 1971, 1982), have stressed the diversity of marriage forms, the various elements involved—sexual,

Ndamba, a Melpa big man, inspects a prohibition sign placed in the track of a bridal party to protect against a supposed infraction of incest rules, Melpa, Papua New Guinea.

economic, legal, and political—and the futility of seeking a universal definition.

Defining "Marriage"

Gough (1959) sees marriage as being, in all times and places, a customary transaction that serves to establish the legitimacy of newborn children as acceptable members of society. Goodenough focuses on contractual rights over a woman's sexuality in trying to reach a universal definition:

> Marriage [is] a transaction and resulting contract in which a person (male or female, corporate or individual, in person or by proxy) establishes a continuing claim to the right of sexual access to a woman—this right having priority over rights of sexual access others currently have or may subsequently acquire in relation to her (except in a similar transaction) until the contract resulting from the transaction is terminated—and in which the woman involved is eligible to bear children. (1970:12–13)

Goodenough's definition is broad enough to fit Nuer "ghost marriage" (the second husband is acting by proxy) and woman-woman marriage. Perhaps it needs to be stretched further to accommodate marriages between male homosexuals (in modern Western societies and some parts of the Muslim Middle East, such as the Siwah Oasis of western Egypt described by Cline 1936), where the legal relationships are modeled on those of male-female marriage. It also needs a corrective to the sexist bias. As Di Leonardo (cited in Quinn 1977) points out, marriage gives a woman rights, sexual and otherwise, over her husband.

Goodenough's comparative analysis is useful not so much because with some expansion it gives us a stretchable and serviceable definition, but because it relates variable cultural and social conventions to fundamentals of human psychology and biology. Leach's and Goodenough's emphasis on variability is also important: we should not see marriage as serving a single function. Marriage is crucial because it ties bundles of rights and relationships into one or several packages (a society can have more than one form of marriage): it regulates sexual relations; it defines the social position of individuals and their memberships in groups; it establishes legal rights and interests; it creates domestic economic units; it relates individuals to kin groups other than their own; and it serves as an instrument of political relations between individuals and groups.

We can set out a series of general premises crucial to understanding marriage in many parts of the world:

1. Marriage is characteristically not a relationship between individuals, but a contract between groups (often, between corporations). The relationship contractually established in the marriage may endure despite the death of one partner (or even of both).
2. Marriage entails a *transfer* or *flow of rights*. The exact set of rights passing from the wife's group to the husband's (or vice versa)—work services, sexual rights, rights over children, property, and so on—varies widely. But if we ask what rights are transferred, and assume that something tangible or intangible passes back in the other direction to balance the transaction, we are well on our way to understanding many otherwise peculiar-looking marriage systems.
3. Though marriage involves rights to priority of sexual access by the husband, it need not, as we have seen, be exercised directly or exclusively. Hence woman-woman marriages, wife-lending, sanctioned love affairs, or alternative partners; in 63 percent of Murdock's (1949) sample societies, for example, sexual relations were permitted between a man and his wife's sister.
4. Marriage need not be monogamous. More than one relationship of marriage can in many societies be contracted at once, and sometimes one contract can involve two or more wives or two or more husbands.

To understand marriage comparatively, then, we need to view it as a legal relationship: to sort out carefully who the parties are, what rights and what valuables are transferred, to whom these are distributed and assigned, and what interests of individuals and groups are advanced by such contractual arrangements.

27. MARRIAGE: CONTRACTS AND TRANSACTIONS

We can usefully begin by looking at contracts between kin groups whereby rights are transferred to the groom's group in exchange for symbolically important valuables: systems of **bridewealth.**

Bridewealth and the Transfer of Rights

Bridewealth is most common among horticulturalists-agriculturalists and pas-

Bridewealth: New Guinea Highlanders (Chimbu) of the groom's subclan present goldlip pearl shells to the bride's kin.

toralists. Among cattle-herders such as the Karimojong (Case 8) or the Nuer of the Sudan, the transfer of cattle in marriage assumes a symbolically and politically central place in the affairs of descent groups. In New Guinea, pigs play the roles fulfilled by cattle in Africa. Bridewealth valuables are striking in their variety, as physical objects marked by scarcity and invested with symbolic prestige value. Brass gongs, ivory tusks, dogs' teeth, fossilized clam-shell rings, strung shell beads, rolls of bird-feather strips, and a host of other valuables have been recorded.

Most commonly, bridewealth occurs in patrilineal descent systems. Here the rights that are transferred to the husband's group centrally include rights over a woman's fertility. If the parties to the marriage "contract" are patrilineages, then what the husband's lineage is acquiring is not simply a woman's sexuality and labor, but the children who will be its future members. Bridewealth is characteristically seen by those who practice it as compensation to her kin group for the loss of her work services and presence, as well as her fertility. Where bridewealth occurs in matrilineal descent systems, this is usually where a rule of postmarital residence takes a woman—and her work services—away from her parents and her matrilineage. Bridewealth is common in Southeast Asian societies organized on cognatic lines, but is likely to be a transaction primarily between families which compensates the bride's kin for the loss of her work and ritualizes the creation of a new domestic corporation (as among the Subanun, Case 25).

The prestige valuables exchanged in bridewealth, however diverse physically, usually have several characteristics in common:

1. They are sufficiently scarce (often coming from external sources) that they cannot easily be obtained by individual effort.

2. Their circulation is controlled by senior men, so that in order to marry, young

men must subordinate themselves, and become obligated, to their elders (and provide labor, political support, bear arms, etc., on their behalf).

3. Through control over these prestige valuables as the means to the circulation of women in marriage, senior men command (in addition to control over young men) the allocation of women's labor power and women's fertility, their capacity as reproducers of humans.

Do senior men use control of prestige valuables and marital politics to accumulate multiple wives themselves at the expense of young men (and hence extract the labor power and fertility of young wives directly)? Or do they assign young women as marriage partners of young men, through whose resulting obligation they extract the labor power of both? Both mechanisms are common, often occurring in the same society. The former pattern is particularly dominant in sub-Saharan Africa, the latter in Melanesia.

Why are bridewealth systems characteristic of cultivators and pastoralists, but not of hunter-gatherers or more complex, class-stratified chiefdoms or states? The nature of labor and surplus production are crucial elements. The production of surpluses men can use to sustain prestige and political operations puts a premium on labor power of young men and women, and on physical reproduction of the labor force. But in societies of this middle-range, surplus production and the embodiments of labor are not accumulated, built up in physical edifices, waterworks, or the like. Among pastoralists, herds—the products of labor—follow cycles of the reproduction of the labor force itself. Recall Lefébure's observations quoted in § 14:

[A man] must be able to maintain the size of his herd and to beget heirs. The controlled

Kwaio bridewealth: Relatives of the groom assess the adequacy of strung shell valuables hung up at a wedding feast.

circulation of women through marriage . . . implies the circulation of the herd through different matrimonial payments [to obtain wives for his sons]. . . . Herd size is a function of the intensity of the technico-economic, matrimonial, political, and symbolic practices designed to ensure the group's reproduction. (1979:3)

For cultivators, surplus produce may be used to achieve male prestige ends, directly through feasting distributions or indirectly through pig herds (as among the Tsembaga Maring). Both women's labor power and male supporters sustain these conversions of surplus into political power and prestige by senior men.

Dowry, which might appear on paper to be the reverse of bridewealth, in fact is characteristic of societies with different economic systems. Such systems, once common among European peasants and widespread in Asia, are characteristic of economies based on fixed-plot agriculture and feudal economic relations. Dowry is, most simply, a payoff to an out-marrying wife of her rights over the family estate. However, dowry provides a mechanism for political alliances between families. As Goody and Tambiah (1973) indicate, dowry is characteristically most important among higher strata of a society, where status and property are centrally at stake. The bride brings into the conjugal relationship her share of her family's estate; the husband brings corresponding wealth, inheritance chances, or high social status (or all three) as his contribution to the newly established family.

Goody and Tambiah note that there is a form of marriage transaction that looks on the surface more like bridewealth but beneath the surface resembles dowry in some respects. What Goody (1973) calls "indirect dowry" entails a contribution by the groom or his close kin to the bride (either directly or through her father). The difference between this and bridewealth is that whereas bridewealth is a payment to a set of men who control rights over a woman by another group of men to whom these rights are transferred, indirect dowry goes to a woman, for her use. (See also Upadhya 1990).

Affinal Relations

A marriage contract, once concluded, does not then simply produce a new domestic group. The corporations or alignments of kin—related as affines—that contracted the relationship continue to have important interests in and through the marriage.

In Case 28, the nature, centrality, and complexity of the affinal relationships between kin groups are vividly illustrated by

the Trobriand system we have already encountered.

Marriage as a Process

Our whole time perspective on marriage is likely to mislead us when we look at affinal rights and relationships in non-Western societies, where marriage is a long, drawn-out process that involves several transactions or stages. The relationships established in the marriage transaction may continue long after the death of one or both parties. Thus among the Kwaio of the Solomon Islands (Case 24), marriage entails an opening payment; then a major feast, which may take place several months later, at which bridewealth is paid; and finally a third transaction where the bride's mother presents her with a married woman's pubic apron. Only then is the marriage physically consummated. And in some of these societies, marriage may become legally binding only after the first child has been conceived or born.

The contract between husband's lineage and wife's lineage may endure even though either he or she dies. If he dies, rights over her sexuality and future children may remain with his lineage, so that the dead husband's brother or some other close kinsman replaces him as husband. This is known as the **levirate.** This is what happens in Nuer "ghost-marriage," except that the dead first husband is still classed as father of the children. If the wife dies, her lineage may be contractually obligated to provide a replacement—her sister, her brother's daughter, or some other close relative. This is known as the **sororate.**

Even where a widow marries a man not in her first husband's lineage, her dead husband's lineage may have some rights and interests. Among the Kwaio, for instance, part of the bridewealth paid for a widow goes to her first husband's relatives. Even

CASE

28

Affinal Relations in the Trobriands

We have glimpsed the system of harvest presentations (Malinowski's *urigubu*) whereby a Trobriand household devotes a large share of its productive energies to exchange gardens. from the time an exchange garden is prepared, the yams in it (growing from cuttings provided by the eventual recipient) belong to the household to which it is presented. The cultivators, husband and wife, are providing their labor.

Most often, a household is paired with the husband's sister's household. Here we can usefully recapitulate the diagram, and example, of Figure 8.2, and build on it (see Figure 10.1).

George will make exchange gardens (in which his wife Sally will work with him) for his sister Mary and her husband Sam. In some contexts, the yams will be spoken of as Mary's; in other contexts, they will be Sam's. The yams go into Sam's yam house, a visible expression of George's generous fulfillment of his obligations. George and Sally also, as we saw in Case 15, present baskets of yams to the household of George's other sisters and other closely related members of his subclan (Figure 10.2).

At a later stage in the cycle, when Sam and Mary's children are grown and have married,

their son Ed and his wife Janet will make harvest presentations to Ed's parents (Figure 10.3).

Powell's Trobriand data from the 1950s indicate that a subclan such as George and Mary's makes collective decisions assigning responsibilities to make exchange gardens to its male members. That is, George will be assigned the responsibility to produce yams for his sister Mary and her husband Sam. George's brothers or matrilineal male cousins will be assigned the obligation to grow exchange gardens for Pam, Wilma, Elizabeth, and Laura and their husbands. Collectively, the *dala* must meet exchange responsibilities to the female members whose fertility will reproduce its membership in the next generation, and do so in public demonstrations of productivity and largesse.

Through Malinowski's writings, the logic of these harvest presentations seemed relatively clear. The adult men lived on the subclan corporation's property; the women through whom descent was traced never lived there. They lived with their fathers before marriage, with their husbands after marriage. Like dowry, these harvest presentations seemed to be a payoff *to* the outmarrying women of the corporation in produce

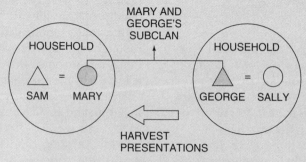

Figure 10.1   Mary's and George's households.

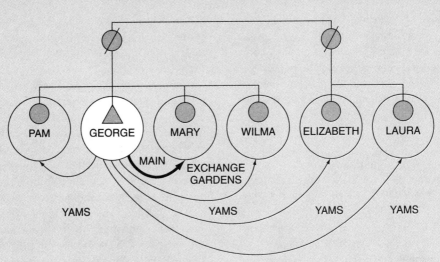

Figure 10.2   George's yam distributions.

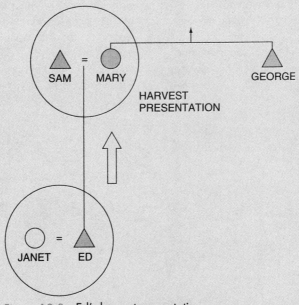

Figure 10.3   Ed's harvest presentation.

Continued

from the land of their *dala*. This interpretation now seems less satisfying. Partly, this is because of the way the yam presentation is in many contexts portrayed as one between male affines (George to Sam) rather than brother to sister (George to Mary). But more importantly, it comes from new evidence on flexible patterns of residence:

Most of the adult males who garden for [women of the subclan] do not reside in their subclan's villages, so that the *urigubu* they provide is not the produce of the land of their, and their sister's, own subclans. (Powell 1969b:581)

But with this evidence has come a realization that subclans are linked together in complex webs of affinal alliance. A marriage is a political act, establishing a formal bond and contractual relationship between corporate subclans that lasts as long as the marriage; and the harvest presentation annually reaffirms it.

Symbolically, the harvest presentations underline both the unity of men of the corporation in meeting their obligations to affines and the unity of male and female corporation members. Moreover, there is an element of subordination implied in these presentations. Symbolically, they imply the dominance of the husband's subclan—

hence, as we will see in Chapter 11, their easy conversion into a more formal tribute to the high-ranking subclan of the husband in a politically strategic marriage.

We have seen in Case 15 how the large-scale and dramatic presentations of yams in the annual presentation are countered by periodic reciprocation of valuables. But these represent only one element of the complex webs of transactions and obligations that bind together the subclans and individuals in a Trobriand marriage. To understand what happens when, and after, a Trobriand young woman marries, we have to think in terms of two different marriages and two affinal relations between subclans (Figure 10.4). Marriage 1 is her parents' marriage, which affinally links her mother's subclan, A, with her father's subclan, B. Then there is marriage 2, her own marriage to a man from subclan C, which affinally links her subclan A with subclan C. At the time of marriage 2, there are eight different presentations of food and valuables to and from the bride's kin. But curiously, most of them are between the C's and the B's; and the A's stay mainly on the sidelines. The B's again play a central part when the daughter becomes pregnant. It is the women of the B's

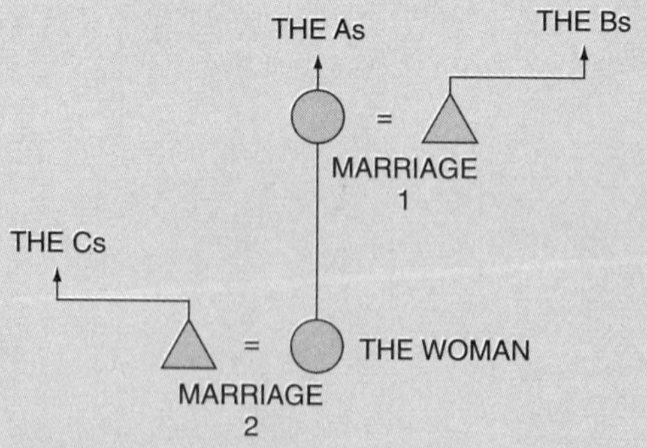

Figure 10.4 Marriage 1, marriage 2, and affinal relations.

who make a pregnancy cloak, the B's who perform magic, the B's who are directly involved in the events of birth of the children, though these children are A's. If marriage 1 is ended by the death of the husband, his wife's relatives, the A's, must prepare the body and conduct mourning rituals; the dead man's subclan members, the B's, must abstain from direct contact. If marriage 1 is ended by the wife's death, the A's must abstain and the affinally related B's take the lead. At the final mortuary rite, the dead spouse's subclan makes large presentations to the survivor's subclan, and the affinal relationship ends. Throughout the cycle of life and death, then, the bonds created through marriages tie households and subclans together in continuing strands of obligation, reciprocation, and mutual dependence.

Women's exchange in the Trobriands: This woman, with shaven head and body painted black, is the sister of the dead man. She directs exchanges and here holds center stage.

after both husband and wife have died, the complex of obligations established in the marriage may endure. Among the Kwaio, the kinsmen who helped to finance a man's bridewealth payment are entitled to a major share of bridewealth when, years later, the daughters of the marriage they helped to finance are married. This also happens in parts of the New Guinea highlands.

Marriage Choice, Preference, and Obligation

Looking at marriage as a contractual relationship between groups helps to free us from our preoccupation with husband and wife. It is useful to ask, in this light, how far marriage in these societies is based on free choice by the marrying pair and how far it is constrained by rules and senior kin.

In some societies, marriage is based on more or less free choice. But when substantial bridewealth is involved, a young man is likely not to have the means to finance his own marriage; hence his personal fancies are likely to be subordinated to the wishes of his elders in choosing a politically and economically appropriate mate. The advent of plantation systems and cash economies has given young men in many of these societies more power and leeway than they had in precolonial times. Leaders may try to recapture power by funneling wealth into inflated forms of exchange (A. J. Strathern 1979).

Choice of a marriage partner may be constrained not only by the politics of affinal alliance but by standards of appropriate or culturally valued marriage. Marriage to a woman in a particular kinship category may be strongly preferred, socially desirable, or a matter of legal right. Thus marriage with mother's brother's daughter or father's sister's daughter or some other relative or category of relative may be the ideal form, with

other arrangements permitted but less favored. Where this occurs, the preferred form may be a way of consolidating property or circumventing the rule of descent or inheritance. When people say it is "best" for a person to marry a particular kind of relative, we can understand them only by asking, "best for whom, when, and why?"

An important preferential form occurs among the Bedouin, other Middle Eastern Arabs, and some other Islamic peoples. This is called *parallel cousin marriage*, where a man has rights to marry his father's brother's daughter or a close paternal cousin classed as equivalent to her. The structural causes and consequences of this peculiar form have been much debated. Marriage with father's brother's daughter implies lineage **endogamy** (in-marriage). That is, given a system of patrilineal descent, a man is expected to marry a woman in his own group. In different places, this marriage system may consolidate group solidarity, may prevent the dispersion of property, and may be a mode of direct exchange of daughters between close male kin. (See also Bourdieu 1977 for a detailed discussion of how the custom may operate in practice.)

"Parallel cousins" are the children of two brothers (as in the Islamic case) or of two sisters. A much more common form of marriage preference is for marriage between "cross cousins," the children of a brother and sister (or second or third cousins classed as equivalent to them), which in such systems may prevent the dispersion of property and maintain close bonds between intermarrying groups. Another common form of preferential marriage is the exchange of sisters between two men of different lineages. We will shortly see how such modes of marriage exchange and strategic alliance are used in some societies in a much more systematic and total way to organize the relationships between groups.

Marriage Stability and Divorce

In some societies, marriage is very fragile, and divorces are common. In others, most marriages are permanent. Americans, for example, concerned about mounting divorce rates, are likely to seek in such variations some secret for reversing this trend. But since divorce in non-Western societies so often involves a contract between corporations, it is hard to understand through Western eyes.

An early line of explanation showed that when bridewealth is high (in terms of the economy in question), marriage tends to be stable; but when bridewealth is low, divorce is common. But that leads to what look like chicken-or-egg questions: Is marriage stable *because* of high bridewealth costs, or can a society afford to have high bridewealth only if it has a stable form of marriage?

One line of approach is to look at the rule of descent. Because the husband-wife and brother-sister ties are in more direct opposition with matrilineal descent, it has been argued that marital instability is a concomitant of corporate matrilineal descent groups. A strong patrilineal descent system, it was argued, would be associated with stable marriage. But as we have already seen, what is really important is the relative strength of the brother-sister and husband-wife ties. When a woman's tie to her natal (birth) group is severed or greatly weakened when she marries, divorce is uncommon. When her affiliation to her natal group remains strong, she may enter into several successive marriages. This still does not fully explain differential marriage stability in patrilineal descent systems, since it only pushes the question one step further back. But it correctly underlines the importance of looking carefully at the relative importance of those two overlapping groupings in a unilineal descent system—the lineage, composed of unilineally related brothers and sisters, and the local group, composed of unilineally related men (or more rarely women) and their spouses. Another important factor to consider is the bonds set up among affines, for example through exchange partnerships.

The causes of divorce in non-Western societies run the gamut from infertility and adultery to quarreling and failure to live up to expected roles (a lazy wife, an improvident husband). Divorce may be highly formalized, or it may be just a matter of one partner ordering the other out or giving public notice that the union is over; a Hopi wife merely puts her husband's things outside her house door. More interesting to the social anthropologist is what happens to bridewealth payments, if any, and what becomes of the contract between kin groups in terms of rights over children, kinship relations, and so on. Sometimes all or some bridewealth must be returned, though this may depend on the cause of divorce, whether the woman has borne children, and so on. This underlies the importance of tracing out how rights are distributed and transferred in a society. It is no accident that some of the best early amateur ethnographers were specialists in jurisprudence who set about to study patterns of the distribution of rights while their contemporary anthropologists were studying patterns of basket-weaving.

Plural Marriage

The most common form of plural marriage in tribal societies is **polygyny,** or marriage of a man to two or more women. In some areas, polygyny is the normal marriage pattern, as in most of Africa, although this does not in itself mean that most men are polygynous at a given time. We will see in discussing family structure that polygynous families pose some difficult structural problems. These have more to do with access to resources, relative power, and conflicts of interest in relation to children, than sexual jealousy. But strong solidarities sometimes develop between cowives as well.

Cowives may be from different lineages, or they may be sisters (in what is called **sororal polygyny**). The latter, at least as a preferred form, avoids some of the conflicts that can disrupt polygynous families. Polygyny may be practiced only by men of wealth or high rank or by most men in the society. It is commonly associated with an age asymmetry between partners, where second and subsequent wives are acquired by men who have gained power and prominence in middle life. In some societies polygyny is correlated with high rates of male mortality in war.

Conflicting interests of cowives in the children each bears by a single father are a major source of division, both within households and within patrilineages. The relations between half-siblings and the distribution of rights to each, in relation to their common father and different mothers, are always important in such systems. Lineage segmentation in a patrilineal system often takes place between half-brothers, with ties through the different mothers (and their lineages or ancestors) reflecting and symbolizing the contrasts between segments.

In a good many societies two or more men may share sexual access to one woman. These arrangements have been called **polyandry.** But it is a delicate problem of definition whether they involve plural marriage or simply the extension of sexual rights by the husband to other men (for various reasons in different societies). Only where fatherhood is assigned to two or more husbands, or is in some sense collective, does this actually involve plural marriage rather than extension of rights of

sexual access. A common form of such plural mating involves a group of brothers (what has been called **fraternal polyandry**). Polyandry is often associated with population imbalance, produced in some places by female infanticide. In the Himalayas, where such systems are concentrated, polyandry is also commonly associated with land shortage. It is one of several alternative marital strategies for adjusting the size of the labor force to the amount of land. Because a woman can only become pregnant, say, once every 2 years—no matter how many husbands she has—fraternal polyandry is an effective way for families to avoid expansion in size while ensuring their perpetuation (Berreman 1978). Polyandry is not characteristically associated with matrilineal descent or an unusually high status of women.

We have seen how, to understand marriage customs that seem strange or exotic at first glance, we must search out their underlying logic. Narrowing marriage down to an intensely personal relationship between husband and wife, on which the rearing of children and so much else depends, places a tremendous burden on people that human frailty very often cannot support. A return to broader contractual relationships would hardly be possible. But as the pressures of life rend more and more families apart, comparative social anthropology can give insights into the structural reasons for the strength and fragility of marriage.

28. INCEST, EXOGAMY, AND ALLIANCE

Incest and Its Prohibition

A central question in social anthropology for decades has been why human societies prohibit matings between siblings, and between parents and children, as incestuous. Why are there **incest taboos?**

There have been partial exceptions. Brother-sister and father-daughter matings were apparently common, and accepted, in Ptolemaic and Roman Egypt; and among the Azande of Africa, some aristocrats are permitted to keep their daughters and sisters as mistresses, though these women are not allowed to bear children. There are several cases of dynastic incest, where—as in ancient Egypt, Peru, and Hawaii—royal brothers and sisters, who approached the status of gods and goddesses, were mated to preserve the sacredness of a royal line.

Though some kind of incest taboo is universal, not even within the range of the immediate nuclear family are these taboos uniformly conceptualized or applied. Thus a Kachin tribesman of Burma cannot have sexual relations with his daughter or his sister because it is sinfully incestuous; but he cannot have sexual relations with his mother because that would be *adulterous*. And half-siblings with the same mother can apparently have sexual relations among the Lakher of Burma. Some societies define incest as a terrible sin that draws the most drastic punishment; others blithely declare that it is unthinkable or nonexistent.

Moreover, the extension of prohibited sex from the immediate family out to more distant relatives follows highly diverse genealogical paths. It may depend on degrees of cousinhood; but it may depend on lineality, so that sex relations within the lineage are defined as incestuous. Thus, though the core of prohibited relatives—parents and children—is almost always the same, the extension of the taboo to wider categories of relatives, and its conceptualization, vary greatly—so much so that Needham (1974) would deny that there is such a thing as *the* incest taboo.

Many theories, psychological, sociological, and evolutionary, have been advanced to explain the universality of the incest taboo. The theory that humans raised together since infancy have less sexual attraction for one another has received recent support in A. D. Wolf's (1966, 1970) Chinese evidence. In some parts of China, poor families transferred very young daughters into other families as wives-to-be—so that as they grew up with the young boys they were to marry, they worked for their mothers-in-law-to-be. Statistical evidence shows that these "little daughter-in-law" marriages were very unsatisfying to the husband and wife who had grown up together as if they were brother and sister. The quasi-sibling bonds between them seemingly blocked sexual attraction. (For review of this and other issues, see Roscoe 1994, Godelier 1990.)

The discovery of psychobiological obstacles to mating between parents and offspring and between siblings, in many mammalian species—including primate species—has cast the whole question of incest prohibition in humans in a new light (Bischof 1974). Presumably the adaptive value of such psychobiological obstacles lies in their consequence of preventing inbreeding and maximizing genetic variability.

But for humans, especially for mother and son and father and daughter, there are vulnerabilities to sexual attachment as well as obstacles—as witness Oedipal and Electra complexes. Cultural reinforcement of psychobiological barriers, and culturally fostered abhorrence of what otherwise might be temptations, have served to rule out incest in most times and places.

Is the threat of inbreeding sufficient explanation for the emotional strength incest prohibitions so often carry? Some theorists have argued that incest is not simply a biological threat, but a challenge to human sociality, hence to society itself.

Incest and Exogamy

In a characteristically brilliant early insight, Tylor suggested the social significance of rules preventing marriage within the group:

> Exogamy, enabling a growing tribe to keep itself compact by constant unions between its spreading clans, enables it to overmatch any number of small, intermarrying groups, isolated and helpless. Again and again in the world's history, savage tribes must have had plainly before their minds the simple practical alternative between marrying out and being killed out. (1889:267)

The evidence from hunting and gathering societies and from early human sites suggests that exchange of mates between bands was binding them into wider networks within which regional cultures could evolve, networks that could provide the basis for temporary crystallization of larger groups.

But Lévi-Strauss's (1949) argument that exogamy and the incest taboo developed as a single complex is speculative. Lévi-Strauss argued that protohumans, living in bands within which they mated and raised their young, were self-sufficient. There was no basis for union of the bands into a wider society. The crucial step toward culture, and hence wider social integration, would have been a renunciation by the males of a band of their own females, so as to obtain as mates the females of other bands. Lévi-Strauss viewed this as a great social gamble, which, once it paid off and established bonds of exchange between bands, was the essential step toward human society. The incest taboo became the rule symbolic of culture itself and the transition from natural to cultural order. It acquires a central fascination in human ideational and emotional worlds. Though he is speculating in linking the evolution of the incest taboo with the evolution of band exogamy, Lévi-Strauss is probably right in stressing (following Tylor and adding the insights of the great French sociologist Marcel Mauss) the symbolic and political importance of exogamy. (Another problem in his theory, however, is its attribution of agency only to males, not females.)

Symmetric Alliance Systems

On this theory of exogamy and exchange, Lévi-Strauss has built a widely influential theory of marriage. Where most anthropologists had focused on descent and kinship, Lévi-Strauss focused on the exchange of women by groups of men as the essential element in social structure. Such systems of exchange are solutions to the "primal" problem of how to get women back from other groups in place of one's own, who are prohibited as mates. Kinship and descent systems, in Lévi-Strauss's view, are primarily devices for defining and regulating the nature of this exchange.

Lévi-Strauss argues that we are misled by the fact that for each of us there is a seemingly endless number of potential mates. For us the gamble imposed by a rule of out-marriage is a statistical one—we renounce our sisters and brothers and have a wide choice of mates in return. This is not necessarily the simplest or safest solution to guarantee the return of a spouse, particularly in the tiny societies characteristic of most human history.

What is simpler and safer, in a society of tiny scale, is to specify a rule for the exchange of women with other groups. Lévi-Strauss calls systems that specify a mode of exchange among groups **elementary systems of kinship**. A society that simply specifies a range of prohibited spouses is a *complex system*. Although elementary systems are rare, they occur in some contemporary societies and, in vestigial form, in the ancient systems of China and India. They may once have been far more widespread, perhaps the characteristic forms of society until the last several thousand years. The simplest system for exchanging women is one where the whole tribe is divided into two exogamous descent categories (our side and their side, with one's side determined by either patrilineal or matrilineal descent). Such categories are called **moieties.** They represent the simplest form of what Lévi-Strauss calls **restricted exchange:** men of each side give their sisters to the other side and get wives in return. In subsequent development of what has come to be known as "alliance theory", such direct exchange of wives between groups—both the simple case of moieties and the much more complicated systems of Aboriginal Australia—has come to be called **symmetrical alliance.**

Australian kinship systems characteristically include quite complicated kinship terminologies, and a prescriptive marriage rule that specifies a single category from which a man must take a wife. Australian kinship is characteristically overlain by, and conceptualized in terms of, what are called **section systems.** In a four-section system, local groups are divided into two kinds. One consists of A's and B's, in alternate generations. (A man who is an A has a father who is a B and a grandfather who is an A.) The second kind consists of C's and D's, again in alternate generations. This scheme fits with (and simplifies) the marriage rule: typically the rule is that an A man must marry a C woman, and their children are B's. Note, then, that this amounts to a slightly more complicated form of direct (in Lévi-Strauss's terms, "restricted") exchange: the A + B's are exchanging women with the C + D's. More complex Australian systems, such as the famous Aranda

(= Arunta) system, have eight sections. Here there are four kinds of groups: A + B's, C + D's, E + F's, and G + H's. In a four-section system a man marries into the same kind of group as his father, but the alternate section (if you are an A man you marry a C woman; your father, a B, married a D woman); the closest permitted wife is a first cousin, a mother's brother's daughter or father's sister's daughter. In an eight-section system, one cannot marry into the same kind of group as one's father, and the closest permitted spouse is a second cousin.

Other systems, like the equally classic Murngin, are even more complicated and are fraught with internal inconsistency. Specialists on Australian kinship are far from agreed that Lévi-Strauss's ingenious interpretation of these as symmetrical alliance systems, and subsequent interpretations by such alliance theorists as Dumont, Maybury-Lewis, and Needham, fit the highly complex facts; or whether the kinship terminologies, marriage systems, and section labels are secondarily and inconsistently interconnected (Hiatt 1965, Keen 1994, Scheffler 1978).

Asymmetric Alliance

Lévi-Strauss interpreted the Australian section systems, however complicated, as still symmetrical or "direct": the group yours gives wives to gives wives back to your own. Lévi-Strauss showed how an alternative form is possible, under a rule that your group gives its women to one set of groups and receives women from a different set of groups. Such a system of **generalized exchange,** Lévi-Strauss argues, risks more in the gamble of renouncing one's own women—but the rewards in terms of social integration are greater. No pair of groups can achieve self-sufficiency and hence social isolation—and this interdependence of social units makes possible a "global integration."

The societies practicing indirect exchange, or as it is now more often called, **asymmetrical alliance,** lie mainly in Southeast Asia—northeast India, Burma, and a few parts of Indonesia. Ideologically they conceive their systems as "marrying in a circle," and phrase their marriage rule in terms of a kinship category, including mother's brother's daughter and many more distantly related women, from which a man must select a wife. Both the "circles" and "mother's brother's daughter marriage" have led to endless confusion and controversy among the scholars who, following Lévi-Strauss's lead, have pored over the meager evidence on these groups.

The picture that has emerged is of systems far more complex and dynamic than marrying in a circle would suggest. These societies are usually composed of many small localized patrilineages. It is these lineages that serve as "alliance groups" in the marriage system. These lineages may be ranked, and may be markedly unequal in status, as with the Kachin of Myanmar (Burma) (Leach 1954), or they may be unranked as among the Purum of northeast India. In either case, marriage becomes an instrument of political negotiation and status. A few marriages in each generation may serve to maintain the political status of lineages. Other marriages are less important and in some societies need not necessarily conform to the marriage rule.

From the standpoint of any single lineage, some women may be nonmarriageable because their lineages share common descent at a higher segmentary level. Some lineages may simply be too far away for marriage to be likely. But there remain two other crucial categories of lineages. There are lineages whose women have married men of one's own lineage (they are "wife-givers") and lineages to which one's own has given women (they are "wife-takers"). The basic marriage rule is that no other lineage can be both wife-giver and wife-taker. While actual patterns of marriage may deviate from the ideal model, most "wrong marriages" (at least those that are politically consequential) are treated as if they were right ones, and hence simply readjust the shifting network of alliances. Such an alliance system is usually prominently reflected in the cosmological scheme of a people. The contrast between wife-givers and wife-takers is mirrored in cosmological dualisms (right-left, sun-moon) and in ritual symbolism. This "global" and encompassing structure has led Needham (1962) to make a sharp distinction between such societies, which "prescribe" marriage into a particular category and others which merely specify "preferred" marriages. This distinction has led to great controversy and to fission between Needham and his students (Korn 1973, Needham 1974) and Lévi-Strauss (1969) himself.

The endless debates in the 1970s about "prescriptive marriage" systems have seemed to outsiders the height of sterile formalism in kinship studies. But beneath the technical argument has lain a central problem we encountered with the Smiths and Joneses, and glimpsed again in discussing kinship and social relations. There is a wide gulf between the ideal conceptual models and ideologies central in people's thought world and real people competing, choosing, and manipulating. Equally, there is sometimes a gulf between anthropological models and people's own ideal models. For a detailed study of both models and practices, see McKinnon (1991) on the Tanimbarese of Indonesia.

Real people live in a world of ecological pressures, economic and political strivings, individual variability, and the whims of life history. A way of life consists, in a sense, of accommodations and adjustments between a lived-in world and a thought-of world. Specialists who focus on the crystalline models of thought-of worlds see neat systems, where specialists who focus on the messy realities of actual choices see complexity and exceptions to supposed rules. This leads to some more general questions about comparative analysis of social structure.

Kinship Structures, Marriage Systems, and Comparative Analysis

Because systems of kinship and marriage lend themselves so neatly to formalisms and diagrams, they tempt us to base comparisons on formal resemblance—even though this leads us to array together societies whose scale and economies are radically different. Thus Goody warns that the organization of kin groups and marriage systems always has directly to do with property and status:

> Then clearly the systems of kinship and marriage must be vitally affected by the type of economy and by the type of stratification. Hence the grouping together of China with the Miwok [California Indians] as systems of generalized exchange, or with the Australian Aborigines as elementary structures, can only be of limited analytical use. (1973:31)

It is a virtue of neoevolutionary theory in anthropology that where comparisons are carefully drawn, they do array together societies with similar economic foundations, similar in scale and the nature of political integration. Once again, then, I must emphasize that my criticisms of "ladder" theories are not intended to dismiss the strengths of careful comparative work in this tradition. My quarrels are with glib classification—for example, placing all "hunters and gatherers" on the same rung

of the ladder, thereby putting sago collectors living in huge New Guinea villages alongside Malaysian forest dwellers, Inuits, and the Paleolithic hunters of the Dordogne—and with the illusion, too common in anthropology texts and popularizations, that the fundamental task is sorting and labeling, putting every society on the right rung or in the right pigeonhole. A comparative theory that arrays together societies similar in scale and economy so as to analyze how they are organized, and looks at actual developmental sequences, not imaginary ones put together from societies widely separate in time and space, is pursuing important questions in strategically useful ways.

29. DOMESTIC GROUPS

We have seen that in societies such as the Maring, Iban, and Trobriands, as in our own society, domestic groups—households—are the primary units in everyday production and consumption. The reason why these basic building blocks of society are most feasibly looked at after, and in terms of, systems of descent and marriage is that it is in terms of these systems that domestic groups are formed, organized, and linked together.

Much ink has been used up, in anthropology and comparative sociology, trying to define "the family." Is the **nuclear family**—a married couple and their children—universally important? Anthropologists have recorded forms of social organization where domestic groups are built on sister-brother ties rather than husband-wife ties. They have also studied communities, notably in the Caribbean, where the most common form of domestic group consists of a mother and her children, with the mother's sexual partners as at most transitory members of the group.

The Mother-Children Unit as Building Block

For comparative purposes, it is useful to distinguish the fundamental unit from which domestic groups are constructed as consisting of a mother and her children. (This analytical step is meaningful in evolutionary terms, since among nonhuman primates units of mother-plus-young are universally important and constitute the building blocks of larger social groups.) How males are attached to these component units, and in what capacities, varies widely from society to society. One man, the mother's mate, may act as father to the children and mother's sexual partner, as is conventional in Western societies; or the roles of providing nurturance, having authority over the children, and being sexual partner can each be assigned to different people. All of them but the sexual element can be provided by mother's brothers; or the functions may be divided between mate and brothers. Viewing mother and children as forming the nucleus of domestic groups enables us to fit into the comparative spectrum some of the arrangements that have grown out of women's liberation movements, particularly ones where sexual bonds between women, and legal and economic independence, have eliminated men from all or most of the roles they have historically played. (See Weston 1991.)

Domestic groups can then be seen as building on the family core—by adding father, by stringing conjugal families together by a rule of descent, by linking several mother-child units to a single husband-father, and so on.

Nuclear Family Households

Where nuclear families, consisting of a couple and their children, stand alone, they can best be understood in terms of the absence of factors that produce more complex forms. They occur where descent does not link unilineally related men together (father and two married sons, married sisters) into larger households and where plural marriage does not produce partial replication (as with three wives and their children, with a common father).

Thus nuclear families, by themselves, tend to occur where descent groups are absent or of lesser importance. In such societies, emphasizing bilateral kinship, nuclear families carry a very heavy "functional load"—as in our own society and among the Inuit. It is not by chance that our examples come from each end of the continuum of societal scale and complexity. It is in the middle that proliferations of more complex households are concentrated.

In bilaterally organized societies such as the Subanun (Case 25), the nuclear family serves as the center of a child's social universe—in it he or she is reared, is cared for, grows up, and learns the culture. Sexual relations and hence reproduction and the continuity of the society are focused in the family. It serves as an economc corporation, owning property and producing (or acquiring) and consuming food. Linkages between nuclear families produce the larger social and political units—bands, villages, and neighborhoods—of a society. However, in other societies nuclear families may be culturally distinguished and socially important, yet be components of larger local groupings that we can also call "households" at a higher level, as we will see shortly.

Complex Households Based on Multiple Marriage

Polygyny is the dominant mode of marriage in parts of Africa and some other areas. Organizationally the problems in such

Polygynous Households Among the Tallensi

The polygynous family among the Tallensi of Ghana (Cases 2 and 19) well illustrates both this mode of domestic organization and the way it can provide building blocks for larger domestic groupings. Most younger Tallensi men have only a single wife. Their domestic family, centered in a small courtyard and a mud-walled sleeping room, with kitchen and granary, may live in a single homestead, enclosed within mud walls. Sometimes the husband's mother would live with them, and as senior woman would have a separate courtyard and living quarters. More often, in this society where local groups are shallow patrilineages, the man with only one wife will occupy an "apartment" within the homestead of a father or an older brother.

By the time he is middle-aged, a man of substance will have acquired two or more wives. He probably will be living in his own homestead. Each wife will have her own little courtyard, her own sleeping room, her own kitchen. She and her children comprise a *dug*, or domestic household group. The senior wife (or the husband's mother) is a kind of leader in the women's realm, but for

each wife her apartment is the center of life, a place where she is in charge and where only her children and her husband have free access.

The male head of the homestead group controls the family granary, which supplies the component *dug* groups, and to which they all contribute the produce of their labor. The importance of the *dug* unit in Tallensi social structure is profound. The lines of lineage segmentation normally do not cut across *dug* units, but divide half-brothers with the same father, and their descendants.

Although relations between cowives are usually fairly amicable due to the separation of their spheres of influence, quarrels over shares of grain, rights of children, and other matters are common. The arrangement of apartments of cowives reflects their social relationships:

Wives who are clan sisters will usually have adjoining quarters; wives who get on badly will be put in well-separated rooms. . . . If a woman has a quarrelsome disposition . . . her quarters will be separated from those of the next-door wife by a low . . . wall. (Fortes 1949:58)

systems lie in cowives' conflicting economic and political interests, especially with regard to their children, their labor, and their allegiances to their kin. The most common solution is for each wife to have her own household. The husband plays a secondary role in each; and where, as is common, a wife is sexually taboo for a long period after childbirth, the isolation of households is increased. The households are seldom fully

independent economically, since a principal motive for polygyny is to create a joint work force and pool the productive efforts (as well as the reproductive efforts) of several women. Case 29 describes polygynous households among the Tallensi.

Each household group may be a partly separate unit in production and consumption. In everyday life those component households are in many respects separate social units. This does not solve all tensions in polygynous households, and the roles of cowives are always a delicate matter: there is, for example, a correlation between polygyny and witchcraft accusations. In some African societies, however, witchcraft accusations are mainly directed by men against women, and seemingly represent a kind of "structural paranoia" in which men fear both women's solidarity and women's sexuality.

When cowives share a single household and hearth, the possibilities of conflict between them—or conversely, solidarity between them—are increased. In some African societies a separate household is established for each cowife except when they are sisters (sororal polygyny)—on the assumption that sisters can manage, as they did in childhood, to coexist in the same household. A senior cowife, with her grown sons, may achieve greater independence over time (Besteman 1995).

As we saw in discussing bridewealth, polygynous households represent a control by established senior men over both the labor power and fertility of women, and over junior men. The structural rivalry between the children's generation and the parents', which dominates and eventually is replaced by it, is expressed in the special rules and rites focused on the first-born Tallensi son (Case 2).

The Tallensi example in Case 29 can serve to underline the dangers of viewing tribal societies as all having the same mode of production (whether we label it "primitive communist" or "lineage" or even "domestic"). A domestic group consisting of one man, a wife, and their children is no more, and no less, "domestic" than one consisting of a man and several cowives. Both may be represented in the same society, either at different stages in a man's career (as among the Tallensi) or among commoners and men of importance or rank (as in the Trobriands). Nonetheless, many societies (such as the Tsembaga Maring or the Kwaio of Melanesia) rule out polygynous marriage, so that a household's pool of labor and scale of production is quite limited in contrast to an African society where half a dozen cowives and their children labor to fill a senior man's granary. To analyze the dynamics of a society in terms of labor, surplus, and relations of production and distribution, we need to probe carefully into how it works and how the system is perpetuated. Broad labels classifying "modes of production" too easily can serve as substitutes for analysis.

Polyandry, where a woman has multiple husbands, cannot entail the creation of separate households of husbands and their children. A woman cohabiting with several men cannot produce a child by each of them at once. Cohusbands, then, share a single household—a household within which the men (who usually are brothers, in any case) pool their labor. Again, however, there are dangers of falling into simple typologies. Berreman (1978) has shown how polyandry among Himalayan Hindus is one of several strategies whereby families adjust their human resources to their land resources. In the same community, polyandrous families, nuclear families, polygynous families, and more complex arrangements may all occur.

Extended Families and Joint Families

Patrilineal or matrilineal descent, and a pattern of residence that aligns a core of lineally related men or women together in a local group, combine to produce many complex family structures. Extended or joint families are produced when, with patrilineal descent, a father and his married sons form a household or two brothers form a household. Often this is a second-order grouping, where the component nuclear families act separately for some purposes and together for others. Extended family households are also possible with matrilineal descent, as among the Hopi (Case 20).

Extended and joint family households take many forms, and can be based on parent-child or sibling-sibling links. Case 30 describes the Tiv arrangement. We best classify them as **extended families** when they are built on parent-child connections. Where complex households are formed on the basis of links between siblings, rather than descent links between parent and child, they are usually classed as **joint families.** Many varieties of joint families have been anthropologically described, most notably those of Hindu India.

Processes and Cycles: The Dynamics of Domestic Groups

The gulf between an ideal household form (nuclear family, extended family household, polygynous household) and the composition of actual households is often very wide. Households are always breaking up due to parental death, divorce, and the like—with widows, orphans, old people, and others attaching to existing households. In some societies, adoption—the assignment of a child to new parents, which may or may not entail breaking ties with the old ones (see also the definition in Carroll 1970: 3)—and fosterage are very common. In parts of Polynesia, adoption is so frequent as to be almost the normal form; on these islands, where land is very scarce, it serves among other things as a way of evening out population imbalance between property-owning groups. If we try to classify the households we actually encounter, we run the risk of defining almost as many types as there are households. A major step in the right direction came from Meyer Fortes (1959b), who showed that many different household types represent the same kind of

family at different stages in a developmental cycle. A household group characteristically passes through a "phase of expansion" during which children are born, a "phase of dispersion" (that may overlap the first) during which children marry, and a "phase of replacement" ending with the death of the original couple. The composition of a household (and hence what type it is according to older theories) depends on what stage of the cycle it happens to be in when we observe it. This approach improved greatly on earlier classificatory efforts, although it is sometimes difficult to establish clearly what the phases of development are.

30. KINSHIP AND COMMUNITY

We have already touched on local groups at several points. In talking about the emergence of food producing, in looking at hunter-gatherers, pastoralists, and swidden horticulturalists, in looking at adaptationist theories of how cultures change, we have glimpsed local groups of varying scale and complexity. In looking at Trobriand production we saw the village as forming the basis for gardening teams; and in this chapter and the last one, we have seen the interplay of descent and kinship in structuring local groups.

In this section we narrow our focus to the community. In doing so, we will add to our understanding of social structure in comparative perspective. And we will add a useful dimension to our understanding of Trobriand society and culture—a goal chosen to illustrate the challenges of entering and illuminating other people's worlds.

Axes of Variation in Community Structure

The kinds of villages and hamlets found in the tribal world represent a mid-range between the shifting camps of hunter-

Patrilineal Extended Families Among the Tiv

Among the Tiv of Nigeria, the domestic unit of production is the compound group. The Tiv compound is an oval or circular arrangement of huts and granaries, with a central open space that is the "center of Tiv family life" (Bohannan and Bohannan 1968: 15). The nucleus of the compound group is a senior man, the oldest in the group, who acts as its head. He arbitrates disputes, controls magical forces, and supervises production.

He has several wives, each of whom would normally have a separate hut in the compound. The compound group typically includes the head's minor children and unmarried daughters and his married sons and their wives and children. To this extended family core may be added a younger brother of the head and his wives and children or a nephew of the head. There may also be outsiders—friends or age-mates of the men at the compound—who live there. The membership of the compound group, especially these others attached to the extended family core, may shift considerably over time. The genealogical composition and spatial arrangement of one Tiv compound are diagrammed in Figure 10.5.

While in a sense each wife who has a separate hut and her children constitute a separate domestic unit, the larger compound group—a patrilineal extended family augmented by outsiders—is the central domestic unit of everyday Tiv life and of collective economic enterprise (Bohannan and Bohannan 1968).

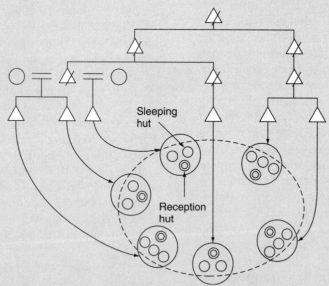

Figure 10.5 Map and genealogy of a Tiv compound. (After a diagram in P. Bohannan 1954).

gatherers and the towns of urbanized societies (with which they have coexisted for several thousand years). Even among societies of what we have been broadly classing as the tribal world, we encounter great variations in the size of communities. Among some shifting horticulturalists, household groups live scattered across the landscape in clusters of two or three or four, or even singly—often being shifted to follow the cycle of swiddens. At the other end of the range are large villages (which in some ecologically rich areas of New Guinea may have over a thousand inhabitants); in parts of Africa, as among the Yakö, we find towns with inhabitants numbering in the tens of thousands.

In looking comparatively across this range of communities, it is useful to ask a number of questions about their internal structure.

1. Is it composed of smaller units that are spatially separate and similar to one another in structure? A village or hamlet may be composed simply of separate households, or it may be some kind of composite. That is, it can be something like an orange in structure, composed of distinguishable segments. Such segments may be clearly visible to an outsider or simply invisible cultural lines between the "pieces." One recurrent pattern is a separation into subhamlets, a cluster of which comprise a village. Another common pattern divides a community into residential areas, or *wards,* with some social and political separation.

2. Are communities or segments associated with descent groups or other kinship units? And if so, is each segment associated with one group, or several? The community may be located in a group's territory and contain its men and their wives. But alternatively, the community may be composed of members of several groups. Whether kin groups are spatially segregated into segments, so that each ward or

subhamlet corresponds to a descent group, is structurally critical. Even where the segments themselves contain more than one descent group, it is crucial whether at the level of individual households there is separation according to **kin group** or whether households are "mixed together." If the latter, the arrangement can usually be interpreted as an expression of the precedence of community over kinship. This has been the trend in societies of increased scale and complexity.

3. Are the communities socially independent? Do most marriages take place *within* the community? In some societies one often finds community exogamy, where each settlement (or cluster of settlements) is associated with an exogamous descent group. Here intermarriage provides a linkage between settlements, and no settlement is in the long run socially self-sufficient. Other communities, especially where they are larger and composed of segments, are largely self-contained. That is, most marriages take place within the village, so that in terms of kinship and other social ties the system is a more closed one. Such relatively self-contained communities—socially, though not economically—are particularly characteristic of peasants. Even in the tribal world, networks of trade and economic specialization are likely to bind communities into wider systems, as in the trade of pots, greenstone, canoe timbers, fibres, and other raw materials and manufactured goods in the Melanesian zone where *kula* exchange takes place.

Kinship, Community, and Symbolic Structure

This usefully leads us back into the Trobriands, where the organization of communities and their articulation with symbolic schemes will reveal further patterns

CASE

31

The Trobriand Village

Recall that the Trobrianders are organized in corporate matrilineal subclans, each of which is associated with a territory by traditions of ancestral emergence. In the simplest case, the Trobriand village is the "headquarters" of a single subclan. This means that all or most of its male members, and their wives, live there, while the women of the subclan live elsewhere with their husbands.

As we noted in Case 22, however, a great many Trobriand villages contain segments of two or more subclans. In these villages, where subclan and village do not coincide, we can see that in many ways the whole village—not the subclan—is the most important social unit. "The whole village is the context of family life" (Powell 1969a: 188), not simply a person's own subclan segment.

The village may have one "owning" subclan and other subclan segments that are attached to it. (Some Trobriand villages are in fact "compound," in that there are two "owning" subclans, each of which may have subclan segments attached to it—a complexity we can ignore.) The importance of the village, as well as the individual corporate subclans based in it, comes to the fore in gardening. As we noted in first glimpsing Trobriand production (Case 14), it is the village, not the subclan, from which gardening teams are constituted.

The spatial arrangement of the Trobriand village reflects both its unity and the partial separation of the subclan segments that make it up.

Figure 10.6 shows the plan of a large and internally complex Trobriand village with a very high-ranking "chief." The arrangement is roughly circular, consisting of a central plaza with dancing ground and burial ground, and two concentric rings of buildings with a "street" between them. The outer ring of buildings consists of domestic dwelling houses. The inner ring consists of yam storehouses and the bachelor houses in which the amorous adventuring of the young is centered.

In this particular village the presence of the very important chief shapes the distribution of residents around the outer circle. Chiefs are entitled to polygynous marriage, and this one had many wives, as well as outsiders resident as his "retainers." In a more typical village each subclan segment would be associated with a sector of the circle. Thus the outer circle of buildings serves to emphasize the partial separation of the segments, while the inner plaza symbolizes the unity of the village.

Such a circular arrangement of the village is not an arbitrary custom. As Lévi-Strauss has shown, the circular villages of Indians in central Brazil and other peoples represent a mapping out of basic principles of cosmology. For the Trobriands he suggests that the concentric rings reflect a series of symbolic polarities in Trobriand culture:

A circular street runs around the storehouses, with the huts of the married couples built at the

of cultural order and social structure, described in Case 31.

One of the most interesting patterns of community organization is that in which the larger communities are modeled on the structure of segmentary lineages. Fustel de Coulanges (1864), in a classic early study of social structure, showed that in ancient Greece and Rome the patrilineal extended family household centering around a sacred

outer edge. This Malinowski called the "profane" part of the village. Not only are there oppositions between central and peripheral and between sacred and profane. There are other aspects too. In the storehouses of the inner ring raw food is stored and cooking is not allowed. . . . Food can be cooked and consumed only in or around the family dwellings of the outer ring. The yam houses are more elaborately constructed and decorated than the dwellings. Only bachelors may live in the inner ring, while married couples must live on the periphery. And finally, the two concentric rings . . . are opposed with respect to sex: "Without overlaboring the point, the central place might be called the male portion of the village and the street that of the women" (Malinowski 1929:1).

In the Trobriands we see, therefore, a complex system of oppositions between sacred and profane, raw and cooked, celibacy and marriage, male and female, central and peripheral. (1963b:137)

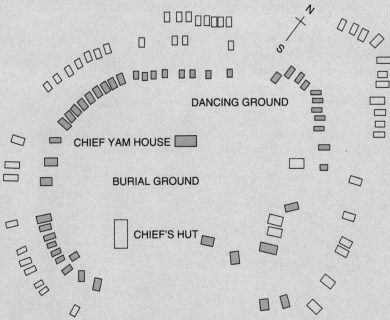

DANCING GROUND

CHIEF YAM HOUSE

BURIAL GROUND

CHIEF'S HUT

Figure 10.6 Plan of a Trobriand village: This village, Omarakana, is the center of the prosperous district and the seat of the most powerful "chief." (After Malinowski)

hearth fire and shrine provided a model that was replicated not only at higher levels of lineage structure (with lineage shrines and sacred fires) but also in the city-state. Thus an ancient city-state had its sacred fire and

shrine symbolizing its unity as though it were a descent group. A strikingly similar pattern has been described by Vogt (1965) among the modern highland Maya of southern Mexico (a pattern we will examine in

Karimojong Age Sets

The Karimojong, pastoralists of Uganda whose cattle-centered economy we glimpsed in Case 8, have an elaborate age-set system.

The general outlines are fairly simple and straightforward. Men are initiated, in young adulthood, into a named age set. Every 5 or 6 years, the age set into which men are being initiated is closed, and a new age set is formally opened. At any time, there will be some six age sets active, spanning an age range from young adulthood to old age.

The age sets are grouped into larger divisions or generation sets. A generation set consists of five age sets and bears one of four names. The arrangement of age sets and age grades is cyclical, as shown in Figure 10.7.

There will at any time be two adjacent generation sets represented among the living—A and

B, or B and C, or C and D, or D and A. One will be senior, the other junior, and this relationship of seniority and juniority is pervasively related throughout the system.

The generation sets are symbolically paired in alternate fashion, so that B and D and A and C are symbolically linked. Members of one pair wear brass ornaments and are symbolically "yellow"; the other pair wear copper and are symbolically "red." The names of the generation sets remain constant, hence "recycle." The names of age sets are chosen from a stock associated with each pair of generation sets, so they reappear, but not in a fixed sequence.

Note that only two generation sets can be actively represented. This occasions no problems halfway through the cycle, when, for example, the last three age sets of the A's constitute the

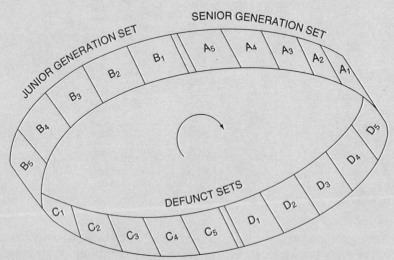

Figure 10.7 The Karimojong age system (schematic). (Adapted from Dyson-Hudson 1966)

senior generation set (A3, A4, A5—though it will mainly be A5's and some A4's who are still alive and active); and the first two or three age sets of the B's (B1, B2, B3) constitute the junior generation set. But 15 years later, almost all the A's will have died, the B's will be chafing at their juniority; and there will be young men who should appropriately be initiated as C's (hence converting B into the senior generation set). At this stage, the A's ritually bow out and retire from the active scene.

The relationship of seniority and juniority is clearly marked between generation sets and is quite explicitly modeled on the father-son relationship. The senior generation set is in charge of initiating new members into the junior, and in ritual and in secular political contexts the power of elders, deriving from their wisdom, is constantly reinforced.

Each age set is similarly in a junior relationship to the ones above it and in a senior relationship to those below it. How this works apparently depends on where the dividing line is between generation sets. Consider the point where the A's have just retired, the B's have become senior and have opened the first of the C age sets. If all the B's exerted their seniority en masse toward the few C's, there would be too many seniors and not enough juniors; so presumably the B1's and B2's exert authority and seniority vis-à-vis the B4's and B5's, as well as C1's. At the other end of the scale, 25 years later, most of the B's will have died and many of the C1's will be acting as senior (to the point that they can if need be initiate C5's, if there are no survivors among those who have gone B4). Each extant age set has a defined part to play in public life. Senior age sets sit together in litigation; appeals are made to their judgment, and they finally deliver a verdict. The junior age set is engaged much of the time in performing services for its elders—collecting wood, serving meat, performing dances. Each age set is, in addition, in a formally subordinate relationship to the one immediately above, whose members are its "masters"; the ornamental insignia worn by members of an age set are established and limited by the one above it. Complex rules about which brothers, or half-brothers, are initiated in what order help to keep age-set relationships parallel to other status relationships.

All this does not imply that Karimojong age sets are tightly organized, corporate groups. Members do not live together, as with the age sets of the Maasai and the military age regiments of the Zulu. They continue to play normal familial roles and to live in local groups or "sections" partly based on shallow ties of agnatic descent. Moreover, these sections or clusters of them, scattered widely across barren grazing lands, conduct their age-set initiations separately. The public affairs in which age sets function as such are local and regional, not tribal-wide. That means that though all sections of the Karimojong are at the same state of the age-set cycle and all members have common insignia and a common name, the corporate nature of tribe-wide age sets is very tenuous. A Karimojong would not know some fellow-members of his age set from other regions, though he would have a close bond with those of his local area. Yet Dyson-Hudson (1966), their ethnographer, suggests that with such a scattered pattern of settlement and so much individual mobility in pastoral resource use, the age sets perform a crucial function of enabling a man to relate to nonkin, even strangers, in patterned ways and to receive hospitality and protection among members of alien groups.

Chapter 18). Vogt suggests that this capacity to replicate a social and ritual pattern at successively higher levels may have enabled the pre-Columbian Maya to create the great temple centers for which they are famous.

31. BEYOND KINSHIP: AGE SETS AND VOLUNTARY ASSOCIATIONS

Before we turn to political processes, it is worth looking very briefly at forms of social grouping based not on kinship but on age or voluntary association.

Age-Set Systems

In many societies, most notably in East Africa, **age sets,** or social groupings based on age, cut across social groupings based on kinship. In age-set systems, young people— usually only men—are grouped together into a named, corporate unit. As they get older, they stay together in the same group. Thus what was a group of young men is 30 years later a group of middle-aged men; and by that time there may be two new age sets of younger men. These systems often are very complicated, particularly in East Africa where they are most common. A distinction has been made between *cyclical* age-set systems, where the same age set appears again every several generations, and *progressive* age-set systems, where a named age set appears only once. The distinction is particularly interesting because cyclical and progressive age-set systems tend to be mirrored in corresponding contrasts in time-reckoning and in the cosmology and world view of a people.

In some African societies, young men of warrior age are separated from normal ties of kinship and community. Most famous anthropologically are the age regiments of the warlike Zulu and warrior age grades of the Maasai, where unmarried men form tightly knit and disciplined segments largely cut off from everyday community

life. The Karimojong in Case 32 illustrate a more typical East African system of age sets. (See also Spencer 1965.)

Age-grades differ from age sets in that they constitute a series of levels through which people, usually men, pass in the course of the life cycle. Thus young people are initiated into one age grade; and then, several years later, collectively or one by one, into the next higher age grade. Such a sequence of age grades often involves progressive revelation of the sacred mysteries commanded by older men.

The social functions of age sets and age grades vary widely. They may fight together, live together, and so on. In view of the preponderant anthropological attention to kinship, it is interesting that age groups sometimes counterbalance kin groups in providing for collective security in blood feuding and protecting age mates' rights vis-á-vis their own kinsmen. The function of age groups as complementary to, or a substitute for, kinship ties has been emphasized by Eisenstadt (1956) in his major study of age as an organizing principle.

Voluntary Associations

Anthropologists—a few of them—have long been interested in voluntary associations, groupings more or less equivalent to the fraternities, clubs, and lodges of Western societies. Thus as early reports came in on spectacular or dramatic secret societies such as the Dukduk and Tamate societies of Melanesia, secret fraternal orders in Africa such as the homicidal Leopards, and Plains Indian military societies, anthropologists tried to sort them out, trace their development, interpret their functions. Webster (1932), Lowie (1920), and Wedgwood (1930) made useful early attempts at synthesis. But though many anthropologists have long taken note of such phenomena, not many of them have been actively interested. In Case 33, a glimpse of

Melanesian Secret Societies

The Dukduk secret society of the Bismarck Archipelago in Melanesia takes into its lower grades of membership virtually all male members of the communities in which it is established. Parents wish their sons to belong for the prestige and privileges membership gives. A man who stays outside would almost certainly run afoul sooner or later of one of its secret rules, and so be subject to fines amounting to more than the "fees" which entrance calls for. The higher grades of the society, however, with their closer relation to the "great mystery," are reserved for important men. Entrance and passage through these grades become progressively more difficult and expensive, especially in terms of ceremonial wealth distribution. The innermost circle comprises the most important leaders in the area. The Dukduk conducts elaborate private and public rituals, notable for their masked figures. The Dukduk society serves subtle political functions by linking together with common rules and rites communities that have no ties other than the periodic arrival of the masked Dukduk figures.

In the Banks and Torres Islands of Melanesia, a number of men's secret societies, or *tamate*, are found on each island. A few major societies occur throughout the area. The clubhouses of these societies are set apart and forbidden to women and uninitiated boys. To become a member, a candidate must meet initiatory expenses, which vary according to the prestige and dignity of the society; and he must undergo fasting and seclusion. Once a member, he uses the clubhouse as a center of leisure-time activity, though as novice he must help to prepare meals. The ceremonial activities of the *tamate* involve festive dancing, but also periods of plundering and license when members in elaborate masks and costumes (Figure 10.8) impersonate ghosts and chase women and children. Each society has certain mysteries such as devices that produce the noises of "ghosts."

Case Update

Codrington's account relates to the late nineteenth century. Versions of these cult practices continue, often with new meanings. See, for example, A. L. Epsterin (1992) and Simet (1992).

Figure 10.8   A *tamate* masquerader (Banks island). (After a drawing by Codrington)

two classic Melanesian "secret societies" illustrates the formal and elaborate voluntary associations found in some parts of the world.

We will encounter another system of secret societies well known in anthropology—the Poro and Sande societies of West African peoples such as the Kpelle and Mende, in Case 39 (Chapter 11). There we will see how secret knowledge provides the means to power. Later, when we look in Chapter 20 at the anthropological study of cities, we will see how secret societies such as the Poro operate in urban situations.

Informal Social Relations

By and large anthropologists have been even more remiss in studying informal relations of friendship and cooperation that crosscut formal groupings based on kinship, or interact with kinship in the formation of everyday action groups. As I have pointed out (Keesing 1972b), anthropologists know a great deal about formally patterned relations of kinship. But they have sometimes ignored or underplayed the role of *friendship* in determining who does what with whom in a small-scale society—though in our own society we are aware of the importance of friendship. The behavior of higher primates and other mammals often can be interpreted only if we infer that the animals that hang around together *like* one another; and that seems to be true of humans in all societies.

Far too little is known about the way friendship and informal partnerships in gardening, trade, or other enterprises are woven into the fabric of everyday social life. One of the side dividends from an increasing anthropological concern with the organization of complex societies is that in them one *must* pay attention to the ways in-

dividual bonds of friendship, economic strategy, and political alliance operate. Anthropologists have tended to ignore them as "outside the system" of descent groups and kinship relations. In modern complex societies, one must deal with their central importance—and that can give new insights into the forces that shape actual behavior elsewhere.

We need now to look at the processes of politics, the structures and uses of power, in comparative perspective. We have seen in the last several chapters quests for prestige in Melanesia, segmentary societies without formal institutions of government, and glimpses of more complex and hierarchical political systems. We turn now to view political systems and the processes of politics in comparative perspective.

=== **SUMMARY** ===

This chapter considers a range of definitions of marriage that enable us to look at customs in a cross-culturally applicable way. In many parts of the world marriage is a contract between groups, and entails transfers of rights over sexual activities and the affiliation of children, with or without corresponding transfers of wealth goods. Marriage also sets up ties of exchange between affinally related families (example: the Trobriands of Papua New Guinea), and these may continue over more than one generation. There can be rules for marriage between certain categories of related persons, citing preferences as well as prohibitions. Plural forms of marriage include polygyny and polyandry. Incest taboos specify ranges of kin who may not be married. There is sometimes a distinction between those with whom sex is prohibited and those whom one may not marry.

Positive rules specifying marriage with categories of persons lead to forms of alliance, either symmetric or asymmetric.

Domestic groups are based on parent-child ties. Nuclear families are found in contexts where wider domestic groups based on unilineal descent are absent. Complex households result from polygyny or polyandry and from the coresidence of siblings and their spouses in extended families. Communities may be built out of several subgroups based on descent or kinship ties. They may also depend on other principles, such as age sets, age grades, and secret societies whose membership is divided along lines of gender. In addition, informal ties of friendship may be important.

SUGGESTIONS FOR FURTHER READING

SECTIONS 26–29

Bohannan, P. J., and J. Middleton, eds. 1968. *Marriage, Family and Residence.* Garden City, N.Y.: Natural History Press.

Comaroff, J. L., ed. 1980. *The Meaning of Marriage Payments.* New York: Academic Press, Inc.

Fox, R. 1967. *Kinship and Marriage.* Baltimore: Penguin Books, Inc.

Goody, J. 1972. *Domestic Groups.* Addison-Wesley Modules in Social Anthropology. Reading, Mass.: Addison-Wesley Publishing Company, Inc.

———. 1977. *Production and Reproduction: A Comparative Study of the Domestic Domain.* Cambridge Studies in Social Anthropology. Cambridge: Cambridge University Press.

Keesing, R. M. 1975. *Kin Groups and Social Structure.* New York: Holt, Rinehart and Winston.

Ogbu, J. U. 1978. African Bridewealth and Women's Status, *American Ethnologist* 5(2): 241–262.

SECTION 30

Hogbin, H. I., and C. Wedgewood. 1953. Local Groupings in Melanesia, *Oceania* 23(4): 241–276; 24(1): 58–76.

Keesing, R. M. 1975. *Kin Groups and Social Structure.* New York: Holt, Rinehart and Winston.

SECTION 31

Baxter, P. T. W., and U. Almagor, eds. 1978. *Age, Generation and Time: Some Features of East African Age Organizations.* New York: St. Martin's Press, Inc.

Hammond, D. 1972. *Associations.* McCaleb Module in Anthropology No. 14. Reading, Mass.: Addison-Wesley Publishing Company, Inc.

Kerri, J. N. 1976. Studying Voluntary Associations as Adaptive Mechanisms. *Current Anthropology* 17(1): 23–47.

Kertzer, D. I. 1978. Theoretical Developments in the Study of Age-Group Systems. *American Ethnologist* 5(2): 368–374.

La Fontaine, J. S., ed. 1978. *Sex and Age as Principles of Social Differentiation.* New York: Academic Press, Inc.

Mendelson, E. 1967. Primitive Secret Societies. In N. Mackenzie, ed., *Secret Societies.* New York: Holt, Rinehart and Winston.

Stewart, F. H. 1977. *Fundamentals of Age-Group Systems.* New York: Academic Press, Inc.

Van Gennep, A. 1960. *The Rites of Passage.* London: Routledge and Kegan Paul, Ltd.

Wedgewood, C. H. 1930. The Nature and Functions of Secret Societies, *Oceania* 1: 129–145.

11

Power and Politics

In every community anthropologists have studied, they have encountered the processes of "politics"—people leading, organizing, and gaining and using power. Yet it is difficult to define what is "political" or to delineate "the political system" in a small-scale society without a government, without a state, without any formal system of centralized leadership.

Looking at societies as stable, isolated systems, we can see certain problems to be solved, by whatever institutional means, if not by formal political organization: maintaining territorial rights, maintaining internal order, allocating power to make decisions regarding group action. We might say that the "political organization" of a society comprises whatever rules and roles are used to manage these problems, whether or not there is any formal kind of government organization. We have already seen leaders at work in a range of settings: from tiny San bands to the nomadic camps of the Basseri and the villages, yam gardens, and overseas *kula* expeditions of the Trobriands. Here we can extend this comparative view of political systems to see a range of institutions and leadership roles.

Having done so, we will need to turn to a broader view of political *processes.*

Anthropologists increasingly encounter political leaders not in traditional settings, but fomenting revolution, organizing a faction, uniting ethnic minorities, or running for political office in a country that had not existed a few years before. We need ways to conceptualize the processes of politics, the nature and uses of power, that allow us to interpret political scenes whether they are enacted in nomad tent, jungle hut, or city.

In taking first a comparative view of political systems in the tribal world we will have to try to go beyond simplistic typological schemes. The knowledge we have built up in the last three chapters will serve us well.

32. POLITICAL SYSTEMS

Political Systems as Superstructure

Before looking at political systems in comparative perspective, it is worth briefly reviewing the theoretical orientation taken in Chapter 8. The economic base of a society, the organization of production and distribution, has a social side—the way humans are organized—and a technological side, the tools, knowledge, and physical resources

Laying out sides of pork for distribution. The pork fat should be plentiful and is displayed clearly. Melpa, Papua New Guinea.

such as land that are deployed to achieve human goals. Together, these social relations and technological resources comprise the *base* or *infrastructure*.

An economic system is maintained and perpetuated by "superstructural" institu-tions that ensure not only the physical repro-duction of a society's members but the *social reproduction* of their relationships to one an-other. Political institutions, in a complex so-ciety, provide the organizational means for defense against invasion; but they also provide a ruling class with means to perpetuate their power, maintaining the relationships of producers and consumers, rulers and ruled. But what about societies without social classes, societies where every able-bodied adult is a producer, societies with no central institutions of government, no rulers?

"Tribes" Without Rulers

This represents a classic anthropological problem. The bands of Australian Aborigines or San were small enough that informal leadership, or the authority of elders, seemed adequate to the scale of organization. But when theoretically minded social anthropologists studied African societies with populations in the tens or even hundreds of thousands, the problem of order loomed large. How do "tribes without rulers" (Middleton and Tait 1958) maintain internal order? How are social relations reproduced across generations? Can we say that people without institutions of government have a "political system" at all (Hindness and Hirst 1975)? Consider a classic case in the history of political anthropology—the Nuer of the Sudan, in Case 34.

The Dynamics of Political Systems

We might, at this stage, look back from the Nuer to the Smiths and Joneses of Chapter 9, in looking at how conflicts and feuds are resolved. Such rifts in social relations of course disrupt the normal run of life. But do they disrupt "the system"? In a sense, they do. But as Max Gluckman and his students have argued, they also maintain and renew it. Beyond the local descent group segment like the Elm Street Smiths, tribespeople seldom unite *for* anything; they unite *against*. Without feuds and conflict, social groupings would be much more atomistic and isolated

from one another than they are. Moreover, the process whereby groups and alliances of groups settle feuds reaffirms their unity within a wider social system and moral order. It is Elm Street Smiths whose mothers were Browns who mediate in a feud between Smiths and Browns; and the resolution of feuds thus underlines the webs of kinship, that bind groups together rather than the lines of descent that separate them.

In such stateless societies, the possibility often lies latent that from the component lineages or local groups some larger and more effective alliance can be crystallized. Sometimes a leader drawing on religious symbols or mystical dreams or visions can unite fragmented and opposed groups in a collective war of liberation or conquest or some other dramatic action. Joan of Arc and El Cid illustrate this theme in European history. The Mahdi who united the feuding lineages of the Sudan in a holy war of liberation provides another example. Among such widely separated peoples as the Assiniboin Native Americans of the eastern Plains and the Iban of Borneo, fragmented local groups have been temporarily united by leaders whose mission of conquest was revealed in dreams.

This usefully turns the process of "social reproduction" around. We cannot assume that it is "natural" for a social or economic system to remain stable across the generations. We ourselves live in a world where economic growth and population increase are taken for granted. What constraints militated against the Nuer developing a more complex and hierarchical political system, against temporary alliances becoming permanent? We have seen the expansion of the Nuer at the expense of the Dinka. Why was this not accompanied by political hierarchy? Why did Nuer leaders (such as Leopard-skin chiefs) not accumulate sufficient cattle—and through them, power—that they controlled political alliances and marriage (and, like Trobriand "chiefs," have trappings of rank and sacredness)? Again, if we view every social system as containing the seeds of its own transformation, then we are led to regard both stability and change as at once natural, and needing explanation.

The dynamic nature of economic and political systems emerges in a volume titled *The Evolution of Social Systems* (Friedman and Rowlands 1978). The evolution of more complex political systems is documented from many parts of Africa, Asia, and the Americas. Our focus on regional systems can well remind us that the transformation of an economic and political system in the direction of greater complexity—a "tribe" to a chiefdom, a chiefdom to a ministate—may be triggered by ideas coming from the neighbors. The spread of Hindu religious and political ideas from India into Southeast Asia similarly catalyzed the emergence of states out of chiefdoms.

Friedman's (1979) analysis of the Kachin of Myanmar (Burma) convincingly argues that an egalitarian lineage-based society may even from "within" have the potential for the emergence of hierarchy, through the concentration of symbolically valued goods and power over marital alliance.

Research in the New Guinea highlands by Jack Golson and his colleagues suggests that the development of more complex economic and political systems need not follow a smooth "upward" course. Golson has uncovered evidence that several times over a span of 6,000 years fragmented local groups may have been united into much larger and more cohesive regional political systems, marked by extensive irrigation and intensification of production—political systems that then disintegrated again into their component elements. (For a recent survey of evidence see Golson and Gardner 1990.)

"Big Men"

This serves as a useful warning against some of the simple typologies that have dominated the literature. The Melanesian "big man," an entrepreneurial leader who commands support through prominence in feast-giving and exchange, has become a stereotyped figure in the literature. But big men in parts of the densely populated New Guinea highlands, with large surpluses of sweet potatoes supporting large pig herds and vast-scale regional exchange systems such as the Hagen *moka* and Enga *tee* (Feil 1978a, 1978b, 1987; Meggitt 1974; A. Strathern 1971, 1982), are very different from their counterparts in many parts of lowland and island Melanesia: much "bigger" and more firmly entrenched as part of the ongoing political structure. Much further down the scale of "bigness" is the big man among the Kwaio of the Solomon Islands, as presented in Case 35.

Where intensified production, increased population density, and control over exchange pigs and valuables increase the power base of the Melanesian big man, as in the New Guinea highlands, such leaders may not only command more power and influence, they may increasingly act as an elite, able to transmit power and influence to their sons. The gulf between big men and ordinary men may widen to the point that they constitute an incipient class.

The Emergence of Hierarchy

Realizing that big men can become more "chieflike" by controlling exchange valuables and the labor of wives and male supporters, by progressively surrounding

Nuer Segmentary Organization

Some 200,000 Nuer live scattered across the swamplands and savanna of the Sudan. Though there is no overarching government, the Nuer maintain a measure of unity and orderly political relations between the territorial divisions, which Evans-Pritchard calls *tribes,* and between segments of them. A Nuer tribe is the largest group whose members are duty bound to combine in raiding and defense. Each tribe has a territory, a name, and bonds of common sentiment. Within a tribe, feuds are supposed to be controlled by arbitration.

A tribe is divided into segments. The relationship between segments is conceived in terms of hierarchies of patrilineal descent, as with the Smiths and Joneses, even though the actual correspondence between descent and the composition of territorial groups is quite messy. The basic principle is contextual opposition and alliance: "We fight against the Rengyan, but when either of us is fighting with a third party we combine with them." (Evans-Pritchard 1940:143). Evans-Pritchard (1940: 143–144) gives the following illustration: "When segment Z^1 fights Z^2, no other section is involved. When Z^1 fights Y^1, Z^1 and Z^2 unite as Y^2. When Y^1 fights X^1, Y^1 and Y^2 unite, and so do X^1 and X^2. When X^1 fights A, X^1, X^2, Y^1, and Y^2 all unite as B. When A raids the Dinka [a neighboring people], A and B may unite" (see Figure 11.1).

Disputes begin over many grievances, having to do with cattle, damage to property, adultery, rights over resources, to name a few. Many disputes lead to bloodshed. Within the same village, Nuer fight with clubs or without weapons. Confrontations between members of different villages can lead to use of spears and to bloody war between men of each village. When a man has been killed, the dead man's close patrilineal kin will try to kill the slayer or one of his close patrilineal kin. The slayer goes to a "Leopard-skin chief" for sanctuary: the latter seeks to mediate and to get the aggrieved lineage to accept "blood cattle" and thus prevent a blood feud. A killing involving members of low-level segments who thus have close social relationships, like Z^1 and Z^2 or even Z^1 and Y^1, is likely to be settled without blood vengeance. The more distantly related are the groups involved, the greater the probability of large-scale fighting between temporary alliances like the X's versus the Y's.

But what about the Leopard-skin chief who arbitrates disputes and provides sanctuary? Does this not indicate some overarching political organization? According to Evans-Pritchard (1940), such a "chief" has ritual powers and a role as mediator and negotiator, but he has no secular

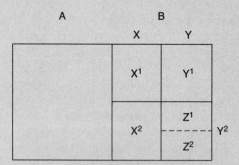

Figure 11.1 Nuer political organization: A and B are the major segments of a Nuer "tribe." X and Y are the major branches of B, and they are in turn divided by segmentation. (From Evans-Pritchard 1940)

authority, no special privileges. His performance in peacemaking is possible because he stands outside the lineage and tribal system, not because he is central in it. He serves an important function which in other segmentary societies must usually be served by persons with conflicting obligations due to cognatic kinship ties that crosscut lineages. His presence enables the Nuer to carry the posturing of hostility and threat further than they otherwise could, because he stands in the way of the actual killings most Nuer hope to avoid.

The Nuer political system is interesting in that changing perspectives on how it works and how it can be understood, in the years since Evans-Pritchard's classic 1940 book *The Nuer,* reveal widening horizons in the study of social and political organization. Evans-Pritchard's view of the Nuer was essentially static: his models show how Nuer society "works" in an ahistorical vacuum where equilibrium prevails. But studies by Newcomer (1972), Haight (1972), Gough (1971), and others have reexamined the Nuer more closely in temporal and ecological context. "Nuer society" emerges as an unstable stage in a process of invasion and assimilation of their cultural cousins, the Dinka, that was modified by colonialism.

For our purposes, it suffices to suggest this change of view by sketching in barest outline an exchange between Greuel (1971) and Haight (1972) regarding the allegedly "powerless" Leopard-skin chief or mediator. Greuel suggested that far from being powerless, the Leopard-skin chief was a wealthy leader, partly because of the cattle he received for his services as mediator, who could mobilize the support of a substantial coalition of followers. If a man murdered a close lineage kinsman, his relatives would offer blood money; if he murdered a dis-

A Nuer Leopard-skin chief.

tant outsider, a blood feud was no threat to community solidarity. But if a man killed a marginally close kinsman or neighbor, where a blood feud would be disruptive of economic and social solidarity, the Leopard-skin chief could often effectively mediate. But he could do so because he could mobilize a dominant coalition with an interest in avoiding internal feuding. Thus, while he had literally no direct power to enforce decisions, he commanded much implicit political power.   *Continued*

Case 34 continued

Haight (1972), invoking a historical interpretation, questions whether the Leopard-skin chief, who emerged to prominence through personal ability from a particular Leopard-skin lineage, usually was the center of a numerically dominant coalition. In many or most areas, the Leopard-skin lineage was not the dominant lineage; and Haight sees the power of the Leopard-skin chief in these areas as more religious than political. Where in some areas the Leopard-skin lineage exercised political dominance, the Leopard-skin chief might indeed mobilize support of a dominant coalition. But both situations, Haight argues, are best understood in terms of the historical process of conquest whereby the Nuer maintained dominance over the Dinka by absorption, and preserved an egalitarian social order while keeping a firm hold on territories.

Case Update

See again works by Kelly (1985), Hutchinson (1996), and also Johnson (1994) for extensive reanalyses of Nuer history, politics, and leadership.

themselves with symbols of their elevated status, and by legitimizing this status in myth and ritual, we can begin to understand how the Trobriand political system, described in Case 36, represents a partial transformation of the big man systems of other peoples of the region.

Chiefdoms and the Legitimation of Power

The hierarchical political systems of Polynesia express further steps toward centralization of authority and its legitimation in terms of sacredness and the gods. Case 37 presents the Hawaiian system.

African Kingship

Africa provides many examples of the emergence of ministates, many of them comprising several ethnic groups. Such systems illustrate how more complex social forms may evolve out of decentralized segmentary lineage systems, which may continue to provide the "building blocks" at a local level. In Africa, as in Southeast Asia, the emergence of more complex state societies was often catalyzed by ideas and organizational models from without, as well as from the accumulation of power from within. In Case 38, the Bunyoro of Uganda provide an instructive example of a small-scale African state.

Rather than extend the survey of political institutions to societies of greater scale and complexity, such as the early states of Mesopotamia and Mesoamerica, we can better turn to look at the nature of political processes. We will need to interpret these processes, and the nature and uses of power, in a range of settings where analysis in terms of political institutions is no longer adequate.

33. THE PROCESSES OF POLITICS

Comparing political institutions inevitably makes assumptions that the societies being compared are relatively independent entities and that the political systems are relatively stable. But these assumptions about discreteness, stability, and integration do not serve us well in understanding the political processes of a rapidly changing and complicated modern world. It is the *processes*, not the institutions, of politics that increasingly command attention. Anthropologists therefore also look at "fields" of political events that cross the traditional boundaries of societies. They look at the way laws, bureaucracies, and political parties impinge on tribal or village peoples; and they observe the "political middlemen" who bridge the gulf between the outside world and their own people. In such settings, one can make no assumptions about stability or equilibrium. Political processes produce new roles, new groups, new conflicts, and new integration. They do not simply keep the system going. Making no assumption that all participants share the same cultural rules or that roles and groups are stable, one can see individuals as shaping and manipulating patterns of social life, not simply following them.

Individuals and Systems

Does this mean that we can view "the system" as the cumulative outcome of individual choices and strategies? Some theorists have taken such a view, as a counter to theories of social systems as transcending and constraining individual actors. A crucial pioneering study here was Barth's (1959a) analysis of political process among the Swat Pathan of northern Pakistan. The political system of this segmentary society was not, he argued, maintained in equilibrium because the component social groups were in balanced structural opposition to one another—as in the classic African studies of Nuer, Tiv, and others. Rather, the system was generated and maintained by individual actors seeking to advance their power by strategic choices and coalitions (Barth 1959a, 1959b).

From this analysis of how individual strategies may cumulatively produce systematic integration and equilibrium, Barth moved toward the study of change. If we see social systems as the outcome of individual decisions, he argues, we are not bound to assumptions of equilibrium: there is no reason that all individuals need pursue the same strategies, and no reason to assume that—even if they did—the outcomes would preserve "the system" rather than progressively transform it (Barth 1966a, 1966b, 1967).

F. G. Bailey, carrying this model further, analyzed the political process in India and elsewhere in several important articles and books. In *Stratagems and Spoils* (Bailey 1969), a major synthesis, he elaborates a model of the way individuals seek to maximize power, and of the common themes of strategy, coalition, and conflict that emerge in competitive struggles for power in different times and places. In *Gifts and Poison* (1971), Bailey and his students turn from the public to the private arena and argue that an informal politics of reputation and status in interpersonal relations is crucial in the European communities they studied. They pay special attention to "people competing to remain equal," and to "the tragedy, the bitterness, which we see in conflict between those who are equal and who therefore might have been friends" (Bailey 1971:19).

The Kwaio "Big Man"

The Kwaio of Melanesia are fragmented into dozens of local descent groups. Each owns a territory, and there is no central government or political office uniting these small groups politically. Influence, authority, and leadership in secular affairs come from success in mobilizing and manipulating wealth. A "big man" in a descent group is a more successful entrepreneur than his fellows—the visible capital being strung shell beads and pigs and the invisible capital being prestige. To acquire renown and be respected, a group must give large mortuary feasts honoring its important dead. If a man from group A dies, the dead man's relative from rival group B may be one of several emissaries allowed to bury him. The big man of group A will take the lead in a great mobilization of wealth by his group. The pallbearers, including the one from group B, will be rewarded with large quantities of valuables. But all this must be reciprocated. When months or years later an equivalent member of B dies, an A relative has the right to bury him and the B's must give as large a presentation to him as was made in the first feast. What looks like an act of kinship obligation is in fact a duel for prestige between big men, on behalf of their groups. A big man becomes "big" by manipulating wealth successfully. To attain great success, he must be an oldest son and he must have a fairly large group of close kin and fellow descent group members to mobilize. His strategy is to make people obligated to him by contributing to their feasts, financing marriages, and otherwise investing his resources.

A big man has no formal authority or powers, no clear-cut position. He is simply a man who leads because people follow, who decides because others defer to him. A big man takes the lead in advancing claims or demands against other descent groups and in settling feuds. He maintains internal stability and direction, Kwaio say, like the steersman of a canoe. A big man's oldest son may have some slight advantage in the quest for prestige and power. But there is no hereditary succession and no position to succeed to. Bigness is a matter of degree, in a society where every man gives some feasts and plays some part in the game of investment; and many descent groups have no clear-cut big man.

Keesing (1978) gives a more detailed account of Kwaio feasting and high finance, as

Viewing individual strategies to maximize and preserve power and reputation as generating "the system" has been highly revealing. We have been led beyond assumptions about stability, led to see how individual motives make sense of collective behavior, led to see informal strategies as well as formal ideologies and rules. But while this reveals one side of politics, it can hide another side.

This distortion is underlined by Talal Asad (1972) in a reinterpretation of Barth's (1959a) Swat Pathan evidence. Asad argues that the decision-makers on whom Barth had focused constitute a landed class whose power over their tenants derives

A Kwaio "big man" in action: 'Elota (Keesing 1978) gives staging instructions to his kin at a mortuary feast (*left*) and puts together shell valuables for a marriage payment (*right*).

introduction to the autobiography of the leading Kwaio big man of recent times. Keesing (1992) pursues the Kwaio history further into colonial and postcolonial times.

from an exploitative economic position with deep historical roots. The system, Asad argues, has been progressively changing. Consolidation of power by landlords, and a polarization between them and the landless peasant class, was accelerated by British colonialism in India and then was stabilized by British military domination of the northern frontier. Asad's critique makes a number of strong points: (1) "A political system" must be seen as part of a wider system, and in a long-range historical perspective: seeming stability may be illusory. (2) Power—who has how much of it and what strategies and options are open for advancing it—is ultimately rooted in control

Trobriand Political Organization

Recall the central elements in Trobriand social organization: the matrilineal subclans, the rule of residence after marriage that brings married men back to their subclan village, and the harvest presentations of yams from these subclan members to the husbands of their out-married female members.

As we have seen, each matrilineal subclan has a village on its land; and some villages also contain a branch of a second subclan. A number of villages in the same area, related by intermarriage and traditional alliance, form a *cluster* (Powell 1960).

Each village has a leader whose role is in many ways similar to that of the Kwaio big man. But there are some crucial differences, for the Trobrianders have a pervasive concept of *rank*. It is not people who are ranked, but subclans. Basically there are two ranks, "chiefly" *(guyau)* and commoner. Any village thus is controlled by a subclan that is either of high or low rank. But the high-ranking subclans are themselves in a long-term competitive struggle for prestige and power; and hence there is a publicly known, if not official, fixed, or clear-cut, ranking of *guyau* subclans.

Now, the leader of a commoner village, attaining his position by manipulating power and wealth and exercising wise leadership, is very much like the Kwaio big man, except that he and his group are pieces in a wider design. The leader of a *guyau* village, however, has an important prerogative: he can take more than one wife. If you were a Trobriand man with six wives, imagine what would happen at harvest time. You would get harvest presentation yams from six different subclans—and yams mean prestige. Harvest presentations become a form

of political tribute. The more powerful a subclan, the more subclans in the same cluster and other clusters are placed in a politically subordinate position to it by strategic and manipulated marriage alliances. Sending a wife is, as it were, the first act of a tribute relationship—although Weiner (1976) makes clear that the leader with multiple wives must provide them with skirts and bundles, so that the tribute relationship is by no means without reciprocation.

Commoners must show formal physical deference to the leaders of the highest-ranking subclans, whose rank is symbolized by the high platforms on which they sit. The leader of a village of high rank symbolizes the status and prestige of his subclan while at the same time steering its decisions and policy and publicly representing it. He may have to mobilize his allies in warfare to maintain or improve its position relative to other important groups. Important leaders take the most prominent roles in *kula* exchanges, so that each flow of armshells and necklaces through the Trobriands validates or adjusts the balance of power and prestige of subclans and clusters.

The leader of the highest-ranking and most powerful subclan in a cluster, by manipulating marriage alliances and effectively distributing wealth, comes to act as leader of that cluster. His role is similar to that of leader of a *guyau* village, but on a larger scale. Once more his authority and powers are far from absolute. They are accorded to him as representative of the will of the subclans in the cluster and because so many people are obligated to support him, or to defer to him, through his manipulations of wealth.

A leader's rank reflects the rank of his subclan, his authority is that accorded to him by his group, and he contracts his marriages and receives his wealth as an expression of his group's power and prestige. Yet the web of strategic marriages must be established afresh by the aspiring leader, and the balance of power is constantly shifting (Powell 1960).

As Weiner (1976:45) notes, leaders of *guyau* rank "share all the difficulties of building and maintaining a constituency that are found among big men in other parts of Melanesia." But she notes that three features set them apart from their counterparts in other Massim societies. First, "the Trobriand 'chiefs' seem to adhere strictly to hereditary claims." (This does not preclude rivalry among potential legitimate claimants, or the need for a successful one to build his power base anew—but it rules out illegitimate claimants.) Second, the separation of high-ranking leaders is marked by "the paraphernalia of decorations and social and physical taboos." Finally, only the few *guyau* men who have actually successfully attained the legitimate status Weiner calls "hamlet manager" are allowed to take multiple wives (so that this is a prerogative, as it were, of "office," not of rank; Weiner 1976:45).

Trobriand "chiefs," Weiner concludes, fit neither into the pattern of Melanesian big men nor Polynesian chiefs, whose authority derives from the sacredness of their genealogically defined rank (Sahlins 1963).

[Such a system] is not to be found in any other Massim island. The style of being a Trobriand chief, however, retains much of Melanesian big man dynamics. . . .[But] the dogma of hereditary right gives only a few Trobriand men potential access to more resources than anyone else. Through these beliefs, Trobrianders grant chiefs this privileged position. (Weiner 1976:46)

The point of drawing such a comparison should not be to plug the Trobrianders in between big men and chiefs on a thin little rung

of an imaginary ladder—but to ask how they got that way. Is it the greater horticultural productivity of the Trobriands that permits the accumulation of yam surpluses? This is very probably a factor. Is it the Trobriands' position in the *kula* exchange? The answers are not clear. One of several interesting hypotheses has been advanced by Brunton (1975), who notes that the concentration of chiefly power in the inland districts of northern Kiriwina is *inversely* correlated to access to *kula* valuables (since coastal districts to the east and southwest have much more direct access to valuables). Brunton suggests that leaders in these agricultural districts, relatively separated from a *kula* exchange system he infers was already in operation through the Massim, were able to participate in the exchange of valuables in a much more monopolistic fashion than their coastal cousins; and that they were able to parlay their monopolistic control of prestige valuables into dogmas of rank, legitimacy, and privileges.

Whether this or some other pattern of transformation occurred in the Trobriands, we can draw some inferences about the processes involved. First, a contingent and transitory power was legitimized in terms of succession and hereditary right. Second, this legitimation of power was apparently achieved (in some way) through an increasing command of surplus produce and exchange valuables. Third, such command entailed control over labor power of others—wives, retainers, and, in the Trobriand case, members of subclans placed in a tributary relationship through marriage. Fourth, such legitimation—where power became converted into rank—entailed the creation of ideas about sacredness (hence, the demanding and observing of deference, symbolically expressed) and the creation of political myths justifying ascendancy in terms of the ancestral past.

The Hawaiian Political System

The Polynesians of the Hawaiian Islands had an exceedingly complex and sophisticated political system based on hereditary rank and classes, and theocracy and divine right; yet at the same time it was flexible and constantly shifting in terms of actual political alignments.

Hawaiian society was based on three major hereditary social classes—commoners, nobles, and inferiors. The commoners, by far the most numerous, were agriculturists, fishermen, and artisans—for the most part self-sufficient, but always living and working in the shadow of nobles to whom their very lives could be forfeit at any time, and supplying them with tribute. The nobles, ranked in sacredness, were occupationally specialized as warriors, priests, and political officials. The hereditary ranking of nobles was based on descent from the gods, genealogically traced; rank of individuals and segments was traced in terms of birth order, with highest rank traced through first-born child (male or female) of the first-born child, down genealogical trees. The

highest-ranking nobles were so sacred that elaborate and extreme deference—for example, prostration—was owed them by lower ranks, under penalty of death.

The islands were divided into chiefdoms, each ruled by a paramount chief whose powers over his subjects were seemingly absolute and were validated by divine right conveyed by his high god. The paramount chief's rule was administered and maintained through a cluster of high-ranking nobles who served as priests, counselors, and military leaders. The districts of his chiefdom were in turn ruled by local chiefs of high rank who exacted tribute and channeled much of it to the paramount chief to support the elaborate religious rites and secular life of the ruling elite. The nobles were supported almost entirely by tribute exacted from commoners in local areas, which in turn were administered by chosen chiefs and overseers of lower rank. The whole system was formally hierarchical, even feudal, in many respects, culminating in the rights of life and death,

over resources and means of production. (3) A class analysis reveals how individual consciousness—and hence individual goals, motives, values, and ideologies—are conditioned by the circumstances of one's social class. To make a general model of human motivation from the strategies of an elite is misleading.

Asad also questions the functionalist assumption that political order is maintained within a society through an implicit convenant of consent regarding legitimate authority. The assumption of consent whereby the governed accept political authority as legitimate is implicit in Barth's interpretation, and explicit within the tradition of political anthropology—from Fortes and Evans-Pritchard (1940), through Smith (1956), Easton (1959), and Swartz and colleagues (1966). Asad, in reinterpreting the Swat Pathan material and his own evidence on the Kababish Arabs of the Sudan (1970), argues that a dominant class or group holds political power over a subordinate class or

and dispossession, the paramount chief exercised over his subjects. Being of the highest rank and sacredness himself, this chief approached the status of the god who conferred on him these divine rights. Secular political powers and ritual relations with the gods were united in his person. Seemingly this almost feudal system was fixed, stable, and immutable.

But in fact it was highly flexible and unstable. The territory of a chiefdom was established and maintained by conquest, and the political fortunes of paramount chiefs waxed and waned with their success or failure in battle and their success in holding their chiefdoms together in the face of insurrection and intrigue. The sacred mandate to rule had continually to be validated by secular success: if a chief lost in battle or a rival successfully challenged him by usurping the paramount chief's sole right to human sacrifice, it showed that he had lost his god's favor or that another's was more powerful. Even if a chief held his chiefdom together or extended its boundaries by conquest, his chosen successor—if there was one—immediately became the focal point of new rivalry and intrigue.

Whole islands were added to chiefdoms, or lost; the political map, as well as its ruling cast of characters, was constantly changing. And with each new paramount chief or territorial conquest, the previous ruling elite lost their jobs—and very often their lives, in sacrifice to the new ruler's god. From the highest to the lowest levels of chiefly rule, office and privilege were conferred by a paramount chief and contingent on his political power. Only rarely, when the paramount chiefdom passed through an orderly dynastic succession, was there continuity of power at the lower administrative levels. As in the Trobriand system, the tides of political fortune were always shifting; gaining and preserving power required skilled direction and manipulation of physical and human resources—and a goodly measure of luck (Davenport 1969).

Case Update
See also Kirch (1989), as well as Sahlins and Kirch (1992), for further information on the historical development of kingship in Hawaii.

group because historical and economic circumstances have given them the means to do it. The very legitimacy of its authority is an ideology created by the politically powerful and imposed on the powerless: the notion of consent becomes meaningless. Legitimacy is not a social contract, but an instrument of power.

Ahmed (1976) has further added to the critique of Barth's work by stressing the importance of religious ideas in the creation of

charismatic leadership and the historical centralization of power. Such an analysis can be added to, rather than simply replacing, Barth's own account.

Barth had made some important conceptual advances over the models that had dominated political anthropology. The classic studies of the Nuer or the Bunyoro had assumed that "the system" was (at least prior to colonialism) in stable equilibrium. Barth's conceptualization, as its

CASE

3 8

The Bunyoro Lineage System and Kingship

The kingdom of the Nyoro of Uganda, who number about 100,000, is believed to comprise three historically separate ethnic groups: an original agricultural people; a pastoral invading group, the Huma; and a more recently invading Nilotic group, the Bito, from whom the kings of modern times trace descent. Although the Nyoro have been much changed by colonial domination, the general outlines of the traditional system can be reconstructed.

The local groupings of traditional Nyoro society were, at least ideally, segments of patrilineal clans. A cluster of extended family households comprise a dispersed community. Just how these local lineages or clan segments were grouped territorially is difficult to reconstruct, since clans are now intermingled. But rituals, marriage transactions, the legal system, and the kinship terminology suggest that patrilineal descent groups may have been more strongly corporate in the past than in the historic period.

On top of this descent system, which fits roughly into the Smiths and Joneses pattern, was a system of kingship and political hegemony that resembled in some ways the feudal system of medieval Europe. At its apex was the king, descended from the traditional dynasty of Bito kings. He exercised formal sovereignty over the entire society and land, expressed both in political authority and in sacredness. His health and well-being were critical for the well-being of his people; if he sickened, the entire country suffered.

Authority to administer territories was delegated by the king to chiefs: great chiefs controlled vast territories; lesser chiefs controlled local areas. But chieftainship at all levels was an appointed, not hereditary, power; though it tended to be passed down in families, it could be withdrawn at the king's pleasure. Chieftainships were not strictly ranked, but varied in importance according to the size, population, and wealth of the territory controlled and the close-

implications were developed in the 1960s, could see cumulative decisions as producing change, as well as reproducing stability. The classic studies, although they recognized that a people might be in conflict with their neighbors, assumed that the boundaries of a political system essentially corresponded to boundaries of language and culture. "The Nuer" or "the Bunyoro" constituted an appropriate unit of analysis. Barth's studies of Swat showed brilliantly how different ethnic groups within a region were tied together into a single political and economic system. The limitations of Barth's point of view, as underlined by Asad, lie in the way it elevates individual choices into systems, and in its relative innocence of history and of the connections between land, social class, and power.

We need to combine the strengths of both approaches. An analysis of politics must be rooted in the historic realities of control over resources and means of production. Analysis of individual choices and strate-

ness of relationship to the king. While the most powerful chiefs were members of the ruling Bito dynasty, most lesser chiefs were Huma cattle herders or peoples of the commoner group, descendants of men who had attracted the favor of a previous king.

The greatest chiefs, mainly Bito relatives of the king, were the "princes" of an aristocracy that commanded deference from commoners and lived from the surplus goods exacted as tribute from these common people. But these great chiefs were potential threats to the king's power, through rebellion and political struggles over succession. Their power was checked by their residence not in the territories they ruled over but in the king's capital; each left the usual affairs of his area in the hands of a deputy. They thus served as links between the king, in whose court they were key figures, and the rural populations that provided foodstuffs, valuables, cattle, and warriors for the king.

Because the king represented, symbolized, and ruled the entire country, it was important that he not be involved primarily with the interests of the Bito. The eldest son of the previous king traditionally held an office as Okwini, the king's "official brother"; and he had primary authority over affairs of the Bito ruling group. A half-sister of the king served as Kalyota, the king's "official sister." She in turn was officially in charge of the aristocratic Bito women, who enjoyed high rank and prestige and were considered to be "like men," in contrast to commoner women with their domestic duties. Formerly, these women of rank were not allowed to marry or have children. The Kalyota's power was in fact considerable: she held estates like male chiefs, deriving revenue and services from them, and she settled disputes among the Bito women.

Thus, among the Nyoro a patrilineal descent system provided the basic corporate groups and shaped organization at a local level. Yet superimposed on this descent system was a feudal hierarchy, a hereditary aristocracy, and a king with sweeping political power and great sacredness (Beattie 1958, 1960).

Case Update
See Uzoigwe (1977) for a consideration of the military basis of power among the Bunyoro and elsewhere in East Africa.

gies must be set within a framework of class analysis, which tells us why individual actors have different values, different interests, and different capacities to choose and act. But a mechanical and doctrinaire Marxist analysis does not deal with individual choices at all, but reifies abstractions such as "the ruling class" into causal agents—as if "it" had motives, made decisions, and invented and used ideologies.

We need to stay close to the realities of humans choosing and acting. But at the same time we need to understand the forces that shape their action. Asad's critique and the neo-Marxist perspective it embodies help us to see the direct connections between political power and economic control. This linkage takes different forms according to the mode of production. Thus men's political power among the Marind Anim of New Guinea rests on their control over women's labor and fertility, on the domination of older males over juniors in the homosexual initiatory grades, and on men's control of sacred rites, knowledge, and cult objects. The political power of the ruling class in ancient Rome or Aztec Tenochtítlan was sustained by state power and conquest that supplied tribute and slaves. But in these or any other societies, we get to the heart of political power by looking at questions of "political economy," at the relations between control over production and control over people.

34. RELIGION, POWER, AND THE POLITICS OF KNOWLEDGE

Religion and Earthly Politics

This representation of worldly power in religious terms demands close theoretical examination. Cultural traditions, such as the one we have encountered in the Trobriands, depict a universe which is closed, eternal, and supernaturally ordained. What in actuality are the cumulative result of generations of sexual politics, adjustment to the practical demands of life, and human symbolic creativity are portrayed as absolute and eternal. Such a representation of the nature of political and economic realities in ideological terms is called, in the Marxist tradition, **mystification.**

Mystification, in some societies, characteristically takes the form of defining earthly realities in cosmic terms: in representing political power in terms of *sacredness*, in populating the universe with ancestors or gods or spirits for whom powerful humans act as intermediaries, in defining human powers as superhumanly conferred, and human rules as imposed by supernatural beings. For such a representa-

tion of earthly realities in cosmic terms, Marx himself introduced the term *celestialization* (Marx 1938, I:367A). This approach draws our attention to the ways in which religious and political power may be intertwined. But we can go further and argue that in many cases there is no distinction made between religious and political power and both are a part of an overall cosmos.

The Politics of Knowledge in Tribal Society

The power of African elders, in controlling marriage and the prestige economy and subordinating women and young men, is based heavily on their control over sacred knowledge. So, too, is the power of men in some New Guinea and Amazonian societies, most strikingly those where secret cults and/or initiation systems progressively conduct young boys from a women's world into an inner sanctum of male secrecy (see Godelier 1986, Herdt 1982). But control over sacredness goes with power in earthly politics—as Case 39 will attest.

The cultural celestialization of the sources and nature of male power over women and juniors has an important consequence. Those who are subordinated are locked into the system not by a political and legal superstructure of state power but by their encapsulation within a closed universe of cosmic power. In such a universe, the subordinate cannot challenge the power that confines them; they have to "believe in" it as well as submit to it. If rules, such as those that exclude women from religious and political realms, were visibly the creations of men, they could be challenged. But if they are imposed by ancestors, who hold powers of life and death over the living, they are beyond challenge.

We need, then, to look *through* cultural conceptualizations as well as *at* them. Beneath symbolic systems, beneath ideas about sacredness and purity and religious duty, we need to see the realities of power: who has it, who uses it, in what ways, to what ends. But this then demands a conceptual clarity we have not yet attained. What *is* power? How can we identify power, and its uses, in a cultural setting such as the Poro society or Trobriand subclan?

What Is Power?

Even after publication of a major comparative volume on the anthropology of power (Fogelson and Adams 1977), and continuing efforts by political scientists and sociologists, the study of power remains conceptually fuzzy. Social scientists characteristically have fairly clear intuitions about power, and difficulty in rendering them precise and explicit. Perhaps this is inevitable: as Balandier has commented, "ambiguity . . . is a fundamental attribute of power" (1970:40). Perhaps it also has to do with the nature of the phenomena for which "power" has provided a label.

Power, virtually all analysts agree, is a matter of *relationships*—relationships between individuals (or units such as corporations or governments) who exert control and those who are controlled by them. Adams (1977:388) defines power as "the ability of a person or social unit to influence the conduct and decision-making of another." Adams conceptualizes the constraints imposed by the powerful in terms of energy (1975, 1977). Distinguishing a series of modalities of power, Adams observes that "when we speak of an individual's power, we are speaking of the totality of influence deriving from the total-

ity of controls that he exercises, directly . . . or indirectly" (Adams 1977:388).

What is important is to see "power" in *relational* terms—in terms of individual A exercising control over individuals B and C (whether the individuals are human beings or corporate entities), such that A constrains their possible options and actions. Moreover, this constraint is always *situational*. In a particular context, in relation to a particular issue, a particular piece of property, and so on, A may impose control over B. In another context, B may impose control over A.

Seeing "power" as situational and relational points to a conceptual problem hidden in our *language*. The key word to describe the relationship of A to B and C is *powerful*. In one context A is powerful in relationship to B and C, in another context C is powerful in relationship to A and B. The problem arises when we try to sum up how much "power" A has. This effort to sum up how much "power" individuals, or classes of individuals, or governments, or companies, "have" reflects a kind of linguistic trap. The morphological particle "-ful" on the end of "wonderful" or "awful" need not imply that there is a substance or entity one is "full" of (to say that something is "wonderful" doesn't mean it is full of "wonder"; to say that something is "awful" doesn't mean it is full of "awe"). But we have somehow gone from the relationship of being "powerful" to trying to measure and define an imaginary substance, "power," that people are more or less "full" of. Academics then exert great ingenuity trying to define what "it" is and to measure who has how much of "it."

Rather, we do better to begin and stay with a relational conception of "being powerful" in relation to particular people (or kinds of people) in relation to particular kinds of things in particular situations. We

Sacred Knowledge, Secrecy, and Power Among the Kpelle and Gola

The Kpelle comprise the largest ethnic group in Liberia. Their economy is based primarily on swidden cultivation of dry rice, which requires heavy labor, male and female. The Kpelle, and other closely related peoples such as the neighboring Gola and the Mende of Sierra Leone, are well known anthropologically because of secret societies into which men and women are initiated. Although there are various subsidiary secret societies, the best known ones are the men's Poro society and the women's Sande society.

Both these societies have long initiation periods, traditionally 4 and 3 years, respectively—periods in which the initiates are "educated" during seclusion in "bush schools." Each society has special areas for meeting:

A traditional village is surrounded by these secret areas carved out of the adjacent forest. The edge of the forest just outside the village is the threshold of a . . . world of hidden spirits and secret activities. (Murphy 1980:196)

The Poro society is concerned primarily with land and its sacredness:

Offenses against the land, such as certain kinds of accidental death, are adjudicated by the Poro society, often in secret meetings outside the village in the "sacred grove" of the Poro. (Murphy 1980:195)

The women's Sande society, counterpart of the Poro, has a complementary function as "ritual custodian" of the land. At some times of the year, the land is placed in the ritual custody of the Sande: "the land belongs to the women," Kpelle say. In this period,

the men's Poro society is not completely inactive . . . : only its ritual activities are subdued. The men still meet in the Poro "sacred grove" to make the important decisions affecting the community. The dominance of the men and the Poro is not affected by turning over the ritual activities to the women. (Murphy 1980:196)

The knowledge controlled by the secret societies is *sále* (the same term Kpelle use for medicine).

The various kinds of important *sále* are owned by the ritual leaders of the respective secret societies. This cultural idea of ownership is expressed by the compound term "medicine owner," which designates those who possess the secret knowledge of a particular "medicine." An owner of the most powerful "medicine" and a leader in the secret societies is called . . . "medicine specialist" or "ritual leader." (Murphy 1980:197)

Another important domain of secret society property is knowledge of history—particularly recent history of individual families, which serves to validate land rights and political claims. Here, for the Kpelle and their close cultural cousins the Gola, present politics are celestialized with reference to ancestors:

Individual interests in property and old feuds depend on . . . validation . . . by reference to the commitments, deeds, and wishes of the ancestors. (d'Azevedo 1962:26)

Thus sacred knowledge, only partly opened to view in public settings, is an important source of political power: "the elders in a community seek to protect and promote their versions of history." (Murphy 1980). When too much is divulged in public, young men among the Gola say, "the old men are wasting their property . . . like a man with a hole in his full sack of rice who does not know why the chickens have come running." (d'Azevedo 1962:19). The elders try to preserve the deeper knowledge of family history as, they say, "truth for grown men that will make them kings in the world" (d'Azevedo 1962:20).

To elders among the Kpelle and Gola, sacred knowledge is both the means to and a celestialization of political power:

Since Kpelle elders stake privileged claim to knowledge of ["medicine"] and history, they have the greatest concern in sustaining the barriers and boundaries which protect their knowledge. . . . The youth learn to honor these boundaries through secret society training which imbuses them with fear and respect for the elders' ownership of knowledge and their prerogatives over its distribution. (Murphy 1980:199)

Through their control over secret knowledge, senior men command the labor, as well as the deference, of young men. As Meillassoux (1960:49) had observed more generally of the power of African elders, "the authority of the elders rests on withholding knowledge, and it is this which supports and justifies the control of youth's labor products."

The political domination expressed in terms of sacredness and secrecy is opened to view if we look at lineage ranking among the Kpelle:

Kpelle elders are differentiated according to their lineage connections. The elders of the landowning lineages—those lineages which "own" the chiefdom's land by exercising primary rights over its use—control the secular and sacred authority of a chiefdom. . . . Control of the "secular" world has its counterpart in control of secret societies. Here again the landowning lineages dominate. The control of secret societies is achieved in large part by filling the high ritual positions, especially in the Poro and Sande societies, with members of these lineages. . . . Since lineages connections prevail over age status, most Kpelle youth cannot simply bide their time until increased age brings them high rank in the secret societies. (Murphy 1980:201)

This inequality of lineage ranking and its disguised consequences for status in the secret societies (among the Kpelle, Gola, Mende, and many other West African peoples) force a reconsideration of the assumption often expressed in the literature that all a young man needs to do to become powerful is get old. "While young men do become old men, not all old men become elders. . . . Most old men, along with women and young men, remain junior, dependents of the elders of the high-ranked lineages" (Murphy 1980:202).

The most crucial point, however, is the way control over the "traditional mystical beliefs of the secret society" goes with elders' control over "important community issues" through "deliberations over pragmatic political and economic affairs" (Murphy 1980:203).

Case Update

For a recent study of the Kpelle, see Lancy (1996).

can assume that imposing constraints on one another—being "powerful"—is a basic and pervasive motive in all human societies. Building up the means and resources that enable one to exercise more constraint over more people in regard to more things in a wider range of contexts is everywhere one of the dynamics of social life. To understand any society—not simply what appears as its "political system," but kinship or religion as well—we must explore these dynamics. If we understand "power" as a shorthand for these relationships and processes, it will serve us well. If we reify it into an imaginary substance people have more or less of, it will serve us badly.

We need now to turn directly to realms where the processes of politics and the dynamics of power are subtle yet pervasive; to the sphere of gender relations.

(example: the Trobriands). Chiefly systems may be more or less hierarchical. They may issue in kingdoms, such as developed in Hawaii in the Pacific or in Africa among the Bunyoro people. Chiefs and kings derive their legitimation from their sacred status. Politics in practice do not follow simply from rules of hierachy and authority. They involve individual strategizing and conflict.

Making those in authority sacred gives them a legitimacy they might otherwise not have. Sacred status may be acquired by either sex through secret initiations. It gives power over others in certain relationships, although not necessarily in others. Two spheres that remain to be considered are those of gender and those between senior and junior males.

SUMMARY

Political systems may be based on segmentary principles in terms of which order is maintained through the balanced interrelations of segments with one another via a hierarchical calculus of unity and difference (example: the Nuer). Leadership may be exercised by elders and other prominent men, or by priests. In Melanesia, we find the type of the "big man" (among other types, such as the "great man"), who generally bases his influence on his prominent part in exchanges of wealth goods and the speech-making that goes with these (example: the Kwaio). Or leaders may be chiefs, who belong to a ranked series of chiefly positions but who must also work hard to maintain their position in exchanges

SUGGESTIONS FOR FURTHER READING

SECTIONS 32–34

Bailey, F. G. 1969. *Stratagems and Spoils: A Social Anthropology of Politics*. Oxford: Basil Blackwell & Mott, Ltd.

Balandier, G. 1970. *Political Anthropology*. New York: Random House, Inc.

Barth, F. ed. 1969. *Ethnic Groups and Boundaries*. Boston: Little, Brown and Company.

Cohen, A. 1969. Political Anthropology: The Analysis of the Symbolism of Power Relations. *Man* (n.s.) 4: 215–235.

Cohen, R., and J. Middleton, eds. 1967. *Comparative Political Systems*. Garden City, N.Y.: Natural History Press.

Fogelson, R. D., and R. N. Adams, eds. 1977. *The Anthropology of Power*. New York: Academic Press, Inc.

Fried, M. 1967. *The Evolution of Political Society.* New York: Random House, Inc.

Hamnett, I. 1975. *Chieftainship and Legitimacy.* London: Routledge and Kegan Paul, Ltd.

Mair, L. 1977a. *Primitive Government: A Study of Traditional Political Systems in Eastern Africa,* rev. ed. London: Scholar Press.

———. 1977b. *African Kingdoms.* Oxford: Oxford University Press.

Shack, W. A., and P. S. Cohen, eds. 1979. *Politics in Leadership.* Oxford: Clarendon Press.

Swartz, M., ed. 1968. *Local Level Politics.* Chicago: Aldine Publishing Company.

12

Gendered Lives

Gender is an important dimension of social classification and action in many societies around the world, defining tasks and roles that people play in several spheres of life. There is considerable variation in the roles that are considered appropriate to males and females in different cultures, and there is also an arena of overlap when individual women and men take on roles that are classified as gender-specific within a particular culture. Men may to some extent take up female roles and vice versa. There are always limitations on the flexibility which applies here, and the domain is marked by ideological justifications which often appeal to putative physiological/anatomical and psychological factors. The cross-cultural evidence, however, shows that we cannot simply deduce gendered roles from physiological universals. Work by female anthropologists has contributed greatly to the understanding of the variability and meanings of gendered roles in different ethnographic contexts. Their enrichment of anthropological viewpoints is paralleled by similar alterations of perspective that have been derived from the work of indigenous anthropologists and gay/ lesbian anthropologists investigating problems both in their own cultures and elsewhere.

35. WOMEN'S WORLDS

Contrasts in women's roles, women's lives, and women's symbolic images in different times and places have come clearly into light after many years of serious ethnography of women's worlds. A number of volumes have sought to generalize from this accumulation of ethnographic accounts—an increasingly difficult task as the literature becomes more and more rich and diverse. As Naomi Quinn expressed it in a notable review article:

> Beginning in the early 1970s and rising to a current crescendo of books and articles, anthropologists representing all theoretical persuasions, most of them American and most of them women, have produced an entirely new literature on the status of women cross-culturally. This literature has proliferated so rapidly that apparently competing views, and in some cases compatible and mutually supporting ones, have gone unacknowledged; publication dates of some works are virtually simultaneous. The result is a bewildering number of disconnected hypotheses about the status of women. (Quinn 1977:181)

Quinn (1977) and Rogers (1978) make noteworthy attempts to sort out these "disconnected hypotheses" and summarize the

A woman counts money she has innovatively collected from other women as a contribution to a *moka* Festival, Melpa, Papua New Guinea. Note that the money is laid on colorful cloths worn by women.

major themes in the literature. Subsequent summaries have been made by Ortner and Whitehead (1981), Sanday and Goodenough (1990), Miller (1992), and others.

Before we survey some of the findings and controversies in this field of study, we need to look at a theoretical and conceptual issue: whether we can correctly say that women in societies such as Maring or Marind Anim are exploited by men—or, another side of the same issue, whether young men are exploited by elders.

The Question of Exploitation

Are women "exploited" in societies where they have been portrayed as symbolically demeaned, politically dominated, and economically controlled by men? Are junior men exploited in African societies, such as the Tiv (Case 30), the Tallensi (Cases 19 and 29) and the Kpelle (Case 39), where political and religious authority is held by male elders who extract the labor and fighting power of young men? The two situations would seem to differ in that subordinate young men, if they live long enough, may themselves become male elders (although lineage politics among the Kpelle indicate that this is not necessarily true); subordinate women never become men. (Read on, however, for a further critique on these matters.)

Those who argue that juniors and women are not, properly speaking, "exploited" generally take the view that exploitation can occur only in a system of social classes—that is, where there is a cleavage between those who control the means of production and those whose productive labor they extract. Social classes, in a technical sense, can never be based on age (since everyone gets older) or on sex, but are defined by contrasting positions within a system of production. Those who argue that African elders exploit juniors, or New Guinea tribesmen exploit women, urge that the concept of exploitation needs to be broadened if neo-Marxist theory is to probe beneath cultural ideologies to analyze the realities of these societies. If the issue were simply one of terminology it would be trivial. But it focuses our attention on the way people who live enmeshed in a system of cultural meanings are committed to this system even where it subordinates and demeans them.

Hence, we find over and over again that cultural ideologies that subordinate and exclude women, extract their labor and child-bearing and child-rearing, and place them under legal control of fathers, brothers, and husbands are supported as vehemently by women as by men. Accepting, as they have to, a celestialized system that consigns them to domestic roles and a regimen of labor that serves male prestige, women portray themselves in terms of virtue and duty. Within the constraints of subordination, women may themselves become important political actors who not only substantially

Women's status: Kwaio (Solomon Islands) women are seemingly demeaned and excluded by an ideology of pollution (see Case 49), but they participate centrally in the prestige economy. Here a young woman contributes to her brother's bridewealth.

influence the public political affairs of men from behind the scenes, but themselves pursue strategies of controlling labor and prestige within the constraints of the system. (See, for example, M. Strathern 1972, Lederman 1986.) Here Bledsoe's observations about the Kpelle, described in Case 40, are also instructive.

This, then, brings us back to the question of "exploitation." The choice presented to us by the comparative facts of anthropology is this. Either we accept a broadened conception of exploitation as a technical term, so that it covers the subordination of women

CASE

40

Women's Strategies Among the Kpelle

Bledsoe (1976:372) begins with the observation that "many African women are just as conservative as men in trying to preserve the institutions which hand the control of women's services to other people." In analyzing her data from the Kpelle, whose secret societies we saw in Chapter 11, she finds that in the course of the life cycle, women can achieve considerable personal autonomy despite their jural (legal) subordination, and that they pursue strategies (especially as they reach middle age and beyond) through which they command labor and services.

Even though unmarried girls "are very much the pawns of their male and female relatives," both before and after arranged marriages, they take lovers relatively freely. "A girl with a handsome lover, or a lover who migrates to work and brings her gifts of clothes, is the envy of her friends." But "though she may have affairs, she remains under the legal control of her relatives or her husband . . . who can collect fines from her lovers" (Bledsoe 1976:378).

Powerful men contract multiple marriages—then may "loan" wives out to unmarried men, who become obligated to provide labor and patronage. "Men try to use . . . rights in women to entice other men into their debt, through bridewealth, brideservice, or clientship" (Bledsoe 1976:377). A woman, dependent on men for labor, "has little means of escaping subordination. . . . The great majority of women lack formal, socially sanctioned power over other

adults. Neither do they often gain legal rights in themselves, much less other people" (Bledsoe 1976:377).

Nonetheless, Kpelle women support the traditional framework (in the face of Western influences) and use it to their own ends. They use their husbands' relationships of clientship to advance their own economic ends, and strategically manipulate their daughters' marriages to command labor in their old age and to achieve political goals.

Most women . . . are quite eager to stay married for economic support, even though marriage subordinates them to a man's legal control. Lacking legal rights in her children . . . she manipulates the disposition of these rights in ways most beneficial to her. Women staunchly support the marriage system, which they use to obtain young people's labor and support." (Bledsoe 1976:380)

Bledsoe suggests that most writings on men and women in African societies, in emphasizing the legal and cultural separation of male and female realms, have overlooked the similarity of men's and women's political strategies: "Both men and women try to use economic and political resources to escape from those who have rights to command them." She points out that the structures of domination, ostensibly so heavily weighted in favor of men, shift our attention from "the group which really shoulders the burden of productive labor in African societies . . . : the young" (Bledsoe 1976:387).

and young men and the extraction of their labor to sustain the prestige and power of others; or we develop a more differentiated conceptual system, with terms alternative to and more apt than "exploitation" to analyze the Kpelle and other peoples.

The arguments for the latter—for developing a less crude terminology—seem strong. Recall from Gudeman's (1978:374) critique of neo-Marxist economic anthropology (§19) his argument that "the Marxian notion of exploitation provides a foreshortened view of the variability of distributive patterns" found in the non-Western world (a similar problem runs through a recent controversy about whether peasants are "exploited").

Just what terms best fit the various phenomena continue to be debated. An array of different terms may be required for different elements of what often is a single complex. A term something like *"cultural subordination"* could be used for celestialized systems of domination in classless societies. For the culturally sanctioned command senior men exercise over the labor power of women and/or young men, a term such as *labor control* may be apt. Where our focus is on the deployment of the products of surplus labor to serve the political-economic ends of those who control it, but where such uses of surplus (in pig exchanges or feasts or rituals) are supported by the producers (in terms of duty, prestige, power from the ancestors, etc.), a term such as *consensual surplus appropriation* may be useful.

Armed with such concepts, we could more effectively analyze classless societies where the "controllers" themselves do productive labor, where one's place in hierarchies of power may shift drastically in the course of the life cycle, and where those who are dominated, whose labor is controlled, may be as committed to cultural values and ancestral rules as those who

exercise earthly powers. What matters is not terminology in itself, but rather the paradox of looking at a way of life from "inside" and looking at it from "outside." If we look at a way of life through the eyes of those who live it, women and men, young and old, may be equally committed to a system of rules and meanings—even though it gives power and advantage to some of them and subordinates others. How legitimately, and with what doubts, can we step outside this system and view it as an ideology—without simply imposing *our* ideology on them? With this question in the foreground, we can now turn to women's worlds in comparative perspective.

The Subordination of Women

In one of the books of the 1970s that examine male-female relations in comparative perspective (Rosaldo and Lamphere 1974), a number of prominent women anthropologists lent support, in different ways, to the argument that women are universally subordinate to men: that in every known society, public and political life had been preeminently in the hands of men. Although the status, independence, and political and economic importance of women is relatively high in some societies and quite low in others, it is never, these authors argue, coordinate with or greater than that of men.

In her introduction, Rosaldo (1974) argues that the assignment to women of the tasks of child-bearing has led in every known society to a separation between the domestic realm and the "public" realm. Women have their major roots and major commitment in the domestic realm: women's roles center around hearth and home. The public realm is preeminently the world of men, though in various times and places women have come to play a central part on the public stage, as well as behind the scenes:

Put quite simply, men have no single commitment as enduring, time-consuming, and emotionally compelling—as close to seeming necessary and natural—as the relation of a woman to her infant child; and so men are free to form those broader associations that we call "society," universalistic systems of order, meaning, and commitment that link particular mother-child groups. (Rosaldo 1974:24})

The question remains why, apparently universally and for both men and women, it is the roles associated with men, and with the public realm, that are most highly valued—roles of warrior, elder, priest, or chief. Women's virtues are virtues of subordination and second-class citizenship. (This whole viewpoint, however, has been challenged subsequently, along with the public- domestic dichotomy on which it is based.)

Can Biological Differences Explain Cultural Subordination?

Rosaldo examines the cultural expressions of female subordination even in societies where women have relatively high status and power and sex role polarization is not extreme—societies such as the Arapesh (Mead 1935), where women were excluded from sacred rites; the Merina of Malagasy (Keenan 1974), where men speak publicly with formal allusion while women are "cultural idiots, who are expected to blurt out what they mean; and the Yoruba, where women control trading and economics yet must kneel to serve their husbands and feign ignorance and obedience" (Rosaldo 1974:20). Can such subordination be accounted for on the basis of "different hormonal cycles, infant activity levels, sexual capacities, or emotional orientations" (Rosaldo 1974:20)?

Will they explain the constant factor in the secret flute cults of the Arapesh, the Merina

woman's lack of subtlety, or the bowing and scraping of the Yoruba wife? Although there is no doubt that biology is important, and that human society is constrained and directed in its development by facts of a physical kind, I find it difficult to see how these could possibly lead to moral evaluations. Biological research may illuminate the range in human inclinations and possibilities, but it cannot account for the interpretation of these facts in a cultural order. It can tell us about the average endowments of groups of particular individuals, but it cannot explain the fact that cultures everywhere have given Man, as a category opposed to Woman, social value and moral worth. . . . Biology. . . becomes significant only as it is interpreted by human actors and associated with characteristic modes of action. (Rosaldo 1974: 22–23)

In another important paper in this volume, Ortner (1974) builds on foundations laid down by Simone de Beauvoir (1953) and Ardener (1972). If men have political control in the public realms of society, there is always one power—the greatest power of all—that remains mysterious and beyond their control: the power of life itself, of giving birth. Men may arrange or exchange legal rights over women's offspring, but the power of creating life (and of sustaining it with breast milk) remains beyond their grasp. Pregnancy and birth are processes that seem dark, mysterious, and threatening—yet are envied. This theme of male envy goes back in anthropological literature to Mead (1949) and has an older history in psychoanalytic theory.

Ardener and Ortner, noting this envy of uncontrollable power by the men who create cultural ideologies, suggest that women are often symbolically linked with the wild world of nature, in contrast to the ordered, controlled world of culture. Woman is symbolically marginal or **liminal,** neither fully in the world of nature or the world of culture. Ortner made this observation:

Woman's body seems to doom her to mere reproduction of life; the male, in contrast, lacking natural creative functions, must (or has the opportunity to) assert this creativity externally, artificially through the medium of technology and symbols. (1974:75)

In one sense, the male creations are sterile and superficial in contrast to the creation of life. But paradoxically, "he creates relatively lasting, eternal, transcendant objects, while the woman creates only perishables—human beings" (Ortner 1974:75). De Beauvoir has suggested that cultural valuation of the taking of life by men (in hunting and warfare) above the creation of life by women reflects a celebration not of destruction but of risking life; and Ortner builds on this to argue that warfare and hunting are social and cultural, while giving birth is natural.

These interpretations represent a considerable advance over earlier attempts to account for universal subordination of women, or their consignment to domestic realms, on the basis of supposed biological differences. There probably are differences in the distribution of behavioral-temperamental predispositions between male and female in our species, as among other primates. But differences do not carry *meanings*—which are a matter of cultural symbols, hence specific to time and place. Moreover, the culture-nature distinction is more a product of European historical categorizations than a cross-culturally applicable notion (see MacCormack and M. Strathern 1980).

Beyond Universals

Critics of Rosaldo's and Ortner's universalization of the public-private, dominant-subordinate, and culture-nature dichotomies have not been slow to rise. Some are scholars in the Marxist tradition, who challenge the use of the "public-private" distinction derived from a capitalist mode of production to apply to the very different conceptions of tribal peoples. Where, in some societies, production takes place primarily within domestic groups, the internal relations within these groups are central and crucial—even though ritual, warfare, and speech-making may be male activities carried out more visibly and dramatically within the community. The "private" realm, if that means what goes on within households, is the economic core of the society. But in a capitalist society, the workplace within which production is centered and in which labor is financially rewarded is outside the domestic realm. Housewives do the unpaid and substantially unrewarded labor of bearing and rearing children; cooking, and housework, in a domestic realm that is peripheral and secondary. To say that women are always consigned to the domestic, "private" sphere and that this is a key to their universally subordinate status blurs the crucial fact that in many societies the domestic sphere *is* the workplace.

Another cornerstone of Rosaldo's position that has been seriously challenged is the question of universal subordination. Eleanor Leacock has particularly questioned the assumption that women are or were subordinate in hunting and gathering societies. Leacock (1978) has argued strongly that the subordinate status of women is a concomitant of changes brought about by food-producing, and the property relationships to which it led. Hunting and gathering peoples, she argues, had fundamentally egalitarian relations between the sexes. Where contemporary hunter-gathers are reported to subordinate women, Leacock (1978) argues that this either reflects biased reporting of the facts or the consequences of Western invasion and colonial subjugation (Etienne and Leacock 1980).

Leacock assembles evidence showing the transformation of male-female relationships among hunter-gatherers to be a consequence of capitalist penetration of the economy and the emergence of new property relations and of subjugation. There is also evidence that among some hunting and gathering peoples, an ethnographic focus on men's activities and male views of "the system" led observers to miss corresponding women's ritual and women's considerable power in arranging marriages and in political decisions (Bell 1980).

But even allowing for the impact of colonialism and ethnographic bias, asymmetries of status and power between men and women seem to be old and basic among many hunter-gatherers. Rosaldo and Collier (1981) explore these asymmetries, suggesting that in a number of hunting and gathering societies, and some that augment food-gathering with horticulture, the tenor of asymmetric male-female relationships is established through young men competing for wives and lovers by soliciting the favor of prospective fathers-in-law through labor and hunting. Meat, which men provide, is a medium for the politics of exchange, redistribution, and marital politics; vegetable foods, gathered by women, constitute the bulk of daily subsistence, but are not accorded a symbolic importance coordinate with meat. Rosaldo and Collier see in this complex a key to the way women in these societies, although accorded substantial autonomy and often sexual freedom, play a subordinate part in political life. In these societies women are largely excluded from the subtle political games of negotiating marital exchanges, securing second and third wives, and competition for leadership. The stakes in these games are not material, but involve control over other people. Here, a complex interplay among the pressures

and demands of subsistence, the organization of production, the tenor and structure of social relationships, and the concerns of ritual and religion is postulated.

Women's Status, Women's Power

Assessing the "status of women" in any society is a complicated business. There is considerable evidence that formal rules and institutional structures which place women under male control and restrict and demean them may be enacted, in everyday life, in ways that give women considerable autonomy and choice. Symbolic systems that would seem to polarize the sexes and demean women may, in some societies, be "lived in" without the strain, conflict, or negative self-images one would expect them to entail. Women may exercise substantial power behind the scenes, and sometimes on center stage as well, in systems where male domination seems clear. Women may be economically central and ritually peripheral.

How are we to determine questions of power when a desert Sheikh in the Middle East presses his counterparts in other groups into a strategic alliance that is in his interests and not in theirs, yet when it is the Sheikh's wife—who is never seen in public—who behind the scenes pressured her husband into taking this course when he was reluctant to do it? How powerful is he, how powerful is she? In Mesoamerican peasant communities, men may take center stage in matters of ritual and community politics, exercising their power in public arenas; and women may exercise power mainly in matters of domestic economy and behind the scenes in community life. As Rogers (1975) points out, the question of who has what power in what context is rendered more complicated in peasant communities where the men of a community may be powerless and subordinate to, and

demeaned by, landlords, government officials, and other outsiders. What looks like
political power from a perspective *within* a
peasant community may be a kind of empty
posturing and pageantry in relation to the
constraints imposed from outside. Rogers
suggests that women's power exercised behind the scenes may in some sense be more
genuine than men's power enacted on center stage. At least, we now know that it is
impossible to make simple assessments of
the status of women on the basis of a people's institutions and ideologies: we must
see how they are "lived in." (See also
Keesing 1985, 1987.)

Male Bias in Anthropology

It is now well documented that because of
the historical biases of our society and of
social science, anthropologists—male and
female—have looked at the events in other
people's worlds, and described them, with
a strong male bias. We need only to think
back to the spectacular women's mortuary
distributions in the Trobriands, which went
virtually unnoticed and undescribed for
years. That dramatic aspects of women's
lives and women's worlds went unnoticed,
in society after society, is hardly surprising.
Male bias in interpretation is a continuous
theme. Thus, as Leacock (1972) points out,
when women go into menstrual huts men
are "excluding them from society"; and
when men go into men's houses, they are
"excluding women from the sacred." In
dealing with pollution systems a focus on
the pollutedness of women has led ethnographers both to overlook parallel pollutedness of men (semen may be as polluting as
menstrual blood: Faithorn 1975) and to
overlook the positive powers that may be
attributed to menstrual blood (Meigs 1978).
There are countless other examples of distortion. But this in turn reflects the way men

have presented themselves to ethnographers, male and female, as spokespersons
and ideologists of the system. Public and official "culture" is primarily a male creation,
it would seem, in society after society. So
anthropologists' theories that lead them to
seek a coherent and articulated cultural ideology and describe "it" put ethnographers
in the position of spokespersons of a society's (male) ideologists.

Through sensitive ethnographies of
women's worlds, and autobiographical accounts, anthropologists have accumulated
evidence that these male-articulated public
versions of "a culture" do not exhaust a
society's symbolic resources or represent
perspectives on "the culture" women necessarily share. Women's counter-cultures,
alternative ideologies, and contrasting
perspectives on—or commitments to—the
"official" versions of a culture are emerging
in the literature. That women have often
been relatively inarticulate spokespersons
and ideologists, with a less "global" view of
"the system" may be true in some societies;
but it is certainly not true in all. In some societies, including ones where women are
seemingly subordinate and excluded from
ritual and political life, they have turned out
to be articulate and forceful counter-ideolo-
gists—once social and political and ethnographic contexts have emerged in which
their perspectives could be expressed.

Women's Power and Women's Economic Roles

Although crudely materialistic theories
would anticipate that women's status and
power are directly shaped by their role in
the economic system, these relationships
are turning out to be indirect and complex.
We have seen enough evidence of how
female labor is extracted to serve men's
symbolic goals of power and prestige to

discount any simple correlation between the work women do and their political status. One might imagine that in a real matriarchy, if one ever existed, men might well have done most of the hard work, to serve women's political and economic ends. So when we find women playing the physically demanding role in production, we cannot assume that this reflects, or is the material basis of, women's power. It is more revealing to look at control over distribution, especially of surpluses.

Where women play a central part in production *and* have substantial influence or control over the distribution of surplus, they characteristically play a substantial political role and are accorded important symbolic recognition. But that cannot, in itself, be an "explanation" of women's status: women's partial control over the distribution of surpluses is an expression, not a cause, of their political importance. But again, where women have high symbolic status and a secure place in the prestige economy and the distribution of surpluses—as in the Trobriands—it may still take them to a point far below parity with men. Recall that in the Trobriands, the

Efe woman, baby on back, tending Lese garden, Ituri, Zaire.

kula is entirely a male enterprise, only men are hamlet managers, and women's performances in the prestige economy are largely financed by men. We will return to the complex integration of men's and women's worlds in the Trobriands when we look at Trobriand religion and symbolic systems.

Women's Worlds: The View From Inside, the View From Outside

Although women in many societies may have counter-ideologies or perspectives on the social order complementary to those of men, they are, in most societies we know about, ultimately committed to cultural rules and meanings. We have seen how, given the illusion of a closed universe, and the celestialization of human rules, a system appears to those who live within it as beyond challenge. Where the weapons of aggression—clubs, bows and arrows, spears—are concentrated in the hands of men, there was very often a threat of violence lying behind religious ideologies.

But the question of our positions as observers remains unresolved. If we are looking at a system that places legal control over a woman in the hands of her father and brothers, then her husband and his lineage, a system that rigidly enforces her chastity, that assigns her to roles of bearing and rearing children and doing the bulk of productive labor—yet takes out of her hands control over what she produces, and excludes her from political and religious life— are we to evaluate her life in her terms, or ours? If we evaluate life in her terms, she may be a pillar of virtue, responsible for the moral order of the community and the well-being of her family through following the ancestors' rules about pollution and observing the standards of chastity. She will be as quick to criticize a daughter or wife who shirks her work duties or has an affair as

any man. She sees her role in child-bearing and subsistence production as fulfillment of her essential nature, and views male political control and religious life and men's rights over her as part of the essential order of the universe. Who are we, then, as observers imbued with values about freedom, equality, and the liberation of women, to tell her that her ideas of virtue are an illusion? Is not the role of the anthropologist to understand other people's worlds through *their* eyes?

There is no simple answer. We need, somehow, to see each culture—ours included—from both inside and outside. If we look at each cultural tradition only in its own terms, understand people's lives only through their own eyes, then we are ultimately limited to a relativism that sees whatever *is* as right. If we apply some set of political and moral standards to other people, uncritically, we too easily lose sight of the fact that this set of standards itself has a history, is ideological, is a product of a Western sociocultural tradition embodying values about individualism, equality, and the nature of work that are far from universal. Much anthropology has stood too far on the side of relativism, and has missed essential outside perspectives. But much that has passed for revolutionary idealism has been uncritical of its own cultural roots and ideological foundations. To see other cultural worlds from both inside and outside is no easy challenge. But it is probably the most fundamental one with which the materials of anthropology confront us.

It is perhaps true that women have been subordinate in some sense in all traditional societies. But there have been enormous differences in the status of women, their economic position in relation to the means of production, and their power in domestic and public realms. To understand the subordination of women, one must look at these variations and have a keen sense of history and process—a sense that is dulled if one emphasizes universals.

Such perceptions are needed if a comparative anthropology of women is to serve the interests of transforming in positive ways the role of women in Western society. And an anthropology of women has been strongly—and, I would say, rightly—motivated not simply by the challenge of understanding the world, but by the challenge of changing it. Reflection on that challenge, to the transformation of women's worlds, will have to wait until Part 4. We need to go on to build further, and reinforce, the theoretical foundations for comparative understanding by now turning more directly to the nature of social hierarchy.

SUMMARY

Gender is an important dimension of description and analysis in many cultures. Historically, the interest in gender has emerged from studies of women in society, including questions to do with domination and exploitation between the genders that emerged from neo-Marxist approaches concerned both with gender and with the control of male juniors by senior men. Women may (or may not) themselves assent to male control, while seeking in practice to exercise influence on their own account (example: the Kpelle). The cultural subordination of women is found in many (but not all) societies and is sometimes (but not always) linked to categorizations that oppose female to male domains in terms of "natural" reproductive functions versus "cultural" capacities. Eleanor Leacock has shown that among hunter-gatherer populations gender relations tend traditionally to be relatively egalitarian. Women ethnographers have been able to highlight the significance of women's economic and ceremonial roles in cases where these were earlier backgrounded (example: Annette Weiner on the Trobriands). In addition, we must recognize that as observers our evaluations of the "ethnographic facts" may be quite different from those of the people themselves.

SUGGESTIONS FOR FURTHER READING

SECTION 35

Ardener, S. 1978. *Defining Females: The Nature of Women in Society*. London: Croom Helm.

_____, ed. 1975. *Perceiving Women*. London: Malaby Press.

Friedl, E. 1975. *Women and Men: An Anthropologist's View*. New York: Holt, Rinehart and Winston.

Hammond, D., and J. Jablow. 1976. *Women in Cultures of the World*. Menlo Park, Calif.: Cummings Publishing Company.

Kuhn, A., and A. M. Wolpe. 1978. *Feminism and Materialism: Women and Modes of Production*. Routledge and Kegan Paul, Ltd.

Mitchell, J. 1971. *Women's Estate*. New York: Random House, Inc.

_____. 1974. *Psychoanalysis and Feminism*. London: Allen Wayne.

Paulme, D. 1971. *Women of Tropical Africa*. Berkeley: University of California Press.

Reiter, R., ed. 1975. *Toward an Anthropology of Women*. New York: Monthly Review Press.

Schlegel, A. 1972. *Male Dominance and Female Autonomy: Domestic Authority in Matrilineal Societies*. New Haven, Conn.: HRAF Press.

CHAPTER
13

Structures of Inequality

At several points, we have touched on social classes—for instance, in looking at early states, and in a negative sense, in looking at the classless societies of the tribal world that for years were the main focus of anthropology. Increasingly, anthropological attention has been directed to peasants, and more recently, urbanities—humans incorporated within class systems. Although our main attention to these class systems will come in Part 4, we need for theoretical reasons to pause briefly to look at systems of hierarchy and inequality in comparative perspective.

36. SOCIAL CLASSES AND STRATIFICATION

Do Trobrianders of chiefly rank and those of commoner rank belong to different classes? What about Polynesian nobles and commoners? Or Aztec warriors and priests? Did slaves in ancient Rome and Greece comprise a class? If so, was it the same, as a class, as that of plantation slaves in the American South and Caribbean?

Conceptualizing Inequality

There are few areas of social science theory as messy as the study of structures of inequality. What is the difference between social classes and occupational groupings? Can we speak of a "ruling class," or should we choose the more neutral term *elite*? Can we legitimately speak of a "middle class" in

modern Western societies? Do broad divisions of a society into kinds of people constitute "classes" when they are ranked in prestige but not clearly separated in economic function? And finally, can we legitimately use the term *caste,* derived from Indian civilization, to designate minority groups excluded from the mainstream of society (as African Americans once were) or consigned to degrading work (as with the *burakumin* in traditional Japan) on the basis of their "impurity"?

When we find divisions of "kinds of people" that cut across a whole society and are ranked in terms of prestige, they do not necessarily constitute classes in a technical sense. For this general phenomenon, the term **social stratification** will suffice; and the ranked divisions can be called **strata** (singular, *stratum*). Strata in a system of social stratification cut across the whole society; hence they are more general than occupational groupings. They are not based on biological characteristics of age or sex. (We have seen that polarization of the sexes, or of young and old, in societies that are technically unstratified and classless, may lead to conflicting interests and contrasting economic roles that manifest some of the characteristics, and have some of the consequences, of class opposition.)

Classes are strata of a special kind. They are interlocking "pieces" within a social system defined according to their economic relationships. It is not that they are necessarily richer or poorer; but that their *function* within a system of production is specialized. It is specialized not in terms of what work people actually *do* (butcher, baker, and candlestick-maker are all members of the same class, as long as they work for wages and do not own the butcher's shop, bakery, or candle factory). Rather, a class is defined in terms of the relationship of people's labor to their sources of subsistence and to the means of production. Class relationships thus lump members of a society together broadly, as workers, owners, artisans, slaves, and so on.

Thus Marx and Engels wrote of the evolution of modern society in terms of a history of class relationships in which those who work have been polarized in opposition to those who control the means of production: "freeman and slave, patrician and plebeian, lord and serf, guild master and journeyman."

> In the earlier epochs of history we find almost everywhere a complicated arrangement of social rank. In ancient Rome we have patricians, knights, plebeians, slaves; in the Middle Ages, feudal lords, vassals, guild masters, journeymen, apprentices, serfs; in almost all of these classes, again, subordinate gradations. (Marx and Engels 1848)

Marx viewed peasants as ambiguous, in terms of such a theory of class. Classes in the full sense are distinguished by consciousness of a common lot, of one's group's place in the scheme of things—in relation to others, one's group's collective solidarity, and common interests in relations of production. European peasants, he observed, do not manifest this commonality that defines classes in the full sense.

> The small-holding peasants form a vast mass, the members of which live in similar conditions but without entering into manifold relations with one another. Their mode of production isolates them from one another instead of bringing them into mutual intercourse. . . . In so far as millions of families live under economic conditions of existence that separate their mode of life, their interests and their culture from those of other classes, and put them in hostile opposition to the latter, they form a class. In so far as there is merely a local interconnection among these small-holding peasants, and the identity of their interests begets no community, . . . they do not form a class. (Marx 1852)

Peasants can, as the experience of the late nineteenth and early twentieth centuries makes clear, crystallize into a class with revolutionary power. We will return in Chapter 18 to the anthropological study of peasants.

Classes in Comparative Perspective

Understanding of class phenomena has advanced considerably in the century since Marx's and Engels's work. Whereas nineteenth-century capitalism showed a widening polarization between the bourgeoisie (as "owners of the means of production and employers of wage labor") and the proletariat (as "the class of . . . wage laborers, who having no means of production of their own are reduced to selling their labor power in order to live"), modern postindustrial society has become much less simple in class terms—with a vast middle class of professional people, who sell their specialist skills and technical and managerial abilities rather than their muscle power. Theories of a "ruling class" controlling subject classes through instruments of state power and ideology have had to be refined: "different types of society conform in varying degrees with Marx's model of a society which is clearly divided between a ruling class and subject classes" (Bottomore 1964:28). The warrior nobility of feudal Europe, "which had securely in its hands the ownership of land, military force, and political authority, and which received the ideological support of a powerful church" (Bottomore 1964:29), approximated closely to Marx's idealized conception of a ruling class (although it was decentralized rather than cohesive); and the ascendant bourgeoisie of the England of Marx's time seemed headed in a similar direction, but with far greater cohesiveness, and with full instruments of state power in "its" hands. But in other social systems, including contemporary industrial societies, the "ruling class" model is less clearly applicable.

The preconquest states of the Americas, and of parts of Africa and Asia, were organized in classes. Among the societies we have looked at, the Aztec (with its artisans, warrior nobles, slaves, priests) and the Hawaiians of Polynesia exhibited class stratification.

Slavery

Slavery becomes more comprehensible if we look at it in terms of class relationships. Here our stereotypes about plantation slavery are misleading. First, it is worth thinking about the centrality of slavery in the Greece and Rome of antiquity:

> It was slavery that first made possible the division of labor between agriculture and industry on a considerable scale, and along with this, the flower of the ancient world, Hellenism. Without slavery, no Greek state, no Greek art, and science; without slavery, no Roman Empire. . . . The increase and development of production by means of slave labor . . . [made possible] extension of trade, development of the state and of law, . . . [the] beginning of art and science. [These were] only possible by means of a greater division of labor between the masses discharging simple manual labor and the few privileged persons directing labor, conducting trade and public affairs, and, at a later stage, occupying themselves with art and science. The simplest and most natural form of this division of labor was . . . slavery. (Engels 1878:205–207)

The slavery of the ancient world, based mainly on the capture of prisoners of war, was quite different in class terms from the plantation slavery of the Americas.

So, too, was the slavery of precolonial African societies. To understand the wide range of phenomena in Africa that have been classed as "slavery," argue Miers and Kopytoff (1977) in their long introduction to a volume on these systems, one must discard some Western premises about individualism and autonomy. Recall that marriage and politics are characteristically matters entailing corporate groups. A descent corporation has rights over its members—so that individuals might be assigned in marriage, given up to be killed, or pawned by the "board of directors" of their corporation:

> Neither the criterion of [individuals as] property nor that of salability can be useful . . . in separating "slavery" from simple "kinship" in African societies, in which rights in wives, children, and kin-group members are usually acquired through transactions involving material transfers and in which kin groups "own" and may dispose of their blood members. (Miers and Kopytoff 1977:12)

Slavery was in many cases a further extension of this corporate control, a transfer of humans in political-economic systems within which labor and an obligated following were means to power:

> The acquisition of people . . . was a process ranging from voluntary or peaceful personal transactions between neighboring groups to bilateral compulsory transfers and, with increasing degrees of coercion and organization, to the large-scale entrepreneurship of raiding and war. . . . Strangers seeking patrons were welcomed; orphans or abandoned children were wanted; captives . . . were eagerly sought. Kidnappers found a ready market for their victims. . . . Acquired persons . . . provided extra wives and children to expand a kin group, labor to till the fields, retainers in the compound, soldiers for warfare, paddlers for trading canoes and war canoes,

trading agents, servants and officials at court, and even victims for sacrifice. Political and social power rested with those who could command a large number of kinsmen and dependents, whether clients, followers, or "slaves." (Miers and Kopytoff 1977:14)

There are several lessons in all this. First, we cannot understand the position of slaves simply by classifying them as such. They occupied a place within a mode of production, a system of classes, a social structure. What rights they had, how they were included in and excluded from the social system, must be understood with reference to the total system.

Second, the "total system" did not necessarily coincide with a particular language group or political entity. Slaves in Africa were captured and traded across wide regions. The chapters in Miers and Kopytoff (1977) describe far-flung regional systems across which slaves were traded and trade goods and valuables flowed. These regional networks were expanded and intensified when Europeans entered—and drastically transformed—the slaving business. It is worth pausing to note that to understand plantation slavery in the Americas requires a global, not local, view as well. We will see how events on the sugar and cotton plantations, the first stages of the Industrial Revolution in England, and the devastation of West and Central Africa were systematically interrelated.

An analysis of class relationships in a complex social system must make no assumptions at the outset about individual classes and their status, except in relation to one another, and no assumptions about the geographical or cultural boundaries of the system. It is worth recalling Asad's critique of writings about the "pastoral mode of production," which is exactly in these terms: class relationships may cut across the boundaries between "societies"; and different "societies" may be tied into a regional political

and economic system. (See also J. L. Watson 1980, an edited collection of studies on the workings of slavery in Africa and Asia.)

Child Labor

Another context in which we can discuss the concept of exploitation is that of child labor. Children are used widely to supplement labor capacities in many economic systems, whether based on kinship or not. Children may be called on to work on a family farm without monetary remuneration. In early periods of industrialization in Europe, poor children were extensively employed as they continue to be employed in other parts of the world still. If the work of women and young men can be viewed as subject to exploitation, so can the work of young children below the age of adolescence.

Once again, the issue is partly one of definition, of what we call exploitation. What level of return would be sufficient for us to say that the relationship is not exploitative? Is there a difference between work in the family and labor in the industrial marketplace? And to what extent do we take into account the feelings and judgments of those that are putatively being exploited? Answers to these questions depend on the observer's set of values and concerns, but the issue is worth raising since the existence of child labor is seen by many as a human rights issue. (See Mendelievich 1980 for a cross-societal survey.)

Caste

A final mode of hierarchical social classification bears mention. This is **caste;** the differentiation of a society (in Hindu India and Hindu-influenced areas of South and Southeast Asia) into endogamous, ranked social categories according to ritual purity and impurity. Castes are ranked, from the most sacred and pure to untouchables who do the most polluting and menial duties.

Local caste groups may perform prescribed, hereditary occupations—menial services such as barbering or sweeping—in exchange for small payments in grain. Are they, then, classes? The general answer is "no." At some time in the ancient past the four *varna* or paths of life—priests, warriors, merchants, and farmers—may have been more classlike. But now, in many parts of India, local caste groups supposed to be of warrior or Brahmin status are preeminently village cultivators. Economic relations do not, in general, correspond to the ideal caste scheme. But it is not these vast-scale caste categories that matter, but rather, local subcastes as corporate groups. These local subcastes may be locked into economic relations that are more classlike—although they are expressed in terms of purity and pollution, hereditary obligation, and Hindu ritual (See F. G. Bailey 1957, 1963).

Inequality and Mystification

The nature of castes raises a more general question. Recall how the domination of women and young men may be disguised by cultural ideologies that celestialize relations of subordination and the extraction of labor. The same is true of class-structured societies. The priesthoods of the ancient states of Mesopotamia and the Americas created religious ideologies that justified and sustained the power of ruling elites.

But here there may be an equally strong consensual commitment from the dominant and the dominated. Here, recall Harris's comment, in response to Sahlins's lyrical depiction of Aztec human sacrifice as the highest form of communion, that "we must reserve the right not to believe ruling class explanations" (Harris 1979a:521). In state societies where priests and rulers lived in an opulence sustained by wars of plunder and the sweat of others, we need to be able to look

at religions as ideologies that reinforce the control of those at the top and instill among those at the bottom a sense of duty and devotion, and a hope for reward in an afterlife for their subservience in this one. That those at the top and those at the bottom may be equally pious and equally committed to devotion of the gods does not prevent us from asking about the political economy of the sacred. In some ways we are in the same position, in looking at a religious system vast in scale, rich in philosophical wisdom, and ancient in its textual bases, as we are in analyzing the sacred flutes and men's cult initiations in New Guinea. We need to enter and understand a world of symbolic meanings—and then to step through it to see how it mystifies and reinforces earthly realities.

Whether we can, and should, ask such questions about caste in Hindu India—or should instead see, in an ancient and rich philosophy of cosmic scale, alternative ways of conceiving of humankind and spiritual being (Dumont 1966)—is an issue on which writers disagree. Many would urge that our challenge is to understand gossamer webs of cultural meaning, not cut through them to seek something more "real" underneath.

In the Marxist tradition, religious ideologies, like political institutions, are said to operate as superstructural systems that sustain—reproduce—a mode of production, and disguise its real nature. The evidence of anthropology does not tell us directly whether we need to take this step. But it tells us that if we do take it, we can legitimately do so only after immersing ourself in a system of cultural meanings from the "inside," and only with self-critical awareness that our ideas and values are themselves products of history and cultural tradition, not absolute ideals.

The systems of law through which societal rules are applied and enforced present us with the same paradox. From the standpoint of the businessman in suburbia, laws are the foundation of orderly society, and those who break them are criminals. From the standpoint of the poor in the inner city, the law is a charade, a way the establishment sustains its own hypocrisy; people who are arrested for breaking it are political prisoners. Which point of view do we take on the systems of law and order in Africa or Polynesia? Do they legitimize, hence maintain, a prevailing system of privilege and power? Or are they the means whereby the integrity of a cultural system and its standards of right and virtue are maintained, and social order preserved?

Once more, as we look at systems of law and social control, we will face the need to situate ourselves both inside and outside a prevailing set of cultural meanings and social relationships.

SUMMARY

This chapter addresses some concepts of inequality and systems of hierarchy that exist in various cultures. Conceptualizing and defining inequality is a difficult task and one that must be examined from inside the culture that is being discussed—that is, the indigenous ideology should be explored. The chapter also discussed ideas of social stratification in which strata (layers) of separate groups of individuals exist, taking into consideration Marxist theory of societal structure. The functioning of class groupings and slavery systems was presented in relation to religious ideologies and the concept of mystification.

SUGGESTIONS FOR FURTHER READING

SECTION 36

Bendix, R., and S. M. Lipset, eds. 1966. *Class, Status, and Power: Social Stratification in Comparative Perspective*, 2nd ed. New York: The Free Press.

Berreman, G. 1973. *Caste in the Modern World.* Morristown, N.J.: General Learning Press.

Beteille, A. 1970. *Social Inequality.* London: Penguin Books, Inc.

Bohannan, P. 1963. *Social Anthropology.* New York: Holt, Rinehart and Winston.

Cox, O. C. 1970. *Caste, Class, and Race.* New York: Monthly Review Press.

De Reuck, A., and J. Knight, eds. 1967. *Caste and Race: Comparative Approaches. London:* J. and A. Churchill, Ltd.

Dumont, L. 1970. *Homo Hierarchicus:* Chicago: University of Chicago Press.

Eisenstadt, S. N. 1971. *Social Differentiation and Social Stratification.* Glenview, Ill.: Scott, Foresman and Company.

Fried, M. 1967. *The Evolution of Political Society.* New York: Random House, Inc.

Klass, M. 1980. *Caste: The Emergence of the South Asian Social System.* Philadelphia: Institute for the Study of Human Issues.

Leach, E. R., ed. 1960. *Aspects of Caste in South India, Ceylon, and Northwest Pakistan.* Cambridge Papers in Social Anthropology, 2. Cambridge: Cambridge University Press.

Mencher, J. P., 1974. The Caste System Upside Down, or The Not-So-Mysterious East. *Current Anthropology* 15:469.

Miers, S., and I. Kopytoff, eds. 1975. *Slavery in Pre-Colonial Africa.* Madison: University of Wisconsin Press.

Ossowski, S. 1963. *Class Structure in the Social Consciousness.* New York: The Free Press.

Plotnicov, L., and A. Tuden. 1969. *Essays in Comparative Social Stratification.* Pittsburgh: University of Pittsburgh Press.

———. 1970. *Social Stratification in Africa.* New York: The Macmillan Company.

Richardson, P. 1971. *Empire and Slavery.* New York: Harper & Row, Publishers.

Singer, M., and B. S. Cohn, eds. 1968. *Structure and Change in Indian Society.* Viking Fund Publications in Anthropology, 47. Chicago: Aldine Publishing Company.

Watson, J. L., ed. 1980. *Asian and African Systems of Slavery.* Berkeley: University of California Press.

Winks, R., ed. 1972. *Slavery: A Comparative Perspective* New York: New York University Press.

14

Law and Social Control

In states—ancient and modern, African, Asian, and New World, as well as European—institutions of courts, often codified in legal statutes, have maintained law and order. The range of legal institutions has been wide; but we recognize them as manifestations of law. But where there are no states, often no political institutions beyond those of local kin groups, legal processes stand out less clearly from the ongoing processes of social relations. When an African lineage negotiates the marriage of one of its members, sealed by the transfer of bridewealth cattle in exchange for rights over progeny, is it a "legal" contract? When Inuit men, quarreling over some grievance, sing insulting songs to one another in front of their neighbors, is that "law"?

Here, as so often in the comparative study of humankind, we find a domain which is clearly defined, institutionalized, and compartmentalized in complex societies, yet in tribal societies is submerged within the structures of kinship and the processes of everyday social life. Are we to say that there is no "law" in such societies? Are we to ask what functions are served by legal institutions in complex societies— settlement of conflict, adjudication of disputes, punishment of offenders, redress of damages, maintenance of contractual

relationships—and label as "legal" whatever processes accomplish the same ends in small-scale societies? We faced the same difficulty in looking at "economic systems" and "political systems." The problem may seem tedious, especially if it leads to endless debate about definitions. But if we worry about matters of substance rather than definition, we can learn much about the organization of society, the range of cultural variation—and about ourselves. And that is what anthropology is about.

Before we look at the processes of dispute settlement and conflict resolution in comparative perspective, it is worth reflecting in more general terms on the forces of social control—some of them subtle—that bind people into ongoing social relations and cultural conventions.

37. SOCIAL CONTROL AND PRESSURES TO CONFORMITY

Norms, Conformity, and Deviance

Writings on "deviance and conformity," especially in sociology, usually begin with a narrow conception of a "norm," as something people say should or should not be done. You violate a norm—whether or not you break a formal law—if you steal, cheat, marry two men at once, go nude to church, or drive through a stoplight. You conform when you follow such norms; you deviate if you violate them.

Some norms are indeed public and are consciously followed or broken. But other "rules," hidden below the surface, have been uncovered by researchers in anthropology following the clues provided by the rules of grammar. These rules are implicit in our behavior, deeply ingrained in habit and unconscious mental processes. Yet our following them lies at the heart of ordered social life. The man who robs a bank is, in sociological terms, criminally deviant. But the anthropologist can perceive him as a routine-bound conformist as well. He comes to the bank appropriately clothed, walking rather than crawling, on the sidewalk rather than the roof or the gutter. He utters or writes his demands in conventional language, and he makes his getaway on the right side of the street. One must conform unconsciously to a myriad of cultural rules and conventions to commit a "grammatical" bank robbery—which is, in fact, a complex act of communication.

The rules we break, or would like to break, lie toward the surface of that complex and intricate system of shared knowledge we call culture. To communicate, we are and must be rule-followers. We will, for ease or explication, refer to those standards of behavior we talk and consciously think about as public norms. Our unconscious rule-following on lower, hidden levels does not explain why we follow public norms as often as we do, but it gives a different perspective on them. Another source of perspectives on conformity and deviance is our growing understanding of our biological heritage. Since the writings of Freud, a conflict between human biological drives and the rules of ordered social life has usually been taken for granted. We are, biologically, animals—and to behave as humans exacts a cost of frustration and repression.

Our views of human biosocial life have changed dramatically with modern animal behavior studies. Freud was imagining the individual animal, driven by its aggressive nature and sexuality and free to express these natural drives. But we have seen animals in *groups*. That primates are "programmed" with drives for dominance, aggression, and sexuality does not imply their free expression: the young baboon may be as thwarted as a Viennese psychiatric patient. Social organization, whether animal or human, requires that individual organisms pursuing their goals mesh together into ordered patterns of communication, acknowledged rights and powers, and collective action.

Moreover, the very notion of our biological drives being "blocked" seems unrealistic at this stage. As we have seen, human biological proclivities are open-ended, depending on the symbolic content of cultural traditions for their content and focus. It is only within a matrix of cultural meanings that human goals and motives make sense: the sense they make is social sense; we are social beings. But in striving for goals we inevitably compete and come into conflict; the codes that make ordered social life possible constrain pursuit of individual goals. What, then, keeps us from cutting corners more often than we do?

Self-Interest and Social Interest

Probably the most compelling pressures to conform come from enlightened self-interest. The cynic who sees humans as motivated only by self-interest and the idealist who sees human destiny in selfless giving and sharing are seeing the grays of social life in black or white. Humans have constructed the mazes of social life—because they have had to—so that the paths through them to individual goals are opened only by cooperation, by sharing, and by rule-following.

Sometimes the rewards of playing the game together and of helping one's fellows are immediate and direct. Sometimes they are long-range, as when a young man willingly serves elders in the expectation that later he will attain such status. Our society is rapidly losing a cycling kind of giving and return that is shaped by the life cycle and often axiomatic in the moral system of some people: parents who care for their children when they are young and helpless may be cared for by them when they are old and helpless. Sometimes the rewards are diffuse, as with family cooperation or the satisfaction of friendship, security, or popularity.

We have seen the peculiar moral force of kinship. Fulfilling obligations to one's relatives would seem to run counter to self-interest. But if kin do not always live up to ideal standards, they meet obligations well enough that kinship seems to have an extraordinary moral force. Why? On closer inspection, following kinship obligations turns out to advance, not conflict with, self-interest; and very often, group interests *are* self-interests.

This can well remind us that a self-interest model of society is in part an expression of a Western economic and political ideology. It is clear that human tendencies to be individualistic and motivated by self-interest are reinforced by childhood experience that emphasizes competitive individualism.

Every way of life, every social system entails internal contradictions and lines of stress. Those people whose cooperation is essential to collective action may be placed in competition over resources, status, or succession. In-marrying wives may be the daughters of enemies; cowives may be placed in conflict in relation to the rights of their children. To expand one's sphere of influence or prestige through exchange, one may have to take the risk that one's rivals will not reciprocate; to succeed too well may put you at risk that they will use magical means to retaliate.

Cultural Channeling of Conflict

One way of letting off pressure at the stress points of a social system is to ritualize the expression of conflict. The Tallensi rite whereby a first-born son is shown his father's granary when the father dies (Case 2) dramatizes the structural conflict between generations, giving public expression in a defined form to private conflicts and resentments. Sexual license in a limited situation, or overt hostility against the rules of the establishment, can be an effective way of "blowing off steam." Privileged sexual access outside of marriage, as between a man and his wife's sister, can relieve potential conflict and tension. **Joking relationships** involving joking and often sexual license between certain classes of relatives have been a classic focus of attention in social anthropology. So, too, have been the opposite side of the same coin, **avoidance relationships,** where strict rules of decorum or even of complete avoidance restrict interaction between a man and his mother-in-law, his sister-in-law, his sister, or some such relative or class of relatives. Avoidance relationships, like joking relationships, occur in the strain points of a kinship system; but they control pressures and tensions by ritualized distance rather than blowing off steam. Case 41 describes privileged joking relationships and avoidance relationships among the Trobrianders.

Witchcraft

Supernaturals often, though not always, keep a close watch on the moral conduct of the living. Moreover, customary rules and

CASE

41

Familiarity and Avoidance in the Trobriands

Trobrianders illustrate both privileged familiarity and avoidance, though neither is in as extreme a form as found in some areas. These customs will prove important in Chapter 16. Though Trobriand brother and sister have common concerns in the subclan, and her sons are his heirs, the gulf of her sexuality separates them. From childhood onward, their relations are marked by distance and avoidance of any close contacts. As the sister begins her amorous adventuring, her brother must refrain from any knowledge of it. Even when she marries, matters surrounding her reproductive life are forbidden territory to him. The tabooed relationship between brother and sister is the most emotionally charged and morally fundamental rule in Trobriand culture.

But a man's father's sister has a very different relationship with him. "Her presence always carries with it the suggestion of license, of indecent jokes and improper stories" (Malinowski 1929:535). She is a kind of prototypical sexual object for him—usually considerably older and hence seldom an actual sexual partner—though that is quite permissible—but treated with sexual familiarity and openness. A man cannot mingle with both paternal aunt and sister at the same time: the rules for each contrast too sharply.

For a discussion of Trobriand sexual taboos from a Freudian perspective, see Spiro (1982).

procedures are very often given a stamp of divine origin that validates them and gives them an aura of being ultimate, absolute, and sacred. To break the rules of social life is very often to break the laws that govern the universe.

A powerful force of social control in many societies is witchcraft—malevolent power that operates through individuals as an involuntary force. Even in the outwardly peaceful and restrained social setting of Pueblo Indians in Zuni or Hopi, violence may erupt with the driving of a witch into the desert. In many societies in Africa, North America, and elsewhere, the deviant who failed to meet the norms of kinship or play by the rules—or simply was more successful than everyone else—would be likely to be singled out as a witch and killed or exiled. Witchcraft accusations, which may in

some societies assign responsibility for every death that occurs, give a splendid means to get rid of those who cheat, deviate, or succeed too much—and a splendid incentive to be an upstanding citizen. (See Case 42.) Fear that witchcraft will be directed against one makes conformity to the norms of social life strategically wise. Equally, accusations of witchcraft may be seen as hostile acts of the powerful against those who appear to threaten their control.

Comparative study of witchcraft has been an important theme in modern social anthropology. The premise that witchcraft accusations will follow the "stress lines" of a social structure underlies most of this research. Are accusations usually directed against kin? against affines? against unrelated neighbors? against cowives? Systematic correlations between forms of social

CASE

42

Kaguru Witchcraft and Social Control

The Kaguru of Tanzania believe that many of their fellows, male and female, possess *uhai*, supernatural powers of witchcraft. Beliefs in witchcraft are conceptually quite separate from Kaguru religious beliefs, which center around propitiation of ancestors.

Kaguru believe that most misfortunes, from death and illness to crop failure, loss of articles, and bad luck in hunting, result from witchcraft. Witches represent an inversion of the moral and symbolic values of the Kaguru, with their evil and antisocial intents and, in the most feared forms of witchcraft, their clan incest, cannibalism, and nakedness.

A Kaguru who believes he is a victim of witchcraft will often suspect who the witch is; but he may go to a diviner to find or confirm the witch's identity. In the past, an accused suspect would be tried by the local community, usually with an ordeal. If found guilty, he or she would be clubbed to death. If innocent, the accuser would pay a large fine. Now public witchcraft accusations are illegal, but the suspected witch may learn of the charge in gossip or through some sign; or that person's garden may be damaged or house burned. A man against whom such accusations are directed several times would probably move somewhere else.

Who is accused? Members of your own matrilineal clan are not supposed to be apt to direct witchcraft at you, but many accusations occur even within the closer bounds of a matrilineage. Although anyone might be a witch, the following are particularly suspect: (1) economically successful persons; (2) powerful chiefs and headmen; (3) nonconformists; (4) a wife whom her husband cannot easily control; (5) a woman envious of her cowives; and (6) people who refuse to meet important obligations to their kin (Beidelman 1963:74).

How does witchcraft serve as a force of social control? Beidelman (1963) notes that the powerful man may in fact encourage beliefs in his powers of witchcraft so as to increase his influence and control. A powerful man might be feared as a witch, but it would take corresponding power to accuse him. It is not clear how successfully, and by what means, witchcraft accusations could be used in olden times to eliminate the strong man who went too far in wealth or power. Certainly political rivalries and disputed succession bring witchcraft accusations and suspicions to the fore. For the man of more limited means and powers, the threat of witchcraft accusations was a strong force for conformity and approved social behavior (Beidelman 1963:96–97). See also Beidelman (1993) for a further discussion on Kaguru ideas.

structure and the nature of witchcraft have supported and reinforced this premise.

Looking at forces of conformity gives us only one side of the picture. Social conflict and its resolution, behavior outside permitted bounds, exist in every society. And thus we are left with the sticky problem of how to distinguish and analyze legal processes in various cultural settings, societies where they do not have the separateness and symbolic trappings that distinguish legal institutions in Western societies.

38. LAW: A COMPARATIVE VIEW

What Distinguishes "Law"?

A few first principles will serve us well in making sense of the range of cultural variation. First, if we start out to find *the* legal system in a society, our quest may be misguided from the outset. There may be several "legal systems" in the same society. Different people may make decisions in different kinds of groups, or cases, or settings, with reference to different sets of standards. The different legal subsystems in a society may involve different spheres of life. They may involve different kinds of violations. Thus our distinction between civil and criminal offenses may be mirrored in a non-Western society with a contrast between "private delicts" and "public delicts." Or they may involve different groups. Thus cases involving members of a lineage may activate one set of legal mechanisms, cases involving members of a larger community another, and cases involving members of different communities a third. In societies without state or centralized law, the distinction between civil and criminal offenses may not operate at all (see, e.g., A. J. Strathern 1970 on state versus tribal law in Papua New Guinea).

But how do we know a legal system, or a legal process, when we find one? Is it because there is a clear and codified (if not written) set of "laws"? No, says Pospisil (1968, 1971, 1978). He argues that such abstract rules are rare and specialized in human societies, mainly limited to Western societies since the codification of Roman law. Legal principles are more often implicit, flexible, and constantly changing. Increasingly, the legal processes and legal principles of a society have come to light by looking at *cases,* at specific instances where conflicts of rights or breaches of rules are socially resolved. The legal principles of a society emerge from the study of decisions in these cases.

Who makes these decisions? In what settings and by what processes? And if there is no formal code of laws, what guidelines, principles, or precedents are used to make them? How are they enforced? Each of these questions, if followed out, would show a wide range of variation. Here we can afford only a quick glimpse at each.

Who makes legal decisions? Where the social organization is simple, as in band societies, they are likely to be made by the leader of the band. What legal powers he exercises may be contingent on his success in leading the hunt, dealing with supernaturals, or maintaining internal or external peace. So, too, the big man of Melanesia has power to make legal decisions only to the extent people defer to his skill and wisdom and his success and power as an entrepreneur.

Even where the leader of a descent group or community has formal rights based on his position, not simply his personal power, these are likely to be binding only to members of his own group. In a segmentary lineage system, who has the right to make decisions may depend on who the contending sides are and what the case is about. Offenses involving members of different corporations may lead to blood-feuding or warfare, or they may be settled according to "legal" principles to avoid or end armed confrontation. In some societies, the settlement of conflicts may lead into positive reciprocal exchanges (A. J. Strathern 1971).

Law and Political Power

This usefully shows that—except to some degree in more complex societies where formal courts and legal specialists have developed—legal action is intertwined with politics. The power to make binding decisions in cases of conflict is, in less complex societies, political power. But for us to try to draw, or erase, a line between legal and political would be a waste of time. It is better to think of the political and legal as two ways of looking at events, sometimes the same events: each point of view illuminates a different facet.

This brings us back to a point raised at the end of the last chapter. The class that holds power in a society has the means to define laws that legitimize its own rights and vested interests, and protect and perpetuate them. (We need to be careful about reifying abstractions: the "it" is a shorthand way of referring to individuals who have a commonality of interests and perspectives; only human individuals make decisions and perform acts—classes or lineages do not.) Thus what is legal and morally binding from the perspective of those who hold power may be an instrument of political oppression from the point of view of those who do not. While this conflict of interest and contrast in perspective is most striking in a class-stratified society, the same questions can be raised in a classless society. It is not so much that might makes right as that power conveys the means to define what is legitimate.

Formal and Informal Mechanisms of Dispute Settlement

The range of settings in which processes of dispute settlement take place covers a span from formal courts with legal specialists as judges to informal gatherings of kin and neighbors. This obviously depends in substantial measure on the scale and mode of political organization of a society. In the complex centralized ministates and chiefdoms of tribal Africa, we find legal institutions as elaborate as those of Western societies. For instance, Case 43 describes the Tswana court system.

Even in a society with elaborated courts, informal litigation may often be used to settle cases out of court. Thus, subtle and undramatic legal processes can be found to exist side by side with more formal legal systems. For example, Case 44 describes the Kpelle **moot** (an anthropological borrowing from legal terminology)—an informally constituted and unofficial gathering of kin or neighbors or other interested parties who hear a case and attempt to work out a solution.

Without Courts: The Range of Legal Processes

Where there is no formal political structure uniting members of different kin groups, mechanisms for managing disputes are likely to be based on negotiation or confrontation between the individuals or kin groups involved. In stateless societies, disputes can easily erupt into feuding. Thus an offense may be managed either through legal negotiation or outside the framework of law. We have already seen some of the mechanisms—such as the Nuer Leopard-skin chief and the intervention of kinsmen with divided allegiances—that militate against open hostility or settle feuds once set into motion.

The range of mechanisms used to resolve disputes in stateless societies includes *ordeals* (which also were once used in Europe). (An example from the Philippines, in a society organized along kindred lines, is presented in Case 45.) The assumption that supernatural beings will mete out justice in ordeals—that the guilty will be found out, the innocent exonerated—itself rests on a special kind of world view. The Kwaio of the Solomon Islands, whose social organization we have viewed at several points, sometimes use ordeals to settle accusations.

But the Kwaio, with a personalized view of ancestors and the powers they convey to favored descendants, add a special twist. If you steal a pig or shell valuables, and are forced to take an ordeal to prove the innocence you are falsely proclaiming, you pray to your ancestor for help: the ancestor will, if suitably disposed, help you to demonstrate your innocence in the ordeal even though you are guilty. (More often, you make a false oath of denial, hoping that the ancestors upon whose sacred altar stones you have sworn your innocence will support you, not punish you.)

Among most hunter-gatherers, we find a range of dispute-settlement mechanisms. One from the Inuit is presented in Case 46.

Norms and the Legal Process

The place of norms in the legal process has been a focus of recent attention. It is the essence of law, as opposed to power politics, that the decisions reached be viewed as legitimate, with reference to moral standards or rules that have some universal applicability. They do not simply reflect accepted common practice in the community, but what Hamnett describes as "a normatively clothed set of abstractions from practice" (Hamnett 1977:7)—abstractions "which the actors in a social situation . . . invest with binding authority" (Hamnet 1975:14).

But this reference to norms in the comparative study of legal processes raises a problem. For in some societies, the actors in litigation make frequent reference to abstract normative principles; in other

CASE

43

The Tswana Court System

The Tswana tribes of south-central Africa have a complex and hierarchical court system, paralleling the political hierarchy. As studied and reported by Schapera (1955), each local patrilineage or "ward" had its own court, with the headman as judge; and each village had its court and judge. These lower courts had jurisdiction in civil cases (that is, cases dealing with status, property, and contracts); but difficult cases could be referred to a higher court. A "criminal" case, involving an offense such as homicide or sorcery, could be reviewed at local levels; but decisions were made by the tribal chief's court, complete with legal specialists and elaborate formal proceedings.

In a Tswana court case, the judge and his advisers faced the litigants. Formal statements by the litigants were followed by testimony by witnesses and examination by the court advisers, deeply steeped in the subtle and detailed principles of Tswana law. The advisers debated the merits of the case, after which the judge summarized the evidence and delivered the verdict.

The complexities and detail of Tswana law, as known by legal specialists who act in the courts, are impressive. Schapera, their ethnographer, had years of experience in Tswana legal matters—yet when invited to act as an adviser to the court, he felt insufficiently versed in the intricacies of Tswana law to do so with the skill of a Tswana specialist.

Case Update

For more current developments in Tswana "people's courts," see Pavlich 1992.

The Kpelle Moot

Among the West African Kpelle of Liberia
(whose secret societies we viewed in Case 39) a
political structure of town, district, and regional
chiefs is paralleled by a hierarchy of formal
courts. However, this formal system of courts and
official legal decision-making has major disad-
vantages for settling disputes among kin, affines,
and neighbors whose social relations must be
maintained after the particular legal issue at
hand has been resolved. The formal courts, coercive in imposing decisions in black-and-white
terms, tend to leave the litigants polarized and
bitter.

A more effective means of settling disputes
among people who need to preserve the fabric of
social relations is the "house palaver," or *moot.*
Among the Kpelle, it is usually domestic problems—martial conflicts, unpaid debts between
kin, quarrels over inheritance—that are settled
through airing of the dispute before a moot. The
group is an ad hoc cluster of interested and concerned parties, mainly kin and neighbors. The
gathering is held at the home of the complainant,
who calls the moot, under the auspices of a kinsman who acts as mediator. The mediator is a respected elder skilled in dispute settlement.

A Kpelle moot: This one differs from the usual moot in that it is being held outdoors,
and involves a dispute between a carpenter and his customer.

societies these principles are implicit in the background, but not cited by the participants. Moreover, there seems to be "no obvious relationship . . . between the clarity with which abstract norms are articulated, the way in which they are employed and their importance in decision-making" (Comaroff and Roberts 1977:79).

Two African peoples, the Arusha (Gulliver 1963) and the Soga (Fallers 1969), will serve to illustrate. Among the Arusha, "norms are often relied on in the course of a dispute"; but "norms are seldom explicitly referred to in Soga disputes: instead, argument and decision-making proceeds through reference to facts, the choice of which implies reliance upon a norm that is mutually understood" (Comaroff and Roberts 1977:79).

Why the greater appeal to abstract normative principles in some societies than in others? Bohannan (1965:39) had suggested that normative principles would be made more explicit in societies with centralized legal systems, where decisions are more often based on adjudication than compromise between the litigants. But Comaroff and Roberts note that this does not fit the range of comparative evidence, such as that from the stateless Arusha, who cite norms with great precision. Moreover, Bohannan's hypothesis "is of little help in relation to those societies, like the Tswana [Case 43], where a hierarchy of dispute-settlement agencies include levels at which settlement by compromise is attempted and ones at which the outcome involves [an imposed] decision" (Comaroff and Roberts 1977:81).

Comaroff and Roberts note that among the Tswana, norms are cited in some contexts of litigation and not in others. Rather than seeking to understand this in terms of different "kinds" of societies, they argue, we should look more closely at the dynamics of the litigation process in particular societies. Among the Tswana, litigation in a particular

case is conducted with reference—implicit or explicit—to a particular framework of norms. Where all participants share general knowledge of this normative framework, "the way in which a party arranges the facts will convey to others present his paradigm of argument": That is, he will implicitly establish the normative framework in terms of which these facts "speak" (Comaroff and Roberts 1977:105). They suggest that norms are explicitly stated when a disputant wishes to redefine the "paradigm" of argument. "When disputes appeal to different orders of norm in opposition to one another, we would expect them to state, and argue over, the priority which they assign to competitive norms" (p. 109). Norms are made explicit by judges "when they are compelled, or feel it necessary, to distinguish or adjudicate between a plurality of paradigms of argument" (p. 107).

Law and Social Relationships

To understand litigation in non-Western societies, we need to realize that we ourselves live in a curious world where social relations are largely cast in economic terms: the terms of property and the marketplace. In a society ordered primarily on kinship lines, litigation may be "over" things such as land; but it is characteristically "about" social relationships. Overtly, the issues at stake may seem trivial; but they have to do, below the surface, with the sorting out or restoration of the social bonds of kinship and community that bind the living to one another and the ancestors.

This raises an interesting theoretical problem in the anthropological study of law. It is true that the legal system comes into play when criminal offenses are committed, rights over people or things are contested, or disputes break out. But the legal systems in Western societies play another less visible but equally important part: creating and

Ordeals Among the Ifugao

Among the Ifugao of the Philippines, criminal cases and such civil cases as property disputes are often settled by ordeals. A person accused of an offense who persistently denies guilt may submit to an ordeal as a challenge; or the accuser may challenge the individual to prove his or her innocence. An accused person or a party to a dispute who refuses to submit to an ordeal is considered to be in the wrong.

There are several forms of ordeals. In the hot water ordeal, a person must reach into a pot of boiling water, pull out a pebble, and then replace it. In other Ifugao regions, a red-hot knife is lowered onto a person's hand. In either case, it is believed that if the party is guilty his hand will be badly burned; if innocent (or in the right, in the case of property dispute), it will not be badly burned, and the accuser or rival must pay compensation. Two parties to a dispute must each have the knife lowered onto both of their hands; the one who is the right will be less badly burned. Finally, there are several forms of duels and wrestling matches where the parties to a dispute put their case to the test. Here, as in the individual ordeals, it is believed that supernatural support swings to the party who is in the right.

The ordeals and contests are supervised by a *monkalun*, or arbiter, a neutral party who in these cases acts as an umpire. In other forms of litigation a *monkalun* acts as go-between and attempts to reach a compromise or bring the facts to light by negotiating with and probing the parties to the dispute (Barton 1919).

preserving an ordered system of mutual expectations and understandings that are intended to avoid conflict. Much of the work lawyers do has to do with *contracts*.

> In civil matters, litigation occurs in only a very small proportion even of disputes, and these in their turn are almost infinitesimally few in comparison with the huge number of interactions where the law serves merely as a consensual and implicit context of transactional discourse. Indeed, what the law . . . principally offers is the crucial advantage of knowing more or less where they and their partners stand. (Hamnett 1977:5)

An anthropology of law that focuses on social control and dispute is hard-pressed to bring into view the expectation-preserving, balance-maintaining aspect of legal principles in tribal societies. For this takes us squarely back into the broad domain of custom, of a shared culture that makes possible a consensual definition of the appropriate. To operate in the world—to garden or build houses or conduct religious rituals—humans need an implicit set of "rules" for acting, doing, and deciding. These need not be completely shared or consistent or neat; they are constantly being changed and adapted to fit changing circumstances. The elaboration of legal codes in complex soci-

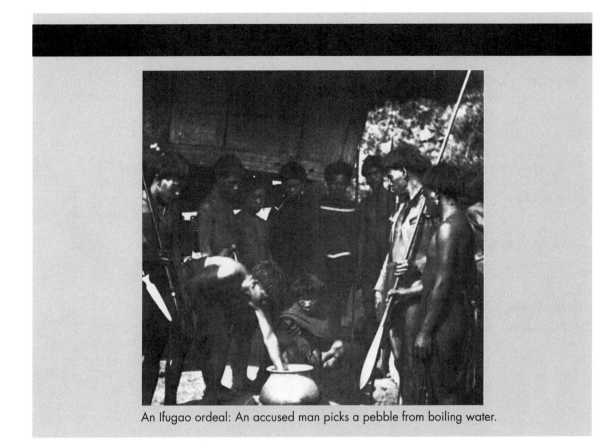

An Ifugao ordeal: An accused man picks a pebble from boiling water.

eties to preserve a universe of shared expectation, amid cultural diversity and the "economization" of social relations, serves this function, but only at great cost. For implicit normative codes are enormously flexible, adaptable to the uniqueness of the situation. In rendering normative codes as explicit legal codes, we "freeze" them. We then need enormous human wisdom and skill to reintroduce this flexibility into a system of courts—to follow the "spirit" of the law rather than the "letter," to recognize and cope with the uniqueness of each case. Where this is not done, the law remains proverbially "a blunt instrument," unable to deal with the complexities of individual disputes—for example, in the realm of family law and divorce cases.

The continuity between "law" and everyday life in tribal societies, the way litigation serves to preserve and rebuild networks of social relations, enables us to understand why

> processes which occur within the legal frame-work do not always concern the actual settlement of disputes. They may . . . provide the context for the public enactment of established relations. . . . [Thus] Barotse* may go to law knowing that they will lose the case or

---

*An African people well known in the anthropology of law from the work of Gluckman (1955).

CASE

4 6

Inuit Song Duels

Among Inuit groups, with no formal mechanisms of government or courts, disputes are resolved with a "court" of public opinion—the small-scale Inuit community. With no formal or codified set of rules, the Inuit are free to treat each dispute over wife-stealing, homicide, or the like, as a unique constellation of people and circumstances (Hoebel 1954).

For disputes less serious than homicide, most Inuit groups have an unusual and effective way of blowing off the steam of hostility while resolving the legal issue: the song duel. Here each party to the dispute composes songs that ridicule his adversary and set out in exaggerated fashion his grievance or his version of the disputed events. Ribald satire, taunts, innuendo, distortion, and buffoonery bring mirth from the

onlookers as the songs go back and forth. By the time the "case" has been made by each party, the litigants have blown off steam and public opinion has swung toward a decision that will redress valid grievances or dismiss weak ones. A perhaps more important function than legal decision-making is that by their song duel the disputing pair have had their say in public and can resume their normal relationship—stung only temporarily by the "little sharp words, like . . . wooden splinters" (Rasmussen 1922:236).

Case Update
More recent studies have also been documented. For a reanalysis of Inuit dueling songs, see Eckert and Newmark (1980).

may commit an offence in order to be taken to court. (Comaroff and Roberts 1977:80)

Legal action is social action, in all its manifold complexity. Frake's vivid picture of litigation among a Subanun (Case 25) group in the Philippines will help to leave us with a view of law as a facet of social life, not a separate compartment:

> Litigation in Lipay . . . cannot be fully understood if we regard it only as a means of maintaining social control. A large share, if not the majority, of legal cases deal with offenses so minor that only the fertile imagination of a Subanun legal authority can magnify them into a serious threat to some person or to society in general. . . . A festivity without litigation is almost as unthinkable as one without drink.

In some respects a Lipay trial is more comparable to an American poker game than to our legal proceedings. It is a contest of skill, in this case of verbal skill, accompanied by social merry-making, in which the loser pays a forfeit. He pays for much the same reason we pay a poker debt: so he can play the game again. . . .

Litigation, nevertheless, has far greater significance in Lipay than this poker game analogy implies. For it is more than recreation. Litigation, together with the rights and duties it generates, so pervades Lipay life that one could not consistently refuse to pay fines and remain a functioning member of society. Along with drinking, feasting, and ceremonializing, litigation provides patterned means of interaction linking the independent nuclear families of Lipay into a social unit, even though there are no formal group ties of comparable extent. The importance of litigation as a social activity makes understandable its prevalence among the peaceful and, by our standards, "law-abiding" residents of Lipay. (Frake 1963:221)

SUMMARY

All societies have ways of exercising social control over their members and of settling disputes, whether we call these ways "legal" or not. All societies, equally, depend on the maintenance of social norms, which may be sanctioned explicitly or implicitly. There are even culturally patterned ways of breaking norms. Pressures to conform may be brought into alignment with self-interest, and tensions between persons may be relieved through either joking or avoidance relationships. Among the Trobrianders, for instance, there is an avoidance relationship between sister and brother based on the sexual taboo between them, but the relationship with the father's sister, who is regarded as a "stranger" and a possible sexual partner, is one of joking.

Ideas of witchcraft may operate to control social relations, discouraging people from greed or cheating. Witchcraft accusations also can express jealousy or hostility, such as between cowives (example: the Kaguru).

It is difficult to give a universal definition of law, and legal action is often intertwined with politics. It may be controlled by those who have political power and can therefore operate in an oppressive manner. In state societies we find separate, complex legal institutions connected with hierarchical power (example: the Tswana). Informal litigation in moots which proceed by discussion and negotiation may coexist with such courts or operate separately from them in noncentralized political systems (example: the Kpelle). Mechanisms such as ordeals may come into play to test truth totally (example: the

Ifugao); or song duels may be used to play out the rivalry between disputants (example: the Inuit). Norms may be explicitly cited in some disputes, in others not.

Law may also preserve order in a more general sense, as by supporting contracts and settlements. In some societies such functions are carried out by diffuse institutions, such as gift-giving. When customs are codified and "frozen," they lose their ability to adapt flexibly to situations of change. Legal action then becomes simplified and loses its complex functions.

SUGGESTIONS FOR FURTHER READING

SECTIONS 37, 38

Bell, D., and P. Ditton. 1980. *Law: The Old and the New; Aboriginal Women in Central Australia Speak Out.* Canberra: Central Australian Aboriginal Legal Aid Service.

Bohannan, P. J., ed. 1967. *Law and Warfare.* Garden City, N.Y.: Natural History Press.

Diamond, A. L. 1971. *Primitive Law, Past and Present.* London: Methuen & Company, Ltd.

Marwick, M. 1970. *Witchcraft and Sorcery.* London: Penguin Books, Inc.

Middleton, J., ed. 1967. *Magic, Witchcraft, and Curing.* Garden City, N.Y.: Natural History Press.

Nader, L., ed. 1965. *The Ethnography of Law.* American Anthropologist Special Publications, Vol. 67, 6, Part 2.

———. 1968. *Law in Culture and Society.* Chicago: Aldine Publishing Company.

———, and H. F. Todd, Jr. 1978. *The Disputing Process in Ten Societies.* New York: Columbia University Press.

Pospisil, L. 1958. *Kapauku Papuans and Their Law.* New Haven, Conn.: Yale University Publications in Anthropology, 54.

———. 1974. *Anthropology of Law: A Comparative Theory.* New Haven, Conn.: HRAF Press.

Sims, M. M. 1995. Old Roads and New Directions: Anthropology and the Law. *Dialectical Anthropology* 20 (3–4): 341–360.

CHAPTER
15

Religion: Ritual, Myth, and Cosmos

We have touched upon religious beliefs and rites at many points in the preceding chapters. We have looked at them, often, as expressions of "something else": as modes of adapting human behavior to the demands of an ecosystem or pressures of demography, as "celestializations" that maintain the power of a ruling class or disguise the subordination of women. Such questions need not be left behind. But we need now to look at religious systems in their own right: to ask why humans have populated their universe with unseen beings and powers, spun out mythic accounts of ancient and wondrous happenings, created elaborate rituals that must be performed correctly if human life is to prosper. What gives religion its emotional power, its central place in human experience? Religions may serve the purposes of adaptation and earthly politics; but they also seem to meet deep needs in relating the lives of individuals and the ways of communities to ultimate concerns, a world beyond that of immediate experience.

39. RELIGION IN COMPARATIVE PERSPECTIVE

Forms of Religion

Anthropologists entering other peoples' worlds have seldom had difficulty recognizing some events and behaviors as "religious": Philippines villagers setting out an extra portion at a meal for an unseen participant; African elders pouring out rice wine or killing a goat while speaking to invisible companions; Trobrianders setting out food portions and building platforms for unseen visitors to the village; Native Americans going alone into the wilderness on vision quests. It is not so easy, however, to define what it is about these and other manifestations of religion that mark them as such and distinguish them from other realms of social life.

Tylor, more than a century ago, defined religion as a "belief in spiritual beings." A number of contemporary social anthropologists have returned to this definition of religion in terms of an extension of "social" relations to superhuman beings or forces. Others follow Durkheim, who located the sacred in the realm of society itself, seen in divinised form. They have sought to find some special quality of "sacredness" that demarcates the religious from the secular.

Religions vary enormously in the powers and agencies they posit in the universe and the ways people relate to them. There may be a range of deities, a single deity, or none—simply spirits or even impersonal and diffuse powers. These agencies may in-

Male participants at a funeral parade with spears on shoulders and bodies caked with yellow mud, Melpa, Papua New Guinea.

tervene constantly in human affairs or be uninvolved and distant; they may be punitive or benevolent. In dealing with them, humans may feel awe and reverence, or fear; but they may also bargain with supernaturals or seek to outwit them. Religions may govern people's moral conduct or be unconcerned with morality.

Studies of comparative religion were for many decades concerned with cataloguing religious systems into "types." In the nineteenth century this was motivated by a concern to discover—by sheer speculation—which was the earliest form of human religion. Was it **animism,** a belief in indwelling spirits—in ghosts, tree spirits, and other spirit beings? Or was it **animatism,** a belief in diffuse, impersonal spiritual power, such as *mana* of Polynesia and Melanesia or *wakan* and *orenda* of North America? Or was it **totemism,** where a mystical relationship connects human groups with animal species or natural phenomena?

Such early typological schemes have proven to be misleadingly simplistic. On closer examination, religions characteristically turn out to be too subtly complicated to fit into such a set of pigeonholes. A single religion may incorporate elements of different "types." Some elements of a people's belief system often seem on the surface to be incompatible with others. Thus the Tallensi (Cases 2 and 29) and some other West African peoples believe that each person's life follows a foreordained destiny. But at the same time they believe that individuals have the power to choose paths of good or evil and that lineage ancestors control and may intervene in the unfolding of a person's life—themes that Fortes (1959c) compares with the ancient themes of Oedipus and Job (see also Fortes 1987). We will shortly see how, in one West African religion, such seemingly contradictory themes are woven into a subtle and complex system of belief.

That does not mean that comparative religion must be bereft of comparison or that any kind of religion will be found in association with any kind of social system in any kind of ecosystem. We will return to modern and more sophisticated attempts to show systematic relationships between thought-of worlds and lived-in worlds.

Why Religion?

It is revealing to ask why humans in all or almost all times and places have created a world of unseen entities and forces—a world that parallels, lies behind, or explains the world perceived directly by human senses. Religions, first of all, *explain*. They answer existential questions: how the world came to be, how humans are related to natural species and forces, why humans die, and why their efforts succeed and fail. Undoubtedly, not all individuals in a society worry about such questions. But every society has its philosophers who seek answers to existential questions, while others carry on assured that there *are* answers, and are more concerned with coping, solving, and striving than with explaining.

Second, religions *validate*. Religions posit controlling forces in the universe that sus-

tain the moral and social order of a people. Ancestors, spirits, or gods reinforce rules and give validity and meaning to human acts. By celestializing rules and relationships that are creations of humans, giving them an aura of being absolute and eternal, religions place them beyond challenge. Later, we will encounter another theme: religious ideas may be revolutionary as well as conservative, may transform social worlds, not perpetuate them.

Third, religions *reinforce* human ability to cope with the fragility of human life—with death and illness, famine, flood, failure. By reinforcing humans psychologically at times of tragedy, anxiety, and crisis, religion gives security and meaning in a world which, "seen in naturalistic terms, appears to be full of the unpredictable, the capricious, the accidentally tragic" (Kluckhohn 1942). And religion also heightens the intensity of shared experience, of social communion.

Clifford Geertz formulated a definition of religions in terms of what they do, and amplified his definition as follows:

> A religion is a system of symbols which acts to establish powerful, pervasive, and long-lasting moods and motivations . . . by formulating conceptions of a general order of existence and clothing these conceptions with such an aura of factuality that the moods and motivations seem uniquely realistic. (Geertz 1966a:4)

Religion, in other words, defines the way the world *is* in such a way that it establishes an appropriate stance to take toward it—a way of feeling, acting, and living in it. Both the nature of the world and human emotions and motives are mutually confirmed and reinforced. It is this double-sidedness, this creation through religions of both "models of" and "models for" that makes them so central in human experience. The way a religion codifies a view of the world, and hence sustains a stance toward life, is vividly illustrated by the view of the cosmos held by the Kalabari of Nigeria, as described by anthropologist Robin Horton and presented in Case 47.

Magic, Religion, and World View

"Magical thinking," which struck early theorists of religion as childlike naïveté, reflects this kind of model of a universe far more deterministic than ours, a universe where things do not just happen by chance or accident. In such a universe, death, illness, and crop failure call for explanation. Such a far-reaching determinism invites people to try to manipulate the course of events in socially approved or socially disapproved ways. A sorcerer who uses fingernail parings of his intended victim, or a magician who draws animals to ensure the abundance of game, is building on a logic quite different from ours—a logic where influences are spread by "contagion" and where like produces like. Such an all-embracing determinism and "magical" pattern of thinking dominate the tribal world.

Magic, then, represents human attempts to manipulate chains of cause and effect between events that to us are unrelated, in ways that to us are irrational. Magic, like prayer, works in the eye of the believer because the system of belief contains an explanation for both success and failure: the magician's beliefs are confirmed whether the garden grows well or dies.

Is magic part of religion, or is it a distinct cultural realm? Where the magician works pragmatically at his routine, recites his spell, and hence "compels" the desired ef-

fects to come about, magic contrasts with the religious mood of supplication and spiritual communion: the magician seems more like a mechanic than a priest. But a hard line between magic and religion is often difficult to draw and culturally meaningless.

Anthropologists have learned the hard way that to understand belief systems they must discard as many rigid definitions and preconceptions as possible and consider the **cosmology**—in other words, find out how another people conceptualize their universe, see the place of humans in it, and relate to and communicate with unseen beings and powers. Striving to understand the religious philosophy of a non-Western people, whether it be from a Zen master, an Indian guru, or a tribal priest, demands every ounce of one's analytical and intuitive powers, and often more.

Thus Australian Aborigines have incredibly subtle, philosophically challenging mystical cosmologies that posit a spiritual plane of existence that was prior to the world of sensory experience (in the "dreamtime") but now lies behind or parallel to it. Mervyn Meggitt (personal communication) describes how the old Walbiri man who was his spiritual guide eventually told him gently that he, Meggitt, had reached his philosophical depth and could follow no further into the mysteries of the cosmos. Probably no Westerner has ever fully penetrated these Aboriginal philosophical realms (see Meggitt 1972; Munn 1973; Myers 1986; Stanner 1956, 1963, 1965). Similarly, the old African hunter and philosopher Ogotemmeli spread out for his ethnographer pupils a vast and incredibly sophisticated vista of the cosmology of his people, the Dogon (Griaule and Dieterlen 1960).

But that is not to say that all peoples are equally concerned with elaborating models

The World View of the Kalabari

The Kalabari, a fishing people who live in the swampy delta of the Niger River in Nigeria, have a highly complicated system of cosmological beliefs. As documented by Robin Horton (1962), three orders of existence are postulated by the Kalabari as lying behind "the place of people"—the observable world of human beings and things. The first level is the world of "spirits." It is the beings of this level with whom the living are most concerned, and with whom they carry on ritualized relations. The spirit world is populated by beings of various sorts. All of them are normally invisible and are manifest, like the wind, in different places. We will glimpse the different categories of spirits that affect human life.

First, every object or living thing has a spirit that guides or animates its behavior. When a person dies, or a pot breaks, spirits and physical form have become separated. More important to people's daily lives are three categories of "free" spirits. First, there are ancestral spirits, dead members of the Kalabari lineages who watch over every member, rewarding them when kinship norms are observed and punishing them when they are violated. Second, there are "village heroes." These formerly lived with the Kalabari, but came from other places bringing new customs. Whereas ancestors are concerned with lineages, village heroes are concerned with the whole village—composed of several lineages—and its unity and community enterprises.

The effectiveness of the village head relies heavily on support by village heroes.

A final category of spirits is the "water people," who are manifest as humans and also as pythons or rainbows. They are identified not with human groups but with the creeks and swamps that are central to Kalabari subsistence. Water people control weather and fishing and are responsible for deviant human behavior, whether positive (innovation or acquisition of unusual wealth) or negative (violation of norms or mental abnormality).

This triangle of spirit forces, interacting with one another as well as with the living, shapes and guides human life. Ritual cycles alternately reinforce relations with ancestors, village heroes, and water people.

But beyond the spirit world, and more abstract and remote from human life, are other orders of existence. A personal creator, shaping each individual's destiny from before birth, lays the design of his or her life. A pattern of power or of failure is preordained for any individual, and the events of life are simply its unfolding. Even the time and manner of a person's death are laid down before birth. Even the destiny of a lineage, or a village, is viewed as laid down, though it has no creator as such.

Finally, on a still more remote and abstract level, Kalabari conceive the entire world and all of its beings as created by a "Great Creator,"

of the cosmos and philosophies of the human condition. Some peoples are relatively pragmatic, down-to-earth, uninterested in ultimate answers and cosmological complexities (see Descola 1996 on the Achuar people of Ecuador and Peru). Moreover, tribal philosophers cannot be lightly assumed to represent "their culture." In

and all the events of the world as the immutable unfolding of an ultimate pattern of destiny. Although offerings are made to one's personal creator, the mood is one of resignation rather than manipulation: "The Creator never loses a case," say Kalabari. The Great Creator is in most respects remote from human life.

The world of the spirits is, in one sense, modeled on the everyday world of Kalabari life. But the spirit world is a transformed and simplified version of the real one. The forces that affect human life are separated out, assigned to different categories of beings operating in different ways in different spheres.

Thus, for example, village heroes appropriately represent the ties of community that transcend the separate loyalties of kinship and lineage. They came from outside places, not Kalabari lineages; they contributed innovations that distinguish the customs of each particular village; they simply disappeared, they did not die; and they left no descendants. They were creatures of community, without any of the ties of human kinship.

The orders of existence postulated by the Kalabari are invoked in different contexts to explain different orders of phenomena, to answer different orders of questions. A temporary success or failure is intelligible in terms of the vicissitudes of relations with spirits; a series of catastrophes or failures is seen as the unfolding of destiny.

Kalabari religion, Horton suggested, is a highly sophisticated philosophical system.

Religious explanations are not as different from scientific ones as they might seem. "As tools of understanding, successive levels of Kalabari reality are committed to explaining more and more in terms of less and less" (Horton 1962). Horton argued that this is as true of the models of atomic physics, with its particles and statistical models, as of the Kalabari conception of Great Creator and cosmic destiny. The difference between religious explanation and scientific explanation lies partly in the demand science imposes for a systematic correspondence between a theory and observed outcomes. Rather than keeping systematic control of the relationship between "the theory" and the evidence of observation, Kalabari allow a complex pattern of secondary and contingent explanation. When sacrifice attains the desired result, this reinforces belief; when it does not, some other explanation—a competing spirit, a ritual mistake, or the like—is invoked. The belief itself is not called into question.

But the cost of scientific explanation, in contrast to that of the Kalabari, is that so much is left unexplained. Our universe is filled with "accidents." Science does not allow questions about why someone got bitten by a snake, or why the light bulb burned out just as I was reading the last page of my mystery novel. But tribespeople such as the Kalabari want to know why the snake and the man arrived at the same point on the path at the same moment, and why it was this man rather than some other.

some cases, their syntheses may be purely personal; and at least, the ordinary man or woman may be quite unconcerned with such matters. The anthropologist straining to conceptualize and codify a belief system may exaggerate systematization and consistency in the process of piecing together individual views of "shared" beliefs.

40. RELIGION AND SOCIAL STRUCTURE

Anthropologists have long perceived that a people's religious beliefs and their social organization are closely interrelated. It is clear that the supernatural order is to some extent modeled on human social relationships. Conversely, religious beliefs validate and regulate social relations.

Religion as Projection of Society

One way to interpret the close relationship between religious and social realms is to view religion as a sort of distortion and projection of the human world. Thus, one can find relationships between the kinds of supernaturals posited by a people and the scale of their political organization. People with fragmented clans often have a cult of ancestral spirits for each clan, and people with a centralized state are more likely to have a high god or centralized pantheon.

But the supernatural world which religions posit is a transformation of the one humans live in, as well as a projection of it. As Leach puts it:

> The concept of the Other World is generated by direct inversion of the characteristics of ordinary experience. This World is inhabited by mortal, impotent men, who live out their lives in normal time in which events happen in sequence, one after another. In this world we get older and older . . . and in the end we die. The Other World is inhabited by immortal, omnipotent [beings] who exist perpetually in abnormal time in which past, present, and future all coexist. . . . "Power," conceived as the source of health, life, fertility, political influence, wealth . . . is located in the other world and the purpose of religious performance is to provide a bridge, or channel of communication, through which the power of the gods may be made available to otherwise impotent men. (Leach 1976:81–82)

Rites of passage have important significance in relating religious beliefs to social life. In a classic study, Van Gennep (1909) noted that many rituals follow the conceptual pattern of initiation. Initiates are ritually separated from everyday life into an excluded, separate realm. After this separation, they are ritually reincorporated back into everyday life, in an altered state. Symbolically, they are *reborn*. Such rites of passage occur in puberty or other initiations to adult status, and at other transition points in life.

In a classic study, the French sociologist Robert Hertz interpreted mortuary rituals reported from Borneo as a symbolic rite of passage. At a first funeral, the dead person was buried and surviving relatives went into a ritual seclusion from social contact. Then the purified skull was exhumed, and a second funeral was staged which sent the spirit to the afterlife and freed the mourners to rejoin normal social life. Hertz interprets this as a treatment of death as a rite of passage to a new status. The afterlife is invented so as to avoid treating death as final; the second funeral reincorporates the living into their world and sends the spirit into its new one. (See Bloch 1972, Huntington and Metcalf 1979, Metcalf 1977.)

The model of a rite of passage has also been drawn on in interpreting sacrifice. Sacrifice has a fairly transparent logic, once a people have posited the otherworld whose controlling powers demand tribute and subordination from the living. Because the supernatural world is immaterial, what is given is converted to ethereal "substance" (while the sacrificers usually eat the material remains). What the supernaturals give in return is similarly intangible. But why the killing of animals, in rites that are so similar in form in widely separated parts of the world? (Sacrifice was not only widespread in the tribal world, but played an important part in the religions of early Indo-European and Semitic-speaking peoples.) Is there a hidden logic in sacrifice? Leach (1976) suggests that by drawing a symbolic equivalence between the sacrificed animal and its owner, sacrifice transforms the donor:

> The procedures [of a rite of passage] separate the "initiate" into two parts—one pure, the other impure. The impure part can then be left behind, while the pure part can be aggregated to the initiate's new status. In the case of sacrifice the sacrificial victim plays the part of the initiate, but since the victim has first been identified with the donor of the sacrifice, the donor is by vicarious association, likewise purified and initiated into a new ritual status. (Leach 1976:84)

Another direction taken by social anthropologists in studying the relationship between the social world of the living and the otherworld is to see supernaturals as projections of the authority of the living. In the functionalist tradition this relationship has been seen as a mirroring on a supernatural plane of the social relations of the living. Punitive ancestors represent the authority of lineage elders, elevated to a supernatural plane (Fortes 1960). Within neo-Marxist theory, this relationship is seen as celestialization as well as projection: ancestors and elders work hand in hand to support one another's authority.

But taking either point of view, we are prone to misunderstand the subjective realities of living in a world controlled by ancestors. Ancestors are not triangles on a genealogical diagram, or part of a "religion" that is separate from everyday life. Rather, they are social actors—albeit invisible ones—in the ongoing life of a community: parties to conversations, recipients of gifts, guests at meals. It often makes better sense of the cultural realities of a society to view lineages as consisting of both living and dead members, in constant interaction. Kopytoff (1971) argues that in many West

African religions, ancestors are defined, treated, and accorded powers as the eldest elders in the lineage system. (See Case 48 to examine in closer detail the religious system of another people, one we have encountered in previous chapters, to see systematic relations between religion and social structure.)

Social Structure and Cultural Meanings

Such interpretations, beginning with the social structure of a people and seeing religious systems as reflections or extensions of the social world, as projections of society on the cosmos, have been highly revealing. But they introduce a characteristic distortion. Our social world is our only vantage point on life. It is inevitable and obvious that our models of the cosmos should be drawn from that world. But one cannot legitimately argue from the resulting parallels and resemblances that religion is "nothing more" than a projection of social life. Why project at all? And as Geertz (1966a) cogently suggested, one could profitably focus on the way the world of the living is transformed in creating a model of the cosmos. Religions must be viewed as ideational systems, and their overall structure mapped. A focus on the parallels between the religious and social has predisposed us to look at those segments of religious experience where the closest parallels occur, at the expense of the rest.

Both the powers and the limitations of a sociological and symbolic approach to religious systems come out clearly in recent concern with cultures in which male and female realms sharply contrast and are believed to be dangerous to each other. We glimpsed such systems in Chapter 7, in considering the relationship of religious beliefs to ecological adaptation.

A number of writers of psychoanalytic bent, for example, have seen a fear of

CASE

48

Kwaio Social Structure and Religion

Recall from Case 24 how the Melanesian Kwaio of the Solomon Islands are organized into small descent groups composed of agnatic and cognatic descendants of the ancestors who founded the territory on which they live. We will see shortly how Kwaio cosmology partitions the world into a sacred realm where ancestors hold sway and from which women are mainly excluded; we will also see the mirror image of the sacred, a realm where women's powers, dangerous to men, hold sway.

Here we will look more closely at the realm of the sacred, the relations of the living with their ancestors, and the linkages between descent groupings and systems of ancestors, shrines, and ritual. Kwaio believe their world to be controlled by ancestral ghosts or *adalo*. *Adalo*, unseen and diffuse "like the wind," communicate with the living. The shades of the living and the dead inter-

act in dreams; the ancestral ghosts convey their displeasure by causing illness or misfortune; and religious officiants, "shrine-men" or priests (who, like Trobriand magicians, are also farmers, not full-time specialists), speak to the spirits on behalf of their descent groups.

The places where this communication between living and dead is centered, priests' men's houses and shrines (which are simply groves where sacrificial oven stones are kept), are especially sacred. It is in these shrines that the men and boys of the group, and other male cognatic descendants of the group's founders, gather to partake of sacrificial communion.

Every adult man and woman, after death, is transmuted into ancestorhood as a ghost. *Adalo*, ancestral ghosts, are distinguished as either "minor" or "important." Minor *adalo* are the ghosts of those one has known in life—close rela-

A Kwaio feast-giver talks to his ancestors while making an offering of taro and coconuts to ensure dry weather.

tives in the parental and grandparental generations, whose activities as ghosts are relevant only to their living close kin. Important ancestors are ghosts that have risen to prominence through the generations; most of them appear on genealogies six or more generations above their oldest living descendants. Minor *adalo* some-times serve as intermediaries on behalf of their living kin, in deal-

ing with important *adalo*. *Adalo,* like living Kwaio men (Case 35), vary in "bigness." There is in practice a large category of *adalo* from previous generations who are not attributed special and dangerous powers and singled out for special sacrifice, but who are in a kind of limbo.

An interesting parallel is thus suggested between ancestors and the kin groups of the living.

Kwaio sacrifice: A priest speaks to his ancestors in a shrine as the smoke of a sacrificial pig rises to them.

Continued

Case 48 continued

Each descent group has a cluster of powerful ancestors, usually two or three, to whom its priest sacrifices pigs. Usually one of these ancestors is primary in power (hence corresponding to a Kwaio big man) vis-à-vis other descent-group ghosts.

A pig sacrificed to the "big" ancestor or ancestors is conceived as going to all of the descent group's ancestral ghosts, through the ancestral big man. While one can conceive of the "ancestral descent group" as a supernatural projection of the social structure, it makes more cultural sense to see the descent group as a single perpetual corporation comprising both the living and their ancestors. Just as the living are fragmented into locally based descent corporations, so the ancestral cults are limited and locally based. Ancestral ghosts are concerned only with their own descendants. The living are concerned only with their own ancestors. The "concern" of ancestors in the affairs of the living is two-sided. Ancestors support and protect the living when they see pigs consecrated in their names, when ritual proce-

dures are carefully followed, and when the living are following rigid rules to contain in proper bounds the potentially polluting powers of women.

The relationships between the living and the ancestors express and reflect the structures of Kwaio kinship. Individuals belong to a number of cognatic descent categories defined by descent from the ancestors who founded descent groups, and to more distant ancestors of the ancient past. It is these ancient ancestors that convey the powers to fight, steal, garden, give feasts, and succeed in other earthly pursuits. When male members of a descent group participate together in sacrifice, cognatic descendants whose primary affiliations lie elsewhere are able to take part. In this respect, the Kwaio resemble the Tallensi (see Case 19; also Keesing 1970).

Case Update
For, a full-length study of Kwaio religion, the reader is referred to later work of Keesing (1982).

menstrual blood as due to male castration anxiety. Mary Douglas, a leading figure in symbolic and sociological approaches to religious ritual and belief, has argued that such a symbolic preoccupation with bodily orifices and substances need not express individual psychic concerns. The concerns and conflicts may be social and collective and public, not psychological and private:

> We cannot possibly interpret rituals concerning excreta, breast milk, saliva, and the rest unless we are prepared to see in the body a symbol of society. . . . It is easy to see that the

body of a sacrificial ox is being used as a diagram of a social situation. But when we try to interpret rituals of the human body in the same way, the psychological tradition turns its face away from society, back toward the individual. Public rituals may express public concerns when they use . . . door posts or animal sacrifices: but public rituals enacted on the human body are taken to express personal and private concerns. (Douglas 1966:138)

In *Purity and Danger* (1966) Douglas examined the ritual use of the human body, particularly in pollution taboos. She notes that the human body is used to symbolize the body politic, the social structure. Powers and dangers focus on the margins of the society—in the anomalous, the marginal, and threatening. And mirroring social threats and dangers, it is the bodily orifices and substances—menstrual blood, spittle, urine, feces—that threaten and pollute. (See A. J. Strathern 1996 for a discussion of Douglas's views.)

The polarization of men and women, and the separation of the social realm into sacred and polluted spheres of life, define categories that must be rigidly kept separate. Case 49 provides an example of how a symbolic division of the cosmos expresses lines of cleavage in the social structure and is reflected in spatial organization and ritual.

There seems little doubt, as such cases accumulate in the literature, that the kinds of symbolic and sociological structuring Douglas and others have analyzed are common. Cosmology and social structure are intimately intertwined, and neither can be understood without the other. But that does not mean that when we have discovered such systematic structure, a sociological and symbolic analysis is sufficient to account for it. Such patterning need by no means rule out the relevance and applicability of psychoanalytic interpretations. Public rites and collective concerns can dramatize private psychological conflicts. If in the past the private fantasies of the individuals who have contributed to the evolution of such ritual and cosmological systems had not struck a responsive chord with their fellows—perhaps articulating and acting out psychic conflicts shared by many of their fellows—they would never have been institutionalized in the first place. If rituals were simply public performances that were no longer meaningful in terms of individual psychic experience, they would not have endured (in the

Kwaio case, they have continued intact despite nearly a century of missionary effort). But conversely, once such a belief system is institutionalized, it perpetuates the anxieties that may have given initial rise to it, and creates new ones. Kwaio men, having given their womenfolk powers of life and death over them, worry continually about being polluted. The point is that psychological and sociological explanations have often been viewed as mutually exclusive; but they should, instead, be viewed as mutually reinforcing.

We may reconsider here the kinds of ecologically adaptive functions of religious behavior we sketched in Chapter 7. Lindenbaum (1972) has argued that **pollution** taboos operate as "supernatural birth control" and occur in Melanesian societies with high population density as a ritual way of maintaining demographic balance. There are also the sexual politics whereby men, in gaining control over things sacred and defining women as polluted, achieve impregnable dominance. Could this dominance— involving as it so often does elaborate ritual mummery, sexual anxiety, initiatory brutalizing, and collective display behavior—disguise and maintain deep-seated male anxiety and feelings of inadequacy? Is male supremacy a hollow and precarious victory when it is achieved at such cost?

Shirley Lindenbaum (1972, 1973, 1976), Michelle Rosaldo (1974), and other authors believe that sexual politics, social structure, cosmology and ritual, and psychology form a tightly knit complex. Though in the past specialists in one or another mode of explanation have tended to dismiss other modes as if they were contradictory, we urgently need less simplistic models that map their interconnectedness.

And if Lindenbaum (1972) is right, ecological factors are crucial as well.

CASE
49

Sacredness and Pollution Among the Kwaio

Kwaio ancestors move in a realm where sacredness prevails. Communicating with *adalo*, sacred and dangerous, is done by men, as priests. All the male cognatic descendants of descent-group ancestors take part in purificatory rites of sacrifice; ritually adult men eat sacred propitiatory pigs as well.

From all these events women are excluded, because women's bodies are considered to be potentially polluting. Urination and defecation by women are polluting. Menstruation is more polluting; and most polluting of all is childbirth. The most common culturally defined cause of illness, death, or misfortune is violation by a woman of the rigid pollution taboos.

The major preoccupations of Kwaio ritual are with keeping sacred and polluted realms properly demarcated from the everyday "mundane"

realm of gardening, eating, talking, and sleeping. As Douglas's analyses would lead us to expect, separation of these categories is ritually central: and it is symbolically expressed in a series of dualistic oppositions:

FEMALE : MALE
POLLUTED : SACRED
DOWN : UP

Thus, men and women have to eat out of separate cooking vessels, drink from separate bamboos, and so on. Male and female, sacred and polluted, are vividly defined as symbolic mirror images of one another.

This symbolic model is mapped onto the spatial layout of a tiny Kwaio settlement (Figure 15.1). At the upper margin of the clearing is

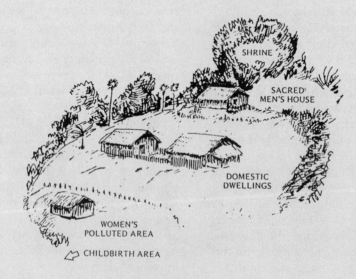

Figure 15.1 A Kwaio settlement.

the men's house where men sleep and eat, and which is sacred and off-limits to women. At the lower margin is the menstrual hut, polluted and off-limits to men. In the central clearing, which is "mundane," are one or more domestic dwelling houses. But even in each house, the uphill side (from the fireplace upward) is for men; the downhill side is open to both men and women. An invisible line runs across mid-clearing, with the uphill side preeminently the province of men. (With characteristic flexibility, male dogma allows Kwaio women to cross this line and go as far as the margins of the men's house to scrape the clearing, pick up pigs' droppings, and carry firewood.) A man may move freely between dwelling house and men's house, and a woman between dwelling house and menstrual hut.

But transitions are carefully observed. A woman must leave pipe and bag behind before she can go into the polluted area. If she takes firewood from the house, she must first light an intermediate stick before lighting a fire in the menstrual hut. If a man is sacred through sacrifice or a woman is polluted by menstruation, more drastic rites of desacralization or purification must be performed before the mundane realm can be entered.

This cosmological and social mirror-imaging of sacredness and pollution is even more dramatically apparent in the most sacred of men's activities and the most polluting of women's: a high sacrifice by cremating a pig, and childbirth. The woman giving birth retires into a hut in the forest below the polluted menstrual area, out of all contact with men, and is attended by a young girl. The priest who sacrifices retires to the men's house near the shrine, out of all contact with women, and takes to his bed, where he is attended by a young boy (see Keesing 1982 for a more detailed account).

Kwaio pollution: A Kwaio girl battens down the thatch on a menstrual hut as gusty winds increase; pieces of the thatch blown into the nearby clearing would cause pollution.

Lindenbaum's argument regarding sexual polarity takes Mary Douglas's ideas in a further direction. If the human body serves as a symbol of the body politic, then what it symbolizes may include a people's perception of their society's demographic state, their relationship to their environment, their relationship to neighboring peoples.

Yet since a people's perceptions of such external problems are often oblique and distorted, their symbolic responses may worsen the problems they seek to deal with. For instance, recall that Fore endocannibalism, which spreads the fatal *kuru* disease (Case 13), may be a symbolic response to perceived demographic decline. And customs, once created, take on a meaning and force of their own; so that even if they were once adaptive responses to a demographic or ecological situation they may continue to be practiced long after they cease to be adaptive. Kwaio pollution taboos, rules enjoining premarital chastity, and customs encouraging late marriage or permanent bachelorhood, may have evolved under circumstances of potential population pressure (although there is no direct evidence of it). But contemporary Kwaio traditionalists, fully aware that such customs limit population at a time when they are dwindling in numbers and beleaguered by Christianity and Westernization, continue to follow ancestral rules. Talking of peoples on surrounding islands whose populations are expanding, a Kwaio man observed that "that's because we live virtuously and they don't."

Ritual behavior and cosmological beliefs that serve ecological ends, cast in cultural terms, undoubtedly evolve. But so do customs and belief systems that have unfavorable social results. A system of pollution beliefs may indeed be in part a means of supernatural birth control; but if so, it is a bitter pill.

41. MYTH AND RITUAL

Myth and ritual have long fascinated anthropologists. Connections have also been made between practices found in tribal contexts and the heritage of early Europe—as witness the continued popularity of Frazer's *The Golden Bough.*

Myths

Myths are accounts about how the world came to be the way it is, about a superordinary realm of events before (or behind) the experienced natural world; they are accounts believed to be true and in some sense sacred. Religious rituals are tightly structured performances of prescribed actions accorded sacred or religious meaning.

Since rituals very often dramatize and act out the stories told in myth, and since the myths correspondingly explain and rationalize ritual performances, anthropologists for many years engaged in a long and fruitless debate about which was a reflection of which. More constructively, social anthropologists have sought to trace the relationships between ritual, myth, and social structure. In the realm of myth, the way was opened by Malinowski's (1925) sociological interpretation of Trobriand myths. He insisted that Trobriand myths made sense not as disembodied texts for the psychoanalyst or Frazerian antiquarian. Rather, they were living social events, intelligible only in the context of real humans in real places involved in continuing political relations (see Case 50).

In seeing myth as an account of the past that serves as charter for the present, though, we can easily distort conceptualizations of a world where past, present, and future are connected; where the ancient past is *lived* in the present; where next year's children are long-dead spirits,

CASE

50

Trobriand Origin Myths

In any Trobriand village, an essential element of life is the recounting of myths. Members of a Trobriand subclan know, mark, and recount the history of the "hole" from which its ancestress and her brother emerged from the underworld. In that underworld, in the days before life on the earth, people lived as they do now. The ancestral brother and sister brought up with them sacred objects and knowledge, skills and crafts, and the magic that distinguish this group from others.

Is this myth an attempt at cosmic "explanation"? Is it an expression of the deep surgings of the unconscious—of incestuous desire? Or is it an encapsulation of actual history? No, says Malinowski. It can only be understood in the rich context of Trobriand life and cultural meaning. Brother and sister emerged because they represent the two essential elements of the subclan; a husband did not emerge because he is, in terms of the subclan, an irrelevant outsider. The ancestral pair lived in separate houses because the relationship of brother and sister is marked by sharp taboos. But why recite the myth at all? Because it validates the rights of the subclan to the territory and encapsulates the magic and skills that make them sociologically and ritually unique. The myth of local emergence is the *property* of the local subclan; it does not float in limbo to be examined by a psychoanalyst, and it can be understood only in terms of how, when, and with whom it is *used*.

Other origin myths known by all Trobrianders relate the emergence of the four clans, legitimizing their food taboos, but, more particularly, matters of rank and precedence. Finally, other local myths deal with the relative rank, position, and dispersion of high-ranking subclans beyond their point of original emergence. Such myths,

Malinowski says, validate the political structure and provide a *mythological charter* to justify and reinforce present social relations. Pulling Trobriand myths out of this social context, we would not understand them (Malinowski 1925).

The political uses of traditions of subclan origins in contemporary Trobriand life have become more clear from other ethnographic studies—which strongly reinforce Malinowski's view of myth as charter:

Origin stories of the founders are among the most coveted and valuable kinds of knowledge. Land disputes can only be settled by a recitation of the genealogies of the land from the time of the founders. (Weiner 1976:40)

A *dala's* [subclan's] claim to land is based on a mythological charter which recounts how matrilineal ancestors came to be associated with the lands. . . . The persons styled *tolipwaipwaiya* ["owners"] of a tract of land, as descendants of the original possessors . . . , bear as a group a responsibility for the land. The *tolipwaipwaiya* relation is a mythological and genealogical relation to the soil. To say of a *dala* with respect to a piece of land, "it is their land," is to recognize the continuity of the *dala* through time such that all members, living, dead, and yet to be born, are conceived of as a single group. (Hutchins 1979)

Each relation between man and land is . . . determined . . . by a man's place in social, historical, and genealogical-mythological events. (Hutchins 1978:55–56, 94)

Trobriand origin myths are the basis not only of the land rights of *dala*, but also of claims to rank. Thus, the entitlement of members of *guyau* [high-ranking] subclans to wear special ornaments, command deference, and occupy special statuses of power and privilege is validated by their special doctrines of emergence (Weiner 1976: 44–45).

returning in new form. Similarly, the **dreamtime** of Aboriginal Australians is both another time long ago and another plane of reality that coexists with one's human experience directly. It is dangerously easy to translate the terms of another people's cosmology into the terms of our own—which we take to be "reality"—and then seek to analyze the constructions that result.

Another influential approach to myth has come from the French anthropologist Claude Lévi-Strauss. Lévi-Strauss sought to explicate the universal workings of the human mind by looking at varied cultural forms as its artifacts. The realm of myth is crucial in this enterprise, according to Lévi-Strauss, because here human thought has its widest freedom. Not every imaginable form of marriage, house style, or residence pattern is actually found; there are too many constraints, too many possibilities that are unworkable for ecological, technological, or purely physical reasons. But humans can *think* all of these possibilities, and in myth their thoughts have freest reign.

Lévi-Strauss (1969, 1971) argued that peoples all over the world are plagued intellectually by the contradictions of existence—by death; by our dual character, as part of nature yet transformed by culture; by dichotomies of spirit and body; by the contradictions of descent from a first man (where did a non-incestuous first mate come from?); and so on. The realm of myth is used above all to tinker endlessly with these contradictions, by transposing them symbolically. Thus the gulf between life and death can be symbolically mediated by rephrasing the contrast mythically as, for example, between an antelope (herbivore) and a lion (carnivore). By introducing a hyena, which eats animals it does not kill, one then in effect denies the contradiction.

Lévi-Strauss's original insistence that a myth, such as the story of Oedipus or of Asdiwal in Northwest Coast mythology (Lévi-Strauss 1967), could be understood by itself was modified considerably in his monumental four-volume *Mythologiques.* In *The Raw and the Cooked* (1969), the first volume, he examined a whole complex of myths among Amazonians of central Brazil, drawing heavily on cultural evidence in his interpretation. His exceedingly complicated and involuted decipherment of their "myth-o-logic" is an analytical tour de force. Subsequent volumes (1971–1974) trace out ever-widening webs of myth through the Americas—for myths and mythic themes and symbols refuse to stay inside societal boundaries. Lévi-Strauss concluded with a sweeping vision of cultures, the mind, and the human condition.

But is he right? Lévi-Strauss was solving puzzles, and often doing it with few clues along the way and little "evidence" at the end that the puzzle had been pieced together correctly. Lévi-Strauss's often daring assumptions about the cognitive worlds of other people have raised many an anthropological doubt. One of the difficult tasks in this whole mode of analysis is to introduce more controls on a method that can discover, or create, structure in any cultural material. Whether Lévi-Strauss's interpretations endure, there is little doubt that myths have a logic, structure, and richness we had not suspected and that most of the work of deciphering them still lies ahead. In this regard Lévi-Strauss's work is to be seen as a major achievement.

Ritual

Anthropological study of ritual, as for the study of myth, has undergone major transformations. Rites had been viewed by Durkheim (1912) and Radcliffe-Brown

CASE
51

Ndembu Ritual Symbols

The key to ritual symbolism among the Ndembu of Zambia is a set of major symbolic objects and qualities that recur in many ritual settings: colors, especially red, white, and black; certain trees and plants; and other "things" accorded central importance in the Ndembu environment. Let us take, for instance, a certain tree, *mudyi*, which exudes a milky sap when cut. The tree is used in several rituals, and we can ask what it "stands for." The answer is that it stands for a wide range of things: a broad fan of conceptually related meanings, from the basic and physiological (breast milk, nursing) to the social (mother-child relations, matrilineal descent) and abstract (dependency, purity). An actual ritual procedure involves not one symbolic object but a series of them in a sequence. What, then, does the ritual "mean," if each object could have such a wide spectrum of possible mean-ings? A sequence of acts involving these objects, like a musical score or a sequence of words, has a *syntax;* and the possible meaning of each is limited and shaped by their combination and arrangement to form a message. But here again the message is not simple and unambiguous, because it is stated on many levels. A rite may at the same time be a statement about mothers and children, men and their matrilineages, and dependency of the living on their ancestors. Moreover, these multiple levels of meaning relate what is abstract and social with the "gut feelings" and emotions of individuals related to their primary experience.

Case Update

Subsequent to Turner's earlier study, there has been further work on ritual. (See also V. Turner 1975, 1985, 1992, and E. Turner 1992.)

(1922) as reinforcing collective sentiment and social integration. The content of rites—whether the priest zigged or zagged, held a stick in his left hand or a leaf in his right—was a secondary and seldom manageable problem.

As the content of cultural systems has been shown to be increasingly systematic, however, with the bits and pieces seemingly less and less arbitrary in relation to one another, such questions seem crucial. The nature of ritual symbols has been revealed dramatically in the work of Victor Turner. Exploring the rituals of the African Ndembu, Turner (1967) mapped an extraordinarily rich structure of symbolism (see Case 51).

In Turner's work are found the beginnings of a theory of symbolism that transcends the Freudian and the crudely sociological: the royal scepter is neither simply a phallic symbol nor a symbol of the power of the state—it is both, and that is why it "works." Individual concerns are systematically related to public concerns; collectively enacted dramas have private and unconscious meanings.

Thus, once more we confront the issue that has run as a theme through the last few chapters. The evidence of anthropology shows how rich and complex are the structures of cultural meaning through which various peoples construe their worlds and their lives. This is nowhere more clear than in religion, where humans act in relation to the unseen beings and powers that lie behind the realm of directly experienced reality. To understand their lives, we must interpret deeply these structures of cultural meaning. A crude Marxism that sees religions as superstructures, as ideologies that disguise and deceive, would dismiss these culturally constructed worlds too quickly without understanding them. The challenge is to understand these cultural meanings, but to step outside them as well—not to dismiss them as "only" ideological mystifications, but to situate them in relation to historical processes and earthly politics and economic relationships. In the next chapter we will pursue further this challenge of attaining both inside and outside views.

We have gone, in the last eight chapters, well beyond the basic theoretical foundations laid down in Part 1 and the preliminary survey of the tribal world of Part 2. Looking at economic systems, descent, kinship, marriage, political systems, male-female relations, social stratification, law, and now religion, we have gained both conceptual and theoretical sophistication and a greatly expanded knowledge of the tribal world. What has been learned cumulatively about peoples such as the Trobrianders, the Tiv, Tallensi, Nuer, Kwaio, and others adds substance to generalizations, deepens perceptions of diversity and underlying similarity.

We are almost ready to turn to the more difficult and more pressing challenge of looking anthropologically at the complexities of societies in global historical change. But first, the theoretical orientation we have gained needs reinforcement. We need to pause to tie together theoretical loose ends, reinforce the analytical powers that will be needed to interpret a more complex and vast-scale world. In doing so, we will pursue a challenge with which this section be-

gan: to find systematic logic and coherence in the bits and pieces of Trobriand culture and society we have examined in these chapters.

SUMMARY

An early anthropologist, Tylor, defined religion as a belief in spiritual beings, and in fieldwork contexts religious actions are recognized as actions directed towards such beings. But there is a huge range of ideas about such agencies, and different ideas may coexist in a given case. Religious ideas work to validate and integrate experience and to provide an encompassing world view (example: the Kalabari).

Religion is connected with magic. Early anthropologists distinguished religion in terms of the approach to spiritual beings, whereas magic was seen as an automatic, coercive act. In practice these elements are often found together. It is often also difficult for the outsider properly to understand people's concepts.

Another way to see religion is in the functionalist tradition, in its role as a projection of society and as supporting the social structure. Social life often requires that people move in a legitimate fashion from one status to another, and this is accomplished by rites of passage. Religion may support the power of elders and males by reference to ancestors and sacrifices to these, defining ideas of gendered pollution and purity in doing so (example: the Kwaio). Cosmology and social structure are therefore closely intertwined. One can also argue that psychology goes hand in hand with cosmology.

Religion may be underpinned also by myth, which validates people's rights by way of identifying origins. The French anthropologist Lévi-Strauss argued that myths have the further function of indicating logical and experiential contradictions, such as life versus death. Myths certainly contain a rich array of symbolism, as do religious rituals. Victor Turner explored the complex world of symbols in rituals of the Ndembu people of Zambia. He found that particular elements in a ritual may have a complex set of messages (may be multivocalic).

We have both to understand such complexities and to situate them in social contexts of power and influence between people.

SUGGESTIONS FOR
FURTHER READING

Section 39

Banton, M., ed. 1966. *Anthropological Approaches to the Study of Religion.* ASA Monographs, 3. London: Tavistock. (See especially articles by Geertz and Spiro.)

Collins, J. J. 1978. *Primitive Religion.* Totowa, N.J.: Littlefield, Adams and Company.

Evans-Pritchard, E. E. 1965. *Theories of Primitive Religion.* London: Oxford University Press.

Leslie, C., ed. 1960. *Anthropology of Folk Religion.* New York: Random House, Inc.

Lessa, W. A., and E. Z. Vogt. 1978. *Reader in Comparative Religion: An Anthropological Approach,* 4th ed. New York: Harper & Row, Publishers.

Middleton, J., ed. 1967. *Gods and Rituals: Readings in Religious Beliefs and Practices.* Garden City, N.Y.: Natural History Press.

———, ed. 1967. *Myth and Cosmos.* Garden City, N.Y.: Natural History Press.

Wallace, A. F. C. 1967. *Religion: An Anthropological View.* New York: Random House, Inc.

Section 40

Douglas, M. 1970. *Natural Symbols: Explorations in Cosmology.* London: Cresset Press.

———, ed. 1977. *Rules and Meanings.* London: Penguin Books, Inc.

———. 1978. *Implicit Meanings: Essays in Anthropology.* London: Routledge & Kegan Paul, Ltd.

Evans-Pritchard, E. 1953. The Nuer Conception of Spirit in Relation to the Social Order. *American Anthropologist* 55: 201–214.

Goody, J. 1962. *Death, Property and the Ancestors.* London: Tavistock Publishers.

Hertz, R. 1960. *Death and the Right Hand.* New York: The Free Press.

Lévi-Strauss, C. 1963. *Totemism.* Boston: Beacon Press.

Lewis, I. M. 1972. *Ecstatic Religion: An Anthropological Study of Spirit Possession and Shamanism.* London: Penguin Books, Inc.

Section 41

Georges, R. A., ed. 1968. *Studies on Mythology.* Homewood, Ill.: Dorsey Press.

La Fontaine, J., ed. 1972. *The Interpretation of Ritual.* Cambridge: Cambridge University Press.

Maranda, P., ed. 1972. *Mythology.* London: Penguin Books, Inc.

Middleton, J., ed. 1965. *Gods and Rituals: Readings in Religious Beliefs and Practices.* Garden City, N.Y.: Natural History Press.

Turner, V. 1969. *The Ritual Process.* Chicago: Aldine-Atherton.

———, 1975. *Revelation and Divination in Ndembu Ritual.* Ithaca, N.Y.: Cornell University Press.

16

The Integration of Societies, the Structure of Cultures

Nineteenth-century anthropology had been devoted largely to armchair speculation about the evolution of society in the ancient past: to schemes depicting how marriage, kinship, and religion progressively evolved. Such speculative reconstructions eventually led to a rejection of "conjectural history," both in England and the United States. The American counter-reaction first took the form of careful historicism, by Franz Boas, A. L. Kroeber, and Ralph Lowie; and then the emergence of a holistic concept of culture, in the work of such scholars (mainly students of Boas) as Kroeber, Ruth Benedict, Ralph Linton, Margaret Mead, Melville Herskovits, and Clyde Kluckhohn.

In England, the counter-reaction to conjectural history took the form of a focus on the organization and integration of societies—the tradition of **functionalism.** The question was not, how did customs evolve?—but, how do the institutions of a society fit together and reinforce one another? In this functionalist tradition the key figures were A. L. Radcliffe-Brown, who followed the theoretical leads of the great French sociologists Durkheim and Mauss and applied them to the study of kinship and ritual; and Polish-born Bronislaw

Malinowski, who brought the Trobriand islanders to the Western world to battle with "economic man," the Oedipus complex, and stereotypes of the exotic and savage, and who sought to show coherence, logic, and interconnectedness in the strange customs of the *kula,* harvest presentations, and matrilineal descent. They were followed by the towering figures of British social anthropology in the middle decades of the century: E. E. Evans-Pritchard, Meyer Fortes, Max Gluckman, Raymond Firth, Edmund Leach.

British social anthropology in the functionalist tradition took the structure and integration of society as the key problems. Ritual, myth, and other symbolic elaborations were seen as reflecting and reinforcing the organization of society. Conceptually, "society" and "social structure" virtually swallowed up "culture."* In the American tradition derived from Boas, "culture" comprised all the learned and socially transmitted ways of a people, thus subsuming their modes of organizing groups as well as their values and belief systems: hence the cul-

---

*Although "culture" had been used centrally in Malinowski's own idiosyncratic theory of the way customs ultimately functioned to meet human needs.

tural tended to swallow up the social. Until the late 1950s, there was a tendency for scholars working in these traditions with different theoretical perspectives to talk past one another.

Since the 1950s, there has been a growing rapprochement between these traditions, an internationalization of anthropological theory and a broadening of theoretical training. By defining the realm of the social rather more narrowly and sharply, by defining "culture" as ideational rather than institutional, we acquire the power to bring the two perspectives into focus at once. As Clifford Geertz expressed it, the integration of a social system is "structural-functional"—the fitting together of institutions and modes of defining social relationships; the integration of a cultural system is "logico-aesthetic"—the coherence and logic of a system of *symbols* (Geertz 1957). In the sections to follow, we will use materials from the Trobriands—adding to the evidence we have already seen—to examine coherence and integration both at the level of social structure and the level of cultural structure.

42. THE INTEGRATION OF SOCIETY

The Logic of Societal Integration

If we take the organization and integration of society as our focus, we can see how systems of social institutions interlock and reinforce one another. We do not, in doing so, ignore cultural belief systems, or patterns of myth and ritual. Rather, we look at them *through* a social structure, asking what the consequences of ritual or cosmological doctrine or value system are for the way social relations are organized. Case 52 illustrates this direction of interpretation, the one developed in the tradition of Durkheim and

Radcliffe-Brown, by setting out some of the Trobriand materials we have glimpsed already, and adding to them selectively.

Social Structure as Lived-in and Thought-of Orders

This perspective does not separate the social—the structuring of social relationships, the organization of groups through kinship, descent, and political hierarchy—from cultural beliefs about conception, the spirits, the origins of rank, and the nature of women and men. But it takes the social world (in Lévi-Strauss's terms, a "lived-in order") as primary, and the cultural symbols (a "thought-of order") as reflecting and reinforcing it.

This vantage point and analytical strategy, previously dominant in British anthropology, has yielded many of the best field studies in the discipline. It is a perspective that encourages careful, detailed study of social relationships and of political and economic systems at community levels. But it exacts costs as well. In stressing how the system fits together, how elements are functionally interconnected, one is prone to stress integration and ignore contradiction and conflict; one is prone to depict "the system" as in timeless equilibrium. We will return to these problems shortly. This perspective on lived-in order as primary, thought-of order as secondary, has been limiting in another respect as well—in impeding our view of the structure of ideational systems.

43. THE STRUCTURE OF CULTURAL SYSTEMS

Cultures as Ideational Systems

Analyses of cultures as ideational systems, looking at "thought-of orders" in their own

CASE

52

The Integration of Trobriand Society

We can begin by setting out a series of what might seem disconnected elements of Trobriand social organization and cosmological doctrine:

1. The doctrine of subclan perpetuity
    a. A brother and sister emerged together from the underworld and founded the subclan.
    b. The spirits of the dead descendants of this ancestral pair continue to be "members" of the subclan, along with the living. Although ·as *baloma* spirits they have moved to a new plane of existence centered in Tuma, the island of the dead, their association with their subclan continues. (We will soon examine the *milamala* festival at which they annually return to visit living members of the subclan.)
    c. New children born into the subclan are reincarnations of subclan spirits. These spirits, after a period as *baloma* in the spirit world, are reborn through women. The subclan existed of old when humans lived underground; and it has always been and will always be the same.
2. The Trobriand theory of conception
    a. Copulation by the father does not "cause" the birth of a child—which is the reincarnation of a spirit of the mother's subclan.
    b. The child's "blood" comes from the mother and her siblings.
    c. The child physically resembles the father, not the mother, because his repeated intercourse with the mother "molds" the child.
3. The avoidance relationship between brother and sister
    a. Brother and sister must avoid close social contact or any intimacy.
    b. The brother must avoid all knowledge of his sister's sexual affairs.
    c. When she marries, he must avoid any direct involvement in her reproductive life.
4. The rule of residence
    a. A Trobriand girl and her brother grow up in their father's household, usually in a different village from her subclan's.
    b. Whereas the brother may return to his subclan village in adolescence, the daughter remains with her father until she marries.
    c. She then goes to live with her husband; thus at no stage in her life cycle does she normally live with her male subclan relatives in their territory.
5. Rules of exogamy
    a. A Trobriand man is forbidden to marry, or have intercourse with, a woman in his subclan.
    b. Though marriage with them is regarded as wrong, sexual affairs with lovers in different subclans of one's own clan are permitted, although they are regarded as naughty and dangerous.
6. The relationship of a father to his children
    a. The father is said to be a "relative by marriage" to his children.
    b. Half-siblings with the same mother and different father are treated as similar to full siblings. Yet half-siblings with the same father and different mothers are treated as nonrelatives.
    c. A daughter belongs to her mother's corporate subclan, which is dependent on her and its other females for members in the next generation. Yet when she marries, it is her father and his subclan—not her own—

with whom her husband's people exchange valuables.

  d. When the married daughter wants to become pregnant, her father asks his subclan ancestors to ask the ancestors of his wife's and daughter's subclan to send a spirit child.

7. The relationship of children to their paternal aunt

  a. For a boy, the aunt is the prototype of a sexually eligible woman, with whom he can joke freely or have sexual intercourse.

  b. Her daughter is said by Trobrianders to be the ideal wife for him.

  c. It is a woman's paternal aunt who takes the lead in events surrounding her pregnancy and childbirth; her aunt, not her mother, makes her a pregnancy cloak.

8. Yam harvest presentations and relations between affines

  a. Yam presentations, in the ideal form, go from a man to his sister's husband.

  b. A second form of yam presentation is from a married son to his father.

  c. Presentation of harvest yams is more widely a relationship between a corporate subclan and its female members' husbands and their subclans.

  d. When a spouse dies, his or her own subclan members cannot have any contact with the body, or outwardly mourn; these things are done by the kin of the surviving spouse, who then receive valuables from the dead spouse's subclan at the mortuary feast.

We could keep widening the circle of social relationships and beliefs and show how they fit together; but at this stage enough elements have been brought out to illustrate their functional interconnectedness.

We view our connectedness to our father and mother in terms of "blood relationship," which extends through them to uncles, grandmothers, cousins, and so forth. The Trobrianders view the connection among subclan members, and most vividly among brother, sister, and the sister's child, in terms of "blood." Blood implies perpetuity and continuity, as in (1) and (2b) in the outline.

Yet if the blood and the immaterial continuity with the spirits give perpetuity and unity to the subclan—as the dogma of conception insists—these cannot make the subclan independent and self-perpetuating. In the brother and sister taboo and rule against subclan incest, blood and sexual relations are inimical and sharply separate. Members of the same clan (*veyola*) may also share blood if they belong to the same subclan as well (Weiner 1976:53–60).

The dogma of subclan perpetuity and conception symbolically asserts that the subclan is self-contained and self-sustaining. But Trobriand ideologists come to terms with ecological, physical, and political necessity and recognize the dependence of the subclan for a complex of services they themselves cannot provide. In the separation of blood and sex, this need for bonds outside the subclan is symbolically expressed.

But Trobriand ideology can define those bonds outside the subclan as radically different from those of blood. They are bonds of influence, but not of substance—as expressed most directly in the father's "molding" of the child (Leach 1961). The bonds outside the subclan are created by marriage, and most of them terminate when the marriage ends. We can view these ties as "affinal," and understand the Trobrianders now when they tell the ethnographer that the father is a "relative by marriage" (6a in the

Continued

Case 52 continued

outline)—that is, connected by bonds of influ-ence but not substance. We can see why they say paternal half-siblings share no common blood (6b).

Because the child's subclan is linked by an "affinal" and hence sexual bond to the father's subclan, father's sister is the prototypical sexual object, with whom a son can joke or have sex-ual relations (7a). Because the mother and her brother are separated by the gulf of taboo (3c), he and other men of her own subclan must avoid involvement in matters connected with her sexuality and reproductive life. Hence it is their "affines," the father's subclan, who receive mar-riage presentations (6c), who assist in her be-coming pregnant (6d), and who provide magical and ritual services connected with her pregnancy and childbirth (7c) (Robinson 1962). When a Trobriander is mourned and buried by his or her spouse's relatives, not fellow mem-bers of his or her own sub-clan (8d), it is be-cause the evil "mist" emanating from the dead could spread to those of common blood; but it cannot pass across the bonds of affinity, where no common substance provides a connection. When the affines have been rewarded for this final service at the mortuary rites, the affinal relation between the two subclans comes to an end.

Thus the men of a subclan must send their sis-ters out for the sexuality, "molding," and child-bearing they themselves can take no part in; and then must get back the sisters' sons who will be their successors. A subclan's dependence on its affines for the services and influences its own members cannot provide is first of all expressed in the relationship of a man to his sister's hus-band, and in the next generation, in the relation of these two brothers-in-law toward children of

the marriage (where the father and his sisters provide services the mother's brother cannot). Because a son is a member of his maternal un-cle's subclan, his relation to his father structurally resembles and continues his uncle's "brother-in-law" relation to his father.

This comes out in yam harvest transactions (8). The transfers of yams can be viewed in part as a contractual obligation whereby a corporate subclan rewards its affines for the services they have provided. That a father can receive harvest yams from his married son as well as (or in suc-cession from) his brother-in-law (8b) makes sense if we see the young man as stepping into his ma-ternal uncle's shoes.

We saw in Cases 36 and 50 how doctrines of subclan emergence reinforce the status of *guyau* subclans and claims to land. A structure of political relationships and powers, organized in terms of strategic marriages and the tribute re-lationships they create, operates through the sys-tem of harvest presentations and mortuary exchanges; and these, in turn, are defined in terms of cultural symbols, ideas about affinal obligation, subclan rank, and obligations to the dead. Trobriand religious beliefs and the rites they motivate create contexts for the display of wealth and power, and for the col-lective action of subclans as corporations. That these corporations consist, in cultural terms, of their living and dead members, that past, present, and future are seen as a continuous process, gives the solidarity of collective action a cosmic dimension. Trobriand beliefs about procreation, blood, and female powers define a province within which women's lives and aspirations are played out, which is substantially separate from and complementary to, that of men (Weiner 1976).

right, have been relatively recent in anthropology. They represent three largely separate streams of thought whose confluence has been a major theme in modern social anthropology.

One of these streams has been the structuralism of Claude Lévi-Strauss, deriving from continental philosophy and structural linguistics. A second stream, largely inspired by the rather different American structural linguistics, has been **cognitive** anthropology, seeking to explore "grammars" of culture. A third stream, most directly brought into anthropology by the American Clifford Geertz, comes from humanistic traditions of literary criticism and philosophy that have explored symbols, meaning, and metaphor. Another look at Lévi-Strauss's approach to cultural structure will serve us well as a starting point.

In Lévi-Strauss's view, the human mind, the instrument through which cultures are created, uses a relatively simple logic to spin out symbolic systems. This logic, like the sound systems of language, is fundamentally *binary* (§6). Symbolic contrasts or oppositions are posed—and often, as we saw in the realm of myth, mediated by some middle term. Some peoples apply this mode or relational thought to the world of sensory experience: the animals, plants, constellations, individuals, and groups that are their direct evidence about the world. Like the handyman who solves infinitely variable repair problems by rearranging the pieces and materials at hand, these peoples endlessly rearrange and classify their universe of experience. The precise arrangements are almost infinitely variable, but the mode of arrangement, the structure of the designs, is repeated over and over. It is as though the human mind were a snowflake machine which never precisely replicated the same pattern, but which always produced the same *kind* of pattern.

Lévi-Strauss did not argue that there is a "primitive mind," a qualitatively different way of thinking, as had Levy-Bruhl (1923). Modern humans live in a conceptual world whose building materials have been enormously expanded by microscope, telescope, the stuff of science, and the language of mathematics; we have also become specialists, more like an electronics expert than handyman. The mode of thought is the same; it is the products of thought that have been transformed.

The same symbolic oppositions—culture versus nature, sacred versus profane, male versus female, right versus left, sun versus moon—run through the domains of all cultures. The same formal arrangements of contrast recur again and again within one culture, and from one culture to another. The differences are in the realm of content, so that it is possible to show how one design is a replica or a transformation of another.

Because the same modes of thinking are applied by tribal peoples to a world of direct sensory experience that is very much the same in jungle or desert, the same elements, themes, and contrasts occur over and over again on different continents: fire, moon, and sun; the contrast between the sexes, between our group and outsiders, between nature and culture; the use of animals and plants to symbolize relations between human groups. Human intellect grapples with the existential contradictions and problems humans face—death, human origin, the contrast between people and animals (and hence culture and nature)—using a logic of polarity and mediation. As we saw in §41, the realm of myth has increasingly preoccupied Lévi-Strauss as a meeting ground where human intellect confronts the paradoxes and contradictions of existence.

These approaches to cultural symbolism—structuralist, cognitive, symbolist, and their possibilities, limitations, and pitfalls—can again usefully be illustrated by looking at Trobriand materials. How does one begin to approach the structure of an ideational system? Trobrianders can tell the anthropologist about their subclans, their property rights, their harvest obligations, and their religious observances. But the ethnographer may not be able to ask Trobrianders what water symbolizes in their myths, or what the basic premises of their philosophy are, or what symbolic structure underlies the arrangement of a village, with any hope of being enlightened, or even understood. Most people are probably as unaware of, or unable to verbalize, the implicit logics and symbolic structures of their culture as they are of the rules of their grammar. How, then, does the analyst uncover these implicit logics and symbolic structures? And how does the analyst know that the inferences drawn are "right"?

Cultures as Cognitive Systems: Toward "Cultural Grammars"

One strategy, which has commanded an optimistic following in American anthropology, has been to seek a "grammar" of a culture through methods and models largely borrowed from linguistics. In that tradition, a culture is viewed as a *cognitive* system, a body of knowledge native actors draw on in understanding their world and one another, and choosing appropriate behaviors. In practice, this has been most seriously pursued through the study of folk classification systems. By analyzing the way Trobrianders categorize the kinds of "things" in their environment, we could not only discover much about how they perceive their environment, natural and social; but could probe the underlying logic of classification, and find out what aspects of perceptual experience they treat as salient.

Though Malinowski gives extensive linguistic materials, the full sets and contextual materials we would need to reconstruct semantic structure are rare. Yet we get a few clues about the sorts of semantic classifications the explorer of Trobriand folk categories would encounter. The fauna of the Trobriands are sparse—reptiles, birds, bats, crabs, and insects. We do not know from Malinowski's writings how the Trobrianders classify different kinds of birds or snakes.

But what concerns us here are two higher-level categories that embrace all of these land creatures: "things of the below" and "things of the above." The former include snakes, crabs, iguanas, and lizards. The latter include birds, bats, and insects. Analyzing these categories in the manner of ethnoscience (§6), we might see the distinction between them in terms of terrestrial versus flying creatures. But what about insects that do not fly? Are they included among "things of the above"? One might discover that "things of the below" are classed together because they come out of holes in the ground, and particularly because they all change their skins. But why class together creatures that change their skins? Why is it logical and meaningful to Trobrianders for the world to be divided into these categories?

The problem is that, having discovered such systems of folk classification, we are left with a partial description of the labeled "things" in the Trobrianders' world, and some evidence on distinctions they treat as important that we do not (and vice versa). But what does this tell us about Trobriand culture as a system? And how do we probe deeper than these labeled categories to find out the implicit conceptions of the world that lie beneath them?

One answer is to go beyond ethnographic semantics in a direction foreshadowed by the earlier cognitive anthropology but seldom pursued very far. One of the ethnographers to have revisited the Trobriands is the linguistic anthropologist Edwin Hutchins. Hutchins recorded, and used computers to store and retrieve, long sequences of Trobriand conversations. The problem to which he directed his attention was not so much what Trobrianders said to one another in naturally occurring conversations, but what they did *not* say: that is, what was taken for granted, the framework of assumption and cultural logic that made what, to the Western observer, seem very truncated and cryptic exchanges comprehensible to the participants. Choosing land litigation as the focus of his doctoral research, Hutchins sought to analyze the logic of argument and the framework of assumption in terms of which Trobrianders advance, understand, and challenge claims over land—a body of knowledge, he suggests, which Trobrianders would need to command to say what they say, and understand one another:

> When Kwaiwai says [in litigation] the garden went to Oyveyova and came back, he has described a series of events in the world which when fully spelled out occupy 16 propositions. Of course, the amount of knowledge the listener needs in order to expand such radical abbreviations is considerable. Here, more than simply the underlying scheme and the inference routines must be shared. In order for such a [statement] to be meaningfully understood, the understander must also share with the speaker [extensive knowledge of] specific historical events. (Hutchins 1980)

How, then, does one represent such knowledge, and express logics and "inference routines"? Are models derived from Western logic appropriate to the task? Hutchins, using computer-based formal systems (and working closely with special-

ists in artificial intelligence and the formal representation of memory at the University of California, San Diego), concluded that the means for such formal representation are rapidly emerging; and that there is nothing so exotic about the logic of Trobriand argument that it resists representation in the tradition of Western logic that comes ultimately from Aristotle:

> The analysis of litigation has shown that a model of folk logic developed from purely Western sources is quite adequate as an account of the spontaneous reasoning of Trobriand Islanders. There is no need to posit a different logic. . . . The clear difference between cultures is in the representation of the world which is thought about rather than in the processes employed in doing the thinking. (Hutchins 1979:236–237)

Both the adequacy of present formal languages to describe cultural knowledge and the possible universals of human thought that underline diversity are questions to which we will soon return. We need now to go back to "things of the above" and "things of the below" (assuming that we had analyzed the semantic structure of Trobriand classifications of the fauna of their island environment). What does that tell us—and not tell us—about the hidden logic and symbolic structure of Trobriand culture?

Hidden Logics: Cultures as Symbolic Structures

Students of symbolism like Leach and Douglas would insist that the anthropologist's job is to go further than just describing the semantics of folk classification. These are cultural creations, and we want to understand their logic—to know *why* as well as *what*. Leach (1965) would have us look very closely at those strange animals that are neither fish nor fowl, that fall in the middle in a scheme of classification. He would have us look carefully at "odd" distinctions like shedding of skin, and would have us note that on the rare occasions when evil spirits take visible form, it is as reptiles. And he might have us note that when women who are witches change their form and become invisible flying *mulukwausi* who prey on men at night and at sea, their presence can be recognized by the smell of decaying flesh—what may be a symbolic transition between life and death. But why are these changes of form and state important? Snakeskins, witches, night, sea—is it all a giant puzzle? And why "creatures of the below"? If there is a structure in all this, it is deeper and more subtle.

The Trobriand material presented in Case 53, though incomplete, is rich and provocative: small wonder that it has stimulated so many attempts at analysis and reinterpretation since Malinowski's day. Tambiah's (1983) analysis of the language of Trobriand magic, for example, hints at the rich symbolic structure in the use of colors, folk botany, direction, and other realms. But, in any case, we have gone far enough to show how such symbolic analysis can bring the structure of a culture to light.

Cultural Structure and Real Life

Can such analysis tell us something about Trobriand life, about the behavior of individual Trobrianders? Can such abstract symbolic interpretations tell us anything about the motives, perceptions, and behavior of real people? Peter Wilson (1969) argues that they can, and illustrates with a Trobriand example, which is presented in Case 54.

As we move to deeper levels of structure, such as those portrayed in Case 54, more elements of a culture fall into place. But the relatively solid foundations of analysis of folk classification have dissolved into something less tangible. How do we know Trobrianders think in terms of these symbolic patterns or use them in ordering their culture? Perhaps the symbolic association between sexuality and water bottles is transparent enough for the average Trobriander-on-the-path to perceive the pattern unconsciously. But is this necessarily true for some of the associations that analysts such as Tambiah and Tooker have distilled from magical spells and myths? How do we evaluate alternative interpretations?

How are we to be sure that we are not interpreting the symbolic systems of an alien culture in terms of the assumptions and logics of our own culture? This danger is reduced somewhat when the ethnographer who knows a language well is doing the analysis. But often, as with Tambiah, Tooker, and Wilson, the interpreter is relying on published sources. Recall that in Wilson's interpretation of Trobriand water bottles, he draws a symbolic equivalence between drinking water and the water of the ocean that serves as medium for pregnancy through the return of *baloma* spirits. But in most of the languages of the Massim, and indeed most Melanesian languages, fresh water and salt water are labeled as separate substances. There is no reason to assume that such peoples regard fresh water and salt water as two versions of the same substance (hence as symbolically interchangeable). Fortunately for Wilson, Kiriwinan seems to be the one language in the area that labels the two "kinds" of water roughly as we do. But still, can one confidently assume that they are symbolically equated in these contexts? Such doubts and dilemmas cut through much anthropological interpretation of symbolism.

CASE

53

The Structures of Trobriand Culture

To try to lay bare the whole structure of Trobriand culture would be far beyond our scope—if indeed it is possible for anthropology at all. But some of the symbolic patterns can at least be glimpsed. We can begin with some basics of Trobriand cosmology. Recall that the ancestors long ago lived underground and then emerged through the subclan holes into the world. The *baloma,* spirits of the dead, live underground as well (Malinowski 1916:170–171). We can draw these dualistic contrasts:

BELOW	:	ABOVE
SPIRITS	:	HUMANS
IMMATERIAL	:	MATERIAL
INVISIBLE	:	VISIBLE

To these further analysis would add such contrasts as:

DARKNESS	:	LIGHT
IMMORTAL	:	MORTAL
DEATH	:	LIFE
MOON	:	SUN

In such a scheme of symbolic dualisms it is worth looking, always, at mediating states and beings. Thus in dreams and visions the living can communicate with the spirits. The subclan holes (and holes in general) are avenues between above and below. But why are evil spirits manifest as reptiles; why changing skins, why "creatures of the below"?

In their earlier existence humans were immortal, and underground. When they aged, they sloughed their skins and grew new ones, as the *baloma* spirits still do. Shortly after emerging from the subclan holes to the world above,

humans lost their immortality in a seemingly trivial incident. But the snakes, crabs, and lizards that emerge from holes and still change their skins are mediators to the underworld and retain the vestiges of immortality; in contrast to humans and to birds, bats, and insects, they are creatures of the BELOW. It is as a creature of the BELOW, a snake or iguana, that an evil spirit becomes visible to humans. Crabs, which brought sorcery to humans from the spirit world, are slow to die, for they too are medial creatures of the BELOW.

But that only takes us into the outermost layers of one sector of Trobriand symbolism.

How in terms of Trobriand cosmology can we "explain" the extraordinary powers attributed to the flying witches, who are on the one hand believed to be deadly dangerous to the *kula* sailors, and on the other hand provide the positive model of imitation for the *kula* deep sea canoe. Aside from the famous . . . myth which treats of flying canoes and witches, canoes are addressed in spells as females and flying witches. Indeed canoes are urged to bind their skirts and fly in imitation of flying witches. . . . Furthermore, just as the flying witch attacks shipwrecked sailors in order to eat their insides, a wrecked canoe at sea turns cannibalistic at the moment the . . . lashings disintegrate. (Tambiah 1983)

To begin to decipher these puzzles leads us into conceptualizations of the male-female contrast in Trobriand culture. For Tambiah, the contrast between witches, who are always female, and sorcerers, who are always male, provides a point of access: "Witchcraft is involuntarily inherited by a daughter from her mother. [The] characteristics of a female witch that have been listed stand in stark comparison and opposition to the features that constitute a male sorcerer" (1983):

Continued

Case 53 continued

MALE	:	FEMALE
SORCERER	:	WITCH
VISIBLE	:	INVISIBLE
NORMAL PERSON	:	INVISIBLE DOUBLE
EXTERNAL PRACTICE	:	INTERNAL TRANSFORMATION
ORDINARY SLOWLY KILLING DISEASES	:	SUDDEN INCURABLE DISEASES
VOLUNTARY TRANSMISSION THROUGH EXCHANGE	:	INVOLUNTARY TRANSMISSION AS HERITAGE

Tambiah notes that this parallels a symbolic association of the *baloma* spirits (as "impersonal ancestral spirits continually reincarnated through women in a cycle of birth and death and rebirth") with women; and the *tabu,* the named ancestors that emerged from the underworld, with men. Thus:

MEN : WOMEN
TABU : *BALOMA*

Tambiah sees the witch as a symbolic transform of the *baloma,* product of both projection and inversion:

While the *baloma* emerge from under the ground to become incarnate as humans on the ground, the witch already a human on the ground becomes disembodied and takes to the air. Thus *baloma, human* and *witch* belong to the three cosmological realms of under the ground, on the ground, and above the ground (sky).

Tambiah notes that the *tauva'u,* nonhuman malignant spirits from whom men acquired powers of sorcery, are to the *baloma* as men are to women:

While *tauva'u* give their sorcery knowledge to men, they copulate with witches; and in their ability to emerge from the ground as reptiles or snakes they are like the *baloma:* underground creatures, who shed skins and are also immortal. But while *baloma* are incarnated through and in women, the *tauva'u* behave like human husbands toward malevolent women in having sexual intercourse with them. (Tambiah 1983)

Tambiah extends his analysis through complex webs of mythic association and cultural logic to seek to explicate the association of conjunction and inversion whereby flying witch and flying canoe are linked. He takes us, in this symbolic voyage, to the *kula.* He seeks to show a logical conjunction between flying witches and overseas canoes (which are magically treated to make them "fly") in the context of the *kula.* The flying witches, involuntary transformations of women, and the flying canoes, cultural constructions by men, are in a curious way symbolic inversions of one another, which come into violent juxtaposition when, during a *kula* expedition, a wrecked canoe is attacked by a witch. Tambiah notes that it is in violent storms, when separate realms of Trobriand cosmology, the sea and sky, come into turbulent conjunction, that "the flying witches descend from up above onto their helpless victims" and the canoe that is victim of this conjunction is jammed by a "turbulent sea . . . against a collapsing sky" (Tambiah 1983).

The *kula* has inspired other symbolic interpretations as well. McDougall (1975) interprets the *kula* as an extended male analogue of women's procreative powers: "*Kula* enables men to act out the procreative role which is sociologically denied, and to act out the fears directly related to their sexual situations." She characterizes the *kula* as a kind of male sexual exchange; and *kula* magic as "akin to love magic," an instrument that "overcomes and wards off dangers of the ocean associated with the female sex."

Another symbolic analysis is contributed by Tooker (1979), who builds on McDougall's insights but fits them into a more global structure of symbolism, in which the "female sea" looms as path of glory fraught with mortal danger. Tooker sets out to explore "the logical order involved in the association of ideas connected with the Trobriand Sea, *Kula,* and male-female relationships" (Tooker 1979:46). Like Tambiah, she sees a symbolic association between women, *baloma,* and the sea—realm with which the *baloma* are associated in myth and magic, and the medium through which these spirits enter the wombs of women to be reborn as humans.

Tooker explores the Trobriand expression of basic ideas about procreation and about maleness and femaleness. Male activity, and the male role in procreation, are conceptualized in terms of *instrumentality* and *externality;* female activity, and the female role in procreation, are conceptualized in terms of *substance* and *internality.* (Note that this expresses in slightly different terms the symbolic contrast Tambiah draws between male sorcerer, as voluntary agent operating on his magical materials, and female witch, involuntary inheritor of malevolent essence; Tambiah contrasted the sorcerer's "external practice" with the witch's internal transformation.") Tooker views the *kula* (carried out on a sea associated with *baloma,* the powers of women, and physical sexuality) as a kind of dramatization of a male counter-ideology of sex and procreation:

We might say that *kula* is a type of "male sex" in opposition to . . . "physical" sex. . . . A man's seduction of his *kula* partner is an acting out of

his basic instrumental role which we also found in procreation. The partner is "opened up" just as the woman is "opened up" in sex. But the *kula* partner is opened up so that the *vaygu'a* (*kula* valuables) will come through rather than *baloma.* These circulating valuables are a kind of male counterpart to the pool of circulating spirits. (Tooker 1979:53)

Such symbolic speculation takes us onto fairly thin ice. How do we know that such interpretations are "right"? What does "being right" mean, when we are interpreting such deep symbolic patterns? We will come back to these questions shortly. We need first to trace out briefly one other expression of Trobriand cultural structure, this one in the dramatizations of ritual.

The climax highpoint of the Trobriand year, the *milamala,* is a harvest festival—a period of dancing, feasting, ceremonial visiting, exchanges of food and valuables, and heightened sexual activity. The *milamala* activities begin after the yams have been harvested, displayed, distributed in harvest presentations, and ceremoniously stored in yam houses. At this point, marking the annual break in the gardening and work cycle, a food distribution and pageantry lead up to the first playing of drums and commencement of dancing. The *milamala* takes place through the first half of a lunar month and ends at the full moon. As the moon waxes, activities become more intense, with dancing going on through the night, organized visits by young people of a village to a neighboring village to enjoy its sexual hospitality, and even organized visits by the whole population of a village to a neighboring village, with accompanying political maneuvering, mock threat, and exchange of ceremonial valuables.

Continued

Case 53 continued

But there are a number of curious features that suggest a more subtle symbolic theme. They suggest that this is a context where symbolic polarities are joined or reversed. Female and male, the spirits and the living, the periphery and the center, the below and the above are united or reversed.

One element in this union of polarities, or reversal, is expressed in the realm of sexuality. Recall that it is the bachelor houses in the center of the village, the male domain, that are the focal settings for premarital sex; and recall the symbolic polarities to which Lévi-Strauss called our attention in his glimpse of the Trobriand village (Case 31):

PERIPHERAL : CENTRAL
COOKED   : RAW
MARRIAGE   : NONMARRIAGE
PROFANE   : SACRED

Trobriand men don women's grass skirts for a dance. Reversal of polarities in the *milamala*.

The symbolic polarity of inner and outer circles of the village may in fact express not a symbolic contrast between MARRIAGE and NON-MARRIAGE, as Lévi-Strauss has argued (see Case 31), but one between REGULATED SEX and UNREGULATED SEX (Boon 1972:127). Premarital sex reaches its height during *milamala* and acquires a kind of overt recognition, cultural embellishment, and collective character in intervillage sexual visiting. The shift of emphasis from individual, regulated, domestic sex to collective, unrestricted, premarital sex and from periphery to center of the village hints that *milamala* is not only a time of liminality (Turner 1967) but a time when polarities are mediated or reversed. Given the polarities between moon:sun and dark:light, the way the *milamala* reaches its climax at full moon probably reflects their symbolic union in this liminal period of heightened cultural intensity. Apparently the dancing in the village center, which attracts men and women around the drums, serves as a medium for the union of dualities. Men wear their festive ornaments emphasizing maleness in the day, during *milamala*, then take them off at night; and in some of the dances the male dancers put on women's grass skirts. Cooked food, symbolic of the women's and domestic realm, is normally taboo within the central plaza. But in the opening feast of *milamala* cooked food is set out and distributed there.

But the most dramatic union of symbolic oppositions in *milamala* is the return of the *baloma* spirits to their village. Through the *milamala* period the spirits are present and are given food offerings and ceremonial valuables (the "spirit" of which they take). The element of symbolic reversal comes out vividly in the high platforms made for *baloma* of high rank—placing them ABOVE rather than BELOW. Moreover the *baloma* enforce the suspension of the normal rules of life. If they are not satisfied with people's conduct, as well as with presentations of food and valuables, they can spoil weather or even the next gardening cycle. "Everybody had to be bound on pleasure, dancing, and sexual license, in order to please the *baloma*" (Malinowski 1916:185). The *milamala* ends at full moon when the *baloma* are ritually sent back to their spirit home.

The inversion where the *baloma*, creatures of the BELOW and symbolically associated with women, with physical sex, and procreative connections of substance, enter the world of the ABOVE, taking part symbolically in the male realm of exchange and politics, is a dramatization in reverse of what happens when men die and enter the symbolically female realm of the *baloma* in Tuma. In this world of the spirits, it is not the men's pursuits of prestige that predominate:

Skill in gardening or carving, outstanding achievements in war or in the *kula*, were no longer objects of ambition to the spirits. Instead, we find dancing and personal beauty celebrated, and these mainly as a setting and a preliminary to sex enjoyment (Malinowski 1929:435)

The *baloma*, in returning to the ABOVE, at once reenter the world of male concerns and bring with them the celebration of beauty and sexuality, the union of male and female, free of their polarization in political and economic life, that is dramatized in *milamala*.

CASE

54

Trobriand Water Bottles

Malinowski (1929:98–99) recounted an event that puzzled him. The son of an important chief discovered his wife in the arms of his half-brother. He reacted with visible anger; but instead of smashing his wife or her lover, he smashed all of his wife's water bottles. And then, seemingly satisfied, he appeared publicly "sitting beside his wife in perfect harmony." Malinowski notes elsewhere that when a husband is angry with his wife he may express this by breaking her water bottles or destroying her grass skirt (Malinowski 1929:21). But this seemed to Malinowski an inadequate and hence idiosyncratic response to his wife and half-brother caught in the act of adultery.

We know enough about displaced aggression to understand that by redirecting anger at the water bottles the husband diverted his aggression from direct assault on the adulterous couple. Redirecting aggression—kicking a wall in frustration—is an old part of our mammalian heritage. But why the water bottles? And is it coincidental

that the wife had taken her water bottles as a pretext to meet her lover? Wilson (1969:287) notes a myth in which women who are raped while getting water are more upset about the breaking of their water bottles than their physical violation. He notes that the waterhole is "the women's club and center of gossip" (Malinowski 1929:17) and that filling water bottles is an exclusively female duty. Moreover, water is the medium through which conception occurs. Not only does a spirit child usually enter a woman's body through water (so that if she wants to avoid conception she stays away from the water); but her brother or mother's brother may facilitate conception by collecting water in a wooden baler (*not* a water bottle) and leaving it in her hut overnight. Wilson argues that there is a symbolic association of water with the reproductive powers of women. He further notes that the symbolic line drawn in Trobriand culture between men's and women's realms centers around the head. Wilson

Access to Meanings and the Distribution of Knowledge

Much work in analysis of symbols builds on the assumption that a culture consists of a system of shared meanings. Assuming that the meanings are shared and public, that the system transcends individual versions and variations, one can piece together clues to symbolism without concern about who knows what.

But it now seems particularly urgent to take into account the way meanings are accessible to individuals—to take a *distributive* view of culture as symbol system. Do all

Trobrianders unconsciously "understand" the symbolic mirror-image relationship between witches and sorcerers, *baloma* and *tabu?* Is it possible that the deepest levels and most global, all-embracing designs of symbolism are understood by only a few folk philosophers? Ethnographers like Malinowski inevitably seek out, and are referred to, the most knowledgeable members of the community. They pass on the myths, ritual accounts, and interpretations that become the texts for symbolic analysis. Do other members of the society command the knowledge they would need to under-

(1969:287) argues that symbolically "A woman's head . . . is that part of her which is the junction and starting point for passion, conception and creation, for the psychological or emotional and physiological process of birth."

That the power of creation symbolically brings together head and water emerges in the Trobriand myth of incest. A woman's brother brings water into her house—but he does so, inappropriately, in water bottles, not a baler. The girl's mother will not bring it to her, so she goes to get it herself; and in doing so, she inadvertently knocks over the coconut shell containing coconut oil brewed by her brother into love potions. Some of it spills on her head; she is seized with desire for her brother and they rush to the sea shore and have intercourse.

Wilson believes that water bottles, also made of coconut shells, symbolically represent the sexual relationship between husband and wife, being carried on women's heads, containers of water as the medium of life, and symbols par excellence of women's domestic role. He argues

that they serve, correspondingly, as symbols of the incest taboo that separates a woman from her brother and matrilineal kin:

To a husband, his wife's water bottles indicate her sexuality and his right to that sexuality. The water within them, and the fact that she carries them on her head, signifies her life-giving powers and her relation to her brother. To a brother water bottles signify the incest taboo and the water within them his rights to her children. To a woman a water bottle is the symbolic nexus of her total social position: her relationship with her husband and thence her sexuality, her relationship with her brother and thence her procreative duties. (Wilson 1969:288)

For the adulterous wife to have taken her water bottles as pretext to meet her lover, for the cuckolded husband to have displaced his aggression by smashing them and not her, and for their fellow Trobrianders to have accepted this as a quite appropriate response is not strange or idiosyncratic, Wilson argues. Rather, these constitute appropriate messages in a symbolic code Trobrianders share and (however unconsciously) "understand."

stand the deepest levels of symbolism? Does one need to understand the symbolism of a ritual such as *milamala* to take appropriate part in it?

Anthropological students of symbolism have often answered such doubts by asserting that "understanding meanings" does not mean being able to explain them—that native actors unconsciously understand a grammar of symbols as they understand the grammar of their language. Symbols, they argue, do not necessarily "stand for" things, but represent relationships. Native actors unconsciously perceive these pat-

terns, expressed in ritual or myth, even though they can offer no interpretations themselves. This is probably true; but it is at best a partial truth.

If we assume that all native actors unconsciously perceive symbolic meanings, we become unable to deal effectively with the many cases where the secrets of symbolic meaning are successively revealed to initiates (as in the Poro and Sande societies of the Kpelle, Case 39, or many systems of male initiatory cults in Amazonia, New Guinea, and Aboriginal Australia). Thus Barth, in his account of the Baktaman of

Papua New Guinea (Barth 1975), describes how the secret knowledge that allows progressively deeper and more comprehensive interpretation of ritual symbolism is revealed to young men step by step as they go through an initiation sequence. The Baktaman have a highly elaborate and subtle system of color symbolism. Knowledge of the keys to this symbolism is acquired as a man progresses through initiatory grades; and this knowledge allows the initiates to understand, in progressive stages, the symbolism of painted shields used in ritual:

> Very few Baktaman bring the necessary knowledge to their reading of the colors on a shield so they can decode the full message. . . . The women will have only . . . public contexts . . . from which to develop their understanding of the color code. (Barth 1975:177–178)

The Political Economy of Knowledge

Understanding how access to knowledge may be controlled, and may serve as a basis for power (as with the Kpelle elders who control the Poro; Case 39), gives further urgency to seeing meanings as distributed in communities. We cannot comfortably assume that symbolic elaborations of Trobriand culture are equally the creation of men and women, or of *guyau* and commoners. The politics of symbols—their creation and deployment—is too easily lost sight of if we conceive anthropology to be a kind of "cultural cryptography." In societies where knowledge conveys power, where magical spells constitute property and knowledge of myth is jealously guarded, we must take seriously into account who commands the keys to symbolic understanding, and what they are used for. Cultural cryptography must at least be complemented by a "political economy of knowledge" that asks who creates secret knowledge, who gains access to it, and how it is used. The Bimin

Kuskusmin of New Guinea, who have an elaborate hierarchy of male initiatory grades, have an apt image for the way esoteric knowledge is progressively revealed to initiates. Symbolic meanings are layered, like an onion: the outer layers are progressively stripped away until initiates are allowed to see the most deeply hidden secrets. It is an image worth remembering when we engage in cultural cryptography. Native actors in a society such as the Trobriands, fully able to participate in the *kula* or the *milamala,* may have access to quite different layers of the onion—may understand the same events in quite different ways.

There is another danger in cultural cryptography. If we try to discover the hidden symbolism of ritual, we are prone to overintellectualize what for the participants is a way of accomplishing collective work. Barth makes the point strongly for the Baktaman:

> Rites . . . *do* something as well as *say* something. . . . It is the *concerns* of Baktaman ritual—taro, growth, pigs—that integrate even the most passive and excluded categories . . . into the cult and make of the whole population one unified congregation with a common purpose. (1975:209–210)

What matters is to perform a rite correctly, hence achieve its desired goals and avoid the wrath of the ancestors or gods; scant wonder that rituals are emotionally powerful collective experiences even though participants may understand the hidden significance of cultural symbols in quite different ways and degrees.

These doubts and concerns will serve us well when we attempt, in the final pages of Part 3, to pull together the strands of the preceding chapters into a coherent synthesis, a formulation of the internal dynamics of small-scale societies. We need to ask, first, whether there are still deeper cultural structures. Are there, underlying the kinds of symbolic structures we have encountered in the Trobriands and other tribal societies, more fundamental premises about the universe and the place of humans in it? Can we characterize ways of life as representing contrasting "world views"?

44. CULTURES, WORLD VIEWS, AND DIVERSITY

World View

In American anthropology, a serious effort was launched in the 1940s and 1950s to characterize the philosophies or world views of non-Western peoples. This had partly been spurred by the effort, in World War II, to analyze the "national character" of Germans, Japanese, and other peoples with whom the United States was engaged as enemies or allies. But a more serious impetus was the dialogue between anthropologists, notably Clyde Kluckhohn, and philosophers, including F. S. C. Northrop, Ethel Albert, and David Bidney. Kluckhohn drew such scholars into close collaboration in looking at the **values,** or "conceptions of the desirable," of non-Western peoples, in contrast to those of the West. Kluckhohn sought himself to characterize the world view and values of the Navaho with whom he worked for years. Among these efforts to characterize the distinctive world views of particular peoples, some of the boldest and most provocative built on the insights of Benjamin Lee Whorf on the way language structures thought (§6). Following Whorf's lead, Dorothy Lee sought to find how a world view is encoded in a language. Like many other anthropologists, she turned to Malinowski's rich linguistic texts. Although she never heard a Trobriander speak, she immersed herself in these texts to try to "think" her way into the Trobriand world

by working through the language. A first attempt to draw the Trobriand world view (Lee 1940) contrasted it with that of an English speaker. But she had misgivings whether one could faithfully render the Trobriand world view in terms of what it was not, in terms of contrasts. In a second paper, Lee (1949:401–415) tried to draw the Trobriand world in its own terms—an immensely difficult challenge when one must write in English about another language. (See Case 55.)

Beneath Diversity

There is a deeper problem about the structure of language, as well as its uses. Modern grammatical theory views languages as having a fundamentally similar, and universal, logical structure underlying the sorts of diversity at the level of surface structure Lee describes for Kiriwinan. The structures, as well as the uses, of language weigh against inferences that the thought worlds of other peoples are radically different from our own.

There are good reasons to expect that human ways of experiencing and reasoning about time, space, and causality are a part of our mammalian biological heritage—however peoples may build on these ways in different cultural idioms. Whatever philosophical elaborations Trobrianders may make on causal relationships, as in their theory of conception and their systems of magic, it seems likely that it is part of their mammalian equipment, on which their ability to learn and survive depends, that they "understand causality": a canoe paddle stuck in the water and pushed in one direction will lead the canoe to go in the other direction; pulling a roasted taro out of the fire leads a hand to be burned; a puncture of the skin with a sharp weapon leads blood to come out. Trobrianders, like other humans, have special linguistic conventions

CASE

55

The Trobriand World View as Structured in Language

Among the Trobriand islanders, as with other peoples, "language . . . incorporates the premises of the culture, and codifies reality in such a way that it presents it as absolute" to its speakers. The speakers of Kiriwinan "are concerned with being, and being alone. Change and becoming are foreign to their thinking. An object or event is grasped and evaluated in terms of itself alone" It is not defined, which implies contrast with other things, but is conceived in terms of what it is. Each event is grasped timelessly, "seen in relation to other things only in that it is part of an ordained pattern."

If I were to go with a Trobriander to a garden where the taytu, a species of yam, had just been harvested, I would come back and tell you: "There are good taytu there; just the right degree of ripeness, large and perfectly shaped; not a blight to be seen, not one rotten spot. . . . " The Trobriander would come back and say "Taytu"; and he would have said all that I did and more. (Lee 1949:402)

History and mythical reality are not "the past" to the Trobriander. They are forever present, participating in all current being, giving meaning to all his activities and all existence. (p. 403)

To be good [an object] must be the same always. . . . Trobriand being never came into existence; it has always been, exactly as now. (p. 405)

To the Trobriander, events do not fall of themselves into a pattern of casual relationships. . . . The magician does not cause certain things to be; he does them. (pp. 400–407)

The Trobriander performs acts because of the activity itself, not for its effects; . . . he values objects because they are good, not good for. (p. 408)

[Yet] being has no independent existence. It is itself only as part of an established pattern. . . . Being is seen . . . as a fixed point in a single, changeless whole. (p. 409)

For members of our culture, value lies ideally in change, in moving away from the established pattern. . . . The Trobriander, on the contrary, expects and wants next year to be the same as this year and as the year before his culture emerged from underground. (p. 413)

Finally, Lee speculates on the level and the relevance of such linguistically structured contrast in world view:

Do we who base our behavior on relationships, read these relationships into reality, or are they given? Which codification is true to reality? . . . Our peculiar codification makes us blind to other aspects of reality. . . . Or makes these meaning-

for talking about these kinds of relationships, ways that may be superficially quite different from our own.

The Trobriand symbolic system and other webs of cultural assumption and conception we have traced show that humans can place very different interpretations on the most basic human experiences of past, present, and future, of the connectedness between events (as witness the logic of contagious magic or explanations for snakebites), of birth and death, illness and health, success and failure. But Lee's misrendering of the Trobriand world view should warn us that it is easy to take linguistic conventions for talking about the

less when presented. But one codification does not exhaust reality. . . . The Trobrianders, according to our view of life, should be bored automatons. Actually they act as they want to act, poised and sure, in activities which hold meaning and satisfaction. (Lee 1949:415)

Lee's intuitions, like Whorf's analyses of the Hopi world view, capture the imagination with their vividness. And they become doubly plausible to many in the West caught up in countercultures that challenge the pervasive and destructive rationality of Western thought and seek a more mystical and holistic vision of the world in the wisdom of other peoples. But was Lee right? It is worth quoting the observations of linguistic anthropologist Edwin Hutchins, who learned Kiriwinan fluently and explored the uses of language in everyday conversation, and the processes of reasoning that underlie Trobriand discourse. Of Lee's claim that "temporality, causation, teleology, and relationship in general have neither meaning nor relevance for Trobriand behavior" (Lee 1949:415), Hutchins had this to say:

Such claims may seem credible when evaluated only in the light of the limited data Lee presents. . . . For one who has lived in the Trobriands, learned the language, and experienced the complexity of everyday life there, however, these claims are absurd. . . . While Trobrianders' beliefs about the world are, in some domains, very different from our beliefs, it is unwarranted to infer from a difference in content that the way Trobrianders reason about what they believe is substantially different from the way we reason about what we believe. (Hutchins 1979:13, 16).

If that is the case, why is it that Lee arrived at such a different conclusion about the nature of Trobriand reasoning? "Even if we ignore the problems Lee faced in working on linguistic data without a knowledge of the language in which it is expressed," Hutchins concluded, Malinowski's data provided the wrong kind of sample of Kiriwinan: mainly magic spells and mythic texts. Such texts, which Malinowski could transcribe with paper and pencil, in the days before tape recorders, are radically different from everyday conversation: "Magical spells . . . are like telegraphic speech, so devoid of overt specification of relations that they often seem cryptic even to Trobrianders" (Hutchins 1979:16).

The logic of syllogistic reasoning, which Hutchins found pervasively expressed in Trobriand land litigation, was missed by Lee because, first, "Malinowski was unable to set down a written record [for want of a not-yet-invented tape recorder] of the sorts of speech in which syllogistic reasoning is made explicit," and second, because "having never lived in the Trobriands, Lee had no access to, and thus could not render explicit, the implicit premises underlying the discourse which was recorded" (Hutchins 1979:16).

world—conventional systems of metaphor, or surface-structure grammatical rules—as evidence of a vast gulf between another people's world and our own. A Trobriand ethnographer roaming the United States might be led to describe a strange conceptual world in which the outcome of events was determined by the meshing of opposing cosmic forces of good luck and bad luck.

The gulfs between cultural models of reality of different peoples cannot be aptly characterized as either superficial or deep. The processes of thought, perception, and memory are very heavily structured by a *Homo sapiens* brain that is the same in

Amazonia or Nigeria or New York or the Trobriand Islands. The range of cultures that are thinkable and learnable by members of our species is probably—in terms of formal organization and logic—quite narrow. But on the other hand, the variation in *content* or *substance* (as opposed to structure and organization) of culturally constructed worlds is striking. If we begin with the "normal" assumptions that humans, as cultural beings, make—that our ways of life and thought are *the* ways, that the things we take for granted are obvious facts of the world—then the diversity of human ways is striking, sometimes staggering.

Having looked at human ways in the broadest comparative perspective, we need to turn from small-scale societies of a vanishing past to the vast complexities and rapid change of the contemporary world. Before we do, it will be useful to pull together the strands of argument and interpretation set out in preceding chapters and try to put them together into a more coherent set of theoretical orientations. Then, conceptually armed, we can turn to the developments that have transformed the non-Western world, and our own.

45. TOWARD A THEORY OF CHANGE

The theoretical framework that was foreshadowed at the end of Chapter 7, introduced in Chapter 8, and developed through the subsequent chapters, proposes a logic of interconnection, an internal dynamic, in the relationships of humans to their environment and to one another, the relationships between social and cultural. Such a theoretical framework is not yet fully developed, particularly in its application to the range of societies anthropologists have traditionally studied. We need now to review this theoretical design, tying together threads left unconnected in the preceding chapters; and

answering more directly the questions posed at the end of Chapter 7, where the solutions proposed by proponents of "cultural materialism" were seen to be inadequate.

Neo-Marxist Foundations of a Composite Theory

A major component of the composite conceptualization of sociocultural process developed in the preceding chapters comes from neo-Marxist theory. This body of theory begins with the assumption that humans engage the world only within social systems. This emphasis on the social side of production, on economy as a sociocultural system rather than on ecology as a biological system, is one of the major contrasts between this neo-Marxist approach and cultural materialism.

> To be human is to be social, for we can reproduce ourselves only through cooperative production of our means of subsistence. . . . There are no autonomous individual subjects, stripped of the accidental accoutrements of culture and history. (O'Laughlin 1975: 346–347)

> Marx's view is . . . quite different from that of most of the cultural materialists and cultural ecologists who insist that the ultimate meaning of history lies in technological processes. The problem here is that technological change becomes an . . . independent variable: ways in which social relations of production affect the development of the productive forces are systematically left unanalyzed. (O'Laughlin 1975:355)

The engagement of a human population with the physical world has both a social, organizational side—**relations of production,** or "relations between people" (O'Laughlin 1975:349)—and a physical, technological side—**forces of production,** or relations "between people and nature." The two-sided interplay between the organization of social relations and the technological side of production means that social change is not simply an adaptive response to ecological or demographic pressures. The organization of social relations structures the encounter between a population and their ecosystem. It is this two-sidedness that rules out any simple environmental determinism. The economic base, the two-sided system of social relations and forces of production, shapes the form of a society. But this, Marx insisted, is determination "in the last instance."

Let us review what this means. In a society with little accumulation of the products of labor, production of surpluses for distribution and exchange depends on control over marriage and fertility. Without classes or centralized political institutions, autonomous local groups provide the settings for production and exchange, and for control over land and resources. Hence we find the centrality of kinship institutions in organizing and reproducing a system of production.

In the Trobriands, subclans control land and magic (crucial resources in the productive process); the avenues of exchange and distribution of surpluses are those of kinship. Even political subordination is expressed in idioms of kinship and marital alliance. In contrast, among the Aztec (Case 11), production was accumulated in the physical structures of a vast city and intensified agricultural systems; and a class system dominated by priests and warrior nobles depended on an expansionist and repressive state and a blood-thirsty religion. Kinship relations were of secondary importance; in family settings, the Aztecs ate, slept, bore and raised children. But neither the organization of the labor force nor control and distribution of surpluses was based on kinship.

It is in this sense that the economic base is "determinant in the last instance" of the fundamental structure of a society—of the kinds of superstructural institutions and ideologies that will develop, and their nature. Thus we find the centrality in the Trobriands of kinship and of a religion defining relations between commoners and chiefs, men and women, ancestors and descendants in an idiom of cyclical descent. Among the Aztec, political institutions of state control and militaristic expansion brought slaves, captives for sacrifice, tribute, and bounty into an economy that could grow only by devouring its neighbors. A priesthood and nobility were buttressed by a state religion that defined warfare and butchery as religious duty.

But this "determination in the last instance" is not a determination by protein starvation. It is not a mechanical process of cultural response to natural demand. And it is not a determination where every detail of ritual or cosmology or kinship pattern has a hidden ecological rationality. A ruling elite among the Aztec could have developed a thousand religions that would have sustained their power and expansionism. We do not have to find a hidden ecological rationality in every belief, rite, and custom; their political and economic "rationality" is determinate in a much less mechanical way, one that leaves ample room for the symbolic elaborations of mind. Ideologies of the ritual danger of women, rituals of male cultism and initiatory secrets, are not reducible to some hidden demographic or ecological purpose. They are at once ideologies that mystify and celestialize, and symbolic creations with a logic and structure such as that we explored in the myths and rites and cosmology of the Trobriands.

Cultures as Ideational Systems in a Theory of Change

The Marxist tradition does not seek to reduce cultural structure to something more "real" external to society. But it does insist that we see in productive relationships the conditions that lead to symbolic elaborations in one realm rather than another, and that we look for the consequences—in control over people and their labor—of ideologies of pollution, subclan perpetuity and reincarnation, and ancestral control.

The Marxist approach would insist that elaborations of cultural symbolism—such as the symbolism of Trobriand sea and land, the above and the below, male and female—be understood in a social and economic context, not simply deciphered as a logical puzzle:

> Cultural representations exist only when they are socially organized. . . . Cultural representations are not logical systems straining toward consistency, for they are ultimately ordered by their social contexts, not by the logic of mind. (O'Laughlin 1975:348)

If we push this mode of analysis to its ultimate implications we are led to see the common commitment of a tribal people to a system of cultural symbols as problematic: these cultural ideologies are mystifications that celestialize and hence disguise political realities.

> If consciousness does not faithfully represent the social conditions of existence [as in a society where women accept the terms of their subordination as laid down and policed by the ancestors with whom the men commune in their men's houses], then we can never fully understand these conditions through the representations of subjective consciousness. . . . The subject's view (whether conscious or unconscious) is quite likely to be a mystification of underlying social relations. (O'Laughlin 1975:348)

That is, from a Marxist point of view we cannot take at face value the commitment a people have to their way of life, cannot analyze a social system only through cultural categories and the meanings of acts and customs to those who perform and follow them.

The View From Within, the View From Without

To look at a way of life through the eyes of native actors, in terms of cultural meanings and values, thus presents us with what are ultimately illusions. These cultural systems depict as eternal and cosmic what have been created by humans in real political and economic contexts and are constantly changing. If we look at a culturally defined world as "real," we are left without a theory of change, or a clear conception of how ideational systems are rooted in social realities. Yet the neo-Marxist view, taken without a complementary view of a cultural world from within, creates this paradox: First, if we treat the view from within as an illusion, we insufficiently appreciate the meanings and motives of native actors, and the richness of cultural structure of the sort we saw for the Trobriands. Second, and more deeply troubling, the analyst who steps outside a people's own world of cultural meanings to treat them as illusions assumes that the realities he or she substitutes for them are absolute. Yet the standards and categories one applies as observer are themselves culturally situated. How do we decide that Aztec commoners, or plantation slaves, were exploited? According to some conception of justice in the relationship between work, control over the means of production, and access to its rewards. This conception is not given to us by the gods, but is itself a human creation, ultimately ideological, a product of the Western intellectual tradition. Can we see Trobriand relations between chiefs and commoners as oppressive? By what standards, if not theirs? Do we not run the risk of engaging in a kind of ideological imperialism ourselves?

There is no easy escape from this paradox. If we take a relativistic stance, treating as valid in its own right each people's cultural definition of values and social relationships, then we are ultimately led into a philosophically and politically untenable position—left defending South African apartheid or Nazi genocide, as well as Marind Anim gang rape. Yet if we take a view from outside a social-cultural system that is not tempered by a view from within, we neither understand nor do justice to other people's worlds.

An adequate anthropological conception must take both a view from within and a view from without. To understand Trobriand life, to understand the motives and meanings that make *kula* exchange, yam presentations, and leaf bundle distributions important to those who enact them, we must see the world in Trobriand terms. We must probe beneath what native participants can themselves tell us to explore a hidden symbolic logic whereby flying witches and cannibalistic canoes have been created and imbued with deep meaning. The fantastic symbolic creativity that has cumulatively constructed such a world cannot be reduced to any hand of "practical reason," whether it be that of the big ecologist in the sky, as cultural materialism would have it, or the cold hand of economic and political advantage, as a simple and "vulgar" Marxism would have it.

There is no alternative, if we are to understand Trobriand life, then to immerse ourselves deeply in these symbols and meanings and, in the process, to take them as our realities. In this task, an ideational conception of culture serves us well. But in doing that, we have situated ourselves in a timeless world where subclan spirits are endlessly recycled, where the *tabu* and *baloma* are participants in social life, where armshells and necklaces are wondrous and

valuable, where magic brings wealth and makes yams grow We must step back out of this frame—but remain conscious that we as observers ourselves see the world through culturally ground lenses we cannot take off. Having done that, we see that the concept of culture is limiting, as well as revealing.

Trobriand men and women, chiefs and commoners, have shared codes of expectation that make ordered social life possible. A commoner shuffles along on his knees with head bowed before a leader of high rank and presents as tribute valuables and yams which the leader will use in ceremonial exchanges and feasting. Both of them share a common culture in the sense that the high-ranking leader knows how to demand and receive obeisance and the commoner knows when and how he has to give it. But to say that those kinds of knowledge, pieced together into a composite, constitute Trobriand culture conveys only part of the picture.

The interests of Trobriand chiefs and commoners, men and women, may be deeply in conflict; and Trobriand culture as pieced together by Malinowski represents a temporary state of the battle lines. That there is no recorded history of the development of social stratification, the *kula* ring, or matrilineal descent in the Trobriands should not mislead us into seeing a spurious unity, integration, or equilibrium of Trobriand society and culture. And that leads us directly into the question of change.

Processes of Change in the Tribal World: Conflict and Contradiction

A cultural materialist position, taking social structures and cultural ideas as adaptive responses to ecological and demographic pressures, is inherently static. To explain why a culture changes, we have to find something in the "more real" physical world which is changing, in response to which human behavior shifts in an adaptive direction (whether by conscious modification or the fortuitous invention of customs with useful consequences).

The neo-Marxist model is inherently dynamic. Every social system incorporates stresslines, conflicts, and contradictions as well as modes of integration and reinforcement.

> In the dialectical working out of the relationship between forces and relations of production in time and space, antagonistic contradictions may develop within the system—think, for instance, of conflict over access to land arising in certain conditions as a swidden system becomes in time a system of intensive cultivation. . . . The system reproduces itself, despite these contradictions, through the mediation of superstructure—juridicopolitical and ideological relations that suppress, displace, or misrepresent basic conflict. (O'Laughlin 1975:349)

But in the neo-Marxist view, these superstructural mediations and mystifications do not eliminate contradictions; "they merely permit their reproduction often in more antagonistic forms" (O'Laughlin 1975:350).

Let us imagine a society with a pollution ideology and cults of male secrecy. By defining male and female realms as separate, and women as inherently dangerous, men create a series of contradictions. First, by denying women coordinate power in the real world, they give women powers to poison and destroy them. Second, creating a secret and sacred realm controlled by adult men, they place young boys in the women's realm—and must invent drastic and psychologically traumatic ways of making men of them. Third, men—in pursuit of symbolic goals—may progressively lose control over, even separate themselves from, the productive processes that sustain them. Hallpike (1977) perhaps overstates the case,

but his argument is a useful corrective to mechanical determinisms:

> Tauade pig-rearing, feasts and dances, fighting and vengeance are not biologically adaptive, or even socially useful in any objective sense. . . . The traditional life of the Tauade was a prolonged fantasy of power, a religion whose rites were burning villages; the cries of warriors and victims; feathers and blood; dying pigs; and the monstrous figures of dancers swaying tumultuously in the darkness of the ranges. These were no sober agriculturalists, making narrow calculations of profit and loss . . . but . . . men in the grip of a collective obsession with blood and death. For them work in their gardens was a boring necessity, to be shifted on to the women as far as possible, valuable only as the foundation of the real business of life—the pursuit of glory. (Hallpike 1977:253)

Such a social system is inherently unstable from within—in separating symbolic pursuits of power from the productive processes that sustain them, in polarizing seniors against juniors, men against women—and from without, in placing local groups in mutually destructive conflict, vulnerable to eventual displacement and absorption by groups with expanding economies and populations.

Such internal contradictions, whether for the Tsembaga Maring, the Tauade described by Hallpike, or the Trobriands, potentially lead to the transformation of a social system. Exchange systems in the New Guinea highlands entail the potential of big men gaining sufficient control over prestige valuables and pig herds that they provide means for the creation of a new regional political order and/or the emergence of an incipient class of big men whose links to one another and collective interest transcend (or at least compete with) the ties to local descent groups that place them in competition with one another. Ideologies may emerge that legitimize their power such that their sons become hereditary successors rather than slightly favored competitors for entrepreneurial power. If things had not gone that far in the New Guinea highlands, they may have been moving in that direction when Europeans entered the scene. Some such transformation of big men into chiefs with hereditary privilege and rank perhaps took place in the very different setting of the Trobriands. (For an assessment of the situation in the New Guinea highlands, see A. J. Strathern 1987.)

Change and Regional Systems

The transition from feudalism to capitalism in Europe entailed thousands of individual properties, hundreds of towns; and of course there was great local diversity in just what happened and when. A class analysis in Marxist terms not only helps us to sort essential processes from the particularities of their local expression, but helps us to relate widespread phenomena within a common framework. But for the smaller scale of Melanesia or tribal Africa or the Kachin hills of Burma such abstraction can be costly. First of all, classing a whole range of societies together as representing the "African mode of production" or the "primitive communal mode of production" lumps together systems whose differences from one another may be what we want to account for. What focus we take will depend on the questions we pose. But if we are asking about, say, the emergence of chiefly hierarchy in the Trobriands, theoretical models must be applied to very specific historical and geographic circumstances. Our questions may be directed, not at broad classes such as feudal lord and serf, but at the Tabalu subclan in northern Kiriwina.

Since our aim when we embarked on our voyage to the Trobriands across the seas of the Argonauts was to develop the means to understand Trobriand society and culture,

we can well end this survey with a glimpse of some very particular questions of Trobriand political history. They will remind us of some important points we can carry into the final section of the book, along with a theoretical perspective we can apply to more complex social systems of the present and recent past.

H. A. Powell (n.d.) looks at his own Trobriand field data from the 1950s in the light of Brunton's speculations (1975; see Case 36) about how the leaders of northern Kiriwina gained ascendancy through monopolistic entry into the *kula* circuit. Brunton had speculated that the northern agricultural areas were marginal to the natural routes of *kula* exchange by virtue of geographical factors. Powell concurs, and adds new evidence to reinforce it. But how, then, did the Tabalu subclan centered in Omarakana enter an exchange circuit from which they were geographically excluded? And if they were able to gain power through doing so, why was their power as limited as it was when Malinowski and later Powell observed them?

> The Sinaketans and Vakutans [see map, Figure 8.1, p. 141] commanded the "natural" route for *kula* articles. . . . The Sinaketans could, and it seems when possible did, cream off the best of the *kula* valuables . . . by exploiting this advantage, and would have been able to monopolize the *kula* exchanges altogether if they could withstand pressure from the other Trobriand communities. . . . But . . . they were unlikely ever to have been able to do this because their population was never large enough by comparison with those of the other districts. The Omarakana Tabalu and their followers would have had no difficulty in dominating the Sinaketans by force but for the need to traverse the territories of some of the intervening communities in order to get at them; but this meant that they had to be able to dominate these communities as well. . . . My guess is . . . that one major reason for the support the Tabalu, and no doubt from

time to time other leaders of Kiriwina district, were able to muster, through the mechanisms of rank, polygyny, and *urigubu* [harvest presentations], was their utility to the rest of the population as foci for the degree of political organization needed . . . to dominate the other communities in order to gain entry into the *kula*. It is, I suspect, this role which is validated and rationalized in the ascription to the Tabalu especially and to the other leading subclans of attributes which in the Kiriwinans' eyes justify their dominance within their own territories. (Powell n. d.)

Whether Powell's speculations are correct is not the important question. What matters more, I think, is to take away some thoughts about the tribal world that will serve us well in looking at the vaster modern one. To imagine "Trobriand society" or "Trobriand culture" as coherent and integrated systems existing in the time-vacuum of the "ethnographic present" would be grossly misleading. "Trobriand society" is an abstraction derived from communities of coastal fisherpeople/traders and inland horticulturalists, large and strong villages and weak subordinate ones. Their political relationships, even on this miniature scale, were fluid and complicated. The communities of the Trobriands were part of a shifting regional system that has had a real (if mainly unknown) history. We can seek in such complex systems, situated in time and space, general models about societal process. But the more closely we look, and the more evidence we gather (and for the Massim area in which the Trobriands are situated, this evidence has expanded enormously), the more we find processes of politics and history, of interconnection rather than isolation, that we will find in the vast-scale world created by European expansion. As we turn to these global systems, it will be well to remember that the processes of domination and absorption, relations between center and periphery, are old, not re-cent. The "traditional" world to which we contrast the "modern" one was not simple, not a mosaic of separate cultures, not ancient and unchanging.

SUMMARY

In British social anthropology key concepts were social structure and function, whereas in American anthropology the key concept was culture. It is possible to combine these two traditions by attending to the social functions of practices and the logical or aesthetic integration of the ideas that inform them. A composite picture of Trobriand social organization is developed to show the possibility for such an analysis, taking into account data on conception ideas, shared blood, rank, succession to chiefship, residence, and many other factors. Ideas can also be presented systematically in themselves, although it is difficult to assess the validity of such synthetic accounts. In this regard we can speak of cultural grammars, the rules in terms of which categories are distinguished from one another and are internally ordered. These rules may be revealed in linguistic practices that govern the operation of arguments—for example, in litigation processes over land, as Hutchins has shown for the Trobriands. Hutchins concludes that although the Trobriands' world view (or ontology) is different from a Western world view, the modes of reasoning and drawing inferences from putative facts are similar. In terms of ontology, a picture of Trobriand categories can be constructed in terms of a table of binary constructs—for example, below/above, spirits/people. Trobriand ideas of witchcraft and sorcery and their spatial and gendered associations can also be explicated in terms of binary opposites and their mediation or their reversibility. For example, when the *baloma*, spirits of below and of the dead, associated with the female realm, reenter the village at the time of harvest rituals, *milamala,* they bring with them a celebration of the union of the sexes rather than their separation.

Symbolic interpretation can also elucidate mundane behavior, as when a Trobriand man smashes his wife's water bottles when he discovers her in adultery. The water in the bottles can be said to stand for her reproductive capacities, which he symbolically destroys in his anger. Such analyses, though, need to be based on accurate semantic knowledge.

Further, it is important also to recognize that cultural knowledge is differentially distributed and is linked to power. Ritual and mythological knowledge may be guarded jealously by elders and experts, for example. World view itself has to be deduced from language uses. Dorothy Lee saw the Trobrianders as concerned with "being" rather than with a sense of the past and present in a historical way. Hutchins, however, refuted this idea, based on his knowledge gained in fieldwork.

Ideas also develop in history and in relation to specific systems of production and of the social relations that underpin these, as neo-Marxist theorists see it. In this viewpoint, then, culture and social structure are brought back into alignment with each other. However, the neo-Marxist approach, which stresses social conditions as seen by the outside observer, also carries with it the danger of ethnocentric misinterpretation of people's practices. Nevertheless, this approach does have the advantage of drawing attention to problems of power, conflict, and change in social systems—for example

between chiefs (and big men) and others. Leaders also operate in contexts of differential ecological opportunities, and every society therefore has its own changing history, whether it has become part of a global historical context recently or not.

SUGGESTIONS FOR FURTHER READING

SECTIONS 42–44

Dolgin, J., et al., eds. 1977. *Symbolic Anthropology: A Reader in the Study of Symbols and Meanings.* New York: Columbia University Press.

Douglas, M., 1970. *Natural Symbols: Explorations in Cosmology.* New York: Pantheon Books, Inc.

Firth, R. 1973. *Symbols, Public and Private.* Ithaca, N.Y.: Cornell University Press.

Leach, E. R., ed. 1967. *The Structural Study of Myth and Totemism.* London: Tavistock Publishers.

Lewis, I., ed. 1977. *Symbols and Sentiments: Cross-Cultural Studies in Symbolism.* New York: Academic Press, Inc.

Sapir, J. D., and J. C. Crocker, eds. 1977. *The Social Use of Metaphor: Essays on the Anthropology of Rhetoric.* Philadelphia: University of Pennsylvania Press.

Sperber, D. 1975. *Rethinking Symbolism.* Cambridge: Cambridge University Press.

Willis, R., ed. 1975. *The Interpretation of Symbolism.* London: Halsted Press.

SECTION 45

Friedman, J. 1975. Tribes, States, and Transformations. In M. Bloch, ed. *Marxist Analyses in Social Anthropology.* New York: John Wiley & Sons, Inc.

Friedman, J., and M. Rowlands, eds. 1977. *The Evolution of Social Systems.* Pittsburgh: University of Pittsburgh Press.

The most urgent reasons for studying the range of human societies and cultures have to do with the precarious and conflict-ridden world we now live in, with the present and the future. Anthropology, if it is to be useful and if it is to survive, cannot simply be a study of ways of life now vanishing or vanished. Anthropologists must study what is happening now—in African towns as well as rural villages, in Chicago as well as on Polynesian islands. And what they learn must be valuable in charting human futures.

Studying the diverse ways of life in small-scale societies has given anthropology special understandings of human diversity and human possibility. But the very social and economic systems of the West that took scholars to the frontiers of "civilization" were subjugating and destroying the peoples along these frontiers. In the era in which anthropology has been a serious academic enterprise, the ascendance and dominance of the West has been complete: hundreds of societies have been obliterated or swallowed up. Even though most of the peoples who once comprised the tribal world have become members of independent countries, many have joined the wider world only to be exploited, pauperized, rendered powerless, marginal, and culturally impoverished. At the same time, such peoples have also been creatively reshaping their lives in hybridized forms that reflect their struggles to deal with new and complex situations.

Part 4

Anthropology and the Present

17

Response to Cataclysm: The Tribal World and the Expansion of the West

Here we will glimpse the cataclysmic impact of European expansion on tribal societies. First, we will briefly introduce a perspective on colonialism that will provide a background for the sections and chapters to follow. Then we will consider the processes of change along the frontiers of colonialism, building on and extending the theory of social process built up in the preceding chapters and summarized in §45. Finally, in a series of subsections, we will examine different facets of the impact of the West on non-Western societies and the response of these societies over time.

46. COLONIALISM AND THE ANTHROPOLOGICAL PERSPECTIVE

To understand colonialism and its historical impact requires a drastic rethinking of many assumptions and myths. It is a rethinking many in Western industrialized societies have already gone through. For others, cherished myths of the West are still accepted, and familiar assumptions remain unchallenged. The pages that follow may be provocative to many, but they will challenge the reader to further thought.

Colonialism and the Myths of the West

Americans brought up on the myths that are a national heritage—George Washington chopping down the cherry tree, Abe Lincoln freeing slaves, and Teddy Roosevelt charging up San Juan Hill—are not likely to have a critical perspective on their own history and the history of Western civilization to which they are joint heirs, unless they have worked very hard to reeducate themselves. (Britons brought up on tales of empire, on myths about Nelson, Kitchener, Livingstone, Gordon, the Black Hole of Calcutta, and the rest, are likely to have a similar difficulty.)

A global understanding of Western expansion and its impact requires a reanalysis of the most sacrosanct institutions of the West. A notable example is Christianity. What began as a religion of the oppressed had, by the Crusades and particularly the age of Spanish and Portuguese "discovery," become the religion of the conqueror.

Female baptismal initiants, Lutheran Church. They wear white uniforms and carefully tonsured hair. Melpa, Papua New Guinea.

Historically, Christianity has been both an imperialist, expansionist force in its own right and a servant of empire in subjugating conquered peoples and organizing them into communities where their labor could be exploited. Thus missionary priests rode beside the *conquistadores* in the Americas and the Philippines, baptizing souls and sending gold to the coffers of Spain and the Vatican—just as, three centuries later, missionaries in "Darkest Africa" brought light to the "savages" and clothed them in raiment from the mills of industrial England.*

A reinterpretation of European history and the systemics of colonialism would take dozens of volumes—volumes that have been written by historians who have broken loose from earlier assumptions of

_____
*Some of the early missionaries were great scholars and humanists, as we will see, but that did not substantially affect the impact of Christianity as an historic force in conquest and subjugation.

empire. It would be presumptuous even to try to sketch the vast intricacies and global systemics of imperialism as it unfolded over 500 years of European expansion.

The Economics of Racism

But what is urgent is that the reader acquire some sense of the way economic strategies dictated ideologies; of the way events in one cluster of far-away islands were tied in with the world economy and events in other corners of the world; of the way peoples were moved around like pawns as sources of slave labor or a cheap equivalent; and of the way fellow humans—whatever their skin color—were accorded or denied humanity depending on the demands of profit.

The latter point will serve as a beginning. Pervasive racism whereby dark-skinned peoples have been despised and treated as lesser beings is a continuing theme of the colonial period. But to see racism primarily in terms of European prejudice against people of different skin colors is far too shallow. A deeper analysis reveals that most often people have been treated as subhuman when it was economically profitable to deny their humanity. Eric Williams, an Oxford-trained black historian who later became Prime Minister of Trinidad Tobago, has argued compellingly that the slave trade whereby Africans were shipped to the Caribbean and the Americas was strongly supported and rationalized by the power of British society as long as the Caribbean sugar plantations were sources of great profit (Williams 1944).

From the royal family down through the highest levels of British society and throughout the merchant class, slavery was rationalized and supported. Humanitarian protests were drowned out by the voices of those pursuing burgeoning profits. The high rungs of British Christianity not only defended the slave trade, but participated actively in it (as did Christians in the British colonies of eastern North America, including many Quakers). Slavery was not hidden from genteel British society: it was displayed on every side as the foundation of prosperity. But when the tide of profit and economic power swung away from the Caribbean sugar plantations to the mills of industrial England, humanitarian voices somehow began to be heard: abolitionism, the ideology of free trade, and shifts in the balance of economic power were closely intertwined. And in 1807 England banned the slave trade to the Caribbean (Williams 1944). But as Williams notes, before African slaves were economically advantageous in the Caribbean, poor whites had been sent from England in virtual bondage and their labor exploited under conditions almost as bad as those endured by the black slaves later. Their humanity as fellow whites had been recognized only when black slaves became more useful with the advent of sugar plantations. In the Americas, an expanding cotton industry made slavery economically advantageous for another half-century. Calls for abolition began to be heard clearly in New England only when the balance of economic power shifted from the agricultural South, which needed slaves, to the industrial North, which needed cheap factory labor.

That racism has been a pervasive and devastating element in colonialism is undeniable. But whether the boundaries of humanity were drawn so as to include or exclude Irishmen or Italians, and whether the inhumanity was focused on black Africans or Chinese, racism was more often based on where profit or economic threat lay than on notions of racial superiority. The latter have been rationalizations for profitable inhumanity. This begins to show—

though inevitably, in overly broad generalizations—the economic roots of the ideologies of colonialism, in its various phases.

Another illustration may be useful. When Spanish power in the New World went through its final disintegration in the Spanish-American War, the United States faced the question of whether to acquire Cuba as a colony or make that island nominally independent as a sugar-producing satellite. The same question arose with the Philippines, where a Filipino independence movement had achieved virtual control by the time Admiral Dewey destroyed the ancient and scarcely operative Spanish fleet based in Manila. Pomeroy (1970) vividly points out how the interests that supported U.S. colonization of the Philippines (mostly northern industrialists anxious for a strong base from which to compete for the vast markets of China and stand against rising Japanese naval power) and the interests opposed to colonial incorporation (mostly southern agriculturalists afraid of cheap competition from a tropical colony) fought a bitter battle through their political spokesmen in Congress. The issue was fought out with noble rhetoric about the rights of brown peoples to freedom versus the responsibilities of the white race to civilize the "childlike Filipinos," but the issues and motives were basically economic. The northern interests supporting colonization won the day, even though this required a bloody war and broken promises.

Colonialism as a Global System

Another urgently needed perspective on colonialism is to see the vast and subtle skein of interconnections which have tied together events and policies in different parts of the colonial world. We will see some elements of this network in the sections to follow.

The flow of raw materials to the burgeoning factories of England, Germany, and New England; the cheap labor of the natives in faraway plantations (and the worldwide relocation of African slaves and of Indians, Chinese, Filipinos, and others to supply cheap labor where needed); the creation of markets in South Asia, Africa, South America, and elsewhere for the cloth and hardware of industry—all tied tribal societies and non-Western states into a worldwide system of exploitation and oppression, in the name of progress and Christianity, and in pursuit of wealth and power.

We will return in Chapter 19 to the nature of this global system and to the historical forces that shaped the contemporary world.

Subjugation and Destruction: An Ancient Process and Its Modern Forms

Before glimpsing the impact of the West on small-scale societies, it is well to underline a point that might otherwise be forgotten. Exploitation, conquest, genocide, and ethnocide—the planned destruction of ways of life—are very old. Europeans did not invent them.

Early military empires spread death and devastation and enslaved neighboring peoples in the ancient Middle East, Mesoamerica, South America, and Asia. Conquering peoples speaking Bantu and Hamitic languages swept across sub-Saharan Africa, imposing conquest states and exterminating, enslaving, or absorbing those who stood in their path. The experience of being enslaved, exploited, subjugated, and forced to change customs to satisfy the designs or customs of the conquerors goes back at least some 5,000 years to the early empires of Mesopotamia. They were a concomitant of the rise of urbanization and social classes that came with the widening gulf between producers and those who controlled surpluses.

Presumably, though we seldom have adequate records, the reactions, adaptations, and transformations of peoples subjugated by early empires parallel those recorded along the frontiers of colonialism. (We do get glimpses of early responses, as in biblical records of Israelite adaptations to subjugation.)

While the human costs of subjugation and exploitation have always been staggering, European imperialism, imposing these costs on a vast scale and in new ways, represents a new phase in human history.

One new element in Western history has been the awesome acceleration of technology since the Industrial Revolution, bringing vast power and affluence to the industrial nations. These nations have had not only an increasingly overwhelming advantage in power, but also an increasing appetite for raw materials and markets and increasingly direct access to remote parts of the world. In the latter twentieth century, technology pushed humans toward a common world culture of airplanes, television, and computers. While polarizing the world into "developed" and "underdeveloped," it has made Western-style development an almost universal aspiration.

The destruction or forced transformation of tribal peoples reached a new scale with the worldwide imperialism of the Industrial Revolution. But ironically both oppression of minority enclaves and the emptiness and alienation of industrial societies re-emerged in the socialist states forged in revolution against capitalist class systems. Thus in the Stalinist wake of the Russian revolution, many thousands of Kazakhs and other minority peoples were exterminated; a socialist police state founded on

terror replaced a czarist one; and Soviet society reconstituted in new form the alienation and bureaucratic emptiness of industrial capitalist society.

In countries that have emerged from colonialism, the record of genocide and oppression against tribal and other minorities is appalling. Capitalist countries built the Industrial Revolution on the blood and sweat of Third World peoples; but in this century Western technology has become a worldwide instrument of power whose use to oppress the weak has known no geographical or ideological bounds. In this chapter we will examine the confrontation between European power and tribal peoples. First, we will relate these phenomena of domination and Westernization to the theoretical foundations built up in Chapter 2 and the model of sociocultural change sketched in §45.

47. CONCEPTUALIZING RADICAL CHANGE

Anthropologists working on colonial frontiers, or with Native Americans, were relatively slow to recognize that the processes of change that were going on before their eyes merited serious study (F. M. Keesing 1952). The task was seen mainly as reconstructing the ways of life of the "ethnographic present," a task in which the changes wrought by colonial administrations, missionaries, and plantations were obstacles to analysis.

Culture and Change

Particularly in the United States, where the concept of "culture" was the main theoretical tool, those who did seek to analyze the processes of change usually conceptualized these processes as a meeting of two cultures. A people confronted with a dominant culture abandoned, modified, reformulated, or clung to their traditional culture. The two cultures might be more or less in conflict, or more or less congruent, in values, norms, and world view—so that the process of **acculturation,** where a traditional culture is progressively modified or replaced, may be relatively easy, quick, and successful, or slow and disruptive. Too often, the two "cultures" were reified into entities that interacted with one another.

In 1957, Clifford Geertz suggested that one reason conceptualizations of change had been relatively unsuccessful was that theorists had not clearly distinguished between a culture, as an ideational system, and a system of social relationships. A **culture** is an organized system of knowledge, more or less shared by individuals, that enables them to communicate, share meanings, and do things together toward common ends. *Social structure* is the network of social relations among the actors on the social stage, in contrast to the scripts they follow and understandings they share. In his case study of a Javanese funeral (see Case 56), Geertz (1957) described what can go wrong when cultural guides to appropriate action no longer fit changed social circumstances due to the impact of Westernization and the new tides of national politics. Distinguishing between a cultural system and changed social realities to which the old system is no longer appropriate, as Geertz would have us do, is a step in the right direction. But it is only a partial step, and it poses dangers.

Beyond Culture

First, there is a danger of idealizing the coherence and stability of an ideational system—which in reality exists only in its varying individual versions, and is constantly changing as humans cope with ever-shifting situations. Thus we may spuriously contrast the kind of conflict Geertz observed in Java with an imagined traditional social world where cultural meanings and social structures fit together in perfect harmony. Our means of conceptualizing radical change must build on the premise that every way of life comprises a dynamic system, a process in time.

Second, Geertz's model—pointing to a lack of fit between culture as ideational system and a changing social system—predisposes us to pay insufficient attention to complex class relationships and political and economic processes. In implying a timelessness, stability, and integration of traditional life, it disguises the dynamics of the situation. "Javanese culture" was the ideology of a sharply stratified social system with its roots in control over land and politics, a system that demanded highly formalized expressions of deference and respect. To talk about "Javanese culture" as a system of meaning disguises the deep conflicts of interest between poor peasant and rich landlord, and between the Javanese and their Dutch colonial masters who were draining the wealth of the "East Indies."

Third, seeing radical social change as a lack of fit between ideational system and social system predisposes us to take as our unit of analysis the local community, or at least the area within which "the culture" is practiced. But the forces that are shaping local events may be far beyond the village.

Case 57, another classic anthropological study of radical social change, takes us somewhat further—but still not far enough. It comes from West Africa, from the Tiv of Nigeria, whose lineage system and domestic groups we have already encountered.

A Javanese Funeral

The Javanese town of Modjokuto in many respects still represents the peasant cultural traditions of rural Java, including a religious system that combines elements of Islam, Hinduism, and the older animistic beliefs. Essential here are communal feasts, *slametan*, where at important

A Javanese funeral *slametan:* Three Islamic priests perform the mortuary rites (Solo, Central Java).

The analysis, by Paul Bohannan (1955), is a landmark in anthropological study of the penetration of cash economy and colonial rule into tribal Africa.

Classes, World Systems, and Change

Is an analysis of changes in the Tiv economy in terms of cultural categories and separate "spheres" adequate? The question leads in several directions. First, we can ask whether—in the Tivland of the early 1950s or today—an idealized composite version of "Tiv culture" is adequate to our analytical task. Among the modern Tiv one could find government officials with radios and trucks, conservative elders, young men employed as entrepreneurs, Christian evangelists, and leftist politicians. A single idealized picture of Tiv culture clearly will not do—it is changing in all directions for different people.

stages in the life cycle members of neighborhood groups gather to make offerings to the spirits and to partake together of the ritual meal. Moslem prayers are part of the proceedings; and Moslem ritual has a particularly central place in the subdued procedure of a funeral, where the living take leave of the social bonds broken by death.

But in the 1950s, political parties, religious fission, and other discordant elements of modern Indonesian life tore the harmony of Modjokuto social life. Particularly important was the split between Masjumi and Permai factions. The Masjumi comprised a national party, militantly Moslem, which pressed for a purified form of Islam as the state religion. The Permai party, strong in Modjokuto, would emphasize the "traditional" Hindu and animistic rites and, being vocally anti-Moslem, would eliminate Islamic prayer and ritual in such affairs as marriage and funerals.

This split precipitated a crisis in Modjokuto when a 10-year-old boy, nephew of a Permai man, died. The *modin*, or religious officiant, remained absent. The ritual washing of the corpse, the quiet and orderly procedure culminating in a *slametan* reaffirming the unity of the community in the face of death, was still not performed. Finally a Masjumi man friendly with the Permai involved tried to conduct the essential rites: In the midst of all this, the grief which the normal funeral rites keep under control burst forth.

Finally the dead boy's parents arrived from the city. Being less committed religiously, the father authorized the *modin* to carry on in the Moslem fashion—though not before the mother had expressed a grief that would normally have remained beneath the surface. By the time the funeral *slametan* had been performed, the unity it was intended to affirm had been badly and publicly torn (Geertz 1957).

Nor can we assume that all the participants in a social system even share the same culture. Consider the market economy in a Nigerian city. Within the physical setting of a marketplace, transactions interlink Tiv traders with Hausa, Ibo, Yoruba, and members of many other African groups, plus Europeans, Arabs, Indians, and others. These participants draw on different cultural traditions that shape decision-making and value commitments, and affect the flow of goods into the market system from rural areas (so that large-scale Tiv refusal to sell foodstuffs or grow beniseed might make a slight ripple in the market). But the patterns of decision and the flow of goods and money depend on a wider worldwide market system that very few Nigerian participants begin to understand—a system within which Nigeria is peripheral. Events that transform the lives of Nigerians emanate from London or New York boardrooms or stock exchanges or oil producers' private jets.

Perhaps it is illusory to imagine that the Tiv ever controlled their own destiny; they have been part of wider systems (social, economic, and ecological) throughout their history. But in the colonial and postcolonial periods, their lives have been progressively pulled further from their own grasp.

CASE

5 7

The Transformation of the Tiv Economy

In the traditional economy of the Tiv, there were three culturally conceptualized categories of "things" over which humans exercised rights. The first category, of subsistence items, consisted primarily of garden foodstuffs (yams, corn, locust bean, etc.), chickens and goats, and domestic utensils and tools. The second category, of valuables, consisted of slaves, cattle, a type of large white cloth, and brass rods. The third category consisted solely of rights over persons, especially over women exchanged in marriage.

Within the first (subsistence) category, barter in the spirit of a "market" prevailed: Tiv sought to secure an advantageous exchange. Valuables could likewise be exchanged for other valuables, though one would do so not for pragmatic value but for advantage in the quest for prestige. Exchanges of women were carried out through a highly intricate system of wards and women-exchanging groups.

The three categories of exchangeables are ranked in moral value, with subsistence at the lower end and women at the higher. Exchange within a category is morally neutral, though ad-

vantageous exchanges are sought. What each Tiv seeks to achieve is *conversion* from a lower category to a higher category: to parlay food into brass rods or cattle, or to parlay the latter into a wife. Such conversions are the main strategic goals of the Tiv, as means to prestige, influence, and dependents. Downward conversion, as from brass to foodstuffs, constitutes a setback, to be avoided where possible. Accumulation within a category, without upward conversion, shows a failure or inability to play the game properly.

Into this system came British administrators, missionaries, traders, money, and the tentacles of a wider economic system (P. Bohannan 1955, 1959). About 1910, slave dealing was abolished. The administration, regarding the brass rods largely as a form of money, over the years replaced them with British currency. This largely emptied the "valuables" category. Moreover, in 1927, a well-intending administration prohibited exchange marriages and substituted a system of cash bridewealth as the legal form—thus essentially eliminating the third and highest category

The theoretical framework sketched in the chapters of Part 3 and summarized in §45 potentially gives means for understanding the phenomena of contemporary Tivland, and Nigeria, that functionalist views of society and culture do not.

First, we make no assumptions at the outset about the boundaries that will be relevant to a particular analysis of a social system. We definitely cannot draw a line around a population speaking the Tiv lan-

guage and considering themselves to be Tiv and assume that this will be strategically useful to account for the phenomena we find in this part of Nigeria.

> It is . . . always methodologically unsound to assume that an ethnic group or political unit (the Nuer, United States society) is an adequate unit of analysis. One must begin by reconstructing the social relations that determine particular subjects or groups. (O'Laughlin 1975:346)

(though modern Tiv marriage retains modes of exchange in covert form).

Meanwhile, many new material items that had no place in the old category system were introduced, and cash began to pervade the Tiv economy. This process was speeded by the imposition of a head tax in British money that forced cash-cropping on the Tiv before 1920. Moreover, the agricultural produce of Tivland flows into market channels that bring foodstuffs to urban areas. The Tiv as primary producers are part of a larger system over which they can exert little control. With pacification and transportation, Tiv men have themselves taken to trading subsistence goods over large distances.

How have such far-reaching changes been conceptualized in Tiv culture? The Tiv have tried to fit money, and the new hardware one buys with money, into a fourth and lowest category. But money will not stay within these conceptual bounds. Most exchanges in and between categories now take place through the medium of money. Women's subsistence trade for money leads to a draining out of foodstuffs and makes it possible to build up cash through which prestige items can be bought. Their prestige value is eroded correspondingly.

Moreover, the bridewealth payment in cash forces the bride's guardian to trade down—to exchange a woman for money. Since the number of women is limited and monetary wealth rises with the export of food, bridewealth has become inflated. "As Tiv attempt to become more and more wealthy in people, they are merely selling more and more of their foodstuffs and subsistence goods, leaving less and less for their own consumption" (Bohannan 1955).

The Tiv are being caught up in a vast system of interconnected events and things, including money, that is changing what they do, what they have, and what they can choose. These new circumstances of life are very difficult for the Tiv to fit into their conceptual scheme. When a Tiv man bemoans the fact that he now has to "sell" his daughter in marriage, hence to trade down from the most valued exchange category to the least valued, we cannot simply talk about "culture change."

Case Update

For a discussion of the image of money as "bitter" in parts of Africa, See Shipton (1989).

Second, analysis must be historical, must see "the social relations that determine particular subjects or groups" as processes in time. We must analyze class relations historically, probing the roots of power in control over land or other means of production. Where colonialism has incorporated classless societies into the world capitalist system, class relationships have been created. In Tivland and other regions of West Africa, cash crops such as cocoa have given opportunities for individual entrepreneurs to divert lineage land for personal use, and to hire fellow tribesmen as wage laborers. Colonial administrations and missions, training clerks and teachers, created the beginnings of what were to become several decades later the "Wabenzi"—the tribe that drives Mercedes-Benzes, a ruling class that controls much of Africa. These class relationships cut across lines of language and nationality. Analyses of change in terms of

A street scene in Lagos, Nigeria. Can cultural analysis capture the complexities of contemporary Africa?

"culture" may obscure the class relationships and economic systems that shape local events.

Third, the perspective we have taken does not assume that within a social system, whatever its bounds, a single mode of production will prevail. The penetration of capitalist cash economy into areas such as Tivland means that peoples may be tied into two or more modes of production—continuing, perhaps, to produce subsistence crops for domestic consumption, producing petty commodities (such as beniseed oil) for market, and selling their labor power as plantation or mine workers. Villagers may engage in circular migration so that as young men they go to urban centers or plantations or oil fields to work, then come back to assume adult responsibilities in a more traditional setting. As we will see in looking at contemporary peasants, the reproduction of relatively traditionally oriented social relations in such communities may be based on very substantial outmigration in each generation or on a flow of

income from city to village through the sending off of successive children for wage employment.

Exactly how best to conceptualize theoretically the relationships between hinterlands communities and urban centers, between a traditional mode of production and the engulfing capitalist mode, have been focal points of debate. We will see some of the issues at stake when we look at peasants and at what has come to be called "dependency theory," in the next two chapters. To give these general theoretical orientations substance, we need to look more closely at the impact of the West on the tribal world.

48. THE IMPACT OF THE WEST ON SMALL-SCALE SOCIETIES

The impact of the West on small-scale societies produced phenomena of physical and cultural destruction that had parallels in earlier empires, as we have noted; but they were in many respects new in human history. What happened to tribal peoples in the path of European expansion depended on a number of factors:

1. The size, political organization, and technology of the society subjugated
2. The time period of initial subjugation (and, consequently, the goals Europeans were pursuing and the technology they commanded)
3. The location of the society, in terms of remoteness or ease of access and of the desirability to Europeans of the territory they occupied
4. The cultural orientation of the subjugated peoples relative to European culture and what Europeans wanted from and demanded of them

Benabena tribesmen from the New Guinea highlands examine the latest transformation in their once-isolated valley. In a period of rapid change, the Benabena have been swept up in an economy of cattle, trucks, and transistor radios.

5. The colonial policy of the colonizers (which has varied in different times and places from ruthless extermination to benevolent paternalism)

We will sketch here a number of the processes that have taken place along the frontiers of colonialism. These are by no means a series of distinct "types" of contact; many peoples subjugated by colonialism were subjected to several of these processes at once or in different stages. They serve to illustrate not types but recurrent themes and processes in different parts of the colonized world.

Physical Decimation by Extermination, Disease, and Enslavement

In many parts of the colonized world, populations of people were decimated early in the contact period. There are many cases where massacres—of Australian Aborigines, North and South American indigenous peoples, and many others— destroyed substantial proportions of aboriginal populations. Systematic extermination ("A good Indian is a dead Indian" or its equivalent on other colonial frontiers) was often a keystone of European policy or the practice of early colonial settlers.

Though adequate statistics are seldom available, European disease was a more devastating blade cutting through populations, often in advance of colonial settlement. Most vicious of the killing diseases was smallpox, accidentally or intentionally spread by Europeans to populations with no immunity. The populations of Aboriginal Australia were decimated by smallpox and other diseases in the early contact period. When European settlement of Australia began in 1788, some 250,000 to 300,000 Aborigines inhabited the continent. By 1798, smallpox epidemics were raging across Australia, reaching far into the interior long before direct contact was made. Tuberculosis, whooping cough, measles, leprosy, influenza, and venereal disease were also spread. Though large numbers of Aborigines were slaughtered by the colonists, most were killed not by guns but by epidemics.

For some North American groups, we have better statistics. Those from the once-rich and powerful Mandan of the upper Missouri are extreme but illuminating. In 1750, at the beginning of the fur trade, some 9,000 Mandan lived in large, permanent villages. Smallpox epidemics, beginning as early as 1764, had by 1782 so reduced and weakened the Mandan that they were vulnerable to raids by the nomadic Teton Sioux on one side and the Assiniboin on the other. By about 1800, the population had been reduced to approximately 1,500. In 1837, when another devastating smallpox epidemic swept through the two villages into which the surviving Mandan had regrouped, the population was almost completely wiped out. The number of survivors was, at most, 63 adults, perhaps substantially less (Bowers 1950, Bruner 1961). Devastation by disease may well have been equally drastic in a number of other parts of North America.

When massive extermination by systematic hunting or massacre and the toll of disease were coupled with enslavement for forced labor in mines or fields, the demographic catastrophes of colonialism were even more staggering. Wilbert (1972) assesses the appalling cost in human life of the Spanish conquest of South America. He estimates that only 4 percent of the pre-Columbian population of some 50 million survived the first few decades after the Spanish conquest:

> Indian populations on Caribbean islands disappeared entirely. New Spain (Mexico) had a dramatic fall in population from approximately 11 million in 1519 to about 1.5 million in . . . 1650. (Wallerstein 1974:89)

Tens of thousands were directly hunted out and massacred. Hundreds of thousands died, broken, enslaved as miners to feed Spanish lust for gold and silver; and millions died of introduced diseases and starvation.

The most tragic and appalling consequence of colonial conquest of tribal societies was thus complete physical destruction or near-extermination. Scattered survivors clustered together as refugees, fleeing beyond colonial frontiers or in despair clinging to bare survival on the periphery of fort, town, or mission. Though cultures and languages may have survived such catastrophic destruction, the patterns of social life they infused with meaning and the lands on which subsistence had depended had been swept away.

Armed Resistance

Where the gulf in numbers and technology between Europeans and others was vast,

The prosperous and powerful Mandan Indians: Here the Bull Dance of the *okipa* ceremony is performed before the earth lodges of a Mandan village. The inhabitants numbered in the thousands.

large-scale resistance was impossible. Yet in some parts of the world, peoples engaged in long and effective armed struggle against invading colonialists. The Hollywood tradition of "whooping redskins" trying to massacre wagon trains and "African savages" threatening intrepid explorers has hardly done justice to these struggles or prepared us to understand them.

The most effective resistance to European conquest did not always come from highly centralized militaristic societies with large armies that could be put into the field. As the fairly rapid collapse of the Aztec and Inca states in the face of Spanish invasion illustrate, highly organized armies were often more vulnerable to dramatic defeat than small, mobile forces. And empires that had held surrounding peoples in subjugation were vulnerable to the uprising of their subjects in support of the invaders.

But even with 300 years of further technological advance at their command, the

Australian Aboriginal prisoners, in the Kimberley area, 1906.

European forces in the Zulu wars and the Ashanti wars were temporarily held in check by tightly organized, mobile resistance by warrior peoples. Even more successful in withstanding imperialist conquest was the brilliant Samory of Guinea (Person 1971). Samory's epic resistance to French invasion is celebrated by the patriots of African independence movements. He achieved among his people a degree of political order that could well be an inspiration:

> In all, he . . . fought 13 major engagements with the French and . . . moved his empire a distance of some 600 km. in the process. He displayed . . . [a] combination of military and administrative genius. . . .

In him we can see the sort of leader who might well have achieved modernization of his own state, independent of European control. That he had the ability and the instinct is clear from his military tactics, his organization of trade, and his spectacular administration of his constantly moving empire. . . . If Samory had not had to face the French there is every indication that he had the organizing genius and sufficient control of his people to have created a state responsive to the needs of the approaching twentieth century. (Crowder 1968:87–89)

Brave resistance against conquest came not only from militarily formidable forces, but also from technologically and numerically weak peoples such as the South

African San, who fought desperately and with surprising success for their hunting territories until their eventual near-extermination. Bellicosity has continued to be a viable foreign policy for a few isolated hunter-gatherers: some Andaman Islanders in the Indian Ocean continue to greet outsiders with a shower of arrows, and retain their independence.

Resistance to invasion in some areas catalyzed a people into united struggle even though there were no overarching political institutions to provide a framework of command. One of the most striking cases was the resistance of the Yaqui of northwestern Mexico. The Yaqui population was about 30,000, living in autonomous communities without centralized political leadership. Yet confronted with the threat of subjugation by Spanish armies and the incursion of a slave trader, the Yaqui put a military force of 7,000 men in the field. In campaigns between 1608 and 1610, Captain Hurtaide and his army of Spaniards and Indian allies were routed three times by well-organized and fierce Yaqui warriors; in the last and largest battle, Hurtaide's forces were crushed and the Spanish captain narrowly avoided capture (Spicer 1961).

In the Pacific, the most dramatic large-scale resistance came from the Maori. In the Maori wars, Polynesian warriors in their palisaded hill forts held British infantry at bay with remarkable success in the face of superior firepower. The Chamorro of Guam fought long and bitterly against Spanish conquest, although in the end they were virtually wiped out. Even in Melanesia, with smaller populations and greater political fragmentation, there were cases of effective resistance—notably in New Caledonia, where in the so-called Kanaka Revolt of 1878, Melanesians killed many settlers and recaptured most of their large island before being crushed.

But however bravely these peoples resisted, they were eventually conquered and subjugated by the increasingly powerful forces of European technology. By the early twentieth century, only marginal peoples maintained political autonomy; and all of them were in remote jungles, deserts, or snowfields around which colonial or national boundaries had been drawn.

European Penetration and the Transformation of Traditional Societies

Even in advance of actual colonial subjugation, the penetration of European power and technology profoundly changed political relationships and balances of power and ecology. In a few cases this resulted in a kind of cultural efflorescence. Most dramatic perhaps was the emergence of nomadic horse cultures on the American plains. In an amazingly rapid burst of cultural adaptation, such peoples as the Cheyenne were transformed from sedentary maize-cultivating villagers into buffalo-hunting nomadic warriors on horseback; and from the other direction, Great Basin Shoshonean hunter-gatherers such as the Comanche underwent a similar transformation. Further to the northeast, at the margins of the plains and woodlands, such people as the Mandan and Assiniboin capitalized on their established position as wealthy traders astride the main trade routes to become purveyors of buffalo hides to European traders further east and purveyors of guns and other European goods to the Plains nomads (see Bruner 1961, Jablow 1951).

Disruptions of the balance of power were often unintentional consequences of European penetration. Thus an enterprising Tongan chief captured a British warship in 1806, killed all the crew other than those he needed to man its cannons, and then—using them—invaded and conquered the Tongan

A rich Mandan leader's earth lodge. The Mandan amassed great wealth and power as middle persons with the flowering of Plains cultures.

capital. The bloody wars and vast-scale cannibalism reported in early nineteenth-century Fiji were drastic escalations of traditional patterns due to introduced firearms and European-fueled conflict. (The presence of Europeans in the armed camps of warring chiefs also contributed. "In the early days many Fijian chiefs had . . . tame white men, regarding them as mannerless but useful; to have one was part of a chief's prestige" (Furnas 1947:215).

The effects of the slave trade on West African peoples, even in advance of colonial penetration of the interior, were disastrous. By setting tribe against tribe, exploiting the gulfs between social classes, draining populations, destroying communities, and creat-ing wealthy African leaders as middlemen, the slave trade nourished inhumanity and human tragedy on a staggering scale.

Syncretism and Cultural Synthesis

Wherever European ways of life have burst upon small-scale societies, cultural borrowing has taken place—both by choice and under duress. Peoples have adopted steel tools and hand-shaking, and have been forced into Mother Hubbard dresses and monogamy.

The synthesis of old and borrowed elements—**syncretism**—has been most striking in the realm of religion, where Christianity has been spread to every continent. Many of the most striking examples come from the New World, particularly from Mesoamerica. Even before the Spanish invaded that part of the world, the processes of conquest, incorporation, and cultural borrowing, from Olmecs through Aztecs, had created complex syntheses of cultural elements. Syntheses of Catholicism with traditional belief systems carried these old processes to much more dramatic degree: there was a vast gulf between the religion of the *conquistadores* and the Mesoamerican priestly cults of war, fertility, sun, and rain; worship of feathered serpent, jaguar, and other gods; and human sacrifice. But striking syntheses were to emerge, sometimes very quickly.

Early sixteenth-century Catholic missionaries had some advantages that fundamentalist Protestants two or three centuries later lacked. Catholicism embodied a rich pageantry and complex ceremonial cycle. It offered roles to men and women, young and old. Its priests, believing in the devil, spirits, and magic, could deal with the older religion in ways Mesoamerican peoples could squarely comprehend. And Catholicism provided, in its multiple manifestations of the Virgin and the Trinity, both an approximation of multiple deities and physical objects for veneration.

Perhaps the most striking example of religious syncretism is the cult of the Virgin of Guadalupe, the patron saint of Mexico, described in Case 58.

In rural communities in Mesoamerica, cultural syntheses of old and new are visible in many realms of life. One is *compadrazgo*, or ritual co-parenthood (to be explored in Case 69), where a Hispanic Catholic pattern has been synthesized with kinship-based social systems of Mesoamerica (Davila 1971). In religion, new beliefs and traditional ones are blended or coexist, as in highland Mayan communities such as Zinacantan in southern Mexico (see Case 59).

Do elements of a culture lie latent, though overt behavior may conform to the demands of the conqueror? The survival of traditional religion in Zinacantan described in Case 59 suggests that overt compliance to the demands of conquest may sometimes mask extreme conservatism. When control is relaxed, latent knowledge may become covert practice; and eventually old patterns may spring forth. Striking illustrations come from the margins of the Caribbean where escaped slaves of Guyana and Surinam (Price 1973) have established communities where African social and religious patterns flowered anew.

Congruence Between Old and New?

Even where new customs and beliefs outwardly replace the old in the course of change, the deeper premises and values of the traditional culture may continue to shape a people's world view and orientation to life. However, this is an elusive question: the very subtlety and depth of these underlying cultural patterns makes them hard to get at and hard to interpret. This then leads to another question: Are there congruences, or lack of them, between the cultures of subjugated peoples and the cultures of the West that make adaptation to new ways more, or less, possible?

Values regarding change and the past have varied widely, and that may be a factor. Thus some peoples have even in precolonial times been receptive to new ideas and new things, while others have hearkened back with solid conservatism to old ways. Receptiveness to change seems particularly characteristic of some New Guinea societies. Many years ago Margaret Mead (1938) described the Mountain Arapesh as having an "importing culture,"

CASE

5 8

The Virgin of Guadalupe

In 1531, 10 years after the Spanish conquest of Mexico, the Virgin Mary appeared to Juan Diego, a Christianized Indian, and addressed him in Nahuatl, the Aztec language. She commanded him, in this and subsequent visions, to have a church built in her honor on the site of their encounter, the Hill of Tepeyac.

This was the site where the Aztecs had worshipped their earth and fertility goddess Tonantzin, Our Lady Mother. The veneration of the Virgin of Guadalupe in the early centuries of the cult was in reality a worship of Tonantzin by a subjugated people, as Spanish churchmen well realized:

Now that the Church of Our Lady of Guadalupe has been built there . . . they call her Tonantzin. . . . It seems to be a satanic device to mask idolatry . . . and they come from far way to visit that Tonantzin, . . . as of old. (Sahagun)

On the hill where Our Lady of Guadalupe is they adored the idol of a goddess they called Tonantzin, which means Our Mother, and this is also the name they give Our Lady. . . . They always say they are going to Tonantzin or they are celebrating Tonantzin and many of them understand this in the old way and not in the modern ways. (Martin de Léon)

Such syncretism persisted in the seventeenth century. "It is the purpose of the wicked to [worship] the goddess and not the most Holy Virgin, or both together" (Jacinto la Serna).

In the seventeenth century, the Guadalupe cult provided a focus for the emergence of Mexican colonial society, and the first emergence of a national culture that offered a place for the oppressed Indian:

To Mexicans [the Virgin] . . . not only . . . is a supernatural mother . . . she embodies their major political and religious aspirations. To the Indian groups the [Virgin] . . . is . . . an embodiment of life and hope; it restores to them the hope of salvation. . . . The Spanish Conquest signified not only military defeat, but the defeat also of the old gods and the decline of the old ritual. . . . [The Virgin] . . . represents on one level the return of Tonantzin. . . . On another level, the myth of the apparition served as a . . . testimony that the Indian . . . was capable of being saved. (Wolf 1958:37)

The Indians were not only exploited and oppressed; their very humanity was denied by many of the conquerors and churchmen, who could absolve themselves of moral responsibility for murder and slavery. Wolf went on to show that the Virgin also served the needs of an emerging group of Mexicans with Spanish fathers and Indian mothers—who, like "half-castes" in so many colonial situations, were denied a place in both worlds.

What had begun as the worship of an Aztec goddess in transformed guise under the swords of the *conquistadores* and the merciless watch of the Inquisition-minded friars thus was transformed into a symbol of the new Mexico rising from colonialism—so that in the war of independence against Spain, and later when the agrarian revolutionary Emiliano Zapata and his men fought against the domination of corrupt landowners and Church, the image of the Virgin of Guadalupe led them into battle (Wolf 1958).

as borrowing customs from the neighbors long before Europeans arrived. The Shimbu of the highlands, and a number of other New Guinea highlands people, seem neither to codify models of the past systematically nor place strong value on old ways. Faced with a bewildering set of changes—from stone tools to transistors, Toyotas, and tourists—the Simbu have been remarkably flexible in their adaptations to a new world of the twentieth century (Brown 1972; see also Brown 1995, A. J. Strathern 1984, on the Melpa and Wiru).

A similarly striking blend of cultural conservatism and radical political and economic reorganization is under way in the modern Trobriands. Though there is an airfield near Omarakana village in the yam-growing heart of Kiriwina Island, *kula* exchange continues and mortuary distributions and yam exchanges flourish. Through traditional political institutions, Trobrianders sought in the 1970s, under the leadership of a radical young university graduate, John Kasaipwalova, to form a cooperative society that controlled tourism and sale of art and craft items. Further, a film made on the Trobriands in the 1990s (with Annette Weiner as consultant)* shows the permutations in women's exchanges that have taken place.

In contrast, conservatism can be a strategy for survival as well as a cultural orientation. One element here is apparently old: some peoples conceptualize time and the past in ways that make change difficult, and have a kind of tight systemic integration that reduces flexibility, pragmatism, and innovation. A second element derives from the impact of the West. As we have

seen, when a people are pressed by the forces of change, a hearkening back to the past may be a crucial—sometimes desperate—way of trying to survive as a people: of preserving identity and integrity in the face of powerlessness, decimation, and degradation.

Congruence between the old and the new, and adaptation to radically changed conditions of life, has also been approached in psychological terms, using instruments of psychological research. Two studies by G. D. and L. S. Spindler (see Case 60) incorporated these methods.

In their subsequent work (Spindler and Spindler 1971, G. D. Spindler 1973) the Spindlers viewed their subjects' differential responses to change more in cognitive terms than in the terms of depth psychology and cultural congruence. In situations of colonial subjugation, people use the best survival strategies they perceive (in terms of the opportunities their subordinate status affords and the cultural materials available for conceptualizing and dealing with them). "Instrumental linkages"—ways of getting to valued goals by cognitively (and economically and physically) available paths—are explored and used to adapt as best possible. The fact that for some peoples this means retaining the traditional language and seeking wages and excitement as cowboys, that for others it means withdrawing into traditional isolation or individual alcoholic escape, and for others that it means adopting the lifestyle of Wisconsin suburbia is not a matter of culture, of personality, of "acculturation," of conservatism, or even of adaptation. It is a matter of survival by the means at hand.

The later work by the Spindlers points to dangers in the anthropological inclination to analyze change—whether rapid and

---

*The Trobriand Islanders of Papua New Guinea, dir. by D. Wason, 1991, a part of the *Disappearing World* series.

Religion in Zinacantan

The casual visitor to the center of the Chiapas *municipio* of Zinacantan is likely, despite the striking dress of its peasant inhabitants, to infer that Catholicism is a dominant force in the community. A church crowned with crosses dominates the central plaza, with lesser churches scattered through the town center and chapels in each of the outlying hamlets. On the steep, surrounding hills are clusters of large crosses. Within the Church of San Lorenzo, candles, altars, and painted figures of Catholic saints further reinforce the impression of a pious Catholic flock.

A Zinacanteco curing ceremony combines traditional Mayan ritual with Christian-derived symbols.

Through years of anthropological study, the external trappings of Christianity have seemed a progressively thinner veneer beneath which lies a complex Mayan religious system (Vogt 1969, 1970, 1976).

The people of Zinacantan, the Zinacantecos, continue to conceive the world as shaped in a large cube. The upper surface of the cube comprises the high mountains and deep valleys of highland Chiapas—with a low earth mound in the ceremonial center of Zinacantan as the center of the world.

The cubical world rests on the shoulders of gods. Beneath it is the "lower world," the shape of an ancient Maya pyramid. Sun and moon, seen as sacred cosmic forces, symbolically male and female, move across the sky above the cube, and humans orient their lives to these movements. The sun is symbolically associated with the Catholic God, the moon with the Virgin Mary; but the Zinacanteco world remains pervasively Mayan.

The universe is inhabited by numerous classes of spiritual beings which play a crucial part in human life. The most important beings are the ancestral gods, who dwell in the mountains around Zinacantan. They are remote ancestors of the Zinacantecos, and were ordered to dwell in the mountains by the gods that support the earth. In their mountain houses, the ancestors survey and confer about the social affairs of their descendants and await offerings of chickens, candles, incense, and liquor. The ancestors not only maintain the rules of proper Zinacanteco social and ritual life and guide the correct behavior of their descendants; they also keep a zealous

Continued

watch over deviations from the straight lines of propriety.

Another deity, the Earth Owner, controls the things and products of the earth on which life depends—the maize crops, rain, the earth, trees, waterholes, and the other sources of subsistence and necessary material props of life. The attitudes toward the Earth Owner, who must be propitiated with offerings when these products of the earth are used, are ambivalent, marked by both danger and dependence.

Since the Spanish conquest, the Zinacantecos have acquired 55 "saints"—carved or plaster images of Catholic saints and other sacred objects. Each saint has a personality and a mythic history. The most important, notably San Sebastian, are the centers of elaborate cults and annual ceremonial activities. The Zinacantecos view them as gods with extraordinary powers, with their "homes" in Catholic churches. Like the ancestral gods, they expect offerings of candles, incense, and flowers. The Zinacantecos view a Catholic mass as a prayer to the saint to whom a fiesta is dedicated. A *Ladino* (Spanish-speaking Mexican) priest is asked to perform the mass. But the position of orthodox Catholicism in Zinacantan is suggested by the reaction if the priest cannot come: the saint is expected to be enraged, but to visit punishment upon the derelict priest, not the community—which has done its part by soliciting the priest.

Zinacantecos have two kinds of "souls." Each person has an "inner soul," located in the heart. This inner soul has 13 components—one or more of which can leave the body in sleep, in fright, in sexual excitement, or when the ancestors cause soul loss due to bad behavior. Shamans play a continuing part in Zinacantan by curing illnesses due to the loss of soul components, restoring the balance with the ancestors and thus reincorporat-ing and reintegrating the patient's inner soul. It is not only humans that have inner souls:

Virtually everything that is important and valuable to Zinacantecos also possesses an "inner soul": domesticated animals and plants . . . ; salt, which possesses a very strong "inner soul"; houses and the household fires; the wooden crosses erected on sacred mountains, inside caves and beside waterholes; the saints . . . ; musical instruments. . . .; and all the various deities in the Zinacanteco pantheon. . . . The most important interaction going on in the universe is not between persons, nor between persons and objects, . . . but . . . between "inner souls" inside these persons and material objects. (Vogt 1970: 10–11)

Every Zinacanteco individual has a second kind of "soul," an "animal spirit companion." The spirit companions of the living, one for each person, live in a mountain that towers above central Zinacantan, in separate supernatural corrals: one of jaguars, another of coyotes, another of ocelots, another of small animals such as opossums. A person's animal spirit companion shares his or her same inner soul, so that one's well-being depends on one's animal spirit companion being properly protected and cared for by the ancestral gods. A person's animal companion may be turned out of its corral by the ancestral gods if that person has transgressed cultural rules; and a shaman must intercede to have the ancestors restore the companion to its corral.

Ostensibly Christian rites, including those that involve cross shrines, turn out on closer inspection to be vehicles for the traditional Mayan religious system. The hundreds of *krus* (from Spanish "cross") shrines, called *kalvario* (from "Calvary"), are in actuality places where the ancestral gods meet, deliberate about the conduct of their descendants, and await ritual offerings. As we will

Case 59 continued

see in Case 68, these shrines are hierarchically ordered in terms of an underlying patrilineage system. The Zinacantecos see the cross altars as doorways to the gods. A set of religious symbols—flowers, incense, and rum—serve to define sacred contexts in which communication with the gods can take place.

What outwardly appears to be a Catholic ceremony thus has a meaning to the Zinacantecos that hearkens back to the religion of their ancestors, and establishes communication with them:

With flowers on the crosses, incense burning. . ., liquor being consumed . . . , and music being played . . . , the stage is set for efficient communication with the supernaturals through prayers and offerings, typically candles, which are regarded as tortillas and meat for the gods, and black chickens whose "inner souls" are eagerly consumed by the gods. . . .

The supernaturals . . . will . . . reciprocate by restoring the "inner soul" of a patient, by sending rain for a thirsty maize crop, or by eliminating . . . evils and setting things right for the Zinacantecos. (Vogt 1970:16)

Cultural syncretism: A Trobriand Islands cricket team dances in traditional dress (in 1973) as it enters the playing field for a game; this team is called "the Airplanes," and their dance imitates a plane banking.

Yam exchange in the contemporary Trobriands: Yams are set out in traditional fashion *(left)* and then loaded on a truck to be presented to another village *(below)*.

CASE

60

The Menomini and Blood Indians

The Spindlers used Rorschach tests and their own culture-specific testing methods to probe the personalities of Menomini Indians in Wisconsin. They divided the Menomini into five categories, ranging from the very conservative native-oriented to those who had fully adopted white middle-class culture. They found that Menomini in each category had a distinctive personality pattern. The native-oriented groups showed a psychological pattern congruent with the restraint and control and dependence on supernatural power appropriate to the old Menomini ways of life: inward orientation, fatalism, lack of overt emotional responsiveness. Those Menomini who adopted white ways achieved a reorganization of personality congruent with the success orientation, competitiveness, and punctuality their jobs demand of them—though not without costs of anxiety. The transitional group in the middle of the continuum of change showed cognitive disorganization and its social expression (G. D. Spindler 1955, L. S. Spindler 1962).

Some are striving for an orderly way of life, toward goals recognizable in the surrounding non-Indian community; others are withdrawn and mostly just vegetate; others go on destructive rampages. (G. D. Spindler 1968:329)

In another study, the Blood Indians of Canada showed marked and significant contrasts. Like the Menomini, they represent a continuum in their adoption of the dominant culture and in their standard of living. Yet the bulk have adopted many white ways without abandoning their identity as Blood Indians. Most still speak their own language and retain many traditional customs and beliefs. Beneath the spectrum of differences between modern Blood in socio-economic status, the Spindlers found a continuum in underlying culture, with evidence of much less psychological reorganization occurring than among the Menomini in adaptation to changed ways of life. Apparently traditional modern Blood culture and the cognitive and emotional organization it fostered were congruent with the alien culture and new alternatives in a way that Menomini patterns were not. The aggressive, competitive, acquisitive way of life of the Blood as hunters of the plains apparently fit sufficiently neatly the modes of life and livelihood whites introduced to the Alberta plains—especially cattle ranching—that the Blood could adopt new ways without fully abandoning old ones, and without a radical shift of psychological integration.

harmonious or slow and disruptive—in cultural terms. Explanation of the "success" or difficulty of change in terms of cultural congruence or lack of it is an easy substitute for careful political and economic analysis. As we will see in more detail in the next two chapters, it is not "Western culture" that has confronted tribal Africans or New Guineans. It is a worldwide economic system of which plantations and colonial administrations were local manifestations. The circumstances of invasion, subjugation, and economic exploitation in which these peoples were transformed, the creation of class systems and the postcolonial hegemony they made possible, are all disguised if we imagine that it has been a collision between two cultures. Peoples who have "adapted successfully" are often ones who have been able, through the circumstances of colonial politics and economy, to exploit opportunities and prosper economically. Peoples who turn in desperation to alcohol or who are "unable to adapt" are characteristically those whose subsistence base has been destroyed, who have been thrust into desperate dependence without land or intact communities, who have been depleted by disease and even genocide. To "explain" despair among those who have been dispossessed, decimated, and rendered powerless and dependent, as a result of "cultural incongruence," is no substitute for analysis.

The Impact of Christianity

Anthropologists and missionaries have, at least in stereotype, been at odds with one another for many decades. The caricatured missionary is a strait-laced, repressed, and narrow-minded Bible thumper trying to get the native women to cover their bosoms decently; the anthropologist is a bearded degenerate given to taking his clothes off and sampling wild rites.

Things are more complicated than that. There is an old and enduring tradition of great missionary scholarship. Though many of the friars that accompanied the *conquistadores* in the Americas and in the Philippines engaged in brutal repression and played an active and often sordid part in the subjugation of conquered populations, there were also many champions of humanism and justice, and there were some great scholars and statesmen like Sahagun and Las Casas and Lafitau who compiled rich records of indigenous cultures and championed the humanity of the conquered. In the nineteenth and early twentieth centuries, such figures as Junod,

Codrington, Leenhardt, and Schebesta enormously enriched anthropological knowledge. And in recent years, missionary ethnographers and linguists have continued to provide valuable evidence.

But there are deep gulfs between the premises, as well as the styles, of missionary work and anthropology that have led to considerable friction and controversy. Here, a critique of missionary work will be set out that takes a direction rather different from the traditional anthropological challenge. Many readers, who accept the missionary's premise that he bears the Divine Word and thus has an urgent duty to spread the faith, will not agree with this critique, but the questions are worth raising even though the answers individuals reach will inevitably differ.

Anthropologists who have contested the work of missionaries through the years have often bolstered their position with a cultural relativism and romanticism about the "primitive" that seem increasingly anachronistic. The anthropologist who finds himself in defense of infanticide, head-hunting, or the segregation and subordination of women, and in opposition to missionization, can well be uncomfortable about the premises from which he or she argues. But if one suspends both the premises of Christian duty and the equally shaky premises of cultural relativism, one can look penetratingly at Christianity and its spread under imperialism as historical phenomena—and one can find stronger grounds for questioning the missionary enterprise.

First, historically Christianity was brought to Latin America, the Philippines, and elsewhere as an instrument of conquest and subjugation. In the sixteenth and seventeenth centuries, Catholicism was literally spread by the sword; and subjugation of conquered peoples and the exacting of tribute and forced labor in mines and fields was as much the work of missionaries as of soldiers. In later centuries, Protestant and Catholic missionaries have been less directly used as instruments of government policy. But they have come under the aegis of colonialism and have been in its vanguard; and in many ways, direct and indirect, they have played a part in the subjugation of non-Western peoples.

Second, a major basis for Christian success, where Christianity has been successful, has been the inference by subjugated peoples that Europeans were rich and powerful because of the supernatural support they enjoyed. The White Man's deity must be the source of the White Man's power. Missionaries seldom tried to dispel this assumption, and in most places consciously exploited it, using sophisticated technology and medical services to attract the people to their cause. From the perspective of the tribal peoples the inference is not surprising. If earth were invaded by an extraterrestrial civilization vastly more powerful and technologically advanced than ours, with a religion of ancestor worship, most Europeans would probably abandon Christianity and become ancestor worshippers. The premise on which any such ideological export rests is fundamentally exploitative.

By imposing European standards and European theology on societies to which they are alien, missionization has been pervasively racist and has eroded the self-conception of subjugated peoples. Colonized peoples have been proffered images of a white-skinned Jesus and a white-skinned God. They have usually, at least implicitly, been promised second-class citizenship in the White Man's heaven. They have been treated as children to be uplifted, not as men and women. They have also re-sponded in their own ways, reappropriating and transforming doctrines, as shown, for example, in Cases 58 and 59.

The most blatant racism and exploitation have been disappearing. Africans, Asians, and Pacific Islanders serve as priests, deacons, or bishops. But paternalism, patronage, and racism remain; Christianity continues in many regions to serve alien interests; and the wounds to peoples' self-conception and to the integrity of their cultures remain deep and unhealed. It is worth quoting from the Declaration of Barbados, which emanated from a 1971 conference cosponsored by the World Council of Churches and the Institute of Ethnology, University of Basel, on the plight of South American Indians:

> Evangelisation, the work of the religious missions in Latin America, also reflects and complements the reigning colonial situation with the values of which it is imbued. The missionary presence has always implied the imposition of criteria and patterns of thought and behavior alien to the colonised Indian societies. A religious pretext has too often justified the economic and human exploitation of the aboriginal population.
>
> The inherent ethnocentric aspect of the evangelisation process is also a component of the colonialist ideology and is based on the following characteristics:
>
> 1. its essentially discriminatory nature implicit in the hostile relationship to Indian culture conceived as pagan and heretical;
> 2. its vicarial aspect, implying the re-identification of the Indian and his consequent submission in exchange for future supernatural compensations;
> 3. its spurious quality given the common situation of missionaries seeking only some form of personal salvation, material or spiritual;
> 4. the fact that the missions have become a great land and labour enterprise, in conjunction with the dominant imperial interests. (Bartolome et al. 1971:5)

It is worth emphasizing as well that despite the enormous power of Europeans, missionization has been less than dramatically successful in many parts of the world. In some parts of Africa where strong missionary effort has been directed for more than a century, only a small percentage of converts have been won. Islam has expanded in Africa, in competition with Christianity; and decades of missionary effort in China and India have had few lasting results. In India, however, it is noteworthy that Christianity has been adopted by those of lower castes, especially untouchables, who wish to contest the indigenous hierarchy.

In the early decades of Christian influence in tribal communities, belief in ancestors or spirits was characteristically retained; and God and the devil were added as new forces in the cosmos. Thus in Papua New Guinea a new Catholic cathedral was opened with appropriate participation by the most powerful sorcerers. In the Solomons an Anglican bishop whose father was a pagan priest drove porpoises ashore in a porpoise drive to obtain the teeth as ceremonial valuables, clutching a crucifix (in lieu of a traditional sacred baton); and he blessed the first kill in traditional fashion—but in Latin. (For a review of materials see Barker 1990.)

We saw from Mesoamerica that the rich pageantry of Catholicism offered rewarding replacement for much that had been swept away. One of the many impediments to the success of fundamentalist Protestant missionaries has been the austerity and emptiness of the new life proffered in place of the old. A pall of Protestant gloom hangs over many a community in the Pacific and tropical South America that once throbbed with life, laughter, and song. The concept of sin must rank with smallpox among our most damaging exports.

Christianity as a worldwide force is also illuminated by examining its ideological and economic roots. Christianity, from its beginnings as a religion of the oppressed, has from the Crusades onward been a religion of expansion and conquest. The treasuries of the Vatican attest to the immense wealth that has flowed directly to the Church from Christianization of the New World and parts of Asia; and the Church in the Third World continues to be an extraordinarily wealthy and powerful force controlling land and resources. Protestantism, as Weber (1956) and Tawney (1926) compellingly argued, has historically been closely associated with the rise of capitalism, supported indirectly by the corporate wealth of Europe and the United States. Spreading Christianity has on the one hand been part of the moral justification Europeans have used to rationalize their subjugation of the world. And on the other hand, it has been a direct instrument of imperialism to spread religion while gaining raw materials, markets, and cheap labor. From the critical standpoint of the student of political economy, who views ideologies as expressing underlying economic and political interests, it is not surprising that European religion has taken these forms. The civilization that produced an insatiable lust for profit has produced a religion with an insatiable lust for souls. And a religion that preaches the nobility of poverty, the virtue of passivity, and the joys of the next world has served rather nicely the interests of colonial powers and modern neocolonialists' pursuit of raw materials, docile cheap labor, and profit.

The conclusions drawn in the Declaration of Barbados are strongly worded, but they bear reflection:

> We conclude that the suspension of all missionary activity is the most appropriate policy on behalf of both Indian society as well as

the moral integrity of the churches involved. Until this objective can be realized the missions must support and contribute to Indian liberation in the following manner:

1. overcome the intrinsic Herodianism of the evangelical process, itself a mechanism of colonialisation, Europeanisation and alienation of Indian society;
2. assume a position of true respect for Indian culture, ending the long and shameful history of despotism and intolerance characteristic of missionary work, which rarely manifests sensitivity to aboriginal religious sentiments and values;
3. halt both the theft of Indian property by religious missionaries who appropriate labour, lands and natural resources as their own, and the indifference in the face of Indian expropriation by third parties;
4. extinguish the sumptuous and lavish spirit of the missions themselves, expressed in various forms but all too often based on exploitation of Indian labour;
5. stop the competition among religious groups and confessions for Indian souls—a common occurrence leading to the buying and selling of believers and internal strife provoked by conflicting religious loyalties;
6. suppress the secular practice of removing Indian children from their families for long periods in boarding schools where they are imbued with values not their own, converting them in this way into marginal individuals, incapable of living either in the larger national society or their native communities;
7. break with the pseudo-moralist isolation which imposes a false puritanical ethic, incapacitating the Indian for coping with the national society—an ethic which the churches have been unable to impose on that same national society;
8. abandon those blackmail procedures implicit in the offering of goods and services to Indian society in return for total submission;
9. suspend immediately all practices of population displacement or concentration in order to evangelise and assimilate more effectively, a process that often provokes an increase in morbidity, mortality, and family disorganization among Indian communities;
10. end the criminal practice of serving as intermediaries for the exploitation of Indian labour. (Bartolome et al. 1971:5–6)

But there is another side. Many Christian missionaries have devoted their lives in ways that greatly enriched the communities where they worked. Many, in immersing themselves in other languages and cultures, have produced important records of ways now vanishing. But more important, in valuing these old ways and seeing Christianization as a challenge to creative synthesis of old and new, the best missionaries have helped to enrich human lives and provide effective bridges to participation in a world community. In a great many colonial regions, missions provided educational systems while colonial governments did not; and consequently, when the stage was set for the emergence of Third World leaders in decolonization, many who took the stage were able to do so because of their mission education. Missionaries, living in local communities where colonial exploitation had tragically disruptive consequences, have often been vocal critics of government policy or practice. No treatment of Christianity in the world could wisely overlook this humanitarian side.

Moreover, as we will see later in this book, anthropologists' critiques of the involvement of missionaries as a part of imperialist design can no longer overlook their own historic involvement as well. It is no accident that after its critique of missionary exploitation, the Declaration of

Barbados goes on to lay bare the exploitative aspects of anthropology.

Anthropological critiques of missionaries have too often been based on a romantic idealism about primitive ways of life, sustained by a philosophy of cultural relativism. Such a relativism denies the very real oppression in these societies and the costs of endemic warfare, fear, and disease. Christian missionaries, in helping to bring medical care, education, and peace to tribal communities, have very often dramatically improved the material conditions of life (even if too often, by condemning customs they have not understood, they have caused needless erosion of social life and its satisfactions). Europeans, as conquerors, have had the power to force change on the conquered; and Christianity has been a more benign and humanitarian force, most of the time, than many other instruments the conquerors have used to impose their will and their standards.

It is urgent not simply to condemn missionary effort retrospectively but to understand its roots and its impact. But it is urgent above all to insist that, while change and the transformation of traditional societies and cultures are inevitable and necessary, the formerly colonized must create their *own* new worlds, their own syntheses of the old and new. If peoples are to emerge from the ruins of colonialism and escape the tentacles of neocolonialism, they must find their own solutions, their own ways to transcend the oppression of the past while drawing on its wisdom and values. In this challenge, Christianity can be either a revolutionary force for liberation and humanization or a force of cultural domination and reaction. In Latin America, the Catholic Church is both a force for social justice and an instrument of an oppressive landed aristocracy, itself owning vast lands and properties that hold impoverished Indians in servitude. In Aboriginal Australia, too, Christianity has been both a force for social justice and an agent of paternalistic oppression and cultural destruction. It is no contradiction that in Melanesia the architect of Vanuatu's independence, Walter Lini, was an Anglican priest. Institutionalized Christianity is, in this view, neither good nor evil; it must be judged by what it does. (For a further review of the work of anthropologists and missionaries, see Salamone 1979.)

Millenarianism, Revitalization, and Anticolonial Struggle

Faced with massive external threat, some peoples made conservatism a stance for survival, a way of preserving cultural and individual identity. With traditional social systems breaking down, they sought to preserve central rites and symbols. As we have seen, the once-numerous and powerful Mandan Indians of the upper Missouri were devastated by smallpox and enemy raids. They were also controlled by a series of fur companies, in the end being controlled and dominated by the American Fur Company. Yet through this period, they struggled to maintain their cultural integrity and identity, even with numbers decimated and autonomy gone, by carrying on their elaborate religious ceremonial. Most notable was the great *okipa* ceremony, requiring scores of participants (Bowers 1950, Catlin 1867). With numbers so far reduced, this required more men than they could muster; so the neighboring Hidatsa, with whom they had coalesced for sheer survival, were incorporated into the rite. And in this period, the Mandan attempted to preserve their culture by adopting into the tribe Indians from surrounding groups,

CASE

6 1

The Ghost Dance Religions

In 1869, a Paiute prophet named Wodziwob had religious visions which foretold the end of the existing world, the ousting of the whites, the return of dead relatives, and the restoration of Indian lands and integrity. These doctrines spread rapidly among Plains tribes

The Ghost Dance: An Arapaho brave in rigid dance position.

and even French trappers and their half-Indian children; the only condition for being a Mandan was raising one's children as culturally Mandan. Yet even this desperate means for survival was to fail: Mandan language and culture have now virtually vanished, driven toward final extinction by a conscious U.S. government policy of assim-

ilation that forced dispersal of the remnant Mandan communities (Bruner 1961). In other cases Native Americans, such as the Huron of Quebec, have been able to reconstitute themselves within a state framework (see Eriksen 1993:67–69).

Subjected to extreme pressures by the onslaught of European power, and forced to

Figure 17.1 "Bulletproof" ghost shirt: This Arapaho (Plains American Indian) shirt was part of the magical equipment of the Ghost Dance adherents, supposedly protecting them against the white man's guns. It is of leather, with both traditional Indian symbols and what appear to be Christian symbols (the cross). (After Mooney 1896)

whose ways of life had disintegrated under white pressure and the extermination of the buffalo. Though attempts at military resistance generated by cult doctrines were smashed, the cult itself spread widely and diversified into local versions.

In 1890, a second Ghost Dance cult inspired by another Paiute prophet, Wovoka, spread eastward across the Plains tribes and even to some Eastern Woodlands tribes. Again the cult stressed return to traditional ways of life that had broken down. If the patterns of traditional culture were purified and restored, the vanishing buffalo would return, the dead ancestors would come back, and the Indians could drive out the whites with magical protection (see Figure 17.1, for example) against the power of bullets (Mooney 1896).

reject their centrality in the scheme of things, tribal peoples often came to view their culture as a "thing." The customs, values and rites that, as in the Mandan case, had been taken for granted as part of human life came to be seen from an external point of view: a peoples' *culture* could become a *symbol*. Once this external view was taken, the old ways could symbolize a golden age of past glories and freedoms; or they could be rejected as delusions, as having kept from one's forefathers the power of the White Man.

Millennial (or **millenarian**) **movements** that promised a future paradise on earth have arisen on many colonial frontiers. Some hearkened back to the glory of the past. Most dramatic were the two Ghost Dance cults (see Case 61) that spread across Plains Indian tribes when their power and independence had been broken and the buffalo on which life depended had vanished.

Millenarian movements that reject a traditional culture and formulate some new social order as a means to a millennium have drawn much attention from anthropologists and other scholars. Most dramatic and intensively studied are the **cargo cults** of New Guinea and neighboring areas of Melanesia (Burridge 1960, Jarvie 1963, Lanternari 1963, Lawrence 1964, Lindstrom 1993, Thrupp 1962, Worsley 1957). In these movements, the material power and prosperity of the White Man are seen as valued goals; and the traditional culture is viewed as an obstacle to achieving them. By

CASE

6 2

The Vailala Madness

As of 1919, the Elema people of coastal New Guinea had experienced the waves of European influence: missionary teachings, early experience as plantation laborers, introduction of the few items of European hardware the Elema could afford, and pacification.

In that year, a movement broke out among the Elema that for a time set whole villages into collective "head he go round," a psychophysical state reminiscent of the dancing mania of plague-ridden medieval Europe. People lost control of their limbs, reeled drunkenly, and eventually lost consciousness. Who formulated the ideology is not clear. Central in it was a belief that the dead would return, bringing with them a fabulous cargo of European material goods—knives, cloth, canned goods, axes, and so on. Sacred bull-roarers and other ritual objects were destroyed in a wave of iconoclasm, in communities where dramatic rituals and spectacular men's houses had been focal points of life. The Elema abandoned normal gardening projects and devoted their efforts to elaborate preparations for the return of the dead (Williams 1923).

Within a year most overt forms of the movement had subsided. When Williams, the government anthropologist, returned in 1933, only a few traces of it remained, though there were vague traditions that some of the prophecies had come true.

following the doctrine of the cult, and (usually) following the leadership of its visionary leader in reorganizing social life, a people expect to achieve the millennium. The "Vailala Madness" of New Guinea (see Case 62) is a dramatic illustration of such movements—sometimes called *cargo cults*—clearly oriented toward a mystical and "irrational" millennium and the acquisition of European material goods and rejecting the religious symbols of the past.

Interpretations of cargo cults and other millennial movements have come not only from anthropologists but from psychologists, historians, sociologists, and students of comparative religion. Many writers have stressed exploitation and economic inequality. Aberle (1962) emphasized relative deprivation, a perceived gap between the desired and possible, between new aspirations and abilities to satisfy them.

Anthropologists have been sensitive to cultural factors as well—congruences between new doctrines and old patterns of belief and magical explanation, relations between the role of cult prophet and traditional leader. But too few analysts of millenarianism in the Pacific have taken a sufficient global view of imperialism, with its racism and exploitation, as the force to which modern millennial movements have been a response (and hence, the experiences of plantation labor, of being "natives," of being caught up in an economy of trade stores, calico, and tobacco).

Most interpreters of cargo cults have also failed to appreciate the extent to which the plantation systems created by capitalist penetration of the southwest Pacific created a vast network through which ideas passed among Melanesian peoples whose home communities were hundreds of miles apart.

The culture of survival that produced the linguae francae of Melanesia created a medium through which ideas about European goods and supernatural means to them could pass. In viewing cargo cults as collective fantasies to which "the Melanesian mind" is prone, Western interpreters have usually viewed as independent, local fantasies the numerous movements that may well have been historically connected through networks of plantation contact. It is a transformation of consciousness, a new vision of one's position in the scheme of things, that opens the possibility of radical change—whether by mystical or political means. It has been the crystallization of a *collective self-identity* that has opened the way for dramatic movements of change. What is needed is for people to perceive their own way of life in a new perspective.

This then leads to another limitation of recent fascination with millenarian movements. Preoccupation with the esoteric, with collective fantasy, has often obscured a continuum between millennial cults and other political responses to colonial subjugation.

In Melanesia itself, there have been more directly political responses to colonial domination, although characteristically these have been cloaked in religious symbols. Such Melanesian movements have painted a much more realistic vision of the new social order: the goal is to transform society and politics by human effort and planning, not supernatural intervention; and this path has been pursued more by political than mystical means. Sometimes, as in the Paliau movement on Manus Island northeast of New Guinea (Schwartz 1962), the plans and methods have been so clearly political that they have become part of the ongoing political process of an emerging nation. In others, such as Maasina Rule in the Solomon Islands

(see Case 63), political action and doctrines for social reorganization have been expressed in religious guise; and too often European observers have exaggerated the millennial content in order to sustain their stereotypes and rationalize their colonialist aims or economic and religious interests.

The continuum from religious millenarianism to political struggle is important and revealing. The deep destruction of identity in colonialism creates an explosive situation. Catalyzed by millenarian vision, it can lead to religious cultism, where people are powerless and the gulf between ways of life is vast. But where people have greater power and a clearer and more global perception of the colonial situation, destruction of identity has led to rebellion, political struggle, or wars of liberation. In retrospect, the Mau Mau movement of Kenya was not a fanatic cult of religious murder as it was painted by the white colonists, but a highly effective war of liberation against an entrenched enemy.

Anthropologists, because of their predilection for studying the exotic and for working among powerless and peripheral small-scale societies have characteristically focused on millennial cults and religious rather than political quests for liberation from colonial oppression. As we will see in Chapter 21, they have found themselves standing apart from—and often rejected by—peoples who have wrested themselves from colonial domination.

The Creation of Colonial Consciousness

In quests for liberation from colonialism— and in the many cases where that liberation has been only nominal or partial—a key factor has been the effect of colonial rule on the colonized. One consequence of colonial subjugation and the incorporation of tribal societies into the world capitalist system

Maasina Rule in the Solomon Islands

The Solomon Islands were the scene of major World War II sea and land battles. The volunteer Melanesian Labor Corps, mainly from Malaita Island, worked with American troops. From their encounter with staggering quantities of military hardware and American egalitarian ideologies, a Malaitan named Nori and a group of compatriots formulated a new doctrine. The different

Prologue to Maasina Rule: A Malaita laborer uses farm machinery on a large-scale agricultural project to feed U.S. troops.

has been a drastic demeaning of people's sense of themselves. The cost for men and women, who have borne the brunt of incorporation into plantation or town economies, has been staggering. Proud people who controlled their destiny, in the center of their universe, have become despised and semihuman "natives" in the colonial situation. "The native" became a scorned creature in his own country; his culture became an object of derision. Proud men were turned into "boys," forced to demean themselves serving and slaving for white "masters" with obeisance. Christian missionaries sought to save their souls by turning them into pious children. Humans were led to

tribal peoples were to join together, united by a council of nine Head Chiefs, to negotiate their demands with the returning British administration (which they hoped might be replaced by Americans). Solomon Islanders were to organize into communal villages, structured on the model of military units—with roll calls, chiefs to supervise communal labor, and drills with wooden rifles. Fragmented local kin groups joined together, building large communal gardens for subsistence and anticipated trade.

Maasina Rule, "The Rule of Brotherhood," was to unite the Solomon Islanders in a new social, economic, and political order in which they would be free of the oppression and racism of prewar colonial rule. Malaitans refused to work on plantations and staged large demonstrations voicing demands to the administration. The British jailed the nine Head Chiefs, but their places were filled again. Eventually, in the face of heavy-handed repression and an old-style "showing of the flag" in which warships and mil-itary aircraft demonstrated British power, the fragile unity of communities gave way and the movement was splintered and driven underground.

Although millenarian doctrines appeared during Maasina Rule, especially when, in the face of repression, leaders sought intervention by the Americans on their behalf, they were clearly subordinate to political aims and community reorganization. European observers were misled into exaggerating the fantasy aspects of the movement, partly because of a very effective veil of secrecy maintained by adherents, partly because many of the adherents still practiced an ancestral religion in which sacrifice, magic, and politics were intertwined—and partly because seeing the movement as collective fantasy sustained European stereotypes of the credulity of "the natives" and made it unnecessary to deal with the movement as an effective demand for a loosening of the bonds of colonialism (Keesing 1978, Laracy 1979).

despise the color of their skin and the ways of their ancestors.

The consequences for the social and psychological integration of colonized peoples have been deep and tragic. The psychology of being a "native" was most searchingly explored by the psychiatrist Franz Fanon (1965), who revealed a cost of colonialism— and a source of anticolonialist rage and frustration—that had remained largely hidden from the colonizers. It was more reassuring to deny the humanity of the indigenous people and decry the barbarism of their customs, and then to seek to uplift them. One could rationalize exploitation with a sense of moral responsibility. A long-range consequence of colonial (or in Latin America, quasicolonial) domination has characteristically been the emergence of class systems among colonized peoples, with the indigenous elites then emulating the values and lifestyles of the former colonists. This has been a theme widespread in Africa, Asia, the Americas, and the Pacific. The political-economic relationships between these elites and formerly colonial powers and transnational corporations will be a theme of Chapter 19. Here,

CASE

6 4

"Crab Antics" in the British Caribbean

Wilson argued that in the formerly British Caribbean, as a historical product of plantation exploitation and the imposition of alien standards, rigid and vicious systems of social stratification emerged. Those who historically acquired land or other sources of wealth, characteristically by serving colonialist interest, constitute an elite—defined in terms of light skin color, Christian virtue, and emulation of British aristocratic ways. "Good" families try subtly to outmaneuver one another in "respectability" as defined in European terms; and this elite, by intermarriage, outside education, and the manipulation of wealth, preserves its hold over the far more numerous poor people who work as laborers, sharecroppers, fishermen, and so on.

Wilson's primary focus was on the small English-speaking island of Providencia, now part of Colombia. He showed vividly the operations of the small "respectable" elite who dominate the economic and social life of the island. But what of "crab antics"? In Providencia,

the term derives from the way that crabs in a barrel, in trying to crawl out, pull one another back down the sides: gains are at someone else's expense. Crab antics are the subtle battles for reputation among the lower-class Providencian men. Unlike the status games enhancing respectability, the quest for reputation is open to the poor. A good man is one who works hard; but most particularly, he exemplifies a set of male virtues: bravado; hard-drinking, and sexual conquests. As in the *machismo* of Mexico and other parts of the Spanish-speaking Americas, material poverty and powerlessness are countered by an ostentatious display of bravado, courage, toughness, and predatory sexual aggression; and relations between the sexes are polarized accordingly. This, in the Caribbean, is the opposite face of the domestic group where women provide strength, continuity, and the means of economic survival, and where men's economic contributions are meager and sporadic.

we need only look in passing at the culture side of this emulation of the colonial rulers.

Peter Wilson (1972), in his study of the scrambling for reputation in the English-speaking islands of the Caribbean (see Case 64), provided a striking example of how social stratification may be defined in the terms of the colonizers. Wilson argued that the two themes of respectability and reputation are pervasive principles of Caribbean social organization. He viewed the quest for respectability as a product of British colonialism, with its racism and its

emphases on class differences, aristocratic manner, Christian virtue, and "breeding." But the quest for reputation, he argued, is an indigenous and egalitarian value system, a creation of the people and an adaptation to adversity. In this, Wilson probably underestimated the degree to which the quest for reputation—a kind of vicious egalitarianism at best—is a product of colonial exploitation and the poverty it produced. It is a status game among those left bereft of power and material reward, a game that exploits women and oppresses the weak. We will return to the debate about the roots of status conflict among the poor and powerless when we look more closely at peasant societies in Chapter 18.

Colonial Policy and the Adaptation of the Colonized

As we noted at the beginning of this section, the adaptation of tribal peoples to colonial subjugation depended in substantial part on where they were, and hence what Europeans wanted from them—whether cheap labor, land, or simply peaceful submission in the wilderness. It also has depended on the colonial policy of a particular country and era, so that it is a gross oversimplification to paint colonialists of all times and places with the same broad brush strokes or to condemn each for the collective sins of all. Europeans were more or less exploitative, more or less ruthless, more or less benevolent, in search of lands and profits; and in different times and places they have pursued different goals for the "natives," running the gamut from extermination to assimilation.

When colonial settlement was the aim—especially in temperate zones of the world, such as North America, Australia, South Africa, and New Zealand—the "natives" had to be removed from the new land that had been "discovered." By extermination and herding of the survivors into barren and unwanted reserves, European settlers could take possession of fertile land and resources in the name of some crown or another.

However, some peoples, instead of succumbing conveniently or disappearing into the wastelands, adopted European ways with apparent ease and enthusiasm and began beating the whites at their own game. The best-known case was that of the Cherokee. Before and after their desperate forced move to Oklahoma, the Cherokee were dramatically successful in adopting white economic patterns, technology, literacy, and customs and reshaping them to their own ends and their own design. Yet the Cherokee Nation was twice destroyed by white greed, land hunger, and fear of Cherokee power and success.

Equally striking, though less well known, was a somewhat similar adaptation by the most populous and politically integrated Australian Aborigines, the "five tribes" of central Victoria. Their story is presented in Case 65.

Where the aim of Europeans was not settlement but pacification, subjugation, and colonial control, the range of options was wider. The first order of the day was to force political capitulation. How that was to be accomplished—whether by conquest, political intrigue, or simply imposition of the *Pax Britannica* or its equivalent—was both a matter of location and a matter of the political organization of the people to be subjugated.

Where a non-Western people had a strong and centralized government, it had to be forced to capitulate to ultimate colonial control within a web of empire. The process of subjugation, and also of cultural misunderstanding by the colonizing power, is vividly illustrated by a famous issue of sovereignty in West Africa: the incident involving the Golden Stool, presented in Case 66.

A characteristic strategy Europeans used to gain colonial control was to support a particular leader fighting with his rivals for power, make him "king," give him the means to conquer other leaders, and then use him to achieve European domination. A classic case was Cakobau of Fiji, chief of the tiny island of Bau, who was armed and supported by the British, was turned into a "king," and then ceded his kingdom to

The Five Tribes and the "Coranderrk Rebellion"

Five Australian language groups or "tribes," the Woiwurrung, Bunurong, Wodthaurung, Jajourong, and Tangerong, had a complex regional system of trade, intermarriage, and ceremonial within a kind of political confederacy (Howitt 1904).

Decimated by disease in the early contact period, the five tribes were deprived of their lands by the sort of deception and broken promises familiar from the American frontier. In 1863, the survivors of the five tribes were given a reservation at Coranderrk, under protection of Queen Victoria.

Many of the Aborigines by then spoke good English; many read newspapers, and some wrote letters to the editors.

In 1874 more than half the population in school was considered "equal to European children of their age." . . . Some were good farmers. . . . They cleared heavy timber, built houses, strung fences, grew saleable crops, and ran some cattle. Many had jobs at European wages; they raised their living standard by craft work for sale, and by wages earned outside the reserve. (Stanner 1973:107)

Coranderrk: Dick and Ellen Richards (right) in front of their houses with their neighbors, about 1876.

Queen Victoria—who guaranteed hegemony of Fiji to his successors.

The people Europeans sought to bring under their control often perceived the political symbols of sovereignty invoked by the whites as quite meaningless, or they manipulated them to their own ends. In Case 67, the Mandan people of the upper Missouri once more provide a striking example.

The Aborigines had European furniture, dishes, bedding, sewing machines, and kerosene lamps. Their reserve had a library for which Aborigines bought novels, magazines, and portraits of Queen Victoria (Barwick n.d., Stanner 1973).

In the first decade, the reserve at Coranderrk was managed by an intelligent and capable man who encouraged the community to work out its own laws and transform its society. The people changed their old prescriptive marriage system, giving young women freedom to choose their own husbands, subject only to the rule of clan exogamy.

Yet by 1875, the Victorian Board for the Protection of the Aborigines was increasingly pressured by whites fearful of the economic success of the Coranderrk Aborigines: they not only held land the settlers wanted and were becoming prosperous, organized, and vocal in their protests against injustice; but they also threatened the stereotype of Aborigines as childlike savages incapable of civilized life—a stereotype white settlers used to rationalize their strategies of extermination and usurpation of land. The Board, itself dominated by self-serving and hypocritical "protectors" of Aboriginal rights, fired the benevolent head of the Coranderrk Reserve and imposed a series of repressive measures designed to wreck the economic and political organization of the Aborigines. In the face of this, the Aborigines did the only thing they could do: they protested, in the form of strikes, demonstrations,

and complaints to authority—though not in violence. Under pressure, factionalism began to split the Aboriginal camp into a "progressive" faction (including a number of half-Aboriginals) bent on assimilation and a "conservative" faction bent on preserving cultural identity.*

In governmental enquiries into the Coranderrk situation a myth was fostered that the reserve had been a den of gambling and prostitution and had been an economic failure. And over succeeding decades the lands of the reserve were broken up and ceded to whites. By the 1920s, only the cemetery and a 500-acre reserve to which the Coranderrk remnants were moved remained from the 27,000 acres given to the Aborigines: the rest was in the hands of whites. Yet Australian histories of Victoria still perpetuate the myth that the Aboriginal reserves, notably Coranderrk, were "failures" and use that to justify their expropriation by land-hungry Europeans (Barwick n.d.; Stanner 1973).

*A similar split among the Cherokee after their tragic forced march along the "Trail of Tears" to Oklahoma, between the conservative Ross Party and the assimilationist Treaty Party, has been a major theme of Cherokee adaptation. White mythologists have attributed the successful adaptation and cultural achievements of the Cherokee—such as the creation of a syllabary by Sequoyah—to the infusion of "white blood"; and have used the division to bolster racism against traditional Native Americans and their culture and the political and economic ascendancy of Americanized Cherokee (see Wahrhaftig and Thomas 1972, Wahrhaftig and Lukens-Wahrhaftig 1977).

In addition to the aforementioned strategies, sometimes subjugation to colonialism was achieved by conquest and naked force (as with the Navaho and Sioux, who were militarily crushed, then herded onto barren reservations) or by less direct imposition of control. In the Pacific and Africa, control was often imposed indirectly through local headmen—sometimes leaders in the traditional political system, but often superimposed for colonialist convenience. Imposition of a head tax was a favorite

A first colonial strategy: Find the "chiefs" and manipulate them. New Guinea chiefs deal with Commodore Erskine on HMS *Nelson* (1884), holding the "emblems of authority" presented to them.

strategy of the colonialists: it forced overt recognition of subjugation, since from the standpoint of the conquered it amounted to the exaction of tribute; but more important, it forced the "natives" to go to work in plantations or mines, or wherever cheap labor was needed. And it brought the colonized regions into a capitalist cash economy, creating markets for cloth, steel tools, sugar, tea, and tobacco. (The spread of tobacco would be a tale in itself; the Germans in New Guinea, for example, conducted schools to teach the "natives" how to smoke.)

Even where colonial administration was relatively benevolent, colonial administrators often rivaled or surpassed missionaries in their misunderstandings of local culture. The reader who has traced in the preceding pages the labyrinths of custom and belief in the Trobriand Islands can appreciate the confusions a well-meaning government administrator there could fall into.

CASE
66

The Golden Stool of the Ashanti

The most sacred symbol of the great Ashanti kingdom of West Africa was the Golden Stool. It had been introduced to the Ashanti by a celebrated magician, who had proclaimed that it contained the *sunsum*, or "soul," of the Ashanti people. He warned that "with it was bound up their power, their honor, their wel-fare, and that if ever it were captured or destroyed the nation would perish" (E. W. Smith 1926). The stool was never sat upon, never allowed to touch the ground; only on great occasions was its sacred power invoked by the Ashanti king.

In 1910, the British governor made a series of demands to the leaders of the Ashanti he had summoned to the fort of Kumasi, to which they had come "outwardly submissive, but inwardly boiling over with indignation" (E. W. Smith

1926:5). His speech stands out as a gem of colonialist history:

Now Kings and Chiefs . . . what must I do to the man, whoever he is, who has failed to give to the Queen [of England], who is the paramount power in this country, the Stool to which she is entitled? Where is the Golden Stool? Why am I not sitting on the Golden Stool at this moment? (Rattray 1923)

The governor, of course, thought the Golden Stool was an "appurtenance of the kingly office," and expected that this symbol of his authority should be given, like the Stone of Scone, to the English monarch.

Within a week the Ashanti nation was at war with England. Perhaps Governor Hodgson suspected his mistake when he and his forces were subsequently besieged at Kumasi by tens of thousands of Ashanti warriors.

Thus Malinowski (1935, I:103) writes of the Resident Magistrate who, in land disputes, "adopted a method natural to the European but fatal in a matrilineal community. He would inquire whose father had cut the disputed plot in olden days, a question which, under maternal descent, was beside the point and usually admitted of no answer, since the fathers of both litigants probably belonged to other communities."

A heavy-handed approach to cultural change marked many colonial situations, but most strikingly in cases where massive settlement by colonists made the surviving indigenous peoples an obstacle, a threat, or an embarassment. Where the indigenous

peoples outnumbered settlers, as in South Africa and Zimbabwe, ruthless separation and brutal exploitation had appalling human costs. But where the surviving indigenous peoples were numerically few and consigned to reservations, paternalism often gave way to pressures for assimilation. Often this meant systematic destruction of Aboriginal cultures. As we have noted, the Mandan Indians, whose desperate efforts for cultural survival we encountered in the preceding pages, were finally destroyed by a deliberate policy that broke up the large village that was the keystone of cultural integration (the remnant of the nine big villages of the early contact period) and forced

CASE

6 7

Mandan Acceptance of European "Sovereignty"

Precontact Mandan trade with the Plains tribes involved partnerships. The important Mandan men were strikingly rich, powerful, and aristocratic. In their trading partnerships with influen-

tial men from other groups, the Mandan ritually defined their partners as "father," fictively incorporating them into the kinship system. They in turn were adopted as the fictive fathers of Plains

The Hidatsa, neighbors of the Mandan, bargain with a royal tourist, Prince Maximilian of Wied, in 1832.

the Mandan to scatter into dispersed homesteads. The language and culture of the once-proud Mandan have been virtually destroyed—a tragic case of forced cultural extinction or ethnocide (Bruner 1961).

The internal colonialism of contemporary nations, Western and Eastern, that has made indigenous minorities an endangered "fourth world" will be a theme of Chapter 21. But first, to pursue these questions more

effectively, we need to look, in the next two chapters, at the global forces that have transformed life in local communities, tribal and peasant.

═════ **SUMMARY** ═════

Ethnographies of particular peoples must be set into the wider context of the global

leaders. This was a means of both strategic alliance and manipulation: "Plains Indian trade was accomplished by barter between fictitious relatives. . . . A vast network of ritual kinship relationships extended throughout the entire Plains" (Bruner 1961:201). When Europeans arrived and demanded sovereignty, what the Mandan wanted from them was trading partnerships and power. La Verendrye, the first European to arrive, was received with ceremonial display and deference: "One of the chiefs begged La Verendrye, whom he addressed as father, to adopt the principal Mandan men as his children. This he did, by placing his hands on the head of each chief. The Mandan replied with shouts of joy and thankfulness" (Bruner 1961:198), and were incorporated (from La Verendrye's point of view) under sovereignty of the king of France.

In 1762, Mandan territory was formally ceded by the king of France to Spain. In 1794, the British built a trading post among the Mandan; but two years later, a Spanish expedition visited the Mandan—who promptly adopted their leader: "He distributed flags, medals, and presents to the chiefs, who promised to follow the counsels of their Great Father the Spaniard " (Bruner 1961:207). Then, in 1803, the area was ceded to the United States under the terms of the Louisiana Purchase; and shortly afterwards, Lewis and Clark visited them: "The American explorers distributed flags, medals, presents, and officers' uniforms to the Indian Chiefs, who now promised to follow the counsel of their Great Father the President" (Bruner 1961:207). However, the Mandan privately observed to a British trader that in the Lewis and Clark expedition there were "only two sensible men . . . , the worker of iron and the mender of guns" (Masson 1889:330, quoted by Bruner 1961).

In this early contact situation, another cultural misunderstanding loomed large. A pervasive principle of Mandan culture was that the power of important men could be transferred to younger and less powerful men through the medium of female sexuality. Thus young men would gain power by sending their wives to sleep with powerful older men. When Europeans arrived, with their obvious wealth and power, the Mandan strategically sent their womenfolk to sleep with the explorers. So in the early literature of the contact period, Mandan women are described as wanton and promiscuous (Bruner 1961).

expansion of the powers of metropolitan societies through the process of colonialism and the resulting postcolonial circumstances of the world. These processes include the expansion of Christianity and the role played by economic interests, for example in creating and supporting slavery as a colonial institution underpinning the cotton industry in America. Western colonialism itself represents only one historical and geographical phase of expansion and subjugation, but capitalist industry intensified such processes further through the exploitation of labor and resources. Underlying the study of historical change is the issue of the role of culture as an ideational system versus social action as a form of negotiated practice, utilized by Clifford Geertz in his study of a Javanese town.

Ideational systems, also, have not necessarily been stable in the past and may reflect ideological interests as well as cognitive principles. Forces that cause change may belong to the switch from a subsistence/prestige goods economy to monetarization, in which cultural separations between domains of exchange activities are broken down (example: Paul Bohannan on the Tiv of Central Nigeria). The switch to money is often accompanied by the development of economically based social classes. European colonial influences on small-scale societies also include the devastations of new epidemic diseases such as occurred in the Pacific, and in North and South America. Indigenous peoples may mount armed resistance to control by outsiders, uniting on a broader front than before (examples: Zulu, Ashanti, Maori). Internal repercussions of external influence also occur, as when indigenous rulers obtain new arms and subjugate their neighbors. On the religious front syncretistic versions of Christianity arise (examples: the Virgin of Guadalupe, Catholicism in Zinacantan). Indigenous peoples do not necessarily resist change, but seek to make use of it as they had in the past (examples: Simbu and Melpa of Papua New Guinea, the Trobrianders). Psychological dimensions of responses to change can be assessed, in tandem with previous cultural patterns (examples: Menomini and Blood Indians).

Missionaries and anthropologists may tend to have different views of these processes of change, since missionaries are change agents while anthropologists may support local cultural forms against introduced ones. However, people themselves make their creative choices over time. The Declaration of Barbados called for the suspension of missionary activity; but missionaries also sometimes devote their lives to the people with whom they work and write in-depth ethnographies about them, and recently independent countries in the Pacific may declare themselves Christian nations. In earlier phases of history anticolonial movements sometimes take a millenarian turn, as in the Ghost Dance movement among the Paiute and in some movements labeled as "cargo cults" in New Guinea (examples: the Vailala Madness and Maasina Rule). Such movements may also take on the symbolism of the oppressors themselves, and new forms of stratification may be defined in the terms of the colonizers (examples: "Crab Antics" in the Caribbean, the "Coranderrk Rebellion" in Australia). At other times, cultural misunderstandings such as a colonial demand for a sacred symbol of authority may promote armed rebellion by the colonized (example: the Ashanti Golden Stool).

SUGGESTIONS FOR FURTHER READING

SECTIONS 46–48

Aceves, J. B., ed. 1972. *Aspects of Cultural Change.* Southern Anthropological Society Proceedings, 6. Athens, Ga.: University of Georgia Press.

Bohannan, P., and F. Plog, eds. 1967. *Beyond the Frontier: Social Process and Cultural Change.* Garden City: N.Y.: Natural History Press.

Eisenstadt, S. N. 1973. *Tradition, Change, and Modernity.* New York: John Wiley & Sons, Inc.

Fanon, F. 1965. *The Wretched of the Earth.* London: Macgibbon & Kee.

Hemming, J. 1978. *Red Gold: The Conquest of the Brazilian Indians.* Cambridge, Mass.: Harvard University Press.

Lang, J. 1975. *Conquest and Commerce: Spain and England in the Americas.* New York: Academic Press, Inc.

Mair, L. 1969. *Anthropology and Social Change.* LSE Monograph, 38. London: Athlone.

Spicer, E. H., ed. 1961. *Perspectives in American Indian Culture Change.* Chicago: University of Chicago Press.

Steward, J. H., ed. 1967. *Contemporary Change in Traditional Societies* (3 vols.). Urbana: University of Illinois Press.

Thrupp, S. L. 1970. *Millennial Dreams in Action: Studies in Revolutionary Religious Movements.* New York: Schocken Books, Inc.

Wallace, A. F. C. 1956. Revitalization Movements. *American Anthropologist* 58: 264–281.

Worsley, P. 1968. *The Trumpet Shall Sound.* 2nd ed. New York: Schocken Books, Inc.

18

Peasants

Peasants have been part of the world scene since the rise of states and urban centers in the Middle East. They have coexisted in time, then, with the tribal ways of life that have spread and diversified in the middle, mainly tropical, zones of the world (Chapters 5 and 6). But anthropology, beginning as a study of the small-scale "primitive" societies encountered along the frontiers of colonial expansion, was slow to turn attention to the vast peasant populations of Latin America, Asia, and Europe. The development of a serious anthropology of peasant societies has taken place mainly since 1950; and since then it has been an expanding theme.

Partly, this reflects a disappearance of tribal societies in the decades since World War II, and the emergence of what was known as the Third World out of the colonial one where anthropologists had mainly worked. Formerly tribal peoples have been transformed by modernization, have been caught up into the world economy and the politics of new nations. Partly the growing attention to peasants reflects a broadened conception of anthropology's scope and goals—a broadening which, as we will see, is now leading to increased study of urban life.

When anthropologists began to study peasant villages, they brought to the task

many assumptions and methods derived from studies in tribal settings. The newer advances in peasant studies have come, as we will see, from seeking wider connections in time and space—from seeing above and beyond the village.

49. WHAT ARE PEASANTS?

The word **peasant** conjures up images of simple, rural farmers, poor people leading lives in backwaters isolated from the mainstreams of society. These images have a partial correspondence with the realities of peasant life; but we need to correct their distortions and gain a more refined conceptualization of peasantries.

Peasant Communities as Closed and Open Systems

An essential element in peasant life is its two-sidedness. On the one hand, peasants characteristically produce much of their own subsistence; and peasant communities characteristically have a self-contained, closed-in sort of orientation. But on the other hand, peasants also produce foodstuffs and other goods that flow into urban centers; they participate economically, both

An old man watched by a grandchild stirs drying coffee on a bag and a wooden plate. Wiru, Papua New Guinea.

as producers and as consumers, in wider economic systems that tie them into cities and national and international markets. This two-sidedness, the paradox of relative self-containedness and self-sufficiency, and at the same time incorporation into wider economic systems, is a dominant theme in peasant life, and peasant studies.

But we need to cast this in theoretical terms. Eric Wolf (1966:3-4) views peasants as cultivators with a special kind of relationship to the world outside: "Peasants are rural cultivators whose surpluses are transferred to a dominant group of rulers that uses the surpluses both to underwrite its own standard of living and to distribute the remainder to groups . . . that . . . must be fed for their specific goods and services." What makes peasants peasants is their existence within a state, where they are subject to "the demands and interests of power holders." Peasants can be defined as such, then, in terms of their position in systems of production.

Are Peasants a Class?

That does not mean that peasants always occupy the same position. We need to make two sorts of conceptual refinement. One is to note that peasants can be incorporated within different modes of production, with differing access to the means of production, and subject to different forms of appropriation of surplus. Peasants can be the *owners* of the tracts of land they cultivate, with their surpluses appropriated by the state (or other outside "power holders") in the form of tax, tribute, and so on. Or peasants can be bound as *serfs* to land held by a feudal lord, who then owns all they produce but gives them the means to subsist physically. Or peasants can be *renters*, who contractually divide their crops with a landowner or must sell a portion to pay their rent. Each of these different relationships of production, and others, can be analytically distinguished.

To analyze a particular system of production, we must sort out carefully the rights and relationships involved; when we do, we find that "peasant" is a sort of umbrella category covering a range of quite different relationships:

> Rural cultivators that we descriptively term "peasants" have existed in very different types of society and in different historical epochs—for example, European and Japanese feudalism, the pre-capitalist agrarian empires of India and China, or the many countries of the Third World today where colonialism has been a major historical force in creating peasantries with specific characteristics. (Bernstein 1979:422)

Even broad categories like "feudal" must be used with care. Economic historians have been vigorously debating about the many forms of feudal relations and how best to conceptualize them. For example, specialists have been arguing about the similarities and differences between the European feudalism of the Middle Ages and the seemingly feudal systems (such as the *encomienda* system of the Spanish-conquered Americas) that developed in the sixteenth century on the peripheries of European expansion. Wallerstein (1974:91) argues that "there is a fundamental difference between the feudalism of medieval Europe and the 'feudalisms' of Sixteenth Century eastern Europe and Hispanic America." He proposes for the second form the term *coerced cash-crop labor,* and points out that the political economy of these later systems is fundamentally different from that of the earlier ones:

> "Coerced cash-crop labor" is a form of labor control in a capitalist and not a feudal economy. (Wallerstein 1974:92)

The point is not simply that there are different forms of feudal relationships between seigneur and serf, but that the nature of the system must be understood in more global terms. This is a point to which we will return in the next chapter. (See Wallerstein 1996 for an update on his ideas generally.)

A second conceptual refinement, building on the first, is to see that the same society may incorporate different classes of peasants. Peasant classes have often been distinguished as rich, middle, and poor. These terms, suggesting simple stratification according to wealth, are misleading: middle peasants do not stand in between rich and poor peasants; analytically, in terms of relation of production, they "belong to a different sector of the rural economy" (Alavi 1973:293). These peasant classes are found, as in South Asia, in circumstances of transition from the dominance of one mode of production to the dominance of another; hence, the "different sectors" of the rural economy:

> First . . . we have the [feudal] sector whose essential distinguishing feature is that the land is owned by landlords who do not undertake cultivation on their own account. Their land is cultivated by landless tenants,

mostly sharecroppers who are classed as *poor peasants*. The second sector is that of independent smallholders who own no more land than they cultivate themselves and enough of it to make them self-sufficient. . . . They are the *middle peasants*. . . . A third sector is that of capitalist farmers [*rich peasants* or *kulaks**], who own substantial amounts of land and whose farming is primarily based on the exploitation of wage labor, although they may participate in farm work themselves. (Alavi 1973:293–294).

We cannot, then, assume that even in a particular society peasants constitute a single class—or, as Alavi's observations can well remind us, that a single mode of production prevails. Analytical untangling of different modes of production, in complex societies undergoing change—especially ones that have gone through a period of colonial domination—is a major challenge in contemporary social theory. (For a discussion on these themes in relation to Papua New Guinea, see Amarshi, Good, and Mortimer 1979; and for one critique of the distinction between tribesmen and peasants, see A. J. Strathern 1982.)

50. PEASANT COMMUNITIES

Anthropologists working in peasant communities in the last 30 years have built up detailed records of the texture of social relations in many parts of the peasant world and have explored economy, religion, and political processes. In seeing peasant communities basically as they had seen tribal communities—as more or less closed and self-contained, and often as devoid of known history—anthropologists have drawn a picture of the peasant condition which is both

*A Russian word that has become a technical term in peasant studies.

vivid and revealing and in many cases inadequate. In the paragraphs to follow, we will present an orthodox picture of the peasant condition. Then we will step back to look at a wider picture of the forces that have created and shaped life in peasant communities, in the centuries before anthropologists arrived as well as in the four or five decades when they have been watching. Like a number of other recent critics, I will argue that the "standard" view of the peasant condition has been inadequate and misleading.

Peasant Social Organization

Many modern peasant communities in New and Old Worlds have patterns of social organization that reflect elements of earlier social systems from which they grew. Unilineal descent groupings may remain important. Thus patrilineages play significant roles in peasant social life in corners of the world as widely separated as Mexico, the Balkans, and China. The Mayan Indians of Zinacantan, whose religious system we examined in the last chapter (Case 59), illustrate unilineal descent groupings in peasant communities. (This system is outlined in Case 68.)

In other peasant societies, as in the southern European agrarian communities that have received increasing anthropological attention, the underlying social systems are the old feudal ones of medieval centuries progressively transformed by emerging modern nations.

Unilineal kin groups are seldom important in such settings, though networks of kinship and intermarriage weave together the households that are the primary constituent groupings. Coalitions of friends and neighbors, formed to pursue collective economic strategies and characteristically temporary, have turned up over and over again in rural European settings—though as

Descent Groups and Zinacantan Social Organization

Zinacantan, whose complex synthesis of Mayan and Catholic religious beliefs we glimpsed in Case 59, is organized in a way that subtly reflects an underlying patrilineal descent system.

Zinacantan has a population of some 8,000, living in a classically Mayan settlement pattern of a ceremonial center and 15 outlying hamlets. The most important social units are domestic groups, composed of families who live in a single

Two Zinacantan women sit in a house compound sorting corn. On the left, with a pot at its base, is the house cross of the domestic group.

house compound and share a single supply of maize (corn). Normally, a compound contains at least two houses, around a central patio. Each domestic group is symbolically centered around a "house cross" that reflects its ritual unity.

Most Zinacanteco domestic groups are patrilocal extended families, the minimal local segments of patrilineages. The essential requirement is that it contain both men and women, so as to be economically viable. The most common pattern—a senior man, his wife, his married sons and their wives, and any unmarried children—reflects the practice of virilocal residence and patrilineal inheritance.

These domestic groups (for which there is no label in their language, Tzotzil) are in turn clustered into larger localized groupings along patrilineal lines. Several patrilineally related domestic groups, living on adjacent lands inherited from their ancestors, comprise an unnamed shallow patrilineage some four generations in depth.

One or several patrilineages (or, rarely, as many as 13 of them) are in turn clustered into ritually defined groupings (Vogt 1969, 1970).

These clusters, ranging from some 15 to 150 people, collectively perform ceremonies for the ancestral gods and Earth Owner (Case 59) twice a year. The senior members and shamans of the component lineages take part in these ceremonies in defined hierarchies of ritual rank. The ceremonies focus around cross shrines that are a formal analogue of the house crosses, on a more inclusive scale (Vogt 1969).

Zinacantan has a complex system of personal naming. One of the three names each individual bears is an Indian surname, of which there are some 70. These names are patrilineally transmitted within lineages, and since there is a rule against marriage between people with the same surname, this produces exogamous groupings Vogt calls "patriclans."

The patrilineage clusters are in turn aligned around particular waterholes, with from 2 to 13 patrilineage clusters using a single water supply for their livestock and household use. There is some seasonal dispersal and regrouping during rainy season and dry season. Each waterhole is highly sacred; its ritual importance is marked by a series of cross shrines, both beside the hole and on a hill above, where the ancestors of the component ritual clusters are believed to assemble. The same twice-annual ceremonial conducted by each cluster is also performed a few days earlier by the whole waterhole group. At these ceremonies, the social and ritual unity of the patrilineages that share a common waterhole, and their collective bonds with their ancestors, are symbolically expressed.

Vogt (1965) has argued that the symbolic complex whereby a patrilineal group is symbolically related to its ancestors through crosses, which constitute an entryway to the sacred, is replicated at successively more inclusive levels of social structure: the domestic group, the cluster, the waterhole grouping. The ritual unity is expressed ceremonially by sacred meals within which the ranking of the human participants is carefully observed—a pattern again repeated on a larger scale at each hierarchical level of the social structure. Vogt suggests that this replication of the same formal pattern at more and more inclusive levels may have provided a mechanism for the symbolic unity of the great temple centers of classic Maya society.

P. Schneider and colleagues (1972) rightly insist, *all* societies are organized in both more formal and enduring groups and *ad hoc* coalitions; it is their relative importance and spheres of relevance that vary.

Fictive kinship ties, relations modeled on parental, fraternal, or grandparental roles, are often important in extending or complementing bonds of kinship and affinity.

Best known is *compadrazgo*, or co-parenthood of Mesoamerica (see Case 69), primarily derived through Catholicism from southern European customs but with roots in Mexican Indian cultures as well. Comparable but historically unrelated systems of fictive kinship have turned up as far away as Japan and Nepal.

Despite wider ties of actual and fictive kinship, the peasant community characteristically differs from its tribal counterpart in the independence of household groups. These may be extended families of various sorts or nuclear family households.

Economically, these family households characteristically act as separate corporations, as units of production, and as competitors for scarce resources and income. In many peasant communities these households stand relatively isolated and are not organized into lineages or other kin groups. The fragmentation into nuclear families, and their economic competition, are very often reflected in the texture of social relations. The competition and hostile distrust that often prevail between families have been described in such terms as "atomism" (Rubel and Kupferer 1968). Here it is worth recalling Bailey's (1971) observations from rural European villages, in *Gifts and Poison*, of subtle struggles for status, the often vicious business of staying even with one's fellows. Similar observations have come from many peasant communities.

Foster (1961) has underlined the emphasis on **dyadic contracts** in peasant life—that is, the way pairs of individuals are, in many different spheres of life, bound into relationships almost similar to contracts, though they are not enforced in law. Ties outside the family are, at least in the Mexican village of Tzintzuntzan, primarily between individuals rather than groups. They persist partly because they are never precisely balanced, and hence call for continuing reciprocity. Some dyadic ties are between persons of equal status; others are with *patrons* of superior status (including deities as well as people), who exploit and are "exploited" by the lower-status clients for mutual benefit. Ties to powerful patrons outside the community help to link its residents into wider social networks.

Peasant Economics

The peasant household head and his wife lead a two-sided existence economically. First, they are primarily **subsistence** cultivators. That is, they and their family subsist primarily on the fruits of their own labor. Their limited technology and resources characteristically force them to scrape by from year to year, vulnerable to crop failure and demands from outside **elites.** Second, they contribute to an outside economy in the form of agricultural **surpluses**—production that exceeds their subsistence needs—or by producing specialized products. Through markets and other networks of transactions, household products go to maintain external elites and the specialists that provide services for elites. But peasants' participation within the outside economy is limited and channeled by the social organization and pressures of the community, which guide economic decisions, as well as by limited means of production. Case 70 describes how these economic forces operate in one Mexican village.

CASE

6 9

Compadrazgo in Mexico

Compadrazgo in Mesoamerica overtly derives from the Catholic institution of baptism: a "god-father" and "godmother" sponsor a child ritually in the baptism; they provide spiritual responsibility for the child complementary to the responsibility of father and mother for the child's physical development. While a child's relationship to *padrino* (godfather) and *madrina* (godmother) is important—marked by respect and obedience from the child and guidance and assistance from the sponsors—it is the relationship between sponsors and *parents* that has received special elaboration in Mesoamerica.

The sponsors and parents establish bonds of ritual co-parenthood which (especially between godfather and father) are important additions to kinship bonds. The reciprocal term *compadre* is used for this relationship, which characteristically has strong associations of sacredness and entails ritual respect and formalized reciprocity.

Mexican and other Latin American elaborations of *compadrazgo* have extended the range and importance of these ties far beyond the original Catholic derivation in the sponsorship of baptism. The relationship may unite the sponsor to the grandparents, as well as parents, of the child or otherwise extend the dyadic relationship into a multiple one. And sponsorship in other ritual events, not simply baptism, may lead an individual to have multiple ritual parents.

The variation in regional forms of *compadrazgo* presumably reflects differences in the pre-Columbian cultures onto which the Spanish

model has been superimposed (Davila 1971). These regional variations in the range of *compadre* relationships, their social entailments and relationships to family structure, and their function in the social life of communities have been extensively studied.

Characteristically, sponsors are nonkin or distant kin. A major function of *compadrazgo* is thus to extend the range of close personal relations beyond the circle of kin. In most communities, fairly free choice of a sponsor is possible. Where the social system is relatively egalitarian, the *compadre* relationship is characteristically symmetrical in terms of status. But where differences in wealth and power are marked, sponsorship by a wealthy or powerful man becomes a political strategy—a way of maintaining status (for the sponsor) and seeking upward mobility (for the son) and patronage (for the father).

The symbolic modeling of *compadrazgo* on kinship is evident not only in terminology and role relationships; it is also apparent in the inalienable, enduring scared nature of the bonds of sponsorship and co-parenthood, the axioms of moral obligation they entail, and the extension of incest taboos to relations of *compadrazgo* (Davila 1971).

Case Update
For a detailed study of *compadrazgo* as "ritual kinship" in Tlaxcala, Mexico, see Nutini and Bell 1980; and for a general theoretical discussion, see Gudeman 1972.

Pottery Production in Amatenango

In Amatenango (Chiapas, Mexico; see Nash 1961), Indian peasant households engage in agricultural pursuits both for subsistence and for trade with neighboring communities. There is a lively trade for foodstuffs between communities, with each one partly specialized in its agricultural output. But Amatenango is more notable within the region for another specialized form of production: pottery making. Within an area nearly 40 miles long by 30 across, it is the only center for pottery production. People in every surrounding village must acquire and use Amatenango

The domestic economy in a Mayan village: Two Zinacantan women, sisters-in-law, work in the house compound spinning and weaving on a backstrap loom. Zinacantan peasants make their own clothes from wool which they spin, dye, and weave themselves.

The relative independence of households as units of production and consumption, in peasant communities such as Amatenango in Case 70, has led to attempts to define a "peasant mode of production." Separate, competing households make allocations of labor and decisions about production which can be analyzed using formal models. This approach, inspired by the work of the early Russian populist economist I. Chayanov, influenced anthropologist Marshall Sahlins, who advanced a parallel theory of the "domestic mode of production" in tribal societies. We will shortly see

pottery. Thus pottery production is economically crucial to the households of Amatenango.

Practically every one of the 280 households in Amatenango makes pottery, through a combination of effort by men and women. The raw materials are freely available, the tools are minimal, and the needed skills are learned in childhood. Yet there is wide variation in the pottery output of the various households. Moreover, although pots are sold for money in markets, no household appears to produce nearly as many pots as it could. Why?

Manning Nash kept detailed records of pottery production in several households. He found that there is a seasonal rhythm in pottery making. Production reaches a peak just before a fiesta in Amatenango or a neighboring community. First, this is because that is when the household most needs cash; second, though the prices are not highest at these times, there is a convenient influx of potential buyers, so marketing is easy. Nash found also that there is a negative association between pottery production and wealth in land. The family with wealth in land can provide more of its own food, hence needs cash less; and more of its productive effort is likely to be devoted to agriculture.

But doesn't a household, like a firm, seek to maximize its gain—whether by pottery or agricultural production? And if so, why is production limited and its peaks seasonal? Because as a unit in a complex system of kinship, local grouping, and religious organization, the Amatenango household is severely constrained by leveling mechanisms. "Getting ahead" of other households is in general neither feasible nor desirable. Household economic gains would in any case be short-lived: movable wealth is quickly consumed, and wealth in land is fractionated by inheritance in each generation. The leveling devices are rather subtle. First, what wealth a family has is drained by the costs of one of the many civil and religious offices in which a man must serve during his adult life. A wealthy household is particularly subject to the financial drain of ritual office. One office, the *alferez* (for which four men are selected each year), is particularly expensive and costs a tremendous amount; a family may take years to recoup. In addition, the household that outdid its neighbors in a quest for wealth would become highly vulnerable to witchcraft or accusations of witchcraft. Thus, the performance of a pottery-producing Amatenango household in the outside market economy is controlled by a series of social forces and mechanisms within the community. Despite the economic advantages on paper, it is not to a family's long-term social advantage to maximize its income by producing as much pottery as it could.

the flaws in a view of peasant households as independent units.

We can usefully go back to the "leveling devices" Nash describes for Amatenango; and in particular, to the way hierarchies of civil and religious offices serve to equalize households and drain off wealth as it accumulates. The operation of such hierarchies of offices as leveling mechanisms has been documented in other highland Mayan communities. The **cargo system** of Zinacantan (see Case 71) is probably the best known.

Other leveling mechanisms in Mayan and many other peasant communities are witchcraft accusations or fear of being bewitched, and malevolent gossip, dwelling

Cargos in Zinacantan

The cargo system in Zinacantan is a hierarchy of religious offices organized around Catholic churches and saints. The system in Zinacantan consists of 61 positions in four levels of a ceremonial ladder.

A major life goal for a Zinacanteco man is to serve for a year at each of the four cargo levels, and hence pass through the whole ladder and become a *pasado,* or honored ritually senior man. When a man holds a cargo, he must move into the ceremonial center and engage in an expensive annual round of ceremonies. The costs of liquor, food, and ritual items such as fireworks, incense, candles, and costumes are enormous, especially for the higher levels of the ceremonial ladder.

At the lower level are 28 *mayordomos,* who serve as caretakers of particular saints or hamlet chapels, and 12 *mayores* who are ranked, and serve as policemen, errand boys, and ceremonial functionaries. At the second level, there are 14 *alfereces,* named for particular saints and organized into two ranked orders, senior and junior. They spend much of the year giving ceremonial meals and dancing for the saints.

The third and fourth level cargo holders are collectively classed as elders. The third level comprises four *regidores;* the fourth and highest level comprises two *alcaldes viejos.* The elders manage the cargo system. An old man who has not been able to get through all levels of the cargo hierarchy can be appointed to a post of terminal cargo seniority. Finally, there are ritual advisers who assist cargo holders at various levels; and there are auxiliary personnel—musicians, scribes, and sacristans—who serve for periods longer than a year. These advisers and auxiliary personnel help to maintain the intricacies of ceremonial in the cargo system despite the annually shifting incumbents.

Whereas in some related Mesoamerican systems a civil hierarchy and religious hierarchy are interconnected into a single complex, with civil and religious services undertaken on an alternating basis, the Zinacantan cargo system is not directly tied to the complicated civil officialdom (Cancian 1965, 1972). Breakdowns in the structure of this cargo system are also described by Cancian (1974).

The cost of holding one of the cargos, especially at higher levels, is so great that an

endlessly upon status and its correlates as part of the deadly game of staying even (Bailey 1971).

In ancient states, and in Europe under feudalism, the agricultural surpluses produced by peasants were appropriated by some form of levy or through ownership of the land. In parts of the contemporary world peasants remain under control of landowners who extract produce by right, giving peasants access to land for subsistence in return for their labor. We will shortly see the gradual transition from semifeudal agrarian economies controlled by landlords and moneylenders in colonial and postindependence India.

More characteristic among contemporary peasants is commodity production for markets, as with pottery production in Amatenango. There are a number of good

The cargo system in Zinacantan: The *alcaldes viejos* examine the lists of those waiting to assume cargos.

individual must save for years, as well as borrow heavily and call on outstanding obligations to kin, to assemble the needed resources. After a year in a cargo, an individual characteristically retires from the limelight with savings spent, heavily in debt, and with outstanding "credit" (in the form of obligations) largely repaid. To build up once more to a position where one can ascend to a higher rung of the cargo ladder is likely to take years of hard work and support of others.

studies of peasant marketing in Central America and Mexico. In most Mesoamerican markets the producer seeks out the most advantageous selling conditions, rather than working through a trader as **middleperson.** Thus the Amatenango potter and the Zinacanteco farmer or weaver (or their spouses) bring their wares to the market—a market most often controlled by Spanish-speaking **Ladinos** who manipulate transactions to their advantage and the disadvantage of Indians. In many parts of the peasant world, the producers live far from the marketplace, and their wares are transported and sold by middlepersons. Thus the Tiv of Nigeria (Case 57) are likely to send their produce to urban markets via trucks operated by Tiv entrepreneurs; and the same patterns have emerged among the Simbu and other New Guinea peoples (see Brown 1995).

CASE

72

Markets in Haiti

There are some 65,000 market traders in Haiti—about 1 person out of 50 in the total population. Fifty thousand are women; in addition, most of the peasants who buy and sell in markets are women. A woman brings her crop to the marketplace, selling some export items like coffee to licensed buyers and selling the rest to *revendeuses,* market traders (Mintz 1959).

There are large market centers in the towns, connected by bus routes to numerous, less permanent rural marketplaces. Within a rural area, alternate marketplaces operate on different days, forming a "market ring" similar to those found in West Africa and Mexico.

Revendeuses can move and manipulate goods between marketplaces so as to buy and sell according to advantageous shifts in supply and demand. Many operate within a narrow geographical range on modest capital.

But larger-scale "operators" may move goods from one region to another or from urban center to countryside. Even larger-scale "operators" may buy manufactured or other goods in the main port and wholesale them to local market traders. Such "operators" obviously need more capital and maneuver financially on a larger scale than local market traders.

Such market operations have not eliminated the interpersonal relations of alliance and obligation as encountered in the Trobriands. For Haitians try to establish a favored trade relationship they call *pratik,* whereby particular partners transact recurrent business according to price or credit concessions (Mintz 1961). Thus there is a personal, not impersonal, relationship, and a sense of mutual obligation. A *revendeuse* tries to establish *pratik* connections, as many as possible, on both ends of her trading, to render supply and sale more secure.

Transactions are based on cash currency according to fluctuating supply and demand. The Haitian system works efficiently because small quantities are traded, crops are diversified (so risks are minimized).

Case Update
See Lundahl (1992) on Haitian markets and "underdevelopment."

An interesting pattern, where women act as entrepreneurs, occurs in Haiti, in the Caribbean. Case 72 describes this system.

The Peasant World View

The social and cultural conservatism of peasant communities, their inward orientation, has often been viewed as a major obstacle to progress. Suspicious of outsiders, hearkening to tradition—and suspicious of one another's means and motives—peasants are seen as prone to resist positive changes even when the means for community transformation are opened to them. Development projects that have attempted to improve the economic lot of peasants, in India, Indonesia, Latin America, and many other regions, have been frustrated by the apparent conservatism, inflexibility, and suspicion of peasant communities. Foster and many others have seen the peasant stance toward life—the world view we will shortly sketch, and the economic and social

CASE

73

CREFAL in Tzintzuntzan

The regional Center for the Development of Fundamental Education in Latin America (CREFAL) attempted to reorganize the economy of Tzintzuntzan by organizing the production of pottery, textiles, furniture, and embroidery for tourists, and introducing chicken ranching. Technicians were brought in. They persuaded potters to experiment with new kilns, created a weaving industry, established a furniture cooperative, and loaned money to begin six chicken ranching businesses. Yet within a fairly short time, these innovations had collapsed. Foster (1967) blames peasant conservatism, suspicion, and lack of motivation for the failure of the development project.

fragmentation—as thwarting effective social change. As presented in Case 73, Foster (1967) cites the example of a UNESCO-sponsored community development program which sought to improve the economic lot of the Tarascan-speaking Indians of Tzintzuntzan in Mexico.

The theme of desperate frustration but inability to transform or break out of the system in which they are enmeshed runs through the anthropological literature on peasants. It was summed up vividly by May Diaz:

> Peasants live in a social world in which they are economically and politically disadvantaged. They have neither sufficient capital nor power to make an impression on the urban society. But they have no illusions about their position. Indeed, often they have no notion at all of that imaginary world which offers social mobility, entrepreneurs . . . , and the possibility of economic growth, rather than a stability fluctuating on the edge of disaster. (Diaz 1967:56)

The morality and value system of peasants, and their view of the world and their place in it, show vividly the pathological side of peasant life. Peasants are locked into a world that has passed them by. It has condemned them to poverty in comparison to urban elites. Their status is demeaned on all sides, and their self-conception is eroded. Pride and achievement, as well as money and the material things it buys, can easily become scarce "goods."

Foster, drawing on his work in Tzintzuntzan, sees the peasant world view as characterized by the "image of limited good." That is, the peasant sees the social, economic, and natural universe "as one in which all the desired things in life such as land, wealth, health, friendship and love, manliness and honor, respect and status, power and influence, security and safety, exist in finite quantity and are always in short supply" (Foster 1965). From this would seem to follow the emphases many have noted in peasant societies: families competing independently against one another, with each seeking to conceal its advances and to guard against loss of relative position to others; competition for friendship and love, within families and outside them; preoccupation with health and illness; and an emphasis on manliness and honor (as with Mexican *machismo*).

The religious ceremonials and ritual offices of Latin American peasants can be seen in part as leveling devices, as in Amatenango and Zinacantan. Ritual office requires the outlay of money in exchange for a prestige that is soon dissipated. By going to the top of the religious ladder, a man slides back down the economic ladder to join his fellows. (But see §51 for a rediscussion on this point.)

51. PEASANT STUDIES: BROADENED PERSPECTIVES

This picture of peasants, some recent critics have argued, is precisely the one an observer gets if for the purposes of study one immerses oneself in a single community and takes the wider society for granted. It sees symptoms, not causes; it sees fragments, not systems; and it sees timelessness, not long-term process. The system to which peasants are adapting, and the strategies they have devised to cope with it, are usually products of centuries of exploitation, in successive modes or phases.

Some of the shortcomings of the conventional picture of peasants can be set out under a series of topical headings. To see others we will need—in the next chapter—to step back and take a still broader perspective in time and space.

Peasant Communities in Regional Systems

Important insights have come from looking at peasant communities not one at a time, but in regional clusters. One line of analysis has been the historical study by G. William Skinner of regional economy and marketing systems in traditional China. Skinner has shown that in rural China, microregions shaped by physical geography comprised systems, with peasant communities tied to one another through focal towns on the basis of markets (Skinner 1964–1965, 1977). This work, carried further by Skinner's students (Smith 1976, vols. I and II), brings anthropologists into close communication with economic geographers.

Integration of peasant communities into regional systems—which the anthropologist working in a single community would inevitably miss—has been recorded in many peasant areas. Thus in Spain, Aguilera (1978) found in the Andalusian province of Huelva a "multicommunity" of 17 peasant communities, linked together by a common cultural pattern, economic linkages, and shared rituals.

The incorporation of peasant communities into wider regional systems has been viewed in a rather different light by Marxist scholars such as the Mexican sociologist Rodolfo Stavenhagen. His reinterpretations give sharp insights into the apparent survival of Mayan culture in communities such as Zinacantan (Cases 59, 68, and 71). Case 74 presents Stavenhagen's regional and historical perspective of relations between Mayan-speaking Indians and Spanish-speaking Ladinos.

Note that in perceiving the importance of regional systems in shaping the place of peasants and the nature of peasant communities, we are expanding our vision in exactly the same way, and the same directions, as we have done earlier with regard to the tribal world (Chapter 5, §45). In fact, the broadening of vision has mainly gone in the other direction, in anthropology. Discovering belatedly that peasant villages were not self-contained, separate, and without histories, anthropologists began to perceive that tribal societies, from which their original expectations had been drawn, were likewise not the separate pieces of a vast mosaic they had seemed to be.

The Internal Structure of Peasant Communities

In looking at the social organization of peasant communities in terms of models derived from the tribal world, anthropologists have been prone to find the remnant traces of lineages or Omaha kinship terminologies, and prone to miss internal class structures or differentials in wealth and status. New perspectives on the cargo systems of such Mayan-speaking communities of Zinacantan (Case 71) will serve to illustrate.

It is becoming clear that although the cargo systems do force the prosperous peasant to redistribute much of his wealth, they do not always cycle him back to the lower levels of the economic ladder. In highland Maya communities, as in peasant communities more generally, there very often is considerable economic inequality between families; and a ceremonial system that is costly but prestigious can be an instrument through which prosperity buys longer-range power, not simply a year's prominence. Anthropologists have often underestimated the economic inequalities in peasant communities (partly because family budgets are so often well hidden).

This can well take us back to the question, raised in the last section, of a "peasant mode of production" based on production, consumption, and economic decision-making within separate households. (Recall pottery production in Amatenango, another Mayan community, in Case 70.) The problem with such a view of households as the separate economic atoms of which peasant society is built is its failure to analyze the system of social relations on which production, appropriation, distribution, and use— as well as the reproduction of the social system—depend.

Analysis of the social relations of production. . . [must] include the relations *between* units of production [that is, peasant households], between various classes [e.g., Amatenango villagers, Ladino shopkeepers, government officials, plantation owners], and the relations of the process of *social* reproduction (no household can satisfy the conditions of its own reproduction . . .). (Bernstein 1979:422)

An analysis that takes the peasant community as "the social system," and its component families or kin group as units, will hide the class structure and dynamics of the system of which peasants are a part. It is likely to blind us to economic and political realities inside, as well as outside, the community.

Peasant Communities in History

Models and expectations derived from anthropological study of tribal societies have often deflected understanding of the historical forces that have shaped peasant communities. Again we can illustrate with the cargo systems of highland Maya communities. Recently discovered historical documents reveal how the cults of saints were specifically created by the Spanish conquerors according to a detailed plan, as one instrument for the subjugation and Christianization of the Indians. It remains true that the Indians turned the cults into their own distinctive cultural design. Yet the tendency to see the cargo systems, and Mayan religious syncretism generally, in cultural rather than historical terms further suggests the cost of bringing to peasant communities the theoretical orientations derived from studying tribal communities. In fact, evidence on the long-term history of Zinacantan (Cases 59, 68, and 71) suggests that far from being a closed little pocket where an ancient Mayan culture survived despite the Spanish conquest and the superficial imposition of Christianity, these

CASE

74

Mayan-Ladino Economic Relationships in Chiapas

San Cristobal las Casas, a town of some 30,000 in a highland valley of Chiapas, southern Mexico, is the center of a regional economy in which the Indians—some 200,000 of them scattered in villages and hamlets in the surrounding mountains (communities such as Zinacantan and Amatenango)—are systematically controlled and exploited by Ladino landowners and merchants. In their studies of the cultural conser-

vatism of the Indian communities, anthropologists have mainly ignored the exploitative class relationships that bind Indians into poverty, and indeed have mainly paid scant attention in their published work to Indian-Ladino relations. As noted by Stavenhagen:

The well-known bargaining of Indian markets is an instrument used by Ladinos in order to

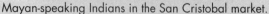
Mayan-speaking Indians in the San Cristobal market.

depress price levels of Indian products. In San Cristobal . . . the Ladino women who place themselves at the city entrance on market days . . . almost violently force the submissive, incoming Indians to sell their wares at prices that they impose and which are lower than those which prevail at the market.

These various forms of exploitation which victimize the Indian trader, both as seller and buyer, are due to economic and political dominance of the urban Ladinos. This power is reinforced by the cultural superiority as expressed by their knowledge of price-building mechanisms, of the laws of the country; above all, of the Spanish language which . . . represents one more factor of inferiority and social oppression. . . . Under these conditions, the Indian has no access to national legal institutions which protect his individual rights. (Stavenhagen 1975:254)

Although at first sight *compadrazgo* [see Case 69] may appear to be an institution in which Indians and Ladinos face each other on a level of equality, in fact it contributes to accentuate the Indians' condition of inferiority and dependence. *Compadrazgo* is one among many institutions in a complex system which keeps the Indian subordinated to the Ladino in all aspects of social and economic life. . . .

[The cargo system in such communities as Zinacantan prevents] economic preeminence of those individuals who for some reason have been able to accumulate a greater amount of goods than their peers. This wealth is not reabsorbed by the community, it is consumed in liquor, ceremonial clothing, firecrackers and fire-works, and in hundreds of articles employed in. . . "institutionalized waste." These expenses required by the ceremonial economy associated with the functioning of the political and religious organizations are transformed into income for those who provide these articles for the community. These purveyors are urbanized Ladinos. . . . We may thus conclude that the structure which maintains equality within the Indian community, preventing the emergence of social classes, also contributes to the whole Indian community's dependence on the city, that is, to the differentiation of social classes between Indians and Ladinos. (Stavenhagen 1975:255, 259)

Stavenhagen argues that the very old relationship of internal colonialism between Ladinos and Indians, whereby Indians maintained relatively closed communities and cultural integrity at a cost of subordination, exploitation, and racism, is being transformed by the emergence of a class system due to the capitalist development of the region. Having lost much of their best land to Ladinos in the process of "land reform," and being threatened by overpopulation and ecological destruction, with erosion of their subsistence base, Indians are increasingly locked into exploitative wage labor on coffee plantations and in other Ladino enterprises. And as they increasingly become plantation laborers, an older system of ethnic domination is being transformed to a class relationship between capitalist and worker (Stavenhagen 1975).

Case Update

For more in-depth information, see Stavenhagen's later work (1990) on the development of interethnic issues in class contexts.

The reader is also referred to the work of Whitmeyer and Hopcroft (1995) on the Chiapas Rebellion.

valleys have been massively affected by, and open to, the world beyond for many centuries. Seven hundred years ago, Zinacantan was an Aztec garrison.

Even Stavenhagen's broadened view of Mayan Indian-Ladino relationships around San Cristobal las Casas (Case 74) does not take sufficient account of the complex regional economic system as it has evolved historically. Studies of communities such as Zinacantan in relation to the economic history of the region show that the orientation of these villagers has changed markedly in the last century. Ironically, the period of the 1960s when these communities were intensively studied by anthropologists was a time when land reform measures and regional economic conditions allowed peasant farmers greater independence from Ladino authorities and landowners than, perhaps, at any time since the sixteenth century. The Zinacanteco farmers of the 1960s had access to sufficient land to enable them to ignore much of the Ladino cultural and political world; the Zinacanteco community of this period looked like a cultural isolate, inwardly oriented. The parents and grandparents of these farmers, however, had been deeply dependent upon Ladino economic institutions for access to the means of a livelihood, and had had to become engaged—personally, and as a community—with the Ladino world; people of these generations often spoke much better Spanish than their children and grandchildren do today, and had traveled more widely and known more people from outside the Zinacanteco community than it was common to do in the 1960s. The cultural conservatism and partial closure of the Zinacanteco community observed by anthropologists was less a continuation of an old tradition, girded against penetration from the outside, than a response to the

opportunity to retreat from disadvantageous participation in Ladino institutions, an opportunity which was structured by changes in economic and political circumstances (Haviland 1979).

Conservatism, Fatalism, and Peasant Struggle

Close immersion in the life of a tribal or peasant community for a year or two, then, has often given a limited view in time as well as in space. Stereotypes of the conservatism, docility, and fatalism of the peasant bear closer inspection from this point of view.

First, peasant hostility and suspicion to outsiders—whether indigenous urban landowner or anthropologist or Peace Corps volunteer or CREFAL technician—is historically well founded and realistic. Centuries of lies, oppression, and forced servitude hardly make either trust of outsiders or the optimism of Protestant ethic entrepreneurship a realistic stance. (See Harris 1971:475–487, Huizer 1970.) Also, the progressive transformation of the modes and structures of exploitation over many decades and centuries has seldom improved the peasant's lot: to be optimistic that well-intentioned programs for education or economic development will markedly improve conditions would hardly be realistic—or wise.

And this leads to a second major inadequacy of the "peasant fatalism" view, emphasizing as it does passive resignation, destructive internal conflict, and ignorance of the wider world. Peasants in certain parts of the world have risen, time and time again, to try to break the bonds of oppression and the chains that tie them in servitude and poverty (see Case 75, for example).

CASE

7 5

Peasant Resistance in Michoacan

In the Mexican state of Michoacan, Tarascan peasants—whose forefathers had resisted Toltec and Aztec domination—rose in the 1920s against oppression by wealthy landowners and their allies in the Church. The Michoacan Socialist Party, some of whose members came from Tzintzuntzan and surrounding communities, demanded land redistribution—and the leaders were liquidated by government forces in 1921. Tarascan peasant villagers, led by Primo Tapia of Naranja (Huizer 1970; Murgica 1946), contin-ued to press their claims for land reform:

In 1923 many peasants from the Liga of Michoacan participated in the 1 Congreso Nacional Agrarista in Mexico City. Primo Tapia brought with him a proposal for a new agrarian law . . . to give . . . workers living on haciendas full rights to petition for land. Another issue was

that large units for the cultivation of sisal, cotton, sugar, henequen, or rice would not be left untouched but given as a whole to the peasants. . . . One of the major manifestations of the Liga was a demonstration of 8,000 peasants at the railway station of Patzcuaro [only a few miles from Tzintzuntzan] when the presidential train passed. (Huizer 1970:453)

Primo Tapia succeeded in forcing some land re-distribution. But in 1926 he was shot by the army.

Case Update

For a report on attempts at agrarian reform in Michoacan during the twentieth century, see the work of Gledhill (1991).

Foster has commented on the wide gulf between the conservative and passive people of Tzintzuntzan (they of the "limited good") and the historically activist peasants of some Tarascan communities, notably Naranja, near Primo Tapia's home village where land redistribution was successfully pressed. But Huizer (1970), citing evidence from Van Zantwijk (1967), suggests that the passivity and conservatism of the Tzintzuntzenos had not prevented their struggling against oppression in the 1920s; rather, he suggests that peasant resistance has been broken under pressure by the Church and wealthy landowners. "The communities where the image of the lim-ited good prevails suffered severe physical

and spiritual repression from a combination of the landed elite and the religious author-ities" (Huizer 1970:304). Conservatism in the face of oppression becomes a survival strategy: "Traditionalism is . . . related to the over-all social structure of the country as a form of protection against the dangers of pauperization."

The "conservatism" of peasants in being unreceptive to development projects is of-ten sound, historically conditioned, politi-cal strategy for peasants who have no reason to trust outsiders who command wealth and power. Even if the aid projects are well conceived and sensitive to cultural nuances (as they most often have not been), they promise piecemeal and gradual improvement. Such piecemeal aid promised by economic development specialists to improve peasant standards of living aims at alleviating symptoms rather than curing causes. Its usual goals, implicit or explicit, have been to decrease peasant unrest by alleviating peasant poverty—and thereby, to reinforce the oppressive structure of landowning elites and foreign investment that keeps peasants in bondage. Small wonder that peasants do not embrace such projects as paths to salvation. Of the abortive CREFAL project in Tzintzuntzan (Case 73), Huizer (1970:305) points to this contradiction: "We can ... ask how the peasants living under these circumstances would have reacted if the visitors from the development agencies had come to help them fight against the repressive system instead of to offer minor improvement schemes which would actually emphasize rather than relieve the state of frustration in which the peasants live."

Peasant Wars and Revolutions

Peasant struggles against oppression, such as that led by Primo Tapia, have occurred in many parts of the world (see, for example, Wolf 1969a). In Mesoamerica, the Mayan Indians of the highlands rose against their oppressors, in the nineteenth century in messianic form, but earlier with guerilla resistance. The lowland Mayans of Yucatan were in revolt and virtual secession through much of the nineteenth century before they were subdued into a system of exploitation in the production of henequen fiber for rope (Reed 1965).

In Indonesia, some 200,000 Javanese died in an unsuccessful struggle for liberation from Dutch rule between 1825 and 1830. The Philippine revolution of 1896 to 1898 was in part, as earlier in South America, a struggle by a local landed aristocracy created by colonialism for independence from a weakened colonial power, Spain. But it was also, in rural areas, a peasant revolt. The Philippine revolution succeeded in wresting power from Spain, only to fall victim to invasion by the United States (Pomeroy 1970). In a bloody war with many parallels to the war in Vietnam, Philippine independence was crushed by the U.S. army at a cost of some 500,000 lives (Pomeroy 1970:96); and the Philippines became an American colony.

The relatively circumscribed and partial view peasants have of their society exacts a cost when they take up arms. Peasant rebellions seldom have turned into successful revolutions without a vanguard of leadership from urban centers. As Wolf observes:

> Where the peasantry has successfully rebelled against the established order—under its own banner and with its own leaders—it was sometimes able to reshape the social structures of the countryside . . . ; but it did not lay hold of the State, of the cities which house the centers of control, of the strategic nonagricultural resources of the society. . . . Thus a peasant rebellion which takes place in a complex society already caught up in commercialization and industrialization tends to be self-limiting, and hence anachronistic. [See Debray 1967 for an argument of the vulnerability of peasant rebellions to outside repression.] The peasant Utopia is the free village, untrammeled by tax collectors, labor recruiters, large landowners, officials. Ruled over, but never ruling, peasants also lack any acquaintance with the operation of the State as a complex machinery. . . . Peasants in rebellion are natural anarchists. (Wolf 1969b:371–372)

Wolf argues, on the basis of comparative study of the revolutions in Mexico, Russia,

China, Vietnam, Algeria, and Cuba where peasants played a central part, that those peasants likely to rise successfully are not the poorest and landless; rather, they are the middle peasants who have sufficient control or leverage over their own resources to rise in challenge to their overlords. Wolf's study also points to another peasant condition likely to breed or catalyze rebellion: relative marginality, and hence relative freedom from outside control, and relative mobility. Wolf points to the participation of a "tactically mobile peasantry" (particularly a peasantry ethnically distinct from more centrally located groups, and with mountain fastnesses to retreat to) in twentieth-century wars of revolution (Wolf 1969a, 1969b).

Peasant Communities in National and International Systems

Peasant communities, especially in these times of multinational corporations, jet tourism, and the worldwide spread of technology, are increasingly caught up in systems far beyond their immediate view. How to conceptualize this incorporation of hinterland communities into the world system poses deep problems.

Peasants from remote villages in the deserts of Rajasthan work on road construction in New Delhi. Turkish villagers build BMW's in Munich. Mexican villagers send their children one after another, to work in Mexico City. How can we conceptualize such connections? How can we conceptualize the flow of knitted shawls or sweaters from a Latin American community into the boutiques of the United States and Europe—or the flow of opium from a peaceful village in the mountains of Burma or Thailand into the ghettos of New York? Peasant villagers in South Korea and Taiwan assemble TV sets and stitch the shirts we wear. All over the world peasants are being incorporated into a global capitalist system, are becoming proletarians as well as peasants. This incorporation does not necessarily entail a transformation from traditional peasant society and culture in the direction of modernization. It can be argued, in fact, that in Latin America, Europe, and other parts of the world where peasant villages and cities coexist, each is dependent on the other. The reason, paradoxically, why peasant villages have remained culturally and politically conservative— why, in Marxist terms, peasant ways of life have continued to "reproduce" themselves—is paradoxically not their isolation *from* urban society and economy but their incorporation *into* it.

There are two sides to this. First, contrary to the stereotypes of the 1960s, peasants need not always abandon traditional ways in order to modernize in some respects or to adapt to a pattern of industrial wage labor in alien settings. There is no necessary contradiction in a Turk working on a BMW assembly line one month and tending his flock the next. Thus:

> Modernization can no longer be equated simply with the destruction of tradition, for the latter is not a prerequisite of modernization. . . . In many instances "traditional" institutions and values may facilitate rather than impede the social changes usually associated with modernization. (Tipps 1973:214)

The second side of this apparent paradox of the coexistence of the old and new, the rural and the urban, is the way that the perpetuation of peasant life may depend on the availability of outside economic opportunities. It may be assembling BMW's that makes herding sheep a viable way of life, given staggering inflation, population increase, and fluctuating economic fortunes in an Anatolian village. Likewise, on the island of Whalsay in the Shetlands, Scotland, crofting can continue only because of its coexistence with expensive, modern ways of fishing (Cohen 1987). Thus, to understand how local worlds and the global one fit together, we need to take a wider field of view, in time and in space.

SUMMARY

Peasants belong both to subsistence economies and to world markets and occupy relatively powerless positions in the market context. The term *peasant* has been used to cover a number of different categories within this broad framework, from landowners to serfs bound in feudal contracts to a lord, so it is risky to generalize about their situation. (Feudal ties also differ in context.) In terms of their social organization, unilineal descent groups may be important (example: Zinacantan), and godparental ties may play a significant role (example: *compadrazgo* in Mexico). Their social organization channels the degree of their participation in a cash economy and the internal stratification patterns that may arise from this (example: pottery production in Amatenango). In Zinacantan the local system of feasting with a hierarchy of religious offices known as "cargos" acts in part to level economic inequalities between persons. Women may be important traders (example: Haiti).

Earlier scholars portrayed peasants as unable to respond to opportunities of modernization because of their inherent conservatism and suspicion of one another, what George Foster called "the image of limited good." More recently scholars have argued that peasants are participants in regional economic networks, in which, however, they may be disadvantaged, a process that intensifies with class relations of production. In peasant communities themselves economic inequalities do arise. Retreating inwards may be a response to stresses imposed from outside rather than a product of tradition or conservatism.

Peasants have sometimes organized resistance and rebellion (example: Michoacan in Mexico). They are more likely to be successful if they are economically reasonably established. They are incorporated into national and global systems nowadays, and are sometimes able to maintain their own ways of living while fully participating in new economic processes. Indeed, money gained from such processes may be used to subsidize their traditional lifestyles.

SUGGESTIONS FOR FURTHER READING

SECTIONS 49–51
Bock, P. K., ed. 1968. *Peasants in the Modern World.* Albuquerque: University of New Mexico Press.
Critchfield, R. 1973. *The Golden Bowl Be Broken: Peasant Life in Four Cultures.* Bloomington, Ind.: Indiana University Press.
Gamst, F. C. 1974. *Peasants in a Complex Society.* New York: Holt, Rinehart and Winston.
Galjart, B. F. 1976. *Peasant Mobilization and Solidarity.* New York: Humanities Press, Inc.
Halperin, R., and J. Dow. 1977. *Peasant Livelihood: Studies in Economic Anthropology and Cultural Ecology.* New York: St. Martin's Press.
Hobsbawm, E. J. 1959. *Primitive Rebels.* New York: The Free Press.
Potter, J. M., M. N. Diaz, and G. M. Foster, eds. 1967. *Peasant Society: A Reader.* Boston: Little, Brown and Company.

Redfield, R. 1956. *Peasant Society and Culture.* Chicago: University of Chicago Press.

Shanin, T. ed. 1972. *Peasants and Peasant Societies.* New York: Penguin Books, Inc.

Stavenhagen, R. 1975. *Social Classes in Agrarian Societies.* Garden City, N. Y.: Doubleday and Company, Inc.

Wolf, E. R. 1966. *Peasants.* Englewood Cliffs, N. J.: Prentice-Hall, Inc.

Worsley, P. 1970. *The Third World.* Chicago: University of Chicago Press.

(See also references for Sections 52–55 for imperialism and its consequences.)

Colonialism and Postcolonialism

In Chapter 17, we looked at the impact of European invasion and colonial domination on tribal peoples. We saw how peoples such as the Tiv, with traditional economies oriented to subsistence and exchange, were caught up into a world capitalist economy. In Chapter 18, looking at peasants in Mayan communities in southern Mexico and in other settings, we saw how peasants are caught up in wider social and economic systems.

We need now to examine the forces of political economy that led to the emergence of the contemporary postcolonial world—what are sometimes called the "underdeveloped countries." To understand how inequalities in wealth and development have emerged and how they are sustained requires that we take a global and historical perspective, although inevitably this must be very brief and partial. Without understanding the creation of this situation, we cannot understand the causes of poverty, hunger, exploitation, and dependency, and thus acquire the power to be positive agents of change and participants in the struggle for human survival.

We need to go back to the view of the world as the system we took fleetingly in §46, and render it more coherent. But first, we need a more clear conception of our goal. It will be useful to set out a series of assumptions about the contemporary world and the causes of underdevelopment that have guided the policies and thinking of the developed Western countries—and then to see how and why we must go beyond them.

52. THE ROOTS OF POVERTY AND UNDERDEVELOPMENT: A CONVENTIONAL VIEW

The postcolonial countries, although diverse, are viewed (in some traditions of Western politics and scholarship) as beset by problems that derive from the nature of the traditional modes of life and society from which they were formed. Although not all these characterizations are true in all cases, they are viewed as a family of problems postcolonial countries will have to overcome as best as possible if they are to develop. We can set them out as a series of assumptions.

The Problems of Postcolonial Countries

1. "Traditional" modes of social organization, values, and customs are by their nature conservative, and retard social change—which requires individual initiative, risk-taking, innovation, and

Young man wearing shirt of a Highlands political party at a funerary occasion. Melpa, Papua New Guinea.

freedom from constraints of kinship or customary obligation.

2. Postcolonial countries, characteristically pieced together from a series of linguistically and culturally disparate societies, are fraught with internal conflict and "tribalism." (Here, Africa serves as the prime and oft-cited example.)

3. In postcolonial countries, rural areas are locked into traditional systems of land tenure and cultivation that are technologically backward, oriented heavily to subsistence, and prevented by the small-scale, inefficiency, and traditional organization of society from achieving intensified production. The

traditional orientation, and large and growing populations, of rural areas bind their inhabitants into perpetual poverty, while at the same time failing to generate, through export, the capital required for economic growth.

The Challenge of Modernization

Seeing postcolonial societies in such terms, one then is led to view them as composed economically of two "sectors"—the *"traditional"* sector, as we have described it, and a *modernizing* sector, characterized by capitalist economic organization, a developing middle class with Western aspirations and values, and economic growth spurred by the export of minerals or other raw materials and/or by industrial development spurred by foreign capital.

The challenge of development, once one takes this view, is clear enough. The modernizing sector is the source of economic growth. The goal must then be to expand this sector—expand it through capital investment (mainly foreign) in towns and cities, expand it into the rural hinterlands by inducing peasants to move into wage labor in cities and factories, and by transforming the technology and economic organization of agriculture so as to intensify production (as in the "green revolution" discussed later in this chapter) and thus generate export revenue and feed growing populations.

> Development is defined as a set of interdependent processes through which a "traditional" social structure is transformed into a "modern" social structure. . . .
> The result has been a pervasive tendency to label as "traditional" any characteristic of the underdeveloped world which has been an obstacle to development. (Rhodes 1970:i)

The implication is that these "traditional" modes of life, structures of economy and society, were there when colonialism began, were only partly transformed in the colonial period, and must now be left behind if modernization is to succeed. When we are able to see what is wrong with these stereotypes, we will be able to see more clearly the realities underlying the myths, to see where the sources of poverty and hunger lie, and thus to see alternative paths.

53. THE DEVELOPMENT OF UNDERDEVELOPMENT

This conventional view of the underdeveloped countries in effect denies them a history:

> To classify these countries as "traditional societies" . . . implies either that the underdeveloped countries have no history or that it is unimportant. (Griffin 1969:69)

But it is increasingly clear that the history of the postcolonial countries has been crucially important in shaping their present underdevelopment:

> The expansion of Europe, commencing in the fifteenth century, had a profound impact on the societies and economies of the rest of the world. In other words, the history of the underdeveloped countries in the last five centuries is, in large part, the history of the consequences of European expansion. . . . The international economy [through which Europe came to dominate the non-European world] first created underdevelopment and then hindered efforts to escape from it. In summary, underdevelopment is a product of historical processes. (Griffin 1969:69)

The most influential proponent of the thesis that European expansion and colonialism created the underdevelopment of these countries has been André Gunder

Frank. Frank's sweeping and provocative interpretations of the colonization of Latin America and its consequences have inspired research and stirred controversy.

Dependency Theory

Frank's thesis is that underdevelopment is not basically a consequence of traditionalism. Rather, he argues that underdevelopment in Latin America—and by extension, parts of Africa and Asia—has been systematically created by colonialist exploitation. Frank has documented "the development of underdevelopment" in Chile, Brazil, Mexico, and Cuba (Frank 1969, 1973, 1978):

> The regions of Latin America which are today the most backward—parts of Central America and the Caribbean, the Northeast of Brazil, the areas in the Andes and in Mexico where the indigenous population predominates, and the mining zones of Brazil, Bolivia, and Central Mexico—have in common the fact that in the early period (and, in many cases, in the present as well), they were the areas where the exploitation of natural, and to an even greater extent human, resources was most extreme. . . . The degree and type of dependence on the metropolis of the world capitalist system is the key factor in the economic and class structure of Latin America. (Frank 1973:21–22)

Frank's studies show how the constant drain of wealth from the areas of Latin America most productive in the colonial and postcolonial periods produced incredible poverty and not only hampered but systematically destroyed indigenous economic development. He also shows how the emergence of a Latin American landowning bourgeoisie was shaped by European interests. What was demanded of Mesoamerican or Andean peoples, how landowning interests operated, and whether exploitation took the form of mining or the production of sugar, coffee, bananas, or other commodities depended on the fluctuations of world capitalism:

> Because of commerce and foreign capital, the economic and political interests of the mining, agricultural, and commercial bourgeoisie were never directed toward internal economic development. The relations of production and the class structure of the latifundia and of mining and its economic and social "hinterlands" developed in response to the predatory needs of the overseas and the Latin American metropolis. They were not the result of the transfer, in the sixteenth century, of Iberian feudal institutions to the New World, as is so often and so erroneously alleged. (Frank 1973:23)

> What happened in the colony was determined by its ties with the metropolis and by the intrinsic nature of the capitalist system. It was not isolation but integration which created the reality of Brazilian underdevelopment. The life of the interior was determined through a whole chain of metropolises and satellites which extended from England via Portugal and Salvador de Bahia or Rio de Janeiro to the farthest outpost of this interior. (Frank 1969:166)

Frank quotes old sources that show clearly how shifts in trade or European politics and economics, and events around the colonial world, affected the systems of exploitation and domination in various parts of Latin America. Thus in 1794, the viceroy of New Spain wrote warning the king about the growth of local manufacture in Mexico that had arisen initially during an economic depression in Spain:

> With no help of any kind . . . they have progressed enormously; to such a degree that one is amazed by certain types of manufactures, principally cottons and cloth for rebozos [shawls]. . . . In these domains it is very difficult to prohibit the manufacture of those things which are made here. . . . The only

way to destroy such local manufactures would be to send the same or similar products from Europe, to be sold at lower prices. This is what has happened to the great factory and guild which existed for all sorts of silk textiles, now barely remembered. (Frank 1973:24)

From Mexico, Frank quotes contemporary assessments of the Mexican peasantry under General Diaz, a period which saw "the systematic organization of capitalist regime":

In a short time, a large number of latifundia were established, and the popular *caudillos* [military leaders] of the Diaz revolution, along with a large number of foreigners, formed a landed aristocracy. At the same time, the Church quickly recovered its former power by purchasing haciendas through intermediaries or inheriting them from the dying, who were terrified by visions of hell's fires. . . . Daily, the consequences of this policy became more evident. Larger harvests were gathered every year, land values rose and labor costs fell steadily, and the wretchedness of the poor deepened as the wealth of the landowners increased. Thus, capitalist organization proved to be the most effective method of increasing the enslavement and poverty of the people and aggravating the inequalities between the poor and the rich. (Gonzalez Roa and Jose Covarrubias, quoted in Frank 1973:39)

Frank argues that "independence" in Latin America accompanied the decline of Spanish and Portuguese power and the increasing power and wealth of the New World creole bourgeoisie who controlled mines and lands but not politics. The liberal philosophy of the eighteenth century, which in Europe had advanced the interests of the industrial bourgeoisie was adopted in Latin America to advance the interests of the landholders and mine owners. The political ascendancy of a landed aristocracy in Latin America, drawing its wealth from export, systematically generated the underdevelopment of rural peasantry and established the structure of class exploitation and internal colonialism that continued into the 1970s.

Frank shows that it has mainly been those regions of the Americas which did not provide the incentive for plantations, mines, or other modes of economic exploitation (because of poor climate, sparse resources, low population, or marginality) that have become most prosperous and developed in the twentieth century. He shows how historically areas such as Cuba, Barbados, and parts of Colombia were prosperous and rapidly developing economically until shifts in capitalist investment and trade brought plantation economies and the destruction of local prosperity.

Frank's theoretical framework is cast in terms of relationships between European centers and the outposts in the colonies, and between the colonial port towns and the hinterland. Frank sees colonialism as creating constellations of economic interest, each with what he calls a "metropolis" at its center and with "satellite" economic regions or sectors; these satellites may, on a smaller scale, consist of a minor metropolis and its satellites. What is a metropolis at one level is thus a satellite of some larger metropolis. (See Frank 1969:15–17; for a later restatement of his views in general, see Frank 1975).

Other, closely related analyses of the historical creation of underdevelopment and dependency in Latin America have been advanced by Celse Furtado, Theotonio dos Santos, and others. What is called "dependency theory," in contrast to orthodox "development theory," has made a considerable impact in academic circles.

Can we extend dependency theory to the analysis of colonial Africa, to South and Southeast Asia? Much rethinking needs to be done. It would seem that a parallel colonialist development of underdevelopment has produced similar class polarization and desperate poverty among exploited peasants in Southeast Asia. Thus we find in Indonesia, Sri Lanka, Malaysia, the Philippines, and other areas the same polarization, the same poverty. The continuous stream of modernization and development in Japan, and its present wealth and prosperity in contrast to its neighbors to the southwest, further supports Frank's interpretation: whereas in most of South and Southeast Asia wealth was drained off for several centuries, Japan remained free of colonial domination and developed on an impressive upward course. The contrast with colonially exploited Indonesia, especially Java—where Dutch investment was greatest—is stark. The disastrous course of what Geertz (1963) called "agricultural

Agricultural involution in Java: The development of underdevelopment through colonial exploitation. The population explosion in colonial Java and the draining off of wealth by the Dutch has left Javanese peasants on a treadmill where more and more people must be fed with less and less efficiency and possibility for economic growth.

involution" in Indonesia, where more and more people have squeezed out a decreasingly adequate subsistence with decreasing efficiency, was the product of a colonialism that poured profits back to the metropolis. (See also Kahn 1993 on such processes in Minangkabau history.)

But while the central tenets of dependency theory are being reinforced by the research and rethinking it has inspired, defects and oversimplifications are also emerging. There are inadequacies in both "ends" of dependency theory: that is, in its conceptualization of the developing world capitalist system that generated expansion and penetration of lands far across the seas from Europe, and in its conceptualization and analysis of the internal structure of colonial societies and economies.

Center and Periphery in the Modern World System

A major view of the dynamics of European expansion was advanced by Immanuel Wallerstein in his analysis, *The Modern World-System* (1974). Wallerstein builds on the work of economic historians in creating a brilliant synthesis. He looks at an economic system centered in Europe, from medieval times on, as a miniature "world system." This world system incorporated separate political entities but was tied together by internal trade and common stances to the other "world systems" centered in the Islamic Middle East and in China. The progressive expansion of the European world, in a quest for wealth, booty, and monopoly by the competing states, penetrated the Americas in the sixteenth century and extended European trade into Asia and Africa.

In his conceptualization of a "world economic system," Wallerstein insists that in the sixteenth and seventeenth centuries the

European world system did not include the whole world. But what, then, were its bounds, and why?

> In the sixteenth century there was a *European world economy*, [but its] . . . boundaries [were] less than the earth as a whole. We cannot simply include in it any part of the world with which "Europe" traded. In 1600 Portugal traded with the central African kingdom of Monomotapa as well as with Japan. Yet it would be . . . hard to argue that either Monomotapa or Japan were part of the European world-economy at that time. (Wallerstein 1974:301)

Wallerstein distinguishes between the *periphery* of a world economy (which is included within it) and its *external arena* (which is tied to it by trade, but not part of it):

> In the sixteenth century, Iberia [Spain and Portugal] establishes *colonies* in the Americas, but *trading-posts* in Asia. . . . The reasons for the two different policies seem to be . . . twofold. On the one hand, the rewards of American colonization were much greater. On the other hand, the difficulties of colonizing Asia were much greater. . . . [Thus] the Americas became the *periphery* of the European world-economy in the sixteenth century while Asia remained an *external arena*. . . . It is only in the periphery that the economically more powerful group is able to reinforce its position by cultural domination as well. (Wallerstein 1974:332–339)

Wallerstein's global analysis of the dynamics of European expansion reinforces the foundations of dependency theory and opens many possibilities for research. But it leaves relatively unexamined the internal structure of the periphery (which initially included the Americas but in the eighteenth and nineteenth centuries extended to incorporate much of Africa and South and

Southeast Asia). Eric Wolf (1982) examines this issue and many others with historical detail in an attempt to "give back" their histories to peoples seen as being "without history."

Economy and Class Relations on the Periphery

Further refinements of dependency theory are coming from closer historical analyses of class relations and internal economy within the colonized periphery. Thus (to take an example from anthropology), Smith examines economy and class relations in Guatemala in terms of dependency theory and Wallerstein's conceptualization of relations between European "core" and colonial periphery.

Smith attempts to build further on the foundations of dependency theory. Frank had taken the organization of economy *within* the periphery to be essentially similar to the relationship between mother country and colony. That is, La Paz was a satellite of Spain but was a metropolis in relation to the satellite towns of the hinterlands. Smith seeks to carry both Wallerstein's and Frank's analyses further. She uses the evidence from Guatemala to argue that kinds of connections of marketing and administration quite different from metropolis-satellite ties linked urban centers to the hinterlands: the organization of colonial peripheries was more complex than Frank's model would suggest. The Guatemalan case shows, moreover, that the economy of the periphery may have an internal dynamic of its own, that is not simply a reflex (as Wallerstein would seem to imply) of what is happening in the European "core." Smith's conclusions, though they push us beyond simple conceptions of the development of underde-

velopment, further reinforce the following viewpoint:

> Capitalism everywhere creates and depends upon the development of some parts [of the world system] and the underdevelopment of other parts. (Smith 1978:611)

Other reformulations of the Frankian view attempt a more complex and sophisticated analysis of class relationships and modes of production in colonial and postcolonial societies. Such analyses link the colonial past with the postcolonial present. They challenge liberal stereotypes of the "traditional sector" (§52), viewing the class relationships within which peasants in the hinterlands are bound as creations of capitalism and colonialism, rather than holdovers from the precolonial past that impede development. Some scholars have argued that the economics of the rural hinterlands are systematically undermined by economic growth, spurred by foreign investment, in the cities. As Smith put it:

> Rural people, rather than being directly exploited as in the . . . earlier . . . system, are simply marginalized—left to fend for themselves in the depopulating rural hinterlands. The economic growth that takes place in the . . . urban centers of Latin America is, of course, funded for the most part by foreign investors, who also take most of the profits. But the most serious problem with this kind of dependency is that it deprives many . . . of the means for achieving even a peasant standard of living. (Smith 1978:576)

Again it will be useful to look beyond Latin America to see the historical roots of postcolonial poverty. Case 76, for example, examines the rural poverty of India and Bangladesh. There is more to it than meets the eye.

CASE

76

Historical Roots of Poverty in India

Here only a few facets of an enormously complex history can be sketched. First, when the British (through the East India Company) gained control of eastern India, very substantial local industries (particularly in textiles) supported tens of thousands of workers. Indian industry was (like the textile industry in Mexico) destroyed by the colonial power.

From time immemorial India had developed cotton manufacture into a great art. It had once found ready vent in Egypt and Imperial Rome, and was no less avidly sought by the Arabs till the sixteenth and the Europeans till the eighteenth century. Spinning and weaving had become a national occupation, peculiarly suited to the tenor of Indian village life. . . . The products satisfied both the cottage and the court and served local as well as foreign needs. The Indian industry . . . lent itself easily to the domestic system of production and was organized under craft guilds. (Majumdar 1963:1103)

Into this system first came the British East India Company, in 1753. The traditional system whereby merchants advanced capital to and bought from the weavers was replaced by an agency system whereby the operatives of the company "lorded it over the looms and defrauded the weavers" (Majumdar 1963:1103).

But the destruction of the Indian textile industry lay in the far-away mechanical looms of Lancashire, in England: "Cheap machine-made muslins flooded the Indian market, while protective duties kept the finer handloomed Indian fabrics at a disadvantage abroad. By 1824 machine-spun twist and yarn began to arrive. . . . The British yarn was being spun at less than half the cost of the Indian yarn and the spinners shared inevitably the same fate as the weavers" (Majumdar 1963:1104).

The case is a complicated, though celebrated, one. It became part of the rhetoric of Indian nationalism (so that the recreation and fosterage of handloom industries has become a symbol of Indian independence). The argument, overstated in terms of colonialist conspiracy, has been challenged by Western scholars such as Morris (1965), and restated in more sophisticated terms by contemporary Indian economic historians. The eventual destruction of the handloom industry in the non-Western world after the Industrial Revolution, except where it has been specially protected, was probably inevitable; and in India an emerging Indian bourgeoisie and merchant class contributed to the process. Yet colonial tariff policies and economic strategies doubtless played a part as well. (There is clear evidence of the quite systematic destruction of handloom industries by European interests in parts of Indonesia and the Philippines—in some cases, by production of machine copies of traditional designs, to put the weavers out of business.)

What is quite clear in the Indian case is that the economic transformations of the nineteenth century were part of a global strategy of empire that defined the relations of colonies to the United Kingdom, and defined India as the jewel in the crown, source of wealth to the conquerors. Exacting tribute from village farmers was part of this strategy. The British reorganizations of land tenure and taxation in the second half of the nineteenth century, ostensibly for the benefit of the farmers, were in reality more efficient means of extracting taxation without causing short-term disasters. In a famous 1875 minute, Lord Salisbury, secretary of state for India, likened this revenue extraction to bleeding—an apt image. "The lancet should be directed to the parts where the blood is congested or at least sufficient, not those which are already feeble for the want of it" (cited in Spitz 1978:880).

This policy of what Pierre Spitz calls an "enlightened form of economic violence," extracting revenue from peasant farmers, was coupled with a policy of transforming agricultural production away from food and into commercial crops:

The encouragement given at the highest level of authority in the colonial state to cultivation of commercially profitable crops, such as cotton, had the effect of reducing the area given over to food crops and thus helped to increase the vulnerability of food-supply systems. [More than 6 million Indians died in the famines of 1876–1878.]

At the same time craftsmen ruined by the competition of British industries were driven to swell the ranks of agricultural laborers. Whereas . . . in 1842, . . . their number [that is, landless laborers] was so small that it was not worth counting them, it emerged from the 1872 census that they represented 18 per cent of the agricultural population. (Spitz 1978:880)

The opening of the Suez Canal in 1870 intensified the pressures of plantation production of cotton, jute, tea, indigo, and other commodities, and for export of grain to England, Belgium, France, and Egypt. The driving of peasants off the land, the destruction of craft industries, and even the impoverishment of tribal areas had the consequences—whether planned or not—of creating the labor force needed for these new systems of production. This begins to give us the means to see how the landless and jobless poor starving on the streets of Calcutta—a city that did not even exist until it was founded by the British in 1690—are the historical heirs not to a "traditional economy" but to one destroyed by colonialism.

Even the flooding which now regularly devastates the plains of Bengal—which we are likely to think of as the epitome of the hopelessness of India and Bangladesh and the cheapness of human life—demands reexamination. Until the massive railroad construction of the nineteenth century, Bengal had an elaborate precolonial system of dikes, channels, and irrigation and overflow canals that seem to have worked quite successfully in preventing disastrous flooding. In the course of building railroads, and in reorganizing land tenure in the interests of revenue extraction, the British destroyed the existing water control systems (Boudhayan Chattopadhyay, personal communication). Ironically, twentieth-century flood control measures do not prevent flooding; they permit a distribution of water so that the poor get flooded and the rich stay dry.

Again, economic historians debate about the extent to which the pauperization of large sections of the Indian population was a consequence of deliberate planning or an incidental result of administrative and economic policies. It is indisputable that the British invested very heavily in railroads and in large-scale commercial agriculture and plantation development and did very little to develop village-level agricultural production. Their strategies and commitments had a consequence of driving millions of people off the land and into wage labor, bonded agricultural labor, or urban poverty—hence did much to create the "backward" India of today.

What about the "traditional" system of castes, the feudal system of landlords and moneylenders that keep the rural poor in desperate struggles for bare survival? In extracting enormous wealth from India through taxes and levies, the British relied heavily on the absentee landlords and moneylenders and gave them greater power as well as legitimacy:

For most of India in the colonial period, a very large proportion of agricultural laborers [were] semi-serfs or . . . tenants; . . . tenancy and a pauperized form of feudal relations were

Continued

Case 76 continued

dominant. Correspondingly, the dominant land-holders in the countryside continued to be non-cultivating landlords and merchant-moneylenders who found it more profitable to live off rent and usury [interest] and sublet their land rather than invest in it. Their political alliance with British imperialism was a major factor in maintaining their power. (Omvedt 1978:387)

As Chattopadhyay observes,

Precapitalist relations . . . [of] parasitic land-lordism, usury, sharecropping, rack-renting, and different forms of servitude of agricultural labor-ers . . . could remain because imperialism pre-served them. (1972:191)

But this was not merely preservation, but transfor-mation, in a direction of integration into the world capitalist system—and hence the develop-ment of underdevelopment:

The British brought India into the world market, introduced and enforced private property in land, and built up railroads and . . . other infra-structural elements (designed primarily for inte-gration into the world market, not integration of India's own economy). The results included a de-struction of traditional handicraft industry and a pauperization of the rural population that left a very high proportion . . . of Indians landless or land-poor and forced to seek work as agricul-tural laborers. (Omvedt 1978:385)

An "Underdeveloped Economy": An Alternative View

We have gone far enough to see that poverty and dependence are neither acci-dental nor simply the residue of "tradi-tional" social systems that impede modernization. Hopkins (1970) character-izes "a tropical African economy" in terms that would apply equally to many other parts of the world:

Its modern sector . . . organized around the production and export of one or a few raw materials . . .

- Dominating the modern sector, . . . the country's principal city. . . . Expatriates . . . control the central operations. . . .
- Private capital . . . goes almost entirely into mercantile or extractive operations, is well serviced by foreign-owned banks, and nets handsome profits that usually leave the country.
- Levels of investment, productivity, and living are all low. . . . Sharply marked dif-ferences in level of living between a tiny

minority of well-to-do, a not much larger middle group, and a very large majority . . . [with] 90-odd percent living in the countryside. (Hopkins 1970:156–157)

Why, then, this economic structure—found over and over again? The answer should by now be clear:

An economy of this sort came into existence . . . [because] it was never supposed to con-stitute the economy of a separate society at all. Its modern sector was to form an integral part of the metropolitan country's economy. (Hopkins 1970: 157)

But if underdevelopment was created by colonialism, how has it been perpetuated? Why are the poor still poor?

54. NEOCOLONIALISM

As they saw the class structures and eco-nomic dependencies and exploitation of the colonial period continuing despite indepen-

Rule Britannia: The flag of colonialism is raised over Port Moresby, New Guinea, in 1884. Papua New Guinea gained its formal independence in 1975, and has subsequently been faced with classic problems of change and development.

dence, scholars began in the 1960s to use the term **neocolonialism** (Alavi 1964). The new colonialism, as viewed by these critics, is a system whereby the metropolitan countries maintain a quasi-colonial relationship with nominally independent states. Heavy overseas investment, characteristically by transnational corporations, extracts minerals and other raw materials from African, Asian, Pacific, and Latin American countries (for example, oil from Venezuela; copper from Chile, Zambia, and Papua New Guinea; bauxite from Jamaica; timber from Indonesia and the Philippines). For such investment, the prime requirements are political stability and a malleable local elite that can be tempted with money and development schemes.

Neocolonial Elites and the Interests They Serve

There are many variations on the theme of neocolonialism. In formerly French West

Neocolonialism and underdevelopment in Brazil: Urban affluence in São Paulo, exploited workers, and hinterland poor peasants are part of a vast system sustained by massive foreign investment.

Africa, in such countries as Senegal and Cameroun, French government advisers and businessmen dominate government policy and public life. Only the fiery patriot Sekou Toure of Guinea resisted French domination and turned down federation with France; and when the French left they ripped out all the telephones and destroyed everything they could. Ruling elites speak French, are French in their values and aspirations, and may still be linked politically to French interests.

The theme is a familiar one around the postcolonial world, whether the elites are speaking French or English, emulating French, British, or American ways (united by a common taste for Mercedes-Benzes). The elites themselves vary in their class interests. In some cases they remain tied to old wealth as a landed class, although they live in the penthouses of Santiago or São Paolo or Bangkok or Manila or Jakarta. Others represent new, urban-based wealth, as with the industrialists of Singapore or Taiwan.

We will see that it is no accident that the postcolonial governments of Africa, Asia, and modern Latin America have so often been repressive dictatorships, and that so often military regimes of right-wing generals or admirals run these countries. Massive foreign investment, the strategic flow of raw materials, the preservation of markets, and a cheap labor force (as well as defense against class revolution by peasants or workers, or outside "subversion") demand stability and massive mechanisms of internal repression.

The stake of the United States in maintaining postcolonial police states has been inescapable even to those who have faith in our role as bulwark of democracy. For instance, recall that in 1973 the popularly elected democratic government of Salvador Allende in Chile was overthrown by a right-wing coup, financed, armed, and planned by the United States, which put General Pinochet and the army in power. The death of democracy in Chile, the slaughter of the intelligentsia, and repression of freedoms that followed, restored the old alliance between the Chilean ruling class and the transnational copper corporations and other foreign interests that extract Chile's wealth. In other examples, the commitment of the U.S. government and corporate interests to keeping the Shah's police state in power in Iran and keeping the Somosa dynasty in power in Nicaragua similarly came to light since their overthrow. This has not meant, of course, that successor regimes have themselves necessarily been "democratic."

Socialist Imperialism

Such a view does not prevent us looking past the myths of the socialist world as well. The former Soviet Union, after World War II, maintained through massive force a quasi-colonial dominance over eastern Europe. A blood-thirsty regime in Ethiopia was sustained by Soviet power, and a Soviet invasion of Afghanistan to support the third in a series of supposedly Marxist coups endangered world peace and served old territorial ambitions from the days of the czars. The political economy of the Soviet-dominated states, maintained in the lip-service of class struggle and socialist equality, for decades gave no cause for optimism and idealism.

Internal Colonialism

One facet of the postcolonial world, a manifestation of neocolonialism of special concern to anthropologists, is what has been called **internal colonialism.** Internal colonialism is the cultural and political subordination and/or economic exploitation of indigenous ethnic minorities. The term has been applied to Australian Aborigines within Australian society, Native Americans within U.S. and Canadian society— that is, to oppression of the original inhabitants, now largely displaced. It has been applied to ethnic minorities in marginal zones of European countries—Lapps in Scandinavia, Basques in Spain, Macedonians and others in the Balkans. But many of the most striking—and destructive—forms of internal colonialism have occurred in formerly colonized areas. The destruction of Amazonian peoples in Brazil, in the name of development and "progress," has attracted worldwide attention (see Davis 1977, Maybury-Lewis 1996, Maybury-Lewis and Howe 1980, Maybury-Lewis et al. 1981). Enormous multinational investment in Amazonia, the construction of the Trans-Amazonian Highway system, and forced relocation of peasants in newly opened areas have cut massively into the remaining rain forest of the world and have

Aborigines in an affluent society: These Arnhem Land Australians live in shattering poverty, with appalling infant mortality, at the margins of a giant mining complex.

led to the virtual disappearance of many Indian populations and the destruction of their cultures.

Another pattern of internal colonialism has emerged in Indonesia, where a Javanese elite dominates the outer islands politically and economically—often in ways as destructive of local social systems and environments as Dutch colonialism ever had been. The wealth and power of the neocolonial elite in Indonesia has been perpetuated through heavy foreign investment in mining, timber, and other forms of resource extraction—in many cases at the expense of indigenous populations. Indonesia, since forcing its claim over Irian Jaya, has ruthlessly controlled indigenous peoples, has brought in large numbers of settlers from other islands who have dispossessed, dominated, and exploited local populations, and has sold off resources to foreign development interests. The revenue generated by the extraction of

The old and the new in Africa. Masai herd with satellite in background.

the resources of the outer islands flows back to Java to sustain the affluence of an elite living in their villas and penthouses. Similar phenomena are found in many parts of Southeast Asia, Africa, and the Pacific.

In many areas, indigenous minorities are more desperately at risk now than they were under colonial regimes. Scenarios such as Irian Jayanese fighting Indonesian helicopter gunships and paratroops with bows and arrows or Afghan tribesmen fighting Soviet tanks with ancient rifles are a commonplace of our time.

Neocolonialism and internal colonialism are two sides of the same coin. To understand what is happening in the formerly colonial periphery, and hence to extend our historical perspective into the present, we need to look at the modern core of the capitalist world system.

55. STRATEGIES OF INVESTMENT: THE MODERN WORLD AS A SINGLE MARKET

The Rationality of the Global Market

The world economic system of the period of capitalist expansion was a "system" in the sense that events around the world were tied together by colonial strategies, market forces, efforts of the nations within it to expand, exploit, and defend their spheres of interest. But as a total system it could not be planned or controlled: vast distances, poor communications, and conflict between nations prevented effective central planning. But in the last years of this century, the dream of a genuinely integrated world system is at hand—not through political unity, which seems as far from reach as it was in the sixteenth century, but through economic unity:

> The men who run the global corporations are the first in history with the organization, technology, money, and ideology to make a credible try at managing the world as an integrated unit. (Barnet and Müller 1974:13)

Barnet and Muiiler (1974:13–15) quote some of the visionary architects of this grand design:

> [The global corporation] is the most powerful agent for the internationalization of human society (director of Fiat and organizer of the Club of Rome).

> Working through great corporations that straddle the earth, men are able for the first time to utilize world resources with an efficiency dictated by the objective logic of profit (former U.S. undersecretary of state).

For business purposes, the boundaries that separate one nation from another are no more real than the equator. They are merely convenient demarcations of ethnic, linguistic, and cultural entities. They do not define business requirements or consumer trends. . . . The world outside the home country is no longer viewed as series of disconnected customers and prospects for its products, but as an extension of a single market (president of IBM World Trade Corporation).

As Barnet and Müller (1974:15) note,

In the process of developing a new world, the managers of firms like GM, IBM, Pepsico, GE, Pfizer, Shell, Volkswagen, Exxon, and a few hundred others are making daily business decisions which have more impact than those of most sovereign governments on where people live; what work, if any, they will do; what they will eat, drink, and wear; what sorts of knowledge schools and universities will encourage; and what kind of society their children will inherit.

These global corporations are not committed to the interests of any country, even though ownership and management is almost always American, British, Dutch, German, French, Swiss, Italian, Canadian, Swedish, or Japanese. Their morality and loyalty is governed by the "rationality" of profit.

In terms of the lives of postcolonial peoples—or indeed, of Americans—that ultimately means amorality. A number of major American-based corporations, for instance, had enormous operations in South Africa long before the end of apartheid. What matters, in the rationality of profit, is a cheap and regimented labor force. If that is a black labor force kept in virtual concentration camps under the previous regime of apartheid and ruthlessly suppressed by a brutal police state, that was someone else's problem. (With the

Apartheid and international investment: The gate of a South African factory, a subsidiary of a giant U.S. corporation.

changeover of regime in South Africa, movements to ameliorate these conditions have been set in motion.)

Rationality, as defined in these terms, demands that each part of the global system do what it does most efficiently. It requires ever-expanding markets for manufactured goods, hence requires that new demands continually be created. These may be demands for cigarettes among the urban poor in South America, even if it means going without food; or demands for soft drinks and tape recorders and denim jeans.

The Terms of an International Division of Labor

These demands of rationality require that the bauxite or nickel or copper or iron or manganese mined in one of the postcolonial countries not be processed there or used to build local industrialization. Rationality means moving raw materials around the globe to feed the industrial giants of Europe,

North America, and Japan; and it means establishing factories wherever the labor force is cheap and kept docile. The epitome of this "rationality" is the creation, especially in Asia, of "free trade zones." What this means is an enclave into which some item for manufacture—say, electronic components—can be brought without customs restrictions so as to be assembled by local workers (usually women) at very low pay, then reexported to Japan or the United States. Such workers stitch American shirts in Mexico and South Korea, assemble Japanese electronic components in Taiwan and the Philippines—without unions or minimum wages or 40-hour weeks. Over time, however, these processes themselves lead to protests and demands for better conditions.

The rationality of the global system demands that underdeveloped countries not be encouraged, or even allowed, to industrialize themselves, or acquire the technology they would need to do so. If a postcolonial country's appointed place in the global scheme of things is to export copper ore, some of its countrymen will be taught the managerial and engineering skills needed to operate copper mines. But the technology to *manufacture* copper *products,* hence to compete with Kennecott and Anaconda and the others, will be kept safely in the industrialized countries. There is, after all, not simply a question of profit at stake: the world's copper ore, bauxite, nickel, iron, and the rest will run out some day. Who will use up what is left is a strategic question that underlies the rhetoric of rationality.

The Impact of Foreign Investment

What does such foreign investment do for postcolonial countries? In some, such as South Korea, living standards in urban and rural areas have been genuinely raised—although at great cost of repression and regimentation of the labor force. But for most such countries (even where gross national product and per capita income may be rising), the gulf between rich and poor is widening. The rich get richer, the poor get poorer; the illusion of improved standards of living comes partly from the fact that the rich are getting richer faster than the poor are getting poorer. For millions of people in rural areas, peripheral incorporation in the cash economy may have meant somewhat greater buying power; but only at the expense of traditional structures of community and with the cost of an ever-widening gulf between rising material aspirations and the ability to satisfy them.

Even in cold economic terms, foreign investment may not be the bargain it seems to the host country—even though it serves the interests of local elites:

> Between 1965 and 1968, 52 percent of all profits of U.S. subsidiaries operating in Latin America in manufacturing . . . were repatriated to the U.S. This means that for every dollar of net profit . . . 52 cents left the country, even though 78 percent of the investment funds used to generate that dollar of profit came from local sources. If we look at the mining, petroleum, and smelting industries, the capital outflow resulting from the operation of global corporations is even worse. Each dollar of net profit is based on an investment that was 83 percent financed from local savings; yet only 21 percent of the profit remains in the local economy. (Barnet and Müller 1974:154)

The icy logic of rationality that governs this "world market," and its appalling consequences for the lives of the poor, is nowhere more clear than in the political economy of food and famine. In this realm as well we see illusions that lead well-meaning people in the developed countries to accept the suffering of others as a natural consequence of traditionalism, underdeveloped technologies, overpopulation, and ignorance.

The Need for a Global View

We might pause, before we look at the political economy of food dependency and famine, to ask what all this has to do with anthropology. The answer is that an anthropology of the present cannot adequately understand social life and economy in hinterland communities, towns, and cities, without taking such a systemic and historic view. The lives peasants lead in Zinacantan or rural India, the lives of urban squatters in the *favelas* of Rio de Janeiro, can be understood only in terms of their place in a scheme of things we cannot see simply by participating as ethnographers in these communities. If we find landless untouchables working in virtual bondage for an Indian landlord, we need not simply to find out about their social organization and kinship and religion; we need to find out how and why their fathers and grandfathers lost their land, how the landlord's wealth was created and how it is sustained. We need to follow the circles of interconnection out in space, and back in time, until they join us to the history of a British past as well as an Indian one, to the political economy of wealth and class as well as caste. Life in an Indian village or on a landlord's estate is inseparably linked to events in Bombay and Delhi, and ultimately to events in New York and London and Tokyo. An anthropology of the present that seeks only local explanations for local phenomena would be both wrong and useless. We will see further in the next two chapters why the perspectives being built

up here are crucial if anthropology is to be both penetrating and relevant.

56. THE POLITICAL ECONOMY OF FOOD AND HUNGER

The Orientation to Export Production

Studies of the political economy of world hunger by Lappé and Collins (1978), George (1977), and Harle (1978a, 1978b) challenge the view that world food production is being outstripped by population growth. They urge that tropical countries are trapped by the demands of the new rationality (imposed on them by the World Bank, Asian Development Bank, and other agencies of Western-style development) into progressively giving up such food self-sufficiency as they may enjoy so as to produce copra or cocoa or coffee or ground nuts for the world market; meanwhile, their waters are being fished out by foreign fleets, often working under local agreements entered into by governments desperate for revenue and jobs. People who used to be able to feed themselves are being encouraged to give up food for money, to grow commodities for export instead of staple foods for internal consumption. The world is to be fed, of course. But rationality demands that this be done by giant agribusiness, using chemical fertilizers and high-yield grains, not by peasant farmers working their own plots. The paper rationality may be compelling; but the political economy of developed and underdeveloped countries is organized in ways that guarantee that the food does not get to many of those who most need it. Grains are more likely to feed steers that end up as steaks on rich people's tables than to feed hungry people. In other circumstances food intended by aid agencies for the poor may fall into the hands of military factions.

Historical Roots of Food Dependency

How did such a situation come about? If there is enough food to feed the world's population, why are so many people hungry? Why do so many starve? Again, we need to look at the roots in history and the spreading branches and tendrils of the modern world economy.

First, in the colonial era, precapitalist economic systems were both denigrated and dismantled:

> Viewing the agriculture of the vanquished as primitive and backward reinforced the colonizer's rationale for destroying it. To the colonizers agriculture became merely a means to extract wealth on behalf of the colonizing power. Agriculture was no longer seen as a source of food for the local population. . . . The colonized society's agriculture was only a subdivision of the agricultural system of the metropolitan country. (Harle 1978b:281)

The creation of plantation economies put the most productive lands into the economic service of the metropolitan country. As Frank would lead us to expect, and as others have concurred, the infrastructures created in the colonial period and perpetuated by neocolonialism were not designed to enable the country to develop internally, but to serve the needs of the countries that fed off them:

> If you examine the transportation network . . . in nearly any poor country, you will see that roads and railways have not been geared to facilitating commerce between neighboring countries or . . . between regions of the same country; but to getting food and other raw materials moved from the hinterlands to the . . . ports and . . . thence northwards. (George 1977:16)

In the late colonial and postcolonial periods, Western experts have pushed these countries further into the production of crops for export. All over the tropical world, planners have been induced or persuaded to plant such cash crops as cocoa, coffee, ground nuts, palm oil nuts, and coconuts (for copra, used in soaps, oils, and explosives). Such specialization in primary products has pitted producers in competition with one another, and rendered them desperately vulnerable to world market prices. The alternative, to diversify local economies to meet local needs and feed local populations, has been hidden from view by development "experts," or depicted as a fatal mistake:

> Many former colonies have "chosen" to continue cash-crop agriculture and have been afraid to take the plunge into diversification because they fear that cash revenues in hard currency will drop so far that they will no longer be able to import any necessities from the industrialized world or pay their increasing debts. Without exception, nations that have opted for continuing and intensifying colonial-type one- or two-crop economies inherited from a world they never made, have lived to rue the day the choice was taken. . . . OPEC has brought higher revenue to [oil] . . . producers because of their remarkable unity and the exceptional Western dependency on the commodity they have to sell . . . but bananas? . . . The producing countries simply do not control the international price for their products—they take what they can get. (George 1977:16–17)

In these neocolonial economies,

> cash crops occupy enormous areas of many countries' best land (55 percent of the cropland in the Philippines, some 80 percent in Mauritius; groundnuts alone occupy 50 percent of all cultivated land in Senegal). (George 1977:19)

Agribusiness in the Global Design

Where, then, is the food to come from that will sustain growing populations, in this "rational" design for a world economy? It is supposed to come in substantial measure from those areas in the developed world where agribusiness—often the transnationals in different guise—can produce with maximum technological efficiency:

> The main characteristic of the underdeveloped continents is a considerable dependence on food imports. . . . From the end of the 1960s until 1974 cereals imports in the underdeveloped continents have on the average increased in quantity two or threefold. (Tuomi 1978:3–4)

Agribusiness has come to operate in some underdeveloped regions where capital and technology from the developed countries can be joined to a cheap and policed labor supply. But this, like assembling electronic components in Southeast Asia "free trade zones" or stitching shirts in Mexico, reflects the global rationality that pours profits back to the transnationals in the developed world, rather than transforming the economies of host countries. Giant cattle ranches in what was once Amazonian rain forest, owned by automotive corporations, are part of the wondrous rationality of our time.

The food dependence created in much of the postcolonial world opens the way to the strategic deployment and political uses of the grain surpluses of the developed countries, principally the United States:

> The U.S. plays a crucial role in world grain trade. The scarcity of grain, the limited number of suppliers, dispersed demands and the relative American independence of action . . . contribute to a political use of food. (Wallensteen 1978:90)

The nature, sources, and potential uses of the United States' "grain power" are discussed at length by Wallensteen. For example, the restriction of grain exports is sometimes threatened as a political instrument. But it is well to remember that the transnational corporations that seek to construct a world of transcendent global rationality have no ultimate national loyalties. In the new rationality, it is ultimately money that matters: nationalism is a relic of tribalism. Yet corporations have to reckon and deal with emergent nationalisms also.

The creation of food dependency entails not simply diversion of countries from self-sufficiency in production, but also the creation of new demands for processed foods. These include soft drinks, canned foods, and—most insidious of all—infant formula, used by mothers persuaded that bottle-feeding is prestigious and modern. The diets of the urban poor around the world are being disastrously eroded by sugar and bleached white flour; destructive diets, and the waste of precious resources to buy processed foods, are spreading into millions of rural households as well. In a capitalist world system the markets must forever expand or the system will collapse. The vision of several hundred million potential Chinese customers is a major force in world politics.

The "Green Revolution"

But if food dependency is being created as part of a global design, what are we to make of the "green revolution" that was to end world hunger by intensifying production through improved seed, fertilizer, and modern technology? First, it is worth going back to Tuomi's (1978:4) observation that "from the end of the 1960s until 1974 cereals imports in the underdeveloped continents have on the average increased in quantity two or three-fold." She continues:

> This increase has taken place concomitant with a major technological reform in agriculture, i.e., the green revolution. It is during this very period that all underdeveloped continents have become increasingly dependent on foreign grain imports, although the . . . revolution was to increase the self-sufficiency in food of the underdeveloped regions. (Tuomi 1978:4)

Second, the green revolution is not simply a matter of improved high-yield varieties of rice, wheat, and other food grains. It is a total technological complex in which petrochemical fertilizers, mechanized farming, and irrigation are required. Hence, except where the country transforming its agriculture is self-sufficient in terms of oil, fertilizer manufacture, and industrial capacity to produce tractors and other machinery, the green revolution creates markets for the industrial countries and plunges underdeveloped countries into deeper and deeper dependency.

Third, and most serious, are the consequences for rural populations. Where green revolution technology has taken hold, as in India and the Philippines, one consequence has been a radical transformation in the agrarian class structure. Even though it is possible in principle to use green revolution technology in small-scale farming, there are cost factors of capital outlay for machinery and fertilizers that favor the large landowner and relatively prosperous peasant farmer. Thus we find a cleavage widening where land-rich middle peasants and rich peasants take the risks of technological revolution and become (if they succeed) highly prosperous, able to employ labor on a substantial scale as capitalist owners of the means of production. Small-scale farmers cannot successfully make the technological transformation, and—unable to compete against more efficient producers—are progressively forced to sell their land to the expanding capitalist farmers and join the labor force. This creates a "rural proletariat"—

> a shift from the quasi-feudal structure of tenancy and sharecropping to a concentration of land in large operational units dependent on wage labor. (Cleaver 1972:193)

Unable to find jobs in the countryside, some of the middle and poor peasants who have become landless are forced to move out of the rural areas into urban squatter settlements. The evidence from India, the Philippines, Pakistan, Thailand, Mexico, and other areas where the green revolution has been "successful" points overwhelmingly to its consequence of driving the poor and marginal off the land, of making the rich richer and the poor poorer.

Where the green evolution has taken hold, it has been in regions where irrigation and large-scale farming are feasible: hence the new technological complex widens gulfs between regions as well as between agrarian classes. Finally, the favored regions and those who work in them bear the brunt of ecological pollution and poisoning inherent in the new technology (see P. Richards 1985, 1986)—a worse problem in the vast ecological complexity of the warmer middle zone of the world than in the temperate zone:

> It is one thing to kill a few bald eagles. It is quite another to poison fish ponds and their protein supply while spraying rice fields. The runoffs from . . . heavy inorganic fertilizer applications . . . result in massive entropication of lakes, streams, and rivers. (Cleaver 1972:195)

All this is not to deny that the green revolution has reduced grain dependency in some countries, and raised the statistical indices of per capita income and "standards of living." But it has further enmeshed postcolonial countries in dependency on the industrialized world, and widened the inequalities between classes: if it is progress, the costs have been staggering. And world "food shortages" and famine remain.

Yet the evidence assembled by Lappé and Collins (1977), George (1977), the authors in Harle (1978a), and others indicate that the problem is not too many people and too little food. It is the structures of inequality and exploitation that govern the production and distribution of the world's foodstuffs. It is also important to realize that if ecology is incorporated into the planning process more sustainable forms of development can be created.

The Political Economy of Urban Malnutrition

The roots of malnutrition in the global economic system emerge clearly in data on the urban poor in West Africa analyzed by anthropologist Filomena Steady (n.d.). She notes how the urban poor, with low and uncertain wages, are forced to survive as best they can in slums and shanty towns: "The peri-urban areas have earned the name of . . . 'septic fringe' because of their high rates of infant and child . . . mortality due mainly to undernutrition and poor environmental conditions." She cites the view of a Nigerian pediatrician that "the problem of malnutrition in Lagos is so grave that it is beyond the scope of modern medicine. According to him, treating malnutrition in Lagos is like mopping a floor with the tap permanently turned on, since only major social and economic change can turn that tap off" (Steady n.d.).

The systemic causes of the influx of peasants into the cities include processes we have already seen: the need for wage labor to sustain poor peasant families in the villages, the emphasis on export cropping, the impoverishment of hinterland areas. Once in town, desperate migrants eat what they can, while working when and as they can, for low wages. Even here the "rationality" of the world economy geared to profit and expanding markets impinges:

> The decline in breastfeeding in developing countries is particularly related to urbanization and the role of the baby food industry in promoting artificial feeding in urban areas [reflecting the] determination of multinational companies to make a profit at all costs. . . .
>
> Perhaps the greatest nutritional crisis in the world today is the decline in human lactation. The nutritional advantages of breast milk, the immunologic and antiallergenic properties, the community contraceptive benefits, the factors ensuring safety [and] cleanliness . . . have all been well documented. Above all the economic advantages especially to the poor mother are immense. . . .
>
> The decline in breastfeeding in Africa is particularly marked in the urban areas [as a result of] . . . the demand for cheap female labor in factories, the need for cash in the urban areas, the constant exposure to high-pressure sales techniques of infant food companies, and the desire to emulate the elite. (Steady n.d.)

Disasters—Natural or Social?

Malnutrition and famine are real enough. But even here, things are not always what they appear to be. Studies of the massive famines of Africa's Sahel region, where vegetation is retreating before the advancing desert (see Case 77), suggest that Western responses to disasters need to be probed carefully to see what lies beneath the surface.

CASE

7 7

The Political Economy of a "Natural Disaster": The Sahel

A classic example of a "natural disaster," and the Western response to it, is the drought of the early 1970s in the Sahel region, an arid belt across north-central Africa. Images of the desert advancing, and of hundreds of thousands of people starving to death, flooded the Western press; and massive relief efforts were mounted.

What kind of a disaster was it? What were the causes? Was the cost in human life as high as we were warned it would be? Is this pattern of drought a new one, or have droughts in the Sahel occurred before?

Anthropologists Ernest Schusky and David Abbott, noting inconsistencies in published casualty figures, were led to wonder if all was what it seemed to be. Their doubts had been kindled by the observation that although a prolonged drought was a major cause of the disaster, experts differed considerably on when the drought had started. They noted, going through the historical, meteorological, and archaeological evidence, that there are records of recurrent periods of drought as far back as 1700 (eleven years), then 1750 and 1790 (six years each), and then in the 1890s and 1911–1914. The decade of the 1960s was drier than the normal, but it showed the usual pattern of great local variation, to which peoples of the area had long adapted. "It is our contention that people had worked out adaptations to such conditions and would not have experienced widespread famine simply because of the vicissitudes of nature" (Schusky and Abbott 1980).

Pastoralism, and the over-grazing it supposedly causes, have been depicted as major causes of environmental disaster in the Sahel. There is no doubt that over-grazing was wide-

spread in the 1970s. But why? And why did pastoralists not survive the drought as they had in the eighteenth and nineteenth centuries? Is pastoralism inherently destructive, as so often claimed? Lappé and Collins make interesting observations:

Nomadic pastoralists have traditionally made efficient use of vast stretches of semiarid land. . . . Their . . . migrations . . . are . . . patterned to take advantage of variations in rainfall and vegetation. . . . Pastoral nomadism . . . is a rational response to an environment characterized by the scarcity of water, seasonal drought, and widely scattered seasonal fodder resources. . . . Traditional pastoralists . . . [keep] a herd that consists of different types of livestock: camels, sheep, goats, donkeys, as well as cattle. A mixed herd can exploit a variety of ecological niches. . . . A varied herd also acts as a walking storehouse for food, either directly or in exchange for grain, during annual dry spells and periodic droughts. (1978:44)

Lappé and Collins point to the close and positive interdependence of settled cultivators and pastoralists, a pattern also noted by Schusky and Abbott in relation to the Tuareg of the desert. Until colonial control was imposed in the twentieth century, a delicate political, economic, and ecological system operated through which Tuareg nomads would live and trade in the desert but, in times of drought, would move south into the settled areas.

The Tuareg . . . had solved the problem of micro-ecological changes through their exchange networks and proved an existence was possible under conditions of greatly fluctuating rainfall. What they had not adapted to was French colonialism. (Schusky and Abbott 1980)

Continued

Case 77 continued

What were these barriers to time-tested adaptations by pastoralists? Lappé and Collins note as follows:

The French colonial administration created arbitrary "national" borders . . . without regard to the need of the nomads to migrate. Endless restrictions have made it increasingly difficult for the nomads to shift their herds in response to the short- and long-term cycles of nature. The French also slapped a head tax on each nomad [which] had to be paid in French francs even though most nomads lived within a barter economy. Most nomads needed, therefore, to raise more livestock, so that some could be sold for cash. (1978:45)

These disruptions were compounded in the 1950s and 1960s by massive "development" projects that induced newly independent countries to shift agriculture to monocropping of export crops, particularly cotton—a process that had begun under the French in the 1920s. Marginal lands were brought into cash cultivation; traditional strategies of food cultivation that rotated crops and left land fallow were abandoned for intensified cultivation that progressively destroyed the soil. The nomads, with fewer places to graze their herds and inducements to expand them beyond the point of prudence, accelerated the process of environmental destruction—so that when the drought of the 1970s hit, traditional means of survival were, for many, no longer possible.

Yet as Schusky and Abbott observe, "the supposed failure of the Sahelian peoples has been greatly exaggerated." They cite evidence from such Sahel peoples as the Dogon, Tamejirt, and Peul that effective local means of maintaining subsistence economies through strategies of cultivation and animal husbandry enabled communities to get through the years of diminished rainfall.

This brings us back to the scope of the disaster. Schusky and Abbott concede that people—perhaps 100,000 of them—did die of famine. "But . . . it was not a lack of rainfall that caused the famine, but major changes in economies and politics." Moreover, they note that in the years when Western relief agencies and governments were focusing on the Sahel, the estimates of the numbers who would die from starvation were grossly at variance with one another. "It quickly became apparent that people had vested interests in mortality rates." They note estimates as high as "more than a million" or higher. *The Washington Post* at one stage pointed to "the gruesome possibility—perhaps even probability—that as many as half of the area's 20 million human inhabitants may be wiped out by the famine." Wildly varying figures continued to be disseminated but eventually, after 1975, they settled down to a conventional figure of 100,000. Schusky and Abbott cite some evidence casting doubt on this figure, and suggesting that the actual death toll may have been 20,000 or less.

They note, as have many critics of the relief effort, the staggering waste, inefficiency, and corruption of the worldwide effort to save the Sahel. But they are more troubled by what they see as the long-term economic and political motives of the developed nations toward the Sahel:

High-level administrators in U.S. AID, and FAO are thinking in terms of major development projects. Large dams for the rivers, deep bore-hole wells, fencing and beef production, capitalization for an infrastructure, and commercialization of the economy are all being seriously discussed as a future for the Sahel. (Schusky and Abbott 1980)

Vast agribusiness and Western technology is being unleashed on the Sahel—with the high probability of pauperization of its inhabitants and dangerous alteration of the ecosystem. The cry of alarm raised by Western leaders and planners may hide sinister motives:

The recurrent drought of the past few years had made clear that the desert is encroaching on a large scale and that food production capacity in western Africa is seriously threatened. . . . What is now needed is a comprehensive international program that, rather than ease the effects of the drought, will help roll back the desert. (Henry Kissinger, 1976, quoted by Lappé and Collins 1978:95)

Space-age farms, modern cattle ranges, and lush market gardens in the middle of the Sahara. . . . This is no mirage. . . . It could eventually turn the rural subsistence economies of the west African nations of Chad, Mali, Mauritania, Niger, Senegal, and Upper Volta into a vegetable garden for Europe and a vast beef belt. (*To the Point International,* quoted by Lappé and Collins 1978:95–96)

For the indigenous inhabitants of the Sahel, the Western planners of salvation have devised plans for resettlement, commercial production of beef, and incorporation into the global scheme of "rationality." Such plans, Schusky and Abbott warn, are missing an important component:

[They] ignore the extreme variability of the region, and the diversity of adaptations which have been worked out by the local people. By combining goats and camels with sheep and cattle, the herding people make it possible to exploit the browsing of the former in dry years while capitalizing on sheep and cattle grazing in wetter years. The animals are also diverse in their reproductive and lactating cycles which complement one another. Further diversity is provided by the fact that many of the nomads also practice some horticulture. . . . Among the groups who do not plant, millet or maize are obtained through trade, often highly dependent on camels. (Schusky and Abbott 1980)

On these diverse and delicate systems for adjusting resources to the pressures of a difficult environment, Western planners would impose "development" schemes. The probabilities of further human disaster if these plans are pursued are high. Peoples who once sustained themselves will be made captive to the world economy, with traditional ways destroyed. The justification for this destruction will be, of course, that the old ways led to the famine.

Anthropology and Global Studies of Political Economy

That it is the peoples anthropologists have traditionally studied, in rural communities, who are being threatened by pauperization, dependency, and the destruction of culture and social structures, is another compelling answer to the question: What has all this to do with anthropology? Anthropologists have what the architects of development usually lack: a knowledge of the textures of social relations and meanings, and of local adaptations, within communities. They often have a clear view of the trees; but can they see the forest?

Is the impoverishment and dependency being forced on the peoples they have studied the concern of anthropologists? Some, like Steady and Schusky and Abbott, clearly think it is—that anthropology must concern itself with the present, and that the present is shaped by the forces of a world economy whose centers lie far from village or nomad camp or shanty town.

At the same time we must continue to be concerned with local meanings, since these do shape people's responses to their problems. We need approaches that combine the study of political economy with the study of local meanings.

SUMMARY

Postcolonial countries have been described as beset by "traditional" practices and "tribalism" that on closer inspection turn out to have been closely influenced by the forces of colonialism. André Gunder Frank argued for Latin America that countries were systematically underdeveloped so as to produce a dependency on metropolitan powers. Exploitation took the form of mining or sugar plantations. Landed aristocracies have excluded peasants from land ownership, and have become the satellites, according to Frank, of metropolitan regimes. Frank's theories apply with varying success to other parts of the world. Immanuel Wallerstein wrote in a similar vein regarding the modern world-system or global economy of extraction and exploitation, developing out of European expansion in the sixteenth century. According to this view the poverty of colonial countries was created by the metropolitan centers. For example, handloom textile industries were destroyed in India by the operations of the British East India Company and the development of factories in Lancashire in the United Kingdom. Even after the political independence of postcolonial countries, metropolitan centers may continue to exert a neocolonial economic influence over them. Neocolonialism may be accompanied by internal colonialism, the subordination of minorities within a postcolonial country.

Global corporations are concerned with profit, not with national boundaries, although they may use national regimes for their own purposes. Foreign investment may raise local living standards, but also may fail to do so. Countries may come to be dependent for food supplies on international sources of aid as a result of the decline of subsistence agriculture. The "green revolution" whereby new forms of cropping were intended to solve food problems and prevent famines has increased prosperity but has also increased underdeveloped nations' dependency on the industrialized world. The successful farmers drive others out, and these displaced persons then become an urban proletariat. The case of the drought disaster in the Sahel in north-central Africa shows how problems were not caused by pastoral over-grazing but rather by the restrictions on movements resulting from new colonial boundaries and from the disruptive effects of agricultural development schemes on nomadic practices. Anthropologists are well equipped to point out the social as opposed to simply the natural causes of such disasters.

SUGGESTIONS FOR FURTHER READING

SECTIONS 52–56

Amin, S. 1976. *Unequal Development*. New York: Monthly Review Press.

Austen, R. A. 1969. *Modern Imperialism: Western Overseas Expansion and Its Aftermath*. Lexington, Mass.: D.C. Heath & Company.

Chilcote, R. H., ed. 1976. *Capitalism in Latin America: The Process of Underdevelopment*. Latin American Perspectives, Vol. III, No. 3, Special Issue.

Frank, A. G. 1979. *Dependent Accumulation and Underdevelopment*. London: Macmillan & International, Ltd.

Horowitz, D. 1969. *Empire and Revolution: A Radical Interpretation of Contemporary History*. New York: Random House, Inc.

Jalee, P. 1970. *Pillage of the Third World.* New York: Monthly Review Press.

Owen, R., and R. Sutcliffe, eds. 1973. *Studies in the Theory of Imperialism.* London: Longman Group, Ltd.

Smith, C. A., ed. 1976. *Regional Analysis.* Vol. I: *Social Systems.* Vol. II: *Economic Systems.* New York: Academic Press.

Taylor, J. G. 1979. *From Modernization to Modes of Production.* London: Macmillan & International, Ltd.

Wallerstein, I. 1979. *The Capitalist World-Economy.* Cambridge: Cambridge University Press.

Wilbur, C., ed. 1978. *The Political Economy of Development and Underdevelopment.* New York: Random House, Inc.

Cities

Anthropologists, with their inclination to study small and isolated societies, were rather slow to tackle complex civilizations in the center—in cities—as well as on the margins, in peasant villages. In Africa, Asia, Latin America, and, on small scales, in the Pacific, villagers have flocked to urban-centers and surrounding slums. Cities are where the action is. An anthropology that aspires to study universals, to see the human condition in the widest possible perspective, cannot study only hamlets and villages. An **urban** anthropology has emerged, taking anthropological researchers to cities in underdeveloped and industrialized countries.

To understand cities we need to place them in a wider context. Just as we could only analyze peasants in terms of their ties to the wider economy and to urban centers, we can interpret the cities, the slums, and shanty towns only in terms of the forces that lead people to migrate from the countryside. The previous two chapters gave us the background we need to understand why villagers are in cities, why they are poor, and what part they play in the urban and international economies. The same perspectives will serve us well in looking at ghettos, ethnic enclaves, and slums in the cities of the industrialized countries.

57. ANTHROPOLOGY OF CITIES, ANTHROPOLOGY IN CITIES

To see urban anthropology as a single subfield or specialization is misleading. Some urban anthropologists are predominantly interested in cities—in how and why urban centers have developed in different times and places, in how variable cities are, in how cities create new modes of human experience. In short, for many, cities are *subjects for study.* But to many other urban anthropologists, cities represent not subjects but *settings:* one studies a neighborhood, a housing project, a street corner, as before one had studied a village or a band—as a microcosm, a social world in miniature.

Cities, East and West

Comparative studies of cities have raised important questions. How much like the cities of the United States or Europe are the cities of Latin America or Africa? Do urban bureaucracies or urban poverty lead to similar patterns in different countries? To what extent do the cities of Japan or India remain distinctively Asian? Do colonial and post-colonial cities contrast with cities that have grown up free of colonial domination? Are rural-urban ties still close?

Comparison of urban experience in underdeveloped countries also throws in question the generalizations sociologists have long made on the basis of studies in Western cities. Do kinship ties shrink in range and importance? Do nuclear families inevitably become predominant? Cast in the crucible of cross-cultural doubt are other widespread assumptions about the stresses of urban life—such as the supposed effects of crowding on aggression and frustration. Thus Anderson (1972) argues, of urban Chinese in Hong Kong, that due to cultural ways of dealing with crowding the supposed pathological effects are minimized. An anthropology that studies urban life in comparative perspective can perhaps fulfill in this new realm the historic role of anthropology in the social sciences: sorting the culture-bound from the universal, and hence pushing toward a genuinely comparative understanding of human ways.

How similar have cities been in different times and places? How similar are Bangkok and Bombay? And how similar to Baltimore? How similar to Babylon?

Gideon Sjoberg has made a noteworthy attempt to pull together the evidence on "preindustrial cities," particularly the cities of antiquity. He arrives at an idealized model of the preindustrial city to which actual cities were an approximation—a kind of composite standard. The ancient city was characteristically the center of government and religion; it housed elites; and it was only secondarily the center of commerce. Ethnic groups tended to form separate enclaves, within which extended family households were strong. Commerce tended to be in the hands of low and outcaste classes; and men, especially elders, of an hereditary elite held political and religious power. Religious ideology and education tended to perpetuate the elite, hence to be conservative forces (Sjoberg 1960).

But as Southall (1973a) and others have pointed out, such an idealized composite hides many of the most interesting variations. Southall cities a number of cases, such as Early Dynastic Sumeria, Aztec Mexico, Damascus, Carthage, and medieval and Renaissance Europe, where merchants were rich and powerful, not polluted or peripheral. For most of the characteristics of Sjoberg's ideal composite, one can find exceptions. And where this is not the case (for example, such characteristics as male dominance or the conservatism and elite-reinforcing functions of education seem to have held true in all preindustrial cities), they hold equally true in tribal societies or rural communities; hence they in no way define the uniqueness of city life.

Technology and industrialization have progressively transformed cities everywhere, creating the possibility of larger populations, more extensive political control, new modes of production, and new class relationships. But is the industrialized city as much of an idealized composite as the preindustrial city sketched by Sjoberg?

Looking at the great cities of Latin America, Asia, or Africa, one sees sharp contrasts with Western industrial cities in the shattering poverty and squalor, and in squatter settlements, as well as similarities in scale and the complexity and fragmentation of social relations. Most of these cities have in varying degrees been created by colonialism, old and new—São Paulo, La Paz, Santiago, Singapore, Bombay, Hong Kong, Calcutta, Manila. It is thus not surprising that the class systems, economic patterns, and relations to the hinterlands of these cities are in some ways similar: tied as satellites to Europe and serving as colonial metropolises in relation to satellites in the hinterlands (to use Frank's terms), they have undergone parallel development. These colonial metropolises all tend to have

CASE
7 8

Urbanization in Japan

In Japan, the first capital city, Heijoku (Nara), was built in conformity to a Chinese model at the beginning of the eighth century; and the subsequent feudal and then industrial cities have evolved in ways distinctively Japanese. After the Meiji Restoration of 1868, Japan industrialized with amazing rapidity—so that by the Russo-Japanese War (1904) Japan had a powerful Western-style war machine and the industrial might to support it. The rise of giant industrial firms and banks, which dominated politics as well as economics, helped to shape the great expansion of such cities as Tokyo and Osaka. By 1920, Tokyo had a population of almost 2 million. The distinctiveness of Japan's cities and urban life has been reconstructed by Yazaki (1963, 1968, 1973), Smith (1973), and others—drawing for recent centuries on detailed census records. Smith

notes that preindustrial eighteenth-century Japanese cities had small individual families, not larger extended families, as crucial constituent units; and these household groups were highly mobile. He argues that rather than nuclear families becoming separate and mobile due to urban industrialization, as urbanization theorists would have it, in the Japanese sequence household independence and mobility apparently preceded industrialization. He suggests that this pattern may have contributed to the remarkably rapid and effective adaptation of Japanese society to industrialization. Smith also suggests that the pattern whereby single heirs inherited control over household property contributed to the emergence of family business firms, some of which grew into the great *zaibatsu* family corporations of industrial Japan (see also Bellah 1957).

squatter settlements, to draw poor wage labor from rural areas, and so on; they evolved to serve the interests of the metropolitan states, under their economic domination.

Striking evidence on the variation in urban patterns comes from those few cases where non-Western countries had precolonial cities and particularly where the path to industrialization was followed substantially free of European domination. Consider, for instance, the urbanization of Japan, described in Case 78.

That Japanese urban society is still distinctively Japanese culturally is reinforced by Thomas Rohlen's study of a Tokyo banking firm. Rohlen found the bank, in its quasi-familial bureaucratic structure and many other respects, to be a kind of microcosm of Japanese culture, Bank trainees, for example, underwent a kind of *zen* job orientation whereby the appropriate humility, respect, and loyalty were instilled (Rohlen 1974; see also Nakane 1970).

Other perspectives on what is distinctive about such *non*colonial cities—and hence, on what is unique to Western urban experience—have come from such settings as Addis Ababa in Ethiopia (see Shack 1973), the Yoruba cities of West Africa (Lloyd 1973), and the old precolonial cities of India (Rowe 1973). These old Indian cities, like ancient Greek or Mayan ones, represent a model of the cosmos. "All the Indian royal cities . . . are built after the mythical model of the celestial city where, in the age of gold, the universal Sovereign dwelt" (Eliade 1959:5). "The symbolism of the house, the temple, and the city are realities in the Hindu scheme of life" (Rowe 1973:211; see also Nas 1993 on urban symbolism in a number of settings.)

The old Yoruba towns had populations of up to 50,000. They contrasted with urban centers in the West in many ways—most notably in the high percentage of subsistence cultivators within the towns. In the twentieth century, modernization has swelled Nigerian populations and increased migration to urban areas, so that Ibadan, with 97 percent Yoruba population, has grown to well over a million. Here the old and the new are joined in revealing ways: "The . . . physical structure and morphology of Ibadan . . . represents a convergence of two traditions of urbanism—a non-mechanistic, preindustrial African tradition more akin to the mediaeval urbanism in Europe, and a technologically oriented European tradition" (Mabogunje 1967:35).

From Village to City

The emergence and growth of cities mean movement from the countryside. Individuals or families flock from villages to the city. So a major challenge to the urban anthropologist is to understand the relationship between rural communities and urban-ites, and to interpret the transformation of rural cultural patterns into urban settings. Do old values, old fabrics of kinship and community, bind people together in urban settings? Pocock (1960) and others have argued that where urban centers have grown up outside a framework of exploitation and colonial domination, rural and urban remain a single system, sustained by the same cultural patterns. When urbanization breaks those bonds of continuity, it is because the fragmentation of wage labor in colonial and postcolonial urbanization has disrupted them—when ties of shared culture are transformed into class relationships; when urban wealth creates rural poverty and draws the poor to the urban margins; and when urban workers, often leaving families behind, are drawn from different ethnic groups and regions. As Southall observes:

> The colonial cities of the nineteenth century were described as parasitic, funneling wanted products out to the West without inducing economic transformation. Now that most of them have become the capital cities of independent countries, local elites have been co-opted alongside the white elites who remain in greater numbers than before, though they have retreated from open political dominance to more subtle diplomatic, commercial, military, and general aid-to-development dominance. Considering that the gap between urban luxury and both urban and rural poverty is also greater than before, and that they serve as channels through which the United States alone consumes 60 percent of the world's natural resources . . . these Asian [and other postcolonial] cities can hardly be considered less parasitic than before. The spatial segregation and social solidarity of the immigrant ethnic communities remain marked and, in the conditions of extreme overcrowding and underemployment, doubtless necessary to survival. (1973a:10)

Within such cities—what might be called neocolonial cities, in contrast to those of the modern West or of Japan and China—traditional bonds of kinship and community may remain strong. In ethnic enclaves, as Southall notes, such cultural patterns may serve as crucial survival strategies whereby identity is preserved and collective action and "belonging" are maintained. (The same is true, of course, of the ethnic enclaves of Western cities.) Kinship ties, both within and between families, may remain more important than the theories of urban sociologists had suggested. Thus Bruner (1973) and others have shown how important and strong are ties of kinship in urban settings, a theme that emerges as well in the autobiographical materials collected from Mexico and Puerto Rico by Oscar Lewis (1961, 1966). And studies of urban ghettos in the United States, notably the work of Carol Stack (1974), have emphasized the centrality and enduring resilience of bonds of kinship, despite the fragmentation, impersonality, and mass scale of urban life. (See also Williams 1981, 1984.)

But in many areas of the postcolonial world, especially neocolonial cities where individuals and families are pulled from rural communities for wage labor, bonds of kinship and community are at least temporarily sundered in urban migration. Here voluntary associations and other institutions, in some ways modeled on the close ties of kin and neighbors (see Case 79), may emerge as sources of strength, identity, and survival—and as ways of incorporating new arrivals in a hostile environment.

In Africa, anthropologists who had first worked in tribal settings followed urban migrants into the shanty towns and slums; and not surprisingly, they looked at the ways old cultural patterns were preserved in new forms, at the ways people from the same village or language group stuck together in their new urban setting in ways modeled on kinship. Critical perspectives on the economic forces that were driving or luring villagers off the land and into the cities in the first place have come only more recently.

Systemic Connections: Rich and Poor, City and Country

We saw in the last chapter some of the pressures and development strategies that have pulled rural peoples into export crop production rather than subsistence, have made them dependent on wage labor in cities, mines or plantations, and have transformed the class structure of rural society. They should make us wary of taking at face value the gulf between the modern and prosperous business districts and affluent suburbs of postcolonial cities and the slums and shanty towns in which the urban poor struggle to survive amid desperate poverty, malnutrition, and disease. Is this simply the gulf between the "developing sector" of the economy where modernization is taking place and the "traditional sector" as it has spilled over into the city? There is a vast physical contrast between the modern skyscrapers, penthouses, and villas, and the miles of cardboard, tin, and board shanties at the outer edges of the smog. Nevertheless the various segments of urban populations are economically linked.

Recent studies of Latin American and cities in other developing areas have uncovered the close and systemic interconnections between the urban rich and the urban poor, the ways in which neocolonial economies and rising middle classes depend on the poor and hungry who emerge by the tens of thousands from the slums and shanty towns at the break of dawn.

CASE
79

The Dancing Compins of Freetown

In the city of Freetown, Sierra Leone, Temne peoples have formed voluntary associations of a sort common in West Africa (Banton 1957, Little 1967). These are known as "dancing compins." Their ostensible function is to perform "plays" of traditional music and dancing. Performances are given for the weddings of members (both men and women), for special occasions such as visits by important people, and to raise funds.

Each compin is tightly organized, with officials, committees, and treasuries to which members contribute weekly and at the death of a fellow member. They maintain close discipline over members and compete for a good reputation for conduct as well as for performances. Fines are levied on members for breaches of rules, and great stress is laid on mutual aid in times of need.

Most members of a dancing compin are migrants from rural towns and villages, and there is a strong local and regional bias in their membership. In many respects they function as an urban counterpart to the kinship-based corporations of traditional Temne society. They also serve to socialize new arrivals to the city in the ways of the world, and provide a closely knit group that contributes to their security in this new and otherwise often hostile setting.

The origin of the dancing compins reveals another side of their importance and appeal. The Temne were long regarded as the "hillbillies" of Sierra Leone by other peoples from less conservative groups. For young Temne, establishment of the first compin by a somewhat revolutionary Temne schoolmaster provided a rallying point around which they could build a new urban identity. As compins became established and acquired prestige, their combination of what was sophisticated and new with what was received from valued traditional elements of Temne culture gave them added influence. Some younger men used them as springboards to political leadership in tribal matters:

Thus, by founding voluntary associations individual Temne raised their prestige and rose in the social scale. These organizations provided new leadership roles. . . . By resuscitating certain aspects of the traditional culture and adapting it to urban needs these young men were able to further their modernist ambitions. (Little 1967:160)

Case Update

In addition to the works cited here, Kenneth Little has published extensively on urban life in Africa (e.g., see Little 1980).

Lomnitz compares the dwellers of a Mexico City shanty town to hunter-gatherers in the urban jungle, who "go out every day to hunt for jobs. . . . Their livelihood is based on leftovers: leftover jobs, leftover trades, leftover living space, homes built of leftovers. . . . They inhabit the interstices of the urban industrial system and feed on its waste" (Lomnitz 1977:208). But despite its marginality this ragged army of the urban poor "performs important though perhaps as yet unrecognized social

Bantu workers in a South African city in the days of apartheid. The sign on the bus: "Non-Europeans only."

functions. In particular, the rise of an urban middle-class in Latin America is greatly indebted to cheap labor and services." The poor work as "domestic servants, gardeners, delivery boys, drivers, and a host of menial helpers of every description. If there is a symbiotic relationship between urban society and marginality, its major beneficiary is undoubtedly the middle class" (Lomnitz 1977:208).

A similar situation is reported by Perlman for the *favelas* or "illegal" slums of Rio de Janeiro. Challenging a "myth of marginality" that views slums as a blight on the urban landscape and a drain on the country's resources, Perlman reports the following:

> Almost everyone who is able works. A third of the men are employed in industry, construction, or transportation, and many more would be if the jobs existed. Only one-tenth work on jobs within the local community,

while all the others contribute their labor directly to the "external city economy." Favelados [the slum-dwellers] not only built the high-rise buildings in which Rio takes such pride, but they also are the ones who maintain and clean those buildings. . . .

About one-third of the favela women are employed in the domestic services which the middle class find so essential. The favelados represent a constant supply of cheap household labor, relieving the upper-class women of the tasks of washing, cleaning, cooking, and child care. . . .

Although some [men] do unskilled factory labor or construction work, most are employed in the service sector as street vendors, garbage men, bus fare collectors, doormen, watchmen, streetcleaners, service station attendants, carwashers, street repairmen, or janitors. These . . . are jobs which need to be done, and which generate income that recirculates throughout the economy. (1976: 152–153)

We will see shortly that stereotypes of the shanty towns as hotbeds of crime, cultural pathology, and social disorganization are similarly challenged by studies such as Perlman's of the actual texture of social life in the slums.

Studying "Urban Problems"

Studies of the lives of U.S. and Latin American or Asian slum-dwellers have often been motivated by liberal humanistic concern; they have also been a response to the availability of research funding to "treat" the social unrest that has exploded into violence. Anthropological studies of the urban poor raise a broad range of questions and doubts. We will return to them in Chapter 21.

Radical critics argue that the roots of urban poverty and crime lie in the political and economic system that has created the pattern of exploitation and discrimination. From this perspective, curing the symptoms by urban renewal projects, "head start" programs, job training, or other piecemeal remedies so as to lift the poor into the mainstream of society can be only partly successful; especially in global perspective, such an approach may only succeed in creating small new elites and widening and polarizing oppressive class relationships.

A Culture of Poverty?

The desperate poverty in which many urban dwellers around the world are trapped can easily be seen as pathological. Thus Oscar Lewis has painted a dramatic picture of an international **culture of poverty,** with many broad similarities that transcend regional and national variations. This picture has been highly controversial. Lewis suggests, and seeks to document with his selected life-history materials, that the poor in Latin American cities pattern their lives partly on, but are largely excluded from, the major institutions of the dominant society. Their social and economic lives and psychological adaptations are shaped by exclusion and deprivation. Socially, the result is a lack of stable marriages and solid family life, with lovers drifting in and out, children leaving home early in search of an adventure that masks their economic frustration, and so on. Psychologically, "a strong feeling of marginality, of helplessness, of dependence and of inferiority" prevails (Lewis 1966:xlvii).

Lewis's writings have provoked a storm of criticism. He has been rightly criticized for underplaying the creative, positive value systems and social relationships that preserve solidarity amid adversity and for a too narrow conception of the roots of poverty. It has been a characteristic strategy of the dominant classes, whether in external or internal colonialism, to caricature the poor as lazy, shiftless, promiscuous, or otherwise lacking in the virtues that would enable them to prosper and get ahead. The problems of the poor are laid at the feet of the poor. Lewis is by no means simplistic, moralistic, and racist, but his picture of urban poverty is too narrow and has been vulnerable to the same critical onslaught (Leacock 1971; Valentine 1968).

Lewis's depictions of the value systems of the "culture of poverty" and the tenor of social life in urban slums have not been borne out by studies-in-depth such as Perlman's documentation of the *favelados* of the slums of Rio. On the basis of participant observation and interview and questionnaire data, she cast doubt on the view that life in the shanty towns is pathological:

> I have found the prevailing wisdom completely wrong: the favelados ... do *not* have the attitudes or behavior supposedly associated with marginal groups. Socially, they are well organized and cohesive and make wide use of the urban milieu and its institutions. Culturally, they are highly optimistic and aspire to better education for their children and to improving the condition of their houses. The small piles of bricks purchased one by one and stored in backyards for the day they can be used is eloquent testimony to how favelados strive to fulfill their goals. Economically, they work hard, they consume their share of the products of others . . . , and they build—not only their own houses but also much of the overall community and urban infrastructure. They also place a high value on hard work, and take great pride in a job well done. Politically, they are neither apathetic nor radical. (Perlman 1976: 242–243)

When gathering their data, neither Lomnitz nor Perlman relied solely on participant observation to document the quality of life of the urban poor and their place within the wider economy: both relied heavily on survey data. Perlman is, by training, an urban sociologist. This raises the question of whether there can be or should be a distinctive "urban anthropology"; and the question of whether traditional anthropological field methods are adequate in urban settings.

Methods of Study in Urban Settings

Are the methods that sufficed in studying a tribal hamlet, and were at least partly successful in a peasant village, adequate to the scale, fragmentation, and diversity of urban social life? Anthropological methodology includes an emphasis on long-term understanding and a focus on questions of culture which are relevant no matter where fieldwork is done but may be difficult to carry out in urban settings.

One strategy has been to take small slices of a vast urban setting and look at them with the closeup lens of anthropological observation over extended time periods. This may involve close participation in small groups, such as gangs, as in Keiser's study of the Vice Lords in Chicago (see Case 80).

Other studies, such as Elliot Liebow's *Tally's Corner* (1967), have taken small slices of life and traced their connections outward. Liebow studied a small and shifting collection of black men in Washington, D.C., whose lives carried them to and clustered them around a particular street corner. He traced their lives outward from it into short-lived jobs, sexual and marital relationships, and webs of friendship. Such studies of small groups or local settings are by no means distinctively new and anthro-

pological: studies of the bank-wiring group in a New England factory and of a street corner gang (Whyte 1955) have been sociological classics for decades. And more recently, sociologists as well as anthropologists have flocked to ghetto housing projects, hippie communes, Divine Light *ashrams,* and other small-scale settings.

Perhaps it is idle to worry about whether participant-observers of small groups carry anthropological, sociological, or some other credentials. But the more urgent question is whether participant observation in small groups, as microcosms of some wider system, is adequate to the complexity of urban life. For characteristically, an urban gang or commune or tenement is the focus for only part of the social life of its participants. For each, daily social life reaches beyond these warm and close settings to the vast impersonal world of jobs and stores and buses and streets. The challenge to systematic exploration of individual social relations in urban settings across this whole range has been faced squarely by British social anthropologists in urbanizing Africa. Particularly anthropologists trained in or influenced by the "Manchester School" of social anthropology—Max Gluckman and his students—have sought to generalize anthropological methodology to deal with the fragmentation of urban life.

Thus Jap Van Velsen, Clyde Mitchell, and others, have developed **situational analysis,** where some collective happening—a dance, a public meeting, a marriage—is analyzed under a close microscope to reveal who participates and why. Such analysis can show how the strategies and conflicts manifest in the particular incident reflect the structures and processes of the wider society. Situational analyses that move from the concrete and immediate to show general processes and networks have developed from strategies first worked out for studying conflict and social relations in African tribal settings—the "structural dramas" examined by Victor Turner (1957) among the Ndembu, the "extended case method" explored by Van Velsen (1967), and others. But in urban settings, particularly where change is rapid, participants are mobile, and ethnic backgrounds are varied, such situational analysis must reveal processes and conflicts against a background of fluidity and diversity, not of shared institutions and values.

A related development has been *network analysis* (Barnes 1972). Here, scholars such as Mitchell, Epstein, Barnes, Kapferer, and Boissevain have sought to trace the activities of individuals as they move through the full range of social relationships. By showing how and why urbanites enter into economic, political, and kinship relationships, and how they strategically use their **networks** of connection, urban anthropologists can move beyond both a static framework of institutional analysis and the distortion that comes from looking only at that portion of each person's life that is spent in the small group—a gang or residence or bar—the anthropologist happens to be observing. Network analysis has been partly successful in mapping patterns of social relations so that the properties of networks can be examined mathematically. But here the formalisms have often been superficial and analogical. There is a danger of becoming carried away with the formal elegance of it all and forgetting what the numbers or diagrams mean—of the usually tenuous relationship between the formalism and the world. (For a set of studies using network analysis among other methods, see Rogers and Vertovec 1995.)

Methods appropriate to research in urban settings will depend on the theoretical framework as well as the phenomena under study. When methods for studying cultures as cognitive systems were developed in studies of Mayan villagers and Philippines tribal communities, some researchers sought to apply them to the subcultures of urban settings. Wherever a subgroup has a distinctive subculture, a set of shared understandings and linguistic usages that makes theirs a private world within the vast impersonality of the city, they can—it was argued—be studied by the methods of cognitive anthropology. By seeing this world through the eyes, and the language, of those who live in it, one can correct distortions that come when middle-class American standards are applied to minorities.

Pioneers in these cognitive approaches to urban subcultures, notably Spradley and McCurdy, have done important studies themselves, and they encouraged their students to turn these methods to familiar settings such as the culture of hitchhikers (see Spradley 1970, Spradley and Mann 1975, Spradley and McCurdy 1977). Spradley's study of "urban nomads" in Seattle, presented in Case 81, illustrates the approach, its strengths, and limitations.

Such studies, although illuminating, pull us back into the old anthropological assumption that people with a common culture provide an adequate unit of analysis, and that a description of this culture adequately describes their life situation: assumptions that may be doubly inappropriate to marginal subgroups in a complex class system. Moreover, there is a deep danger in theories that—in whatever formal guise—see "the system" as generated by the acts and choices of individuals, or by their "culture." The forces that shape the decision of a poor mother in the slums of Lagos to use the handful of coins she has to buy white bread or ice cream for her child,

The Vice Lords

The Vice Lord Nation comprises a union of local black youth gangs in Chicago, studied by anthropologist Lincoln Keiser (1969). The Vice Lords originated in a reformatory in 1958; and by the mid-1960s their original nucleus had expanded to a wide range of neighborhoods—originally filling a temporary vacuum in the power struggles of local youth gangs (the Clovers, the Imperial Chaplains, the Cave Men), and eventually attracting established fighters from other gangs and recruiting local strength.

What had begun as a small social club, giving parties and providing neighborhood solidarity, had under the pressures of surrounding youth gangs become a formidable fighting gang. It was organized in a series of noncontiguous territories, streets within which the Vice Lords had primary power. The Vice Lord Nation was divided first of all into "branches" (The Albany Lords, the Madison Lords, the Maniac Lords, the War Lords, and so on), with the City Lords as the original and most powerful subgroup. Each branch had a particular set of officers and a territory. The formal offices provided a structure of leadership when a particular leader was arrested. The City Lords are in turn segmented into local "sections." These sections are subordinate to the City Lord officers; but the junior branches likewise ac-

knowledge the seniority of the City Lord leaders. It is only they who call the infrequent meetings of the entire Vice Lord Nation. Finally, each branch or section is divided into small "cliques" with strong internal solidarity; these, too, are usually named (Gallant Men, Rat Pack, Magnificent Seven).

If all this sounds reminiscent of a segmentary lineage system, it is. When the gang fights or "gangbangs" that are a focus of group prestige and solidarity break out, they operate in a way not unlike our hypothetical Smiths and Joneses in Chapter 9 or the Nuer of the Sudan (Case 34, Chapter 11). Thus:

If the Vice Lords involved in the gangbang are members of the same section, then it is section membership that will be significant; if the Vice Lords are members of different sections, but the same branch, then it is branch membership that is significant; and if the Vice Lords are members of different branches, it is club membership that will be significant. (Keiser 1969:31)

Within a branch or section, there is also a kind of age-grading (Seniors, Juniors, Midgets). Each local grouping also has a kind of women's auxiliary, girls who are known as Vice Ladies. This does not imply necessarily that Vice Ladies are the mates of particular Vice Lords, and does

or formula for her infant, are not centered in those slums, but far away. The forces that lead an Indian peasant, forced into debt by trying to compete with his tractor-and-fertilizer-using rich neighbor, to sell his plot of land and move into the squatter settle-

ments around Le Corbusier's shining city of Chandigarh, are not to be explained simply by network diagrams or analyses of cultural categories. An analysis of class relationships and global economic processes will tell us what a focus on the lives, deci-

not imply that they are more or less passive and subservient toward the men: one of Keiser's informants recounted vividly how a group of Vice Ladies bashed up a group of Lords with bricks, knives, and clubs when a youth and his Vice Lady girlfriend came to blows.

Fights occurred in planned and unplanned encounters and confrontations (for example, at a dance, a party, a game) or as operations of invasion and defense of club territory. Fights often trigger cycles of feuding. All this is a fairly rough business, when the weapons might include guns and knives as well as fists: killings were not infrequent.

Vice Lord groups also engaged in other operations—"hustling" (begging, stealing, or gambling), "wolf packing" (beating up passersby), "pulling jive" (drinking wine), shooting craps, or simply informally cruising together. Keiser vividly analyzes the ideologies central in the culture of such black youth gangs that give meaning to their actions: a valuation of "soul"(see also Keil's 1966 study of the Urban Blues), a "brotherhood," of "heart" (bravery and daring) and of playing the "game" successfully (that is, conning people, getting the best of interpersonal encounters, beating the system).

Personal status within the Vice Lords and similar gangs depends on displaying virtues of loyalty, bravery, and sheer audacity—but particularly of success and courage in fighting. Note here a partial convergence to the values of *machismo* and "crab antics" (Case 64, Chapter 17).

This usefully reminds us that the Vice Lords and their rivals do not exist in a social vacuum, and that—unlike the precolonial Nuer—they are not ultimately in control of their own territories and their own social system. They have been economically in an often desperate plight, surviving in a world of armed robbery and drug use against which the wider society wages war through police repression. The bravery and violence of black youth gangs have been nurtured by desperate anger and frustration fomented by poverty, alienation, and brutalization in reform schools and prisons.

It is noteworthy that in the latter 1960s the Vice Lords were undergoing a dramatic transformation under the impact of black nationalism and an influx of community-development funds. As economic opportunities opened and a sense of black identity was strengthened, gang fighting was giving way to political unity, militancy, and economic gain.

Case Update

For a study on gangs in contemporary Papua New Guinea, see Trompf (1994) with references.

sions, and social relations of individuals or their cultural conceptualizations does not (although class relationships are themselves also sustained by cultural factors).

Anthropological interpretations of social relations, whether in rural communities or urban enclaves, are always in danger of myopia—of seeing phenomena within too narrow a frame, of being naive about the wider-shaping forces of economic systems and of historic processes. Explanations for what goes on in the narrow frame are

Urban Nomads: "Tramps" and Drunks in Seattle

James Spradley decided that with a mountain of publications on "urban problems" that had accumulated in the 1960s, the anthropologist had a unique contribution to make: *"discover the native point of view"* (Spradley 1970:6). He suggested that methods worked out in tribal and peasant communities for analyzing folk classification, eliciting conceptual schemes and cultural "rules," and hence writing "cultural grammars" of how to reside postmaritally, stage weddings, or make gardens, could potentially provide a means for analyzing the distinctive cultures of urban minorities.

Spradley chose to focus on the culture of people classed as "bums," "tramps," or alcoholics on Skid Road in Seattle (this is the actual street from which the term "Skid Row" is derived). He studied them on the streets, in the courts, and in an alcoholism treatment center. Spradley's perceptions of the plight of urban nomads—condemned by society's rejection and the legal system to drift, to be demeaned and degraded, and to spend much of their lives in jail—are vivid and enlightening:

The urban nomad culture is characterized by *mobility, alienation, poverty,* and a unique set of *survival strategies.* Some men enter this way of life by choice, others are pushed toward it by personal problems, and some others are drawn. . . . because that is where the action is. Whatever the initial impetus, once a man moves to the edge of this world he will be thrust to its center. . . .
 The tramp is on a perpetual journey and the trip is more important than the destination. (Spradley 1970:253–254)

Spradley depicts the way that this mobility is forced by cycles of arrests that compel the urban nomads to keep moving on, yet trap them into the same scenarios wherever they go. Yet in their rejection by, and alienation from, society lies a curious solidarity: on Skid Road, if not elsewhere in the city, one lives in "a world of strangers who are friends" (Spradley 1970:255).

To characterize this world from the inside, Spradley analyzes folk taxonomies—the ways urban nomads classify one another and the scenes, settings, and events of their lives. Thus, he formulates a taxonomy of the "tramp domain," the way kinds of tramps are classified by one another (Table 20.1) Here many of the terms are unfamiliar: a "ding," for example, is a beggar. Spradley then analyzes the eight "core terms" of this "domain" using a kind of componential analysis such as we sketched in Chapter 3 to show how one might distinguish chairs, stools, and benches (Table 20.2). He uses similar formal devices to describe alternative outcomes of court hearings, parts of the "bucket" (the Seattle city jail), kinds of "flops" (places to sleep), and so on. Spradley uses a componential analysis to distinguish, in this domain of "flops," such alternative places as "trash box," "park bench," "brick yard," and "weed patch" according to such dimensions or criteria as atmospheric conditions (out of the wind and rain/snow versus out of the wind versus out of the wind, rain/snow, and cold) and body position (may lie down versus must sit up).

Case Update

In recent years, the topic of the homeless generally has been much studied. For instance, the reader is referred to work by Shanks and Stephanie (1995), Fitchen (1992), and Mathieu (1992).

Table 20.1 Taxonomic Definition of Tramp Domain

TRAMP		
Working Stiff	Mission Stiff	
Construction tramp		
Sea tramp		
Tramp miner		
Harvest tramp		
Fruit tramp		
	Nose diver	
	Professional nose diver	
Bindle stiff		
Airedale		
Rubber tramp		
Home guard tramp		
Box car tramp		
Ding		

Table 20.2 Componential Definition of Tramp Domain

	MOBILE	MODE OF TRAVEL	HOME BASE	LIVELIHOOD
Working stiff	Yes	Freight—Commercial	Job	Specialized—Works
Mission stiff	Yes	Commercial	Mission	Specialized—Missions
Bindle stiff	Yes	Freight	Pack	Generalized
Airedale	Yes	Walk	Pack	Generalized
Rubber tramp	Yes	Car	Car	Generalized
Home guard tramp	No	Ø	Town and Kinsmen	Generalized
Box car tramp	Yes	Freight	None	Generalized
Ding	Yes	Freight	None	Specialized—Begs

sought within the frame, not outside it; and that often leads to misleading and partial interpretations. It is the special and perhaps deepest dilemma of anthropological method that in viewing human life from close up, anthropologists see a richness of everyday experience other social scientists characteristically miss; but they are perhaps in danger of local, partial understandings of events shaped by outside forces. Most contemporary scholars recognize the need for a combination of methods and perspectives that will enable us to see the interrelationship of local and global factors in any given context, whether urban or rural.

SUMMARY

Sjoberg produced a model of the preindustrial city, depicting it as divided spatially and symbolically into rulers and ruled and ethnic and religious enclaves. These structures resemble those of hierarchical rural societies. Industrial technology has produced large cities with populations of the poor and squatters. Japan had preindustrial cities and then rapidly industrialized. Such cities show a blending of old and new features, as do African cities. Urbanized peoples in Africa often form voluntary associations that help migrants adapt to urban life (example: the Temne of Freetown, Sierra Leone). People in slums find their own ways of creating their lives, and the rich depend on the poor for a host of services. Crime emerges as a problem when this political economy breaks down. Social organization similarly is affected, but there is still the possibility for creative adaptations. R. Lincoln Keiser's 1960s study of the Vice Lords in Chicago shows such processes at work. Anthropologists have also used network analysis to elucidate how

urban poor people manage to survive. Anthropologists have studied the cognitive systems that underpin such strategies (for example: Spradley's work on self-classifications by tramps and homeless people in Seattle). Such cognitive approaches are valuable, provided they do not obscure the wider causes of urban poverty.

SUGGESTIONS FOR FURTHER READING

SECTION 57

Barnes, J. A. 1972. *Networks in Social Anthropology.* Reading, Mass.: Addison-Wesley Modules in Anthropology.

Basham, R. 1978. *Urban Anthropology: The Cross-Cultural Study of Complex Societies.* Palo Alto, Calif.: Mayfield Press.

Boissevain, J., and J. C. Mitchell, eds. 1973. *Network Analysis: Studies in Human Interaction.* New York: Humanities Press, Inc.

Eames, E., and J. G. Goode. 1977. *Anthropology of the City: An Introduction to Urban Anthropology.* Englewood Cliffs, N.J.: Prentice-Hall, Inc.

Eddy, E. M., ed. 1968. *Urban Anthropology: Research Perspectives and Strategies.* Southern Anthropological Society Proceedings, 2. Athens, Ga.: Southern Anthropological Society.

Foster, G. M., and R. V. Kemper, eds. 1973. *Anthropologists in Cities.* Boston: Little, Brown and Company.

Fox, R. G. 1972. Rationale and Romance in Urban Anthropology. *Urban Anthropology* 1: 205–233.

————. 1977. *Urban Anthropology: Cities in their Cultural Settings.* Englewood, Cliffs, N.J.: Prentice-Hall, Inc.

Friedl, J., and N. J. Chrisman, eds. 1975. *City Ways: A Reader in Urban Anthropology.* New York: T. Y. Crowell Company.

Gmelch, G., and W. P. Zenner. 1980. *Urban Life: Readings in Human Ethology.* New York: St. Martin's Press, Inc.

Gutkind, P. C. 1974. *Urban Anthropology: Perspectives on Third World Urbanization and Urbanism.* New York: Barnes & Noble, Inc.

Keish, R. L., and D. Jacobson, eds. 1974. *Urban Socio-Cultural Systems.* New York: Holt, Rinehart and Winston.

Mangin, W. P., ed. 1970. *Peasants in Cities: Readings in the Anthropology of Urbanization.* Boston: Houghton Mifflin Company.

Mitchell, J. C., ed. 1970. *Social Networks in Urban Situations.* New York: Humanities Press.

Spindler, G. D., and L. S. Spindler. 1978. *Anthropology in the U.S.: Four Cases.* New York: Holt, Rinehart and Winston.

Weaver, T., and D. White, eds. 1972. *The Anthropology of Urban Environments.* Boulder, Colo.: Society for Applied Anthropology.

Social Science and the Postcolonial World

What can anthropologists, and other social scientists, contribute to transforming the postcolonial nations—those sometimes referred to as the Third World? Can there be an effective "applied anthropology" or "development anthropology"? The view of the creation of the postcolonial world we have taken can well make us wary of Western plans for improving the standard of living of underdeveloped hinterlands communities. And what is to be the political relationship of anthropologists toward postcolonial peoples? Has past anthropology been an unwitting instrument of colonialism? And is present anthropology to be an unwitting instrument of neocolonialism and dependency? The questions to which we now turn are difficult and deep.

58. ANTHROPOLOGY AND COLONIALISM

Anthropologists on the Colonial Frontier

The successive waves of European expansion that engulfed the non-Western world brought to the frontiers a number of astute,

sympathetic observers of peoples and customs. Gifted missionaries, soldiers, explorers, and other pioneer scholars of the colonial frontiers created the foundations on which later theorists such as Morgan, Tylor, Frazer, and Durkheim built. One could trace connections between colonial expansionism and ethnographic observation as far back as the Spanish conquest of Mexico, or perhaps as Tacitus among the Germanic tribes, or even Herodotus.

But since it is the relationship between anthropology as a professional discipline and colonialism that has been searchingly reexamined, it is most useful to begin at about the turn of the twentieth century, when amateur ethnologists began to give way to professionals.

Whether and in what ways anthropologists have been instruments of colonial domination could be asked of South Asia or the Pacific, but it has been raised mainly in connection with North America, and with Africa.

Vine de Loria's (1969) hilarious but biting attacks on the anthropology of Native Americans, intentionally overstated, have boldly forced a rethinking. Anthropologists seeking to reconstruct and preserve vanishing ways of life had seen themselves as champions of the Native Americans. They cared when no one else did, valued what no one else did. That the still-viable Pueblo societies had closed ranks to exclude anthropologists and preserve their sacred secrets had seemed a local anomaly; elsewhere elders unfolded the ways of a remembered past, grateful that someone would listen, care, and perhaps pay a little.

But then the anger and the pride of the Pueblos spread on all sides, as once-broken and powerless peoples began to rise up. The friendly anthropologist had too often looked away when confronted with years of broken treaties, oppression, and shattering poverty, and had gone on piecing together remembered fragments of the old days. The summer visitors from universities and museums often left cumulations of bitterness building up behind them. And some anthropologists, working with the Bureau of Indian Affairs, had actively implemented policies of assimilationism whose cost is now being realized, policies which have become a target for the rhetoric of Red Power. Anthropologists therefore became political symbols and foils for rhetoric, and were caricatured into a kind of composite villain. The criticisms are only partial truths—but they hit close enough to home to force a rethinking, a new awareness, and soul-searching that have long been needed.

Other radical critics of anthropology and colonialism have charged that the social anthropologists, mainly British and South African, who studied British colonial Africa in the 1930s were instruments of colonial policy who developed their models of lineage structure and politics to establish and maintain colonial control. Thus it has been pointed out that functionalist studies of tribal politics served the interests of colonial administration through "indirect rule." Many studies of political and kinship insti-

tutions were funded by a government whose administrators needed to know how these institutions could be used to maintain colonial control within a framework of local custom. It has been suggested that in coming to live with a tribal people and record their social life, the anthropologist used "his people's" subordinate position to intrude upon them and gain their cooperation; and it has been argued that anthropologists were assuming their own niche in the hierarchy of colonial control that included district administrators, missionaries, planters, and traders. Finally, the roles of particular anthropologists vis-a`-vis colonial regimes and their relationship with their subjects have been harshly judged.

It is important to remember that anthropologists were genuinely concerned with what they perceived to be the well-being of the human beings in the communities they knew—and it seemed much better for well-intentioned administrators to understand local social structures than to act in ignorance. What was seldom if ever questioned in the Africa of the 1930s or 1940s was the inevitability of colonial rule. Independence seemed, to most, to be many decades away, if it was ever to come. Colonialism was an established fact and even a moral responsibility. The challenge was to rule well, not badly; and anthropologists did what they could to make colonialism benevolent. Moreover, their appreciation of their subjects as human beings, and their sympathy for different values and ways of life, set them off from most other whites in colonial settings.

Extreme condemnations of functionalist anthropology as a handmaiden of colonialism or of such leading figures as Evans-Pritchard or Nadel as instruments of colonial domination are too simplistic. The question of individual commitment should be treated with particular caution. The comments of Saudi Arabian–born Marxist anthropologist Talal Asad are worth quoting:

I believe it to be both mistaken and unjust to attribute invidious political motives to anthropologists studying primitive societies. . . . Most social anthropologists held and still hold radical or liberal political views. Nevertheless, it remains true that classic functionalism prevented them from effecting a fruitful conjunction between their political commitments and their sociological analysis. (Asad 1970:10)

Rather, the critique must be more global. Asad's later observations are incisive:

The basic reality which made prewar social anthropology . . . feasible and effective . . . was the power relationship between dominating . . . and dominated . . . cultures. We then need to ask . . . how this relationship has affected . . . the uses to which . . . knowledge was put; the theoretical treatment of particular topics; the mode of perceiving and objectifying alien societies; and the anthropologist's claim of political neutrality. . . .

The general drift of anthropological understanding did not constitute a basic challenge to the unequal world represented by the colonial system. Nor was the colonial system as such . . . analyzed. . . .

The scientistic definition of anthropology as a disinterested (objective, value-free) study of "other cultures" helped to mark off the anthropologist's enterprise from that of the trader, the missionary, the administrator . . . ; but did it not also render him unable to envisage and argue for a radically different political future for the subordinate people he studied and thus serve to merge that enterprise *in effect* with that of dominant status-quo Europeans? If the anthropologist sometimes endorsed or condemned particular social changes affecting "his people," did he, in this ad hoc commitment, do any more than many colonial Europeans who accepted colonialism as a system? If he was sometimes accusingly called "a Red," "a socialist," or "an anarchist" by administrators and settlers, did this not merely reveal one facet of the hysterically intolerant character of colonialism as a system, with which he chose nevertheless to live *professionally* at peace? (Asad 1973:17–18)

As Jacques Maquet (1964:260) put it, "What matters is that anthropology was oriented as though it wanted to preserve the existing situation." Though neither a condemnation of individual anthropologists nor a blanket dismissal of "functionalism" is justified or illuminating, it is important that the relationship between theory and its wider historical and ideological context be understood (here, Maquet's critique is highly illuminating). The balanced discussion by Richard Brown (1973) of the work of a brilliant humanistic scholar, Godfrey Wilson, in the setting of a government-sponsored institute in colonial northern Rhodesia well illuminates the complex interplay of theory and application, and of personal commitment and colonial policy.

It is too simple to attack past anthropologists for not condemning the evils of colonialism more globally and more insistently. Had they done so, they would not have run the gauntlet of colonial administrations whose permission and support they needed to get where they were going. In the 1930s, a vocally anticolonial anthropologist would have been an armchair scholar. Nor was it likely that many anthropologists would have been able to step outside the framework of their institutions—despite all the insistence about cross-cultural perspectives —to take a systemic, critical stance toward worldwide imperialism.

Contradictions of the Present

Finally, it is worth pointing out that the contradictions in the stance of many a humanistic anthropologist in the 1930s who accommodated to the realities of a colonialist system were no more stark than those of today's humanistic academic who serves as well-paid consultant to an international development agency.

But by the same token, anthropologists should not be surprised that newly independent peoples have often turned on their benevolent anthropological "friends" and condemned them as another bunch of colonialists—as wolves in sheep's clothing. Above all, the anthropological challenge is not to condemn errors of the past but to learn from them: to redefine the premises of fieldwork. One way in which this has been done is to carry out genuinely collaborative research, involving the host community in an active role (Stull 1987).

Now that the systemics of worldwide domination are opened to view, the nature of this domination has changed. No longer are colonialists "clothing and civilizing the savages"; now neocolonialists are developing the underdeveloped. The anthropologist who wants to do fieldwork in a remote tribal pocket must run the gauntlet of an independent postcolonial government likely to be hostile to what is seen as a holdover from colonialism (the missionary may well have the same problem). But often, the anthropologist (or other social scientist) is there sponsored by the United Nations or Ford Foundation to study or guide "modernization" or "development," and the postcolonial African or Asian elites the researcher deals with are enmeshed in a neocolonial system through which metropolitan countries continue to control and exploit their countries. Rhetoric about anthropology and the old colonialism will only dimly illuminate the ties between anthropology and the new colonialism. It is to these that we now turn.

59. APPLIED ANTHROPOLOGY, DEVELOPMENT STUDIES, AND NEOCOLONIALISM

British anthropologists became seriously and closely involved in colonial administration, and hence the practical application of anthropological knowledge, in the 1920s and especially the 1930s. There had been earlier links with government anthropologists in New Guinea and Africa, and a long tradition of colonial administrator-ethnologists. In United States anthropology there had been a long involvement in Native American affairs, including a tradition of government through the Bureau of American Ethnology that produced distinguished scholars such as Powell and Mooney. But the United States had no colonial empire other than the Philippines and a few scattered islands, and the practical problems of administration there received only limited anthropological attention.

World War II changed the face of American anthropology as dozens of anthropologists sought to assess the character of the enemy or played a part in the liberation and administration of Pacific and Asian regions. After the war, with Americans administering the Micronesian islands of the northern Pacific, anthropologists became centrally involved in the practical problems of administration and policy. Through the late 1940s, the 1950s, and the early 1960s, U.S. investment in rebuilding the war-torn world and aiding developing countries in modernization brought many scholars into **applied anthropology.**

Applied Anthropology

Scholars seeking to apply anthropological knowledge to community development or directed social change have often had mixed feelings about transforming old and valued ways: somewhat romantic appreciation of traditional cultures runs very deep in anthropology. But in general, "applied anthropologists" have accepted the inevitability of change and the desirability of improved education, community health, and participation in government. And in general, they have accepted the colonial or postcolonial social and political system that impinged on the community they were working in (in India, Peru, Mexico, or Micronesia) as inevitable, if not necessarily as benevolent. They sought to make the impact of a wider system on local communities less disruptive and painful than it would have been without their intermediation, or to shape local reform and revitalization. (A classic case of anthropological involvement in cultural change is the Cornell Peru Project in the Vicos Valley, presented in Case 82.)

At times anthropologists have had great surges of optimism about what they could tell governments and colonial administrators, or do themselves, to bridge cultural boundaries and make change more smooth or less costly in human terms. At other times the enormity and complexity of the problems and the inadequacies of their knowledge and theories have raised grave doubts and discouragement. The truth of what can and might be accomplished through applied anthropology lies somewhere between these poles of optimism and pessimism.

The optimism is generated by the fact that an anthropologist who has lived in a local community, who knows its leaders, its language, its details of custom, can very often see what is going wrong and how it might be set right. Many changes, procedures, laws or policies that seem sensible enough to the administrator, the mission-ary, or the doctor may lead to problems the anthropologist can foresee immediately.

Administering, converting, educating, or ministering to the health of a tribal or peasant people involves communication across cultural boundaries, in both directions. Misunderstandings run rampant on both sides, as messages in one cultural code are interpreted in terms of another. The anthropologist, specialist in the nature of cultural codes and conversant with each one, has often been able to serve as "cultural interpreter" or anticipate what messages would be misread and why.

Anthropologists have sometimes been able to suggest creative syntheses between the cultural traditions of a people and the changed situations and demands of modern life. A constitution may be possible that recognizes and builds on the authority of traditional leaders rather than bypassing them. A business cooperative might be formed in which the pattern of rights and responsibilities is modeled on traditional corporate or work groups (such as the Trobriand subclan or gardening team). Schools might teach the traditions, arts, and skills of a people—instead of European history—helping to foster the pride and cultural identity so crucial to a people as they undergo sweeping changes.

Why, then, the pessimism? Basically, because anthropologists are no better than other social scientists in predicting and anticipating human behavior, in all its manifold complexity. When communication takes place between peoples, we are prone to view this as *two cultures interacting*. But cultures do not interact; individual human beings do, with all their idiosyncrasies and unpredictability. An anthropologist might, for example, persuade the government to build a well in the villages he studied—and seemingly have anticipated and guarded against cultural misunder-

CASE

8 2

The Cornell Peru Project

A Peruvian anthropologist trained at Cornell had done field research from 1950 to 1952 in the Vicos Valley of Peru. Vicos was a manor or large estate with a population of about 1,700 monolingual Quechua-speaking Indians. Since early colonial times they had been bound as serfs or peons to the land.

Vicos was a public manor, owned by the Public Benefit Society (like many such manors) and providing revenue (at least in theory) to state charities. An individual or company rents such a manor, at auction, for 5 or 10 years. The renter, inevitably a Spanish-speaking *mestizo,* acquires the rights of a feudal lord over the serfs: he can not only demand farm labor to work the best lands commercially, but can demand household and other services as well. In "return" the serfs are given enough of the poorer agricultural land to eke out a marginal subsistence.

The Vicos serfs, like the villagers of Zinacantan (Chapter 18), had a religious hierarchy wherein respected elders who had given a life service to a scattered "community" took center stage in religious ritual for a year. But the *mestizo patron* and his agents had ultimate power over the peons. All efforts to break out of this desperate exploitative system had been ruthlessly crushed by a coalition of landlords, clergy, and police.

When the industrial firm renting Vicos went bankrupt in 1952 with 5 years of its lease remaining, Cornell University—through the leadership of anthropologist Alan Holmberg—stepped in and subleased the property. Their goal was to try to implement a bold and ambitious program of social change, in the role of *patron* into which they had stepped.

The Cornell Peru Project lasted 5 years. In this period, new farm technology and improved crops were able to lift agricultural production sharply, hence improve diet and bring an inflow of money for further capital improvement. With the aid of Peruvian authorities, education was improved. The work of peons in commercial production was channeled toward collective goals, and their manor services were paid. (Cornell enlisted the existing overseer into the operation, but in pursuit of the project's goals.) Political decision-making was increasingly passed to a committee of the former straw-bosses, progressively replaced by younger men committed to development goals.

When the 5 years were completed, Cornell sought to enable the peons to purchase the manor from the Public Benefit Society. For 5 years, power elites in the region and powerful government figures who themselves were absentee landlords sought to block the freeing of the serfs and their control over their own destiny. Through political pressure from the United States and sympathetic Peruvian intellectuals, the Vicos community finally became independent in 1962—though Cornell continued to play a supervisory role.

The transformation of Vicos, through a program that was unabashedly paternalistic, was viewed by Holmberg (1965:7) in retrospect as a bold demonstration that Peru's "serf and suppressed peasant populations, once freed and given encouragement, technical assistance, and learning, can pull themselves up by their own bootstraps and become productive citizens of the nation." He was optimistic that the Peruvian government's programs of land reform would "go a long way towards a more peaceful and rapid development of the country as a whole" (Holmberg 1965:7).

standing. Yet the project might be rejected because political rivalry between two local leaders leads one to condemn the well, or because someone put a curse on it during a quarrel with his wife. Such turns of events are no more predictable in a village setting than they are in a modern nation. (On community-centered praxis as a response to this problem, see Singer 1994.)

There is another and related problem. When an anthropologist penetrates into another way of life, he or she does so in layers or stages. After several months of fieldwork, a researcher learns the formal rules and groupings that lie on the surface of a society and its culture. At this stage one may feel a confidence and understanding that later evaporates into a feeling of ignorance as one penetrates to a deeper level. Such alternating stages of insight and impotence continue as one probes further. Those who have penetrated most deeply into another way of life are more often left with a feeling of how complex it is and how profound and unpredictable are the ramifications of any decision or event than they are with a feeling that all is known, that prediction is possible.

Yet too often attempts at applied anthropology have been made in the flush of superficial understanding. Particularly when administrators need answers, they are not likely to want to wait years. Too often the role of consultant has taken the anthropologist into an area just long enough for the formal outlines to come into focus, and not long enough for them to dissolve into a blur again. This premature feeling of confidence has also been fostered by the involvement of partially trained or inexperienced anthropologists. Saving the world by anthropology, as by any other means, looks easier to the idealistic neophyte than to the experienced and battle-scarred campaigner.

A final problem in applying anthropological knowledge to practical policy is that very often the choice is between a set of dismal alternatives. It is often not a question of which course of action will work best; but rather, which will work less badly than the others. A people whose old order is breaking down, yet who if they opt for Western ways will be condemned by geography and resources to a life of poverty and isolation, have no desirable alternatives. They are the victims of a world that oppressed, exploited, impoverished, and isolated them; they can neither fully join nor ignore it. In such situations, the satisfactions of applied anthropology are few and the successes are still failures.

Beyond Applied Anthropology

Applied anthropology has been questioned by a number of anthropologists of varying persuasions. Glynn Cochrane (1971), for example, has called for a more broadly conceived "development anthropology"; and he has argued that the anthropologically sophisticated administrator, with more practical approaches and more decisive commitment to development goals, can often do better as an agent of change than the professional anthropologist. (There is something to be said for this criticism: academics are notoriously wishy-washy and slow in making decisions; but on the other side, administrators in cross-cultural situations have a strong record for making bad decisions quickly.) Other criticisms have come from such scholars as Sol Tax, calling for a more bold, decisive, and politically conscious "action anthropology" that would seek to challenge the wider system that is oppressing local communities and to tackle urgent human problems directly rather than, as has usually been the case, as a by-product of fieldwork directed to other goals.

As events in the late 1960s were to make dramatically clear, we need to go further still. With Project Camelot, an abortive attempt to use social science to enable the U.S. government to manipulate the course of politics in Latin American countries, the uses and abuses of applied anthropology began to emerge (see Horowitz 1965). Subsequent revelations about CIA and Defense Department funding behind seemingly innocuous research on the northern frontier of India brought a storm of protest from the Indian government and bitter division among the anthropologists involved (Berreman 1969). Participation of anthropologists in the forced resettlement of Vietnamese villagers and the manipulation of Montagnard tribesmen—often under a cloak of deception—cast a further pall on applied anthropology at a time when opposition to the Vietnam War had polarized the country, alienated millions of Americans from the policies of their government, and shattered the credibility of the myths of the Cold War. The bitterest and most disruptive division in American anthropology focused on clandestine participation of scholars in secret U.S. government programs to reinforce a pro-American regime in Thailand and prevent the tide of revolution from spilling over from Indochina. (See Hamnett 1978 for an evaluation of issues of this kind.)

Meanwhile, in Latin America, U.S.-financed programs of economic development and "land reform"—Kennedy's Alliance for Progress and subsequent programs—sought to create stability, reduce peasant unrest, and erode support for revolutionary movements in Bolivia, Ecuador, Colombia, Brazil, Peru, Chile, Paraguay, Guatemala, Nicaragua, and other areas. And anthropologists found themselves studying ways to alleviate the symptoms of suffering in oppressed rural communities while reinforcing the ruling classes and systems of economic domination that were causing the suffering.

Anthropologists doing applied research in poor American communities similarly found themselves being paid to find out what was wrong with some families or why some people drank all the time instead of working—to find cures for local symptoms that would settle community unrest. The social and economic system that generated oppression in minority enclaves was the very system government and foundations sought to preserve and strengthen.

Anthropology and Liberation?

Realization by many individuals within anthropology that the system they were serving was oppressing the people whose lives they sought to improve has placed the tradition of applied anthropology in a harsh new light. It has been one element in a transformed consciousness about the role of the United States, England, France, Japan, Germany, and other industrial nations in the postcolonial world—about the global economic system and the structures of neocolonialism and dependency. The understandings of this global system and its consequences for postcolonial peoples built up in Chapter 19 will serve us well.

Thus, for example, in Brazil, staggering overseas investment in the development of the interior went hand in hand with sordid political repression and the massive arming by the United States of a military dictatorship—guaranteeing political and hence economic stability at the expense of freedom, and rewarding a small millionaire aristocracy amid vast poverty, squalor, and suffering. The same theme is repeated on a lesser scale over and over in Latin America.

The threat to this system is that poverty and repression often lead to revolution. So aid projects to "develop" rural areas, and token land reform that does little or nothing to redistribute wealth or power, are undertaken to create hope among the hope-less and powerless. Token development is replacing religion as the "opium of the people."

And there in the village has been the an-thropologist or the Peace Corps volunteer trying to teach people to use tractors in-stead of water buffaloes, to raise slightly the productivity of miserable and overworked landholdings, to read and write, or to im-prove village sanitation. The elites that con-trol the most productive land and rake the benefits from foreign aid are far from view, in the cities, behind high walls, in glittering villas, in penthouses. (And their children are likely to be at Harvard or Oxford.)

One irony, as Kathleen Gough (1968) pointed out, is that the anthropologist—if allowed to do research in postcolonial countries at all—is likely to be welcome only in those countries that are client states of the West. Where independence and sov-ereignty have been genuine, not nominal, Western anthropologists have usually been excluded as imperialists in yet another guise. And given the historic role of anthro-pologists, however naive and innocent they may have been about its implications, such a stance is often sensible enough.

Gough's conclusion, one that a number of her colleagues came to share, was that the anthropologist's role as a champion of freedom and dignity for common people should be to support social revolution in neocolonialist countries. If anthropolo-gists do not stand with the oppressed, she argued—if they accept the status quo in the countries where they work, despite political repression and gross inequalities in power and wealth—then they themselves are op-pressors.

Such rhetoric, urging as it does support of socialist revolution, resistance to world capitalism, and active political involve-ment, goes too far for many—most—students or anthropologists to accept. To people who have been brought up to think that fighting back the forces of communism is the historic destiny of the United States and that capitalism and democracy go hand in hand, such talk is downright heretical if not treasonous. But the challenge to ques-tion assumptions and dogma is squarely laid down, for those bold enough to under-take it—whatever the outcome.

The "Neutrality" of Social Science

At least, the bitter political debate in anthro-pology has given the lie to the widespread assumption that social science can be objec-tive and neutral—that it can be free of ideo-logical and political commitments and can seek truth without involvement. It has been realized that not taking a political position, not making a moral commitment, is not neutral: it *is* making a commitment—to the support and continuation of the system of which one is a part and within which one is working anthropologically. If one does not "notice" oppression or injustice or ex-ploitation because one is "only a scientist" and science does not concern itself with po-litical issues, then one is being myopic and self-deluding about objectivity. Ultimately amorality is immorality. At the same time the social scientist needs to show balance. There is no imperative to espouse a revolu-tionary, but only a concerned, stance or position.

The myth of scientific objectivity has also begun to fall apart through an awareness of the ideological bias implicit in social science theory. Theories that seem to build on com-mon sense in fact build on the premises of the economic and political systems of the theorist. Thus the assumptions that the in-dividual is the appropriate locus of expla-nation, that social systems are created and maintained by cumulative individual acts of maximization and self-interest, and that the roots of such self-interest lie deep in human nature are premises of Western capitalist ideology that have been promulgated since Adam Smith's time to rationalize and explain the political economy of Western nations. The anthropologist or sociologist or economist who uses such models may take these premises to be obvious, objective, and beyond question. The rise of radical counter-interpretations within Western social sciences (including a belated discovery of the extensive body of Marxist scholarship) has given new insight into the ideological biases of "establishment" social science. Yet, equally, the denial of all "individuality" to persons outside the capitalist world may perpetuate a falsely romanticized picture of the world.

All this points to a need to broaden and generalize the intellectual base of anthropology and other social sciences—the need for a "critical and self-reflexive" study of human assumptions and the distortions in our special view of the world (Scholte 1972). It also points to a need to redefine the relationship of anthropology to the postcolonial world, a need for decolonization of anthropology both at the level of theory and at the level of practice. It is to these problems that we now turn.

60. DECOLONIZING ANTHROPOLOGY

Anthropology has aspired to be a general study of human condition, ranging widely in time and space to see contrasts and similarities. But the kind of perspective we have taken underlines the fact that a Chinese anthropology or an ancient Indian anthropology or a Trobriand anthropology might have begun with very different premises, and achieved very different perspectives. (Seeing anthropology as a product of colo-

nial expansion, and of the romantic quest for the "primitive" as a recurrent Western fantasy, helps us to understand why Chinese, Indians, and Trobrianders did *not* elaborate anthropological theories—for this version of the enterprise was peculiarly Western.) A different approach is taken by anthropologists who use ethnography itself to articulate protest (Brodkey 1987).

The Insider's View, the Outsider's View

All this underlines an urgent need for one kind of decolonization of anthropology, at an intellectual level. Scholars studying human behavior in comparative settings—perhaps most urgently in Western industrialized countries—could contribute crucially to the emergence of a genuinely universal and generalized study of human ways. As debates and discussion (see, for example, Lewis 1973 and Caulfield 1973) have underlined, there needs to be a decolonization of anthropology that yields both the insights that come from studying one's own culture, and the insights that come from an outsider studying another people's way of life.

The central theme of Lewis's argument, building on other critiques, is that in a decolonized anthropology the anthropologist would always belong to the same ethnic or local category as those studied (Lewis 1973).

But, as Caulfield and others have countered, there are some flaws in this approach. One flaw is that an anthropologist with a university Ph.D. who happens to be a Native American, for example, who grew up in a middle-class suburban setting, although he may be defined *politically* as an "insider," is probably separated by wide gulfs of social class from Native American groups living on reservations whose traditional culture he is attempting to study—and thus may be as much "outside" in terms of culture and class as an "outside" anthropologist who came from some other ethnic background or culture. Second, the anthropological cost of an inside view is at least as great as the benefit. A corollary of Lewis's view would seem to be that only white middle-class ethnographers should study American suburbia. Yet they may be precisely the wrong ones to do it, because they take too much for granted, accepting strange behavior (like clipping grocery coupons or taking pet dogs to doctors) as commonplace and undeserving of comment. The heightened perception of a Trobriand anthropologist or a Kachin anthropologist would be likely to cast more vivid comparative light on American upper-middle-class behavior than an anthropologist who grew up in these settings. Unfortunately, when scholars from India, Indonesia, the Philippines, or Nigeria have been trained anthropologically, they have usually been indoctrinated with the technical jargon and theoretical prejudices of Anglo-American or continental anthropology. In the process of acquiring a Ph.D. from Oxford, Chicago, the Sorbonne, or Leiden, an anthropologist is likely to be so indoctrinated in the traditional assumptions of the discipline that he or she emerges perceiving the world in the manner of its leading academics. Part of the challenge in decolonizing anthropology is for students to be encouraged to question and challenge the premises and categories of Anglo-American or French anthropology, not simply apply them in emulation of their teachers.

At the same time, there is some power in an inside view as well: intuitions can be brought to bear, and native actors can often see the oversimplifications in anthropological descriptions. Conventional anthropological descriptions may be possible only because of the ethnographer's limited evidence and relative ignorance of how subtle and complicated another people's social world really is. As I have observed, "The anthropologist who can confidently write about 'the lineage' in an African tribe would be hard-pressed to write in a similar vein about 'the department' in his university—because he [or she] knows too much" (Keesing 1972c:38). The inadequacies, oversimplifications, and distortions of fieldwork—the costs of an "outside" view—have become clear as students in formerly colonial areas learn what anthropologists have written about their people. In Papua New Guinea, for example, there is a body of critical commentary from Trobrianders, Dobuans, Enga, Arapesh, and other students from anthropologically classic societies on the flaws of ethnography and the frailties of ethnographers. These commentaries proceeded both from genuine inside knowledge and from a sense of rivalry towards the outside scholar. In some cases there has been appreciative collaboration also. These obvious benefits of an insider's perspective highlight the need for and value of a dialectic between insider's and outsider's views, so that benefits of each can be achieved and the limits of each can be transcended. It seems more appropriate to recast Lewis's critique.

The Powerless as Partners

What is needed is a genuine decolonization of anthropology; and having anthropologists study only people of their own culture or skin color gives only a partial and illusory decolonization. The colonialism in anthropology has come from the rich, powerful, and dominant studying the poor, powerless, and subordinate; and racism has been more symptom and by-product than cause of this exploitation. (As we noted, the boundaries between oppressed and oppressor, between the victims and perpetrators of racism or its equivalent, have shifted historically with tides of economic exploitation: poor whites and southern Europeans and Irish have been victims, as well as Africans and Asians, when it was economically advantageous to deny them full status.) A decolonized anthropology will have to balance this asymmetry of power and seek to create a dialectical and symmetrical relationship between the studier and the studied.

As we will shortly see, this means a new ethic of fieldwork where subjects are accorded full rights, where they participate as collaborators in the process of ethnography and its rewards. But it also means that anthropology can no longer concern itself only with powerless, poor, marginal communities far from where wealth and power are manipulated. An anthropology not only of suburbia but of bureaucracies, corporations, governments, and legal systems is urgently needed. As we have seen in previous sections, the anthropologist's view from a small marginal community often leaves hidden the wider systemic forces of economy and politics that shape local events. Anthropologists—including both those from postcolonial nations and Anglo-American anthropologists who can look critically at their own institutions—need to be where decisions are made, as well as in distant communities where their impact is felt.

61. STUDYING UP

Can a discipline that has historically studied the remote and powerless peoples now productively begin to "study up," to study the centers of power in contemporary society?

Where the Power Is

Laura Nader made the first clear call in anthropology for a study of Western elites, transnational corporations, and state institutions:

> We anthropologists have studied the culture of the world only to find in the end that ours is one of the most bizarre of all cultures and one, by virtue of its world influence for "bad" or "good," in urgent need of study. (Nader 1964:302)

A social science that "studies up," to the extent that studies are effective and penetrate layers of secrecy and press agents' propaganda, is likely to meet opposition and hostility. Scant wonder, when the interlocking structures of international finance, corporate investment, development policy, and government have such a strong vested interest in preserving myths and hiding their connections. Thus, for instance, Dutch activist social scientist Gerrit Huizer, who worked for years mobilizing Latin American and Indian peasants, noted the following about his own country:

> The Royal Institute for the Tropics in Amsterdam . . . , a major agency for sponsoring fundamental and development research and completely subsidized by the Dutch Ministry of Development, has a board of directors with five of its seven members being top managers of Dutch multinational corporations with considerable investments in the Third World. (Huizer 1979:38)

If "studying up" means studying the Ford Foundation or the World Bank or the International Monetary Fund, should one be surprised that research quickly turns into a kind of detective work of unraveling hidden connections and penetrating layers of secrecy and deception? Huizer made this observation:

CASE

83

Agribusiness and the Sahel Famine

One of the startling facts that came to light in the detective work of Lappé and Collins on the Sahel was the extent of food *exports* from the Sahel in the peak period of drought and famine:

[There were] vast amounts of agricultural goods sent out of the region, even during the worst years of drought. Ships in . . . Dakar . . . bringing in "relief" food departed with stores of peanuts, cotton, vegetables, and meat. Of the hundreds of millions of dollars' worth of agricultural goods the Sahel exported during the drought, over 60 percent went to consumers in Europe and North America and the rest to elites in other African countries. . . . (Lappé and Collins 1978:89)

French corporations were making vast profits in the height of famine. But Americans were on the scene as well. Lappé and Collins discovered that a California-based agribusiness corporation, the world's largest iceberg lettuce grower, had in 1972—at the height of its difficulties with Cesar

Chavez and his United Farm Workers of California seeking to unionize farm labor—established a giant agribusiness subsidiary in Senegal, West Africa:

The Senegalese government, the German foreign aid agency and [the] World Bank . . . put up most of the capital. The Senegalese government helpfully supplied police to clear away villagers who had always presumed the land was theirs for growing millet for themselves and the local market. The Peace Corps contributed four volunteers. (Collins and Lappé 1977:27)

They note that the height of the Sahel famine, the corporation's Senegal subsidiary was exporting large quantities of vegetables to Europe. Collins and Lappé (1977:27) find similarly complex global connections in looking at other agribusiness multinationals: one of them, also California-based, "operates farms, fisheries, and processing plants in more than two dozen countries."

Agencies which are determining development policies concerning . . . peasants, such as the World Bank and the International Monetary Fund, . . . are closely related to Western economic and political interests in ways which are not easy to unravel. What is the significance of the fact that the director of the World Bank . . . was formerly a chairman of the Ford Motor Company and later United States Secretary of Defense, and that [the] . . . director of the International Monetary Fund . . . [and] his predecessor were both advisers to the Anglo-Dutch Unilever Company, one of the fifteen largest multinational corporations. (Huizer 1979:30–31)

Social scientists who work in universities need not dig very deeply to discover ways in which their own institutions are engaged in international big business and politics (through their investments, through their dependence on government and foundation grants, through the power of trustees and boards of regents, and the like). Academic freedom has sharply defined limits, as scholars who have become "too political" have often discovered. It is no coincidence that much of the best "studying up" has come not from university academics but from research groups outside institutional structures and more freedom from their constraints.

Studying Transnational Corporations

Excellent research on transnational investments and development strategies in the postcolonial world has been done by groups such as the North American Congress on Latin America (NACLA) and the Pacific Studies Center. Here again, considerable detective work is often needed to penetrate the layers of disguise and find subtle connections—such as interlocking boards of directors, subsidiary companies, and movements of funds between countries, not to mention hidden political influence. (Some may recall the record of massive international bribery used by an American aircraft corporation to try to sell its products around the world—a practice that company executives sometimes sought to justify on grounds that such bribery is common practice among corporations operating internationally.)

"Studying up" is not, of course, something only anthropologists can or should do. Lappé and Collins pursued studies of the political economy of food by looking at corporate investment and agribusiness in the postcolonial world (through a research group called the Institute for Food and Development Policy. Their studies of drought in the Sahel region of Africa (Case 77, Chapter 19), its causes and consequences, led them into detective work to find out what corporate interests were at work. Their findings are presented in Case 83.

Thus, "studying up" would lead us to look not only at foundations and corporations, but at government bureaucracies, at judicial systems, at police systems, at communications media, and so on. Again, anthropologists have no special mandate to study the centers of power. But their traditional role of studying remote communities, and studying through close participation in people's everyday lives, may give them special perspectives and insights. The view from within and the view from below can perhaps be joined (Huizer 1979:23–29). More recently, Laura Nader (1980, 1996) has continued to work on these themes.

62. ANTHROPOLOGY AND THE "FOURTH WORLD"

We noted (§54) that the oppression of tribal and other ethnic minorities within postcolonial states puts in jeopardy peoples anthropologists have studied. Such tribal or ethnic minorities, threatened by internal colonialism, have been recently depicted as constituting an oppressed "Fourth World," within the "Third." What stances can and should anthropologists take toward powerless peoples threatened by cultural extinction (ethnocide) or even extermination (genocide)? The problem applies not only in postcolonial circumstances, but globally—as, for example, in Yugoslavia and the countries it formerly included.

Speaking Out

One clear responsibility of the social scientist who (by virtue of research in such an area) has specialist knowledge of what is happening is to make that information public, as clearly and forcefully as possible. Thus American anthropologist Shelton Davis, working in a research group investigating the oppression of Brazil's Amazonian Indians, writes:

> The basic responsibility of anthropologists who possess knowledge of the situation of Indian peoples in Brazil is . . . to document just what is happening . . . , to counter the

CASE

8 4

Destruction of the Yanomamö?

The 8,500 Yanomamö Indians of Amazonia, whose homeland is divided by the Brazil-Venezuela border, comprise one of the last strongholds of traditional subsistence economy and intact community organization in Amazonia. They have fiercely defended their autonomy—while fighting one another (Case 10)—for the centuries since Europeans invaded South America.

Now the Northern Perimeter Highway, part of Brazil's new network of highways through Amazonia, and massive mineral development, threaten to destroy this autonomy, and the Yanomamö themselves (Davis 1980).

Although the . . . highway is still not completed, one section has been built along the southern fringe of Yanomamö territory. Diseases carried by highway workers have already destroyed 15 Yanomamö villages along the first 100 kilometers of the new road. Brazilian anthropologist Alcida Ramos, who was present at the time of the initial invasion by highway workers, witnessed Indians in a state of misery, sickness, and shock. The Indians refused to speak their language, their gardens had been uprooted by bulldozers, and they were wearing ragged clothing given to them by highway workers and infested with influenza, tuberculosis, measles, and other germs. (Davis 1980:20–21)

The agency which supposedly protects Indian rights, FUNAI, which in fact works closely with development interests, proposed creation of 21 small Indian reserves for the Yanomamö in Brazil. But these enclaves would leave out 2,900 living in 58 villages (Davis 1980:21).

In addition, highway and settlement corridors are planned to run between almost all of these reserves and no provisions have been made for satisfying the demographic, ecological, and subsistence needs of the tribe. (Davis 1980:21)

In response, a group of prominent Brazilians proposed to the government the creation of a 16 million acre Yanomamö Indian Park, that would at least give the Indians the chance of viable future life. The government countered by appointing to the presidency of FUNAI a retired army officer with no experience with Indian affairs, who previously had been chief of security and information for the mineral corporation that is seeking mining rights in Yanomamö country.

Case Update

For the later history of FUNAI, see the work of Oliveira (1988).

fallacious claims of governments and other agencies, and to raise to public and international attention the real conditions of native peoples. (Davis 1979:217)

As anthropologists, . . . our primary contribution to the rights of indigenous peoples lies in independently and publicly documenting the social realities that these people face.

Given the nature of political repression in contemporary Brazil, this . . . is a vital task. Political secrecy and repression have become institutionalized aspects of both the Brazilian government and my own, and we can do no less, as scientists and citizens, than make known what our governments would wish left free from public scrutiny, action, and debate. (Davis 1979:223)

What price progress? Brazil's Trans-Amazon Highway network is being carved out of rain forest at a cost of ecological devastation, the destruction of Indian populations and their cultures, and the forced resettlement of thousands of poor farmers along the highway margins.

Davis's account of the ethnocide, desperate poverty, and in some areas virtual extermination to which Brazilian Indians have been subjected in the name of development, progress, and "integration into the national society" (Davis 1977) has helped to bring the truth to light. His most recent warnings point to the threat to the Yanomamö and their neighbors (see Case 84), whose patterns of feuding we glimpsed in Chapter 7.

Such cynical greed as reported in Case 84 is not confined to any particular part of the world. Aboriginal Australians whose aspirations to community control and development, recognition of rights to ancestral lands, and the preservation of sacred sites are all recognized in the rhetorical pronouncements of state and federal governments, were cynically manipulated, deceived, intimidated, and invaded when they stood in the way of mineral explorations. Recognition of Aboriginal rights in

the abstract is a convenient rhetorical stance for Australian politicians; but particularly in the most conservative states, Queensland and Western Australia, these rights are trampled whenever money is at stake. (For further studies see Beckett 1995, Keen 1993, Merlan 1995.)

The political stance appropriate to the anthropologist in the face of ethnocide, genocide, or the oppression of powerless minorities in pursuit of profit is clear enough. But a problem emerges if this stance is elevated into a general commitment to the autonomy and cultural integrity of tribal minorities.

The Argument for Cultural Autonomy

Is it sufficient for anthropologists, as a general commitment, to argue that tribal peoples should be left alone to practice their traditional cultures? Have they thought through the full implications of principles of cultural pluralism and the relative autonomy of traditional societies? In an important paper, Terence Turner (1979) argues that they have not. Characterizing this position as a commitment to "cultural autonomy," Turner notes that it portrays "cultures" as essentially static, and that it denies to a people themselves the power to act, choose, and change in the face of oppression. He would have us substitute for the romantic naïveté of a universal support for cultural autonomy a commitment to the

> optimization of people's ability to control, create, reproduce, change or adopt social and cultural patterns for their own ends. (Turner 1979:12)

This requires that we replace a fuzzy belief in the superiority of the "primitive" and the sanctity of culture with a critical view of "traditional" ways of life, such as we have taken in this book. Turner notes that a

CASE

85

The Balante of Guinea-Bissau and National Goals

The Balante [comprise] one of the two major indigenous peoples of the country and . . . the least integrated, economically, socially, and politically, into the national society. It is a patrilinea, segmentary lineage-based society with an age-set system. Political and economic power is firmly in the hands of the senior men who act as lineage heads and preside over the age-set organization. They use their position in the lineage and age systems to accumulate surplus agricultural produce, which they reinvest in wives. Control of the marriage system, expressed in the institution of polygamy, also allows them to control younger men. An elaborate system of funerary rituals and mortuary feasts also serves as a vehicle for their dominance of the society as a whole. (Turner 1979:14–15)

Following the independence of Guinea-Bissau in 1974, after a 10-year struggle, the ruling PAIGC party rejected development in the neocolonial Western mold:

It has instead embarked upon a popularly based socialist model of development. . . . The political basis of this program is a system of local institutions: Village Committees and People's Courts (both elected, and both with a mandatory representation of women), . . . health clinics and schools. . . . The basic economic program is . . .

based on heightened productivity by the peasant population as a whole, partly based on positive economic incentives and partly on their understanding and ideological support of the goals of national development. (Turner 1979:14, citing Aaby 1978)

Faced with conservatism by Balante elders against changes that would undermine their domination of the traditional society, PAIGC did not use repression but sought "to induce the Balante themselves to overthrow [those] aspects of the traditional system" that subordinate women and young men and extract their labor for investment in wives and mortuary feasting:

The social and political pattern of domination of women and younger men by senior men supported by the traditional economic and sociocultural pattern is . . . incompatible with the . . . goals of PAIGC, which emphasizes egalitarian cooperation and the participation of all sections of the population, explicitly including women, in the productive and distributive aspects of the accumulation process. (Turner 1979:15)

Case Update
See Bigman (1993) for a further review of Guinea-Bissau history and agriculture.

commitment to "cultural autonomy" often entails another assumption:

The way of life [of] . . . whatever indigenous or tribal groups the anthropologist happens to be defending is actually superior, either in terms of ecological adaptation or some general notion of the authentic cultural potential of the human species, to that of the more technologically advanced, Westernized societies

that currently dominate and oppress them. (1979:8)

Turner does not question the destructive effects of the dominant society in situations such as the one in Amazonia (where he himself worked) where Indians are being threatened with pauperization and extermination. These Indians need desperately to have their plight recognized internationally, since the forces deployed against them include not only a repressive government quite prepared to sacrifice them to "progress," but some of the world's largest corporations, which are investing hundreds of millions of dollars in the transformation of Amazonian rain forest into mines, agribusiness development, and other sources of profit. But in the general case, what indigenous minorities desperately need is power to speak and choose for themselves as well as protection from the devastation of their environments and engulfment in cash economy and national society. They have in fact begun to organize themselves into local movements for their own empowerment over ecological issues.

It is not participation in the national society *in itself* that necessarily erodes the quality of life in hinterlands communities. It is incorporation into global and national economy as poor plantation laborers, or massive internal colonialism in the form of immigration and/or resource extraction (as in Irian Jaya). Turner notes that the quality of life in traditional society may have been a good deal higher for male elders than for women or young men. In romanticizing traditional cultures we are blinded to the oppression they entailed.

When some members of a traditional culture are oppressed, as described, for example, in Case 85, an anthropologist arguing for the preservation of the traditional system in the name of "cultural autonomy" would be allied with male elders in maintaining the subordination of women and young men. We must, Turner argues, support the right of peoples in traditional societies to liberate themselves, even when that means overturning systems that are undeniably imbued with symbolic meaning and are the product of human cultural creativity.

63. THEORY AND ACTION: THE CHALLENGE OF SOCIAL CHANGE

"Applied social science" has often had second-place status because it has been contrasted with "pure" research, which is supposed to demand and advance theory. But the genuine transformation of social systems—not simply the cosmetic treatments that often pass for "development"—places the ultimate demands on the adequacy of our theories. Commitment to improving the world is no substitute for understanding it. That is why, in the foregoing chapters, I have placed such emphasis on a theoretical framework for understanding. If we do not have the power to see beneath the surfaces of things, to see processes rather than symptoms, to see whole systems rather than separate parts, then our individual efforts and energies will be dissipated; our voices will add to the confusion that surrounds us.

Let me illustrate. The oppressive systems of landownership of such countries as India, the Philippines, Bolivia, Chile, Colombia, Uruguay, and other parts of Latin America are a major obstacle to the liberation of the rural poor and the transformation of production. "Land reform" is a crucial step, before production can be reorganized. But how is this to be achieved? What are the roots of the problem?

Urban Bias: A Correct Analysis?

Michael Lipton (1977) argues that the roots of rural poverty in the Third World lie in what he calls "urban bias." Political decision-making and allocation of resources are controlled by an urban elite who systematically discriminate against rural areas. Thus capital is generated in rural hinterlands, by export crop production or mining; and it gets spent in cities, rather than in improving infrastructures of transportation, communication, education, and health in the countryside. Lipton's analysis suggests that to redress this imbalance and urban bias would require concerted "rural power": An alliance and united front of rural people—of poor farmers and rich ones, landless laborers and their employers—so as to demand their fair share of development resources.

Is this the right answer? Byres (1979) argues convincingly that Lipton is wrong in his analysis—and that he thus points to the wrong solution. Reanalyzing the statistics Lipton himself had presented, Byres shows that if anything, there is a *rural* bias. Where does rural bias come from? In countries such as India or the Philippines, the elites who control political power may live in the cities; but their wealth and power bases are very often rural, sustained by vast landholdings. Rural class systems deeply divide landless workers from kulaks (rich farmers employing labor) and subsistence farmers, and divide sharecroppers from absentee landlords. In suggesting an alliance to combat "urban bias," Lipton would have those divided by opposed class interests join against an imaginary common enemy:

> The divisions which actually exist in the countryside of the Third World are both far deeper than Lipton suggests and developing irreversibly with a speed and ferocity which make nonsense of the idea of a single rural class. (Byres 1979:235)

Instead, he says, rural areas of the contemporary Third World are characterized by

> polarization along class lines . . . , with a class of kulaks growing immensely in power, a poor peasantry cut off from the fruits of technical advance and the advantages of . . . high food prices, and rising numbers of landless laborers. (Byres 1979:235)

What Are the Class Relations?

The same issue was debated by Marxist scholars in India, through the 1970s, in slightly different form. Is the dominant mode of production in postindependence rural India quasi-feudal, based on absentee landlords and merchant moneylenders? Or is it, increasingly, capitalist, with kulaks employing landless labor as the dominant class? The question is not merely academic:

> The mode of production in agriculture is vitally connected with the question of *who is the main enemy*, and how to orient rural organizing strategy. (Omvedt 1978:383)

Omvedt argues that in postindependence India, capitalist relations of production have increasingly become dominant:

> With independence and coming of power of the national bourgeoisie, limited antifeudal land reforms and a limited but significant investment by the state [and, we might add, the impact of the green revolution and the massive influence of the World Bank and other forces of "development"] there has been an increasing development of capitalist relations in agriculture. . . . [This] has not led to any sustained growth in agricultural production, but rather to an increased marginalization as well as proletarianization of the rural population. . . . [Thus] the focus of conflict in rural areas has shifted, . . . so that now the main contradiction is between poor peasants and laborers on the one hand, and rich peasants and landlords on the other. (Omvedt 1978:385)

A further analysis of the Indian situation would take us into deeper complexities—for example, the way rich farmers and landlords use caste divisions to set the poor against one another, and prevent exactly these class alliances from being effective. Thus, poor farmers from cultivator castes are played off against landless untouchables, and castes are played off against one another. To mobilize the poor in India would require somehow cutting through deep layers of religious ideology as well as mobilizing groups across traditional local and regional boundaries.

The point is not that fomenting agrarian revolution is necessarily to be our goal, or that the same analysis could be applied both to rural India and to rural Uruguay. Rather, the important point is that whatever sorts of social change we seek to bring about (whether it be spreading literacy, improving public health, or helping landless peasants to acquire land and power), the first prerequisite is to analyze the realities of the social system in which we are operating—realities which are often hidden in veils of disguise. To discover them requires not simply facts, but theories and analytical concepts.

The Limitations of Cultural Explanation

The concept of "culture," as it has emanated outward from anthropology into popular thought, has too often served as a way of avoiding explanation in historical and economic terms. Thus, for instance, Aboriginal Australians beset by staggering rates of infant mortality, malnutrition, and disease, and economically oppressed by state and private interests, are often depicted as prevented because of *culture* from being able to stay sober, live in neat houses, or settle down and earn a living. Their "culture," it is said, keeps them in a dreamtime which the standards of white society cannot penetrate. (A similar nonexplanation used to be proffered for the failure of African Americans to "succeed" and "adapt" to the standards of white society; but too many of them have now done so to give this even superficial plausibility.)

The resurgence of militant Islam evoked a series of similar "cultural" explanations in the popular press. If one can depict "the Islamic mind" as fundamentally tribal, fanatical, given to frenzied religious worship and medieval customs such as chopping off the hands of thieves, then one can avoid the need to analyze the way the Islamic counterreaction against the West has been shaped by centuries of oppression and invasion from Europe and decades of subjugation and exploitation. One needs, to account for the Islamic counterattack against Western domination, not glib "cultural" explanation in terms of the Arab mind or of Islam as a religion, but a perspective such as that of the social historian Eric Hobsbawm. As he wrote in 1962:

> By 1848 [an] extraordinary future reversal of fortunes was already to some extent visible. Admittedly, the world-wide revolt against the West . . . was as yet barely discernible. Only in the Islamic world can we observe the first stages of that process by which those conquered by the West have adopted its ideas and techniques to turn the tables on it. (Hobsbawm 1962:20)

The process whereby the Ayatollah Khomeini could challenge President Carter in 1979 was foreshadowed by the middle of the nineteenth century by the beginnings of westernizing reform in the Turkish Empire and the career of the Egyptian leader Mohammed Ali. We need such a perspective to understand the way symbols of traditional Islam, and old religious rules, are being used to fight Western domination. Having seen in previous chapters how political symbols from the past can be put to new uses—for example, in the way an ancient Aztec goddess, in her guise as the Virgin of Guadalupe, led Mexican revolutionaries into battle (Case 58)—we should by now be able to probe beneath the symbols, to analyze why and how they are being used, to see what social realities they express, and disguise. We also, however, have to come to terms with the fact that cultural symbols do become foci for the expression and creation of power, so they too cannot be ignored.

To understand such phenomena of our time, we need theories that account for class conflict and the political economy of world capitalism, and we need a historical perspective on the expansion of the West and the struggles by postcolonial peoples against domination and engulfment. The theoretical perspectives built up earlier, and applied in the preceding chapters to the historical creation of the contemporary world system, give us the means to such understanding.

SUMMARY

Anthropologists have made studies in both colonial and postcolonial situations. In colonial times they depended on colonial administrations for access to their field areas and in some cases worked with colonial agencies. Often, however, they were concerned for the welfare of the people they studied and disagreed with colonial practices. Structural-functional theory in social anthropology was well adapted to studying order, but less to studying change. Anthropologists who act as consultants on development schemes today also are at risk of accusations that they are supporting an unjustifiable status quo. In some cases such projects may have beneficial results (example: the Cornell Peru Project), in others not. Knowledge is always partial and provisional, and deeper knowledge of an area goes with the realization that much is not known.

Anthropologists may also be excluded in independent countries on grounds that they are associated with imperialism—although some scholars have suggested

that they should be champions of revolution. Social science, in any case, is not empty of ideological content or implications, and there is a constant need to guard against ethnocentrism masquerading as common sense.

One way forward is to combine insights of both insiders and outsiders in the study of a local context, so that the strengths of different perspectives can be brought together. Postcolonial peoples should participate in the study of their societies; and anthropologists should try to study the elites in their own societies, and institutional corporations also.

Another contribution anthropologists of whatever political persuasion can make is to inform the public of events that happen in their areas that threaten the survival of the people with whom they work (example: studies of the Yanomamö). Anthropologists have reported on the struggles of Australian Aboriginal peoples in relation to mining corporations, for example. This does not mean that cultures either are or should be static, or that life in the past was perfect. Elders may resist changes that threaten their position in society.

One topic that has emerged is the issue of social class and the extent to which in formerly precapitalist societies capitalist relations of production have come to predominate. Another issue has to do with the role of culture in change and persistence. Weighing cultural factors against political and economic factors requires a sense of intellectual balance.

SUGGESTIONS FOR FURTHER READING

SECTIONS 58–62

Barnes, J. A. 1967. Some Ethical Problems in Modern Field Work. In D. Jongmans and

P. Gutkind, eds., *Anthropologists in the Field.* New York: Humanities Press.

Clifton, J. A., ed. 1970. *Applied Anthropology: Readings in the Uses of the Science of Man.* Boston: Houghton Mifflin Company.

Foster, G. M. 1973. *Traditional Societies and Technological Change.* New York: Holt, Rinehart and Winston.

Goodenough, W. H. 1963. *Cooperation in Change.* New York: Russell Sage Foundation.

Huizer, G., and B. Mannheim, eds. 1979. *The Politics of Anthropology: From Colonialism and Sexism Toward a View From Below.* The Hague: Mouton and Company.

Hymes, D., ed. 1973. *Reinventing Anthropology.* New York: Random House, Inc.

Idris-Soven, A., E. Idris-Soven, and M. K. Vaughn, eds. 1978. *The World as a Company Town: Multinational Corporations and the Social Sciences.* The Hague: Mouton and Company.

Leacock, E. B., ed. 1971. *The Culture of Poverty: A Critique.* New York: Simon & Schuster, Inc.

Nash, J. 1975. Nationalism and Fieldwork. In B. J. Siegel, ed., *Annual Review of Anthropology,* 4. Palo Alto, Calif.: Annual Reviews, Inc.

Rynkiewich, M. A., and J. P. Spradley, eds. 1976. *Ethics and Anthropology: Dilemmas in Fieldwork.* New York: John Wiley & Sons, Inc.

Sanday, P. R., ed. 1976. *Anthropology and the Public Interest: Fieldwork and Theory.* New York: Academic Press, Inc.

Spicer, E. H., ed. 1952. *Human Problems in Technological Change: A Casebook.* New York: Russell Sage Foundation.

Valentine, C. A. 1968. *Culture and Poverty: Critique and Counter-Proposals.* Chicago: University of Chicago Press.

Valentine, C. A., and B. Valentine. 1971. *Anthropological Interpretations of Black Culture.* Reading, Mass.: Addison-Wesley Modules in Anthropology.

Weaver, T., ed. 1973. *To See Ourselves.* Glenview, Ill.: Scott, Foresman and Company.

CHAPTER

22

Toward Human Survival

This book has been written in the conviction that if there are to be safe and fulfilling human futures, we must seek them and work for them, individually and collectively.

One source of guidance in the search for human futures is human pasts: ways of life that have provided coherence, warmth, a sense of value and meaning. Anthropologists, by virtue of being there, sharing these meanings, caring about these values, and writing down what they could, have become chroniclers of cultures now gone or vanishing. The records anthropologists have preserved, the understandings they have built up, can become valuable resources in the quest for survival.

But how directly, and in what ways, can we learn lessons from past worlds where humans lived in smaller groups, closer to one another and to forces of nature they could not control? At what level are we to seek lessons from other peoples? Are they to be lessons about world view and values? Here we can refer to the observation of the distinguished geneticist J. V. Neel:

In the most sophisticated way we can summon, we must return to the awe, and even fear, in which primitive man held the myste-

rious world about him, and like him we must strive to live in harmony with the biosphere. (Neel 1970:805)

Are they to be lessons about patterns of social relations? Anthropologist Steven Polgar, shortly before his death in 1978, wrote this:

We cannot return to the mode of production used by such gatherer-hunters as the Bushmen of the Kalahari desert, Ituri Forest pygmies, or the Australian Aborigines, but the goal of building a society as egalitarian as theirs is within the reach of humanity in the next 50 to 100 years. (Polgar 1979:264)

Are we to find in the tribal world models for social relations that would render more close and human the vast, bureaucratic systems in which we live? Might we find such models in, say, the Kpelle moot or communal work groups in the Trobriands? Or, rather than seeking to graft borrowed models onto our own, do we seek to foster cultural pluralism, try to stem the tides of world culture that would obliterate the remaining subcultural traditions in industrialized countries and cumulated heritages of postcolonial peoples?

64. ANTHROPOLOGY AND THE QUEST FOR HUMAN FUTURES

The Scale of the Problems

We need to be clear at the outset about the scale of the problems. That was further reason for looking at the global "rationality" of transnational corporations, and the enormously powerful vested interests of those who profit from the world as it is. These include not only the rich and powerful in the United States, Germany, England, France, Japan, and other countries of the industrialized world, but their counterparts in Singapore, Bombay, Jakarta, Manila, Lagos, Bangkok, and other emerging centers of commerce. The industrialized nations were using the rhetoric, in 1979 and 1980, of being "held to ransom" by the OPEC countries who could control oil prices and affect oil supplies; but they were not saying that they were being held to ransom by the giant corporations which, with no loyalties but profit, could bring governments to their knees with their control over prices, profits, supplies, and the flow of capital. Experiments in social and economic change which did not fit the interests of global "rationality" were cynically undermined and destroyed.

The former Soviet-bloc countries were ultimately no more receptive to social change that did not fit Soviet strategic interests. If the United States destroyed Chile's attempt to find an independent alternative, so the former Soviet Union destroyed Czechoslovakia's. Soviet military might attempted to crush the aspirations of Eritreans in Ethiopia, Somalis in the Ogaden desert, Kurds in Iraq, and Afghan tribes: condemning any attempt at autonomy as "reactionary" justified using tanks and napalm against warriors on horseback, or snuffing out glimmers of political freedom. If China had been less cynically expansionist, the people of Tibet can attest to the destruction of culture and autonomy that comes from being "liberated."

The vastly powerful forces at work in the world make it naïve to believe that experiments in rehumanization can flourish freely. It is hard enough to imagine ways of rediscovering the quality of life in close, egalitarian communities where social relations are based on caring and sharing—when there are so many millions of humans who must work and eat. It is harder still to imagine how such rediscoveries of our lost humanity would be given room to grow and spread, with powerful forces seeking to turn the world into a global marketplace governed by the "rationality" of profit, and other equally determined attempts to "liberate" the oppressed into new forms of military and bureaucratic bondage under foreign hegemony.

This is not to say that the struggles for cultural autonomy all over the world, which spread during the 1970s, would—if successful on a wide scale—lead to viable human futures. Those who tried to assert their "independence" from existing state structures include groups as widespread and diverse as Basques in Spain, Croatians and Macedonians in the Balkans, Kachins in Burma, Eritreans in Ethiopia, Ainu in Japan, Kurds and Armenians in the Middle East, and Papuans in Papua New Guinea. (In 1973, I heard a student at the University of Papua New Guinea introduce himself, in a political debate, as from "The Republic of the Trobriand Islands." From 1988 onward, the Bougainville Revolutionary Army actually did announce its secession from the state of Papua New Guinea and did battle to pursue its aims.) This resurgence of nationalism, tribalism, and ethnic separatism is an important historical phenomenon that requires to be understood and reckoned with.

A Crumbling World System?

Can we, individually and collectively, transform the global political and economic system that pushes humans all over the world into more and more mindless consumption, a system that has to use more and more energy and scarce raw materials, that must expand or collapse? We have seen, in looking at the creation of the post-colonial world and the political economy of hunger, how vast and powerful are the corporate giants that each year push the world further into a spiral of consumerism, production, and pollution from which there is no return. Can a system so vast and powerful be stopped by a lot of individuals growing a bit wiser?

There are signs of cracks and contradictions in this system. The vulnerability of energy resources, the limited world distribution of rare metals used in the most advanced technologies, the tottering world currency system, as well as the old specters of capitalism, inflation, and depression, make the foundations of the global economic system seem less solid today than they did in 1970. Yet the capitalist systems of the West have continued in operation beyond the collapse of the Soviet bloc and its "planned economies."

The global economic system depends on the internal stability of the countries that supply raw materials and cheap labor, and provide markets for baby food and infant formula, grain surpluses, tractors, cars, and radios. This internal stability, in turn, depends on repressive state power and oppressive class structures that keep the rural and urban poor powerless, and keep the rich powerful. The revolutionary potential of the poor makes the rich vulnerable—and, with them, the global economic system. If one by one the pieces of the system free themselves from it (as Guinea-Bissau and Nicaragua and Mozambique have done), a system that must ever expand to stay alive will begin to contract—and fall apart. The global system *is* vulnerable, because of the aspirations of the world's poor for autonomy and justice.

Building a new society requires a reorganization of production, a reorientation of class relations, a new relationship between men and women, and a restructuring of social relations of community. Where there are modes of community organization from the tribal past, a mixture of new technology and old, production for subsistence and for trade, the challenge of building a new social order may be closer to people's grasp. There are fewer people, better able to feed themselves and survive without massive technological systems and state structures, less intricately tied than we into systems of national and international interdependence. But in such countries also the military conflicts provoked by rival warlords can and do promote havoc.

What steps, then, can we realistically take? And what can we learn from anthropology? A first and urgent step is for us to develop a humility and sense of doubt about "standards of living" as conceived in materialistic and technological terms. Is it a higher "standard of living" to have a car rather than to have a bicycle? To have a color TV set than to have a radio? Or even, necessarily, to have a solid roof rather than a thatch one?

We need "standards of living" defined in human, not material, terms. The quality of life is contingent on having enough food to eat, food that meets nutritional needs. But beyond that, it depends more on the rewards of fulfilling work and sustaining social relationships than on more and more hardware. The social solidarity and sense of community we find in Trobriand villages is more likely to be found, ironically, in the streets of Harlem or the *favelas* of Rio de Janeiro than in affluent Connecticut suburbia or the elegant villas of Rio.

With a heightened sense of the one-sidedness of Western materialism and affluence, and the erosion of fulfilling social relations in modern industrial societies, we can well reflect on the destruction of the natural environment, the plundering and polluting of our planet, that has been a consequence of our commitment to "progress." A looming ecological crisis is a real threat, not the hollow rhetoric of conservationists and radicals. We may already have passed the point of no return. Yet insights derived from anthropology on peoples living in nature, not trying to control and dominate it, might help us to seek understanding of balance and harmony in the ecosystem of which we are a part.

In thinking about human futures, it is useful to counterpose some aspects of life in societies such as the Trobriands to the life of urbanites in Western societies. We can then ask if—across the vast gulfs in scale and technology—there are lessons to be learned. Before we look at these contrasts between small-scale societies and contemporary industrialized ones, we need a sobering reminder that these societies were not paradises, need to remember deception and gang rape, symbolic denigration and physical abuse, sorcery and witchcraft accusations, feuds and bloody warfare. We are not romanticizing a "noble savage" or depicting idyllic ways of life. We are looking at organizational principles in small-scale societies from which we may be able to learn.

Let us look, then, at a series of contrasts between tribal and industrialized societies:

1. *The Organization of Work*
   For most people in industrial societies, the workplace and "home" are sharply separated. The small and fragile families in which we live are not the settings where we gain our livelihood. Work done in the domestic setting (mainly by women) is unpaid and—in the wider society—largely unrecognized. In contrast, work in the tribal world is done within the framework of kinship and community; there is no comparable gulf between "home" and "work," or between remunerative work and unpaid domestic "housework"—although in the tribal world, as we have seen, female labor may be appropriated to further male quests for prestige.

2. *Kinship and Community*
   Increasingly in industrial societies, especially for urbanities and suburbanities, nuclear families have become isolated from one another, in their separate physical compartments—homes or apartments. Mobility has left relatives scattered. The kinds of support networks, mutual assistance in childcare, and collective work and reciprocal obligation that sustain everyday social life in tribal societies such as the Trobriands are relatively uncommon and (lacking institutional reinforcement) usually fragile.

3. *Continuity in Life Trajectory*
   We can begin by noting that the kinds of interpersonal bonds that sustain social relations in a Trobriand village exist in the play groups of children in the schools and neighborhoods of New York and Chicago. It is the circumstances of "growing up"—going off to

college, getting jobs, getting married—that break the close bonds of childhood. In the small-scale communities of the tribal world, the close ties of childhood continue into adulthood. The neighbors and kin you work with and exchange with are likely to be those you grew up with. The same continuities follow adults into old age, or to ancestorhood. Adults care for aged parents as the parents cared for them. For us, old people are often seen to have outlived their usefulness, to have become economic burdens families cannot maintain.

4. *Continuity in Culture*
In traditional Trobriand society, valued goals in a new generation were the same as those of the previous generation—making *kula*, growing yams, making harvest presentations, giving feasts, distributing skirts and leaf packets. Parents could teach children, grandparents could teach grandchildren; elders were repositories of an accumulated knowledge and wisdom which was a crucial resource for the young to draw on. In Western societies, rapid "progress" and a cultural valuation of the new and denigration of the old mean that the old are seen as repositories of anachronisms, not wisdom and valued knowledge.

5. *Personalized Politics and "Law"*
In tribal communities, the political decisions that shape group and individual action are made in settings where personal relations prevail, a give-and-take of discussion is possible, where consensus is usually reached. Leaders are directly accountable to, and accessible to, the led. Conflict resolution is likely to be similarly personal, fitted to the circumstances of the case and the social relations between the individuals concerned. In the vast bureaucracies of complex societies, rules are made and invoked by faceless, nameless cogs in the machinery. Political decisions are made far away in ways that allow little room for discussion, direct accountability, or consensus. Legal processes are impersonal and bureaucratic: "the state" versus an accused, a corporation against a claimant.

6. *Personalized Economic and Exchange Relations*
Products of human labor, in tribal societies, are either consumed by the producers or exchanged along paths of kinship or other mutual obligation. Transactions are social as well as economic; they make statements about interpersonal relationships. The satisfactions of work for one's own needs—of building the house you will live in, making the canoe you will paddle, planting the yam cutting that will later provide a meal—are strong and compelling. So are the satisfactions of reciprocal work (you help me build my house and I feed you a meal; when you need a house built, I'll help you and you'll provide a meal for me). Where we exchange valuables, or yams, or barter baskets for adze blades or taro for fish, we cement our personal ties and reinforce networks of interdependence.

But when I use money my work has earned to buy groceries wrapped in plastic at the supermarket, or to get my car repaired, I am taking part in a vast economic system held together by the impersonal medium of money. The work I do, the work of the people who produce the items in the supermarket, is separated, depersonalized, dehumanized. I, as modern urbanite, can scarcely make myself any of the commodities I need: I cannot build a car, make a tool, build a house, manufacture a radio or the batteries that power it; I could scarcely grow my own food if I had the means and place to do it. The satisfactions of producing and exchanging have largely vanished, for the person who puts together a tiny piece of a car on an assembly line, or wraps the plastic around some item that will be sold in a supermarket—if, indeed, it is still a human, and not a machine, that does it.

Is There a Way Back?

What humans have lost in the passage from garden to factory, village to city, may emerge in all this. But are there paths back to some of the rewarding social bonds that have been broken? Or are there simply too many of us, too interdependent already in a vast worldwide network?

First of all, there is ample evidence that a spirit of community can rise, that towns or neighborhoods can transform themselves. In the face of scarcity, or mass economic disruption, or natural disaster, sharing and collective concern emerge: a company town in the midst of a strike, a community after a natural disaster, acquires temporarily the internal solidarity of a Trobriand village. A humanity in our social relations lies close to the surface; we need to find ways to bring it out.

Second, collective consensual, personalized political processes have reappeared in many Western communities, in protest movements, in consumer and ecological activism. The "new populism" may not be an avenue toward social change on the needed scale. But it does show that when we become committed collectively to a cause, the modes of political action commonplace in Melanesia can reappear in a city meeting hall.

Some lessons from the tribal world could be learned only if we discard some of our values about change and progress. Old people could be, as in the Trobriands, teachers of the young: but only if we concede that they have something to teach. Perhaps they do, especially if we are going to have to adapt to the depletion of resources and technological devolution. Skills of greater self-sufficiency, skills of making things and growing things and cooking things that were commonplace 75 or 100 years ago, may be needed again; they are evaporating each year with the passing of old people, put in institutions to die.

I have written, in a vein of more radical futurology:

If our human potential for self-realization and collective commitment is to be [fulfilled], it will have to come in part from restructuring the experience of work . . . whether by evolution or revolution. . . . To evoke in ourselves the human potentials realized in the small worlds of hunting/gathering societies will require the rebuilding of communities—inevitably larger than 50 people, but perhaps in some way modular so as to achieve something of the small-scale intimacy of the hunter-gatherer band. Only in such restructured communities can work become once more a part of life-in-groups, not a compartmentalized job-one-does. There are two sides to this reorganization of life. . . . First, a reorganization of the mode of production, however revolutionary, does not *in itself* humanize social relations. The re-humanization of social relations is *dependent on,* but not *produced by,* a revolution at the level of economic institutions and class relations. Second, this re-humanization, as perhaps the radical side of the women's movement has argued most cogently, requires a revolution in the integration of labor with domestic and community life. In trying to reconstitute the wholeness of social life, to re-articulate what we do as mates and parents and as neighbors with what we do as workers, and in trying to make work itself more fulfilling in a vast-scale society, we can learn much from the so-called primitives, for whom family, community, and work are a single flow: continuous, interpenetrating elements in the daily round of life. (Keesing 1979:7)

The challenge of building a new mode of life that not only ensures our survival but enriches our experience may be beyond us because of the massive forces that keep us on our present course. But the experience of tribal peoples shows that humans *can* adapt to changes more cataclysmic than those we are likely to face: "A final lesson from the tribal world is the fantastic human ability to change, the incredible resilience we have to become new beings . . ." (Keesing 1979:8).

This takes us back to the challenge to postcolonial peoples to find syntheses of the old and new that preserve what is of value from the past. It is ironic that the industrialized countries continue to send "experts" to teach postcolonial peoples how to adopt Western technology and achieve Western goals. We may well have more to learn than to teach. B. M. Narokobi, who emerged from a New Guinea society studied by Margaret Mead to become a brilliantly able lawyer, has written this:

[We can] build a new society based on communal sharing, interdependence, mutual trust, self-reliance, and love. We cannot hope to build a new society by being half committed to the imperialistic and capitalistic lifestyles. We have arrived at the point where the only honest road to choose is a total commitment to the ideology of human development. Let those who believe take the first step and build our nation based on interdependent communities. . . . I am convinced we can build a new society . . . free . . . of many constraints of . . . past societies. . . . Modern civilization is yet to answer many basic needs of

humans everywhere. There is no harm in trying an alternative which might answer our true needs. (Narokobi 1974:2)

Perhaps this is an unrealistic optimism. But at this point, new modes of political and economic organization are urgent not only for nations like Papua New Guinea but for humans everywhere.

The challenge, somehow, is to achieve for the industrial nations what their massive invasion has forced on less powerful peoples—a radical restructuring of world view and experience, and a new integration. Whether that is possible can well be doubted. Collective exploration of new visions, and the transformation or dismantling of established systems and vested powers, will be extraordinarily difficult, perhaps impossible.

An understanding of human diversity is urgent if such visions and transformations are to be possible. Much of the wisdom which anthropology has gleaned in its sweeping study of human ways is wisdom about diversity—its extent, its nature, its roots. That wisdom, used wisely, can be a crucial human resource: for in understanding human differences we can glimpse new human possibilities. Visions of society must be broadened, but they must be wisely constrained. If they are not illuminated by sound understanding of human nature—biological, social, and cultural—and of the limits of human possibility, they could speed disaster, not avert it. We have no better source of wisdom about human possibilities than the diverse ways of life anthropology has helped to explore and chronicle.

SUMMARY

This chapter considers the forces of change in the world at large, stressing the power of international capitalism on the one hand and the development of movements for cultural and political autonomy on the other (i.e., the coexistence of globalism and localism). Global stability depends on the stability of both producing and consuming countries. It is argued that we may learn from the cultures studied by anthropologists alternative and more humane ways of organizing work, kinship, life trajectories, politics, law, and economic and exchange relations; and that it may be possible to reintroduce such values in today's contexts. At any rate, the historical understanding of human cultural diversity is a vital means whereby we can also imagine possible better futures.

Postscript

In the years since the second edition of this book appeared, several important shifts have taken place within anthropology as a discipline and in the world at large. Here we pick out two such shifts which are highly relevant to the themes and the orientation of the book itself. The first is the shift from "grand theory" approaches to a congeries of positions usually labeled postmodernist. The second is the shift in global politics from the monolithic stereotypes and rhetoric of the Cold War to the breakdown of the Soviet Union and the growth in postcolonial and other movements for achieving separatist identities under the rubrics of ethnicity and nationalism. These two shifts, the first within anthropology and the second in the world, are not unconnected. The switch from grand theory towards first deconstruction and then to modestly reconstructive modes of argumentation in cultural anthropology reflects the various impasses of theorizing in the general mode which were reached as both the world and people's perceptions of it altered. The disillusionment with or rejection of general, encompassing theories of social life has extended to the Marxist and neo-Marxist projects which made an input into the theoretical framework of this book without dominating its overall perspectives or obliterating structuralist and linguistically oriented approaches. Marxist theory as a theory of history in general has suffered a decline in its overall image as a result of its association with Soviet Communist ideology, although here too it is important not to equate Marx's ideas with Soviet Communist political and bureaucratic structures.

Along with the breakup of the onetime politically unified units in the former Soviet Union, the resurgence of varieties of separatist-oriented movements in Western European countries (for example, within the United Kingdom), and the attempts to reshape government and its borders in many parts of postcolonial Africa, there has been a countervailing tendency, already pointed to in this book, toward a certain globalization of social and economic effects and processes. Globalization theory, which attempts to synthesize knowledge of such processes, is the successor to world systems and dependency theories, but tends to have a cultural as well as an economic focus. At its broadest it has to do with the dynamics of diffusion of ideas, objects, and practices and the different power that goes with and is created by these in the world as a whole.

Globalization theory in this sense stands in strong contrast to the long-standing traditions in anthropology of making in-depth local studies. At one extreme we would find an attempt to explain global macro-patterns of change, while at the other we would be dealing with a highly specific ethnography of a single local group of a few hundred persons. As many anthropologists and others have pointed out, however, anthropology does not have to aspire to either extreme. We occupy in our writings, rather, a middle ground, recognizing that in order to explain many locally situated phenomena we need to understand how they are intertwined with wider phenomena and may be profitably seen as the hybrid historical products of regional interactions by which the local is ultimately connected to the global. It is a matter of pragmatics, not of principle, where we stop in a given analysis, with regard to both space and time. One matter on which anthropologists of different theoretical persuasions are widely agreed upon is that we must cast our discussions firmly into a historical mode, as a means of avoiding the artificialities of the "ethnographic present." This stress on history is at least partly a result of the demise of the structural-functionalist framework and of the criticisms of it by neo-Marxist writers in the 1960s and 1970s. We see therefore that while the Marxist program—as a kind of encompassing theory—has, like other projects, run into difficulties, it has nevertheless contributed to the development of current non-Marxist approaches, which stress the importance of understanding local systems in regional and wider terms and of casting our arguments in historical time as well as in geopolitical space.

Postmodernist approaches in anthropology began as negative, deconstructionist exercises, and are generally contrasted with modernism and modernization theory, although it is not really possible to date the emergence of forms of thinking called postmodernist in any exact way. Modernism is associated with grand theory, deriving from Enlightenment views of progress in knowledge and rationality. Modernization theory dealt with the trajectories of emergence of economic and political change toward putative "Western models" in postcolonial countries. Postmodernist approaches challenged both of these trends on grounds that history was not proceeding in directions that substantiated them.

In its questioning mode, postmodernist theory may be seen as injecting a healthy note of scepticism into our accounts of the world. It questions the epistemological basis of our knowledge, both of ourselves and of others. This act of questioning is associated, somewhat paradoxically, with a strong emphasis on interpretation, on the notion that the knowledge we produce is a set of interpretations of events and processes, and that these interpretations vary with the interpreter. More abstractly, in some approaches, there is a questioning of the idea of the author as the producer of a fixed text. Even a text, it is argued, may be seen as many different texts in accordance with the different readings given to it. We are left therefore, in this version of postmodernism with an indeterminate "text" as well as many different "readings" of it. The "text" may be a constructed ethnography, or it may be a segment of social life which is under observation. Anthropologists such as Clifford Geertz, who pioneered in America the interpretation of cultural systems, and David Schneider, who "deconstructed" the idea of kinship by separating its cultural manifestations from any putative universal psychobiological bases, were succeeded by others who argued for the indeterminacy and ambiguity of cultural categories and the uncertainty of our knowledge of them. Geertz's stress on "local knowledge" threatened at times to become more like a "cloud of unknowing."

Critics of the more negative versions of postmodernism argued that its skepticism promoted political disengagement and ultimately solipsism. Most such critics also argued that we needed not to deconstruct but to reconstruct anthropological theory, and that the processes of doing so have always been a part of the history of anthropology. Reconstructive theories, in turn, have either drawn on parts of previous grand theories (for example, semiotics, structuralism, cultural materialism), or have re-created a space for theorizing by drawing on alternative traditions of thought (for example, theories of consciousness and embodiment derived from phenomenological philosophy). Reconstructive work has proceeded also within the expanding sphere of gender studies, moving from an earlier set of concerns with the cross-cultural position of women (in terms of domination and exploitation) to a more nuanced understanding of the varying and complementary roles that are gender-inflected in various societies. Gender studies have moved to the center, or close to the center, of the stage in many spheres of analysis of politics, kinship, economics, and symbolism. (For a survey see Knauft 1996:219–248; and for an assessment of current issues in this arena see di Leonardo 1991.) Such reconstructive theorizing has been undertaken alongside more deconstructive exercises since at least the early 1980s.

George Marcus and Michael Fischer set the tone for a whole decade of studies in American anthropology with their 1986 book *Anthropology as Cultural Critique: An Experimental Moment in the Human Sciences.* They began with the idea of a "crisis of representation," that is, with the uncertainty induced by skeptical questions of theoretical positions. They turned this sense of crisis, however, into a sense of opportunity, of how uncertainty can itself produce experimental ways of writing that can creatively open up new perspectives. They stressed also the crucial role of a long-established genre of writing in anthropology, the ethnographic study, and gave examples of new versions of ethnography using interpretive, reflexive, dialogic, and rhetorical effects to highlight arguments and descriptions. These ethnographies situate themselves firmly in the realm of subjectivity rather than in objectivist versions of knowledge production. But they are to be evaluated in terms of the insights they provide.

Overall, Marcus and Fischer stressed two themes that had tended to be developed separately and which they urged should be aligned and unified: first, the interpretation of culture, seen in terms of studies of the emotions and constructions of personhood as well as autobiographical accounts and psychological profiles; and second, world political economy. They suggested that interpretive accounts must be situated within the study of political economy in a broad unification of culturalist and what we may call post-Marxist approaches. They also noted that anthropology cannot restrict itself to "exotic" societies, but must be involved with studies "at home" and with "studying up" as well as "studying down."

This reconstructive program of combining studies of local meanings with studies of regional and wider processes has generally been accorded validity in much work that has been done since the mid-1980s as well as before that time. One sphere into which anthropologists have increasingly moved has been that of ethnicity, nationalism, and questions of historical consciousness and identity in general. A balanced treatment of many of the issues here is found in Thomas Hylland Eriksen's book *Ethnicity and Nationalism* (1993). Eriksen starts from ethnicity and moves to nationalism, whereas other studies begin with the level of the nation, as in Benedict Anderson's *Imagined Communities* (1991). Both *ethnicity* and *nationalism* are terms that are hard to define and a movement labeled as "ethnic" at one moment in time may become "nationalist" at another. The fusion of ethnic and nationalist concerns which has become a focus of studies may be called the study of *ethnonationalism.*

Ethnicity itself is a term that refers on the one hand to cultural ideas of shared descent based on ideologies of "blood" and the like, and on the other to shared cultural practices, values, and traditions. Often there is a combination of such ideas, as when the propensity to follow certain practices or ways of behaving is said to be "in the blood." As a blended ideology of descent plus custom, ethnicity clearly can provide a "naturalized" basis for solidarity between people. Custom provides a framework of shared practices, while descent provides a boundary in terms of legitimate membership of the group or category to which such practices are said to belong. The two criteria may be desegregated or re-aggregated over time and the contents of custom referred to may change. Retrospective reformulations of both shared descent and shared customs are frequently made, especially in the context of shifts in boundaries and in historical opportunities. Ethnic identifications are made usually and most clearly in the context of self-differentiating from others and therefore enter as constitutive forces of historical consciousness. Viewing ethnic identities as historical products and as elements of consciousness in this way enables us to mediate between two extreme positions: one, the primordialist position, in which it is argued that ethnicity refers to anciently established identities that are historically resurgent; and second, the instrumentalist position, in which it is stressed that such identities may be creatively formulated or invented as means of dealing with new historical situations, usually those of conflict or opportunity. The instrumentalist position, related to the idea of the "invention of tradition" (Hobsbawm and Ranger 1983), has generally prevailed. But it is important also to recognize that instrumental needs are best served by symbolic appeals that resonate with consciousness and that they make selections from existing cultural repertoires or create surface forms that correspond to deeper historical complexes of ideas. Primordialist elements thus appear as historically reformulated ideologies in instrumentalist contexts.

In his treatment of themes, Eriksen stresses the study of ethnicity in action, as a factor in social relations, thus showing his ties with British social anthropology and the work of Fredrik Barth. But he does not neglect cultural factors, recognizing the power of cultural classifications in the processes of boundary creation and maintenance. He discusses "minorities" and the "plural societies" to which they may belong—that is, multiethnic societies that may not have internally shared foci of value.

When he discusses nationalism Eriksen similarly takes culture into account, stressing the importance of the political use of cultural symbols, as with national flags and their symbolic construction. He notes Ernest Gellner's definition that links nationalism directly with ethnicity by defining the nation in ethnic terms (Eriksen 1993:99). Benedict Anderson's definition is a little broader: the nation is an "imagined community," and the act of imagination could take place in more than one dimension, just as ethnicity itself may be a complex notion in practice (Anderson 1991). In practice, however, nations have tended to imagine themselves along dimensions of ethnicity and what anthropologists call "metaphoric kinship" (i.e., extended notions of common descent). One point here is that while nations may claim to be anciently based, nationalist ideology is relatively modern (Eriksen 1993:101) and is associated with the violent conflicts and world wars of the twentieth century as well as with the formative forerunning events of the eighteenth and nineteenth centuries. Nationalism is also linked by some theorists with industrialization and the need to coordinate large numbers of mobile workers into the organization of the state. It thus becomes an instrument of state organization. In other contexts a nationalist movement may represent an attempt to break away from an existing state structure through rebellion or secession, or to create a new form of representation in which only the ethnically qualified have full political rights.

These observations lead easily into an understanding of the historical contexts in which both ethnicity and nationalism are tied to violence, as became abundantly evident in the late twentieth century. Ethnicity and nationalism are historical and ideological constructions based on attempts to define boundaries and access to rights through group membership. In contexts of rivalry, splitting, suppression, rebellion, class conflict, racial conflict, and territorial competition, ethnicity and nationalism supply the ideological fuel that leads to the fires of violence. And this has become one of the prime problems both for anthropology and the worlds that anthropologists study. Violence itself is, of course, a permanent part of human history. Its particular shape today, however, takes on characteristics of its own, formed by the conflicts between localism and globalism. Two different examples can be given.

The first is violence associated with "the troubles" in Northern Ireland within the United Kingdom. This has its roots in what

some observers have called "internal colonialism" within the United Kingdom and the growth of a Protestant landowning class in a previously Catholic context. It is therefore rooted in political economy. The cultural elaborations of conflicts that have emerged from this context have been explored by Allen Feldman in his *Formations of Violence* (1991). Feldman uses an extensive panoply of theorizing from the psychology of Jacques Lacan to the classificatory approach of Mary Douglas as well as an approach through phenomenology and embodiment to discuss a number of powerful themes: political torture, the creation and violation of local political spaces by the marking of boundaries and their transgression, and the significance of narratives of resistance. His approach goes beneath the surface categories of Protestants versus Catholics to reveal both more abstract and more concrete material processes at work.

Shifting to quite a different part of the world, Amazonia, we may cite R. Brian Ferguson's study of Yanomamö warfare (Ferguson 1995). Ferguson begins with an approach through cultural materialism with its stress on infrastructural factors and their causative role in processes, but he greatly enriches this with an emphasis on historical processes that occurred in the context of colonial influences on the Yanomamö. In contrast to certain sociobiological approaches that have stressed biologically conditioned modes of aggression as basic to Yanomamö life, Ferguson argues that violence has been historically induced, through the depletion of game reserves and the effects of introduced diseases. Not violent psyches as such but disturbed ecologies have therefore influenced Yanomamö warfare. His position is part of a broader one advanced by himself and Neil Whitehead in their edited volume *War in the Tribal Zone* (1992), in which the contributing authors all argue for a complex interrelationship between "tribes" and "states" over time, giving agency to both sides. This approach amounts to a reformulation of how we are to view the colonial and postcolonial circumstances of peoples called "tribal": as players in wider arenas of relationships.

While the emphases in Feldman's work are very different from those of Ferguson and Whitehead, in both cases we see anthropologists creatively reworking the idea that identities are made through conflict in historical circumstances, without appealing to an innate drive for aggression (although they do not necessarily refute such a theory in general).

Studies of this kind need to be brought to bear on the questions of local violence and global processes that beset the world, particularly in such a way that they throw light not only on the persistence of violence, but also, through their stress on contingency, history, and the creativity of symbolization, on the prospects for conflict resolution and the achievement of peace. Theorizing the bases, as well as the dangers, of ethnicity and nationalism is one of the tasks of what we may call a post-postmodernist anthropology.

Andrew J. Strathern
Pamela J. Stewart
1997

SUGGESTIONS FOR
FURTHER READING

ON POSTMODERNISM AND
RECONSTRUCTIVE APPROACHES:

Marcus, George E., and Michael M. J. Fischer. 1986. *Anthropology as Cultural Critique: An Experimental Moment in the Human Sciences.* Chicago: University of Chicago Press.

Rosenau, Pauline Marie. 1992. *Post-Modernism and the Social Sciences: Insights, Inroads, and Intrusions.* Princeton: Princeton University Press.
Smart, Barry. 1993. *Postmodernity.* London: Routledge.

ON ETHNICITY, NATIONALISM,
AND VIOLENCE:

Anderson, Benedict. 1991. *Imagined Communities.* London: Verso.
Eriksen, Thomas Hylland. 1993. *Ethnicity and Nationalism: Anthropological Perspectives.* London: Pluto Press.
Feldman, Allen. 1991. *Formations of Violence: The Narrative of the Body and Political Terror in Northern Ireland.* Chicago: University of Chicago Press.
Ferguson, R. Brian. 1995. *Yanomamö Warfare.* Santa Fe: School of American Research Press.
Ferguson, R. Brian, and Neil L. Whitehead, eds. 1992. *War in the Tribal Zone: Expanding States and Indigenous Warfare.* Santa Fe: School of American Research Press.
Gellner, Ernest. 1983. *Nations and Nationalism.* Oxford: Blackwell.
Giddens, Anthony. 1985. *The Nation-State and Violence.* Cambridge: Polity.
Herzfeld, Michael. 1992. *The Social Production of Indifference: Exploring the Symbolic Roots of Western Bureaucracy.* New York: St. Martin's Press.
Hobsbawm, Eric. 1990. *Nations and Nationalism Since the 1780s: Programme, Myth, Reality.* Cambridge: Cambridge University Press.
Hobsbawm, Eric, and Terence Ranger, eds. 1983. *The Invention of Tradition.* Cambridge: Cambridge University Press.

ON GENDER STUDIES:

di Leonardo, Micaela, ed. 1991. *Gender at the Cross-Roads of Knowledge: Feminist Anthropology in the Postmodern Era.* Berkeley: University of California Press.
Knauft, Bruce. 1996. *Genealogies for the Present in Cultural Anthropology.* New York and London: Routledge.

Glossary

Aboriginal: If capitalized adjective: pertaining to Australian Aborigines. If uncapitalized adjective: pertaining to an indigenous population.

aborigine, Australian: A member of the indigenous population of Australia.

acculturation: Culture change due to contact between societies; most often used to refer to adaptation of subordinate tribal societies to domination by Western societies.

affines: An in-law: parents-in-law, siblings-in-law, and other relatives by marriage; may refer to groups related to one another by a marriage.

affinity: Relationship by marriage. May include the relationship between corporate groups linked by marriage among their members.

age grade (= age class): A social category based on age, within a series of such categories, through which individuals pass in the course of the life cycle.

age set: A category (or corporate group) based on age, within a hierarchy of such categories. Differs from age grades in that one remains in the same age set as it becomes progressively more senior rather than moving up a ladder of categories.

agnate: A person related by patrilineal descent.

agnatic descent: See *patrilineal*, q.v.

agriculture: In general sense, cultivation of crops; in narrow and more technical sense, cultivation using plows or other nonhand tools, as contrasted with horticulture, in which only hand tools—digging sticks, hoes, etc.—are used. (Cf. *horticulture*.)

alliance: A system whereby descent groups or other kin groups are linked by a rule of prescriptive or recurrent marriage so that the groups remain in an affinal relationship to one another across generations.

ancestor worship: The worship or propitiation of ancestors, particularly characteristic of societies organized in terms of corporate descent groups.

animatism: A belief that the natural world is pervaded or animated by impersonal spiritual force(s), such as Melanesian *mana* or North American Indian *orena*.

animism: A belief in indwelling spirits in natural objects and phenomena.

applied anthropology: The use of anthropological knowledge and expertise to deal with problems in the "real world," e.g., the introduction of technological innovations, public health, or economic development schemes.

association: A social group based on shared interest or voluntary participation.

asymmetrical alliance: In alliance theory, a marriage system involving indirect exchange. (Patrilateral alliance is considered by some theorists to be nonexistent or impossible, so matrilateral alliance—marriage with MBD or a girl classed with her—is the form commonly referred to as asymmetrical.)

avoidance relationship: A patterned social relationship whereby individuals in a particular kinship relationship (e.g., mother-in-law–son-in-law, brother–sister) must avoid social contact or behave in formal and constrained ways.

avunculocal: Postmarital residence of a person with mother's brother (since characteristically this entails residence of a couple with the husband's maternal uncle, the terms *viri-avunculocal* or *avuncu-virilocal* are more precise).

base (or infrastructure): In Marxist theory, the economic system, conceived as comprising social relations of production and distribution, as well as technological factors; contrasted with *superstructure* (q.v.), the political, jural, and ideological institutions and processes that sustain and *reproduce* a prevailing social system.

big man (system): A mode of leadership found in Melanesia (including New Guinea), whereby the leader ("big man") commands a following by manipulation of wealth; the leader's powers depend on personal skill and continuing entrepreneurial and political success, and are not hereditary.

bilateral (kinship): Kinship traced to relatives through both father and mother (= consanguineal kinship).

bride price: See *bridewealth,* q.v.

bride service: A pattern whereby husbands or potential husbands acquire rights by working for the wife's parents (or other close relatives), characteristic of some hunting-gathering and hunter-horticulturalist societies.

bridewealth: Marriage payments from the husband and his kin to the bride's kin. Characteristically these payments balance a transfer of rights over the wife's sexuality, work services, residence, fertility, etc.

cargo cult: A millennial movement, of a sort characteristic of Melanesia in the southwest Pacific, marked by the expectation that Western material goods will be received by supernatural means.

cargo system: In Mesoamerica, a Spanish-derived hierarchy of religious offices, or religious and political offices, through which individuals pass as temporary holders of these offices (cargos).

case: In grammatical theory, a categorization of the nouns (or pronouns) of sentences according to the functional role they play in the sentence: as subject of an intransitive verb, agent or direct object of a transitive verb, object of a preposition, etc. (Latin: nominative, accusative, dative, etc.)

caste: In the Indian subcontinent, an endogamous social group incorporated within the stratified hierarchy of Hindu ideology. Some sociologists would apply more generally to endogamous, ranked social classes.

chiefdom: A political system in which kin groups are linked together through a hierarchy of political and/or religious leadership.

civilization: A term used to characterize a complex society (usually a state) that has achieved a high order of cultural complexity (usually a literate tradition, a state religion, specialist arts and crafts, etc.).

clan: A unilineal descent group or category whose members trace patrilineal descent (patri-clan) or matrilineal descent matri-clan) from an apical ancestor/ancestress but do not know the genealogical links that connect them to this apical ancestor.

cognate: A bilateral (consanguineal) kinsman or kinswoman.

cognatic descent: (1) A mode of descent reckoning where all descendants of an apical ancestor/ancestress through any combination of male or female links are included (preferred sense). (2) Synonymous with *bilateral* or *consanguineal* (q.v.), as in "cognatic kinship" (= "bilateral kinship").

cognition: The processes of thinking and memory.

cognitive: Related to the processes of cognition, the processes of *thinking* and *knowing* (in contrast to emotions and motivation).

compadrazgo: In Latin America and other Spanish-influenced areas (e.g., Guam), ritual co-parenthood, where godparents play roles complementary to parents in relation to children.

componential analysis: A mode of analysis, originally used for phonological systems but later used for defining the meanings of sets of contrasting words (notably kinship terms), whereby several dimensions of contrast (high vs. low, male vs. female, etc.) intersect to define the uniqueness of each phoneme or each word in the set, in terms of their contrast with the rest.

consanguineal: A relative by birth (i.e., a "blood" relative), as distinguished from in-laws ("affines") and step-relatives.

corporate group: A social group whose members act as a legal individual in terms of collective rights to property, a common group name, collective responsibility, etc.

cosmology: A people's beliefs and assumptions regarding the world—what entities and forces control it, how the universe is organized, and what humans' role and place within the world are.

cultural anthropology: The field of anthropology concerned with the study of human customs—that is, the study of cultures and societies.

cultural ecology: The study of human populations and their culturally patterned behavior, within ecosystems.

cultural materialism: The position, argued most forcefully by Marvin Harris, that cultures represent primarily adaptive solutions to the material circumstances of life, and hence that peoples with similar technologies in similar environments will tend to evolve similar modes of social grouping, similar belief systems, etc.

culture: The system of knowledge variably shared by members of a society.

culture and personality: The attempt, most characteristic of American anthropology in the 1940s and 1950s, to find regalities in the relationship between a people's child-rearing practices (and the personality configurations they tend to produce through childhood experience) and their cultural beliefs and institutions.

culture of poverty: The theory, initially advanced by Oscar Lewis, that a generally similar way of life (marked by exploitative and fragile sexual relations, psychological stress, and fragile family structures) occurs among the urban poor in many parts of the world.

deep structure: In transformational linguistics, the underlying syntactic pattern of a sentence that conveys meaning.

descent: A relationship defined by connection to an ancestor (or ancestress) through a culturally recognized sequence of parent–child links (from father to son to son's son = patrilineal descent, from mother to daughter to daughter's daughter = matrilineal descent).

descent group: A kin group whose membership is based on a rule of descent. Appropriate descent status (patrilineal, matrilineal, or cognatic, depending on the society) entitles a person to be a member of the group.

dialect: A variety of a language characteristic of a particular geographic region or social class.

distinctive features: In phonology, semantics, or symbolic analysis, two-way contrasts (high vs. low, front vs. back, right vs. left, nature vs. culture); a set of contrasting items (phonemes, words, etc.) are defined by combinations of these distinctive features (e.g., a phoneme is defined as vowel-front-high-tense, in contrast to the other phonemes in the set).

domestic mode of production: Term used by Sahlins and Meillassoux about economic systems where the bulk of production takes place within the domestic family.

double descent: A system whereby two systems of social groups or categories exist (for different purposes) in the same society, one based on patrilineal descent and the other on matrilineal descent (so a person belongs to his/her father's patrilineal group and his/her mother's matrilineal group).

dowry: The valuables or estate transferred by a bride's relatives to her, her husband, or her children in connection with her marriage.

dreamtime: In Australian Aboriginal cosmology, a mode of existence believed to have preceded the visible mundane one (a time of sacred beings and events celebrated in ritual and myth) and to lie behind that realm of perceptible events in the present.

dyadic contract: Enduring obligations entailing exchanges of goods and services between two individuals; especially important, according to George Foster, in some peasant communities.

Electra complex: In psychoanalytic theory, ambivalence and hostility between mother and daughter in relation to the father's sexuality.

elementary system (of kinship): In Lévi-Strauss's theory, systems of kinship and marital alliance where all members of one's society are potentially incorporated in kinship categories and where these categories serve to define a system of marital alliance (exchange of women between groups).

elite: The dominant class or classes in a complex stratified society, with political power and a prestigious lifestyle sustained by strategic control, direct or indirect, over resources and the means of production.

endogamy: A requirement for marriage within a defined category or range or group or community ("in-marriage").

ethnocentrism: Viewing other peoples and ways of life in terms of one's own cultural assumptions, customs, and values.

ethnographic present: The hypothetical time baseline where (in various parts of the world, at different times) Europeans first intruded on the tribal world.

ethnography: The documenting and analysis of a particular culture through field research.

ethnology: The study of human cultures in historical and comparative perspective.

ethogram: The behavioral patterns or propensities of a species that are transmitted genetically.

exchange: Reciprocal transfer of valuables, rights, commodities, etc., between individuals or groups.

exogamous: Of a kinship group (e.g., a lineage or clan), subject to a rule of exogamy, or out-marriage.

exogamy: A requirement for marriage outside a particular social group or range of kinship.

extended family: A domestic group or composite of domestic groups consisting of two or more nuclear families linked together through parent and child (patrilineal extended family, matrilineal extended family) or through siblings (fraternal or sororal extended family).

fictive kinship: Relations, such as *compadrazgo*, between nonrelatives whose nature, affective content, and social obligations are modeled on those appropriate to blood relatives.

fieldwork: A broad term for research in which social/cultural anthropologists (and other social scientists) engage, involving close study of partial participation in the life of a community or group (characteristically in a setting that contrasts culturally with that in which the observer normally lives).

filiation: Relationship to or through one's father and one's mother; the relationship between parents and children, or the basing of rights on this relationship.

folk taxonomy: A system used by a people to classify natural (or culturally created) phenomena that is organized hierarchically, in "kind of" relationships of class inclusion.

forces of production: The technology and physical resources used in production (viewed, in Marxist theory, as comprising, along with social *relations of production*) q.v., the economic base of a society.

formalist: In economic anthropology, the premise that if they are rendered sufficiently broad and abstract, the models of (neoclassical) economic theory can be applied to all human societies. (Cf. *substantivist.*)

fraternal polyandry: Marriage of a woman to two or more brothers.

functionalism: Modes of theoretical interpretation in social science that search for the interconnections between social institutions—how they fit together and what they *do*—rather than seeking causal explanations.

generalized exchange (*échange géneralisé*): A system of alliance (prescriptive marriage) whereby kin groups exchange wives indirectly, so that a man must marry his actual or classificatory mother's brother's daughter (matrilateral alliance), so that wife-givers cannot be wife-takers.

horticulture: Cultivation of crops using hand tools (e.g., digging stick or hoe). (Cf. *agriculture.*)

hunter-gatherers: Human populations that rely in subsistence exclusively or almost exclusively on wild foods, hunted and collected. Some modern hunter-gatherers receive subsistence food from governments or missions or do minimal cultivating.

hunting and gathering: A mode of subsistence based on hunting and collecting of wild foods.

ideational: Pertaining to the mental realm of ideas rather than to the physical world of things and events. (Cf. *phenomenal.*)

identity: A sense of one's self as an individual (personal identity) or as a bearer of a particular cultural heritage (cultural identity). See also *social identity.*

idiolect: The special version of a language known and used by each individual speaker.

incest taboo: A rule prohibiting sexual relations between immediate kin (father and daughter, mother and son, brother and sister) and others culturally defined as in an equivalent relationship. Differs from *exogamy,* which prohibits marriage but not necessarily sexual relations.

internal colonialism: Within an ethnically diverse nation-state, cultural domination, and economic and political domination and exploitation of minorities.

joint family: Often used as equivalent to *extended family;* may have specialized meaning with reference to specific societies, notably Hindu India, to indicate a particular complex of legal relationships between, e.g., father and married sons who comprise a corporate group.

joking relationship: A relationship of privileged familiarity or license between kinsmen or affines in a particular relationship.

kindred: A category comprising a person's relatives, or relatives within a certain range of distance, from which groups are formed, where ego is born, marries, gives a feast, and so on.

kin group: A social group whose members define their relationship (or their eligibility for membership) on kinship or common descent.

kinship: Relationship based on or modeled on the culturally recognized connection between parents and children (and extended to siblings and through parents to more distant relatives).

kinship terminology: A system of linguistic categories for denoting kinds of relatives.

kuru: A neurological disease occurring among the Fore of the Eastern Highlands of Papua New Guinea and transmitted by ritual consumption of the brains of the dead.

Ladino: In southern Mexico and Guatemala, a Spanish-speaking participant in the national culture (in contrast to a person who is culturally and linguistically Indian).

language: (1) A code for symbolic communication consisting of a set of symbols and a set of rules for constructing messages. (Thus a computer uses a man-made artificial language of digital signals.) (2) A naturally evolved human code for vocal communication or a

system (e.g., of hand signs) based on a natural language.

levirate: A system where a dead man's brother (or equivalent close male relative) succeeds to his status as husband by marrying his widow.

lexicon: A dictionary. In linguistic theories of grammatical competence, the mental "dictionary" in which words (and wordlike elements), their meanings, and their grammatical possibilities are assumed to be organized.

liminal: In symbolic analysis, a state or category that is in between or outside normal states or categories. This may be a state of transition between social categories (as when initiates are taken off into seclusion or when on a honeymoon bride and groom go off together) or a category that is outside a normal framework (hermaphrodites, in relation to men and women).

lineage: A unilineal descent group based on patrilineal descent (patrilineage) or matrilineal descent (matrilineage) whose members trace descent from an apical ancestor/ancestress by known genealogical links.

lineage mode of production: Term used in neo-Marxist anthropology for a subsistence-oriented system of production (characteristically horticulturalist or pastoralist) where domestic groups that are the primary producing units are grouped into corporate lineages or clans with substantial collective rights and interests.

machismo: A quest for manly honor and reputation, marked by bravado, sexual predation, etc., characteristic of men in many Latin American societies.

market: The abstract relationship of supply and demand in the buying and selling processes of a money economy.

Marxist: Pertaining to the theories of Karl Marx regarding socioeconomic systems, social change, and class struggle and the body of scholarship derived from these theories.

marriage: An institutionalized form of relationship in which sexual relationships and parentage legitimately take place.

matrilateral: Based on relationship on the mother's side.

matrilineage: See *lineage.*

matrilineal descent: A principle of descent from an ancestress through her daughter, her daughter's daughter, etc. (in the female line).

means of production: In Marxist analysis, the resources used in the process of production (tools, land, technological knowledge, raw materials, etc.); *social classes* are defined with reference to their differential relationship to the means of production (e.g., owners vs. wage laborers).

messianic (movement): A social movement with a doctrine of a new world, to be accessible to members of the group by the leadership of a spiritual intermediary (a messiah).

metacommunication: Term coined by Gregory Bateson for "messages about messages"—that is, for messages (between animals, humans, machines) that define the premises according to which messages are to be interpreted (seriousness, play, threat, etc.) and/or define the relationship between the communicators.

middleperson ("middle man"): A go-between, particularly someone who mediates in economic transactions (e.g., who buys from A, then sells to B, C, D, . . .).

millenarian movement: See *millennial*, q.v.

millennial movement: A social movement with a doctrine of a new world (a millennium) to be attained at least in part by spiritual means.

mode of production: In Marxist theory, a complex of productive relationships—e.g., *capitalist*, entailing relationships between wage laborers and employers; or *feudal*, entailing relationships between serfs and lords, etc. Two or more modes of production may coexist within the same society (in Marxist theory, a *social formation*).

moiety: A division of a society into two social categories or groups, characteristically by a rule of patrilineal descent (patri-moiety) or matrilineal descent (matri-moiety).

moot: An informal hearing of a legal dispute by peers and neighbors.

mortuary (feast, rite): Having to do with funerals or more generally with the disposal of the dead or the relationship of the living to the recently deceased.

mystification: In Marxist theory, the process whereby, through ideologies, social and economic relationships are disguised (e.g., the power of a king or chief is defined as ordained by the gods; workers are persuaded by ideologies of "free enterprise" that high productivity is in their own interest).

natal: Pertaining to the group or kinship connections of one's birth (as opposed to those acquired in marriage).

nature (vs. culture): In symbolic analysis, especially as pioneered in the work of Claude Lévi-Strauss, a polarity between the realm of plants and animals and the world of humans.

neoevolutionary: In anthropology, revival in sophisticated form (especially by the American scholar Leslie White and his students) of the theory that societies can be viewed as representing successive levels of efficiency in technology and the harnessing of energy.

neo-Marxism: The body of theory developed (mainly in the second half of the twentieth century) to extend and build on the theoretical foundations established by Karl Marx, to deal with advanced capitalism, non-Western social formations, and problems (e.g., the state, imperialism) beyond those on which Marx focused.

neocolonialism: The process whereby industrial nations control the political and economic life of nominally independent countries through investment and support of local elites.

neolocal: Residence of a couple after marriage in a new household not linked spatially to that of the groom or the bride. (Cf. *virilocal, uxorilocal.*)

network: In sociological analysis, a mode of tracing and analyzing the relations between individuals as though they formed a pattern of connected points, whose nature and arrangement can then be studied. More loosely in folk sociology, the friends and associates who provide contacts and support for a person.

nonunilineal descent: An alternative term to "cognatic descent." Since cognatic descendants *include* patrilineal descendants and matrilineal descendants, this usage is unfortunate. The term can be used in societies that recognize a unilineal core within a cognatic descent category to denote descent status through at least one alternate sex link (i.e., nonagnatic where descent includes at least one female link, nonuterine where it includes at least one male link).

nuclear family: A family unit consisting of parents and their dependent children.

Oedipus complex: In psychoanalytic theory, the relationship of conflict and ambivalence between father and son in relation to the sexuality of mother.

parallel cousin: Ego's father's brother's child or mother's sister's child, or more distant cousin classed terminologically with these first cousins.

pariah: In India, an outcaste, an untouchable; more generally, a member of a member of a social group or category excluded from normal participation and rights in a society.

pastoralism: A mode of life where herding (of cattle, sheep, camels, goats, horses, etc.) provides the major subsistence.

patrilateral: Based on relationship through the father's side.

patrilineage: See *lineage.*

patrilineal descent: Descent traced through a line of ancestors in the male line. (Also known as *agnatic descent.*)

patrilocal: See *virilocal,* q.v.

patrilocal band: A mode of social organization believed by some scholars to have been characteristic of most hunting and gathering societies, where men remain in their territories and wives marry in—hence where men tend to be related in the male line.

peasant: A member of an agrarian social class or estate whose productive labor supports an elite (characteristically urban) as well as providing for subsistence.

personality: The biological/psychological characteristics of a particular human individual, viewed as a relatively stable and integrated system.

personal kindred: See *kindred,* q.v.

phenomenal: Pertaining to the realm of observable phenomena—things and events. (Cf. *ideational.*)

phoneme: In linguistics, a distinctive unit of sound contrasting with other such units.

Whether phonemes exist as psychologically real or linguistically salient elements, or simply represent stages in the application of phonological rules, has been much debated by specialists.

phonetic(s): In linguistics, the sound patterns of speech and the notations used for describing these acoustical patterns. Since phonetic description includes many contrasts that are irrelevant to speakers and hearers of a language, the linguist moves toward a *phonemic* notation that includes only the contrasts the linguistic code defines as relevant.

phonology: In linguistics (the study of) sound systems of languages.

pollution (symbolic): A belief that some state, substance, or class of persons is dirty, defiled, or virtually contaminating.

polyandry: Marriage of a woman to two or more men.

polygyny: Marriage of a man to two or more women.

prehistory: Study of the ways of life and sequences on processes of cultural development prior to the advent of written records. (Also known as *prehistoric archaeology.*)

prescriptive marriage: In alliance theory, a requirement that marriage be with a partner in a particular kinship category. Even where "incorrect" marriages occur, they are likely to be classed as if they were correct and kinship relations readjusted accordingly.

primary bond: The close psychoattachment of an infant to mother (or mother-surrogate) established in the first year of life; a central element in psychological development and in formation of adult personality.

psychodynamics: The psychology of motivation, emotion, and unconscious mind (in contrast to cognition, the psychology of learning, thinking, and remembering).

reciprocity: A mode of exchange marked by continuing obligation to reciprocate, particularly in kind.

redistribution: A mode of distribution of surplus commodities whereby they flow upward through a political hierarchy (as taxes, tribute, etc.) and are then redistributed downward.

relations of production: In Marxist theory, the social relationships through which production (and distribution and consumption) are organized in a society (relations of production and *forces of production*, q.v., together define a *mode of production*, q.v.)

reproduction, social: The process whereby a particular system of production is perpetuated across generations. This entails physical reproduction and regeneration of the labor force and tools, seed, gardens, and other productive resources. It also entails the perpetuation of the political institutions, religious beliefs, etc., that sustain this system of production.

residence rules: Cultural principles for deciding residential affiliation. Most commonly, *postmarital* residence rules, defining where and with whom a couple should reside after they marry.

restricted exchange (*échange restreint*): A system of alliance (prescriptive marriage) whereby two kin groups exchange wives directly (so that wife-givers are the same people as wife-takers).

rite of passage: A ritual dramatizing the transition from one social state to another (e.g., a wedding, a bar mitzvah, an initiation).

ritual: A stylized, repetitive pattern of behavior (in humans, in most cases culturally patterned collective behavior). Often used only of religious ritual, i.e., stylized behavior deemed to be sacred.

role: The behavior patterns appropriate to an individual acting in a particular social capacity. (See *social identity*.)

Rorschach: A projective test in which a subject reports what he or she "sees" in a standard set of inkblot cards; used in psychiatric diagnosis and cross-cultural research.

section system: In alliance theory and Australian kinship studies, division of a society into two, four, or eight social categories through rules of descent and alliance. Symmetrical rules of marital alliance, enjoining marriage with a member of one of the sections, are a normal accompaniment of such systems.

segmentary: Of descent systems, defining descent categories with reference to more and more remote apical ancestors so that the descent categories form a treelike structure (including successively wider ranges of descendants).

semantics: The study of linguistic meaning: how "words" represent meanings, and how their arrangement in sentences conveys propositions.

shifting cultivation: See *swidden cultivation*.

sister-exchange: Exchange of sisters in marriage by a pair of men (as seen from the male perspective).

situational analysis: In social anthropology, analysis of social relations in a complex society by taking a particular social event as the focus and tracing out the wider ties of the participants, and how and why they play the parts they do.

social anthropology: The area of "cultural anthropology" concerned with comparative study of human social institutions.

social class: A division of society, defined in terms of its relationship to the means of production, within a system of such classes, hierarchically ordered, and marked by a consciousness of their collective identity and interests.

social group: A plurality of individuals who recurrently interact in a system of interlocking *social identities* (q.v.).

social identity: A social position or capacity (e.g., salesperson, customer, physician) that a person assumes in a particular setting. (See *role*.)

social reproduction: See *reproduction, social*.

social stratification: Division of society in terms of inequality; differential ranking or status of social groups, classes, or categories.

social structure: The organization of a group or society seen in terms of structures of positions and roles; a formal abstraction from the ongoing social relations within communities.

social system: A system of ordered social relations maintained over time.

society: A population marked by relative separation from surrounding populations and a distinctive culture (complex societies may include two or more distinctive cultural groups incorporated within a single social system).

sociocultural system: The patterns of behavior characteristic of a population sharing a distinctive culture within an ecosystem.

sororal polygyny: Marriage of a man to two or more sisters.

sororate: A form of secondary marriage whereby, upon the death of a wife, her sister or some other close relative marries the surviving husband. This perpetuates the marital contract between groups.

speech acts: Acts in which speech is used to convey information, give orders, ask questions, etc., or to define situations or change them ("I now pronounce you man and wife").

strata: The levels in a system of *social stratification* (q.v.).

structuralism: The theoretical tradition, most closely associated with the French anthropologist Claude Lévi-Strauss, that seeks to find, beneath cultural phenomena, the structures of mind—particularly the logic of opposition—they express.

subsistence economy: The technical processes and social relationships whereby the foodstuffs and other physical means of life are produced and consumed.

substantivist: In economic anthropology, the stance that the models of (neoclassical) economics properly apply only to capitalist economies where the market principle is pervasive (hence that tribal societies where other modes of production and redistribution predominate must be analyzed in terms of different models). In substantivist theory, economics is properly concerned not with maximizing behavior but with the ways in which humans produce and distribute the material goods that sustain their existence.

superstructure: The institutional and ideological apparatus that, according to Marxist theory, functions to sustain and justify a set of economic arrangements.

surface structure: In transformational linguistics, the syntactic string that is converted into sound by phonological rules, in the derivation of a sentence.

surplus: In economics, production that exceeds the subsistence needs of the producers.

swidden cultivation: Gardening in which forest is cleared and burned, crops are planted and harvested, and the land is then allowed to lie fallow and develop secondary growth before it is cultivated again. (Also known as *shifting cultivation.*)

symmetrical alliance: In alliance theory, a marriage system involving direct exchange, q.v.

syncretism: Synthesis of the elements of two or more cultures, particularly religious beliefs and ritual practices.

syntax: The formal system whereby linguistic elements (words and wordlike elements) are constructed in sentences.

systems theory: A body of theoretical models for dealing with the organization of complex natural (or artificial) systems, in terms of cybernetic regulation, information, and bioenergetics. The formal study of biological (and quasi-biological) systems.

taboo: Sacred; forbidden, especially by religious sanctions (from Polynesian *tapu*).

temperament: The personality dispositions of individuals in a population, which differ considerably, apparently reflecting genetic predispositions as well as differential experience.

totemism: Symbolic association between a social group (e.g., a lineage or clan) and a kind of bird, plant, or natural phenomenon. In "classic" forms, a member of the social group has some special religious relationship (e.g., a food taboo) toward members of the natural species.

trade: The transfer of commodities by purchase, barter, or other modes of transaction.

transhumance: Seasonal movement of peoples according to the availability of pasturage.

tribal: Pertaining to small-scale food-producing societies without centralized political organization.

tribal communal mode of production: Term provisionally suggested for subsistence-oriented systems of production in tribal societies in which labor, distribution, and consumption take place primarily within structures of kinship and community and in which surplus labor is directed to communal ends and kinship obligation.

tribe: A small-scale society characterized by a distinctive language and culture with a political identity but not central, hierarchical institutions.

ultimogeniture: A rare pattern of inheritance in which the appropriate family heir is the youngest son or youngest sibling.

unilineal descent: Patrilineal (agnatic) or matrilineal (uterine) descent.

urban: Pertaining to cities or life in cities.

uterine: See *matrilineal,* q.v.

uxorilocal: Residence of a married couple with the wife's kin (formerly called "matrilocal").

values: Theories of the desirable principles that guide human choice.

virilocal: Residence of a married couple with the husband's kin (formerly called "patrilocal"). Residence rules can be further distinguished as viripatrilocal (with the husband's father—patri-virilocal expresses the same pattern), viri-avunculocal (or avunculo-virilocal—residence with the husband's maternal uncle).

Bibliography

Aaby, P. 1978. What Are We Fighting For? 'Progress' or 'Cultural Autonomy'? *Transactions of the Finnish Anthropological Society,* No. 2.

Aberle, D. 1962. A Note on Relative Deprivation Theory as Applied to Millenarian and Other Cult Movements. In S. L. Thrupp, ed., *Millennial Dreams in Action: Comparative Studies in Society and History,* Supplement 2. The Hague.

Adams, R. M. 1966. *The Evolution of Urban Society.* Chicago: Aldine Publishing Company.

Adams, R. N. 1975. *Energy and Structure: A Theory of Social Power.* Austin: University of Texas Press.

———. 1977. Power in Human Societies: A Synthesis. In R. D. Fogelson and R. N. Adams, eds. *The Anthropology of Power.* New York: Academic Press.

Adams, W. Y. 1983. Once More to the Fray: Further Reflections on Navajo Kinship and Residence. *Journal of Anthropological Research* 39(4): 393–414.

Agar, N. 1973. *Ripping and Running: A Formal Ethnography of Urban Heroin Addicts.* New York: Academic Press.

Aguilera, F. E. 1978. *Santa Eulalia's People: Ritual Structure and Process in an Andalucian Multicommunity.* St. Paul: West Publishing Company.

Ahmed, A. S. 1976. *Millennium and Charisma Among Pathans.* London: Routledge and Kegan Paul.

Alavi, H. 1964. Imperialism: New and Old. *Socialist Register.*

———. 1973. Peasants and Revolution. In K. Gough and H. P. Sharma, eds. *Imperialism and Revolution in South India.* New York: Monthly Review Press.

Allen, F. J. 1976. Comment on K. Hutterer, *An Evolutionary Approach to the Southeast Asian Sequence. Current Anthropology* 17.

Amarshi, A., K. Good, and R. Mortimer. 1980. *Development and Dependency: The Political Economy of Papua New Guinea.* Melbourne: Oxford University Press.

Anderson, E. N., Jr. 1972. Some Chinese Methods of Dealing With Crowding. *Urban Anthropology* 1: 141–150.

Ardener, E. 1972. Belief and the Problem of Women. In J. LaFontaine, ed., *The Interpretation of Ritual.* Cambridge: Cambridge University Press (reprinted with new Introduction in S. Ardener, 1975).

Ardener, S., ed. 1975. *Perceiving Women.* London: Malaby Press.

Arens, W. 1979. *The Man-Eating Myth: Anthropology and Anthropophogy.* New York: Oxford University Press.

Asad, T. 1970. *The Kababish Arabs: Power, Authority, and Consent in a Nomadic Tribe.* London: Conrad Hurst and Company.

———. 1972. Market Model, Class Structure, and Consent: A Reconsideration of Swat Political Organization. *Man* (n.s.) 7: 74–94.

———, ed. 1973. *Anthropology and the Colonial Encounter.* London: Ithaca Press.

———. 1979. Equality in Nomadic Social Systems? Notes Toward the Dissolution of an

Anthropological Category. In *L'Equipe Ecologie et Anthropologie des Sociétés Pastorale*. Pastoral Production and Society. Cambridge: Cambridge University Press.

Aschmann, H. 1959. The Central Desert of Baja California: Demography and Ecology. *Ibero-Americana* 42: 316.

Bailey, F. G. 1957. *Caste and the Economic Frontier: A Village in Highland Orissa*. Manchester: Manchester University Press.

———. 1963. *Politics and Social Change: Orissa in 1959*. Berkeley: University of California Press.

———. 1969. *Strategems and Spoils: A Social Anthropology of Politics*. New York: Schocken Books, Inc.

———. 1971. *Gifts and Poison*. Oxford: Basil Blackwell & Mott, Ltd.

Balandier, G. 1970. *Political Anthropology*. New York: Random House.

Banton, M. 1957. *West African City: A Study of Tribal Life in Freetown*. London: Oxford University Press.

———. 1973. Urbanization and Role Analysis. In A. Southall, ed., *Urban Anthropology*. London: Oxford University Press.

Barker, J., ed. 1990. *Christianity in Oceania: Ethnographic Perspectives*. ASAO Monograph #12. Lanham: University Press of America.

Barnes, J. A. 1967. *Inquest on the Murngin*. Royal Anthropological Institute of Great Britain and Ireland. Occasional Paper No. 26.

———. 1972. *Networks in Social Anthropology*. Reading, Mass.: Addison-Wesley Modules in Anthropology.

Barnet, R. J., and R. E. Müller. 1974. *Global Reach: The Power of the Multinational Corporations*. New York: Simon & Schuster.

Barth, F. 1956. Ecological Relationships of Ethnic Groups in Swat, North Pakistan. *American Anthropologist* 58: 1079–1089.

———. 1959a. *Political Leadership Among Swat Pathans*. London: Athlone Press.

———. 1959b. Segmentary Opposition and the Theory of Games: A Study of Pathan Organization. *Journal of the Royal Anthropological Institute* 89: 5–21.

———. 1961. *Nomads of South Persia: The Basseri Tribe of the Khamseh Confederacy*. Boston: Little, Brown and Company.

———. 1966a. *Models of Social Organization*. Royal Anthropological Institute Occasional Papers, No. 23. London: Royal Anthropological Institute.

———. 1966b. Anthropological Models and Social Reality. *Proceedings of the Royal Society* 165: 20–25.

———. 1967. On the Study of Social Change. *American Anthropologist* 69: 661–669.

———, ed. 1969. *Ethnic Groups and Boundaries*. Boston: Little, Brown and Company.

———. 1975. *Ritual and Knowledge Among the Baktaman of New Guinea*. Oslo: Universitets Forlaget; New Haven: Yale University Press.

———. 1981. *Features of Person and Society in Swat: Collected Essays on Pathans*. New York: Routledge.

———. 1992. Towards Greater Naturalism in Conceptualizing Societies. In A. Kuper, ed., *Conceptualizing Society* (pp. 17–33). London and New York: Routledge.

Bartolome, M. A., et al. 1971. *Declaration of Barbados: For the Liberation of the Indians*. Copenhagen: International Work Group for Indigenous Affairs. (From proceedings of the Barbados symposium, January 1971, sponsored by World Council of Churches Programme to Combat Racism and University of Berne.)

Barton, R. F. 1919. Ifugao Law. In *American Archaeology and Ethnography*, 15. Berkeley, Calif.: University of California Press.

Barwick, D. 1972. Coranderrk and Cumaroogunga: Pioneers and Policy. In T. S. Epstein and D. H. Penny, eds., *Opportunity and Response*. London: C. Hurst & Company.

———. n.d. Rebellion at Coranderrk. Unpublished Ms.

Basso, K. 1976. 'Wise Words' of the Western Apache: Metaphor and Semantic Theory. In K. Basso and H. Selby, eds. *Meaning in Anthropology*. Albuquerque: University of New Mexico Press.

Bateson, G. 1955. A Theory of Play and Fantasy. *Psychiatric Research Reports* 2: 39–51. American Psychiatric Association. (Reprinted in Bateson 1972.)

———. 1972. *Steps to an Ecology of Mind*. San Francisco: Chandler Publishing Company.

———, and M. Mead. 1942. *Balinese Character: A Photographic Analysis*. Special Publications, 2. New York: New York Academy of Sciences.

Beattie, J. 1958. *Nyoro Kinship, Marriage, and Affinity*. London: Oxford University Press.

———. 1960. *The Bunyoro: An African Kingdom*. New York: Holt, Rinehart and Winston.

Beckerman, S. 1978. Comment on B. R. Ross, *Food taboos, Diet, and Hunting Strategy. Current Anthropology* 19: 17–19.

Beckett, J. 1995. National and Transnational Perspectives on Multiculturalism: The View From Australia. *Identities: Global Studies in Culture and Power* 1(4): 421–426.

Beidelman, T. O. 1963. Witchcraft in Ukaguru. In J. Middleton and E. Winter, eds., *Witchcraft and Sorcery in East Africa*. London: Routledge and Kegan Paul Ltd.

———. 1993. *Moral Imagination in Kaguru Modes of Thought*. Bloomington: Indiana University Press.

Bell, D. 1980. Desert Politics: Choices in the 'Marriage Market.' In M. Etienne and E. Leacock, eds., *Women in Colonization*. New York: Praeger.

———, and P. Ditton. 1980. *Law: The Old and the New: Aboriginal Women in Central Australia Speak Out*. Canberra: Central Australian Aboriginal Legal Aid Service.

Bellah, R. N. 1957. *Tokugawa Religion: The Values of Pre-Industrial Japan*. New York: The Free Press.

Bellman, B. L. 1979. The Social Organization of Knowledge in Kpelle Ritual. In R. B. Jules and J. W. Fernandez, *The New Religions of Africa*. Norwood, N. J.: Ablex.

Belshaw, C. S. 1965. *Traditional Exchange and Modern Markets*. Englewood Cliffs, N.J.: Prentice-Hall, Inc.

Bernstein, H. 1979. African Peasantries: A Theoretical Framework. *Journal of Peasant Studies* 6, (4): 421–443.

Berreman, G. D. 1969. Academic Colonialism: Not So Innocent Abroad. In *The Nation*, Nov. 10, 1969. (Reprinted in T. Weaver, ed., 1973, *To See Ourselves*. Glenview, Ill.: Scott, Foresman and Company.)

———. 1978. Ecology, Demography, and Domestic Strategies in the Western Himalayas. *Journal of Anthropological Research* 34: 326–368.

Besteman, C. 1995. Polygyny, Women's Land Tenure, and the 'Mother–Son Partnership' in Southern Somalia. *Journal of Anthropological Research* 51(3): 193–213.

Béteille, A. 1986. The Concept of Tribe With Special Reference to India. *Archives Européennes de Sociologie* 27(2), pp. 297–318.

Bettelheim, B. 1954. *Symbolic Wounds*. Glencoe, Ill.: Free Press.

Bigman, L. 1993. *History and Hunger in West Africa: Food Production and Entitlement in Guinea-Bissau and Cape Verde*. London: Greenwood Press.

Binford, L. R. 1968. Post Pleistocene Adaptations. In L. R. and S. Binford, eds., *New Perspectives in Archaeology*. Chicago: Aldine Publishing Company.

———, and W. J. Chasko, Jr. 1975. Nunamiut Demographic History: A Provocative Case. In E. Zubrow, ed., *Demographic Anthropology*. Albuquerque: University of New Mexico Press.

Birdwhistell, R. L. 1970. *Kinesics and Context: Essays on Body Motion Communication*. Philadelphia: University of Pennsylvania Press.

Bischof, N. 1974. Comparative Ethology of Incest Avoidance. In R. Fox, ed., *Biosocial Anthropology*. London: Malaby Press.

Black, M. 1959. Linguistic Relativity: The Views of Benjamin Lee Whorf. *Philosophical Review* 68: 228–238.

Bledsoe, C. 1976. Women's Marital Strategies Among the Kpelle of Liberia. *Journal of Anthropological Research* 32: 372–389.

Bloch, M. 1971. *Placing the Dead: Tombs, Ancestral Villages, and Kinship Organization in Madagascar*. London: Seminar Press.

Blue, A. V., and A. D. Gaines. 1992. The Ethnopsychiatric Repertoire. In A. D. Gaines, ed., *Ethnopsychiatry: The Cultural Construction of Professional and Folk Psychiatries* (pp. 397–461). Albany: State University of New York Press.

Bock, P. K. 1988. *Rethinking Psychological Anthropology: Continuity and Change in the Study of the Human Action*. New York: W. H. Freeman.

Bohannan, L. 1958. Political Aspects of Tiv Social Organization. In J. Middleton and D. Tait, eds., *Tribes Without Rulers*. London: Routledge and Kegan Paul Ltd.

————, and P. Bohannan. 1968. *Tiv Economy.* Evanston, Ill.: Northwestern University Press.

Bohannan, P. 1954. *Tiv Farm and Settlement.* London: H. M. Stationery Office.

————. 1955. Some Principles of Exchange and Investment Among the Tiv. *American Anthropologist* 57: 60–70.

————. 1959. The Impact of Money on an African Subsistence Economy. *Journal of Economic History* 19: 491–503.

————. 1965. The Differing Realms of Law. *American Anthropologist* 67: 33–42.

Boissevain, J. 1968. The Place of Non-Groups in the Social Sciences. *Man* (n.s.) 3: 542–556.

Bolton, R. 1973. Aggression and Hypoglycemia Among the Qolla: A Study in Psychobiological Anthropology. *Ethology* 12: 227–257.

————. 1976. Aggression in Fantasy: A Further Test of the Hypoglycemia Aggression Hypothesis. *Aggressive Behavior* 2: 251–274.

————. 1978. *Aggression and Hypoglycemia in Qolla Society.* New York: Garland STMP Press.

Boon, J. 1972. *From Symbolism to Structuralism: Lévi-Strauss in a Literary Tradition.* New York: Harper & Row, Publishers.

Bordes, F. 1968. *The Old Stone Age.* New York: McGraw-Hill, Inc.

Boserup, E. 1965. *The Conditions of Agricultural Growth: The Economics of Agrarian Change Under Population Pressures.* Chicago: Aldine Publishing Company.

Bottomore, T. B. 1964. *Elites and Society.* London: Watts.

Bourdieu, P. 1977. *Outline of a Theory of Practice.* Trans. by Richard Nice. Cambridge: Cambridge University Press.

Bowers, A. W. 1950. *Mandan Social and Ceremonial Organization.* Chicago: University of Chicago Press.

Bowlby, J. 1969. Attachment and Loss, Vol. I: *Attachment.* London: Hogarth Press.

Brace, C. L. 1968. Ridiculed, Rejected, But Still Our Ancestor, Neanderthal. *Natural History,* May.

Brenner, R. 1977. The Origins of Capitalist Development: A Critique of Neo-Smithian Marxism. *New Left Review* 104: 25–92.

Bronson, S. 1975. In S. Polgar, ed., *Population, Ecology, and Social Evolution.* The Hague: Mouton.

————. 1976. Comment on K. Hutterer, ed., *An Evolutionary Approach to the Southeast Asian Cultural Sequence. Current Anthropology* 17(2): 230.

Brose, D. S., and M. H. Wolpoff. 1971. Early Upper Paleolithic Man and Late Middle Paleolithic Tools. *American Anthropologist* 75: 1156–1194.

Brown, J. 1975. Iroquois Women: An Ethnohistoric Note. In R. Reiter, ed., *Toward an Anthropology of Women.* New York: Monthly Review Press.

Brown, P. 1972. *The Chimbu: A Study of Change in the New Guinea Highlands.* Cambridge, Mass.: Schenkman Publishing Company.

————. 1995. *Beyond a Mountain Valley: The Simbu of Papua New Guinea.* Honolulu: University of Hawaii Press.

Brown, R. 1973. Anthropology and Colonial Rule: Godfrey Wilson and the Rhodes-Livingston Institute, Northern Rhodesia. In T. Asad, ed., *Anthropology and the Colonial Encounter.* London: Ithaca Press.

Bruner, E. M. 1961. Mandan. In E. H. Spicer, ed., *Perspectives in American Indian Cultural Change.* Chicago: University of Chicago Press.

————. 1973. Kin and Non-Kin. In A. Southall, ed., *Urban Anthropology.* London: Oxford University Press.

Brunton, R. 1975. Why Do the Trobriands have Chiefs? *Man* (n.s.) 10: 544–558.

Buchbinder, G. 1973. *Maring Microadaptation: A Study of Demographic, Nutritional, Genetic, and Phenotypic Variation in a Highland New Guinea Population.* Unpublished Ph.D. dissertation, Columbia University.

————. 1977. Nutritional Stress and Postcontact Population Decline Among the Maring of New Guinea. In L. S. Greene, ed., *Malnutrition, Behavior, and Social Organization.* New York: Academic Press.

Burridge, K. 1960. *Mambu, a Melanesian Millennium.* London: Methuen.

Butzer, K. W. 1971. *Environment and Archaeology: An Ecological Approach to Prehistory,* 2nd ed. Chicago: Aldine Publishing Company.

Byres, T. J. 1979. Of Neo-Populist Pipe-Dreams: Daedalus in the Third World or the Myth of Urban Bias. *Journal of Peasant Studies* 6: 210–244.

Campbell, B. 1970. The Roots of Language. In J. Morton, ed., *Biological and Social Factors in Psycholinguistics.* Urbana: University of Illinois Press.

Cancian, F. 1965. *Economics and Prestige in a Maya Community: The Religious Cargo System in Zinacantan.* Stanford, Calif.: Stanford University Press.

———. 1972. *Change and Uncertainty in a Peasant Economy.* Stanford, Calif.: Stanford University Press.

———. 1974. New Patterns of Stratification in the Zinacantan Cargo System. *Journal of Anthropological Research* 30(3): 164–173.

Caplan, A., ed. 1978. *The Sociobiology Debate.* New York: Harper & Row Publishers.

Carneiro. 1970. A Theory of the Origin of the State. *Science* 169: 733–738.

Carroll, V., ed. 1970. *Adoption in Eastern Oceania.* Honolulu: University of Hawaii Press.

Carsten, J., and S. Hugh-Jones, eds. 1995. *About the House: Lévi-Strauss and Beyond.* Cambridge: Cambridge University Press.

Catlin, G. 1867. *O-Kee-Pa.* Philadelphia. (Republished as *George Catlin's O-Kee-Pa.* J. Ewers, ed. 1954. New Haven, Conn.: Yale University Press.)

Caulfield, M. D. 1972. Culture and Imperialism: Proposing a New Dialectic. In D. Hymes, ed., *Reinventing Anthropology.* New York: Random House, Inc.

———. 1973. Participant Observation or Partisan Participation? In G. Huizer and B. Mannheim, eds., *The Politics of Anthropology.* The Hague: Mouton.

Chagnon, N. A. 1968. Yanomamö Social Organization and Warfare. In M. Fried, M. Harris, and R. Murphy, eds., *The Anthropology of Armed Conflict and Aggression.* Garden City, N.Y.: Natural History Press. (Page reference is to reprinting in M. Fried, ed. 1973. *Explorations in Anthropology.* New York: Thomas Y. Crowell Company.)

———. 1977. *Yanomamö: The Fierce People.* 2nd ed. New York: Holt, Rinehart and Winston.

———, and R. B. Hames. 1979. Protein Deficiency and Tribal Warfare in Amazonia: New Data. *Science* 203: 910–913.

———, and W. Irons, eds. 1979. *Evolutionary Biology and Human Social Behavior: An Anthropological Perspective.* North Scituate, Mass.: Duxbury Press.

Chattopadhyay, P. 1972. Mode of Production in Indian Agriculture: An Anti-Kritik. *Economic and Political Weekly,* December.

Chodorow, N. 1974. Family Structure and Feminine Personality. In M. Z. Rosaldo and L. Lamphere, eds., *Woman, Culture, and Society.* Stanford, Calif.: Stanford University Press.

———. 1979. *The Reproduction of Mothering: Psychoanalysis and the Sociology of Gender.* Berkeley: University of California Press.

Chun, A., J. Clammer, P. Ebrey, D. Faure, S. Feuchtwang, Y. K. Huang, P. S. Sangren, and M. Yang. 1996. The Lineage-Village Complex in Southeastern China: A Long Footnote in the Anthropology of Kinship. *Current Anthropology* 37(3): 429–440.

Claessen, H. J. M., and P. Skalnik, eds., 1978. *The Early States.* The Hague: Mouton.

Clarke, W. C. 1971. *Place and People.* Berkeley: University of California Press.

Cleaver, H. M., Jr. 1972. The Contradictions of the Green Revolution. *American Economic Review* 62(2): 177–186.

Cline, W. 1936. *Notes on the People of Stwah and el-Garah in the Libyan Desert.* Menasha, Wis.: George Banta, Inc.

Cochrane, G. 1971. *Development Anthropology.* New York: Oxford University Press.

Cohen, A. P. 1987. *Whalsay: Symbol, Segment, and boundary in a Shetland Island Community.* New York: St. Martin's Press, Inc.

Cohen, R. 1978a. State Foundations: A Controlled Comparison. In R. Cohen and E. Service, eds., *Origins of the State: The Anthropology of Political Evolution.* Philadelphia: Institute for the Study of Human Issues.

———. 1978b. State Origins: A Reappraisal. In H. J. M. Claessen and P. Skalnik, eds., *The Early States.* The Hague: Mouton.

———, and E. R. Service, eds. 1978. *Origins of the State: The Anthropology of Political Evolution.*

Philadelphia: Institute for the Study of Human Issues.

Cole, M., and S. Scribner. 1974. *Culture and Thought: A Psychological Introduction.* New York: John Wiley & Sons, Inc.

Cole, S. 1965. *The Prehistory of East Africa.* New York: New American Library, Mentor Books.

Collier, J. F., and M. Z. Rosaldo. 1981. Politics and Gender in Simple Societies. In S. Ortner and H. Whitehead, eds., *Sexual Meanings: The Cultural Construction of Gender and Sexuality.* Cambridge: Cambridge University Press.

Collins, J., and F. M. Lappé. 1977. Still Hungry After All These Years: The Not-So-Grand Opening of the Global Supermarket. *Mother Jones* August: 27–33.

Colson, E., G. Foster, T. Scudder, and R. van Kemper. 1979. *Long-Term Field Research in Social Anthropology.* New York: Academic Press.

Comaroff, J. L., and S. A. Roberts. 1977. The Invocation of Norms in Dispute Settlement: The Tswana Case. In I. Hamnett, ed., *The Anthropology of Law.* London: Academic Press.

Conklin, H. C. 1957. *Hfanunóo Agriculture.* Rome: FAO.

Converse, H. M. 1908. *Myths and Legends of the New York State Iroquois.* In A. C. Parker, ed. New York State Museum Bulletin No. 125. Albany, N.Y.

Cook, S. 1973. Economic Anthropology: Problems in Theory, Method, and Analysis. In J. J. Honigmann, ed., *Handbook of Social and Cultural Anthropology.* Chicago: Rand McNally & Company.

Coon, C. S. 1971. *The Hunting Peoples.* Boston: Little, Brown and Company.

Coursey, D. G. 1978. Some Ideological Considerations Relating to Tropical Root Crop Production. In E. K. Fisk, ed., *The Adaptation of Traditional Agriculture.* Development Studies Centre Monograph No. 11. Canberra: Australian National University Press.

Crawford, M. A., and J. P. W. Rivers. 1975. The Protein Myth., In F. Steel and A. Bourne, eds., *The Man/Food Equation.* New York: Academic Press.

Crowder, M. 1968. *West Africa Under Colonial Rule.* London: Hutchinson Publishing Group, Ltd.

———, ed. 1971. *West African Resistance: The Military Response to Colonial Occupation.* London: Hutchinson Publishing Group, Ltd.

Curtin, P. D., S. Feierman, L. Thompson, and J. Vansina. 1978. *African History.* Boston: Little, Brown and Company.

Dahl, G. 1979. Ecology and Equality: The Boran Case. In l'Equipe Ecologie et Anthropologie des Sociétés Pastorales, eds., *Pastoral Production and Society.* Cambridge: Cambridge University Press.

———. 1987. Women in Pastoral Production. *Ethnos* 52 (1–2): 246–279.

———, and A. Hjort. 1976. *Having Herds: Pastoral Growth and Household Economy.* Stockholm Studies in Social Anthropology 2. Stockholm: Department of Social Anthropology, University of Stockholm.

Dalton, G. 1961. Economic Theory and Primitive Society. *American Anthropologist* 63: 1–25.

———. 1965. Primitive Money. *American Anthropologist* 67: 44–65.

———, ed. 1972. *Studies in Economic Anthropology.* Washington, D.C.: American Anthropological Association.

Damasio, A. R. 1994. *Descartes' error: Emotion, Reason, and the Human Brain.* New York: G. P. Putnam.

Danks, B. 1887. On the Shell-Money of New Britain. *Journal of the Royal Anthropological Institute* 17: 305–317.

Davenport, W. 1969. The Hawaiian Cultural Revolution: Some Political and Economic Considerations. *American Anthropologist* 71: 1–20.

Davidson, B. 1959. *The Lost Cities of Africa.* Boston: Little, Brown and Company.

———. 1966. *A History of West Africa to the Nineteenth Century.* Garden City, N.Y.: Anchor Press, *imprint* of Doubleday & Company, Inc.

———. 1969. *A History of East and Central Africa to the Late Nineteenth Century.* Garden City, N.Y.: Anchor Press, *imprint* of Doubleday & Company, Inc.

Davila, M. 1971. Compadrazgo: Fictive Kinship in Latin America. In N. Graburn, ed., *Readings in Kinship and Social Structure.* New York: Harper & Row, Publishers.

Davis, S. H. 1977. *Victims of the Miracle: Development and the Indians of Brazil*. London and New York: Cambridge University Press.

———. 1979. The Social Responsibility of Anthropological Science in the Context of Contemporary Brazil. In G. Huizer and B. Mannheim, eds., *The Politics of Anthropology*. The Hague: Mouton.

———. 1980. Mining Projects Endanger Amazon's Yanomamo Tribe. *Multinational Monitor* 1(1) February: 20–21, 28.

D'Azevedo, W. 1962. Uses of the Past in Gola Discourse. *Journal of African History* 3: 11–34.

de Beauvoir, Simone. 1953. *The Second Sex*. Trans. and ed. by H. M. Parshley. New York: Alfred A. Knopf, Inc.

DeBernardi, J. 1994. Social Aspects of Language Use. In T. Ingold, ed., *Companion Encyclopedia of Anthropology* (pp. 861–890). London and New York: Routledge.

Debray, R. 1967. *Revolution in the Revolution? Armed Struggle and Political Struggle in Latin America*. Trans. by B. Ortiz. New York: Grove Press, Inc.

Deevey, E. S., Jr. 1960. The Human Population. *Scientific American* 203: 195–204.

de Heinzelin, J. 1962. Ishango. *Scientific American* June: 105–116.

De Loria, V. 1969. *Custer Died for Your Sins: An Indian Manifesto*. New York: The Macmillan Company.

Dentan, R. K. 1968. *The Semai: A Nonviolent People of Malaya*. New York: Holt, Rinehart and Winston.

Descola, P. 1992. Societies of Nature and the Nature of Society. In A. Kuper, ed., *Conceptualizing Society* (pp. 107–126). London and New York: Routledge.

———. 1996. *The Spears of Twilight: Life and Death in the Amazon Jungle*. New York: The New Press.

De Sonneville-Bordes, D. 1963. Upper Paleolithic Cultures in Western Europe. *Science* 142 (3590): 347–355.

Devereux, G. 1953. Why Oedipus Killed Laius: A Note on the Complementary Oedipus Complex. *International Journal of Psycho-Analysis* 34: 132–141.

———. 1967. *From Anxiety to Method in the Behavioral Sciences*. Preface by W. LaBarre. The Hague: Mouton and Company.

———. 1975. *Fantasy as a Reflection of Reality*. Paper presented at 46th ANZAAS Congress, Canberra, Australia. January.

———. 1978. The Works of George Devereux. In G. D. Spindler, ed., *The Making of Psychological Anthropology*. Berkeley: University of California Press.

Diaz, M. N. 1967. Introduction: Economic Relations in Peasant Society. In M. J. Potter, M. N. Diaz, and G. M. Foster, eds., *Peasant Society: A Reader*. Boston: Little, Brown and Company.

Divale, W. T., and M. Harris. 1976. Population, Warfare, and Male Supremacist Complex. *American Anthropologist* 78: 521–538.

Douglas, M. 1966. *Purity and Danger*. Baltimore: Penguin Books, Inc.

———. 1970. *Natural Symbols: Explorations in Cosmology*. London: Cresset.

Dumont, L. 1966. *Homo-Hierarchicus: Essai Sur le Systeme des Castes*. Bibliotheque des Sciences Humaines. Paris: Gallimard.

Dundes, A. 1976. A Psychoanalytic Study of the Bullroarer. *Man* 11: 220–238.

Dupré, G., and P. P. Rey. 1973. Reflections on the Pertinence of a Theory of the History of Exchange. *Economy and Society* 2: 131–163.

Duranti, A. 1990. Politics and Grammar: Agency in Samoan Political Discourse. *American Ethnologist* 17: 646–666.

Durkheim, E. 1912. *Les Formes Elementaires de la Vie Religieuse: Le Systeme Totemique en Australia*. Paris: Presses Universitaires.

Dyson-Hudson, N. 1966. *Karimojong Politics*. Oxford: Oxford University Press.

Dyson-Hudson, N., and R. Dyson-Hudson. 1970. The Food Production of a Semi-Nomadic Society: The Karimojong, Uganda. In P. F. M. McLoughlin, ed., *African Food Production Systems*. Baltimore, Md.: The Johns Hopkins Press.

Dyson-Hudson, R., and N. Dyson-Hudson. 1969. Subsistence Herding in Uganda. *Scientific American* February: 76–89.

Easton, D. 1959. Political Anthropology. In B. Siegel, ed., *Biennial Review of Anthropology* 2.

Eckert, P., and R. Newmark. 1980. Central Eskimo Song Duels: A Contextual Analysis of Ritual Ambiguity. *Ethnology* 19(2): 191–211.

Edgerton, R. B. 1964. Pokot Intersexuality: An East African Example of the Resolution of Sexual Incongruity. *American Anthropologist* 66: 1288–1299.

Eibl-Eibesfeldt, I. 1968. Ethological Perspectives on Primate Studies. In P. Jay, ed., *Primates: Studies in Adaptation and Variability*. New York: Holt, Rinehart and Winston.

———. 1989. *Human Ethology*. New York: Aldine DeGruyter.

Eisenstadt, S. N. 1956. *From Generation to Generation*. New York: The Free Press.

Ekholm, K. 1977. External Exchange and the Transformation of Central African Social Systems. In J. Friedman and M. J. Rowlands, eds., *The Evolution of Social Systems*. London: Duckworth.

Eliade, M. 1959. *Cosmos and History: The Myth of the External Return*. New York: Harper & Row, Publishers.

———. 1970. Cargo Cults and Cosmic Regeneration. In S. L. Thrupp, ed. *Millennial Dreams in Action: Studies in Revolutionary Religious Movements*. New York: Schocken Books, Inc.

Endicott, K. A. L. 1979. *Batek Negrito Sex Roles*. Unpublished M.A. thesis, Department of Prehistory and Anthropology, The Australian National University.

Endicott, K. M. 1974. *Batek Negrito Economy and Social Organization*. Unpublished Ph.D. thesis, Harvard University.

Engels, F. 1878. *Origin of the Family, Private Property, and the State*. New York: International Press, 1942.

Epstein, A. L. 1963. Tambu: A Primitive Shell Money. *Discovery* 24: 28–32.

———. 1968. Power, Politics, and Leadership: Some Central African and Melanesian Contrasts. In M. J. Swartz, ed., *Local Level Politics*. Chicago: Aldine Publishing Company.

———. 1969. *Matupit: Land, Politics, and Change Among the Tolai of New Britain*. Berkeley, Calif.: University of California Press.

———. 1979. Tambu: The Shell-Money of the Tolai. In R. Hook, ed., *Fantasy and Symbol*. New York and London: Academic Press.

———. 1992. *In the Midst of Life*. Berkeley: University of California Press.

Epstein, T. S. 1964. Personal Capital Formation Among the Tolai of New Britain. In R. Firth and B. Yamey, eds., *Capital, Saving, and Credit in Peasant Societies*. Chicago: Aldine Publishing Company.

l'Equipe Ecologie et Anthropologie des Sociétés Pastorales. 1979. *Pastoral Production and Society*. Cambridge: Cambridge University Press.

Eriksen, T. H. 1993. *Ethnicity and Nationalism. Anthropological Perspectives*. London: Pluto Press.

Etienne, M., and E. Leacock, eds. 1980. *Women and Colonialization: Anthropological Perspectives*. New York: Praeger.

Evans-Pritchard, E. E. 1940. *The Nuer*. Oxford, England: Clarendon Press.

———. 1951. *Kinship and Marriage Among the Nuer*. Oxford, England: Clarendon Press.

———. 1956. *Nuer Religion*. Oxford, England: Clarendon Press.

Fage, J. D. 1978. *A History of Africa*. New York: Alfred A. Knopf, Inc.

Faithorn, E. 1975. The Concept of Pollution Among the Kafe of the Papua New Guinea Highlands. In R. R. Reifer, ed., *Toward an Anthropology of Women*. New York: Monthly Review Press.

Fallers, L. A. 1969. *Land Without Precedent*. Chicago: University of Chicago Press.

Fanon, F. 1965. *The Wretched of the Earth*. Preface by J. P. Sartre. Trans. from French by C. Farrington. London: Macgibbon & Kee.

Feil, D. K. 1978a. Women and Men in the Enga *Tee, American Ethnologist* 5(2): 263–279.

———. 1978b. Enga Women in the *Tee* Exchange. In J. Specht and J. P. White, eds., *Trade and Exchange in Oceania and Australia. Mankind* 11, 3. Sydney: University of Sydney Press.

———. 1987. *The Evolution of Highland Papua New Guinea Societies*. Cambridge: Cambridge University Press.

Fenton, W. N. 1957. Locality as a Basic Factor in the Development of Iroquois Social Structure. In W. N. Fenton, ed., *Symposium on Local Diversity in Iroquois Culture*. Bureau of American Ethnology Bulletin No. 149. Washington, D. C.: U. S. Government Printing Office.

Ferguson, R. B. 1989. Game Wars? Ecology and Conflict in Amazonia. *Journal of Anthropological Research* 4S(2): 179–206.

———. 1995. *Yanomami Warfare.* Santa Fe: School of American Research Press.

———, and N. L. Whitehead, eds., 1992. *War in the Tribal Zone: Expanding States and Indigenous Warfare.* Santa Fe, New Mexico: School of American Research Press.

Fernandez, J., ed. 1991. *Beyond Metaphor: The Theory of Tropes in Anthropology.* Stanford: Stanford University Press.

Fillmore, C. 1968. The Case for Case. In E. Bach and R. T. Harms, eds., *Universals in Linguistic Theory.* New York: Holt, Rinehart and Winston.

———. 1977. The Case for Case Reopened. In P. Cole and J. Sadock, eds., *Syntax and Semantics: Grammatical Relations,* Vol. 8. New York: Academic Press.

Fischer, J. L. 1964. Solutions for the Natchez Paradox. *Ethnology* 3: 53–65.

Fishman, J. A. 1960. A Systematization of the Whorfian Hypothesis. *Behavioral Science* 5: 232–239.

———. 1969. Origins and Ecological Effects of Early Domestication in Iran and the Near East. In P. J. Ucko and G. W. Dimbleby, eds., *The Domestication and Exploitation of Plants and Animals.* Chicago: Aldine Publishing Company.

Fitchen, J. M. 1992. On the Edge of Homelessness: Rural Poverty and Housing Insecurity. *Rural Sociology* 57(2): 173–193.

Flannery, K. V. 1969. Origins and Ecological Effects of Early Domestication in Iran and the Near East. In P. J. Ucko and G. W. Dimbleby, eds., *The Domestication and Exploitation of Plants and Animals.* Chicago: Aldine Publishing Company.

———. 1972. The Cultural Evolution of Civilizations. *Annual of Ecology and Systematics* 3: 399–426.

Fogelson, R. D., and R. N. Adams, eds. 1977. *The Anthropology of Power.* New York: Academic Press.

Forde, C. D. 1950. Double Descent Among the Yakö. In A. R. Radcliffe-Brown and C. D. Forde, eds., *African Systems of Kinship and Marriage.* London: Oxford University Press.

Fortes, M. 1945. *The Dynamics of Clanship Among the Tallensi.* London: Oxford University Press (for International African Institute).

———. 1949. *The Web of Kinship Among the Tallensi.* London: Oxford University Press (for International African Institute).

———. 1959a. Primitive Kinship. *Scientific American* 200(6): 146–157.

———. 1959b. Introduction. In J. Goody, ed., *The Developmental Cycle in Domestic Groups.* Cambridge Papers in Social Anthropology, 1. London: Cambridge University Press.

———. 1959c. *Oedipus and Job in West African Religion.* Cambridge: Cambridge University Press.

———. 1960. Ancestor Worship in Africa. In M. Fortes and G. Dieterlen, eds., *African Systems of Thought.* London: Oxford University Press (for International African Institute).

———. 1969. *Kinship and the Social Order: The Legacy of Lewis Henry Morgan.* Chicago: Aldine Publishing Company.

———. 1974. The First Born. *Journal of Child Psychology and Psychiatry* 15: 81–104.

———. 1978. An Anthropologist's Apprenticeship. In B. J. Siegel, ed., *Annual Review of Anthropology,* Vol. 7. Palo Alto, Calif.: Annual Reviews, Inc.

———. 1987. *Religion, Morality, and the Person: Essays on Tallensi Religion.* Cambridge: Cambridge University Press.

———, and E. Evans-Pritchard, eds. 1940. *African Political Systems.* London: Oxford University Press.

Fortune, R. 1932. *Sorcerers of Dobu.* London: Routledge and Kegan Paul Ltd.

Foster, G. M. 1961. The Dyadic Contract: A Model for the Social Structure of a Mexican Peasant Village. *American Anthropologist* 63: 1173–1192.

———. 1965. Peasant Society and the Image of Limited Good. *American Anthropologist* 67: 293–315.

———. 1967. *Tzintzuntzan: Mexican Peasants in a Changing Community.* Boston: Little, Brown and Company.

———. 1972. A Second Look at Limited Good. *Anthropological Quarterly* 45: 57–64.

Foulks, E. K. 1972. The Arctic Hysterias of the North Alaskan Eskimo. *Anthropological Studies,*

No. 10. Washington, D.C.: American Anthropological Association.

Fox, R. 1967. *Kinship and Marriage: An Anthropological Perspective.* Harmondsworth: Penguin.

Frake, C. O. 1960. The Eastern Subanun of Mindanao. In G. P. Murdock, ed., *Social Structure in Southeast Asia.* Viking Fund Publications in Anthropology, 29. New York: Wenner-Gren Foundation for Anthropological Research.

———. 1963. Litigation in Lipay: A Study in Subanun Law. In *Proceedings of the Ninth Pacific Science Congress of the Pacific Science Association* 3: 217–222. Bangkok (1957).

Frank, A. G. 1969. *Latin America: Underdevelopment or Revolution.* New York: Monthly Review Press.

———. 1973. *Lumpenbourgeoisie, Lumpendevelopment: Dependence, Class and Politics in Latin America.* New York: Monthly Review Press.

———. 1975. *On Capitalist Underdevelopment.* Bombay: Oxford University Press.

———. 1978. *World Accumulation, 1492–1789.* London: Macmillan.

Freedman, D. G. 1974. *Human Infancy: An Evolutionary Perspective.* New York: John Wiley & Sons, Inc.

———, and M. M. De Boer. 1979. Biological and Cultural Differences in Early Child Development. In B. J. Siegel, ed., *Annual Review of Anthropology,* Vol. 8. Palo Alto, Calif.: Annual Reviews Press.

Freeman, J. D. 1955. Iban Agriculture. *Colonial Research Studies,* No. 18. London: Colonial Office.

———. 1958. The Family Structure of the Iban of Borneo. In J. Goody, ed., *The Developmental Cycle in Domestic Groups.* Cambridge Papers in Social Anthropology. Cambridge: Cambridge University Press.

———. 1960. The Iban of Borneo. In G. P. Murdock, ed., *Social Structures in Southeast Asia.* Chicago: Quadrangle Press.

———. 1974. Kinship, Attachment Behaviour, and the Primary Bond. In J. R. Goody, ed., *The Character of Kinship.* Cambridge: Cambridge University Press.

Fried, M. H. 1967. *The Evolution of Political Society.* New York: Random House, Inc.

———. 1975. *The Notion of Tribe.* Menlo Park, Calif.: Cummings Publishing Company.

———. 1978. The State, the Chicken, and the Egg: Or, What Came First? In R. Cohen and E. Service, eds., *Origins of the State: The Anthropology of Political Evolution.* Philadelphia: Institute for the Study of Human Issues.

Friedman, J. 1975. Tribes, States, and Transformations. In M. Bloch, ed., *Marxist Analyses and Social Anthropology.* New York: John Wiley and Sons, Inc.

———. 1979. System, Structure, and Contradiction: The Evolution of 'Asiatic' Social Formations. *Social Studies in Oceania and South East Asia,* 2. Copenhagen: National Museum of Denmark.

———, and M. J. Rowlands. 1978. *The Evolution of Social Systems.* Pittsburgh: University of Pittsburgh Press. London: Duckworth.

Friedrich, P. 1965. A Mexican Cacigazgo. *Ethology* 4: 190–209.

———. 1978. *Agrarian Revolt in a Mexican Village.* Chicago: University of Chicago Press.

Frisch, R. E. 1974. Critical Growth at Menarche Initiation of the Adolescent Growth Spurt and Control of Puberty. In *Control of Puberty.* New York: John Wiley & Sons, Inc.

———, and J. McArthur. 1974. Menstrual Cycles: Fatness as a Determinant of Minimum Weight for Height Necessary for Their Maintenance or Onset. *Science* 185: 949–951.

Furnas, J. C. 1947. *Anatomy of Paradise.* New York: William Sloane Associates.

Fustel de Coulanges, N. D. 1864. *La Cité Antique.* (Trans. as *The Ancient City.* 1956. Garden City, N.Y.: Doubleday & Company, Inc.)

Gaines, A. D., ed. 1992. *Ethnopsychiatry: The Cultural Construction of Professional and Folk Psychiatries.* Albany: State University of New York Press.

Gardner, B., and R. A. Gardner. 1971. Two-Way Communication With an Infant Chimpanzee. In A. Schrier and F. Stollnite, eds., *Behavior of Nonhuman Primates,* Vol. 4. New York: Academic Press, Inc.

Gardner, R. A., and B. T. Gardner. 1969. Teaching Sign-Language to a Chimpanzee. *Science* 165: 664–672.

Geertz, C. 1983. Common Sense as a Cultural System. In *Local Knowledge: Further Essays in Interpretive Anthropology.* New York: Basic Books, Inc.

————. 1973. The Impact of the Concept of Culture on the Concept of Man. In *The Interpretation of Cultures: Selected Essays by Clifford Geertz.* New York: Basic Books, Inc.

————. 1957. Ritual and Social Change: A Javanese Example. *American Anthropologist* 59: 32–54.

————. 1960. *The Religion of Java.* New York: The Free Press.

————. 1963. *Agricultural Involution.* Berkeley: University of California Press.

————. 1966a. Religion as a Cultural System. In M. Banton, ed., *Anthropological Approaches to the Study of Religion.* A.S.A. Monographs, 3. London: Tavistock Publications.

————. 1966b. The Impact of the Concept of Culture on the Concept of Man. In J. R. Platt, ed., *New Views on the Nature of Man.* Chicago: University of Chicago Press.

George, S. 1977. *How the Other Half Dies: The Real Reasons for World Hunger.* Montclair, N.J.: Allanheld, Osmun and Company.

Geschwind, N. 1967. The Neural Basis of Language. In K. Salzinger and S. Salzinger, eds., *Research in Verbal Behavior and Some Neurophysiological Implications.* New York: Academic Press, Inc.

————. 1970. The Organization of Language and the Brain. *Science* 170: 940–944.

————. 1974. *Selected Papers on Language and the Brain.* Dordrecht, Holland: D. Reidel.

Gibbs, J. L. 1963. The Kpelle Moot: A Therapeutic Model for the Informal Settlement of Disputes. *Africa* 33: 1–11.

Gledhill, J. 1991. *Casi Nada: A Study of Agrarian Reform in the Homeland of Cardenismo.* Austin: University of Texas Press.

Glickman, M. 1972. The Nuer and the Dinka: A Further Note. *Man* (n.s.) 7: 586–594.

Gluckman, M. 1940. The Kingdom of the Zulu of Southeast Africa. In M. Fortes and E. E. Evans-Pritchard, eds., *African Political Systems.* London: Oxford University Press.

————. 1955. *Custom and Conflict in Africa.* Oxford: Basil Blackwell & Mott, Ltd.

————, ed. 1962. *Essays in the Ritual of Social Relations.* Manchester, England: Manchester University Press.

————. 1963. *Order and Rebellion in Tribal Africa.* London: Cohen and West.

————. 1965. *The Ideas in Barotse Jurisprudence.* New Haven, Conn.: Yale University Press.

————, J. C. Mitchell, and J. A. Barnes. 1949. The Village Headman in British Central Africa. *Africa* 19: 89–106.

Godelier, M. 1974. Anthropology and Biology: Towards a New Form of Co-operation. *International Social Science Journal* 26(4): 611–635.

————. 1977. Politics as 'Infrastructure': An Anthropologist's Thoughts on the Example of Classical Greece and the Notions of Relations of Production and Economic Determination. In J. Friedman and M. J. Rowlands, eds., *The Evolution of Social Systems.* London: Duckworth.

————. 1978. Infrastructures, Society, and History. *Current Anthropology* 19(4): 763–768.

Godelier, M. 1986. *The Making of Great Men: Male Power and Domination Among the New Guinea Baruya.* Cambridge: Cambridge University Press.

————. 1990. Inceste, Parenté, Pouvoir. *Psychanalystes* 36: 33–51.

————. 1996. *L'Enigme du Don.* Paris: Fayard.

Golson, J., and Gardner, D. S. 1990. Agriculture and Sociopolitical Organization in New Guinea Highlands Prehistory. *Annual Review of Anthropology* 19: 395–417.

Goodenough, W. H. 1957. Cultural Anthropology and Linguistics. In P. Garvin, ed., *Report of the Seventh Annual Round Table Meeting on Linguistics and Language Study.* Monograph Series on Language and Linguistics, 9. Washington, D.C.: Georgetown University.

————. 1961. Comment on Cultural Evolution. *Daedalus* 90: 521–528.

————. 1970. *Description and Comparison in Cultural Anthropology.* Lewis Henry Morgan Lectures, 1968. Chicago: Aldine Publishing Company.

————. 1990. Evolution of the Human Capacity for Beliefs. *American Anthropologist* 92, pp. 597–612.

Goody, J. R. 1962. *Death, Property, and the Ancestors: A Study of the Mortuary Customs of the LoDagaa of West Africa.* London: Tavistock.

————. 1973. Bridewealth and Dowry in Africa and Eurasia. In J. R. Goody and S. N. Tambiah, eds., *Bridewealth and Dowry.* Cambridge Studies in Social Anthropology, 7. Cambridge: Cambridge University Press.

———, and S Tambiah. 1973. *Bridewealth and Dowry.* Cambridge Papers in Social Anthropology, 7. Cambridge: Cambridge University Press.

Gough, E. K. 1959. The Nayars and the Definition of Marriage. *Journal of the Royal Anthropological Institute:* 23–34.

———. 1961. Variation in Matrilineal Systems. In D. Schneider and K. Gough, eds., *Matrilineal Kinship,* Part 2. Berkeley: University of California Press.

———. 1968. World Revolution and the Science of Man. In T. Roszak, ed., *The Dissenting Academy.* New York: Random House, Inc. (Reprinted in M. T. Weaver, ed. 1973. *To See Ourselves.* Glenview, Ill.: Scott, Foresman and Company.)

———. 1971. Nuer Kinship and Marriage: A Reexamination. In T. Beidelman, ed., *The Translation of Culture.* London: Tavistock.

Gray, S. J. 1994. Comparison of Effects of Breast-Feeding Practices on Birth-Spacing in Three Societies: Nomadic Turkana, Gainj, and Quechua. *Journal of Biosocial Science* 26(1): 69–90.

Gregory, R. L. 1969. On How Little Information Controls So Much Behaviour. In C. H. Waddington, ed., *Towards a Theoretical Biology,* Vol. 1. Chicago: Aldine Publishing Company.

———. 1970. Information Processing in Biological and Artificial Brains. In H. E. Von Gierke, W. D. Keidel, and H. L. Oestreicher, eds., *Principles and Practice of Bionics* (pp. 73–80). Slough, England: Techvision.

Greuel, P. J. 1971. The Leopard-Skin Chief: An Examination of Political Power Among the Nuer. *American Anthropologist* 73: 1115–1120.

Griaule, M., and G. Dieterlen. 1960. The Dogon of the French Sudan. In C. D. Forde, ed., *African Worlds.* London: Oxford University Press.

Griffin, K. 1969. *Underdevelopment in Spanish America.* London: Allen and Unwin.

Grinder, J. T., and S. H. Elgin. 1973. *Guide to Transformational Grammar: History, Theory, Practice.* New York: Holt, Rinehart and Winston.

Gross, D. P. 1975. Protein Capture and Cultural Development in the Amazonian Basin. *American Anthropologist* 77: 526–549.

Gudeman, S. 1972. *The Compadrazgo as a Reflection of the National and Spiritual Person.* Proceedings of the Royal Anthropological Institute for 1971: 45–71.

———. 1978. Anthropological Economics: The Question of Distribution. In B. J. Siegel, ed., *Annual Review of Anthropology,* 7. Palo Alto, Calif.: Annual Reviews Inc.

Gulliver, P. H. 1963. *Social Control in an African Society.* London: Routledge and Kegan Paul Ltd.

———. 1965. *The Family Herds.* London: Routledge and Kegan Paul Ltd.

Haight, B. 1972. A Note on the Leopard-Skin Chief. *American Anthropologist* 74: 1313–1318.

Haiman, J. 1980. Dictionaries and Encyclopedias. *Lingua* 50: 329–357.

Hall, E. T. 1959. *The Silent Language.* Garden City, N.Y.: Doubleday & Company, Inc.

———. 1966. *The Hidden Dimension.* Garden City, N.Y.: Doubleday & Company, Inc.

———. 1972. Art, Space, and the Human Experience. In G. Kepes, ed., *Arts of the Environment.* New York: George Braziller, Inc.

Hallpike, C. K. 1977. *Bloodshed and Violence in the Papuan Mountains: The Generation of Violence in Tanade Society.* London: Oxford University Press.

Hamnett, I. 1975. *Chieftainship and Legitimacy.* London: Routledge and Kegan Paul Ltd.

———. 1977. Introduction to I. Hamnett, ed., *Social Anthropology and Law.* ASA Monograph 14. London: Academic Press.

———, ed. 1977. *Social Anthropology and Law.* A.S.A. Monograph 14. London: Academic Press.

Hamnett, M. P. 1978. *Ethics and Expectations in Cross-Cultural Social Science Research.* Presented at the Annual Speech Communication Association Summer Conference on Intercultural Communication. Tampa, 1978.

Harding, T. G. 1967. *Voyagers of the Vitiaz Strait.* American Ethnological Society Monograph 44. Seattle: University of Washington Press.

Harlan, J. R., J. M. J. De Wet, and A. B. L. Stemler. 1976. *Origins of African Plant Domestication.* The Hague: Mouton (World Anthropology).

Harle, V., ed. 1978a. *The Political Economy of Food.* Westmead, Farnborough, Hants.: Saxon House.

———. 1978b. Three Dimensions of the World Food Problem. In V. Harle, ed., *The Political*

Economy of Food. Westmead, Farnborough, Hants.: Saxon House.

Harner, M. 1970. Population Pressure and the Social Evolution of Agriculturalists. *Southwestern Journal of Anthropology.* 26: 67–86.

———. 1977. The Ecological Basis for Aztec Sacrifice. *Ethnology* 4: 117–135.

Harre, R., and P. Secord. 1973. *The Explanation of Social Behavior.* Oxford: Blackwell.

Harris, M. 1968. *The Rise of Cultural Theory.* New York: Thomas Y. Crowell Company.

———. 1971. *Culture, Man, and Nature: An Introduction to General Anthropology.* New York: Thomas Y. Crowell Company.

———. 1974. *Cows, Pigs, Wars, and Witches: The Riddles of Culture.* New York: Harper & Row.

———. 1975. *Culture, People, Nature: An Introduction to General Anthropology.* New York: Harper & Row.

———. 1977. *Cannibals and Kings.* New York: Random House.

———. 1979a. *Cultural Materialism: The Struggle for a Science of Culture.* New York: Harper & Row.

———. 1979b. Cannibals and Kings (letter to the editor). *New York Review of Books,* June 28: 51–52.

Hassig, R. 1992. Aztec and Spanish Conquest in Mesoamerica. In R. B. Ferguson and N. L. Whitehead, eds., *War in the Tribal Zone: Expanding States and Indigenous Warfare.* Santa Fe: School of American Research Press.

Haugeland, J. 1974. Comment on C. H. L. Dreyfus, *What Computers Can and Cannot Do.* In *New York Review of Books* 21(11)27: 33.

Haviland, L. 1979. *Social Relations of Production in a Mexican Peasant Village.* Unpublished Ph.D. dissertation. Cambridge, Mass.: Harvard University.

Helman, C. G. 1994. *Culture, Health, and Illness: An Introduction for Health Professionals,* 3rd. ed. Oxford; Boston: Butterworth-Heinemann.

Herdt, G. H., ed. 1982. *Rituals of Manhood.* Berkeley: University of California Press.

Herskovits, M. J. 1937. African Gods and Catholic Saints in New World Religious Beliefs. *American Anthropologist* 39: 635–643.

———. 1955. *Culture Anthropology.* New York: Alfred A. Knopf, Inc.

Hertz, R. 1907. Contribution a une Etude sur la Representation Collective de la Mort. *Annee Sociologique* 10: 48–137. (Trans. in *Death and the Right Hand.* 1960. New York: The Free Press.)

———. 1909. La Prééminence de la Main Droite: Etude sur la Polarité Religieuse. *Revue Philosophique* 58: 553–580. (Trans. in *Death and the Right Hand.* 1960. New York: The Free Press.)

Hewes, G. W. 1973. Primate Communication and the Gestural Origin of Language. *Current Anthropology* 14: 5–24.

Hiatt, L. R. 1965. *Kinship and Conflict: A Study of an Aboriginal Community in Northern Arnhem Land.* Canberra: Australian National University.

Hide, R. L. 1974. *On the Dynamics of Some New Guinea Highlands Pig Cycles.* Unpublished Ms., deposited at Department of Primary Industry, Kundiawa, Papua New Guinea.

Hindess, B., and A. Q. Hirst. 1977. *Mode of Production and Social Formation.* London: Macmillan and Company.

———, and P. Q. Hirst. 1975. *Precapitalist Modes of Production.* London: Routledge and Kegan Paul Ltd.

Hobsbawm, E. J. 1962. *The Age of Revolution 1789–1848.* New York: Mentor Books.

Hockett, C. F. 1960. The Origin of Speech. *Scientific American* 203: 88–111.

Hoebel, E. A. 1954. *The Law of Primitive Man: A Study in Comparative Legal Dynamics.* Cambridge, Mass: Harvard University Press.

Holloway, R. J., Jr. 1969. Culture: A Human Domain. *Current Anthropology* 10: 395–407.

Holmberg, A. R. 1965. The Changing Values and Institutions of Vicos in the Context of National Development. *American Behavioral Scientist* 8: 3–8.

Holy, L. 1976. Kin Groups: Structural Analysis and the Study of Behavior. In B. J. Siegel, ed., *Annual Review of Anthropology* 5. Palo Alto, Calif.: Annual Reviews Press.

Hook, R. H., ed. 1979. *Fantasy and Symbol: Studies in Anthropological Interpretation.* London and New York: Academic Press.

Hopkins, T. K. 1970. On Economic Planning in Tropical Africa. In R. I. Rhodes, ed., *Imperialism and Underdevelopment.* New York: Monthly Review Press.

Horowitz, I. L. 1965. The Life and Death of Project Camelot. *Trans-Action,* December.

(Reprinted in M. T. Weaver, ed., 1973. *To See Ourselves*. Glenview, Ill.: Scott, Foresman and Company.)

Horton, R. 1962. The Kalabari World View: An Outline and Interpretation. *Africa* 32: 197–220.

Howell, F. C. 1969. Foreword to R. H. Klein. In *Man and Culture in the Late Pleistocene*. San Francisco: Chandler Publishing Company.

Howitt, A. W. 1904. *The Native Tribes of South-East Australia*. London: Macmillan and Company.

Huizer, G. 1970. 'Resistance to Change' and Radical Peasant Mobilization: Foster and Erasmus Reconsidered. *Human Organization* 29(4): 303–313.

———. 1979. Anthropology and Politics: From Naivete Toward Liberation? In G. Huizer and B. Mannheim, eds., *The Politics of Anthropology*. The Hague: Mouton.

———, and B. Mannheim, eds., 1979. *The Politics of Anthropology*. The Hague: Mouton.

Huntington, R., and P. Metcalf. 1979. *Celebrations of Death: The Anthropology of Mortuary Ritual*. Cambridge: Cambridge University Press.

Hutchins, E. L., Jr. 1979. Reasoning in Trobriand Discourse. *Quarterly Newsletter of the Laboratory of Comparative Human Cognition* (Center for Human Information Processing, University of California, San Diego), 1(2): 13–17.

———. 1980. *Reasoning in Discourse: An Analysis of Trobriand Land Litigation*. Cambridge, Mass.: Harvard University Press.

Hutchinson, S. 1996. *Nuer Dilemmas: Coping With Money, War, and the State*. Berkeley: University of California Press.

Hutterer, K. L. 1976. An Evolutionary Approach to the Southeast Asian Cultural Sequence. *Current Anthropology* 17: 221–242.

Isaac, B. L. 1993. Retrospective on the Formalist-Substantivist Debate. *Research in Economic Anthropology* 14: 213–233.

Jablow, J. 1951. *The Cheyenne in Plains Indian Trade Relations 1795–1840*. Monographs of the American Ethnological Society, 19. Locust Valley, N.Y.: J. J. Augustin, Inc.

Jarvie, I. C. 1963. Theories of Cargo Cults: A Critical Analysis. *Oceania* 34(1): 1–31 and 34(2): 108–136.

Johanson, D. C., and T. D. White. 1979. A Systematic Assessment of Early African Hominids. *Science* 203: 321–330.

Johnson, D. 1994. *Nuer Prophets: A History of Prophecy From the Upper Nile*. Oxford: Oxford University Press.

Johnson, M. 1987. *The Body in the Mind: The Bodily Basis of Meaning, Imagination, and Reason*. Chicago: University of Chicago Press.

Jolly, M. 1992. Banana Leaf Bundles and Skirts: A Pacific Penelope's Web? In J. G. Carrier, ed. *History and Tradition in Melanesian Anthropology*. Berkeley: University of California Press.

———, and M. MacIntyre. 1989. *Family and Gender in the Pacific: Domestic Contradictions and the Colonial Impact*. Cambridge: Cambridge University Press.

Jones, D. J. 1970. Towards a Native Anthropology. *Human Organization* 29(4): 251–259.

Jordan, D. K., and M. J. Swartz, eds. 1990. *Personality and the Cultural Construction of Society: Papers in Honor of Melford E. Spiro*. Tuscaloosa: University of Alabama Press.

Jorgenson, J. G. 1972. *The Sun Dance Religion: Power for the Powerless*. Chicago: University of Chicago Press.

Kahn, J. S. 1993. *Constituting the Minangkabau: Peasants, Culture, and Modernity in Colonial Indonesia*. Providence, R.I.: Berg.

Kahn, S., and J. R. Llobera, eds. 1981. *The Anthropology of Pre-Capitalist Societies*. London: MacMillan Press.

Kakar, S. 1991. Western Science, Eastern Minds. *The Wilson Quarterly* 15(1), pp 109–116.

Keen, I. 1993. Aboriginal Beliefs vs. Mining at Coronation Hill: The Containing Force of Traditionism. *Human Organization* 52(4): 344–355.

Keen, I. 1994. *Knowledge and Secrecy in an Aboriginal Religion*. Oxford: Oxford University Press.

Keenan, E. 1974. Norm-Makers, Norm-Breakers: Uses of Speech by Men and Women in a Malagasy Community. In R. Bauman and J. Sherzer, eds., *Explorations in the Ethnography of Speaking*. Cambridge, England: Cambridge University Press.

Keesing, F. M. 1952. *Culture Change.* Stanford, Calif.: Stanford University Press.

Keesing, R. M. 1966. Kwaio Kindreds. *Southwestern Journal of Anthropology* 22(4): 346–353.

———. 1968a. On Descent and Descent Groups. *Current Anthropology* 9: 453–454.

———. 1968b. Nonunilineal Descent and the Contextual Definition of Status. *American Anthropologist* 70: 82–84.

———. 1970. Shrines, Ancestors, and Cognatic Descent: The Kwaio and Tallensi. *American Anthropologist* 72: 755–775.

———. 1971. Descent, Residence, and Cultural Codes. In L. Hiatt and C. Jayawardena, eds., *Anthropology in Oceania.* Sydney: Angus and Robertson.

———. 1972a. Paradigms Lost: The New Ethnography and the New Linguistics. *Southwestern Journal of Anthropology* 23: 299–332.

———. 1972b. Simple Models of Complexity: The Lure of Kinship. In P. Reining, ed., *Kinship Studies in the Morgan Centennial Year.* Washington, D.C.: Anthropological Society of Washington.

———. 1972c. The Anthropologist's Dilemma: Empathy and Analysis Among the Solomon Islanders. *Expedition* 3: 32–39.

———. 1974. Transformational Linguistics and Structural Anthropology. *Cultural Hermeneutics* 2: 243–266.

———. 1975. *Kin Groups and Social Structure.* New York: Holt, Rinehart and Winston.

———. 1978. *'Elota's Story: The Life and Times of a Solomon Islands Big Man.* New York: St. Martin's Press: St. Lucia, Queensland: University of Queensland Press.

———. 1979. Linguistic Knowledge and Cultural Knowledge: Some Doubts and Speculations. *American Anthropologist* 81: 14–36.

———. 1982. *Kwaio Religion: The Living and the Dead in a Solomon Island Society.* New York: Columbia University Press.

———. 1985. Kwaio Women Speak: The Micropolitics of Autobiography in a Solomon Island Society. *American Anthropologist* 87: 27–39.

———. 1987. Ta'a Geni: Women's Perspectives on Kwaio Society. In M. Strathern, ed., *Dealing With Inequality: Analysing Gender Relations in Melanesia and Beyond.* Cambridge: Cambridge University Press.

———. 1989. Exotic Readings of Cultural Texts. *Current Anthropology* 30: 459–479.

———. 1990. Kinship, Bonding, and Categorization. *Australian Journal of Anthropology* 1(2–3): 159–167.

———. 1992. *Custom and Confrontation: The Kwaio Struggle for Cultural Autonomy.* Chicago: University of Chicago Press.

———. n.d. Cultural Symbols and the Political Economy of Knowledge: Some Problems in Analyzing Kwaio Religion. Unpublished Ms.

Keil, C. 1966. *Urban Blues.* Chicago: University of Chicago Press.

Keiser, R. L. 1969. *The Vice Lords: Warriors of the Streets.* New York: Holt, Rinehart and Winston.

Kelly, R. C., and M. Verdon. 1983. A Note on Nuer Segmentary Organization. *American Anthropologist* 85(4): 905–906.

Kelly, R. L. 1995. *The Foraging Spectrum.* Washington: Smithsonian Institution Press.

Kelly, R. C. 1985. *The Nuer Conquest: The Structure and Development of an Expansionist System.* Ann Arbor: University of Michigan Press.

Kemp, W. B. 1971. The Flow of Energy in a Hunting Society. *Scientific American,* September.

Kipp, R. S. 1984. Terms for Kith and Kin. *American Anthropologist* 86(4): 905–926.

Kirch, P. V. 1984. *The Evolution of the Polynesian Chiefdoms.* Cambridge: Cambridge University Press.

———, and M. Sahlins. 1992. *Anahulu: The Anthropology of History in the Kingdom of Hawaii.* Chicago: University of Chicago Press.

Kluckhohn, C. 1942. Myths and Rituals: A General Theory. *Harvard Theological Review* 35: 45–79.

———, and W. H. Kelly. 1945. The Concept of Culture. In R. Linton, ed., *The Science of Man in the World Crisis.* New York: Columbia University Press.

Knauft, B. 1993. *South Coast New Guinea Cultures: History, Comparison, Dialectic.* New York: Cambridge University Press.

Kopytoff, I. 1964. Family and Lineage Among the Suku of the Congo. In R. F. Gray and P. H. Gulliver, eds., *The Family Estate in Africa.* London: Routledge and Kegan Paul Ltd.

———. 1965. The Suku of Southwestern Congo. In J. Gibbs, Jr., ed., *Peoples of Africa*. New York: Holt, Rinehart and Winston.

———. 1971. Ancestors as Elders in Africa. *Africa* 41(11): 129–142.

Korn, F. 1973. *Elementary Structures Reconsidered: Lévi-Strauss on Kinship*. Berkeley: University of California Press.

Kortlandt, A. 1973. Comment on G. Hewes 'Primate Communication and the Gestural Origin of Language.' *Current Anthropology* 14(1–2): 13–14.

Kracke, W. 1978. *Force and Persuasion: Leadership in an Amazonian Society*. Chicago: University of Chicago Press.

Krader, L. 1968. *The Formation of the State*. Englewood Cliffs, N.J.: Prentice-Hall, Inc.

———. 1979. The Origin of the State Among the Nomads of Asia. In l'Equipe Ecologie et Anthropologie des Societes Pastorales, eds., *Pastoral Production and Society*. Cambridge, England: Cambridge University Press.

Kroeber, A. L. 1948. *Anthropology*. New York: Harcourt Brace and Jovanovich.

———, and C. Kluckhohn. 1952. *Culture: A Critical Review of Concepts and Definitions*. Peabody Museum Papers 47, 1. Cambridge, Mass.: Harvard University Press.

Kummer, H. 1971. *Primate Societies: Group Techniques of Ecological Adaptation*. Chicago: Aldine & Atherton, Inc.

LaBarre, W. 1967. Preface to G. Devereux, *From Anxiety to Method in the Behavioral Sciences*. The Hague: Mouton and Company.

———. 1970. *The Ghost Dance: The Origins of Religion*. Garden City, N.Y.: Doubleday & Company, Inc.

———. 1978. The Clinic and the Field. In G. D. Spindler, ed., *The Making of Psychological Anthropology*. Berkeley: University of California Press.

Lakoff, G. 1987. *Women, Fire and Dangerous Things: What Categories Reveal About the Mind*. Chicago: University of Chicago Press.

———, and M. Johnson. n.d. Toward an Experientialist Philosophy: The Case From Literal Metaphor. Unpublished Ms. Department of Linguistics/Department of Philosophy, University of California, Berkeley, April 1979.

Lancaster, J. B. 1968. Primate Communication Systems and the Emergence of Human Language. In P. Jay, ed., *Primates: Studies in Adaptation and Variability*. New York: Holt, Rinehart and Winston.

Lancy, D. F. 1996. *Playing on the Mother-Ground: Cultural Routines for Children's Development*. New York: Guilford Press.

Landa, J. T. 1994. *Trust, Ethnicity, and Identity: Beyond the New Institutional Economics of Ethnic Trading Networks, Contract Law, and Gift Exchange*. Ann Arbor: University of Michigan Press.

Lanternari, V. 1955. L'Annua Festa 'Milamala' Dei Trobriandesi: Interpetazione Psichologica e Functionale. *Revirta di Antropologia*. 42: 3–24.

———. 1963. *Religions of the Oppressed: A Study of Modern Messianic Cults*. New York: Alfred A. Knopf, Inc.

Lappé, F. M., and J. Collins. 1978. *Food First: Beyond the Myth of Scarcity*. Boston: Houghton-Mifflin. (Revised ed.: first edition published 1977).

Laracy, H. 1979. Maasina Rule: Struggle in the Solomons. In A. Mamak, A. Ali, et al., eds., *Race, Class and Rebellion in the South Pacific*. Sydney: Allen and Unwin.

Lawrence, P. 1964. *Road Belong Cargo: A Study of the Cargo Movement, Southern Madang District, New Guinea*. Manchester: Manchester University Press.

Leach, E. R. 1954. *Political Systems of Highland Burma*. Cambridge, Mass.: Harvard University Press.

———. 1955. Polyandry, Inheritance, and the Definition of Marriage, With Particular Reference to Sinhalese Customary Law. *Man* 55: 182–186.

———. 1957. Aspects of Bridewealth and Marriage Stability Among the Kachin and Lakher. *Man* 57: 59.

———. 1958. Magical Hair. *Journal of the Royal Anthropological Institute*. 88: 147–164.

———. 1959. Concerning Trobriand Clans and the Kinship Category Tabu. In J. Goody, ed., *The Developmental Cycle of Domestic Groups*. Cambridge Papers in Social Anthropology 1. London: Cambridge University Press.

———, ed. 1960. *Aspects of Caste in South India, Ceylon, and Northwest Pakistan*. Cambridge Papers in Social Anthropology 2. London: Cambridge University Press.

————. 1961. *Pul Eliya, a Village in Ceylon: A Study of Land Tenure and Kinship.* London: Cambridge University Press.

————. 1962. *Rethinking Anthropology.* London: Ahtlone Press.

————. 1965. Anthropological Aspects of Language: Animal Categories and Verbal Abuse. In E. Lenneberg, ed., *New Directions in the Study of Language.* Cambridge, Mass.: M.I.T. Press.

————. 1969. *Genesis as Myth, and Other Essays.* London: Gossman Publishers.

————. 1970. *Lévi-Strauss.* London: Fontana.

————. 1971. Marriage, Primitive. *Encyclopaedia Britannica:* 938–947.

————. 1976. *Culture and Communication: The Logic by Which Symbols Are Connected.* Cambridge: Cambridge University Press.

————. 1982. *Social Anthropology.* New York: Oxford University Press.

Leach, J. W., and E. R. Leach, eds. 1983. *The Kula: New Perspectives on Massim Exchange.* Cambridge: Cambridge University Press.

Leacock, E. B., ed. 1971. *The Culture of Poverty: A Critique.* New York: Simon & Schuster, Inc.

————. 1972. Introduction to F. Engels. *Origin of the Family, Private Property and the State.* New York: International Publishers Company, Inc.

————. 1974. Review of S. Goldberg, *The Inevitability of Patriarchy* (New York: Morrow and Company, 1973) *American Anthropologist* 76(2): 363–365.

————. 1978. Women's Status in Egalitarian Society: Implications for Social Evolution. *Current Anthropology* 19(2): 247–276.

————. 1981. *Myths of Male Dominance: Collected Articles on Women Cross Culturally.* New York: Monthly Review Press.

————. 1983. Interpreting the Origins of Gender Inequality: Conceptual and Historical Problems. *Dialectical-Anthropology* 7(4): 263–284.

Lederman, R. 1986. *What Gifts Engender: Social Relations and Politics in Mendi, Highland Papua New Guinea.* Cambridge: Cambridge University Press.

Lee, B. M. 1987. *Control of Children in a North Carolina Milltown: Parents, Professionals, and the State.* Doctoral dissertation, Department of Anthropology, University of North Carolina at Chapel Hill.

Lee, D. D. 1940. A Primitive System of Values. *Philosophy of Science* 7: 355–378.

————. 1949. Being and Value in a Primitive Culture. *Journal of Philosophy* 46(13): 401–415.

Lee, R. B. 1968a. What Hunters Do for a Living. In R. B. Lee and I. DeVore, eds., *Man the Hunter.* Chicago: Aldine Publishing Company.

————. 1968b. Comments. In L. R. and S. Binford, eds., *New Perspectives in Archaeology.* Chicago: Aldine Publishng Company.

————. 1969. !Kung Bushman Subsistence: An Input-Output Analysis. In A. P. Vayda, ed., *Environment and Cultural Behavior.* Garden City, N.Y.: Natural History Press. (Revision of a paper originally published in D. Damas, eds., 1969. *Ecological Essays.* Ottawa: Queens Printer.)

————, and I. DeVore, eds. 1968a. *Man the Hunter.* Chicago: Aldine Publishing Company.

————, and ————. 1968b. Problems in the Study of Hunters and Gatherers. In R. B. Lee and I. DeVore, eds., *Man the Hunter.* Chicago: Aldine Publishing Company.

————, and ————, eds. 1974. *Kalahari Hunter-Gatherers.* Cambridge, Mass.: Harvard University Press.

Lefébure, C. 1979. Introduction: The Specificity of Nomadic Pastoral Societies. In l'Equipe Ecologie et Anthropologie des Societés Pastorales, eds., *Pastoral Production and Society.* Cambridge, England: Cambridge University Press.

Leroi-Gourhan, A. 1968. The Evolution of Paleolithic Art. *Scientific American,* February.

Lévi-Strauss, C. 1945. L'Analyse Structurale en Linguistique et Anthropologie. *Word* (Journal of Linguistic Circle of New York) 1(2).

————. 1949. *Les Structures Elementaires de la Parenté.* Paris: Plon. (Trans. as *The Elementary Structures of Kinship.* 1969. Boston: Beacon Press.)

————. 1962. *La Pensée Sauvage.* Paris: Plon. (Trans. as *The Savage Mind.* 1966. Chicago: University of Chicago Press.)

————. 1963a. *Structural Anthropology.* New York: Basic Books, Inc.

————. 1963b. Do Dual Organizations Exist? In C. Lévi-Strauss, ed., *Structural Anthropology.* Paris: Plon.

———. 1967. The Story of Asdiwal. In E. R. Leach, ed., *The Structural Study of Myth and Totemism*. A.S.A. Monographs. London: Tavistock Publications.

———. 1968. The Concept of Primitiveness. In R. B. Lee and I. De Vore, eds., *Man the Hunter*. Chicago: Aldine Publishing Company.

———. 1969. *Mythologiques III: L'Origine de Manières de Table*. Paris: Plon.

———. 1969. *The Raw and the Cooked*. New York: Harper & Row, Publishers. (Translation of *Le Cru et le Cuit*, 1964. Paris: Plon.)

———. 1971. *Mythologiques IV: L'Homme Nu*. Paris: Plon.

———. 1973. *An Introduction to the Science of Mythology, Vol. II: From Honey to Ashes*. New York: Harper & Row, Publishers (Translation of *Mythologiques: Du Miel aux Cendres*.)

Levy-Bruhl, L. 1912. *Les Fonctions Mentales dans les Sociétés Inférieures*. Paris: F. Alcan. (Trans. as *How Natives Think*. 1966. New York: Washington Square Press.)

———. 1923. *Primitive Mentality*. London: Allen & Unwin. (Trans. by L. A. Clare.)

Lewis, D. K. 1973. Anthropology and Colonialism. *Current Anthropology* 14: 581–602.

Lewis, O. 1961. *The Children of Sanchez*. New York: Random House, Inc.

———. 1966. *La Vida*. New York: Random House, Inc.

———, and V. Barnouw. 1956. Caste and Jajmani System in a North Indian Village. *Scientific American* 83(2): 66–81.

Lieberman, P., and E. S. Crelin. 1971. On the Speech of Neanderthal Man. *Linguistic Inquiry* 2: 203–222.

———, ———, and D. H. Klatt. 1972. Phonetic Ability and Related Anatomy of the Newborn and Adult Human, Neanderthal Man, and the Chimpanzee. *American Anthropologist* 74(3): 287–307.

Liebow, E. 1967. *Tally's Corner*. Boston: Little, Brown and Company.

Lindenbaum, S. 1972. Sorcerers, Ghosts, and Polluting Women: An Analysis of Religious Belief and Population Control. *Ethnology* 11(13): 241–253.

———. 1976. A Wife Is the Hand of Man. In P. Brown and G. Buchbinder, eds., *Male and Female in the New Guinea Highlands*. American Anthropological Association Special Publication.

———. 1979. *Kuru Sorcery: Disease and Danger in the New Guinea Highlands*. Palo Alto, Calif.: Mayfield Press.

Lindstrom, L. 1993. *Cargo Cult: Strange Stories of Desire From Melanesia and Beyond*. Honolulu: University of Hawaii Press.

Linton, R. 1940. Acculturation. In R. Linton, ed., *Acculturation in Seven American Indian Tribes*. Gloucester, Mass.: Peter Smith.

Lipton, M. 1977. *Why Poor People Stay Poor: A Study of Urban Bias in World Development*. London: Temple Smith.

Little, K. 1965. *West African Urbanization: A Study of Voluntary Associations in Social Change*. London: Cambridge University Press.

———. 1967. Voluntary Associations in Urban Life: A Case Study of Differential Adaptations. In M. Friedman, ed., *Social Organization: Essays Presented to Raymond Firth*. Chicago: Aldine Publishing Company.

———. 1980. *The Sociology of Urban Women's Image in African Literature*. Totowa, N.J.: Rowman and Littlefield.

Livingstone, F. B. 1958. Anthropological Implications of Sickle-Cell Gene Distribution in West Africa. *American Anthropologist* 60: 533–562.

Lizot, J. 1977. Economie Primitive et Subsistance. *Libre* 4: 69–113.

Lloyd, P. C. 1973. The Yoruba: An Urban People? In A. Southall, ed., *Urban Anthropology*. London: Oxford University Press.

———, A. Mabogunje, and B. Awe, eds. 1967. *The City of Ibadan*. London: Cambridge University Press.

Lomnitz, L. A. 1977. *Networks and Marginality: Life in a Mexican Shanty Town*. New York: Academic Press, Inc.

Lounsbury, F. G. 1965. Another View of the Trobriand Kinship Categories. In E. A. Hammel, ed., *Formal Semantic Analysis*. American Anthropologist Special Publication 4(67), part 2. Menasha, Wis.: American Anthropological Association.

Lowie, R. H. 1920. *Primitive Society*. New York: Liveright.

Lucy, J. A. 1992a. *Grammatical Categories and Cognition: A Case Study of the Linguistic*

Relativity Hypothesis. Cambridge: Cambridge University Press.

———. 1992b. *Language Diversity and Thought: A Reformulation of the Linguistic Relativity Hypothesis.* Cambridge: Cambridge University Press.

Lukens-Wahrhaftig, A., and J. Lukens-Wahrhaftig. 1977. The Thrice Powerless: Cherokee Indians in Oklahoma. In R. D. Fogelson and R. N. Adams, eds., *The Anthropology of Power.* New York: Academic Press, Inc.

———, and R. K. Thomas. 1972. Renaissance and Repression: The Oklahoma Cherokee. In H. M. Bahr, B. A. Chadwick, and R. C. Day, eds., *Native Americans Today: Sociological Perspectives.* New York: Harper & Row, Publishers.

Lumholtz, C. 1889. *Among Cannibals.* New York: Charles Scribner and Sons.

Lundahl, M. 1992. *Politics or Markets? Essays on Haitian Underdevelopment: Introduction.* London: Routledge.

Mabogunje, A. L. 1967. The Morphology of Ibadan. In P. C. Lloyd, A. L. Mabogunje, and B. Awe, eds., *The City of Ibadan.* London: Cambridge University Press.

———. 1968. *Urbanization in Nigeria.* London: University of London Press.

MacCormack, C. P., and M. Strathern, eds. 1980. *Nature, Culture, and Gender.* Cambridge: Cambridge University Press.

MacNeish, R. S. 1964. The Origins of New World Civilization. *Scientific American.* November. (Page citations in J. Jorgenson, ed., 1972. *Biology and Culture in Modern Perspective.* San Francisco: W. H. Freeman and Company.)

———. 1971. Early Man in the Andes. *Scientific American* 224: 36–46.

———. 1969. The Paranoid Streak in Man. In A. Koestler and J. R. Smythies, eds., *Beyond Reductionism: New Perspectives in the Life Sciences.* London: Hutchinson and Company.

———. 1970. The Triune Brain, Emotion, and Scientific Bias. In *The Neurosciences: Second Study Program.* F. O. Schmitt et al. New York: Rockefeller University Press.

———. 1973. A Triune Concept of the Brain. In T. J. Boag, et al., eds., *A Triune Concept of the Brain and Behaviour.* Toronto: University of Toronto Press.

Majumdar, R. C., ed. 1963. *British Paramountcy and Indian Resistance. The History and Culture of the Indian People,* Vol. 9. Bombay, India: Bharatiya Vidya Bhavan.

Malinowski, B. 1916. Baloma: The Spirits of the Dead in the Trobriand Islands. *Journal of the Royal Anthropological Institute* 46: 353–430. (Reprinted in *Magic, Science, and Religion.* 1954. Boston: Beacon Press.)

———. 1919. Kula: The Circulating Exchange of Valuables in the Archipelagoes of Eastern New Guinea. *Man* 20: 97–105.

———. 1922. *Argonauts of the Western Pacific.* London: Routledge and Kegan Paul Ltd.

———. 1925. Magic, Science, and Religion. In J. Needham, ed., *Science, Religion and Reality.* London. (Reprinted in *Magic, Science, and Religion,* 1954. Boston: Beacon Press.)

———. 1926. *Myth in Primitive Psychology.* London. (Reprinted in *Magic, Science, and Religion,* 1954. Boston: Beacon Press.)

———. 1927. *Sex and Repression in Savage Society.* London: Routledge and Kegan Paul Ltd.

———. 1929. *The Sexual Life of Savages in Northwestern Melanesia.* London: Routledge and Kegan Paul Ltd.

———. 1935. *Coral Gardens and Their Magic.* 2 vols. London: Allen and Unwin Ltd.

Maquet, J. 1964. Objectivity in Anthropology. *Current Anthropology* 5: 47–55.

Marshack, A. 1964. Lunar Notation on Upper Paleolithic Remains. *Science* November 6: 743–745.

———. 1972. *The Roots of Civilization.* New York: McGraw-Hill, Inc.

Marshall, L. 1959. Marriage Among the !Kung Bushmen. *Africa* 29: 335–364.

———. 1960. !Kung Bushmen Bands. *Africa* 30: 325–355.

———. 1965. The !Kung Bushmen of the Kalahari Desert. In J. Gibbs, Jr., ed., *Peoples of Africa.* New York: Holt, Rinehart and Winston.

Martin, P. S., and H. E. Wright, eds., 1967. *Pleistocene Extinctions: The Search for a Cause.* New Haven, Conn.: Yale University Press.

Marx, K. 1852. *The Eighteenth Brumaire of Louis Bonaparte.* (Page reference is to 1963 edition, New York, International Press.)

———. 1938. *Capital* (2 vols.) London: George Allen & Unwin. (Trans. of *Das Kapital.*)

———, and F. Engels. 1848. *The Communist Manifesto*. (Page reference is to Marx and Engels, Selected Works. New York: International Publishers, 1968.)

Mathieu, A. 1993. The Medicalization of Homelessness and the Theater of Repression. *Medical Anthropology Quarterly* 7(2): 170–184.

Maybury-Lewis, D. 1996. *Indigenous Peoples, Ethnic Groups, and the State*. Needham Heights, Mass.: Allyn and Bacon, Inc.

———, and J. Howe. 1980. *The Indian Peoples of Paraguay: Their Plight and Their Prospects*. Cambridge, Mass.: Cultural Survival Inc.

———, J. W. Clay, D. Price, D. Moore, B. M. Lafer, and C. Junqueira. 1981. *In the Path of Polonoroeste: Endangered Peoples of Western Brazil*. Cambridge, Mass.: Cultural Survival, Inc.

McArthur, M. 1974. Pigs for the Ancestors: A Review Article. *Oceania* 45(2): 87–123.

———. 1977. Nutritional Research in Melanesia: A Second Look at the Tsembaga. In T. P. Bayliss-Smith and R. G. Feachem, eds., *Subsistence and Survival: Rural Ecology in the Pacific*. New York: Academic Press, Inc.

McDougall, L. 1975. The Quest of the Argonauts. In T. R. Williams, ed., *Psychological Anthropology*. Paris: Mouton and Company.

McElroy, A., and P. K. Townsend. 1985. *Medical Anthropology in Ecological Perspective*. Boulder: Westview Press.

McKinnon, S. 1991. *From a Shattered Sun: Hierarchy, Gender, and Alliance in the Tanimbar Islands*. Madison: University of Wisconsin Press.

McLean, P. D. 1964. Man and His Animal Brain. *Modern Medicine*. February: 95–106.

———. 1968. Alternative Neural Pathways to Violence. In M. L. Nag, ed., *Alternatives to Violence*. New York: Time-Life Books.

Mead, M. 1935. *Sex and Temperament in Three Primitive Societies*. New York: William Morrow and Company, Inc.

———. 1938. The Mountain Arapesh. Part 1: An Importing Culture. *American Museum of Natural History Anthropological Papers* 36: 139–349.

———. 1949. *Male and Female*. New York: William Morrow and Company, Inc.

Meggers, B. J. 1971. *Amazonia: Man and Culture in a Counterfeit Paradise*. Chicago: Aldine-Atherton, Inc.

Meggitt, M. 1964. Male-Female Relationships in the Highlands of Australian New Guinea. In J. B. Watson, ed., *New Guinea: The Central Highlands*. American Anthropologist Special Publication 66, part 2.

———. 1965. *The Lineage System of the Mae Enga of the New Guinea Highlands*. Edinburgh: Oliver & Boyd.

———. 1972. System and Subsystem: The Te Exchange Cycle Among the Mae Enga. *Human Ecology* 1: 111–123.

———. 1974. Pigs Are Our Hearts: The Te Exchange Cycle Among the Mae Enga of New Guinea. *Oceania* 44.

Meigs, A. S. 1978. A Papuan Perspective on Pollution. *Man* (n.s.) 13: 304–318.

Meillassoux, C. 1960. Essai d'Interpretation de Phénomène Economique dans les Sociétés Traditionelles d'Autosubsistance. *Cahiers d'Etudes Africaines* 1: 38–67.

———. 1975. *Femmes, Greniers et Capitaux*. Paris: Francois Maspero.

Mendelievich, E., ed. 1980. *Children at Work*. Geneva: International Labour Office.

Merlan, F. 1995. The Regimentation of Customary Practice: From Northern Territory Land Claims to Mabo. *Australian Journal of Anthropology* 6(1–2): 64–82.

Merton, R. K. 1968 (1957). *Social Theory and Social Structure*. New York: Free Press.

Metcalf, P. 1977. The Berawan Afterlife: A Critique of Hertz. In G. Appell, ed., *Studies in Borneo Societies*. Dekalb, Ill.: Northern Illinois University.

Meyers, J. T. 1971. The Origins of Agriculture: An Evaluation of Three Hypotheses. In S. Struever, ed., *Prehistoric Agriculture*. Garden City, N.Y.: Natural History Press.

Michels, J. W. 1972a. *Dating Methods in Archaeology*. New York: Seminar Press.

———. 1972b. Dating Methods. In *Annual Reviews of Anthropology*, 1. Palo Alto, Calif.: Annual Reviews Press.

Middleton, J., and D. Tait. 1958. *Tribes Without Rulers: Studies in African Segmentary Systems*. London: Routledge and Kegan Paul Ltd.

Miers, S., and I. Kopytoff, eds., 1977. *Slavery in Africa*. Madison: University of Wisconsin Press.

Migliore, S. 1987. The Language of Secrecy: Symbols and Metaphors in Poro Ritual.

Canadian Review of Sociology and Anthropology 24(2): 292–294.

Miller, B. D., ed. 1992. *Sex and Gender Hierarchies.* Cambridge: Cambridge University Press.

Mintz, S. W. 1959. Internal Market Systems as Mechanisms of Social Articulation. In V. F. Ray, ed., *Proceedings of the American Ethnological Society.* Seattle: University of Washington Press.

———. 1961. Pratik. Haitian Personal Economic Relationships. In *Proceedings of the 1961 Annual Spring Meetings of the American Ethnological Society.* Seattle: University of Washington Press.

Mitchell, J. 1974. *Psychoanalysis and Feminism.* London: Allen Wayne.

Mitchell, J. C. 1969. The Concept and Use of Social Networks. In J. C. Mitchell, ed., *Social Networks in Urban Situations,* 2nd ed. Manchester, England: Manchester University Press.

Montague, S. 1971. Trobriand Kinship and the Virgin Birth Controversy. *Man* 6: 353–368.

Mooney, J. 1896. *The Ghost Dance Religion.* Bureau of American Ethnology, Annual Report 14. Washington, D.C.: U.S. Government Printing Office.

Moore, O. K. 1957. Divination—A New Perspective. *American Anthropologist* 59: 69–74.

Morris, M. D. 1965. *The Emergence of an Industrial Labor Force in India: A Study of the Bombay Cotton Mills,* 1854–1947. Berkeley: University of California Press.

Morton, K. L. 1978. Mobilizing Money in a Communal Economy: A Tongan Example. *Human Organization* 37(1): 50–56.

Munn, N. 1973. *Walbiri Iconography.* Ithaca: Cornell University Press.

Murdock, G. P. 1949. *Social Structure.* New York: The Macmillan Company.

Murgica, A. M. 1946. *Primo Tapia: Semblanza de un Revolucionano Michaocano,* 2nd ed. Mexico.

Murphy, R. F. 1959. Social Structure and Sex Antagonism. *Southwestern Journal of Anthropology* 15: 89–98.

Murphy, W. P. 1980. Secret Knowledge as Property and Power in Kpelle Society: Elders Versus Youth. *Africa* 50(2): 193–207.

Murphy, Y., and R. F. Murphy. 1974. *Women of the Forest.* New York: Columbia University Press.

Myers, F. R. 1986. *Pintupi Country, Pintupi Self.* Washington and London: Smithsonian Press.

Nader, L. 1972. Up the Anthropologist—Perspectives Gained From Studying Up. In D. Hymes, ed., *Reinventing Anthropology.* New York: Random House, Inc.

———, ed. 1980. *No Access to Law: Alternatives to the American Judicial System.* New York: Academic Press.

———, ed. 1996. *Naked Science: Anthropological Inquiry into Boundaries, Power, and Knowledge.* New York: Routledge.

Nakane, C. 1970. *Japanese Society.* Berkeley: University of California Press.

Narokobi, B. M. 1974. To Build a New Society We Must Build From the Base. *Papua New Guinea Post Courier.* October 22.

Nas, P. J. M., ed. 1993. *Urban Symbolism.* Leiden: E. J. Brill.

Nash, M. 1961. The Social Context of Economic Choice in a Small Society. *Man* 61(219): 186–191.

———. 1966. *Primitive and Peasant Economic Systems.* San Francisco: Chandler Publishing Company.

Needham, R. 1962. *Structure and Sentiment: A Test Case in Social Anthropology.* Chicago: University of Chicago Press.

———. 1971. Remarks on the Analysis of Kinship and Marriage. In R. Needham, ed., *Kinship and Marriage.* A.S.A. Monographs, 11. London: Tavistock.

———, ed. 1973. *Right and Left: Essays on Dual Symbolic Classification.* Chicago: University of Chicago Press.

———. 1974. *Remarks and Inventions. Skeptical Essays About Kinship.* New York: Barnes & Noble, Inc.

Neel, J. V. 1970. Lessons From a 'Primitive' People. *Science* 170: 805–822.

Newcomer, P. J. 1972. The Nuer Are Dinka: An Essay on Origins and Environmental Determinism. *Man* (n.s.) 7: 5–11.

Nietschmann, B. 1975. Beyond the Bizarre With Rumplestiltskin. *Reviews in Anthropology* May: 157–168.

Nutini, H., and B. Bell. 1980. *Ritual Kinship: The Structure and Historical Development of the Compadrazgo System in Rural Tlaxcala.* Princeton: Princeton University Press.

Obeyesekere, G. 1981. *Medusa's Hair: An Essay on Personal Symbols and Religious Experience.* Chicago: University of Chicago Press.

———. 1984. *Medusa's Hair.* Chicago: University of Chicago Press.

O'Laughlin, B. 1975. Marxist Approaches in Anthropology. *Annual Review of Anthropology,* Vol. 4 (B. J. Siegel, ed.). Palo Alto, Calif.: Annual Reviews, Inc.

———. 1977. Production and Reproduction: Meillasoux's *Femmes, Greniers et Capitaux. Critique of Anthropology* 2(8): 3–33.

Oliveira, R. C. 1988. *A Crise do Indigenismo.* Campinas, Brasil: Editora da Unicamp.

Omvedt, G. 1978. Women and Rural Revolt in India. *Journal of Peasant Studies* 5(3): 370–403.

Oomen, H. A. P. C. 1970. Interrelationship of the Human Intestinal Flora and Protein Utilization. *Proceedings of the Nutritional Society (Great Britain)* 29: 197–206.

Ortiz de Montellano, B. R. 1978. Aztec Cannibalism: An Ecological Necessity? *Science* 200: 611–617.

Ortner, S. B. 1974. Is Female to Male as Nature Is to Culture? In M. Z. Rosaldo and L. Lamphere, eds., *Woman, Culture, and Society.* Stanford, Calif.: Stanford University Press.

———, and H. Whitehead, eds. 1981. *Sexual Meanings: The Cultural Construction of Gender and Sexuality.* Cambridge: Cambridge University Press.

Pavlich, G. 1992. People's Courts, Postmodern Difference, and Socialist Justice in South Africa. *Social Justice* (19) 3: 29–45.

Perlman, J. E. 1976. *The Myth of Marginality: Urban Poverty and Politics in Rio de Janeiro.* Berkeley and Los Angeles: University of California Press.

Person, Y. 1971. Guinea-Samori. In M. Crowder, ed., *West African Resistance: The Military Response to Colonial Occupation.* London: Hutchinson Publishing Group Ltd.

Peters, C. R. 1972. A New Start for an Old Problem: Evolution of the Capacity for Language. *Man* 7: 13–19.

Peterson, J. T. 1978. Hunter-Gatherer/Farmer Exchange. *American Anthropologist* 82: 335–351.

Piaget, J. 1970. Piaget's Theory. In P. H. Mussen, ed., *Carmichael's Manual of Child Psychology,* vol. 1., 3rd ed. (pp. 703–732). New York: John Wiley & Sons, Inc.

Pilbeam, D. 1972. *The Ascent of Man: An Introduction to Human Evolution.* New York: The Macmillan Company.

Pocock, D. F. 1960. Sociologies: Rural and Urban. *Contributions to Indian Sociology* 4: 63–81.

Polanyi, K. 1957. The Economy as Instituted Process. In K. Polanyi et al., eds., *Trade and Market in the Early Empires.* New York: The Free Press.

———. 1959. Anthropology and Economic Theory. In M. H. Fried, ed., *Readings in Anthropology,* Vol. 2. New York: Thomas Y. Crowell Company.

Polgar, S., ed. 1971. *Culture and Population: A Collection of Current Studies.* Cambridge, Mass.: Schenkman.

———. 1975. *Population, Ecology, and Social Evolution.* The Hague: Mouton.

———. 1979. From Applied to Committed Anthropology: Disengaging From Our Colonialist Heritage. In G. Huizer and B. Mannheim, eds., *The Politics of Anthropology.* The Hague: Mouton.

Pomeroy, W. J. 1970. *American Neo-Colonialism: Its Emergence in the Philippines and Asia.* New York: International Publishing Company.

Pospisil, L. 1968. Law and Order. In J. A. Clifton, ed., *Introduction to Cultural Anthropology.* Boston: Houghton Mifflin Company.

———. 1978. *The Ethnology of Law.* 2nd ed. Menlo Park, Calif.: Cummings Publishing Company.

Powell, H. A. 1960. Competitive Leadership in Trobriand Political Organization. *Journal of the Royal Anthropological Institute* 90: 118–145.

———. 1968. Correspondence: Virgin Birth. *Man* 3: 651–652.

———. 1969a. Genealogy, Residence, and Kinship in Kiriwina. *Man* 4(2): 177–202.

———. 1969b. Territory, Hierarchy, and Kinship in Kiriwina. *Man* 4(4): 580–604.

Premack, A. J., and D. Premack. 1972. Teaching Language to an Ape. *Scientific American* 227: 92–99.

Premack, D. 1971. Language in Chimpanzee? *Science* 172: 808–822.

Price, B. J. 1971. Prehispanic Irrigation Agriculture in Nuclear America. *Latin American Research Review* 6(3): 3–60. (Reprinted in abridged form in M. Fried, ed., 1973. *Explorations in Anthropology*. New York: Thomas Y. Crowell Company.)

———. 1978. Demystification, Enriddlement, and Aztec Cannibalism: A Materialist Rejoinder to Harner. *American Ethnologist* 5(1): 98–115.

Price, R. 1973. *Maroon Societies*. Garden City, N.Y.: Doubleday & Company, Inc.

Quinn, N. 1977. Anthropological Studies on Women's Status. *Annual Review of Anthropology*, Vol. 6 (B. Siegel, ed.). Palo Alto, Calif.: Annual Reviews Press.

Radcliffe-Brown, A. R. 1913. Three Tribes of Western Australia. *Journal of the Royal Anthropological Institute*. 43: 143–194.

———. 1922. *The Andaman Islanders*. Cambridge, England: Cambridge University Press.

———. 1951. The Comparative Method in Social Anthropology. *Journal of the Royal Anthropological Institute*. 81: 15–22.

———. 1952. *Structure and Function in Primitive Society*. London: Cohen and West.

Randle, M. C. 1951. Iroquois Women, Then and Now. In W. N. Fenton, ed. *Symposium on Local Diversity in Iroquois Culture. Bureau of American Ethnology Bulletin*, No. 149. Washington D.C.: U.S. Government Printing Office.

Rappaport, R. 1967. Ritual Regulation of Environmental Relations Among a New Guinea People. *Ethnology* 6: 17–30.

———. 1968. *Pigs for the Ancestors: Ritual in the Ecology of a New Guinea People*. New Haven, Conn.: Yale University Press.

———. 1970. Sanctity and Adaptation. *Io*, Winter (Special Oecology Issue): 46–70.

———. 1971a. Ritual, Sanctity, and Cybernetics. *American Anthropologist* 73: 59–76.

———. 1971b. The Sacred in Human Evolution. *Annual Review of Ecology and Systematics* 2: 22–44. Palo Alto: Annual Reviews Press.

———. 1971c. The Flow of Energy in an Agricultural Society. *Scientific American*, September. (Page references are to reprinting in J. G. Jorgenson, ed., 1972. *Biology and Culture in Modern Perspective*. San Francisco: W. H. Freeman and Company, Publishers.)

———. 1971d. Nature, Culture, and Ecological Anthropology. In H. Shapiro, ed., *Man, Culture, and Society*. London: Oxford University Press.

Rasmussen, K. 1922. *Grønlandsagen*. Berlin.

Rattray, R. S. 1923. *Ashanti*. Oxford: Clarendon Press.

Read, D. W., J. Atkins, I. R. Buchler, M. Fischer, G. DeMeur, E. Lally, B. Holbrook, D. B. Kronenfeld, H. W. Scheffler, S. Seidman, and W. Wilder. 1984. An Algebraic Account of the American Kinship Terminology. *Current Anthropology* 25(4): 417–440.

Reed, N. 1965. *The Caste War of Yucatan*. Stanford, Calif.: Stanford University Press.

Rey, P. P. 1971. *Colonialisme, Néo-Colonialisme et Transition au Capitalisme*. Paris: Maspero.

———. 1973. Las Alliances de Classes: sur L'Articulation des Modes de Production. *Suivi du Materialisme Historique et Luttes de Classes*. Paris: Maspero.

Reynolds, P. C. 1976. The Emergence of Early Hominid Social Organization: I. The Attachment Systems. In *Yearbook of Physical Anthropology*, Vol. 20. New York: American Association of Physical Anthropologists.

Rhodes, R. I., ed. 1970. *Imperialism and Underdevelopment: A Reader*. New York: Monthly Review Press.

Richards, A. I. 1950. Some Types of Family Structure Amongst the Central Bantu. In A. R Radcliffe-Brown and C. D. Forde, eds., *African Systems of Kinship and Marriage*. London: Oxford University Press.

Richards, C. 1957. Matriarchy or Mistake: The Role of Iroquois Women Through Time. In *Cultural Stability and Cultural Change* (Proceedings of the 1957 Annual Meeting of the American Ethnological Society). Seattle: University of Washington Press.

Richards, P. 1985. *Indigenous Agricultural Revolution: Ecology and Food Production in West Africa*. London: Westview Press.

———. 1986. *Coping With Hunger: Hazard and Experiment in an African Rice-Farming System*. London: Allen and Unwin.

Riley, C. L., J. C. Kelley, C. W. Pennington, and R. L. Rands, eds., 1971. *Man Across the Sea: Problems of Pre-Columbian Contacts*. Austin: University of Texas Press.

Robinson, M. 1962. Complementary Filiation and Marriage in the Trobriand Islands. In M. Fortes, ed., *Marriage in Tribal Societies*.

Cambridge Papers in Social Anthropology, 3. London: Cambridge University Press.

Rogers, A., and S. Vertovec, eds. 1995. *The Urban Context: Ethnicity, Social Networks, and Situational Analysis.* Oxford: Berg Publishers.

Rogers, S. C. 1975. Female Forms of Power and the Myth of Male Dominance: A Model of Female/Male Interaction in Peasant Society. *American Ethnologist* 2(4): 727–756.

———. 1978. Women's Place: A Critical Review of Anthropological Theory. *Comparative Studies in Society and History.* 20(1): 123–167.

Rohlen, T. 1974. *For Harmony and Strength: Japanese White-Collar Organization in Anthropological Perspective.* Berkeley, Calif.: University of California Press.

Rosaldo, M. Z. 1974. Woman, Culture, and Society: A Theoretical Overview. In M. Z. Rosaldo and L. Lamphere, eds., *Woman, Culture, and Society.* Stanford, Calif.: Stanford University Press.

———, and J. Collier. 1981. Politics and Gender in 'Simple' Societies. In S. Ortner and H. Whitehead, eds., *Sexual Meanings.* Cambridge: Cambridge University Press.

———, and L. Lamphere. 1974. *Woman, Culture, and Society.* Stanford, Calif.: Stanford University Press.

Rosch, E. 1974. Universals and Cultural Specifics in Human Categorization. In R. Breslin, W. Lonner, and S. Bochner, eds., *Cross-Cultural Perspectives on Learning.* New York: Russell Sage Foundation.

———. 1978a. Human Categorization. In N. Warren, ed., *Studies in Cross-Cultural Psychology,* Vol. 1. London: Academic Press.

———. 1978b. Principles of Classification. In E. Rosch and B. B. Lloyds, eds., *Cognition and Categorization.* Hillsdale, N.J.: Lawrence Erlbaum Associates.

Roscoe, P. B. 1994. Amity and Aggression: A Symbolic Theory of Incest. *Man* 29(1): 49–76.

Ross, B. R. 1978. Food Taboos, Diet and Hunting Strategy: The Adaptation to Animals in Amazon Cultural Ecology, *Current Anthropology* 19: 1–36.

Rowe, W. L. 1973. Caste, Kinship and Association in Urban India. In A. Southall, ed., *Urban Anthropology.* London: Oxford University Press.

Rowley, C. D. 1970–1971. *Aboriginal Policy and Practice.* Vol. 1: The Destruction of Aboriginal Society; Vol. 2: Outcasts in White Australia; Vol. 3: The Remote Aborigines. Canberra: Australian National University Press.

Rowthorn, R. E. 1974. Neo-Classicism, Neo-Ricardianism and Marxism. *New Left Review* 86: 63–87.

Rubel, A. J., and H. J. Kupferer. 1968. Perspectives on the Atomistic-Type Society—Introduction. *Human Organization,* 189–190.

Rubin, J. 1968. *National Bilingualism in Paraguay.* Janua Lingaurum, Series Practica 60. The Hague: Mouton and Company.

Russell, W. M. S. 1988. Population, Swidden Farming, and the Topical Environment. *Population and Environment* 10(2): 77–94.

Sackett, J. R. 1968. Method and Theory of Upper Paleolithic Archeology in Southwestern France. In L. R. and S. Binford, eds., *New Perspectives in Archeology.* Chicago: Aldine Publishing Company.

Sacks, K. 1974. Engels Revisited: Women, the Organization of Production, and Private Property. In M. Rosaldo and L. Lamphere, eds., *Women in Culture and Society.* Stanford, Calif.: Stanford University Press.

Sahagun, B. De. 1951. *The Florentine Codex: General History of the Things of New Spain.* Trans. by A. J. P. Anderson and C. E. Dibble. Santa Fe, N.M.: Museum of New Mexico.

Sahlins, M. 1961. The Segmentary Lineage: An Organization of Predatory Expansion. *American Anthropologist* 63: 322–343.

———. 1963. Poor Man, Rich Man, Big Man, Chief: Political Types in Melanesia and Polynesia. *Comparative Studies in Society and History* 5: 285–300.

———. 1968. *Tribesmen.* Englewood Cliffs, N.J.: Prentice-Hall, Inc.

———. 1972. *Stone Age Economics.* Chicago: Aldine-Atherton, Inc.

———. 1976. *The Use and Abuse of Biology: An Anthropological Critique of Sociobiology.* Ann Arbor, Mich.: University of Michigan Press.

——. 1977. *Culture and Practical Reason.* Chicago: University of Chicago Press.

——. 1979. Reply to Marvin Harris, *New York Review of Books,* June 28: 52–53.

Sahlins, M., and P. V. Kirch. 1992. *Anahulu: The Anthropology of History in the Kingdom of Hawaii.* Chicago: University of Chicago Press.

Salamone, F. A. 1979. Epistemological Implications of Field Work and Their Consequences. *American Anthropologist* 81: 46–60.

Salisbury, R. F. 1966. Politics and Shell Money Finance in New Britain. In M. Schwartz and A. Tuden, eds., *Political Anthropology.* Chicago: Aldine Press.

——. 1970. *Vunamami. Economic Transformation in a Traditional Society.* Berkeley: University of California Press.

——. 1975. Non-Equilibrium Models in New Guinea Ecology: Possibilities of Cultural Extrapolation. *Anthropologica* 17(2): 127–147.

Sanday, P. R., and R. G. Goodenough, eds. 1990. *Beyond the Second Sex: New Directions in the Anthropology of Gender.* Philadelphia: University of Pennsylvania Press.

Sanders, W. T., and B. J. Price. 1968. *Mesoamerica: The Evolution of a Civilization.* New York: Random House, Inc.

Sapir, E. 1949. *Selected Writings of Edward Sapir in Language, Culture, and Personality.* D. G. Mandelbaum, ed. Berkeley: University of California Press.

Schaller, G. B. 1963. *The Mountain Gorilla: Ecology and Behavior.* Chicago: University of Chicago Press.

Schapera, I. 1955. *A Handbook of Tswana Law and Custom.* 2nd ed. London: Oxford University Press.

Schebesta, P. 1954. Die Negrito Asiens. *Ethnographie der Negrito,* Band 2/1. Wien-Mödling: St. Gabriel.

Scheffler, H. W. 1970. 'The Elementary Structures of Kinship' by C. Lévi-Strauss: A Review Article. *American Anthropologist* 72: 251–268.

——. 1972a. Kinship Semantics. In B. Siegel, ed., *Annual Reviews of Anthropology.* Palo Alto, Calif.: Annual Reviews, Inc.

——. 1972b. Systems of Kin Classification: A Structural Semantic Typology. In P. Reining, ed., *Kinship Studies in the Morgan Centennial Year.* Washington, D.C.: Anthropological Society of Washington.

——. 1973. Kinship, Descent, and Alliance. In J. J. Honigmann, ed., *Handbook of Social and Cultural Anthropology.* Chicago: Rand McNally.

——. 1978. Australian Kin Classification, *Cambridge Studies in Social Anthropology.* New York: Cambridge University Press.

Scheflen, A. E. 1973. *How Behavior Means: Exploring the Contexts of Speech and Meaning; Kinesics, Posture, Setting and Culture.* New York: Gordon and Breach.

Schlegel, A. 1973. Adolescent Socialization of the Hopi Girl. *Ethnology* 12: 449–462.

——. 1974. Review of M. Rosaldo and L. Lamphere, eds., *Women, Culture, and Society. Reviews in Anthropology* 1.

——. 1977. Male and Female in Hopi Thought and Action. In A. Schlegel, ed., *Sexual Stratification.* New York: Columbia University Press.

Schneider, D. M. 1961. Introduction. In D. Schneider and K. Gough, eds., *Matrilineal Kinship.* Berkeley: University of California Press.

——. 1972. What Is Kinship All About? In R. Reining, ed., *Kinship Studies in the Morgan Centennial Year.* Washington, D.C.: Anthropological Society of Washington.

——. 1976. Notes Toward a Theory of Culture. In K. H. Basso and H. Selby, eds., *Meaning in Anthropology.* Albuquerque: University of New Mexico Press.

——. 1984. *A Critique of the Study of Kinship.* Ann Arbor: University of Michigan Press.

Schneider, H. K. 1974. *Economic Man: The Anthropology of Economics.* New York: The Free Press.

Schneider, P., J. Schneider, and E. Hansen. 1972. Modernization and Development: The Role of Regional Elites and Non-Corporate Groups in the European Mediterranean. *Comparative Studies in Society and History* 14: 328–350.

Scholte, B. 1972. Toward a Reflexive and Critical Anthropology. In D. Hymes, ed., *Reinventing Anthropology.* New York: Random House, Inc.

Schusky, E., and D. Abbott. 1980. Misperception and Misdirection in the Sahel. Paper presented at symposium on "Hunger, Work, and the

Quality of Life" Xth ICAES Post-Plenary Session, Hyderabad, December 1978.

Schwartz, T. 1962. *The Paliau Movement in the Admiralty Islands, 1946–1954*. New York: American Museum of Natural History Occasional Papers, Vol. 49, Part 2.

———. 1963. Systems of Areal Integration: Some Considerations Based on the Admiralty Islands of Northern Melanesia. *Anthropological Forum* 1: 56–97.

———. 1978. Where Is the Culture? Personality as the Distributive Locus of Culture. In G. D. Spindler, ed., *The Making of Psychological Anthropology*. Berkeley: University of California Press.

———. 1992. Anthropology and Psychology: An Unrequited Relationship. In T. Schwartz, G. M. White, and C. Lutz, eds., *New Directions in Psychological Anthropology* (pp. 324–349). Cambridge: Cambridge University Press.

Service, E. R. 1975. *Origins of the State and Civilization: The Process of Cultural Evolution*. New York: W. W. Norton and Company, Inc.

———. 1978. In. R. Cohen and E. R. Service, eds., *Origins of the State: The Anthropology of Political Evolution*. Philadelphia: Institute for the Study of Human Issues.

Shack, W. A. 1973. Urban Ethnicity and the Cultural Process of Urbanization in Ethiopia. In A. Southall, ed., *Urban Anthropology*. London: Oxford University Press.

Shanks, M., and L. Stephanie. 1995. Tell Them Who I Am: The Lives of Homeless Women. *Journal of Contemporary Ethnography* 23(4): 516–520.

Sherzer, J. 1987. A Discourse-Centered Approach to Language and Culture. *American Anthropologist* 89: 295–309.

Shillinglaw, J. 1870. *Journal of the Rev. Knopwood: Historical Records of Port Phillip*. Melbourne, Australia: Government Printer.

Shipton, P. M. 1989. *Bitter Money: Cultural Economy and Some African Meanings of Forbidden Commodities*. Washington, D.C: American Anthropological Association.

Sider, K. B. 1967. Affinity and the Role of the Father in the Trobriands. *Southwestern Journal of Anthropology* 23: 65–109.

Silverman, J. 1967. Shamans and Acute Schizophrenia. *American Anthropologist* 69: 21–31.

Simet, J. 1992, *Tabu*. Ph.D. dissertation. Anthropology Department, Australian National University.

Simons, E. L. 1972. *Primate Evolution: An Introduction to Man's Place in Nature*. New York: The Macmillan Company.

———. 1977. Ramapithecus. *Scientific American* 236(77): 28–35.

Sims, M. M. 1995. Old Roads and New Directions: Anthropology and the Law. *Dialectical Anthropology* 20(3–4): 341–360.

Singer, M. 1994. Community-Centered Praxis: Toward an Alternative Nondominative Applied Anthropology. *Human Organization. Winter 1994:* 53(4): 336–344.

Siskind, J. 1973. Tropical Forest Hunters and the Economy of Sex. In D. Gross, ed., *Peoples and Cultures of Native South America*. New York: Doubleday & Company, Inc.

Sjoberg, G. 1960. *The Preindustrial City*. New York: The Free Press.

Skinner, G. W. 1964–1965. Marketing and Social Structure in Rural China. Parts I and II. *Journal of Asian Studies*. 24: 3–43, 195–228.

———. 1977. Regional Urbanization in Nineteenth-Century China. In G. W. Skinner, ed., *The City in Late Imperial China*. Stanford, Calif.: Stanford University Press.

Sloan Foundation. 1978. *Cognitive Science, 1978*. Report of the State of the Art Committee to the Advisors of the Alfred P. Sloan Foundation.

Smith, C. A., ed. 1976. *Regional Analysis*. Volume I: Social Systems. Volume II: Economic Systems. New York: Academic Press, Inc.

———. 1978. Beyond Dependency Theory: National and Regional Patterns of Underdevelopment in Guatemala. *American Ethnologist*. 5(3): 574–617.

Smith, E. W. 1926. *The Golden Stool: Some Aspects of the Conflict of Cultures in Modern Africa*. London: Holborn Publishing House.

Smith, M. G. 1956. On Segmentary Lineage Systems. *Journal of the Royal Anthropological Institute* 86(2): 39–80.

Smith, R. J. 1973. Town and City in Pre-Modern Japan: Small Families, Small Households, and

Residential Instability. In A. Southall, ed., *Urban Anthropology.* London: Oxford University Press.

Southall, A. 1973a. Introduction to *Urban Anthropology.* A. Southall, ed., London: Oxford University Press.

———. 1973b. The Density of Role-Relationships as a Universal Index of Urbanization. In A. Southall, ed., *Urban Anthropology.* London: Oxford University Press.

———, ed. 1973c. *Urban Anthropology: Cross-Cultural Studies of Urbanization.* London: Oxford University Press.

Specht, J., and J. P. White, eds. 1978. Trade and Exchange in Oceania and Australia, *Mankind* 11(3). University of Sydney Press.

Spencer, P. 1965. *The Samburu: A Study of Gerontocracy in a Nomadic Tribe.* Berkeley: University of California Press.

Spicer, E. H., ed. 1952. *Human Problems in Technological Change: A Casebook.* New York: Russell Sage Foundation.

———. 1961. Yaqui. In E. H. Spicer, ed., *Perspectives in American Indian Culture Change.* Chicago: University of Chicago Press.

Spindler, G. D. 1955. *Sociocultural and Psychological Processes in Menomini Acculturation.* Berkeley: University of California Publications in Culture and Society, 5.

———. 1968. Psychocultural Adaptation. In E. Norbeck et al., eds., *The Study of Personality.* New York: Holt, Rinehart and Winston.

———. 1973. *Burgbach: Urbanization and Identity in a German Village.* New York: Holt, Rinehart and Winston.

———, ed. 1978. *The Making of Psychological Anthropology.* Berkeley: University of California Press.

———, and L. S. Spindler. 1971. *Dreamers Without Power: The Menomini Indians.* New York: Holt, Rinehart and Winston.

Spindler, L. S. 1962. *Menomini Women and Culture Change.* American Anthropological Association, Memoir 91. *American Anthropologist* 64(1), part 2.

Spiro, M. E. 1966. Religion: Problems of Definition and Explanation. In M. Banton, ed., *Anthropological Approaches to the Study of Religion.* A.S.A. Monographs, 3. London: Tavistock Publications.

———. 1978. Culture and Human Nature. In G. D. Spindler, ed., *The Making of Psychological Anthropology.* Berkeley: University of California Press.

———. 1982. *Oedipus in the Trobriands.* Chicago and London: University of Chicago Press.

Spitz, P. 1978. Silent Violent: Famine and Inequality. *International Review of Social Science* 30(4): 867–892.

Spradley, J. P. 1970. *You Owe Yourself a Drunk: An Ethnography of Urban Nomads.* Boston: Little, Brown and Company.

———, and B. J. Mann. 1975. *The Cocktail Waitress: Women's Work in a Man's World.* New York: John Wiley & Sons, Inc.

———, and D. W. McCurdy, 1977. *The Cultural Experience—Ethnography in Complex Society.* Chicago: Science Research Associates.

Stack, C. B. 1974. *All Our Kin: Strategies for Survival in a Black Community.* New York: Harper & Row, Publishers.

Stanner, W. E. H. 1956. The Dreaming. In T. A. G. Hungerford, ed., *Australian Signpost.* Melbourne, Australia: F. W. Chesire.

———. 1963. On Aboriginal Religion. *Oceania Monographs,* No. 2. Sydney.

———. 1965. Religion, Totemism, and Symbolism. In R. M. Berndt and C. H. Berndt, eds., *Aboriginal Man in Australia.* Sydney: Angus and Robertson.

———. 1973. Fictions, Nettles, and Freedoms. *Search* 4(4): 104–111.

Stavenhagen, R. 1975. *Social Classes in Agrarian Societies.* Garden City, N.Y.: Anchor Press, imprint of Doubleday & Company, Inc.

———, ed. 1976. *Capitalismo y Campesinado en Mexico: Estudios de la Realidad Campesina.* Mexico: Inst. Nacional Antropol. Hist.

———. 1990. *The Ethnic Question: Conflicts, Development, and Human Rights.* Tokyo: United Nations University Press.

Steady, F. 1980. Urban Malnutrition in West Africa. In *The International Congress of Anthropological and Ethnological Sciences (10th): 1978.* New Delhi: Concept.

Steward, J. H. 1938. Basin-Plateau Aboriginal Sociopolitical Groups. *Bureau of American Ethnology Bulletin* 120. Washington, D.C.: Government Printing Office.

———. 1955. *Theory of Culture Change.* Urbana, Ill.: University of Illinois Press.

Strathern, A. J. 1971. *The Rope of Moka.* Cambridge, England: Cambridge University Press.

———. 1972. The Supreme Court: A Matter of Prestige and Power. *Melanesian Law Journal* 2: 23–28.

———. 1979. Gender, Ideology, and Money in Mt. Hagen. *Man* 14: 530–548.

———, ed. 1982. *Inequality in New Guinea Highlands Societies.* Cambridge: Cambridge University Press.

———. 1984. *A Line of Power.* London: Tavistock Publications.

———. 1987. Social Classes in Mt. Hagen? The Early Evidence. *Ethnology* 26(4): 245–260.

———. 1996. *Body Thoughts.* Ann Arbor: University of Michigan Press.

Strathern, M. 1972. *Women in Between; Female Roles in a Male World: Mount Hagen, New Guinea.* London: Seminar Press.

Strouse, J. 1974. *Women and Analysis: Dialogues on Psychoanalytic Views of Femininity.* New York: Grossman.

Stull, D. D., and J. J. Schensul, eds. 1987. *Collaborative Research and Social Change: Applied Anthropology in Action.* Hartford, Conn.: The Institute for Community Research, Inc.

Sukhatme, P. V. 1975. Human Protein Needs and the Relative Role of Energy and Protein in Meeting Them. In F. Steel and A. Bourne, eds., *The Man/Food Equation.* New York: Academic Press, Inc.

Swartz, M. J. 1968a. Introduction to *Local Level Politics.* M. J. Swartz, ed. Chicago: Aldine Publishing Company.

———, 1968b. *Local Level Politics.* Chicago: Aldine Publishing Company.

———, V. Turner, and A. Tuden, eds., 1966. *Political Anthropology.* Chicago: Aldine Publishing Company.

Talmon, Y. 1962. Pursuit of the Millennium: The Relation Between Religious and Social Change. *Archives Européennes de Sociologie* III: 125–148.

Tambiah, S. J. 1969. The Magical Power of Words. *Man* 3(2): 175–208.

———. 1983. On Flying Witches and Flying Canoes: The Coding of Male and Female Values. In E. R. Leach and J. W. Leach, eds., *New Perspectives on the Kula.* Cambridge: Cambridge University Press.

Tawney, R. H. 1926. *Religion and the Rise of Capitalism.* London: John Murray (Publishers) Ltd.

Terray, E. 1972. *Marxism and 'Primitive' Societies.* New York: Monthly Review Press.

Testart, A. 1988. Some Major Problems in the Social Anthropology of Hunter-Gatherers. *Current Anthropology* 29(1): 1–31.

Thrupp, S., ed. 1962. Millennial Dreams in Action: Essays in Comparative Study. *Comparative Studies in Society and History.* Supplement No. 2. The Hague: Mouton. (Reprinted in 1970 as *Millennial Dreams in Action: Studies in Revolutionary Religious Movements.* New York: Schocken Books, Inc.)

Tipps, D. C. 1973. Modernization and Comparative Study of Society. *Comparative Studies in Society and History* 15: 199–226.

Tooker, D. E. 1979. Some Basic Trobriand Attitudes About Sex as Expressed in the Kula Trade. *Cambridge Anthropology* 5(1): 44–65.

Trabasso, T., C. Riley, and E. Wilson. 1975. The Representation of Linear Order and Spatial Strategies in Reasoning: A Developmental Study. In R. J. Falmange, ed., *Reasoning: Representation and Process.* Hillsdale, N.J.: Lawrence Erlbaum Associates.

Trautmann, T. R. 1987. *Lewis H. Morgan and the Invention of Kinship.* Berkeley: University of California Press.

Trigger, B. 1972. Determinants of Urban Growth in Pre-Industrial Societies. In P. J. Ucko, R. Tringham, and G. W. Dimbleby, eds., *Man, Settlement, and Urbanism.* London: Gerald Duckworth & Company, Ltd.

Trompf, G. W. 1994. Gangs and Politics. *Current Affairs Bulletin,* September 1994: 32–37.

Tuomi, H. 1978. Food Import and Neo-Colonialism. In V. Harle, ed., *The Political Economy of Food.* Westmead, England: Saxon House.

Turnbull, C. M. 1961. *The Forest People: A Study of the Pygmies of the Congo.* New York: Simon & Schuster, Inc.

Turner, E., ed. 1985. *On the Edge of the Bush: Anthropology as Experience.* Tucson: University of Arizona Press.

————, ed. 1992. *Blazing the Trail: Way Marks in the Exploration of Symbols.* Tucson: University of Arizona Press.

————. 1992. *Experiencing Ritual.* With W. Blodgett, S. Kahona, and F. Benwa. Philadelphia: University of Pennsylvania Press.

Turner, T. S. 1979. Anthropology and the Politics of Indigenous Peoples' Struggles. *Cambridge Anthropology* 5(1): 1–43.

Turner, V. 1957. *Schism and Continuity in an African Society.* New York: Humanities Press, Inc. (Reprinted 1972.)

————. 1964. Betwixt and Between: The Liminal Period in Rites de Passage. In J. Helm, ed., *Proceedings of the 1964 Annual Spring Meeting of the American Ethnological Society.* Seattle: University of Washington Press.

————. 1966. Colour Classification in Ndembu Ritual. In M. Banton, ed., *Anthropological Approaches to the Study of Religion.* A.S.A. Monographs, 3. London: Tavistock Publications.

————. 1967. *The Forest of Symbols: Studies in Ndembu Ritual.* Ithaca, N.Y.: Cornell University Press.

————. 1968a. Mukanda: The Politics of a Non-Political Ritual. In M. J. Swartz, ed., *Local Level Politics.* Chicago: Aldine Publishing Company.

————. 1968b. *The Drums of Afflication: A Study of Religious Processes Among the Ndembu of Zambia.* Oxford, England: Clarendon Press.

————. 1975. *Revelation and Divination in Ndembu Ritual.* Ithaca, N.Y.: Cornell University Press.

————. 1978. Encounter With Freud: The Making of a Comparative Symbologist. In G. D. Spindler, ed., *The Making of Psychological Anthropology.* Berkeley, Calif.: University of California Press.

————. 1992. In E. Turner, ed., *Blazing the Trial: Way Marks in the Exploration of Symbols.* Tucson: University of Arizona Press.

Tylor, E. B. 1871. *Primitive Culture: Researches Into the Development of Mythology, Philosophy, Religion, Art, and Custom.* London: John Murray, (Publishers) Ltd.

————. 1889. On a Method of Investigating the Development of Institutions; Applied to Laws of Marriage and Descent. *Journal of the Royal Anthropological Institute* 18: 245–269.

Uberoi, J. P. Singh. 1962. *Politics of the Kula Ring.* Manchester, England: University of Manchester Press.

Ucko, P. J., and A. Rosenfeld. 1967. *Palaeolithic Cave Art.* London: Weidenfeld and Nicolson.

Udall, L. 1969. *Me and Mine: The Life Story of Helen Sekaqueptewa.* Tucson: University of Arizona Press.

Upadhya, C. B. 1990. Dowry and Women's Property in Coastal Andhra Pradesh. *Contributions to Indian Sociology* 24(1): 29–59.

Uzoigwe, G. N. 1977. The Warrior and the State in Precolonial Africa: Comparative Perspectives. *Journal of Asian and African Studies* 12(1–4): 20–47.

Valentine, C. A. 1968. *Culture and Poverty: Critique and Counter-Proposals.* Chicago: University of Chicago Press.

————, and B. Valentine. 1971. *Anthropological Interpretations of Black Culture.* Reading, Mass.: Addison-Wesley Modules in Anthropology.

Van Baal, J. 1966. *Dema: Description and Analysis of Culture* (South New Guinea). The Hague: Martinius Nijhoff.

Van Gennep, A. 1909. *Les Rites de Passage.* Paris: Libraire Critique Emile Nourry. (Trans. as *The Rites of Passage.* 1960. London: Routledge and Kegan Paul Ltd.)

Van Ginneken, J. K. 1974. Prolonged Breastfeeding as a Birth-Spacing Method. *Studies in Family Planning* 5: 201–208.

Van Lawick-Goodall, J. 1968. Expressive Movements and Communications in Chimpanzees. In P. Jay, ed., *Primates: Studies in Adaptation and Variability.* New York: Holt, Rinehart and Winston, Inc.

Van Valin, R., and W. Foley. 1980. Role and Reference Grammar. In E. Moravcsik, ed., *Syntax and Semantics, Vol. 13: Current Approaches to Syntax.* New York: Academic Press, Inc.

Van Velsen, J. 1967. The Extended-Case Method and Situational Analysis. In A. L. Epstein, ed., *The Craft of Social Anthropology* (pp. 129–149). London: Tavistock Publications.

Van Zantwijk, R. A. M. 1967. *Servants of the Saints: The Social and Cultural Identity of a Tarascan Community in Mexico.* Assen, Holland: Van Gorcum.

Vayda, A. P., A. Leeds, and D. B. Smith. 1961. The Place of Pigs in Melanesian Subsistence. In V. E. Gorfield, ed., *Proceedings of the 1961 Annual Spring Meeting of the American Ethnological Society.* Seattle: University of Washington Press.

———, and R. Rappaport. 1968. Ecology, Cultural and Noncultural. In J. A. Clifton, ed., *Introduction to Cultural Anthropology.* Boston: Houghton Mifflin Company.

Verdon, M. 1982. The Dynamics of Dynamics, or the Tallensi in Time and Numbers. *Journal of Anthropological Research* 38(2): 154–178.

Vogt, E. Z. 1965. Structural and Conceptual Replication in Zinacantan Culture. *American Anthropologist* 67: 342–353.

———. 1969. *Zinacantan: A Maya Community in the Highlands of Chiapas.* Cambridge, Mass.: Harvard University Press.

———. 1970. *The Zinacantecos of Mexico: A Modern Maya Way of Life.* New York: Holt, Rinehart and Winston, Inc.

———. 1976. *Tortillas for the Gods: A Symbolic Analysis of Zinacanteco Rituals.* Cambridge, Mass.: Harvard University Press.

Wallace, A. F. C. 1956. Revitalization Movements. *American Anthropologist* 58: 264–281.

———. 1960. Mental Illness, Biology, and Culture. In F. L. K. Hsu, ed., *Psychological Anthropology.* Homewood, Ill.: Dorsey Press.

———. 1978. Basic Studies, Applied Projects, and Eventual Application: A Case History of Biological and Cultural Research in Mental Health. In G. D. Spindler, ed., *The Making of Psychological Anthropology.* Berkeley: University of California Press.

Wallensteen, P. 1978. Scarce Goods as Political Weapons: The Case of Food. In V. Harle, ed., *The Political Economy of Food.* Westmead, England: Saxon House.

Wallerstein, I. 1974. *The Modern World-System: Capitalist Agriculture and the Origins of the European World-Economy in the Sixteenth Century.* New York: Academic Press, Inc.

———. 1979. *The Capitalist World-Economy: Essays by Immanuel Wallerstein.* Cambridge: Cambridge University Press.

Washburn, S. 1973. Primate Field Studies and Social Science. In L. Nader and T. Marctzki, eds., *Cultural Illness and Health: Essays in Human Adaptation.* Anthropological Studies 9.

———, and C. S. Lancaster. 1968. The Evolution of Hunting. In R. B. Lee and I. DeVore, eds., *Man the Hunter.* Chicago: Aldine Publishing Company.

Wasserstrom, R. 1977a. White Fathers and Red Souls: Indian-Ladino Relations in Highland Chiapas (1528–1973). Unpublished Ph.D. dissertation, Harvard University.

———. 1977b. Land and Labor in Central Chiapas: A Regional Analysis. *Development and Change* 4: 441–463.

———. 1978. The Exchange of Saints in Zinacantan: The Socioeconomic Bases of Religious Change in Southern Mexico. *Ethnology* 17(2): 197–210.

Watson, J. B. 1977. Pigs, Fodder, and the Jones Effect in Postipomoean New Guinea. *Ethnology* 16: 57–70.

Watson, J. L., ed. 1980. *Asian and African Systems of Slavery.* Berkeley: University of California Press.

Weber, M. 1956. *The Protestant Ethic and the Spirit of Capitalism.* New York: Charles Scribner's and Sons.

Webster, H. 1932. Primitive Secret Societies. Rev. ed. New York: The Macmillan Company.

Wedgewood, C. 1930. The Nature and Function of Secret Societies. *Oceania:* 129–145.

Weiner, A. 1974. *Women of Value: The Main Road of Exchange in Kiriwina, Trobriand Islands.* Unpublished Ph.D. Dissertation, Bryn Mawr College.

———. 1976. *Women of Value, Men of Renown.* Austin: University of Texas Press.

Westen, D. 1984. Cultural Materialism: Food for Thought or Bum Steer? *Current Anthropology* 25(5): 639–656.

Weston, K. 1991. *Families We Choose: Lesbians, Gays, Kinship.* New York: Columbia University Press.

Wheatley, P. 1975. Satyanrta in Suvarnadvipa. In J. A. Sabloff and C. C. Lamberg-Karlovsky, eds., *Ancient Civilization and Trade.* Albuquerque: University of New Mexico Press.

White, J. P., and J. F. O'Connell. 1978. Australian Prehistory: New Aspects of Antiquity. *Science* 203: 21–28.

Whiteley, P. M. 1985. Unpacking Hopi 'Clans': Another Vintage Model Out of Africa? *Journal of Anthropological Research* 41(4): 359–374.

Whiting, J. W. M. 1964. Effects of Climate on Certain Cultural Practices. In W. Goodenough, ed., *Explorations in Cultural Anthropology*. New York: McGraw-Hill, Inc.

Whitmeyer, J. M., and R. L. Hopcroft. 1995. *Community, Capitalism, and Rebellion in Chiapas*. Paper presented to the American Sociological Association.

Whorf, B. L. 1956. *Language, Thought, and Reality: Selected Writings of B. L. Whorf*. J. B. Carroll, ed. Cambridge, Mass., and New York: MIT Press and John Wiley & Sons, Inc.

Whyte, W. F. 1955. *Street Corner Society: The Social Structure of an Italian Slum*. Rev. ed., Chicago: University of Chicago Press.

Wierzbicka, A. 1972. *Semantic Primitives*. Frankfurt: Athenaeum Verlag.

———. 1991. *Cross-Cultural Pragmatics: The Semantics of Human Interaction*. Berlin: Mouton de Gruyter.

Wikan, U. 1990. *Managing Turbulent Hearts: A Balinese Formula for Living*. Chicago: University of Chicago Press.

Wilbert, J. 1972. *Survivors of Eldorado: Four Indian Cultures of South America*. New York: Praeger Publishers, Inc.

Williams, E. 1944. *Capitalism and Slavery*. Chapel Hill: University of North Carolina Press.

———. 1966. *British Historians and the West Indies*. London: Andre Deutsch.

Williams, F. E. 1923. *The Vailala Madness and the Destruction of Native Ceremonies in the Gulf Division*. Territory of Papua Anthropological Reports, 4. Port Moresby, New Guinea.

Williams, M. D. 1981. *On the Street Where I Lived*. New York: Holt, Rinehart and Winston.

———. 1984. *Community in a Black Pentecostal Church: An Anthropological Study*. Prospect Heights: Waveland Press.

Wilson, E. O. 1975. *Sociobiology: The New Synthesis*. Cambridge, Mass.: Harvard University Press.

Wilson, P. 1969. Virgin Birth: A Comment. *Man* (n.s.) 4(2): 287–290.

———. 1972. *Crab Antics: The Social Anthropology of English-Speaking Negro Societies of the Caribbean*. New Haven, Conn.: Yale University Press.

Wittfogel, K. A. 1955. Developmental Aspects of Hydraulic Societies. In J. Steward, ed. *Irrigation Civilizations: A Comparative Study*. Washington, D.C.: Pan American Union.

———. 1957. *Oriental Despotism: A Study in Total Power*. New Haven, Conn.: Yale University Press.

Wolf, A. D. 1966. Childhood Association, Sexual Attraction, and the Incest Taboo: A Chinese Case. *American Anthropologist* 68: 883–898.

———. 1970. Childhood Association and Sexual Attraction: A Further Test of the Westermarck Hypothesis. *American Anthropologist* 72: 503–515.

Wolf, E. R. 1957. Closed Corporate Peasant Communities in Mesoamerica and Central Java. *Southwestern Journal of Anthropology* 13: 1–18.

———. 1958. The Virgin of Guadalupe: A Mexican National Symbol. *Journal of American Folklore* 71: 34–39.

———. 1959. *Sons of the Shaking Earth*. Chicago: University of Chicago Press.

———. 1966. *Peasants*. Englewood Cliffs, N.J.: Prentice-Hall, Inc.

———. 1969a. *Peasant Wars of the Twentieth Century*. New York: Harper & Row, Publishers.

———. 1969b. On Peasant Rebellions. *International Social Science Journal* 21(2): 286–294.

———. 1982. *Europe and the People Without History*. Berkeley: University of California Press.

Worsley, P. 1957. *The Trumpet Shall Sound: A Study of 'Cargo' Cults in Melanesia*. London: MacGibbon and Kee. (2nd ed. 1968. New York: Schocken Books, Inc.)

Worthman, C. M, C. L. Jenkins, J. F. Stallings, and D. Lai, 1993. Attenuation of Nursing-Related Ovarian Suppression and High Fertility in Well-Nourished, Intensively Breast-Feeding Amele Women of Lowland Papua New Guinea. *Journal of Biosocial Science* 25(4): 425–443.

Yap, P. M. 1969. The Culture-Bound Reactive Syndromes. In W. Caudill and T. Y. Lin, eds., *Culture and Mental Health Research in Asia and the Pacific*. Honolulu: East-West Center Press.

Yazaki, T. 1963. *The Japanese City: A Sociological Analysis*. Tokyo: Japan Publications.

———. 1968. *Social Change and the City in Japan*. Tokyo: Japan Publications.

———. 1973. The History of Urbanization in Japan. In A. Southall, ed., *Urban Anthropology*. London: Oxford University Press.

Zelenietz, M., and S. Lindenbaum, eds., *Sorcery and Social Change in Melanesia*. Adelaide: *Social Analysis, 8*, special issue.

Acknowledgments

Text

Excerpts from *Global Reach* by Richard J. Barnet and Ronald E. Muller, reprinted by permission of Simon & Schuster. Copyright © 1975 by Richard J. Barnet and Ronald E. Muller.

Excerpt from *Social Classes in Agrarian Societies* by Rodolfo Stavenhagen, reprinted by permission of Doubleday, a division of Bantam Doubleday Dell Publishing Group, Inc.

Excerpts from *Women of Value, Men of Renown, New Perspectives in Trobriand Exchange* by Annette B. Weiner, copyright © 1976. By permission of the University of Texas Press.

Excerpts from *Lumpenbourgeoisie, Lumpendevelopment (1973), Latin America: Underdevelopment or Revolution (1969)* by Andre Gunder Frank. Copyright © 1973 by Andre Gunder Frank. Reprinted by permission of Monthly Review Press.

Excerpt from *The Political Economy of Food* by V. Harle, ed. Reprinted by permission of Gower Publishing Company Limited.

Excerpt from *Anthropology and the Politics of Indigenous Peoples* by Terence Turner. Reprinted by permission of the author. Appeared in Cambridge Anthropology, 5(1).

Excerpt from *Declaration of Barbados: For the Liberation of the Indians* by M. A. Bartolome, et al. Reprinted by permission of the International Work Group for Indigenous Affairs. IWGIA Document no. 1.

Excerpts from *Being and Value in a Primitive Culture* by D. D. Lee. Reprinted by permission of Journal of Philosophy. (From Vol. XLVI, No. 13, pp. 401–415.)

Excerpt from *Culture and Communication* by E. R. Leach. Reprinted by permission of Cambridge University Press.

Excerpt from "Nonunilineal Descent and the Contextual Definition of Status" by R. M. Keesing. Reprinted by permission of the American Anthropological Association. Appeared in *American Anthropologist* 70(1): 82–84, 1968.

Excerpts from *Slavery in Africa* by Miers, S. and I. Kopytoff, eds. Copyright © by the Board of Regents of the University of Wisconsin System. Reprinted by permission of the University of Wisconsin Press.

Excerpts from "Marxist Approaches in Anthropology" by B. O'Laughlin. Reprinted by permission of Annual Reviews, Inc. from *Annual Review of Anthropology*, vol. 4, 1975.

Excerpts from *The Myth of Marginality: Urban Poverty and Politics in Rio de Janeiro* by J. Perlman. Reprinted by permission of the University of California Press.

Excerpts from "Where Is the Culture" by T. Schwartz in *The Making of Psychological Anthropology*, G. D. Spindler, ed. Reprinted by permission of the University of California Press.

Excerpts from "Women's Marital Exchange Among the Kpelle of Liberia" by C. Bledsoe in *Journal of Anthropological Research*, 32: 372–389 (1976). Reprinted by permission of the copyright holder, *Journal of Anthropological Research*.

Excerpts from *Coral Gardens and Their Magic* (Vol. 1) by B. Malinowski. Reprinted by permission of Paul R. Reynolds, Inc.

Excerpts from *How the Other Half Dies: The Real Reasons for World Hunger* by S. George. Copyright © Susan George, 1976, 1977. Reprinted by permission of Penguins Books Ltd.

Excerpts from *Argonauts of the Western Pacific* (1922) by B. Malinowski. Reprinted by permission of Routledge & Kegan Paul Ltd.

Quotations from Asad, Dahl, Krader, and Lefebure from *Pastoral Production and Society* by l'Équipe Ecologie et Anthropologie des Sociétés Pastorales, eds. Reprinted by permission of Cambridge University Press.

Excerpt from *Sorcerers of Dobu* (1932) by R. Fortune. Reprinted by permission of Routledge & Kegan Paul Ltd.

Excerpts from *The Sexual Life of Savages in Northwestern Melanesia* (1929) by B. Malinowski. Reprinted by permission of Routledge & Kegan Paul Ltd.

Excerpt from "Non-Equilibium Models in New Guinea Ecology : Possibilities of Cultural Extrapolation" by R. F. Salisbury from *Anthropologica*, 17(2): 127–147 (1975). Reprinted by permission of *Anthropologica* and the author.

Excerpt from "Women and Rural Revolt in India" by G. Omvedt from *Journal of Peasant Studies*, 5(3): 370–403, 1978. Reprinted by permission of Frank Cass & Co. Ltd., London.

Excerpt from "Iroquois Women, Then and Now" by M. Randle from *Symposium on Local Diversity in Iroquois Culture*, W. N. Fenton, ed., BAE Bulletin No. 149. Reprinted with the permission of the Smithsonian Institution.

Excerpt from "Simple Models of Complexity: The Lure of Kinship" by R. M. Keesing from *Kinship Studies in the Morgan Memorial Year*, P. Reining, ed., 1972. Reprinted by permission of the American Ethnological Society.

Photos

Photographs by Andrew J. Strathern unless otherwise noted.

12   Art rendered from photo supplied courtesy of Phoebe Ottenberg Miller

54   Photograph courtesy of David and Judith MacDougall

57   Reprinted by permission of the publisher from *East Is a Big Bird* by T. Gladwin, Cambridge, Mass.: Harvard University Press, copyright © 1970 by the President and Fellows of Harvard College.

58   David S. Boyer © National Geographic Society Image Collection

61   Courtesy of Meyer Fortes

66   Art rendered from photo supplied courtesy of Karen and Kirk Endicott

83   Both photographs courtesy of Robert Edwards

84   Courtesy of Karen and Kirk Endicott

87   Medford Taylor / National Geographic Society Image Collection

88   Courtesy of Department of Library Services, The American Museum of Natural History

92   Both photographs courtesy of Roy D. Rappaport

95   Roger M. Keesing

96   Hedda Morrison

101   Bruce Dale / National Geographic Society Image Collection

108   Courtesy of Roy D. Rappaport

109   Courtesy of Roy D. Rappaport

121   All photos courtesy of Koninklijk Instituut voor de Tropen, Amsterdam

126   Photographs courtesy of D. G. Gajdusek. In *Tropical Neurology* by John D. Spillane, ed. By permission of Oxford University Press

127   Reprinted by permission of the publisher from "Kuru: Clinical, Pathological, Epidemiological Study of an Acute Progressive Degenerative Disease of the Central Nervous System Among Nations of the Eastern Highlands of New Guinea" by D. C. Gajdusek and V. Zigas, American Journal of Medicine: March 1959, p. 446, copyright 1997 by Excerpta Medica Inc.

130   Photograph courtesy of Douglas L. Oliver

136   Art rendered from photo supplied courtesy of Karen and Kirk Endicott

142   Courtesy of Jerry W. Leach

143   Shirley Campbell

154 Courtesy of Jerry W. Leach
156 Courtesy of Barry Shaw
157 Courtesy of Department of Foreign Affairs, Australia
162 Shirley Campbell
163 Shirley Campbell
164 Shirley Campbell
165 Shirley Campbell
189 Courtesy of Meyer Fortes
206 Hedda Morrison
207 Hedda Morrison
210 Both photos courtesy of Roger M. Keesing
211 Both photos courtesy of Roger M. Keesing
219 Courtesy of Department of Foreign Affairs, Australia
220 Roger M. Keesing
225 Courtesy of Annette Weiner
253 Photograph by E. E. Evans-Pritchard, courtesy of the Clarendon Press, Oxford
257 Both photos courtesy of Roger M. Keesing
272 Roger M. Keesing
279 © Edward Troncik/ Anthro Photo
296 Courtesy of James Lowell Gibbs, Jr.
299 Courtesy of Phoebe Apperson Hearst Museum of Anthropology and the Regents of the University of California
310 Roger M. Keesing
311 Roger M. Keesing
315 Roger M. Keesing
334 Courtesy of Department of Foreign Affairs, Australia
350 Art rendered from photo courtesy of UN/DPI Photo
358 Courtesy of Masri Singarimbun
362 UN/ DPI Photo
363 Courtesy of Department of Information and Extension Services, Papua, New Guinea
365 National Museum of American Art, Smithsonian Institution, Gift of Mrs. Joseph Harrison, Jr.
366 Photograph by Professor H. Klaatsch, courtesy of Australian Institute of Aboriginal and Torres Strait Islander Studies
368 From a painting by Carl Bodmer. Courtesy of Department of Library Services, The American Museum of Natural History
372 Courtesy of John Haviland
374 Courtesy of Jerry W. Leach
375 Both photos courtesy of Barry Shaw
382 National Museum of Natural History, Smithsonian, NHB MRC 152, Washington, DC 20560
386 Roger M. Keesing
390 Photograph by Friedrich Kruger, copyright The Museum of Victoria
392 Courtesy of Department of Foreign Affairs, Australia
394 National Museum of Natural History, Smithsonian, NHB MRC 152, Washington, DC 20560
402 Courtesy of John Haviland
406 Courtesy of John Haviland
409 Courtesy of Frank Cancian
414 Both photos courtesy of Roger M. Keesing
427 Courtesy of Masri Singarimbun
433 Courtesy of Department of Foreign Affairs, Australia
434 (top left) © Paulo Fridman/Gamma Liaison
434 (top right) © Yuen Lee/ Gamma Liaison
434 (bottom) © Ricardo Beliel/ Gamma Liaison
436 All photos courtesy of B. Wongar
437 © Adrian Arbib/ Anthro Photo
438 UN/ DPI Photo
456 UN/ DPI Photo
481 © Antonio Ribeiro/ Gamma Liaison

Index